D1085052

Arguing Americanism

NEW STUDIES IN U.S. FOREIGN RELATIONS

Mary Ann Heiss, editor

Arguing Americanism

Franco Lobbyists, Roosevelt's Foreign Policy,

and the Spanish Civil War

✳ ✳ ✳

Michael E. Chapman

The Kent State University Press
Kent, Ohio

Part of this manuscript previously appeared in a different form in the following article and is republished with permission: "Pro-Franco Anti-communism: Ellery Sedgwick and the *Atlantic Monthly,*" *Journal of Contemporary History* 41, no. 4 (2006): 641–62.

LIBRARY OF CONGRESS CATALOGING-IN-PUBLICATION DATA
Chapman, Michael E.
Arguing Americanism : Franco lobbyists, Roosevelt's foreign policy, and the Spanish Civil War / Michael E. Chapman.
p. cm. — (New studies in U.S. foreign relations)
Includes bibliographical references and index.
ISBN 978-1-60635-078-2 (hardcover : alk. paper) ∞
1. Spain—History—Civil War, 1936–1939—Foreign public opinion, American.
2. Spain—History—Civil War, 1936–1939—Diplomatic history. 3. Spain—History—Civil War, 1936–1939—Participation, American. 4. Spain—History—Civil War, 1936–1939—Propaganda. 5. Anti-communist movements—United States—History—20th century. 6. Public opinion—United States—History—20th century. 7. National characteristics, American. 8. United States—Foreign relations—Spain. 9. Spain—Foreign relations—United States. I. Title.
DP269.8.P8C43 2011
946.081'2—dc22
2011000681

British Library Cataloging-in-Publication data are available.

15 14 13 12 11   5 4 3 2 1

Contents

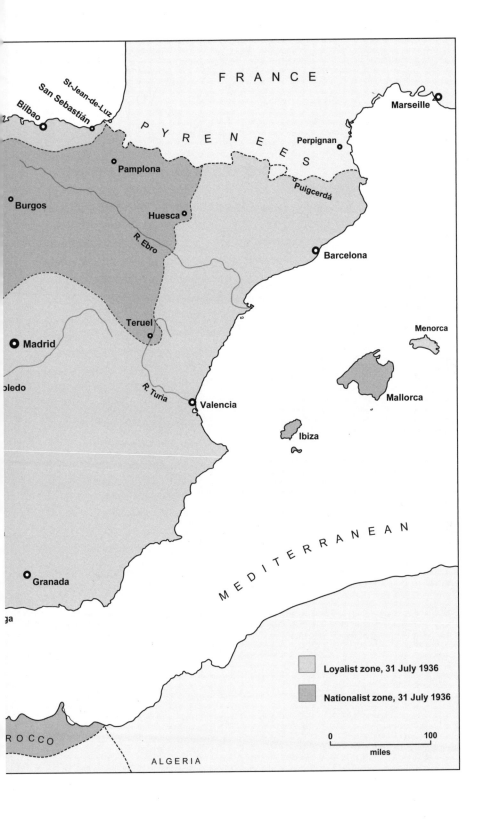

F R A N C E

Marseille

P Y R E N E E S

Bilbao

St-Jean-de-Luz

San Sebastián

Perpignan

Pamplona

Puigcerdá

Burgos

Huesca

R. Ebro

Barcelona

Menorca

Teruel

Madrid

Mallorca

oledo

R. Turia

Valencia

Ibiza

Granada

M E D I T E R R A N E A N

ga

ROCCO

ALGERIA

Loyalist zone, 31 July 1936

Nationalist zone, 31 July 1936

0   100

miles

Acknowledgments

This project began in 2000 when I wrote a paper for an undergraduate class on the Spanish Civil War, a topic that first caught my imagination in 1968 when reading George Orwell's *Homage to Catalonia* while attending a Protestant boarding school similar to the one Orwell attended. But the following year, when I was developing a senior honors thesis based on the paper, the story took an unexpected turn. I had intended to expose a scheme by Catholic clergy to divert aid from U.S. donors to Gen. Francisco Franco's war chest using the mechanism of foreign exchange controls, but in the last hour of a three-day research trip to the *America* magazine archive at Georgetown University, I blinked at a document that refuted my argument. Yet once I turned my thesis on its head, the evidence made sense. In the archive, I had noticed letters mailed from an address in Pittsfield, Massachusetts, my home state, so later, enrolled in graduate school and casting around for a dissertation topic, I inquired there and was amazed to discover the existence of some 1,800 documents spanning three generations. My first thanks, therefore, are to Frances Kelly, John Eoghan Kelly's cousin, not only for hanging on to a barnful of musty old family papers but also for all her gracious hospitality during my several visits—bless you Frances.

To paraphrase the Vietnamese proverb, it takes an entire department to educate a historian. There can be few scholarly environments as supportive as Boston College (BC), where Kevin Kenny, David Quigley, and my adviser Seth Jacobs have been towers of inspiration and encouragement. At Suffolk University, Bob Hannigan's commitment to this project is a testament to the academic process, as well as to our friendship. It was with John Cavanagh that I studied the Spanish Civil War, and through his urging, and that of my mentor, Joe McCarthy, that I plunged into graduate school. John and Joe, your boundless enthusiasm and scholarly example will always drive me. BC's interlibrary loan staff rendered sterling service in procuring rare manuscripts and articles. There is not space here to list the many archivists, librarians, and history buffs without whom this project would be a hollow shell, but I would like to mention Scott Taylor, Bob Clark, Mike Gibson, Charles Lamb, Joe Hovish, John Lynch, Mike Hussey, Leslie Farkas, Abbott Combes, Dan Benedetti, Ron Marsh, and John Michalczyk. All who read drafts of chapters—Peter Weiler, Rob Niebuhr, Frank Costigliola, Stanley

Payne, Patrick Maney, Ken Shelton—and the anonymous readers at the *Journal of Contemporary History* and the Kent State University Press (KSUP) have been of considerable assistance. A George C. Marshall/Baruch Dissertation Fellowship put a spring in my stride and provided funding for several research trips. Five people—Terry Liebman, Dorothea Straus, Louise Dunn, Gen St. George, Pablo Franky—agreed to take part in oral history interviews, which not only brought to life historical actors who would otherwise have been blank faces but also provided valuable insights. Louise Dunn's involvement, furthermore, made possible the sections on her mother, just as it convinced me of academic history's wider relevance. It has been a joy to work this project through to publication with the staff at KSUP, particularly series editor Ann Heiss, acquisitions editor Joyce Harrison, managing editor Mary Young, and my superhuman copy editor Joanna Craig. To all of you my sincerest thanks.

Introduction

After the outbreak of the Spanish Civil War in July 1936, the leaders of Britain and France organized a twenty-seven-nation Non-Intervention Committee, which included Italy, Germany, and the USSR, in the hope that they could contain the fighting. Across the Atlantic, where isolationist sentiment was at a historic peak after the one-two shocks of the Great War and the Great Depression, President Franklin D. Roosevelt followed Britain's lead, agreeing to his State Department's "moral embargo" to Spain, which then became law on 1 May 1937 when Congress passed an amended Neutrality Act. These attempts at containment notwithstanding, Soviet Russia pocketed Madrid's extensive gold reserves in return for shipping matériel of supposedly equal value to the Loyalists, while Italy and Germany armed Gen. Francisco Franco's Nationalists. Spain's civil war quickly became an international cause. Some 35,000 idealistic foreign volunteers flocked to the Loyalist zone claiming that they were defending democracy against fascism. In several countries, an argument developed between partisans, dividing along ideological lines, with Loyalist supporters slurring their detractors as anti-Semitic fascists and Nationalist supporters damning pro-Loyalists as godless Reds. This "Great Debate"—to borrow from F. Jay Taylor's influential *The United States and the Spanish Civil War*—became particularly intense in the United States, where it reappeared in a different guise following Roosevelt's interventionist support of Britain in 1939–40, was hushed after Pearl Harbor, and did not reach an accommodation until the cold war liberal consensus.[1]

Rigid policies that barred arms shipments to Spain effectively disadvantaged the Loyalists of Madrid's Second Republican government. Whereas the Nationalists' high-quality supplies originated from ports such as Hamburg or Genoa, Loyalists either bought shoddy equipment at high cost on what had become a black market or were dependent on periodic Soviet shipments from Murmansk, above the Arctic Circle. Loyalists lost control of the skies in part because of their inability to buy U.S. aircraft and especially Curtiss-Wright engines for their existing Douglas transports and the roughly 1,400 fighters and bombers that began arriving from the USSR.[2] Non-Interventionists, moreover, isolated Loyalists diplomatically and debilitated their morale. Historian Helen Graham insists that "what destroyed the Republic was the long-term impact" of the "absolutely devastating"

Non-Intervention Committee's embargo. Graham's charge has a wider implica-tion than the fate of Spain. Official U.S. support of the Loyalist cause in 1938 would have waved a threat card at Adolf Hitler's expansionism, prompting English and French parliaments to show greater resolve and encouraging hesitant Nazi mili-tary leaders to question the timing if not the inevitability of their Führer's next step. Why did Roosevelt—a president with unprecedented potential to influence foreign policy, if not always to make it—sidestep such a crucial issue?[3]

Historians have blamed America's Catholic hierarchy and congregants. Allen Guttmann is typical of those who cite the diary of Interior secretary Harold L. Ickes, which recorded that Roosevelt held back because lifting the embargo "would mean the loss of every Catholic vote" in the November elections. Leo V. Kanawada Jr. is one of many who note that in May 1938 alone, "the White House, the State Depart-ment, and members of Congress received thousands of messages" from Catholics "denouncing any attempt to lift the embargo." Yet evidence presented here shows that while Roosevelt did read a few messages from pro-Loyalist Catholics asking him to lift the embargo, he saw none from denunciatory pro-Franco Catholics, and ranking State Department officials read only four. Indeed, through Popular Front organizations and fellow-traveling journalists, Soviet communists exerted far greater pressure on Roosevelt and his State Department to lift the embargo than Roman Catholics ever did to retain it. While it may be convenient to blame Catholics for U.S. appeasement of Hitler, it is time to seek new explanations.[4]

Despite talking in terms of a Great Debate, it is odd that historians have dwelled on only half of the argument, that made by America's pro-Loyalists, while show-ing distaste for the other side, the pro-Nationalists, whom they snub as either the "Catholic hierarchy" or "fascist crackpots." There was on the one hand a heroic throng of fascist-fighting interventionists and on the other a tiny "lunatic fringe" of isolationist appeasers. Revisionist studies are suggesting fresh approaches by recasting the Spanish generals' insurgency as a valid military response to incipient communist revolution. Yet the received wisdom of honest-to-goodness folks bat-tling fascist evil in Spain, reinforced by popular culture and public history (most obviously in film, from *Casablanca* [1942] to *Pan's Labyrinth* [2006] and the Mu-seum of the City of New York's *Facing Fascism* exhibition and book [2007]), still limits discussion.[5] Many pro-Loyalist activists were of course socialists, pacifists, liberal intellectuals, and even anticommunists. A majority—at least two-thirds—of Americans who fought in Spain were nevertheless American Communist Party (CPUSA) members, albeit ones who temporarily shrouded their radical ideol-ogy with Joseph Stalin's Popular Front, maintaining that they were saving de-mocracy by fighting fascism. Acknowledging, therefore, that communists sought the revolutionary overthrow of the capitalist state and the imposition by force of a workers' dictatorship will make it easier to understand the rationale of the ac-tors discussed here. Accepting, too, that Franco lobbyists might have been just as thoughtful and diverse as their pro-Loyalist counterparts, with the same human complement of biases and inconsistencies, allows for a more objective historiographical interpretation of late-1930s sociopolitical ideologies.[6]

This study employs new archival sources to document a small yet effective network of lobbyists—including engineer-turned-writer John Eoghan Kelly, progressive humanist Ellery Sedgwick, homemaker Clare Singer Dawes, art deco muralist Hildreth Meière, philanthropist Anne Tracy Morgan, and libertarian pundit Merwin K. Hart—who successfully capitalized on the inertia of a weak, distracted, and divided administration to promote Nationalist Spain. Franco lobbyists provide an interesting cultural study, for they revered the exceptionalism of America's founding principles while advocating modern, progressive solutions to pressing socioeconomic problems. They are politically important too, for they influenced not only public opinion but U.S. foreign policy as well.

What drove these Americans to work so hard and to sacrifice so much to back an unpalatable dictator in distant Spain during a time of economic and social crisis at home? Sources indicate that they found unity of purpose in their loathing of international Marxism. Given America's subsequent role as global cold war hegemon, this observation might not seem surprising, but it is necessary to stress that the pro-Franco anticommunism of 1937–43 differed from its bookends, the 1920s Red Scare and 1950s McCarthyism. Far from being a confident harbinger of capitalist boom, Franco lobbyists saw their anticommunism as confronting socialist euphoria over the Great Depression's apparent vindication of Karl Marx. For them, it was not the product of an exaggerated threat but, rather, a balanced riposte to a serious Comintern (the Soviet Union's Third Communist International) thrust. Most importantly, their anticommunism was not a state initiative but a minority sentiment that acted in opposition to the New Deal state, which they judged to be soft on communism while favoring Franco's Soviet-backed Loyalist enemies. Consequently, their critique of the Roosevelt presidency attracted Justice Department ire and a conviction for principal activist Kelly in 1943 under the Foreign Agents Registration Act. At a time of ideological disjuncture, pro-Franco anticommunists were patriots to themselves but un-American to their state.

Exposing and thus halting communist influence in the United States was the Franco lobbyists' primary motivation. This study nonetheless hypothesizes that a greater project lay behind their activism, even if they never acknowledged it as such. During a period of national crisis unmatched since their own civil war in 1861, American Franco lobbyists seized the example of Spain's civil war to bolster what they believed was their country's unique historic legacy of Enlightenment liberalism and republican governance. Their argument during the Great Debate was not really over Spain. Pro-Nationalists were arguing with their pro-Loyalist counterparts about who should define America's national ideology and what that definition ought to be. At home, they believed that hundreds of Comintern agents strove to sweep away the nation-state in favor of an international repub-lic of workers, and they feared that the double-dip recession of 1937–38, which was once again pushing unemployment over 20 percent, was creating the kind of conditions for social unrest that radicals eagerly exploited. For evidence that their fears were rational, they pointed abroad to mayhem wrought by Spain's rev-olutionaries, which they contrasted with Franco *The Christian Soldier,* as Kelly entitled one pamphlet, and, by extension, the civilizing order of American prin-ciples. Arguing, through the Great Debate over U.S. neutrality toward Spain, that communism was un-American had unintended consequences both for American ideology and prospects for global peace. Despite falling foul of their own gov-ernment, American Franco lobbyists ultimately won the argument, yet, to their surprise, the resultant cold war liberal consensus was not what they envisaged.[7]

Because these anticommunists supported Franco, their argument from the outset proved as contentious as it was anachronistic. Evidence presented here em-phasizes how most Americans in 1938, along with their president and his White House staff, had succumbed to sophisticated Popular Front propaganda about fascist aggression in Spain and sided, at least emotionally, with Madrid's Loyal-ists. This was, after all, the CPUSA's zenith, a time when, in the celebratory words of cultural historian Michael Denning, "'politics' captured the arts, when writers went left, Hollywood turned Red, and painters, musicians, and photographers were 'social-minded.'" Pilloried by such a broad coalition of social-minded intel-lectuals—from movie producers to journalists—anticommunism seemed vulgar, reactionary, the vain pursuit of mavericks like Representative Martin Dies Jr. (D-TX) and the hired guns of Chicago's Memorial Day Massacre.[8]

Franco lobbyists—at a subliminal if not an outwardly manifest level—read their unpopular stand as a declaration of their Americanism, as an opportunity for the Catholic American editor Francis X. Talbot, the Jewish-American brewer Philip Liebmann, or the Irish-German-American Kelly to cast aside hyphenated identities and claim the high ground of an all-American citizenship. Neither were old stocks immune from concerns over their identity as genuine Americans. Sedgwick and Meière, who loudly traced ancestry back to the *Arbella* or *Mayflower* on one side of their families, kept awkwardly silent about a hyphenated cousin or grandparent on the other. Determined to convince skeptics that the Comintern really did intend to build a workers' dictatorship on the ruins of U.S. capitalism, lobbyists toured Spain's Nationalist zone, publishing travelogs such as *America: Look at Spain!* In part be-cause their activism caused compatriots to look and then argue with them over what they saw, Americans after 1945 committed to a massive forty-year ideological mission to make Americanism impregnable by battling communism worldwide. Just as Franco became a cold war bulwark, it is ironic that the un-American Kelly found rehabilitation in 1949 as a patriotically American cold warrior, lobbying Con-gress for the strategic utilization of domestic mineral resources.[9]

When pro-Franco lobbyists took issue with their pro-Loyalist counterparts over the extent of communist or fascist influence in Spain, or which side committed the worst atrocities, or whether to embargo U.S. arms, the heated argument they created drew thousands of otherwise unconcerned Americans into the debate. Lobbyists accordingly thought it best to present their cases in black-and-white terms, yet that very simplification of the situation in Spain focused attention on complex moral issues and political philosophies at home. At the core of this larger argument over Americanism in 1938—the year around which this study pivots—lay the definition of *democracy*. For the pro-Loyalists of the Popular Front, the term meant the pure democracy of the ballot box, for they believed that in an increasingly industrialized economy, especially at a time of global recession and high unemployment, the working class enjoyed a majority and could therefore impose a socialist state. For pro-Franco lobbyists, the term meant the checks and balances of indirect democracy, for they believed that the success of America's republican experiment depended on the kind of meritocracy envisaged by Founding Fathers Thomas Jefferson and James Madison to counter the dictatorial tendencies of factions, or foreign *isms* in contemporary parlance. When these actors decided to defend Americanism against communism by pointing to what was happening in Spain, the argument they intensified became the critical precursor of a fundamental change in that Americanism: the Founders' meritocratic form of democracy survived, perhaps even becoming further removed from popular sentiment, but only at the expense of other founding principles, as evidenced by the illiberal repression of McCarthyism, the arbitrary government of the national-security state, and the entangling political alliances of the cold war.[10]

Two Spains

Spain has always occupied a special place in the American psyche, just as it has served a special purpose. On subjects from Christopher Columbus (an Italian) to the Inquisition (which executed less than six heretics a year on average), legend has invariably trumped reality, which is why Spain has proved so useful. Until the 1960s, when it became a popular tourist destination, few Americans visited Spain. Before Dwight D. Eisenhower's meeting with Franco in 1959, only five Americans who would become or had been presidents ever ventured south of the Pyrenees: John Adams and his son, John Quincy, traveled through Galicia and the Basque Country in 1780 en route to Paris; Ulysses S. Grant and Franklin Pierce took post-presidential European tours in 1858 and 1878, respectively; and Herbert Hoover went to Spain in 1917 because U-boats made a crossing to Britain risky. For Adams, the poverty of Catholic Spain's peasantry, the backwardness of its industry, and the self-indulgence of its nobles and clergy served to demonstrate the enlightened progress and civilization of Protestant America. "I see nothing," Adams wrote, "but Signs of Poverty and Misery." Spain, he observed, was a fertile enough country, yet it was only half cultivated. Spaniards were "ragged and dirty, and the Houses universally nothing but Mire, Smoke, Fleas and Lice." There was nothing "rich but the Churches, nobody fat, but the Clergy." "This Country," Adams complained, "is an hundred Years behind the Massachusetts Bay." Still, even in so bleak an account, there were inconsistencies. While he could find "no Simptoms of Commerce, or even of internal Traffic, no Appearance of Manufactures or Industry," two weeks later he came across "great Numbers of Mules loaded with Merchandizes from Bilbao," including mass-produced horseshoes "to sell in various Parts of the Kingdom." On reaching Bilbao, a prosperous port with three hundred registered merchant ships, Adams had to admit there were "several Stores and Shops [for books, glass, china, trinkets, toys, cutlery] pretty large and pretty full." Not that Massachusetts in 1780 had much in the way of industry, cities, or roads, especially in comparison with the efficient factories, teeming metropolises, and advanced infrastructure of rival Britain, but that was precisely why a primitive yet decadent Spain was so useful to Adams as a counterpoint to the virtues of American republicanism.[11]

Yankee doyen Whig senator Daniel Webster (MA) visited neither Spain nor Latin America, yet in his two most famous public orations, delivered at the commencement (1825) and completion (1843) of the Bunker Hill Monument, he conjured up vivid stereotypes of Spaniards. When patriots fought the Battle of Bunker Hill in June 1775, South America was hardly visible to the civilized world, weighed down as it was by Spanish "colonial subjugation, monopoly, and bigotry." When English colonists arrived in the New World, they were already prosperous, free, and "trained for the great work of introducing English civilization, English law, and what is more than all, Anglo-Saxon blood, into the wilderness of North America." These "industrious individuals" made their own way in the wilderness, "defending themselves against the savages, recognizing their right to the soil, and with a general honest purpose of introducing knowledge as well as Christianity among them." Spanish colonists, by contrast, emulating their behavior at home and greedy for gold, subjugated native peoples with "every possible degree of enormity, cruelty, and crime." They acquired territories by fire and sword, destroyed cities by fire and sword, and "even conversion to Christianity was attempted by fire and sword." Whereas "England transplanted liberty to America," Webster made clear, "Spain transplanted power." Generations of young Americans absorbed Webster's Spain when studying his orations for the College Entrance Examination, at least until 1911.[12]

In 1898, when many of the policy makers and lobbyists discussed in this book were impressionable teenagers, newspapers drooled over the sinking of USS *Maine* in Havana's harbor and the ensuing Spanish-American War. Cartoonists portrayed Spaniards as sword-wielding conquistadores ravishing Cuban maidens, while commentators relished the opportunity to contrast American good-ness with Spanish evil. "The record of the Spanish Nation," noted William E. Ma-son (R-IL) in a widely reported Senate debate, was one "of continuous treachery." Mason regretted his inability to join a negotiating committee, for he "would not sit at a table with a Spaniard who might have a stiletto under his clothes." When Cardinal James Gibbons conducted a requiem mass for *Maine* victims, Gibbons gave thanks that America was "too just to engage in an unrighteous war" and praised the "calmness and tranquility, the self-control, and the self-possession" of Washington's leaders. "Let us remember," he cautioned, "that the eyes of the world are upon us." While Gibbons hoped that the *Maine*'s destruction was an accident, he hinted nonetheless that a "fiendish Cuban" or "fanatical Spaniard" had "per-petrated this atrocious crime." Spain in 1898 served not only to deflect attention from the corruption and crime endemic to cities like New York and Chicago but also to justify colonization of the Philippines on humanitarian grounds.[13]

When Spaniards chose violence in 1936 to resolve their differences over class, religion, ethnic separatism, and political philosophy, Americans found a mythical Spain especially useful, for they too were struggling with ideological confusion and economic recession. Those who had joined Popular Front organizations because they thought socialism would cure the Great Depression used the presence of Ger-man and Italian units in Spain to argue that an international fascist conspiracy was trampling liberal democracy and workers' rights. Those who still trusted capitalism but worried that continued unemployment would lead to societal breakdown used the murder of clergy by Spanish militia to argue that an international communist conspiracy was subverting progressive democracy and middle-class values. Once they had committed to being pro-Loyalists or pro-Nationalists, honor demanded they stick to their guns, which required bringing as much ammunition to the argu-ment as credibility allowed. For every point they wished to make, debaters could find evidence in Spain. Look at the poverty of Spanish peasants, pro-Loyalists said, to see how aristocrats siphoned profits that should be fueling industrialization. Look at the rapid collapse of once-profitable Spanish factories, pro-Nationalists countered, to see how selfishness, not social uplift, was behind spiraling demands by trade unionists. Because their understanding rested on legends, debaters found that a little substance could support a large myth. At the same time, those legends exposed inconsistencies in debaters' arguments, which, when sufficiently blatant, left denial as the only recourse. Pro-Nationalists, for instance, needed to argue that the descent into anarchy following the February 1936 election of a Popular Front government forced Franco to restore order by military means, so they cited the murders of civilians by leftists as evidence. But when Nationalists bombed civilians in Guernica, they risked losing credibility as the defenders of order, especially when pro-Loyalists seized on the raid to demonstrate fascist aggression. With the legend of Spanish brutality suggesting that an atrocity must have occurred, they did not attempt to justify the bombing on strategic grounds, so they accepted Franco's lie that retreating Basques had torched their own town.

Just as each side in the Great Debate claimed to speak for the true Spain, so the compelling mix of fact and fancy propagandized by the opposing side forced debaters to acknowledge the existence of another, false Spain. Pro-Nationalists confronted the fascist Spain created by pro-Loyalists, characterized by medieval Catholicism, vast estates owned by absentee aristocrats, the execution of leftists and dissidents, the indiscriminate bombing of civilian centers, contingents from Nazi Germany and Fascist Italy, and military rule. Pro-Loyalists confronted the Red Spain created by pro-Nationalists, characterized by the redistribution of land and property, atrocities against respectable civilians and clergy, spiraling inflation, immorality and lawlessness, and an influx of Soviet officials and international communists. Debaters on both sides sought to show contented workers sharing in the profits of busy factories; yet in their propaganda, they tended to ignore industry to present instead a romanticized portrait of traditional farming. From *Blockade* and *The Spanish Earth* (Loyalist) to *Spain in Arms* (Nationalist), films featured ox-drawn carts, primitive irrigation ditches, peasants scything wheat, and quaint shepherds tending flocks of goats. Legends of a backward, feudal Spain helped to support a paradox that was in both sides' interest to perpetuate. For pro-Loyalists, bucolic Spain highlighted the iniquitous sharecropping that socialist land reforms would eradicate, while for pro-Nationalists, old-style farming identified the traditional values of Franco's true Spain with the yeoman farmers of New England and the Midwest.[14]

Historians, too, have struggled to objectify modern Spain. One scholar notes how during 1917–29, iron and steel production doubled, "strong labor organizations kept up wages in a period of falling world prices," and there was "a remarkable expansion in the field of light industry." Another stresses that "Spain entered the 1930s a backward state, still largely agricultural with levels of poverty equaled only by . . . Greece or Sicily." Pessimism is understandable in the context of the Spanish Civil War, for liberals hope to show how, in Paul Preston's words, "reactionary elements" always resort to "political and military power to hold back social progress." This study does not presume to add to the shelves of works that debate what happened in Spain. Rather, it is concerned with how U.S. lobbyists for Franco's Nationalists understood Spain and communicated their understanding to other Americans. When it does reference Spain in an objective sense, it is broadly optimistic. As David Ringrose contends in his explanation for the dual "Spanish miracles" of rapid industrialization and democratization in the post-Franco years, those miracles built on "generations of cultural, institutional, and economic experience," on modernizing and progressive trends in place long before 1900.[15]

Historical analysis of foreign policy making invariably ignores long-run structural factors to concentrate instead on the immediate, nip-and-tuck world of realpolitik, an approach that minimizes the role of individual agency with its attendant psychosocial and cultural determinants, which is my interest here. A useful influence is Michael Seidman's *Republic of Egos,* which downplays grand strategy, power politics, and even ideological motivation to argue instead that events in Spain were as much to do with efforts by individuals to survive and feed themselves. "Acts of acquisitive, entrepreneurial, and subversive individualism," Seidman writes, often upset the collectivist plans of anarchist or communist ideologues to establish a wartime economy or mobilize against the better organized, motivated, and disciplined Nationalists. Political ideology, as well as the ideology of national identity, may well have been of less interest to Spaniards than historians have assumed, but it was fundamental to the thousands of Americans who volunteered to fight in Spain and the millions more who argued about the Spanish Civil War at home.[16]

Concepts

Many of this study's actors traveled abroad, but their trips were not so much for relaxation or even enlightenment as they were for legitimation. When Franco lobbyists who had visited Nationalist Spain talked about the destruction of churches by Loyalists or the building of affordable housing by Nationalists, they could do so with the authority of direct experience. Traveling qualified their arguments. Inevitably, the Spain of their writings and lectures was a different Spain from the one that existed for Spaniards, or even from the one that the travelers encountered. Alan K. Henrikson's concept of cognitive geography, or "mental mapping," offers an apt interpretive schema. In the context of Americans' mental map of Spain in 1938, I employ Henrikson's term to intend a conception more imagined than a *National Geographic* but less ethereal than a *Weltanschauung.*[17]

Our identity—who we are—is a crucial component of our psyche. Sociologist Johan Galtung values it alongside freedom, welfare, and survival as one of the four basic human needs. At least since the Peace of Westphalia laid the foundations of international law, the nation-state paradigm has offered a seductive enhancement to the organic identities of tribe, clan, family, and self. If earthy patriotism identifies us with farmstead or village, supporting us with the resources of family or community, then modern nationalism identifies us with metropolis or nation, empowering us with the resources of an entire militarized state. As a kind of turbocharged patriotism, nationalism is a powerful and compelling ideology.[18]

A current survey indicates that Americans are among the most nationalistic people on Earth, a distinction explicable in part by the observations that they are a settler community, of recent origin, convinced of their own rectitude and grown powerful beyond compare. Yet this does not mean that Americans are necessarily comfortable within themselves. Indeed, their very exceptionalism has been a constant source of anxiety and guilt. According to political scientist David Campbell,

Americans have an exceptionally fragile sense of national identity, which explains why they attempt to secure the boundaries of their state by exaggerating danger through foreign policy. Nor should it imply that Americans have felt uniformly nationalistic over time. Nineteen thirty-eight was a particular nadir, when Americans troubled as much by social discord as a broken economy looked abroad for inspiration, whether to international communism, transnational Catholicism, or authoritarian fascism.[19]

Americanism—the ideal tenets of American nationalism—was a term used throughout the 1920s and 1930s, as when Kelly wrote to a friend in January 1938 that he was coming to the "defense of Americanism." It represented a consensus across old-stock elites and immigrants aspiring to citizenship, which both groups articulated through the Americanization programs of the 1910–20s. By virtue of their Puritan inheritance, Americans could expect a life of goodness and greatness, providing they adhered to a bundle of traditional core values, including but not limited to Protestant ethics, Lockean liberalism, Jeffersonian producerism, and the sanctity of the Constitution at home and the Monroe Doctrine abroad. Historian Samuel P. Huntington terms this package *Anglo-Protestantism,* an alluring and pervasive identity-building ideology adopted, often unconsciously, by immigrants, regardless of their ethnicity or religion. Huntington's Anglo-Protestantism makes for an informative if static analytical model. This study considers Americanism more broadly and dynamically as a disputed ideology of empowerment. For Spanish Civil War partisans, it could be a derogatory term as well as a badge of honor, but it was always a national soul to argue over, possess, and then appropriate.[20]

After researching Chinese society in the first decades of the twentieth century, Michael H. Hunt concludes that climactic moments in the gradual and contested process of national identity formation can arise when intellectuals and elites—often those with a heightened appreciation of and a yearning for robust nationalism—respond to a foreign affairs crisis, yet their historically rooted patriotism may limit the scope and appropriateness of their responses. There is resonance here with this study's concerned, argumentative Americans, for whom pro-Franco anticommunism became a path for the affirmation of their deep-rooted core values, which a sense of insecurity had rendered fragile. Historian Prasenjit Duara believes that citizens construct their national psyche on a foundation of fluid relationships, so their composite national identity "both resembles and is interchangeable with other political identities." During the Great Debate of 1937–38, a fierce argument over political ideology between pro-Loyalists and pro-Nationalists forced participants to think what being an American meant and to "take sides," as debaters said. By focusing so much attention on Americanism, and then fighting over its ownership, Great Debaters not only elevated the importance of national identity for all U.S. citizens, but they also altered its core values. Franco lobbyists, though small in number, were the necessary other half of the debate; it was against the arguments of lobbyists such as Kelly that thousands of Popular Fronters in meeting rooms, during street parades, and through the mass media directed their anger.[21]

U.S. policy makers talk in terms of "traditional values" but less often list them, just as they proudly refer to an American "way of life" yet rarely say what that entails. Pressed for specifics, they might first insist that the meaning of these phrases is as obvious as apple pie or the Fourth of July, and then perhaps mention self-reliance, rugged individualism, level playing fields, free-market capitalism, republican democracy, freedom of speech, and a shared belief in the Supreme Being. To whatever extent the tenets of Americanism are obvious, the shift from an abhorrence of tyrannical government, standing armies, and high taxes in 1775 to the enthusiasm of the cold war onward for an ever more powerful military and mushrooming federal budget begs a paradox. Since *Arbella* dropped anchor in Massachusetts Bay in 1630 with John Winthrop's band of Puritans, an overarching characteristic seems to have infused the American psyche, which may solve the riddle. It stems from an organic, perhaps spiritual certainty in right thoughts and right actions. It extends to a well-meaning urge to impart that rectitude to others and set them straight. And it manifests itself daily in earnest debate and anxious activity, as well as intense introspection when utopian dreams turn to nightmares. It is evident in Winthrop's embittered decision to emigrate and in his 1683 expulsion of Anne Hutchinson, an upstart minister he judged to be a latter-day Jezebel. "You have suffered yourselves to be so divided for so small matters," one church council lamented in 1772 after settling an acrimonious conflict over preachers' salaries in Concord, Massachusetts. Indeed, Concord's yeoman farmers bickered so much over trivial issues that their frustration drove them to bear arms against Redcoat police at Lexington in April 1775. Moralistic preoccupation with social reform (prisons, poor houses, prohibition) and religious purity (anti-Masonry, anti-Irish nativism) came to a head in 1861 in a civil war over the ethics of work and citizenship. More recently, it has popped up in dramatic quests for a New Deal, a New Frontier, or a New World Order and in wars on poverty, drugs, or terror.[22]

This restless American angst was the predominant characteristic of and driving force behind the arguments that suffused the Great Debate. Danish philosopher Søren Kierkegaard developed the "concept of anxiety" to explain the "dizziness of freedom," the chronic insecurity commensurate with a growing sense of liberty, especially among Protestants, who consequently lived in fear that they would fail in their moral duty to God. If democracy is about the freedom to have an argument, then Americanism describes a collective will that is about being on the same page. There has always been an inherent tension—an angst—in American society between healthy debate and stifling conformity. Because liberty-loving Americans believe their brand of republican democracy to be exceptional, they are watchful of experiments to replicate it abroad and fearful of threats to its existence at home. In Germany, Italy, and Japan of the 1930s, where confidence in parliamentary democracy was still consolidating, citizens turned to authoritarian regimes and militarization to rejuvenate their economies, sanction their nationalism, and end the dizziness. Central planning and a workers' dictatorship had apparently created an economic miracle in the Soviet Union. Significantly, in Spain—from which Columbus sailed to discover the New World and where inquisitorial churchmen, ruthless conquistadores, and corrupt aristocrats ever since served to demonstrate to Americans the merits of their own Anglo-Protestant civilization—the short-lived Second Republic of 1931 flirted with socialist revolution before collapsing into civil war.[23]

Scope and Sources

Because this study's purpose is to document and explain the activism of American lobbyists for Franco's Spain, it ignores pro-Loyalists, who have already received extensive historiographical treatment. Ignored, too, are many important and no doubt interesting Franco lobbyists, such as Edward J. Heffron, secretary of the National Council of Catholic Men, or William H. McCarthy, postmaster of San Francisco and promoter of Pacific Coast baseball. In the interests of a compact, coherent narrative, executive membership in the American Union of Nationalist Spain (AUNS), the most influential and previously unstudied pro-Nationalist lobbying organization, provides my primary selection criterion, while Kelly, both in his capacity as AUNS secretary and as an independent activist, is a focal point for the story.

Sources should drive historiographical analysis, and I hope this study is no exception. Kelly's collected correspondence, writings, speeches, and memorabilia, comprising some 12,000 document pages, plus an uncensored Federal Bureau of Investigation (FBI) dossier of 1,800 pages, allow for a breadth and richness of interpretation that is unusual for a grassroots actor from the 1930s. At the same time, Kelly was an opinionated individual, which is why I have tried to balance his views against those of other lobbyists from a range of political-cultural backgrounds. Because my intention is to portray these actors as they saw themselves, this account is necessarily as sympathetic of pro-Franco Americans as it will be disturbing for those who hold to the prevailing interpretation about Spain's 1936 Popular Front government and the CPUSA members who organized volunteers in its defense. While faith in the meaning—as opposed to the politics—of objectivity suggests to me that historiographical treatment of the Spanish Civil War and the U.S. foreign policy pertaining to it has been a tad myopic, it does not follow that my actors' opinions are my own.

1

Pro-Franco Anticommunism

There was a one-column hint of trouble on 14 July 1936. Under the headline "Monarchist Chief Murdered in Spain," *New York Times* correspondent William P. Carney, a Catholic whose sympathies were not with Madrid's Popular Front government, wired that at 3:00 A.M. uniformed police in an official car arrested rightist opposition leader José Calvo Sotelo and then delivered his bayoneted body to a cemetery at 3:45.[1]

As a band of cooler, rainy weather broke the Northeast's record heat wave, four days passed with little to report, although a "clubfooted writer with a grudge against society" narrowly missed assassinating Britain's King Edward. Then, on 19 July, the longest-running, most widely reported, and politically stimulating news saga of the decade erupted. "Spain Checks Army Rising" spanned two *Times* columns; the 20 July edition ran "Rebels Gain in South Spain" across three columns, and by 23 July, "Rebel Success Reported in Spain" covered half of the paper's eight columns. It might never have garnered one of the rare full-width banners, as did "Roosevelt Sweeps Nation" and "Hindenberg Burns in Lakehurst Crash," but from July 1936 to March 1939, the Spanish Civil War was rarely out of the news. With 1,069 column inches (8.9 percent), the *Times* devoted more front-page headlines to Spain than to unions and strikes (7.5 percent), New York politics (7.4 percent), violent crime (6.7 percent), or even Nazi Germany (6.7 percent).[2]

An ideological lightning rod, Spain's civil war simultaneously energized and split opinion—although, as in 1776, when a third of Americans were ambivalent about independence, there were always those who opened newspapers at the sports section or classified advertisements. Generously funded by the Comintern and the Spanish embassy and professionally organized through existing Popular Front structures, pro-Loyalists presented a coherent, vocal lobby from the outset. Lobbyists for Gen. Francisco Franco's Nationalists, by contrast, who first had to identify and then find themselves, operated autonomously throughout 1936–37, coalesced through informal networks, and did not build a national association until the end of 1938.

This chapter introduces the central actors in these overlapping pro-Nationalist circles, and shows how pro-Franco anticommunists influenced public opinion by intensifying an argument over U.S. foreign policy. It begins with John Eoghan Kelly, whose experience, efficiency, and productivity made him a surprisingly effective lobby-of-one, and ends by documenting the Franco advocacy of two old-stock elites, public administrator W. Cameron Forbes and *Atlantic Monthly* editor/publisher Ellery Sedgwick.

Cultured if understated, moneyed though careful, informed yet discreet, politically ambitious but from an ethic of public service, upper-crust Yankees typically learned Latin at Groton School, studied law at Harvard College, worshiped at an Episcopal church, connected in exclusive clubs, and gleaned opinion from literary journals like the *Atlantic* or *Harper's Weekly*. As exemplified by Secretaries of State Henry L. Stimson and Dean Acheson and that most interventionist of presidents, Theodore Roosevelt, throughout the 1890s to 1950s these elite Northeasterners were disproportionately influential in Washington, especially in foreign policy making, where by reputation they favored Britain over Germany in the West, China over Japan in the East, and intervention over isolation, given an opportunity for advancing their liberal exceptionalist ideology and Open Door commercial interests. For otherwise liberal Yankee republicans, therefore, the foreign policy positions of Forbes, Sedgwick, and other like-minded Boston Brahmins in 1938 may seem unusual. Sedgwick's circle, representative of an important segment of elite opinion, admired authoritarian regimes in Germany and Italy, supported Japan over China, and—when they argued that Franco, by confronting atheistic communism in Spain, was restoring much-needed order to the civilized Christian West—aligned themselves with the isolationists.[3]

This chapter highlights the Great Debate's polarized Red-fascist rhetoric, which backed liberal progressives into the conservatives' corner and laid the discursive groundwork for 1950s McCarthyism. It posits that Forbes and Sedgwick were not interested in Franco per se but promoted his cause because they sought to demonstrate the danger that international communism posed to Americanism during a period of crisis and insecurity. Yet theirs was neither an irrational response nor merely an informational campaign. Rather, it was an educated, if unconscious, effort to emphasize and enforce their particular definition of Americanism. Franco lobbyists mentally mapped Spain onto the United States to contrast what they saw as the amoral anarchy of encroaching foreign Marxism with the civilizing order of traditional American core values. Like later cold warriors, Franco lobbyists confronted the paradox of the necessary enemy. International communism represented the ultimate danger for a nation-state founded on Puritan ethics and the sanctity of private property. Defending the nation against that danger provided the perfect opportunity to strengthen national identity while establishing themselves as guardians and interpreters of national values; but defeating an ideology with the power and appeal of 1930s communism necessitated hard-nosed tactics that risked undermining the very values they aimed to defend.[4]

Kelly Family Activism

Spain's conflict was of professional interest to U.S. Army Intelligence personnel, particularly those stationed in the soft-coal counties of the Appalachians where armed clashes between rival unions and with nonunion miners resembled small wars. When Assistant Chief of Staff Col. William A. Alfonte heard about a reserve officer in West Virginia who was an authority on Central American military history, fluent in Spanish, and a mining engineer with prior experience of monitoring subversives ("un-American Reds," in army parlance), Alfonte asked him to find out all he could. By the end of 1936, Captain Kelly was lecturing groups of officers across the United States on the Spanish Civil War, a subject that came to define his life. Yet, ironically, Kelly's strident anticommunism and unwavering support of Spain's Nationalists would cost him his commission and land him in federal court in 1943 on a charge stemming from un-American activities.[5]

John Forrest Kelly, born in Ireland in 1859 to schoolteachers Jeremiah and Kate Kelly, emigrated to Hoboken, New Jersey, in 1873 with his mother to join his father, a Fenian who had fled Ireland a few years earlier. John earned a bachelor's degree at nineteen and a PhD in electrochemical engineering after three years at the Stevens Institute. By 1886 he was chief electrician for the U.S. Electric Lighting Company. While living in Manhattan with his sister, Gertrude Bride Kelly, a pediatric surgeon, John was involved with the Knights of Labor and presided over a mass protest meeting in the aftermath of Chicago's Haymarket Square riot. Passionate about political philosophy, John and Bride, as she was known, were individualist anarchists, advocating a kind of free-market socialism that stressed personal responsibility, privately funded education, and nonviolent political action through local yet federated societies.[6]

It was probably through anarchist circles that John met Helen Tischer, who was also the daughter of German political exiles, republicans of 1848 from the Silesian border town of Görlitz. Helen was born in 1866. Shortly after Prussia forced Saxony into the North German Confederation in 1867, the Tischers emigrated to St. Louis, Missouri. In about 1885, Helen went to Manhattan as a social worker. After marrying in 1892, Helen and John moved to Pittsfield, Massachusetts, where John formed a partnership with William Stanley Jr. and Cummings C. Chesney. A pioneer of high-voltage alternating current transmission systems with seventy patents to his credit, John installed a 16,700-volt line from a generating station on the Yuba River eighteen miles to Marysville, California, in 1898 and then proved the feasibility of a 60,000-volt line from Electra, near San Andreas, 120 miles to Oakland. General Electric bought Stanley Electric in 1903, and John left to develop other ventures, including an electric player piano, oil exploration in the South, and the Cooke-Kelly process for dehydrating vegetables, with a manufacturing plant in Humboldt, Tennessee. In 1912 he took Helen and their two sons, John Eoghan (pronounced ŌWĬN) born 4 May 1896 and Domnall Forrest born in 1898, for a year-long tour of Asia and Europe; this was when seventeen-year-old Eoghan first experienced Spain. An indefatigable campaigner for Sinn Féin and Irish independence, John presided over the Massachusetts Friends of Irish Freedom, was the anonymous writer of much of the *Irish World*'s most politically influential content during 1919–22, and orchestrated a nationwide Irish American boycott of British goods. When he died of angina in October 1922, the *World* eulogized that Ireland had lost "her ablest champion on this side of the Atlantic."[7]

John Eoghan Kelly evidently absorbed his parents' views about radical action in the defense of republicanism, arguing with his eighth-grade teacher at Pittsfield High School that the French Revolution was "*perfectly* justified" and bringing his father's copy of *The Reds of the Midi* by Felix Gras to prove it. An avid reader, he made full use of the 4,000-title family library—a rich resource for medicine, philosophy, or literature, from Cicero (in Latin) to Ibsen, Wilde, Faulkner, Shaw, and Forrester. At Rensselaer Polytechnic Institute, he studied chemical engineering, qualified for the ice hockey team, and was an associate editor of *The Polytechnic*. A scrapper on the ice and "an absolute authority on college fraternities," according to Rensselaer's yearbook, Kelly "of the silver skates" enjoyed a reputation as "silver tongued." But after overexerting himself in hockey training, he developed tubercular laryngitis—or at least that was the diagnosis of his aunt, who recommended he head to a dry climate to recover. This was opportune, since his father had business connections in Chihuahua, Mexico, outside the U.S. War Department draft board's jurisdiction. While Kelly agreed with his father's principled refusal to fight in the cause of British imperialism against Ireland's ally, Germany, military life appealed to him. He first tried registering for the draft in 1917 and then applied for a commission with the Texas National Guard the following year, but his father refused to certify his American birth for the necessary passport application.[8]

In Chihuahua, Kelly worked for American Metals Company, added fluency in Spanish to that of French and German, and completed University of Mexico correspondence courses. With the Great War over, he went to help build his father's dehydration plant in Tennessee and began dating Frances "Fanny" Mae Jeffries, a schoolteacher. Eager for further immersion in Spanish culture, he took a position as resident manager for a sisal plantation in Tegucigalpa, Honduras, returning briefly in March 1921 to marry Fanny in Chicago. It was the start of a passionate though stormy marriage, with Fanny admitting the following day she had married a Texan named McBee in 1911 but had divorced him, an action Kelly later discovered was invalid. Over the next few years, he helped Fanny McBee's family, buying her brother a truck, purchasing a house for another relative, and bailing a brother-in-law out of jail for bootlegging. They were "typical poor white trash," he belatedly realized. McBee, moreover, who, it became clear, married him for his inheritance, was thirty, not twenty-five, as she had said, and while he found her passion exciting he discovered she was unstable and vindictive. Until his father's death forced their return to the States, they lived in Honduras, where he also acted as the *New York World*'s Central American correspondent.[9]

As with his father, whatever his business involvements, he never neglected political activism. He wrote to a friend in Chihuahua during the revolution in 1919 that he was lobbying against U.S. interventionists because of his "passionate attachment" to Mexico. Among other endeavors, Kelly tackled the editor of *Leslie's Weekly* over an article entitled "What's the Matter with Mexico." Many of the mining concessions granted to American interests by President Porfirio Díaz in the 1900s, he noted, had no legal standing. It was therefore hypocritical of Americans, who "stood for honesty and fairness of dealing with all peoples," to demand millions from President Venustiano Carranza in compensation for the nationalization of those concessions when they held foreign companies operating on their soil accountable to U.S. law. Anti-imperialist philosophy, learned no doubt from his father's abhorrence of British colonialism in Ireland, was a common theme in Kelly's articles on U.S. foreign affairs, although he never singled out German imperialism or Franco's neoimperialism in the Maghreb.[10]

Kelly's anti-imperialism went hand in glove with republicanism. Felix Gras's *Reds of the Midi* stuck with him, for he cited Gras in a 1922 article for *The Nation* entitled "White Reaction in Ireland," which attacked Arthur Griffith for deserting the republican principles of Sinn Féin and Michael Collins for selling out to the British, perhaps to the extent of becoming a double agent. Kelly identified the Catholic Church as a leading force for the conservative, white reaction he had condemned in the article, opposed "as ever . . . to freedom and the progress of the Irish nation." Church hierarchy banned the Fenians in 1867, fought the Land League, and forbade the teaching of Irish history and Gaelic, although Kelly shifted some blame onto bishops appointed by the British. After Ireland's hierarchy issued a pastoral letter condemning guerrilla warfare, Kelly wrote an even more trenchant critique of the "Catholic church machine" for the *Irish World*. With English soldiers, Irish patriots at least knew what they faced, but the Roman Church, in a "most hypocritical and cowardly manner," had "sneaked into the houses of the Irish nation" in order to "stab in the back" its most devoted followers. Going back to Pope Adrian IV, who sanctioned Henry II's occupation of Ireland, Kelly noted how Rome always sacrificed the Irish to gain influence in England. It was time for the Irish to throw off the "hierarchical yoke," to trample that "serpent on their hearths." Irish folk were quite capable of managing their own affairs, and the longer they allowed Rome to "intrigue, meddle and betray the cause of freedom," the longer they would have to wait for their republic. Despite Kelly's claims to be a Presbyterian during his later support of Franco, his papers offer no evidence of church attendance or religious faith. Pittsfield had Lutheran as well as Catholic churches, but his parents advantaged themselves of neither priests nor burial plots. They were atheists, as were both their children.[11]

Issues drove Kelly, underscoring a concern for social justice if not always human rights. As he showed with his later support of regimes that abused the rights of communists, his judgment was selective, differentiating between those he felt deserving of rights versus those who abused the rights of others. In "Glimpses of the 'Klan'" by the Passerby, an article probably published in St. Louis in 1923, Kelly attacked "cowardly, hypocritical lawless bands" of Ku Klux Klansmen who "drape themselves in the American flag and prate of law and order, while they spread ruin and death about them." After working in Oklahoma's oil fields, where Klan murders were so common that the few opposition newspapers barely mentioned them, he felt safer with the savages of the Amazon. In Tulsa, Greek Americans ran the best restaurant in town, but Klansmen cast them as "vile foreigners" and tried to prevent anyone from patronizing these proud "sons of Hellas" who had fought with the Allies in the Great War. Pointing to a double murder in Mer Rouge, Louisiana, Kelly identified simple jealousy as the motivation for Klan hatred, "driving out workers whose places they coveted and the Jewish merchants whose success they envied," as well as a fundamental immorality that encouraged a Klansman to "ravage with impunity his Jewish neighbor's wife" while "hooded bands" stood ready to maltreat the husband should he dare to complain to the police. This indictment of Klan anti-Semitism would also be at odds with Kelly's later elision of Jews with communists, yet he seems not to have been racist per se. Willie Francis was a black man convicted of murdering a white drugstore owner. When the electric chair failed to snuff out Francis's life in 1946, Kelly sent a telegram petitioning Louisiana governor James H. Davis for commutation of the death sentence; a trivial anecdote perhaps, but Kelly had a half-hour walk to Pittsfield's downtown telegraph office.[12]

He was always active politically, from writing letters to editors, of which the *New York Times* printed seven during the 1920s, to becoming a grassroots activist for Robert M. La Follette's 1924 presidential campaign. In addition to canvassing and distributing leaflets, Kelly addressed several La Follette rallies up and down the East Coast, including a crowd of three thousand at Newark, New Jersey, when he spoke from the platform alongside La Follette's running mate, Senator Burton K. Wheeler (D-MT). Support for Battling Bob's blend of agrarian populism and progressive socialism might seem out of character for someone who would become America's leading Franco lobbyist. Yet Kelly was something of a latter-day mugwump, picking and choosing among issues then voting for whichever party came closest to his shopping list. He surely appreciated La Follette's scientific approach to reform, his determination to separate the federal government from corporate trusts, and his no-nonsense rhetorical style. It may be, too, that Calvin Coolidge's Calvinistic piety scared Kelly and that Democratic candidate John W. Davis was a product of the kind of machine politics he had censured in his draft *Irish World* article. For the election of 1928, Kelly supported Democrat Alfred E. Smith, and, as he made plain in a *Times* letter to the editor, he was critical of Herbert C. Hoover's alignment with "coal barons" and lack of sympathy for unemployed miners.[13]

After reorganizing the family's businesses, Kelly sailed with McBee for Guatemala in 1925, where he consulted for the Sociedad Petrolera Izabal oil concessionaire and helped draft the Guatemalan Petroleum Code. Back in the States in 1926, Kelly received a first lieutenant's commission in the U.S. Army Reserve Corps, Military Intelligence Branch, and throughout 1927–28 he and McBee traveled Central America. In 1929 he became an executive for a subsidiary of investment bank E. R. Diggs & Company, purchasing natural gas fields in West Virginia, Ohio, Kentucky, Tennessee, and Pennsylvania. He was soon running four operating companies spread over 38,000 acres with 356 gas wells, closing one deal in July 1930 worth $2 million ($60 million in 2011 dollars).[14]

He thought he was flying high, but his world was about to fall apart. After a stormy scene, no doubt, at their home in Queens, McBee tried to murder him, but the pistol's hammer hit an empty chamber. Some weeks later, she tried again, with a razor while he was asleep. Then, the following month, Diggs went bankrupt, and of the $150,000 Kelly had earned with Diggs, he was surprised to realize that McBee had spent her way through $140,000. Unable to stand the violent scenes and shocked to learn of McBee's adultery, Kelly moved to a New Jersey hotel, made a trip to Honduras, and then lived in his mother's Pittsfield home for a year, obtaining a divorce in 1932 in Nevada on the grounds of cruelty. By then, his $13,317 investment in blue-chip stocks was worthless, and the once-promising orders for dehydrated vegetables from the armed forces, arctic explorers, backpackers, and innovative homemakers across the country met with strong competition from food-processing conglomerates.[15]

With the Great Depression having sapped his wealth and dented his enthusiasm for mining engineering, Kelly turned to writing for financial support as well as intellectual enrichment. His fascination with history and his adopted Spanish identity prompted his first book-length project, *Pedro de Alvarado, Conquistador* (1932), which revealed a biographer's empathy for this conqueror of Guatemala but did not hide Alvarado's ruthlessness. Neither did Kelly try to smooth over the Inquisition or *encomienda,* although he did question whether U.S. historians worked to a double standard, hinting at the Protestant Black Legend that depicted Catholic Spaniards as depraved torturers. English colonists in North America, Kelly noted, massacred indigenous peoples, lynched blacks, and did not abolish slavery until 1863, while in

Ireland colonists committed terrible atrocities. Having halted the barbarous practices of the Aztecs, Spanish colonists, by contrast, abolished Indian slavery in 1546,
thereafter intermarrying to create a thriving heterogeneous culture. New York's
Herald Tribune thought *Alvarado* "well fitted to stand on a shelf" next to the prolific
works of R. B. Cunninghame Graham, while Albany's *Knickerbocker Press* called it a
"first class adventure story." Although Kelly did complete another academic history,
the unpublished "William Walker: A Biography," adventure fiction was his favorite
genre. He began perfecting the short story format, typically in borderlands or mining settings and with plenty of action and romance, although he would not see one
in print until 1948, when he became popular with readers of *Zane Grey's Western
Magazine*. Despite titles like "The Stewardess Wore Furs" or "Sandy McGrew's War,"
he did more than rattle out pulp fiction. Good triumphed over evil just as the right
man always won the girl's affections, yet he avoided preachy moralizing and portrayed his characters warts and all. On his death in 1954, he had written a hundred
short stories and published at least twenty. And as the mood took him, he would
pen a poem, sixteen of which are extant.[16]

Kelly's Anticommunism

"I am painfully aware of how far I fall short of [my father's] great attainments in
every field of endeavor," Kelly wrote dejectedly to his mother. Still, now that he
was free of the twelve-hour corporate days and the weeks spent moving from
one hotel room to another, he had more time to think. Talented, experienced,
in his midthirties with the reputation of an overachieving father to live up to, he
was not about to let a failed marriage or a pending bankruptcy hold him back. If
the American system that had treated his family so well was out of sorts, then it
was his duty to help find a cure. Rooted in a world economy halved by imperialism and quartered by socialist revolution and shackled by protectionist tariffs,
America's ills were intractable; indeed, it would take another hot war to regain
parity, followed by four decades of cold war to globalize trade. But in 1932—four
years before revolutionary civil war struck Spain—Kelly decided that Soviet communism was the most debilitating problem facing his homeland. A dozen years
earlier, during negotiations with Soviet commerce officials over the exportation
of Cooke-Kelly dehydration technology, Kelly probably shared his father's respect
for the USSR's socialist ideals and commitment to workers' rights. What happened to switch this left-leaning liberal to such strident anticommunism?[17]

   Reaction, rather than *conservatism*, was his term of choice in *The Nation* article. His early political writings show that he used *conservatism* as a synonym for
American-style capitalism in the context of the fight against communism, while
liberal became synonymous with *pink*, or soft on communism. These distinctions

are more than semantic, for Kelly was intrinsically liberal, and several of his ideas for reforming American society were socialistic. Even though his activism for Franco, combined with opposition to the New Deal state, would force him ever further to what most commentators would term the political Right, in 1940 he was still calling for a government-mandated ceiling of 8 percent on corporate profits, with the excess going directly into workers' paychecks. So in June 1932, when he wrote "Wanted: A Conservative Counter Attack," his targets were communists, not reformist liberals or progressives.[18]

Kelly observed in "Counter Attack" how historians criticized the citizens of overthrown civilizations throughout the ages for their apathy in defending their institutions, concluding that such "supine-ness" justified the upheaval. How would historians judge Americans were their nation to become a Soviet satellite? Kelly identified a world split between two competing ideologies: "Sovietism" versus "Capitalism, or Conservatism." Just as in the past, when America could not exist "half slave and half free," neither could these ideologies exist side by side. "One or the other must perish." He blamed Russian revolutionaries for prolonging the recession through the closing of trade, the skewing of their internal market, and the cut-price dumping of raw materials mined by gulag slaves. Neither would Washington's current initiative to recognize the USSR help, he argued, for Moscow lacked the capital to pay for imported U.S. machinery. With the exception of Benito Mussolini's Italy, European countries had become "fertile breeding grounds for the Communist germ." And in America, midwesterners—not just laborers but middling folks who had seen their savings swept away—were now so despondent that they would embrace a communist form of government. Yet such a government was fast becoming a reality, with "regulatory legislation taxing and restricting individual initiative," while the hordes of bureaucrats prying into every private effort were "cousins but once removed from the Commissar." Democracy, Kelly admitted, had failed to provide for the needs of a modern industrialized nation, except perhaps in Switzerland, which was sufficiently small and endowed with a high percentage of intelligent and industrious conservatives. While he was sure the communist movement "must in time fail of itself," that did not lessen the immediate danger, as Marxist doctrines were so enticing. He described a theoretical state capable of fighting communism, "a bulwark of conservatism against chaos." In order to offset "the absolutism of the Communist movement," it would necessarily have to be a "benevolent autocracy," for how else to avoid "the endless discussions, factions and 'isms' of a democratic form of government."[19]

Here, then, is the most compelling explanation for what would become Kelly's pro-Franco brand of anticommunism. His background—multiethnic, anarchist parents, his father's library, liberal education, global travel—emphasized the imperative of individual liberty and the futility of absolutism, yet he evidently understood the intrinsic problem of both communism and anticommunism: they were absolutist arguments. Still, as he would stress after 1936, if Americans learned to understand the chaos that revolution in Spain had caused and realized that Franco's response was necessary to restore order, then perhaps they would re-embrace traditional American values, thereby avoiding authoritarian absolutism at home. As Kelly intimated in "Counter Attack," when a mass movement occurred in a democratic society, short of allowing a revolution of some sort, curtailment of the movement required the suspension of democracy. Yet his mention of "factions and 'isms'" pointed back to a founding principle of Americanism. Far from advocating a democracy for the new United States, Thomas Jefferson and James Madison envisaged a meritocracy, or "benevolent autocracy," as Kelly put it.[20]

Secondary explicators of Kelly's anticommunism are, first, that he had absorbed from his individualist anarchist parents and aunt a distrust of collectivists, whose ideology in practice always restricted individual liberty. Second, as with conservatives who once had been enthusiastic communists, such as George E. Sokolsky, Kelly no doubt reconsidered his sympathies on learning of the Soviet gulags and Joseph Stalin's purges.[21]

Kelly developed his anticommunism in revolutionary Latin America, and his experiences there may explain why he was so quick to tout the Spanish Civil War as an example of what he believed was coming to the United States. Estimating the extent of Kelly's extrabusiness activities during his years in Central America is problematic, but the U.S. Army apparently encouraged certain officers to act in their country's best interests as they saw fit. In 1934 Kelly either coauthored or ghostwrote *The Incurable Filibuster: Adventures of Col. Dean Ivan Lamb,* a chronicle of Lamb's extraordinary exploits so realistically told as to beg the question of Kelly's own activities while a reserve officer. Lamb's preface, which served as his mission statement, affirmed this four-part code: "I do not make war upon noncombatants, betray a cause once chosen, oppose the United States, or serve communism." Lamb noted that his warring in Nicaragua received Washington's "blessing"; his service in Mexico and Guatemala had the "well-nigh unanimous" backing of public opinion; and his presence in Rio Grande do Sul was in response to a massacre of women and children by Brazilian government forces to which Lamb was an eyewitness. It was only in Paraguay, he suggested, that his filibustering lacked in fundamental significance.[22]

Although Kelly may not have fought with Lamb, who flew a biplane from one trouble spot to the next (he shot down five German aircraft during World War I), Kelly assisted U.S. Army Intelligence in some capacity, for his correspondence mentions working with Luke E. Hart, later Supreme Advocate of the Knights of Columbus, St. Louis, "on the investigation of communism in Mexico in 1934." He gave a talk to an army group in January 1936 entitled "Personal Reminiscences of a Soldier of Fortune in Carranza's Army," so it appears he filibustered in Mexico in 1918. But as he indicated in "The Monroe Doctrine," a letter to the *New York Times* in 1929,

Kelly believed that while Old World powers must keep out of Latin America, it was unethical for the United States to meddle in the affairs of other nation-states, even when it came to protecting U.S. interests. It is likely, therefore, that he would have limited his ad hoc activities in Mexico to anticommunism, to keeping Soviet influence out of the Western Hemisphere.[23]

When not drumming up mining consultancy work or fighting communism in Mexico, Kelly was courting Celia M. Cameron, the daughter of a Parkersburg, West Virginia, mine operator. They married on 5 June 1935, traveling to Guatemala for their honeymoon before renting a home in Charleston, West Virginia. When McBee heard of the marriage, she threatened Cameron, hired detectives to tap Kelly's telephone, and even attempted to kidnap him in New Jersey. McBee claimed that Kelly married Cameron for her money (an unlikely charge, since Kelly regularly sent Cameron the bulk of his income, including $5,062 [$151,860] during the first year of their marriage). Now at the rank of captain, Kelly transferred his U.S. Army Reserve posting to the Fifth Corps in Charleston, where his fellow officers so admired his enthusiasm and organizational skills that they elected him president of the Kanawha Chapter of the Reserve Officers Association (ROA). By 1936 he headed the Fifth Corps's ROA Committee on Subversive Activities. Through socializing with army officers, he met a chemical engineer named George E. Deatherage, who had just formed a nationalist organization called the Knights of the White Camellia. In 1938 Deatherage tried to recruit officers to serve under Maj. Gen. George Van Horn Moseley in the event that communists took over the federal government. While Deatherage did contribute $750 to the ROA fund in support of Kelly's investigations, there is no evidence that Kelly took Deatherage's counterrevolutionary schemes seriously.[24]

Hayes Pickelsimer, a banker at Charleston's Kanawha Valley Bank, told FBI agent Andrew K. Ugden in mid-December 1941 that Kelly visited the bank with Deatherage in 1937–38 to raise support for the Knights. But when Agent Ralph V. Reed interviewed him again in August 1943, Pickelsimer could not remember meeting Deatherage and recalled that Kelly came to the bank with others seeking a loan to buy guns so that independent miners could protect themselves against "labor trouble." Nat Deutsch, a clothing store owner who had known Cameron for years, reported to Ugden in 1941 that he stopped round the house where Cameron and Kelly were living, probably in late summer 1935, and that Cameron mentioned her husband was in the office over the garage, so Deutsch walked in without knocking, whereupon he saw that Kelly had "a number of large bundles [of] Nazi circulars and literature" on the floor. Yet as with the Pickelsimer stories, when Reed interviewed Deutsch in 1943 he was "unable to definitely describe the circulars as being 'Nazi circulars,'" adding that on mentioning them to Cameron, she said they were not "Nazi circulars." An explanation for the discrepancies in both sets of interviews is that the witnesses, who no doubt heard accusations on

Walter Winchell's popular *Jergens Journal* radio show that Kelly was a Nazi agent, were responding to leading questions by Ugden. When Reed asked specific, probing questions thirty months later, neither witness could remember what they had earlier imagined. If their surnames are any guide, then Pickelsimer and Deutsch were both German Americans, and it is likely that immediately after Pearl Harbor in December 1941, they would have been trying to impress their neighbors—and an aggressive FBI agent—with their loyalty. What better way than to expose a Nazi agent distributing anti-Semitic propaganda?[25]

Still, in 1935 Kelly did admire Nazi Germany and despise Jewish communists, yet qualifying those positions is as problematic as it is context dependent. Writing to his mother in October 1933 to thank her for homemade cookies and to apologize that he could not send her more money for coal, Kelly was pleased to note that "Hitler is doing very well and exposing the shocking hypocrisy of the [Washington] 'disarmament conference' [of 1922]." Other than a *German Short-wave Station: North America Program* booklet for May 1938, indicating that Helen listened to Berlin radio, there is no record of his mother's view, though it was probably positive, for German radio successfully projected Nazism's attractions. As one radio program director noted in 1946, few international broadcasters were "ardent Nazis," while many were "very critical of the Party line." Neither is there much to grasp in Kelly's writings over the next ten years to clarify his opinion of Nazi Germany. At the end of November 1937, he spent three weeks in Berlin on business, but besides implying that Nazism trumped communism, he made no mention of Adolf Hitler's regime on his return. Following the Spanish Civil War, if not before it, whatever animus Kelly felt toward Jews apparently stemmed from his observation that many Soviet communists as well as communist radicals in the Western Hemisphere were Jews. If his prejudice was racist rather than ideological, then it is difficult to explain his expressions of disgust at the persecution of Jews by Klansmen in his "Glimpses of the 'Klan'" article.[26]

By the summer of 1936, Cameron and Kelly were no longer sharing their Charleston home. She moved back to her parents' house while he divided his time between his Manhattan office and trips to see her in Parkersburg. Physical intimacy waned, but love did not. They maintained close contact until Cameron's death, with Kelly sending her gifts of clothes or books and visiting whenever he could. No doubt they struggled with the practicalities of the relationship. Kelly alternated periods of typing or reading at home with geological surveying or socializing in the city. In keeping with Theodore Roosevelt's "doctrine of the strenuous life," in which he had immersed himself as a youth, Kelly's world was intense, active, and masculine. Cameron, a West Virginia girl with little interest in bright lights and hurly-burly, was dying of tuberculosis, and her mother, a chronic diabetic, was almost blind. He saw hers as a feminine world of coping and care giving, no less active but one at which Kelly surely chafed.[27]

Since 1930, consulting for the growing natural gas industry accounted for the bulk of Kelly's income. To the New Deal state, though, utility companies were monopolistic, while interstate grids of gas pipelines were easy targets for regulation. In 1934 the Securities and Exchange Act made it hard for companies to raise funds for exploration; after the Federal Trade Commission reported that eleven holding companies owned a quarter of U.S. pipelines, Congress passed the restrictive Public Utility Holding Company Act (1935); finally, in 1938, the Natural Gas Act gave the federal government full regulatory powers, from prices to pipelines. This string of measures ruined Kelly's consultancy enterprise; ironically, he earned his last fees by testifying as an expert witness for companies such as United Fuel Gas Company in rate cases brought by the government. He felt that the government was guilty of unnecessary—and counterproductive—meddling in the affairs of private business, and he never forgave the Roosevelt administration, not so much for his financial loss but for damaging an industry that produced a natural resource of value to all Americans.[28]

Kelly Networks Talbot and Cárdenas

Kelly's turn to writing, lecturing, and political activism was a perfect match for his talents and interests. After responding to Colonel Alfonte's request for research on Spain's civil war, he was soon presenting his findings at meetings of U.S. Army officers, initially in the South and Midwest but then, by the spring of 1937—following his transfer to Washington and then Manhattan's Governor's Island army base—up and down the East Coast. His first lectures in December 1936 stressed the importance of studying Popular Front propaganda techniques. "Abetted by radical columnists," the Comintern, Kelly explained, had blanketed popular opinion, convincing Americans that Franco was slaughtering innocent children in Madrid—a theater of war, he lamely suggested, the Loyalists themselves selected—while stories of Loyalist atrocities could only be "Fascist or Catholic propaganda."[29]

Until he could no longer make rent in mid-1937, Kelly kept up appearances for his engineering consultancy from an office at 17 Battery Place, a magnificent art deco building at Manhattan's southern tip, while lodging in a clapboard row house on a leafy side street in the Bergen section of Jersey City. It was a tedious commute by trolley and ferry, but the affordable and quiet lodgings kept him out of the jurisdictional clutches of McBee's detectives, who were always hounding him for alimony. New York City was the hub of Spanish Civil War activism, so it was inevitable that he would make contact with Nationalist campaigners, whom he evidently impressed. One of them, Manuel Alonso, arranged for him to address a group of elites vacationing in Bar Harbor, Maine. After traveling there at his own expense, Kelly spoke at a theater owned by George McKay, a local business and civic leader. Many attendees came at the recommendation of Rev. Dr. Guy Wilson, pastor of the Clark Memorial Methodist Episcopal Church, so it was far from being a Catholic audience.[30]

Although the meeting's coordinator, Thomas P. Abello, introduced him as a captain in the U.S. Army Reserve, Kelly stressed that he spoke in a private capacity, as an "American citizen who hates and loathes Communism." He had not traveled to Bar Harbor to defend Franco but to explain the perils of ignoring Spain's fate. Complacent Americans might snub Spain, but it was a matter "of vital, indeed frightful importance to us that our American traditions, that our form of government, that our democracy be maintained unimpaired." "It cannot happen here" was the most dangerous phrase in any language, and Spaniards had said as much in February 1936. Now they suffered "a struggle of the best elements against the worst—of Government against Anarchy—of Christianity against atheistic Communism." Americans must learn to comprehend the insidiousness of the Popular Front. "Red propaganda," Kelly stressed, "has been vociferous, overwhelming and well financed." Numerous "Red agencies, committees, boards, associations, and other gatherings of the devil's brood" were swinging their "high powered publicity machines" into the Comintern's service. Some six hundred "red and pink newspapers and magazines" in America were shrieking about an assault on democracy in Spain. Through their constant war coverage, Popular Front journalists had cleverly sugarcoated the word *communism,* turning it into a respectable defender of republicanism and democracy. Yet what was at stake was "Red democracy," and the Comintern's ultimate aim was not Spain but capitalism's powerhouse, the United States. While there were only fifty thousand CPUSA members, these were essentially the "officers of the Red movement," Kelly explained. To receive a membership card, a communist apprentice "must demonstrate his fanaticism and his hatred of tradition and religion." Already, two million Americans sympathized with Stalin's aims, though they did not hold CPUSA cards. In 1918 Russia had fallen to 79,000 communists; 1.5 million party members now controlled a population of 180 million. Kelly's message was plain: Americans who love true democracy must learn from Spain and do their utmost to fight communism.[31]

According to Abello, there was "nothing but praise" for Kelly's carefully scripted, clearly delivered speech, which had to win over "a very skeptical audience." Kelly "proved to be a great speaker" who talked like a diplomat, handled questions deftly, and knew "more about the Spanish tragedy than any other American I have heard before." Several of the attendees—including Mrs. W. S. Moore, daughter of Joseph Pulitzer, founder of the *New York World*—asked if Kelly could speak again to a "private reunion of prominent people" summering in Bar Harbor. Consequent to the speech, via either Alonso or Abello, Kelly made contact with Father Francis X. Talbot, through whom he would tap into a wellspring of sympathy among Catholics for the Nationalist cause, sympathy that his articles and speeches over the next two years would conflate with anticommunist Americanism.[32]

Born into an Irish American family in Philadelphia in 1889, Talbot joined the Society of Jesus in 1906, received ordination in 1921, and became a literary editor of the influential Jesuit weekly magazine *America* two years later. He accepted Catholicism as fundamental, sought knowledge in God's service, and strove to make his writings a vehicle for Christ's message of salvation to Americans. An interest in colonial history prompted him to study the Huron, a confederation of four Iroquoian tribes inhabiting the region between Lakes Huron and Ontario. Yet in *Saint Among Savages: The Life of Isaac Jogues* (1935), the Huron served to demonstrate Catholicism's civilizing power. Jogues, a Jesuit missionary full of youthful enthusiasm, arrived among the Huron from Renaissance France in 1636, just as the savages were grappling with a deadly mix of smallpox and typhus. Working to understand native culture and master a new language while enduring a litany of privations, he eventually won some converts, but this exacerbated intertribal tensions at a time of turmoil. Captured during the ensuing conflict, Jogues watched his new charges tortured to death before suffering himself; later, a hatchet blow to the skull dispatched him to martyrdom. Talbot described the fate of Jogues and his converts in the goriest of detail, contrasting savage heathens with civilized European colonists. *Saint Among Savages* was really a study into the virtuous origins of a Catholic American identity.[33]

In 1936, the Jesuit hierarchy rewarded Talbot's bookish endeavors by promoting him to the editor's office. Taciturnity never inhibited Talbot from politicizing *America*, perhaps because he drew so much credence from his unshakeable faith. Of all the causes he tackled during his eight-year tenure, none compared to his championship of Nationalist Spain. With the civil war coinciding with his promotion, he no doubt sensed God's purpose, although Spanish history and culture had long enthralled him. One of his first endeavors was to form the America Spanish Relief Fund (ASRF) to provide aid to the Nationalist zone through Spain's primate, Cardinal Isidro Gomá. Because public opinion was "almost wholly in favor" of the Loyalists, he explained to Gomá, agencies "in close alliance with Spanish Communists" received the bulk of aid contributions, which they forwarded "solely to the areas in Spain controlled by the Socialists, Communists and anarchists." This was "a most distressing situation for us Catholics," and one he intended to remedy. Talbot's ASRF was by far the most successful pro-Nationalist aid organization, collecting $73,500 ($2.2 million), which he wired to Gomá's London bank for fear that America's pro-Loyalist Red Cross would misdirect the aid. Still, ASRF aid was paltry compared with Loyalist fund-raising, which exceeded it twenty-five-fold. Humanitarian fund-raising, it is sad to observe, was no less partisan than lobbying over foreign policy, so when a mailing solicited contributions for Spanish orphans, potential donors generally understood that the orphans in question were strictly those on a particular side of the front line.[34]

Talbot found Franco's liberation of Toledo's besieged Alcázar early in the war so morally inspiring that he prepared a gushing foreword for *The Cadets of the*

Alcazar, published by the Paulist Press as a translation of a French original. Since February 1936, a "growing dominance of foreign propaganda" had been throttling the very "soul of Spain," Talbot asserted. Once a "Communist minority" had usurped its government, a Christian majority had no other course but an appeal to arms to save itself from "foreign aggression." Thus, Franco led "the counter revolt" against the junta of labor leader Francisco Largo Caballero. With anarcho-communist militia from Madrid advancing on unprepared Toledo, two thousand terrified men, women, and children fled to Col. José Moscardó's fortress. For sixty-eight days they were "torn by airbombs, battered by artillery, sprayed by bullets." Moscardó even refused to ransom his post for his beloved son, whom the militia had captured and later executed. Massive mines reduced the ancient masonry to rubble. With capitulation imminent, Franco arrived to lift the siege, so out of the civil war's tragedy was "born one of the most heroic exploits of all Spanish history." But as with the Huron, Toledo's noble defenders were really serving Talbot's Catholic American agenda. Just "as in our own West Point," the Alcázar's young cadets, pledged to an "unbreakable fidelity to their country," had "gloriously sacrificed their lives for their fatherland." Though its mighty towers crumbled, its defenders' faith stood resolute. For Talbot, Spain's Alcázar epitomized the triumph of civilizing Christianity over the godless savagery of communism.[35]

Talbot made his program for a Catholic America clear during an address at the Poughkeepsie Civic Forum in April 1938 on the role of organized religions within democratic societies. He observed that the previous two speakers were a Jew, who represented "a religion and a race that has kept its identity" throughout history, and a Protestant, who represented some three hundred denominations that "preserve their complete identity and do not accept a centralized authority." As a Catholic, he represented something quite different. His Catholicism included "all known races" and gloried in their embrace. Insisting on a "single code of doctrine and morality," it spanned every nation: Catholicism was a "supranational" identity. Defining his attitude toward government was easy, for Christ had defined it: "Render, therefore, to Caesar the things that *are* Caesar's, and to God the things that *are* God's." For two thousand years, governments had come and gone, yet the Church always prevailed, for it was God's church. All Talbot asked from government was the freedom to worship. He had no more difficulty with Italy's Fascist dictatorship than he had with American democracy, because Mussolini "recognized the place of God" in his regime. Neither was Germany's dictatorship a problem for Catholicism, "except in so far as Nazism invades the spiritual supremacy of the Church," creating an idolatry of state and Führer while suppressing the free exercise of worship. But the Church did have a problem: "For the first time in Christian history," man had erected a government "on the principle of atheism." Consequently, "in the three Communist States [of] Russia, Mexico and Loyalist Spain," the Church confronted its potential doom. Spanish communists, not only as "irresponsible fanatics" but also through the "direct action of a Government that misrepresented the will of the Spanish people," destroyed churches, banned religious observance, and now were busy rearing a new generation to atheism. When irreligious dictatorships trampled organized religion, God's faithful must resist by all spiritual means, protest by all legitimate means, and pray that God will save his people, and, when these means fail, they must—like Jogues—choose "Martyrdom" in defense of God.[36]

At the start of his address, Talbot expressed satisfaction with the meeting's format, because panelists were "explaining [their] positions, not debating them"; it was a true forum, whose purpose was "to clarify issues" rather than "intensify discords." Talbot was mincing words. As an Irish Catholic American, Talbot was arguing with a Jewish American and a Protestant American over the right to define Americanism. Despite Talbot's claim that Catholic identity was supranational, the very act of arguing the point at a civic forum in Poughkeepsie—significant for its proximity to Roosevelt's country estate—was itself a project in national identity construction. Historian Eric J. Hobsbawm charts the emergence of antifascist nationalism in the context of the Great Debate's "international ideological civil war." Hobsbawm theorizes that French, British, or Italian workers and intellectuals who sided with Spain's Loyalists "made an international choice," but one that "happened to reinforce national sentiment" at home. What works for pro-Loyalist socialism in European nation-states should serve as well—if not better—for modeling pro-Franco Catholicism in America. During the troubled times of the Great Debate, the anxious argument over national identity was not really about specific attributes of language, music, history, festivals, or, as Talbot would have it, religious denomination. Nor was it a matter of state sovereignty, for America was intrinsically safe, bounded by vast oceans and tamed neighbors. It was about political identity, which, as Karl Marx prophesied, once seemed so solid but now threatened to melt into air.[37]

Talbot professed to be supporting Nationalist Spain because Franco was crusading for supranational Catholicism, but the preservation of nationalistic Americanism was his underlying intent. Kelly was no Catholic, yet he shared Talbot's political faith. Indeed, despite dissimilar backgrounds and personalities, Talbot and Kelly had much in common. Both prized learning and enjoyed writing. Both claimed Irish heritage, and were fascinated with Spanish culture and history. From a shared love for their adopted homeland, both feared for its health. Hence, nothing troubled them more than the advance of international communism. "I have studied intensively the inroads of Communism," Kelly wrote later, "which I regard as a major menace to the American way of life." Common cause united their trajectories, which, in concert, developed a reciprocal dynamism. If Talbot understood that Kelly was an atheist, then he conveniently forgot the fact. For his part, Kelly could draw on his mother's Lutheran upbringing to promote himself as a Protestant, the ideal credential for a Franco lobbyist.[38]

At the same time as Kelly was meeting pro-Franco Catholics through his association with Talbot, he was developing another network via Juan Francisco de Cárdenas, who had earlier been Spain's ambassador in both Washington and Paris but now ran an unofficial embassy for Franco's Nationalist government from a suite at the Ritz-Carlton Hotel overlooking Manhattan's Central Park. In mid-April 1937, Cárdenas sent Kelly literature on Spain, and the two became acquainted a short time later. Production of the English translation of *Cadets of the Alcazar* was Cárdenas's idea, and Kelly was able to suggest a bookshop on Wall Street for local distribution, one owned by a Mrs. Evelyn Newkirk, who had "very good contacts with people who would naturally be sympathetic to the Nationalist cause."[39]

Building an effective network through influential elites was one of four features of Kelly's activism, along with writing, speechmaking, and personal initiative. In this latter category during the first half of 1937, he worked to hamper the progress to Loyalist Spain of International Brigade volunteers, as well as trying to expose Loyalist propagandists who entered America as aliens. Whether his leads came from operatives in army intelligence or unofficially through his own anticommunist grapevine is unclear. One source was J. G., who sent Kelly several lists of Cuban and Italian Americans to whom the Spanish consul general in New York was issuing false passports under assumed Spanish names in full knowledge that the recipients would be traveling through France to the Loyalist zone for enlistment. Kelly then transmitted the names to his State Department contact, Ruth B. Shipley, chief of the Passport Division. During March, as he informed Shipley, New York's Italian Anti-Fascist Committee selected eleven recruits, obtained illegal Spanish passports, and paid their passage to France; none of the eleven spoke Spanish, and all held U.S. passports, which would otherwise have precluded their transit to Spain. In this case, Kelly's information came too late for Shipley to act. A note attached to Kelly's letter in State Department files indicates that all eleven received tickets from World Tourists, Inc. (a Moscow-owned travel agency operated by Comintern agent Jacob Golos), sailed on the *President Harding,* and disembarked at Le Havre on 31 March. CPUSA leader Earl Browder later stated that he was "the chief organizer" of the U.S. volunteers who formed the Abraham Lincoln Brigade (ALB), a name he chose to emphasize "the political aim to preserve the republic, not to turn the war into a socialist revolution."[40]

Kelly also tried to make life difficult for Loyalists entering the United States. He wrote to Secretary of State Cordell Hull, pointing out that Americans who enlisted in a foreign army or swore allegiance to a foreign government automatically forfeited citizenship. Immigration officials should therefore classify ALB veterans returning from Spain as aliens. In June he received information that "a notorious anarchist named Pena" had left Paris traveling on a false Italian passport issued to Luigi Bianchi, with the "avowed intention of 'liquidating' enemies of the red Spanish regime" in America. Shipley sent the information to the Immigration and Naturalization Service, which posted lookout notices but did not apprehend the suspect. Kelly also used Shipley as a funnel for general information. On 24 June 1937, he told her that a Soviet embassy official, who had been drinking vodka with one of his contacts, boasted how Russian pilots, acting independently of the Loyalist government, had flown the Tupolev bombers that attacked the German battleship *Deutschland,* anchored at Ibiza on 26 May, killing more than thirty sailors. Eighteen Soviet bombers, flown by Soviet pilots, were on station at Valencia, and Kelly's source even named three of the pilots. While this story has an anecdotal ring, accounts written in the 1970s prove its accuracy, suggesting that Kelly rarely shot from the hip.[41]

In mid-1937, Cárdenas decided to finance a pro-Nationalist monthly magazine, and he introduced Kelly to its staff, publisher Miguel Echegaray, treasurer Javier Gaytan de Ayala, and editor Joseph M. Bayo. Unlike its politicized pro-Loyalist counterpart *News of Spain,* Echegaray's *Spain* was an attractive glossy publication with articles on Spanish culture and history to interest a general reader. From the first edition in October 1937, Kelly was responsible for "Military Operations," which tracked the course of the war itself. Material for this column came in the form of reports from Luis María de Lojendio in the Nationalist zone, which Kelly then translated and adapted to suit *Spain's* American readership. In addition to nineteen "Military Operations," Kelly wrote forty-one articles for *Spain* on subjects ranging from sixteenth-century conquistadores to postwar reconstruction. Also in October, Kelly published his first article in Talbot's *America,* "Foresworn Americans Serve Red Cause in Spain," which built a case for the traitorous duplicity of ALB volunteers. Continuing on a regular basis until the end of 1941, *America* carried twenty-seven articles by Kelly.[42]

Forbes and Sedgwick Tour Nationalist Spain

In the fall of 1937, Cárdenas invited W. Cameron Forbes to lunch at the Ritz-Carlton. A sagacious, private, and competitive bachelor of sixty-seven, Forbes had retired from a frustrating public service career to socialize in Boston's elite clubs and train polo ponies at his Norwood farm, although he retained directorships in several U.S. conglomerates, including United Fruit, Stone & Webster, and AT&T (which his father, railroad tycoon William Hathaway Forbes, had bankrolled). Cárdenas had a proposition for Forbes, whom he had met through diplomatic circles when Forbes was governor of the Philippines (1903–13) and later ambassador to Japan (1930–32). As Forbes said in his memoir, the press, "honeycombed" with "Communistic agents working under cover," was cleverly misinforming the American public to the effect that Madrid's Republic was "fighting the battle of democracy," whereas, in truth, Loyalists were ruthless Marxists "indulging in unheard of atrocities and wholesale slaughter of the bourgeois class." If a group of "responsible Americans sufficiently well known so that their testimony would carry weight" were to tour Spain as Franco's guests, then they might be able to redress the misperception by explaining how Franco was simply attempting to rid Spaniards of a "hideous Soviet-directed government then running wild in their country." Cárdenas proposed Forbes—a fluent Spanish speaker—to head the tour.[43]

With his railroad magnate father on one side and his grandfather Ralph Waldo Emerson on the other, Forbes had the right family background. A Brahmin traditionalist turned economic technocrat—to borrow historian Emily S. Rosenberg's term—his governorship of the Philippines promoted modernization with a legacy of schools, macadam roads, telephones, and accountancy systems. From smallpox vaccinations to irrigation projects to freedom of speech, he devoted his administration to the Filipinos' well-being. But as his magisterial *The Philippine Islands* (1928) indicates, his larger mission was establishing an ordered world—made safe for U.S. trade—while solidifying American identity through imprinting it onto an Americanized Filipino Other. A quarter of the 600-page first volume covers the imposition of order through police, courts, and prisons. It dwells on tribal peoples and is intent on proving that the natives' inherent backwardness advanced only through the efforts of altruistic Westerners. "Philippine history," Forbes professed, "beg[an] with the death of Magellan," as if the archipelago came as an empty slate primed for civilizing Western chalk. Yet Forbes's oft-stated public policy of postponing independence alienated Manila's elites and hampered his administration. Perhaps he appreciated the value of maintaining an extension of the civilized American self on primitive foreign soil, a living example of order through progress, an opportunity to contrast the goodness of Americanization against the propensity of non-Americans to revert to a state of nature. He vindicated his rationale—that Filipinos were insufficiently advanced along civilization's road to go it alone—when, as chairman of President Herbert Hoover's commission to Haiti in 1930, he recommended rapid Haitianization of government before a phased U.S. withdrawal, reluctantly choosing self-determination for Haitians over the interclass bloodshed that he knew would ensue.[44]

Forbes never mentioned why he accepted Cárdenas's offer, although loyalty to a friend and a love of Spain, to which he had not traveled since 1915, were reasons enough, as was the fact that Loyalist revolutionaries now controlled much of Spain's telephone system, which was built and hitherto run by International Telephone and Telegraph (ITT), an AT&T subsidiary, of which Forbes was a director and shareholder. Yet it was probably Forbes's educated faith in progress as challenged by Soviet-directed forces of international communism that propelled him to Nationalist Spain. To accompany him, Forbes asked his friend Ellery Sedgwick, who "jumped at the chance."[45]

Moral condemnation of the Sacco-Vanzetti verdict and promotion of the presidential candidacy of a Catholic, Alfred E. Smith, were but two of the causes championed by Sedgwick during his formative editorship of the *Atlantic Monthly* (1908–38). During the period relevant here, 1936–39, Sedgwick published more than four hundred writers, including E. M. Forster, Bertrand Russell, Robert Frost, Klaus Mann, W. B. Yeats, Antoine de Saint Exupéry, Gertrude Stein, Virginia Woolf, and John Steinbeck, while maintaining a loyal readership of 135,000. Influential and respected, the liberal-progressive *Atlantic* defined intellectual discourse in the 1930s much as the *New York Review of Books* would do later. Many readers were therefore shocked when Sedgwick made Franco his last great cause. In addition to an abhorrence of communism held naturally by old-stock Yankees, Sedgwick would seem to have had four further motivations for visiting Spain: a desire to unearth "the facts" behind press stories of Nationalist atrocities; a translation of his Episcopalian piety into sympathy with the plight of persecuted Spanish clergy; the need to distance himself from the recent loss of Mabel Cabot, his wife of thirty-three years; and a desire to investigate whether authoritarian rule facilitated progressive reforms.[46]

Intent on immersing himself in the undertaking, Sedgwick reread *Don Quixote,* Miguel de Cervantes's story of a marvelous quest for goodness in a corrupt society that all too often reduces individual heroism to acts of madness, and contacted learned friends for advice. Seeking information on Franco's relationship with the Catholic hierarchy, he wrote to Boston's Cardinal William O'Connell, stressing confidentiality, for nothing was "more distasteful" than seeming to be "connected with any form of propaganda." In a letter to Manhattan attorney John E. Lockwood, Sedgwick emphasized he was going as a nonpartisan observer with a dislike for "both parties to the quarrel" in Spain. And to *New York Times* editor-in-chief John Finley, after claiming that his mind was "altogether open," Sedgwick even evoked Mercutio's dying curse on "both their houses." He also contacted several Harvard professors, including historian Roger Bigelow Merriman, and, of most interest to this study, romance language chair Jerry D. M. Ford. Indicative of a tacit support for Franco among American elites—which I argue was more widespread than prevailing historiography allows—Ford confessed to Sedgwick, "My own sympathies have been from the start with Franco," but in deference to pro-Loyalist colleagues at Harvard, "I have kept absolutely quiet," refusing "again and again to sign [pro-Franco] manifestoes of any kind."[47]

Having pulled strings with Undersecretary Sumner Welles at the State Department, which was then prohibiting travel to Spain, Forbes procured visas for Sedgwick and himself. Steamer trunks packed, the adventurous duo stepped aboard an Italian ocean liner in early January 1938. After a fast, five-and-a-half-day Atlantic crossing, they disembarked at Gibraltar, where their tour guide around southern Spain, Carlos Ferrendez of the Tabacalera Company, met them. Forbes noted proudly the next day that of the cars parked outside their Málaga hotel, four were American made. And it may have been in Málaga—peaceful at last after six thousand executions by both sides and twelve months of Nationalist control—that the avowedly nonpartisan Sedgwick had an epiphany. He was thrilled to witness a progressive's dream come true: the bulldozing of slums and the construction by the state of affordable housing, which the local government either rented to workers for a low rate or, with a small premium, as a lease-purchase option. Next, they toured Tabacalera olive refineries and soap manufacturing plants in Seville, where a manager explained how loyal workers were now "overjoyed and relieved" that they no longer had to pay a weekly tribute to the old Republic's anarchist factory syndicates. At lunch at the Hotel Andalucía, the province's military governor, Gonzalo Queipo de Llano, a competent soldier, voluble radio broadcaster, and corporatist administrator who had earned the nickname "the Social General," joined them. To a question by Forbes, Queipo acknowledged a still "virulent" "Red menace," but felt that a combination of good leadership and just treatment was the remedy. "Given justice in regard to wages and improved living conditions," common people would shun communism and return to the capitalist fold.[48]

Sedgwick insisted on visiting Badajoz near the Portuguese border, the scene of a reputed massacre of civilians by the Moors of Col. Juan Yagüe's Nationalist army, accounts of which had received extensive U.S. press coverage. After interviewing eyewitnesses, Sedgwick and Forbes inspected the walls of the bullring (the purported scene of the crime), where they found traces of bomb damage but no scarring from machine gun bullets. Although they uncovered evidence of executions by "the Reds" and accounts of Nationalist bombing, they concluded that "the Whites" had killed more than four hundred combatants and a few civilians during the battle for the city but had not perpetrated an atrocity. Over the next ten days, they toured Nationalist Spain, discussing Forbes's famous treatise *As to Polo* (1919) with cavalry officers, enjoying their hosts' excellent hospitality, and marveling at the country's speedy return to order, industry, and economic prosperity.[49]

Back in Boston, the travelers could not contain their enthusiasm for Franco's Spain. Forbes gave a rosy press interview that offended pro-Loyalist sensibilities. *Time* magazine's pro-Loyalist editor complained that William Randolph Hearst's *New York Journal* had "favored" Forbes with its striking headline, "EX-ENVOY FORBES HAILS FRANCO RULE—People Happy and Have Plenty in Nationalist Spain"—yet had rejected as leftist propaganda a piece in Walter Winchell's syndicated column by Hollywood's Lillian Hellman, who had recently returned from Loyalist Madrid. Uncomfortable with the media spotlight, the reserved Brahmin switched to behind-the-scenes networking of sympathetic elites, a more efficacious tactic anyway, given the weight that President Franklin D. Roosevelt placed on leading opinions. Forbes prepared a glowing lecture that he delivered with much acclaim to august audiences at a dozen venues, including Baltimore's University Club, three gatherings in Georgia, and one in Manhattan, probably at the Harvard Club, India House Club, or Yacht Club, where he held memberships. He also gave a modified version of his speech to 2,000-plus attendees of a fund-raising event for the Spanish Nationalist Relief Committee at Boston's Symphony Hall, extracts of which made the *Boston Globe*'s front page. With only Forbes's self-effacing letters to Sedgwick to draw on and without attendance lists, it is difficult to assess the impact of these lectures, but they may well have been significant.[50]

As Cárdenas had appreciated, Forbes was both a responsible and a respected American figure. Though small in stature, as befits a polo jockey, he approached the podium with a substantial reputation for ethical practice. Since his retirement, Forbes had been no less dedicated to the spirit of public service through various trusteeships, especially as board chairman of the Carnegie Institution. His Baltimore lecture stressed Franco's aims for law and order, protection of private property, religious toleration, social justice, and diplomatic neutrality—issues that lay close to the hearts of concerned elites. Preferring the ballot to the coup d'état, and with no record of political ambition, Franco had only acted after concluding that "Reds" planned a "Soviet Spain" and the liquidation of the upper classes. Nationalist officials throughout the country had reiterated this motive of freeing Spain from a foreign "Soviet-directed oligarchy," while their victory would ensure that "Spain is for the Spaniards." Forbes believed that Franco was the kind of God-given leader who so often appeared in a nation's hour of crisis, as had Julius Caesar, George Washington, Giuseppe Garibaldi, Porfirio Díaz, and "shall we say Mussolini?" How many University Club attendees nodded approval is unknowable, but even in the spring of 1938 a majority of elites presumably still respected Italy's fascist dictator, otherwise Forbes would never have posed that question. By 24 May, when Forbes reported to Sedgwick on his lecture tour, he could relate a meeting with Boston's Cardinal O'Connell, who was convinced that public opinion had begun a distinct "swing toward Franco . . . due in important measure to what you [Sedgwick] and I were doing." While Forbes admitted his audiences had been small, people had come up afterward to say they now had a "clear understanding and appreciation" of the Spanish conflict. Each of these persons, Forbes was convinced, would go home and correct the "misapprehension of their neighbors" whenever the subject of Spain came up. "So, from these little contacts, I don't doubt a spreading influence radiates out."[51]

Forbes also tried to influence his State Department contacts. On 16 March, his earliest opportunity, he visited Stanley K. Hornbeck, Far Eastern adviser on political relations, whom he had known since his ambassadorship to Japan. His choice was a poor one, as Hornbeck, along with Assistant Secretary George S. Messersmith, was one of State's most outspoken realists, favoring an interventionist role not only against Japan but also in Europe to block fascist aggression. Hornbeck, moreover, had opposed the embargo to Loyalist Spain since August 1936. During their conversation, Forbes stressed the necessity of establishing trade relations with the Nationalist zone and, to that end, affording recognition to Franco. He also expressed frustration that the postal service was hindering mail to Nationalist territory. After listening patiently without expressing his own opinion, Hornbeck promised to communicate Forbes's view to Hull. Presuming that Hornbeck kept his word, he likely tempered it with his own view that public opinion had swung in favor of intervention, which in the case of Spain meant lifting the embargo, while those isolationists who wanted to keep the embargo were an unrepresentative if vociferous minority. Yet there was a tension here. No isolationist, Forbes was a realist, like Hornbeck, only for Forbes this equated boosting U.S. foreign trade, which in Spain meant favoring the Christian corporatism of Franco's Nationalists over the revolutionary communism of Madrid's Loyalists.[52]

Sedgwick, though, had no inhibitions in his forthright and sustained public praise of Franco. Using his extensive media contacts, he unleashed a blizzard of press releases that appeared in newspapers coast to coast in varying forms, depending on editorial bias. Editor John Finley at the *New York Times* was friends with Sedgwick, and the *Times* was unusual for trying—if failing, for, William Carney's reportage notwithstanding, it still held a pro-Loyalist bias—to play both sides of the Spanish drama, so Finley gave Sedgwick free rein. In an eighty-column-inch, two-part report, Sedgwick enthused over Nationalist Spain's civic duty, business confidence, and full employment. "Cabinet members take no pay, and countless civilians and officers serve only for the love of serving. Rich men make gifts. Everybody works." Here, to a tee, was the Yankee spirit of public service and honest labor. There were, though, elements of Nationalist ideology that Sedgwick found troubling, "conservative elements" of which some were "sharply reactionary." Sedgwick had spoken with monarchists, great landowners, and rich manufacturers, yet his impression was that they comprised "but a fraction" of Franco's support. Indeed, putting Franco's "political acumen" to the test was an "extraordinary diversity" of opinion among his followers. Great numbers of Spanish "progressives" followed Franco, as did "tens of thousands of genuine radicals." By radical, Sedgwick did not mean radical socialist but the "'falange Espanola'— the Spanish phalanx." (Members of the Falange Española Tradicionalista y de las JONS cloaked a spiritual though aggressively anticommunist form of Catholic Social Action in fascist trappings and garnered support from women in Puerto Rico and New Mexico as well as Spain.) Yet Sedgwick prophesied—correctly, as it happened—that "after the victory is won," pressure from conservatives, along with Franco's own "judicial intelligence," would ameliorate these extreme elements. On balance, Sedgwick felt that "the liberal spirit" was "clearly in the ascendant" throughout Franco's zone.[53]

New York's *Herald Tribune,* with obvious skepticism, quoted Sedgwick's wonder at conditions "in 'White Spain.'" "Everything was well ordered and everyone appeared contented." Governance "appeared perfect," exports were booming, prices were reasonable, taxes were low, food was plentiful, and "Franco has an ambitious program of slum clearance." Some editions approvingly emphasized Sedgwick's censure of foreign communism, the war being not one of "Spaniard against Spaniard but Spaniards against the Reds," as the *Spokane Catholic* put it. South America was the real reason why the Russians were so interested in Madrid, Sedgwick reasoned, for "if they could get a Red Spain, they could get all to the south of us. They've already got Mexico." Boston's *Sunday Globe* even gave the local boy front-page headlines: "Franco Efficiency Amazes Sedgwick." Perhaps Sedgwick's greatest press coup came in May, when the mass-circulated *Reader's Digest* ran a condensed version of his *Times* report, albeit under a byline linking "famous American editor" Sedgwick's finding of "peace and prosperity" to Franco's "rebels' rule." With Sedgwick's message receiving such widespread press coverage, and set against the stark domestic backdrop of renewed economic downturn and a return to rising unemployment, many elite—and not a few middle-class—readers must have noted the contrast between Franco's corporatist Spain and Roosevelt's struggling New Deal.[54]

Of those who read Sedgwick's paeans to Franco, sixty-six members of the League of American Writers penned a *New York Times* letter expressing total disbelief that the editor of such a "liberal, impartial American magazine" as the *Atlantic* could possibly find anything good to say about "fascist Spain." One hundred and fifteen outraged educators also attacked Sedgwick through the *Times,* calling attention to "the facts . . . of Spanish [Loyalist] democracy" at a dangerous time when "the Catholic hierarchy, the meetings of diplomats and the partisan reports of certain newspapers" were attempting to mold public opinion in favor of a "fascist internationale," to which Brazil and other "neighbors to the south" were invitees. After sixty-one Episcopalian and Methodist bishops issued a bitter denunciation through an open letter, Sedgwick fired back via press interview from his Beacon Hill townhouse. An annotated map of Spain spread before him, this "professing Episcopalian" and hitherto discreet "leader in the New England intellectual group," charged Protestant clergy with flirting with communism and succumbing to Marxist propaganda. "As an American Protestant, with firm convictions on the right of a free conscience to worship God," he declaimed flatly, "I protest against the revolutionary social doctrines fostered by theological leaders in American Protestantism." How would these smug clerics feel if it were Protestant clergy who had been "beaten to death before their altars" by bloodthirsty mobs? For sure, there had been "cruelties enough practiced by both sides" in Spain, and the European conflict between fascism and communism was only worsening, but "Fascism was born of the fear of Communism. Kill Communism and Fascism will fade out." Writers, educators, bishops, and Sedgwick alike actually understood little of Spain's sociopolitical milieu, which only served to vociferate their argument.[55]

Carried prominently in dailies around the nation, the sharp exchanges drew considerable public attention, although their net effect was to polarize debate rather than sway mass opinion toward Franco, as Sedgwick intended. Seven letters printed by the *Washington Post* under the heading "Symposium on Spain" employed a binary discourse of fascism versus democracy and communism versus Christianity, with each term sounding like a cudgel. Six of the bludgeoners were pro-Franco, although whether this reflected editorial selectivity or letter-writer majority is unknowable. But public spats were unseemly, and Forbes's and Sedgwick's primary concern was to influence elites, the sector of opinion that policy makers, many of whom were old stock like themselves, judged to be the most weighty. One of the *Post*'s letters raised this point, wondering how editor Sedgwick, ex-governor Forbes, and two other ardent Franco supporters, ex-ambassador Ogden H. Hammond and Middlebury College professor Robert Davis, could possibly be antidemocratic "fascists" when in fact they were "good American citizens, widely respected for truth-telling and love of civil liberty." Shelving his high-profile crusade in the mass media, Sedgwick returned to more subtle suasion through the *Atlantic.*[56]

"Leaning Toward a Dictatorship"

At first glance, the *Atlantic*'s 717 essays and poems from 421 contributors during the civil war period suggest no particular agenda. Most pieces are on apolitical subjects, ranging from landscape gardening to child rearing to the fall of Troy, and a high proportion, for a magazine of the time (18 percent), were written by women. A closer reading indicates that of 190 political articles, only ten are leftist, while a third convey a rightist message and a majority of the rest espouse right-of-center positions, a contention supported by the thirty-two articles from the three most prolific contributors, anti-Marxist philologist Wilson Follett, Jeffersonian educator Albert Jay Nock, and militant conservative George Sokolsky. Follett made plain in his October 1938 "Letter to a Communist Friend" why it was "a moral monstrosity" for anyone to "dream of procuring 'social justice' by putting the bottom layer on the top" so that the trampled could in turn do the trampling. Not that Follett lacked sympathy for the downtrodden; rather, he considered all Americans to be greedy capitalists, given half a chance. As the author of *Our Enemy, the State,* and a later inspiration for William F. Buckley, Nock's rightist credentials seem solid. Yet this aristocratic Yankee who detested popular culture was no modern American conservative. His freethinking political ideology was anarchistic, viewing the state as anathema to truth and to the aesthetics of a cultured, civil society, and he drew from the libertarianism of John Stuart Mill rather than the cynicism of Edmund Burke. Above all, Nock abhorred meddlers and improvers, those with a "monstrous itch for changing people." Although Nock made little comment on Spain's civil war, he admired Spanish philosopher José Ortega y Gassett, who, after supporting Spain's Second Republic in 1931, came to despise mass movements for their threat to cultural values and failure to produce leaders who could keep society from lapsing into riotousness. That Ramón Serrano Súñer, Franco's brother-in-law and an extreme Falangist, proposed Ortega for inclusion in Spain's government of 1945 is an indication of Ortega's ideological U-turn.[57]

Old-stock Protestant subscribers were probably unaware that the *Atlantic*'s most featured contributor—Sokolsky—was the son of a Polish rabbi who had traveled to Petrograd as an idealistic supporter of Alexander Kerensky and spent 1917 editing the *Russian Daily News* before taking up the torch of capitalism. As he made clear in *Labor's Fight for Power* (1934), a book dedicated to Ellery Sedgwick, Sokolsky was not above meddling, but only when necessary to uphold "conservative characteristics," those three American pillars—in slender, libertarian profile—of "capitalism, democracy, and the Constitution." Not merely a "one-man intellectual front for conservative capital," as *Time* magazine demonized him in August 1938, Sokolsky also fretted over America's global mission. A foreign-policy realist who appreciated America's innate security, Sokolsky saw Secretaries Stimson and Hull pursuing moralistic policies that had "no grounding in fact, no relationship to reality, no specific and definable aim" and that, in the Far East, were inexorably driving Japan to war. For Sokolsky, the fundamental problem was policy makers' assertion that the United States was the lone "arbiter of right." Sokolsky, nevertheless, was quite capable of drawing pragmatic distinctions between major military "entanglements" with the old imperialist powers and limited insurgencies to protect U.S. business interests of the kind Woodrow Wilson had favored in the Western Hemisphere. It is important to note that nonentanglement ideology, rooted in America's near-impregnable strategic geography, was not limited to isolationists like Charles Lindbergh and "Radio Priest" Charles E. Coughlin or to conservatives such as Senator Robert A. Taft and Sokolsky but, rather, as historian Richard M. Ketchum puts it, was "a habit of thought that came naturally to millions" of Americans in 1938.[58]

Just as it proves hard (on first reading) to distill anything of political import from Sedgwick's waggish memoirs, aptly entitled *The Happy Profession* (1946), so it is with his own contributions to the *Atlantic*. His only article on Spain, appearing four months after the tour, described Gen. Queipo de Llano's administration of Seville under the innocuous-sounding title "The Patron Saint of Andalusia." Writing from a Spaniard's viewpoint, Sedgwick avoided injecting his own opinion, yet his lucid prose leaves little doubt as to where his sympathies lay. After admitting Queipo's personal faults as well as cataloging his civic successes, Sedgwick closed with an old tale: For as long as "uninstructed people [the masses]" preferred the "irregularities of Robin Hood [Reds] to the virtues of the excellent Sheriff of Nottingham [Queipo, Franco]," then for so long would "Queipo the Sinner be enshrined as Don Gonzalo the Saint in the hearts and minds of every freeborn Andalusian." By turning the tale inside out, Sedgwick was challenging his readers to balance the net worth of law and order—with all its potential for venality—against its derivative core value of real freedoms. What was Robin

Hood but a bandit out to steal from the rich, ostensibly to give to the poor but only by violating property rights; as any freeborn American surely appreciated, a benevolent corporatist sheriff is far better than an irregular communist robber.[59]

A 1936 essay on Japan sheds light on Sedgwick's support of Franco, suggesting that his motivation for writing travelogues was to reinforce a traditional sense of American identity. His two-step method was first to describe primitive yet romantically outlandish foreigners only to reveal later how they actually held superior values to supposedly more civilized Americans. Having inherited "primitive instinct[s]" from the "vast Oriental tide from China" in the sixth century, individual thought "in the Western sense" was difficult for the Japanese. Still, whereas one might be "incompetent," a group of Japanese could multiply "individual inefficiencies" into a miracle of "superlative efficiency." After romanticizing a primitive Samurai with a "hawk's beak" nose and a "venomous slit" for a mouth, Sedgwick noted that these ferocious warriors carried a fan—symbolizing "civil obedience and social order"—in addition to their sword of "dominion [and] power." Noteworthy, too, was Japan's constitution of A.D. 604, which entreated public officials to make "decorous behavior their guiding principle." Sedgwick admired the "coarse-fibred and violent" sixteenth-century warlord Hideyoshi for instituting the tea ceremony, and he praised the daily instruction by schools of manners and etiquette. "Neither native nor natural," American feminism had filtered from Paris to 5th Avenue to "all points west," but in Japan women still considered the house their domain and sat "sweet and silent" while their husbands recollected the day's travails. Americans could learn much from Japan's "ancient simplicities," just as they could from Franco's outlandish Carlists, who shared "spiritual stock" with Scottish clansmen. These Spanish *traditionalistas,* with their "country, bread and justice" war cry, were actually "brothers in a common cause." Like strong anticommunist Americans, Sedgwick implied, Carlists were "a simple people, strong in faith" and "clear in their conception of duty."[60]

On the sole occasion, in March 1938, when Sedgwick ran overtly political articles on Spain, he juxtaposed John Langdon-Davies's "The Case for the Government" with Ian D. Colvin's "The Case for Franco" and left it to the reader to decide. Colvin's piece, presented first, argued that Nationalist officers had intervened with reluctance to halt a revolution in progress. Only after Spain had descended into chaos following the Popular Front's election in February 1936, only after 209 murders, 1,287 assaults, and the whole or part destructions of 411 churches, did Franco, "who had always set his face against military intervention," agree to take up arms to restore order. Franco was no fascist at the head of a military dictatorship but a "regular soldier" backed by the "greater part of the Spanish nation." In his defense of "law, order, and civilization," Franco's acceptance of Italian and German assistance was pragmatic and temporary. With the cause won, an independent Spain would emerge "in possession of her own territory—and her own soul." Langdon-Davies's case painted Franco's fascists as the real murderers, and, with all its talk of the feudal Church, atrocities by Catholics, and *autos de fe*, it even revived the Black Legend of the Inquisition, presumably for the benefit of the *Atlantic*'s Protestant readership. A few wayward anarchists may have burned some churches, but so had "Fascist *agents provocateurs*." In his closing remarks, Langdon-Davies also looked past victory. Franco's rebellion had ironically accelerated social change, and the Left had learned how to discipline its anarchist elements. With the fascist legions defeated and order restored, Spain's "liberal Government" would henceforth be the beneficiary of a responsible Left.[61]

Both articles underscored the bifurcated discourse of isms then in vogue. Colvin used *fascism* once but *communism* and *Red* sixteen times (plus four instances of *Soviet* and *Moscow*), while Langdon-Davies used *fascism* seven times and *communism* only twice, plus once in scare quotes. Both writers (who were British, as were many *Atlantic* contributors) also played on the emotive Whiggish tropes of order, government, civilization, private property, worship, liberty, tyranny, and privilege. Indicative of the importance Sedgwick attached to events in Spain, during January 1936 to July 1939, the *Atlantic* published more pieces on Spain (twelve) than it did on Germany (ten).[62]

Readers' letters can be revealing of an editor's hand. Sedgwick generally printed few—none from January through May 1938—but in June, with tensions mounting over worsening unemployment at home and "aggression" abroad, he solicited essays from young "men and women, from those with degrees and those without, from all walks of life." Of the nine essays featured in the *Atlantic*'s "Under Thirty" column from June to August, four debated the overheating sociopolitical climate, and each was supportive of fascistic authoritarianism as a palliative measure.[63]

Ella Tambussi, a Mount Holyoke honors student, wrote about a photograph on her desk of Paolo, an Italian boy in a fascist uniform standing proud and ready to die in defense of "ideals far higher than those which prompted the desire to make the Yangtze safe for Standard Oil," a pointed reference to the December 1937 sinking of the U.S. gunboat *Panay* by Japanese aircraft (an act that newspapers unanimously condemned as unprovoked "aggression" without giving a thought to the right of America's Yangtze patrol to police China's inland waterways). As Tambussi watched her young cousins growing up in the old country with the "opportunity and education that monarchist Italy" had never provided, she felt confident that "the true Fascism of [leading ideologist Giovanni] Gentile will succeed." While Tambussi feared the "ruthless coercion of a dictatorship," she nonetheless advocated the planned economy of fascist socialism as an antidote to the complacency of American capitalists, who mouthed "life, liberty, and the pursuit of happiness" and watched one third of their fellows going destitute. It is notable that in 1975, Ella Grasso, née Tambussi, a liberal democratic politician in Connecticut, became the first woman elected to a state governorship.[64]

In a similar vein, Robert James, a UCLA political science major, asked how Americans could hate Italians, Germans, and Japanese for turning in desperation to a form of government that was curing their economic woes when American greed had fueled the international depression and then American selfishness withheld aid to poorer nations. How could it be "moral to subjugate half of the peoples of the world" or "democratic to use force to maintain [Versailles's] unjust peace?" Once again, James predicted, warmongering "elders" would commit their sons to battle to uphold foreign trade and the world's "democracies." John Claiborne Davis, an open-minded and well-traveled Princeton graduate student, also appealed for greater understanding and less belligerence. As a younger man, Davis had visited Germany "intent on discovering the right and wrong of National Socialism," only to find divided opinions and both good and bad policies, On realizing that issues were never black and white, he had since striven to find a middle way. Elizabeth (no last name given), a twenty-seven-year-old graduate of Smith College, was one of the more liberal yet potentially un-American of Sedgwick's respondents. What kind of world did she wish for her newborn son? "Certainly not the capitalistic society of to-day," with all its unemployment, inequality, and lack of values, yet mob rule would be just as untenable. Caught between the two fires of rampant materialism and overbearing government, Elizabeth nonetheless found herself "leaning toward a dictatorship." She envisaged not a "Hitler or a Mussolini" but a leader capable of imposing public education and equitable living standards while encouraging intellectual freedom—essentially, Sedgwick's idealized Franco and Nationalist Spain's benevolent corporatist state.[65]

Advocacy of corporatist or fascist dictatorship in the late 1930s was evidently not the sole preserve of isolated crackpots, members of the lunatic fringe, or the Catholic hierarchy. Sedgwick's young letter writers were mainstream liberal intellectuals. Historian Benjamin L. Alpers documents a "cautious optimism about dictatorship" at the Depression's outset, but by the time Studebaker rebadged its six-cylinder Dictator model as a Director in 1937, Alpers sees a "nearly universal condemnation of the phenomenon"; by spring 1933, "calls for dictatorship" in America were "rare except on the political fringes." To whatever extent calls were rare, my sources indicate that optimistic thinking about dictatorships was more common, at least until Pearl Harbor.[66]

Sedgwick's selections for the *Atlantic*, along with his own writings during 1938, suggest three related conclusions. First, although he was an old-stock traditionalist who valued the rule of law, his angst was no mere crotchety negativism (anticommunism, anti–New Deal, anti-intervention). Rather, he was a proponent of salient, modern issues, from slum clearance and public housing to state-sponsored workers' rights. Second, and in spite of being a standard-bearer for American-ness—or, at least, an inheritor of Yankee-ness—he was open to discussing alternative forms of government, even those that were incompatible with the Constitution. Whether he could have stomached such alternatives in Washington or saw them only as restoratives for disorderly foreigners is unclear, although his first publication as a twenty-seven-year-old had been a biography of the Revolutionary ideologue Thomas Paine. Third, Sedgwick was sufficiently upset with sociopolitical trends to challenge openly—at great risk to his wealth and reputation, vested as they both were in the *Atlantic*—the full weight of both public opinion and state power. As historian Alan Brinkley has argued for Huey Long and Father Coughlin, Sedgwick was surely not acting out of irrationality or iconoclasm but, as Brinkley puts it, from a compelling, all-American life force: the defense of individual autonomy and community independence against the encroaching modern state, the necessity of maintaining a society "in which the individual retained control of his own life and livelihood; in which power resided in visible, accessible institutions; in which wealth was equitably (if not necessarily equally) shared." Sedgwick's activism, then, fell within the historically informed project of U.S. nation building, albeit with a dash of *Don Quixote*'s romantic, tragic idealism.[67]

While Sedgwick, with refined subtlety, was doing his utmost to edify *Atlantic* readers of Franco's merits, he was also lobbying for State Department recognition of the Nationalist regime. Former senator George H. Moses (R-NH) advised him that the best chance of forcing Roosevelt's hand was through a congressional resolution proposed by "some person of character," such as John J. O'Connor (D-NY) or John W. McCormack (D-MA). In case Sedgwick was ignorant of diplomatic procedure—unlikely, given his association with Forbes—Moses spelled out the prerequisites for formal recognition: a government with authority over designated territory; the maintenance of order; and functional administration, including courts, postal services, banks, and commerce. It is interesting to observe the frequency with which Sedgwick, Forbes, and other advocates for recognition evidence these conditions throughout Nationalist Spain in their writings. Sedgwick's discussions with Moses were productive. In April 1938, Sedgwick informed Cárdenas that Irwin Laughlin, former ambassador to Spain and former secretary to Moses when he was minister to Greece, was tapping his State Department contacts. Laughlin, as he indicated in a *Washington Post* report, felt in common with many Hispanophiles that the "extreme individualism" of the "Spanish race" valued monarchy over democracy and would never tolerate foreign fascism. But campaigners for recognition faced an uphill struggle.[68]

With the exception of State, Roosevelt's administrative departments backed Madrid's Loyalists, most notably Justice, Interior, Labor, and Treasury. Within State, though, officials held divided opinions, with a majority at least being anti-communist like Hull if not necessarily pro-Franco like Laughlin, William Phillips (ambassador to Italy since November 1936), or Robert Murphy (chargé d'affaires for William C. Bullitt's important Paris embassy). But Franco lobbyists could draw little comfort here, for Claude G. Bowers, Roosevelt's friend and ambassador to

Spain, was outspokenly pro-Loyalist, and John C. Wiley at the Spanish desk was convinced that muddle-headed anarchists rather than disciplined Soviet communists had been behind Spain's social unrest. Roosevelt, moreover, bypassed State Department functionaries "from Cordell Hull downward," as historian David Mayers has noted. Ideology notwithstanding, there was also a pragmatic consideration, one neglected by historians but perhaps uppermost in the minds of several State Department officials and surely Forbes's. Direct foreign investments in Spain amounted to $81 million ($2.4 billion), of which ITT's telephone infrastructure accounted for $64 million. To put this figure in perspective, it equaled one-fifth of America's entire investments in Asia, and only in Britain, Germany, and France did U.S. investments in Europe exceed it. This capital was lost to a communist regime, but a Franco government would provide hope of restitution. Still, with Messersmith and Hornbeck pushing Hull toward a more interventionist line against fascist aggression in Europe, the realist approach to foreign policy cut both ways in the case of Nationalist Spain.[69]

By June 1938, Sedgwick's Franco lobby, which had grown to include international affairs scholar Philip M. Brown and renowned Harvard geographer Alexander Hamilton Rice, was working to garner signatures for a recognition petition. Sedgwick, who raised support among fellow Episcopalian members of Boston's exclusive Tavern Club, was excited that petitioners would be Protestants, for the public, "particularly the radical public," was convinced that the Catholic hierarchy was the sole torchbearer for Nationalist Spain. In addition to the elite Bostonians who put their signature on the line, there were pro-Nationalists who did not want to upset pro-Loyalist colleagues or stand out as nonconformists and so held back. Industrial chemist and interrelated Brahmin Samuel Cabot expressed his "sympathy with the Rightists in Spain" and wished to support them "in every legitimate way" but demurred from signing a blanket petition that was critical of federal government policy.[70]

Red-Fascist Discourse

Sedgwick was proud of his stand for what he judged to be the righteousness of Franco's Spain, but he found the character of the argument he promoted through the *Atlantic*'s cultured pages to be altogether larger, uglier, more public and yet more personal than any of his prior causes. Whereas Sedgwick liked to develop a case through artistic prose and humanistic sidebars, Spanish Civil War antagonists cuffed each other with crass Red-fascist epithets. After experiencing the furor in the newspapers over his anticommunist stance, he then faced the correspondence in the *Atlantic*'s mailbag. Sedgwick's files preserve 117 letters voicing opinions about his support of Franco, running at a pro–con ratio of about two to three, although for every reader threatening to cancel a subscription there was another ordering two years in advance or recommending the *Atlantic* to a friend. From the pro side, Frank Schoonmaker, a Manhattan wine merchant, considered Sedgwick's "courageous" articles in the *New York Times* to be the "first really intelligent summary" of conditions in Spain since the conflict erupted. Having lived in Spain while writing a guidebook in collaboration with Lowell Thomas, and then touring the Nationalist zone the previous summer, Schoonmaker was convinced that those who criticized Franco did so from ignorance. Schoonmaker had recently dined with *Times* publisher Arthur Hays Sulzberger, taking the opportunity to congratulate Sulzberger for "at last" printing "something accurate on the Spanish war." J. J. Hibbard of Michigan, who made sure to mention he was a Protestant, felt that by "masquerading under the names of Liberty and Democracy," the communists were fooling Americans. Protestant clergy, along with college professors, were "impractical fellows" easily duped by sentimental theories like communism.[71]

Many of the con letters were acid, and Sedgwick's restrained replies barely conceal his anguish. Bryan Allin of Chicago lamented that the *Atlantic* had "fallen on evil days and into incompetent hands." Creighton J. Hill of Washington, DC, likened Sedgwick to a mad dog, infected with "pipsqueak ideas" and running amuck. What would "Emerson or Thoreau" make of Sedgwick's "Fascist poison-pen utterances," Hill wondered. Tucson doctor William L. Holt berated Sedgwick for his "un-American, Fascistic espousal of the damnable cause of the Spanish Rebels and that arch baby-killer, Francisco Franco." In April 1938, at the height of his pro-Franco activism, Sedgwick chastised one irate letter writer, Mrs. Richard Edsall of Boston, for speaking of Loyalist Madrid's democracy when the "whole basis" of the Spanish Civil War arose from an "infection of communism." He thought it "rather foolish" of her to call him a fascist with sympathies for Hitler and Mussolini when, for thirty years as *Atlantic* editor, he had been a "thoroughgoing democrat, further to the left than to the right."[72]

Sedgwick's Americanism had always been transatlantic, progressive, and liberal—further to the left than to the right. Yet there would be no room for thoroughgoing Yankee democracy in Red-fascist discourse. Cultural critic Robert Warshow might have been writing about Sedgwick in observing that the Sacco-Vanzetti trial was the "last strong expression of uncorrupted radicalism" in the United States. During the 1930s, by contrast, the CPUSA so dominated intellectual life that it forced friend and foe alike to operate at its level: "Everyone became a *professional* politician." Now an "end in itself," political activity came at the detriment of a liberal's quest for truth. Following Warshow's analysis, Sedgwick's activism confronted him with the reality of an irreversible leveling down of high culture and a concomitant deliberalization of intellectual thought. Once so self-assured, he faltered, for his elitist cultural milieu now seemed unsettlingly outmoded. Two letter writers said as much in response to his "Patron Saint" article. Edward C. Jacobs of New York detected an "Opera Bouffe spirit" that "today seems archaic," while Dr. G. G. Holdt of Oregon considered Sedgwick to be an "aged gentleman" embracing the miracles of a "bygone age." Not only did communism pose an ideological challenge to Sedgwick's civilized Americanism, but the politicization by communists—by the "*laboring*" of the leftist "cultural front" so well portrayed by Michael Denning—had created a brash new public culture that, ironically, Sedgwick's participation in the Great Debate had exacerbated.[73]

In January 1938, when Forbes had proposed the tour, Sedgwick sensed that Americans' argument over Spain was, like with Sacco-Vanzetti, as much a test of personal conscience as it was of national principles, which he must approach as he had all his prior issues—with an open, interested mind. He conducted background research. He went to Spain to look for himself. Yes, at Badajoz, his hosts duped him, and if he had spent more time in tapas bars than posh restaurants, then he might have acquired from locals a less favorable assessment of Franco's ruthless regime. But when Sedgwick decided to make Nationalist Spain his last great cause, he at least did so with a concern for injustice and a measured truthfulness. He could not have thrown his support behind Nicola Sacco, Bartolomeo Vanzetti, or Alfred Smith without recognizing their faults, as he no doubt did in the case of Franco. To Sedgwick, these were all equally valid causes with broad-based implications for American society, which a good liberal humanist should be concerned to bring to public debate. This time around, though, he found a different set of rules: forensic evidence had become immaterial, values were bunk, and the verdict a foregone conclusion. Had he checked back through his writings, he would have realized how a new discursive convention had dragged him down to the Comintern's level, for he too was stacking his prose with Marxist–fascist, Red–White polar opposites. As the communists had hoped, the Center could not hold in such a rhetorically vituperative atmosphere. Being "further to the left than to the right" was now an untenable position: Sedgwick could be either on the left or the right, but no longer in between.

Spain was the perfect metaphorical location on which to imprint Red-fascist discourse or present the utility of liberal governance. Unlike Italy or Germany, few Americans had vacationed in Spain, in part because even fewer were Spanish American. But where it was a blank slate experientially, as a trope it came preloaded with a rich grab bag of historic symbols: Reconquista for Catholics, Inquisition for Protestants and Jews, Moorish harems for orientalists, Columbus for adventurers, Cuban repression for anticolonialists, the USS *Maine* or San Juan Hill for jingoes. *Spain* could be masculine or feminine, Western or Eastern, Christian or Islamic. More relevantly, for politicos, its *marqués* could be as pretentiously aristocratic as its *jornaleros* were pathetically poor, and it had the longest of traditions for both liberalism and anarchism. Unknowably alien yet familiarly *Spanish,* Spain for 1930s Americans became a mythical land on which to ascribe one's own mores without fear of contradiction. Yet vehement contradiction was bound to ensue, for if one pundit could cloak Spain in democracy, then another could just as naturally press her calves into jackboots.

2

Defending Americanism

At the end of 1937, John Eoghan Kelly returned from a business trip to Berlin convinced that Europeans were in the final throes of a death struggle with communism, worried that communist propaganda would provoke revolution at home, and determined to defend America from what he believed was impending Red peril. Kelly's fears might seem silly, even paranoid, yet to him and the hundreds of Americans who joined him in lobbying Capitol Hill to back Spain's Nationalists they were real. Just as Popular Front activists evinced Gen. Francisco Franco's coup of July 1936 as the first stage of a worldwide fascist plot, so Franco lobbyists pointed at Spain's murdered clergy and syndicalist communes to demonstrate the Bolshevik threat. For both sides, reality became a zero-sum argument to define democracy. In Kelly's case, his fears sent him dashing from typewriter to lecture hall to meeting room, a single-minded effort to intensify the Great Debate over arms to Spain and thereby sway public opinion, affect U.S. foreign policy, modify Americanism, and turn anticommunist patriots who supported Franco into enemies of their state. During January–August 1938, while he was developing his counterpropaganda campaign, Kelly wrote more than twenty articles, delivered at least a dozen speeches, and pulled off a front-page *New York Times* exposé. His message was consistently simple: Soviet communism—a foreign menace "boring from within" to first undermine existing structures and then build on the ruins a workers' dictatorship—was the doctrinal enemy of Americanism. Agents of Joseph Stalin's Comintern, Kelly was certain, were intent on overturning the American system and destroying Americans' very identity as God-fearing practitioners of capitalist endeavor and republican governance, and if Americans needed proof of this, then they only had to look at Spain. *America, Look at Spain!* became a campaign slogan for Franco lobbyists, cropping up in articles and speeches as well as in the titles of a radio address and a book.[1]

When Franco lobbyists gave speeches against international communism, they spoke with authority, for most of them had toured Nationalist Spain and felt they had experienced firsthand the consequences of proletarian revolution. But when they staked out their opposition to New Deal liberalism, they rarely defined their conservatism. When they talked approvingly of Christian corporatism or author-itarian rule abroad, they did not specify whether they advocated those systems of governance for Washington. Most glaringly, when they stated their intention to act in the defense of Americanism, they never clarified what they meant by such an ideology. That Franco lobbyists—and most other Americans, for that matter—had difficulty defining their politics in 1938 was in part because the core values of their civil religion were the subject of such heated debate. Popular Fronters and Franco lobbyists claimed to be debating whether to send arms to Spain, but they knew that their real disagreement was over the extent to which American society should turn socialist or remain capitalist. They blamed sinister, alien forces for the Spanish conflict, although their anxiety really stemmed from the disorienting rate of change—or progress at home, which they had a hand in creating, whether in mass media, communications, transportation, finance, or state power. They said they were fighting to save democracy in Spain, yet their argument was over what *democracy* meant for Americans, an argument the democratic process itself made possible. In part, too, it was because Franco lobbyists found it easier to stress something simple called *Americanism* than to confront the complex inconsisten-cies inherent in their unbending anticommunism and promotion of an authori-tarian regime in Spain. *Americanism,* of course, was in play for both sides. "Com-munism is twentieth-century Americanism," puffed the Comintern clarion.[2]

Activists on both sides of the Great Debate were well-meaning, if idealistic, Americans concerned about solving the world's problems and making it a better place, but their concern over distant Spain would have unintended consequences for world peace. As their rhetoric sharpened, they forced the uncommitted to take sides, shamed isolationists into the open, and made compromise untenable. As their lobbying of Capitol Hill intensified, their angst unnerved policy makers, pressuring them into decisions that exacerbated rather than diffused global tensions.

In documenting Kelly's tactical lobbying for Franco during the first half of 1938, this chapter lays groundwork for my thesis that Kelly's project, in a subliminal sense, was not so much the defense of Americanism as its restructuring—its adap-tation to troubling times—through an argument over foreign policy with Ameri-can supporters of Spain's Loyalists. His writings and speeches indicate that he knew what the structure ought to be—republican, secular; ordered, cultured; technolog-ical, entrepreneurial; progressive, cosmopolitan—but the Great Debate's corrosive political climate reformulated these ingredients during the process. In addition to the Red–fascist rhetoric, there was a second polarizing discourse, Roosevelt's dis-course of liberalism. Concerned Americans, especially disillusioned progressives like W. Cameron Forbes, Ellery Sedgwick, and Kelly, could hardly support Franco's fight against communism while still claiming the high ground of reformist liberalism, and so both these powerful discourses backed them into the conservatives' corner. Hence, the Americanism that emerged by 1946—statist, God-fearing; celebratory, brash; managerial, consumerist; conservative, nativist—was a different edifice from the one Kelly had in mind and worked so hard to defend. For sure, the cold war consensus would be thoroughly anticommunist, but it came with a troubling set of new precepts that, in honest conversation, Kelly would never have countenanced.

"The Issue in Spain Is Communism"

Publishing articles in pro-Franco magazines like *Spain* and *America* generated $80–$130 a month ($2,400–$3,950), but that was insufficient to cover Kelly's office and secretarial overhead once his income from mining consultancy dried up. In November 1937, California geologist Dr. E. U. von Buelow, whom Kelly had known since 1923, asked if he would travel to Germany, expenses paid but on a contingency fee, in an attempt to free up assets owned by a group of West Coast investors. Kelly jumped at the chance. He was determined to make the best of this opportunity to revisit Europe, which he had not seen since he was seventeen, but he had little time to prepare and political tensions complicated travel arrangements. Through Talbot, he made plans to continue from Berlin to Spain as a freelance reporter for *America,* and he must have contacted someone in the army, because in his capacity as a reserve army captain he carried a War Department letter to Berlin's U.S. military attaché. But Buelow's failure to join the Nazi Party while he was still living in Germany stymied Kelly's business negotiations on his behalf, and a miscommunication between Berlin's consulate and Ruth B. Shipley at Washington's passport office stalled Kelly's visa for Spain. Still, as he explained to Talbot in a letter he mailed from his hotel in Berlin's fashionable Charlottenburg district, the visit had allowed him to gather "much data on communism, both Spanish and worldwide."[3]

After a swift crossing from Hamburg to the Port of New York in mid-December aboard the SS *Bremen,* Kelly wrote "World Revolution's Next Objective." He sent the article to Talbot with a covering letter explaining how he regretted his inability to visit Spain, where he could more fully have appreciated communism's "worldwide offensive" and better noted the striking parallels "between red action there and in this country." Yet now that he was back, and with America's fast-growing "radical movement" so patently "rushing toward an open break" with democratic society, he would have hated to be away when even in an "infinitesimal manner" he could assist the "defense of Americanism by my presence." This was no time for "just lamenting the red offensive." Although Americans were "beginning to awake to the danger" of Stalin's Comintern, they were neither sufficiently informed about nor united against its insidiousness. This was a time for concerted "action." Talbot, though in agreement that a "seething" Popular Front presented dangers, found Kelly's letter "rather alarming." A "break" must come, Talbot sensed, but not immediately, for "our side" would "muddle along" until some "startling and explosive accident rouses us" to the true state of affairs. Talbot's lukewarm response—he declined the article for his 35,000-subscriber *America*—emboldened Kelly's resolve.[4]

"World Revolution" soon found publication in the smaller-circulation *Sign*. Communism, Kelly surmised, was on the defensive in Europe, but therein lay increased danger for Americans. Barring "unforeseen catastrophe," such as the lifting of the arms embargo, Franco's army would "sweep the last red resistance over the frontiers" by the summer of 1939. In France, Léon Blum's "Alice-in-Wonderland" financial policies had terminally discredited his "communist-led" government. With the Rome-Berlin Axis a foil to their Soviet military alliance, Czechs exhibited a "strengthening of anti-communist sentiment." Informed by communism in action across their frontiers, "strong rightist governments" in Portugal and Turkey knew better than to shelter radicals. Fearful of Russia, as well as out of economic necessity, Yugoslavs, Hungarians, and Romanians were "veering toward the anti-communist bloc." And while the "red grip on Russia" itself appeared unchanged, "factional quarrels" between the Kaganovich ruling clique and surviving Old Bolsheviks, compounded by a "purge of ruthless executions," had rendered the Red Army temporarily powerless for any cross-border sorties. Yet the more defensive the communists became in Europe, "the greater effort they make here," Kelly warned, for world revolution's ultimate objective, as stated "ad nauseam" from Comintern platforms, was "the conquest of the United States." Russia's Kerensky government had fallen to 79,000 Bolsheviks, but the CPUSA now counted "two million followers and affiliates, led by fifty thousand card-holding Party members." Kelly actually underestimated, for in January 1938 the CPUSA membership reached its zenith at about 75,000.[5]

On Sunday, 13 February 1938, a Works Progress Administration–sponsored radio forum provided a rare opportunity (albeit limited to the war's causes and with religious issues off limits) to Kelly, as New England's foremost pro-Nationalist, to air his half of the Spanish case via New York's nationally syndicated WEVD. Perhaps he had shamed the station's producer into allotting him a slot for debate. A couple of weeks earlier, he had given an address that singled out WNYC and WEVD (named after Socialist Party leader Eugene V. Debs) for making free speech the "private property of the reds," because he had noticed how the stations would overwhelm with "gutter language," or tar with a fascist brush, anyone who dared to criticize the leftist bias of their programming.[6]

Spain's present "trial at arms," Kelly began, would determine whether Spaniards enjoyed their own government "untrammeled by foreign interference" or whether they would enter Moscow's orbit, "sink to the cultural and economic level of Soviet Russia," and become the locus for the "spread of communist doctrines" throughout France, North Africa, and Latin America. Listeners must harbor no doubts; "the issue in Spain is communism." Claiming that Spain's February 1936 election had given the Right a 500,000-vote majority distorted the facts, but Kelly's presentation of systematic efforts by Spain's Communist Party (PCE) officials—trained in and financially backed by Moscow—to foment armed revolution since 1919 was otherwise well informed.[7]

Communist leader Dolores Ibárruri, known as La Pasionaria for her rousing orations, boasted in her 1966 autobiography of a hitherto undocumented episode, the PCE's national leadership decision in the summer of 1921 "to organize an armed insurrection." Yet most who listened to Kelly's radio address in February 1938 were accustomed to the popular media's pro-Madrid bias—the *"laboring of American culture,"* as Michael Denning puts it—most consciously by glancing at the front page of newspapers like New York's *Post* or *Daily News* but also more subliminally after hearing, say, Archibald MacLeish's widely aired 1937 Columbia Workshop radio drama "The Fall of the City" or perhaps a passerby singing a line or two of Woody Guthrie's alternative "Jarama Valley" lyrics to the catchy "Red River Valley" folk ballad. They therefore would have been inclined to believe Kelly's pro-Loyalist opposite, Dr. Juan Ortiz González, a former professor of Spanish at Vanderbilt University, to the effect that Republican Madrid's democratic governance had fallen victim to fascist aggression. Still, several listeners did write to WEVD requesting copies of Kelly's talk. Mrs. Herbert N. Dawes in distant Boston was the most congratulatory: "Yours was the finest, the most convincing factual presentation of the 'Issues Behind the Conflict' in Spain that I have ever heard." Dawes compared Kelly to the mesmerizing radio sermonizer Monsignor Fulton J. Sheen, whom she had heard at 6:00 the night before: Sheen was "good, but your speech stirred me much more." Kelly must have been in fine oratorical form that evening. Dawes, who herself lectured to society groups in the Northeast and Midwest on what she judged to be a mounting communist menace, pleaded with Kelly to undertake a speaking tour in Boston, which he did the following year, at such venues as the Engineers' Club, Women's National Republican Club, Florence Crittenden League, and Boston College.[8]

If attendance at his engagements is any guide, Kelly's reputation as a stirring orator grew quickly. He was principal speaker at the 23 May Fourth Annual Communion Breakfast of the Holy Name Society of the Board of Transportation and Independent System Employees at Manhattan's Hotel Astor. After Mass at St. Patrick's Cathedral, nine hundred of New York's most anticommunist trade unionists marched to the hotel behind an honor guard of a hundred police officers, the American Legion's drum and bugle corps, and the Clann Éireann Irish pipe band. Kelly told his audience, which included the former president of the Catholic Actors' Guild and both the president and commissioner of the Board of Transportation, that he spoke neither as a representative of the War Department nor as a Catholic but "as a private citizen." In claiming—although he was an atheist—to speak as a Presbyterian, moreover, he rebuked Bishop Francis J. McConnell, singling out the Methodist educator and Chautauqua trustee as a leader of New York's anti-Catholic establishment.[9]

Kelly first explained how Russia had been plotting the Spanish revolution for nineteen years. Spain's war, he made clear, was one of civilization against anarchy, of Christianity against communism, "of the Spanish people against Soviet Russia and the red scum from all the world." For much of his forty-minute address, he argued, "What has happened in Spain can also happen in our own country," for he had found frightening parallels. Red propaganda was rampant, with more than six hundred American magazines advocating communism. Loyalist Spain's ambassador, Fernando de los Ríos, had lavished $15 million of the Spanish people's gold reserves on propaganda and International Brigade recruitment. Miners and steelworkers carried arms. Just three weeks before at a May Day union parade of 300,000 in Manhattan, "communist bystanders" had "cheered placards demanding intervention in Spain and the Soviet flag" while bands played "The Internationale." But, Kelly asserted, defending Nationalist Spain—and the world—was the Catholic Church, making it the target of Marxists. And stifling Loyalist Spain was the U.S. arms embargo. Hence, those who demanded the embargo's lifting cared "more for communism than for involving us in another world war." There could be no doubt, he concluded, that "if the reds' propaganda wins in this country, we will have Spain all over again here." What had happened in Spain "must not happen here."[10]

On 6 August 1938 Kelly addressed a community forum of more than three hundred Philadelphians organized by St. Stephen's Protestant Episcopal Church. He began by stressing the power of modern propaganda to cloud the truth, evident nowhere more than in the United States, which the Comintern was exposing to its "full blast." Indeed, communist propaganda had proved so effective that "without reasoning why," most Americans were "sympathetically inclined" toward Madrid's "so-called 'Loyalist' government," which he noted was remarkable given the negative connotation of the word since America's own Revolutionary War. Americans, though, must not allow party line rhetoric to fool them, for, he emphasized, "*the issue in Spain is communism.*" Kelly described for his audience how even before the final tally of voting in Spain's February 1936 election, Popular Front legislators opened the jails, releasing thousands of "convicted communist rebels" with "orders to burn churches" and "create a reign of terror." A wave of strikes swept the country, with more than three hundred in June alone. In Zaragoza in May, communists and anarchists held a joint convention whose openly published proceedings called for "a communist revolution that should sweep away the last vestiges of western civilization and erect on the smoking ruins a frankly soviet state." On 13 July 1936 rightist leader José Calvo Sotelo read from the floor of the Cortes (Spain's parliament) a list of political murders and church burnings committed by organized mobs and condoned by the government, advising that unless the government controlled the mobs, the mobs would soon control Spain. La Pasionaria arose from her seat, "pointed a grimy finger," and screamed, "That man has made his last speech." Two days later, government Assault Guards murdered him. All this, Kelly suggested sarcastically, was the work of the "'legally constituted, democratic' government" so loved by American "pinks." Mercifully for Spain—and Western civilization too—Franco's armed intervention had checked the revolution. A Soviet Spain, Kelly felt, would become a "stepping stone to a Soviet France, a Soviet North Africa," and on to Spanish-speaking countries in the New World.[11]

Franco was not fighting Spaniards, Kelly explained, rather Spaniards in welcome alliance with Franco's army were fighting communists. Leaving aside the communist-run industrial centers of Barcelona and Madrid, Franco's Nationalists were immensely popular, as evidenced by the notable absence of guerrilla warfare behind his lines. Whereas Moscow-backed Loyalists outlawed religion, killed business, and mocked morality ("as a bourgeois virtue"), in Franco's zone "peace and order prevail." Yes, he admitted, Franco enjoyed foreign aid too. German technicians provided assistance, and 29,000 Italians had volunteered for service, just as there were tens of thousands of foreign revolutionaries aiding the Loyalist side. Yet Franco, Kelly implied, was far too Spanish to tolerate foreign intervention long term. Kelly concluded by speculating on Franco's plans. Following a short period of military rule necessary to bring to trial fugitive anarchists and communists, Kelly expected there would be an authoritarian civilian government resembling that of Portugal's Christian corporatist state. Americans were rightly proud of their unique democratic system, but they should not presume it could work in every country. Franco's regime, then, would never be "Fascist, nor National Socialist" but thoroughly "Spanish, desired by and fitted to the needs of its people." As Kelly folded his notes and left the podium, there was thunderous applause and cries of "hear, hear!"[12]

Kelly had given this speech at least once before, in July, to five hundred Rotarians at Manhattan's Hotel Commodore, so it was no doubt a polished performance. But it was neither flashy nor egotistical; Kelly seemed more comfortable playing second fiddle rather than taking center stage, working unglamorously in the background ghostwriting other people's books and speeches. Like all consummate public speakers, he had a knack for bonding with his audience, fine-tuning his speeches for particular interest groups. To the Rotarians, he stressed the growing interconnectedness of world trade and Spain's importance to U.S. markets. Apart from the $34 million owed to American firms in accounts frozen by Madrid's Loyalist government, with Franco's victory Spain would need building materials and manufactures galore, for which it could trade olive oil, wine, sardines, cork, mercury, and copper. But unless Washington changed its attitude and ceased its "outspoken declarations of sympathy for the Spanish communists," the British, whose greater pragmatism had disregarded the "clamor of their left-ist parties and press," would take the lion's share. If Manhattan Rotarians wanted Spanish trade, he challenged, then they must lobby their government to be a real "good neighbor." Washington should cleanse its mind of communist propaganda and show the "Spanish people the respect due a race that has fought for its exis-tence against desperate odds—and WON."[13]

Although sometimes a church or association did pay Kelly a lecturer's stipend of $20–$40, he delivered most of his addresses without remuneration, which meant he was out of pocket for travel expenses. And while he had certainly developed a fascination for political and military events in Spain, he had not toured that country since the extended family trip he took as a seventeen-year-old. Indeed, his primary interest and scholarly expertise lay in the history and culture of Central America, Guatemala in particular. So Kelly's motivation for lecturing on the Spanish Civil War was neither financial nor personal but, rather, rhetorical. Spain, Spaniards, and their troubles were talking points. In Spain he could find evidence for his argument with Popular Fronters over the meaning of *Americanism*.[14]

Christian Corporatism, Authoritarian Rule, Anti-Semitism

Manhattan Rotarians understood the importance of friendly governments and free trade and, along with Philadelphia Presbyterians and the other mostly middle-class and elite audiences Kelly addressed, many of them would have also appreciated the basic tenets of Christian corporatism. As associated with António de Oliveira Sala-zar's Portugal and Franco's Spain, and enlightened by Pope Pius XI's call for Catholic Social Action in *Quadragesimo Anno*, Christian corporatism was analogous to later state-industry-labor triumvirates of European statist socialism and Middle Eastern étatism, the difference being its prerequisite of a Catholic polity. Promoted as an antidote to both rapacious capitalism and godless communism, and emphasizing nation building in a regulated, cooperative environment, it was a Christianized ver-sion of Benito Mussolini's *Stato sociale*, whereby an authoritarian yet benevolent government aimed to maximize economic output for the good of the nation, in-dustrial profit, and—its primary goal—the well-being of workers without recourse to radical unionization and labor disruptions. According to historian Fredrick B. Pike, it was a potentially equitable system, playing a "striking" role in improving income distribution under Franco during the 1950s, although this rosy picture begs the counterpoint of detractors like Sebastian Balfour, who observes that Franco's administration tended to fall back on autarkic import substitution industries when-ever economic conditions deteriorated. Howard J. Wiarda sees corporatism as an "Iberic-Latin counterpart to the great isms of liberalism and socialism."[15]

Christian corporatism also became state policy in North America. It was the central platform of Premier Maurice Duplessis' National Union Party in Quebec, from where its ideology trickled south. A November 1937 *New York Times* article quoted Tim Buck, general secretary of the Canadian Communist Party (CCP), who bemoaned the success of Duplessis' policies, for while the CCP did have 15,000 members, only 1,500 of them were in Quebec with a mere 500 in Montreal. Bostonians who tuned in to the so-called Yankee Network, NBC's affiliated WNAC radio station, on Sunday, 29 May 1938, had the opportunity to hear about "Portugal's Progress." Jesuit priest George T. Eberle explained how Christian corporatism in Salazar's Portugal had rejuvenated the economy, brought full employment, obviated strikes in favor of arbitration, and created a climate of social progress and dignity through spiritualism in the workplace. Corporatism, moreover, opposed communism without being fascistic, and because it was "a cure for economic and social chaos" without sacrificing spirituality to a materialistic worldview, it had papal backing.[16]

Catholic scholars—Jesuits in particular—took political ideology seriously in the late 1930s. They worked hard to evaluate the competing isms so that, on one hand, they could combat threats and, on the other, recommend enhancements to Christian America. Marxism fell squarely in the former category while corporatism had potential for the latter. On the basis that nothing "renders a defense so inadequate as misunderstanding the position and under-estimating the strength" of one's opponent, Charles J. McFadden conducted a rigorous analysis of dialectical Marxism in *The Philosophy of Communism*. Unsurprisingly, McFadden's opponent turned out to be CPUSA leader Earl Browder, who was on record for urging that America's communist revolution would not "simply *happen;* it must be *made.*" McFadden gave communists credit for not idealizing bloodshed; yet, he said, because the ruling class would always fight desperately to retain power, the essential characteristic of the proletariat's "coming revolution will be its *violence.*" In common with many political commentators of the 1930s, McFadden liked to add emphasis to his writing, but then he knew the violence that had befallen Catholic priests during Spain's revolution just two years earlier, and he no doubt feared for the well-being of America's clergy should Spanish anticlerical ideology cross the North Atlantic. In the preface, radio preacher Monsignor Sheen observed that long before Karl Marx thought out his dialectical materialism, he had become an atheist. "Once man lost his God," he lost his soul, his "value as a sovereign being," Sheen contended, thus exposing the absurdity of Marx's claim that a worker's value could somehow lie in the collectivity of a proletarian dictatorship. As systematic as McFadden, Joseph Patrick Dalton at Boston College's affiliated Jesuit seminary embarked on a scholarly critique of corporatism. Though Dalton found much to admire in Mussolini's version, he ultimately dismissed it as insufficiently Christian. In Portugal, though, he not only discovered corporatist utopia but also evidence that a genuinely Christian brand was compatible with American democracy. Few outside Dalton's advisory committee read his thesis, but his work legitimated corporatism for interested faculty, from whom its most appealing aspects filtered out to the classroom and on into New England's politico-business world through well-placed alumni.[17]

Kelly and his audience members were American individuals who tended to be curious, innovative, and well-read. Their political system of federated yet quasi-autonomous states had long taught them that experimentation engendered success as well as failure. If the greed of robber barons and stock speculators had tarnished the producer ethic, especially when so many family farms and small companies had lost their competitiveness to the agribusinesses and conglomerates favored by New Deal policies, then perhaps it was time to look across the Atlantic for workable alternatives. Many Americans, moreover, especially those who considered that they already had a dictatorship in the White House, spoke openly about the merits of authoritarian governance.

Throughout the winter of 1937–38, Fulton Oursler's *Liberty*, a weekly magazine with a middle-class readership of two million, featuring romance stories interspersed with political comment and strategies for playing contract bridge, presented a twelve-part serialization of Emil Ludwig's *Life of Roosevelt: A Study in Fortune and Power*. Its 5 February edition posed the "still-debated" question: "Did the new President, in '33, seek to be a dictator?" After focusing on Roosevelt's threat in his inaugural address to "seek" the kind of "broad executive power that would be given to me [in times of war]," Ludwig argued that it was "both fair and historically intelligible" to liken Roosevelt's "assumption of great powers reaching in the direction of a dictatorship" to Adolf Hitler's. It is notable that just nine months before Kristallnacht, a renowned Jewish author who had fled anti-Semitic persecution in Nazi Germany was prepared to extol the virtues of dictatorship for America. Dictatorship was a charge to which Roosevelt himself was especially sensitive. On 31 March a three-column *New York Times* headline blared "PRESIDENT HAS NO INCLINATION TO BE A DICTATOR" and quoted a letter Roosevelt had written to a friend justifying his pending Reorganization Bill. Roosevelt regretted that for "over forty years," the executive branch had been grappling with congressional inertia. A legislative conspiracy, he implied, sought "deliberately to wreck the present Administration." He had found legislative "bogies under every bed," which had "hamstrung" one of his initiatives and "damaged beyond repair" another. He could cite examples "of a score of equally silly nightmares conjured up" by a Congress determined to revert to the 1920s. All he asked in the bill, as "President, as Chief Executive," was "the authority to make certain adjustments and reorganizations by Executive order." Despite his "I have no inclination" rebuttal, he could not disguise his disdain for the Constitution's checks and balances.[18]

A transatlantic climate of uncertainty and fear was concentrating power in fewer hands, yet in the process, complex agendas such as foreign policy making, which whole departments of experienced professionals sometimes misconstrued, were slipping through presidential fingers. A paradox of late-1930s authoritarianism would be its empowerment of political activists, whose positions became more radical as they fought over the windfall. Increasingly confident were pro-Franco anticommunists like Kelly, who found it tempting to talk out both sides of their typewriters: Americanism was obviously good, but Americans had a shattered economy to rejuvenate or else underemployed mobs would clamor for Red revolution; all foreign isms were bad, but some isms were battling communism while rebuilding their economies and so might well have useful lessons for the United States. A logical extension of Franco lobbyists' doublespeak was the so-called defense mechanism argument: fascism abroad, as a benign polity that had so successfully restored order, rejuvenated depression-ravaged economies, and resuscitated national pride only arose as a welcome antidote to godless communism.

During a May Day speech to the Knights of Columbus (K-of-C) in the Bronx, Kelly listed America's enemies, including "those who denounce Fascism and do not mention communism." Surely, he reasoned, such people "betray their allegiance," for fascism had only ever appeared in countries as a reaction to communism's excesses. Kelly was addressing a predominantly Catholic Irish American crowd that would have included anticommunist trade unionists and Italian Americans, a crowd predisposed to holding sympathies with Nazi Germany and Fascist Italy, although his scripted remarks were not off the cuff and he gave the same speech that evening to a large gathering at St. Joseph's College in Philadelphia. Like all good orators, Kelly played to his audience, and there were probably few present in the K-of-C hall, Kelly noted, who could honestly say that they did not harbor anti-Jewish feelings. Historian Ronald H. Bayor's *Neighbors in Conflict* shows how metropolitan New York of the late 1930s seethed with interethnic rivalries, which invariably fragmented along interreligious fault lines. And in Leonard Dinnerstein's view, "It was the Spanish Civil War that had the most profound effect on Catholic–Jewish relations." New York's Jewish rabbis could be as antipapist as its Catholic priests were anti-Jewish, while old-stock Protestant ministers, who represented an ideal of Americanism to which many immigrant groups aspired, tended to be nativist.[19]

Two Brooklyn weekly newspapers with influence outside their locales, Rabbi Louis D. Gross's *Jewish Examiner* (circulation 29,000) and Patrick F. Scanlan's *Brooklyn Tablet* (circulation 99,000), were particularly combative. In June 1938, after physicist Albert Einstein insisted that the U.S. government must lift its arms embargo on Loyalist Spain, Scanlan took issue with aliens who used their prestige to promote seditious Comintern ideology and suggested that Einstein should leave the United States. Gross editorialized that Scanlan had unburdened himself "of a sentiment which for unadulterated malice and astounding cruelty ranks with the choicer abominations of [Nazi propagandist Joseph] Goebbels." Scanlan and

Gross were soon slinging linotype at each other, with readers waging in with letters to their editors. Charging hypocrisy, Scanlan identified an "anti-Christian campaign" conducted through *The Nation, New Republic,* Musicians Union Local 802, the International Garment Workers Union, and radio station WEVD, all of which were run by "Jewish interests—and interests which specialize in denouncing anti-Semitism."[20]

Kelly was typical of pro-Franco Americans who associated Jewish New Yorkers with enthusiasm for both communism and Madrid's Loyalists, especially the Abraham Lincoln Brigade volunteers. Generalizations being the mechanism through which a populace simplifies societal complexity, one can see how Kelly and those like him conflated Jews with communists and ALB volunteers. Historians concur with Nathan Glazer that "a large proportion" of the CPUSA was Jewish—Glazer suggests a figure for Brooklyn's CP of 77–90 percent—and, according to the ALB's first historian, "some 30 per cent of the Lincolns came from Jewish homes." Yet, given that, for Kelly, a stereotypical American communist as well as a Loyalist volunteer in Spain was Jewish, he made surprisingly few anti-Jewish remarks. Rather, his was the anti-Semitism of omission. When Kelly returned from Berlin, his letters to Talbot did not mention the official persecution of the city's Jews, a pertinent topic to which his fluency in German could hardly have left him oblivious. Conspicuous signs, which the authorities removed for the 1936 Berlin Olympics but then quickly reinstated, banned Jews from public parks as well as the Zoologischer Garten adjacent to his hotel on Fasenenstrasse. In his scores of magazine articles and letters to editors, he never commented on what he had witnessed during his business trip to Nazi Germany, although his blind spot was more likely to have been a German American's embarrassment over the sins of the fatherland than an Irish American's resentment of Jewish successes in the new country. His argument for sympathy with authoritarian regimes abroad—boldly stated, at least until spring 1939—was that of the defense mechanism: nothing in Franco's Spain or even in Hitler's Germany could ever be so bad as in communist Russia, where, as he charged in his K-of-C speech, Bolshevik Party leader Vladimir Ilich Lenin had "deliberately starved five million of his subjects to death" for harboring differing political opinions. Fascist regimes were harsh, he was saying, but at least they were fighting the ungodly Reds.[21]

Before the Spanish Civil War, there was little in Kelly's writings to indicate that he would have welcomed authoritarian governance for the United States, even as an antidote to communist revolution. To the contrary, he valued individual autonomy and had nailed his business career to the mast of laissez-faire. Still, times had changed. From what Kelly learned in newspapers and in his travels around the country, Roosevelt's double-dip recession, with its eleven million unemployed, had just given the lie to five years of New Dealing. International communism, Kelly reasoned, was on the march, and military dictatorships were the only regimes so far that had mustered the resolve to block its path; producerist capitalism was broken, labor was discontent, and Christian corporatism was the only system so far that had revived economies while accommodating trade unionism. Roosevelt was both dictatorial and corporatist, but for Kelly—in addition to his personal grudge against New Deal conglomerates for bankrupting his natural gas business—foredooming Roosevelt's administration were what he saw as its left-leaning credentials: it had extended diplomatic recognition to the Soviet Union, formed an unholy alliance with Earl Browder's Popular Front, and knowingly or otherwise employed CPUSA members, and, furthermore, the First Lady regularly socialized with members of the American Youth Congress, American Student Union, and other communist-controlled groups. From this perspective, Christian corporatism had its attractions, at least to cure the ills of far-away Europe if not necessarily for application at home.[22]

Americanism

When Kelly addressed nine hundred New York trade unionists, three hundred Philadelphia Presbyterians, and five hundred Manhattan Rotarians in those anxious months of 1938, theories of Christian corporatism, nods and winks at fascist dictatorships, and critiques of New Deal liberals were debating points in a collective discussion over something far more fundamental. What drew speaker and audience members together was a shared understanding that their brand of Americanism was in jeopardy. Communists from abroad, they believed, were exploiting economic collapse at home to foment social unrest. Because it seemed to them that Roosevelt's administration was incapable of ending the recession, and was encouraging rather than silencing the communists, many—especially Kelly, who had studied the Mexican and Spanish revolutions—feared an imminent sociopolitical crisis with attendant violence.

In asking, what was this Americanism, why were Americans so anxious about it, and why did so many European societies turn to socialism while Americans persisted with their trust in free-market consumerism, I suggest that the answers are mutually explanatory. Arguing obsessively over Americanism reinforced Americans' belief that just as Providence had guided the Founding Fathers, so destiny was still guiding them as dutiful Americans; because the Constitution already enshrined an ideal set of values, they had a special responsibility to reject competing political philosophies. Thomas Jefferson liked to talk in universal terms, yet he did so nevertheless as an American. That philosophers could not agree on something as fundamental as the origins of human morality, Jefferson wrote to a friend, made clear "how necessary was the care of the Creator in making the moral principle" so integral to man's psyche so that "no errors of reasoning or speculation might lead us astray from its observance in practice." "I have sworn upon the altar of god," he wrote to another friend, an "eternal hostility against every form of tyranny over the mind of man." After observing in a bill to establish religious freedom how "Almighty God hath created the mind free," he averred that "all attempts to influence it" would be "a departure from the plan of the holy author of our religion." "We hold these truths to be self-evident," his Declaration of Independence famously stated, that all men were "endowed by their Creator with certain unalienable Rights." American principles, Jefferson was certain, conformed to a providential design, and genera-tions of Yankees upheld his conviction. America, British author G. K. Chesterton observed in 1922, "is the only nation in the world that is founded on a creed" as "set forth with dogmatic and even theological lucidity" in the Declaration.[23]

Commentators like Samuel P. Huntington agree with Chesterton that Americans' national creed is a unique concept. Indeed, citizens of other countries have rarely articulated such an exceptionalist national ideology as Americanism, let alone leg-islated for a body to investigate and prosecute insufficiently national behavior. That Congress chose to do this in May 1938 when it created the Special House Commit-tee for the Investigation of Un-American Activities (HUAC; renamed the House Un-American Activities Committee in 1945), indicates the insecurities prevalent in American society. Although HUAC under the chairmanship of Martin Dies was an investigative body, it nonetheless had teeth, recommending prosecutions for in-come tax evasion and especially for breaches of the Foreign Agents Registration Act (FARA), which Congress passed in 1938. Huntington asserts that this un-American corollary is unique, though his proposition only holds for the West. Japan and Brit-ain, two countries on American minds at the time, make for a revealing compari-son. Whereas the Japanese state during the 1930s similarly arrested and imprisoned a number of citizens it judged to be insufficiently Japanese, or *hikokumin* (literally, not a member of the nation), English Parliamentarians tended to dismiss radicals as amusing eccentrics who exemplified Britishness; it was not until 1940 that the government proscribed Sir Oswald Mosley's British Union of Fascists.[24]

Late-1930s Americans understood their national ideology on three broad levels. First, on a subconscious level—as articulated by the American Legion, that bastion of "100% Americanism"—their native ideology was so obvious as to be indefinable, but, if pushed, it meant simply the rejection of foreign isms, for there was only one true spirit. As the mayor of Portland, Oregon, equivocated in a letter to *Life* in Au-gust 1938, his city was "against all 'isms' except Americanism." Second, on a personal level, they experienced their Americanism through a set of traditional ideals or core values, including but not limited to Enlightenment rationalism, Lockean liberalism, Jeffersonian producerism, and Jacksonian frontier individualism; justice, freedom, and democracy; to the kind of integrity at home and fair dealings abroad as en-shrined in foundational documents like the Constitution and Washington's Fare-well Address; to a manifest design or providential destiny that all true Americans were, by virtue of their Puritan inheritance, potentially cut out for a life of goodness, greatness, and, of course, expansion westward.[25]

Third, on a public level, Americanism as a quasi-official doctrine grew out of the Americanization programs of the 1910s and 1920s that aimed to transform a massive influx of European immigrants into proud and productive citizens. At the same time, the programs reinforced nationalism and encouraged exemplary behavior among the elites who promoted them. City councils, chambers of commerce, big corporations, veterans' associations, benevolent clubs, and religious organizations (none more so than the Catholic Church) were at the forefront of proselytizing Americanism through school textbooks, primers, periodicals, and evening classes. Old-stocks and immigrants alike developed an innate sense of what Americanism meant, even if they had difficulty putting it into words. Handbooks often began by explaining how "Americanism is an attitude of mind upholding certain principles," just as they were careful to stress its exceptionalist nature, akin to a state religion: "Americanism is a matter of the spirit, to be regarded and approached in a spirit of truth." One of the more systematic primers was Emory S. Bogardus's *Essentials of Americanization* (1919), which laid down four "fundamental sets of characteristics" defined as "liberty and self-reliance, union and co-operation, democracy and the square deal, internationalism and brotherhood." This latter set was the projection abroad of the first three with a view, naturally, toward advancing America's "commercial interests" through open-door trade policies while holding "aloof from entangling alliances." These bibles of Americanism authenticated the absolutism of the core values. They encouraged appropriate legislation, such as a Massachusetts statute of 1935 compelling public school teachers to lead their pupils in a weekly salute to the flag and a pledge of allegiance; and they created a set of revered iconic symbols through the mythicizing of history (Washington's Valley Forge), the guardianship of objects (the Washington Monument), and the celebration of festivals (Washington's Birthday), reinforced through public performance and photographs of these events. At Ford Motor Company's English-language school graduation of 1916, two hundred workers gathered on stage around a twenty-foot melting pot set against an ocean liner backdrop. Workers carrying European flags descended from a gangplank into the pot only to emerge holding American flags, while a banner unfurled, proclaiming, "E pluribus unum," out of many, one. An Americanization pageant in a Milwaukee auditorium in 1919 featured a tableau of immigrants and their children in East European garb facing the Statue of Liberty, while an immigrant dressed as Abraham Lincoln outstretched his hand. A placard declared, "The Wanderer finds Liberty in America." Throughout the interwar period, city mayors and state governors across the country encouraged patriotic exercises on Americanization Day, staged originally on either George Washington's or Ulysses S. Grant's birthday, but then moved celebrations to May Day as counterpoints to the parades of unionists and communists.[26]

These three definitional approaches shared the assumption that Americanism was as immutable as it was timeless, that it was as powerful as it was perfect, and that it was as achievable as it was essential for all immigrants. It also was as assimilationist to those who approached the Anglo-Protestant ideal as it was exclusionary to those who had the wrong, or inassimilable, cultural attributes. Americanism was the "great Melting-Pot," as Israel Zangwill had his young Russian Jewish immigrant hero David Quixano explain in the famous play of that name. It was "God's Crucible" through which "all the races of Europe are melting and reforming" into the sublime. "God," David confidently affirmed to thousands of theatergoers in his slight German accent, was "making the American" presumably in his own (fixed) image. Writing in the *Catholic Mind* in July 1939, Jesuit thinker C. C. Chapman similarly placed Americanism on a level with natural law, elevating it to "a *way of life*" that involved "man's right relationship to God." He averred that Americanism was not perfect but was nonetheless "as close to fool-proof as any system ever established."[27]

Yet these unassailable truths belied both the social crisis through which Americanism was evolving and the mutated ideology that would emerge during the cold war. Looking back on 1930s Americanism reveals that it was less of a closed ideology and more of an open forum for public debate. To paraphrase historian Prasenjit Duara, it was an arena where two quite different ideas of national identity contested and negotiated with each other. Without realizing that they were so doing, anticommunist Franco lobbyists took the stage of Americanism, where they argued its meaning—and hence its future—with their pro-Loyalist counterparts, many of whom were communists. For those Americans who saw anticommunism as a key component of their providential way of life, the cauldron that was the Great Debate over the Spanish Civil War did brew for them a foolproof national ideology: the McCarthyist repression, military-industrial complex, and statist consumerism of the cold war liberal consensus.[28]

Their self-confidence already shaken by the collapse of American laissez-faire capitalism, Kelly and his audiences did more than fear communism as a foreign ism; they understood it to be the embodiment of everything that would destroy Americanism and, hence, their identity, insecure as that so often was in a land of opportunistic newcomers. Revolutionary communism had every opportunity to pervade the senses of Franco lobbyists during 1938. Kelly, in Manhattan, probably heard marchers cheering the Soviet flag and singing "The Internationale" during the massive May Day parades of 1937 and 1938. In many parts of the country, street-parade vocalism crossed over into picket-line violence. Radical intimidators of John L. Lewis's United Mine Workers of America and Joe Ozanic's rival Progressive Miners of America carried firearms and bombed homes, newspaper offices, and mine workings. During his field trips to the soft-coal mines of Kentucky and West Virginia, Kelly had met frightened nonunion miners and mine operators, many of whom worked in cooperative ventures to keep open so-called submarginal pits whose revenue could not support the overhead of unionization. When Kelly explained during his lectures on the spread of communism, how an official in Paul Blanshard's New York Commissioner of Accounts department openly sold fifty-cent fund-raising stamps bearing a "soviet star, hammer and sickle, and the legend 'For a soviet America,'" he spoke as someone who had gone to city hall to see them for himself. For skeptics, Kelly could cite Manhattan borough president Stanley M. Isaacs's recent appointment to his staff of Simon W. Gerson, a CPUSA state executive committee member. But if, for Kelly and his audiences, there was still any doubt that international communism was just a mild scare, then their proof was not rumor of famine or purge in the far-off Eastern Russia but close-to-home fact in the Western Spain, where organized, Soviet-backed revolutionaries had murdered 6,800 religious, destroyed cultural artifacts, collectivized industry and farms, and persecuted property owners as well as petty entrepreneurs and shopkeepers whose work ethics they judged to be insufficiently working class.[29]

"The Power of Protest"

It seemed to Kelly that every newsstand and bookstore was rife with pro-Loyalist propaganda. To whatever extent he exaggerated, literary scholars agree with Kelly's findings. John M. Muste emphasizes the strength of communist influence in the late 1930s, noting how "American writers were virtually unanimous in sympathizing with the Loyalists." In Frederick R. Benson's analysis, the "literary response was overwhelming," with the "vast majority" of American writers defining the conflict as "a graphic struggle between the defenders and the destroyers of democracy." Benson, who admires the Comintern's "skilful propaganda machine," leaves no doubt that "many" of the radicals he discusses were "active members or sympathized with the anarchist, socialist, and communist organizations." To remedy the imbalance, Kelly intended a two-prong strategy: expose negative propaganda to the unwitting public and fight it directly with positive propaganda of his own, wherever he could find a willing publisher.[30]

By the summer of 1938, Kelly was a regular contributor to Catholic periodicals like *America, Sign, Catholic World, Catholic Mirror,* and *Wisdom,* and he was writing several articles each month for the glossy magazine *Spain* on topics from South American history to Spanish culture to military analysis. As Franco's U.S. organ, *Spain* was a rejoinder to the (Loyalist) Spanish Information Bureau's *News of Spain,* but because Washington policy makers denied the Nationalists official recognition, it required publication by a private corporation, Peninsular News Service. Financial underwriting came from Juan Francisco de Cárdenas, with whom Kelly was now meeting regularly for a free lunch and *conversación confidencial* at the Ritz-Carlton. Also during the summer, Mrs. Dawes of Boston commissioned Kelly to write a pocket history of Franco, *The Christian Soldier,* which she published in the form of a smart, red-covered five-cent booklet and then distributed her first print run of a thousand copies through clubs and churches.[31]

As well as serving on its editorial board, Kelly wrote the leader for the first edition of R. Caldwell Patton's *Patriot Digest,* a sophisticated quarterly that attracted respected writers such as H. L. Mencken, cofounder of the *American Mercury* literary magazine, who had become one of America's shrillest Roosevelt critics. In "Should Relief Vote?" Kelly tackled the thorny issue of representation in a democracy, pointing out that the current system sidestepped a significant part of the citizenry, including Native Americans on reservations, many in the armed forces, 35,000 Americans living abroad, 650,000 citizens of the District of Columbia, and some 4.3 million (mostly blacks) on the grounds of illiteracy. Because Roosevelt received the support of around six million voters in families reliant on federal handouts, Kelly argued that New Deal welfare would self-perpetuate. He then linked the administration's expansion of relief to its shackling of private enterprise, which he blamed for causing further deterioration of the economy. Washington's New Deal "high command" was only adding muster to "the desperate, the hopeless, the drifting," to those who found uplift at the sound of the demagogue and promise in communism. Such an "invertebrate mass of voters" dependent on welfare and voting "*en bloc* for the perpetuation in office of incumbent politicians" would destroy the "American tradition of self-reliance, individualism, and hard work." Communists would find it easy to preach class hatred. "Americanism and democracy will sink *spurlos* [without trace] in chaos." With no end to the recession in sight, Kelly's warning to the *Digest*'s elite Protestant readership was plain: The "great mass of conservative Americans" must "arouse themselves from their lethargy, overcome their instinctive distrust of politics, and restore the American system," or else the "sovietized relief" of the New Deal would do what "bread and circuses" did for Rome.[32]

When he was not battling mass media pro-Loyalist writers through low-volume pro-Nationalist publications, Kelly lost no opportunity to question his opponents' methods. Two days before his February radio broadcast, the *New York Times*'s front page featured his exposé of Ambassador Ríos's abuse of the diplomatic franking privilege. At a publicity meeting attended by a *Times* reporter, Kelly exhibited a bundle of pamphlets whose wrapper bore the label "Spanish Embassy, Washington" and the stamp "Diplomatic Mail, Free" as evidence of "thousands" of such "packages of propaganda" mailed by the embassy with a postal value of twenty-five cents ($7), a considerable "burden to American taxpayers." All pro-Loyalist propagandists were fair game. In June, Kelly even went after Alfred P. Sloan Jr., chairman of General Motors.[33]

Time magazine had run a sensational, full-page advertisement in the *New York Times* featuring an American waving his fist at a pair of low-flying bombers. Under the slogan "Cadillac knows that American anger can help sell cars," the ad explained how a survey had proven that Cadillac buyers were discerning newsreaders—they read *Time*. To make the point, streaming out from the Cadillac's hood were suggestive tickertape messages: "Barcelona—rebel bombers spread destruction"; "bombing of civilian centers protested by Washington"; "prime minister Chamberlain seeks end to Spanish war"; "18 indicted in Nazi spy case—Catholic Churc_," obscured by the angry American's business suit. Kelly's letter to Sloan was scathing. Although the "radical" *Time* placed the ad, surely Sloan's advertising manager had approved it? This "most glaring mistake" in "a generation" of GM advertising had already caused protest selling of GM stock by elites in Kelly's network, and Kelly had forwarded the ad to contacts in Nationalist Spain, where GM products were popular. Unless *Time* had somehow "hoodwinked" GM, the ad showed a deliberate advocacy of communism. "Understand," he cautioned Sloan, "you help communists just as much by an advertisement of this kind as if you yourself mounted barricades in Union Square." Sloan's reply was blushingly apologetic: *Time* copy artists had indeed hoodwinked him by adding the offensive tickertape to an innocent proof. But he had personally telephoned *Time*'s editor to demand the ad's discontinuance and now wanted to assure Kelly that he was "quite the contrary to a communist." On relating the story to Talbot, Kelly observed how it illustrated "the power of protest." Indeed, it illustrated the ability of an individual to influence elite opinion on key issues through a carefully channeled complaint.[34]

When it came to the Spanish Civil War, Kelly's assessment of the popular *Time* as radical was not so far off the mark. During the cold war years, if not by the early 1940s, Henry Robinson Luce's magazines were essentially conservative, and, as historian Seth Jacobs has shown, *Time* was congenial to authoritarian Catholic regimes, at least in Asia. Yet it is worth noting here that during the late 1930s many of *Time*'s journalists, editors, and evidently copy artists toed the Comintern line; they were products of the "*laboring* of American culture" described by Michael Denning. Luce endeavored to cast *Time/Life* publications as centrist, with *Time*'s trademark front covers featuring graphic illustrations of leaders from across the political spectrum. Yet under its affable skin, a "surprising number," according to Denning, "of Popular Front" staff managed to project considerable Loyalist support. In the 14 February 1938 issue, which featured "Spain's Leftist General Pozas" on the cover, *Time* quoted "the latest civil war statistics." At 2 percent of its 800,000 armed forces, Loyalist Spain had only 16,000 "non-Spaniards," but the Nationalist army of 450,000 had 35 percent, the implication being that 157,500 Fascist Italians and Nazi Germans were fighting for Franco. In fact, discounting Moors from Spain's North African protectorate and including Loyalist aid workers, some of whom—such as Eleanor Roosevelt's close friend Joseph Lash, who wrote that he was "training with the 1st Company, but as an observer"—took part in combat, the two sides were close to parity on foreign fighters. Judging by its photographic captions and leaders, *Time*'s editorial policy was to label the two sides "Leftists" and "Rightists," although its foreign news editors often managed to gloss those labels into "Republicans" and "Fascists," such as on 28 March, when quotations from *Chicago Daily News* reporter Richard Mowrer spoke of "a whole division of Republican forces" and "the Fascists' great superiority in arms." At *Fortune*, Luce's sister publication, two fellow travelers, Archibald MacLeish and Ralph Ingersoll, were at the helm. MacLeish's outspoken Loyalist partisanship alienated him from his friend Luce; he quit the paper in summer 1938 to devote his literary skills to Popular Front causes. Ingersoll left in early 1939 to found *PM*, a Popular Front workers' daily tabloid that aimed for a half-million circulation in metropolitan New York and which, though it projected a liberal socialist image, followed a rocky path between CPUSA and Socialist Party lines.[35]

Roosevelt's Discourse of Liberalism

Red–fascist discourse was not the only powerful construction with which Franco lobbyists had to contend and, in contending, did so much to reinforce. Nineteen-thirty-eight saw the flowering of Roosevelt's discourse of liberalism. As a durable engine of power and control by and within a society, an effective discourse requires official legitimation as well as broad participation. Far more than a set of linguistic symbols, its politico-social utility reaches peak effectiveness when it ceases to be the subject of debate and enters mainstream thought as a "depoliticized" standard, to borrow Jenny Edkins's conception, even though its ideology may only be a "social fantasy." Roosevelt's powerful and enduring discourse of big-government liberalism satisfied these theoretical criteria. Theorists would also be pleased to note that Roosevelt was not so much its originator but rather its discoverer in the mass media as a debate in progress. Once he had commandeered it, though, redefined its agenda, and then given it his presidential endorsement, it became the de facto system; anyone who disagreed became a political pariah rather than a concerned dissenter. And with unprecedented access to the influential new media of radio, Roosevelt could easily propagate its social fantasy.[36]

Roosevelt had occasionally dropped the word *liberal* during the 1930s, deploying it as a trope for his New Deal. Its first appearance in one of his legendary fireside chats came on 9 March 1937 when he was selling his plan to stack the Supreme Court. "Today's recovery," he reminded radio listeners, "proves how right" New Deal policies were. Unfortunately, because only two of the "three-horse team" of government—the executive and legislative branches—were pulling in unison, the recovery was jeopardized by the third horse, the judiciary. If Americans would back the immediate authority he sought to appoint one extra judge for every judge over seventy years of age, then all three horses could pull the country back to prosperity.

Rest assured, he told listeners, appointing six new justices would "not infringe in the slightest" on civil liberties, for his long record in public office had already proven his devotion to liberty and the "heritage of freedom." Only speedy legislation to change the Court could provide the kind of "reinvigorated, liberal-minded Judiciary" necessary for the continued passage of New Deal reforms.[37]

By the following year, though, with Roosevelt's court-packing scheme an embarrassing defeat and "today's recovery" mired in a deepening recession, critics became more vocal and, in their stridency, debated the meaning of the New Deal's ideological double, liberalism. Americans struggled for the high ground of liberalism in the mass media, evidenced in May 1938 when *Time* magazine, with its circulation of 600,000, began a six-week debate argued through readers' letters. Letter writer Edward McArdle of Toronto postulated that Roosevelt was a model liberal because he believed in "the increasing freedom of the individual in relation to his government." Conservatives, McArdle reasoned by contrast, such as political philosopher and former socialist Walter Lippmann, who had taken a right turn, were "opposed to change in existing institutions" and were always "harking back" to prior regimes like free trade. McArdle also considered a third category, reactionaries, such as southern racists or columnist Dorothy Thompson. (It is ironic that Thompson, though a reactionary, actually supported Loyalist Madrid and the lifting of the U.S. arms embargo, and Lippmann dedicated his 1937 espousal of "radical conservatism" as the key to "liberal reform" to Sedgwick, even though as a socialist in the 1920s Lippman had concurred with the Sacco-Vanzetti verdict.) *Time*'s editor then asked readers whether they agreed with McArdle that their president was a liberal.[38]

Time received 180 letters, of which only forty-eight (27 percent) judged Roosevelt a liberal, and not all of those were flattering. Lindsey C. Foster, of Pennsboro, West Virginia, defined liberals as having an eye to see how "trees grow better in sunlight" and an eye to observe how "all men are *not* created free and equal." Maurice C. Latta, of Olivet, Michigan, thought Roosevelt was a liberal when he spoke yet in any "historic" sense was illiberal when he acted to strengthen the controls of government over the actions of individuals. Most of the published letters in disagreement with McArdle saw Roosevelt's liberalism as insincere "window dressing" or "blab sounds," as two writers put it. James Aswell of Venice, Florida, went the furthest, accusing Roosevelt of being a "rock-ribbed conservative" who sought only to retain his "powers, perquisites and glories" by any means at his disposal. Economics professor Elmer Pendell of Uniontown, Pennsylvania, was one of several writers to debate the meaning of the word itself. Based on sampling his students' opinions over many years, Pendell concluded that *liberal* was "merely a word of approval, like 'good' and 'beauty.'"[39]

Yet *liberal* had always been much more than a blab sound or word of approval, as evidenced by *Time* printing so many letters devoted to the concept. Liberalism was not only a term denoting a primary American core value extending back

past the Founding Fathers to the Enlightenment and John Locke, but it was also a
discursive vehicle fueled with charge and purpose. Before 24 June 1938, Roosevelt
had rarely used *liberal* (or its derivative, *liberalism*) stressing *social* instead. In a
six-page extract of his "Own Story of the New Deal," published in *Liberty* magazine on 12 March, Roosevelt wrote *liberal* once (indirectly, at that) and *social* (social justice, social reform) eight times. He said *liberal* once in twelve previous fireside chats but used it eight times during his chat of 24 June, the week after *Time*'s
letter forum. With his administration under critical assault and midterm elections looming, it seems likely that Roosevelt and speechwriter Stephen T. Early
had been following the debate and saw an opportunity to jump into the driver's
seat. It is also notable that in 1941, when he collaborated with the publication of
his addresses, Roosevelt subtitled the 1938 volume *The Continuing Struggle for
Liberalism*. Just as Red–fascist discourse permitted no middle way, so Roosevelt's
struggle for the soul of liberalism polarized Americans between good pro-state
liberals and bad antistate conservatives and, by inference, between those who
would either lift or retain the Spanish arms embargo. As an oppositional construction, it forced participants to take sides. In its official monopolization of the
high ground, it backed opponents into dark corners. Roosevelt—never much of
an ideologue—explained something of what he understood his 1938 liberalism to
mean in *Continuing Struggle*'s introduction.[40]

First, it was populist and inclusive, representing "the wisdom and efficacy of
the will of the great majority" of Americans. Because the great majority of Americans were good liberals, Roosevelt did not need to say who those Americans were;
rather, all he needed to do was identify the bad opposition. Those who would
"strike down liberalism" were a "small minority of either education or wealth." They
were the "big guns" of conservatism, representing the interests of "wealth, privilege, economic power, political power," whom in one paragraph Roosevelt slurred
as a "'putsch.'" Second, it was "militant" and go-ahead, dealing in "remedies" and
"progressive reforms." Liberalism was the "only path of true recovery and the only
assurance" of the American way of free enterprise. Conservative big guns, by contrast, did nothing, letting Americans sink unless private initiative could somehow
save them at the last minute. Third, it was good and social-minded (Roosevelt
was careful not to say *socialist*), for "true" liberalism assured an "equitable distribution of income," combated "social problems with new social controls," and
even tackled soil conservation and sweatshop labor. Conservatives, though, only
created the "abuses, evils, and widespread maladjustments" that had brought the
country to the "very brink of destruction." Fourth, it was all-American, ensuring
rights to "economic and political life, liberty, and the pursuit of happiness." Liberalism was the way of all good presidents, and here Roosevelt invoked Jefferson,
Abraham Lincoln, Theodore Roosevelt, and Woodrow Wilson, all of whom had
battled evil conservatives, presumably Alexander Hamilton, Jefferson Davis, Wil-

liam Howard Taft, and Henry Cabot Lodge, respectively. True liberalism, in short, was Roosevelt's good New Deal package, and any big gun who would strike down even a small part of it was a bad, un-American conservative.[41]

In 1938, when there were sixty million radio sets in American homes and popular shows such as *Amos 'n' Andy* reached a third of listeners, Roosevelt's fireside chats commanded a 70 percent rating. His 24 June chat devoted a third of the broadcast to a newfound struggle for liberalism. Americans, he wanted it "clearly understood," must realize there were now two opposing schools of thought. Those who held to the "progressive principles" of the liberal school successfully solved problems through "democratic process instead of Fascism or Communism." Whoever would place any kind of "moratorium" on his "new remedies" and beneficial reforms was a reactionary. So anyone who opposed his liberal reforms, those who would "go back" to the gold standard, say, or abolish unemployment insurance, believed in the "conservative school of thought." When Father Charles E. Coughlin, himself a master of the ether, heard Roosevelt's chat, he had no doubt about its thesis, which he paraphrased as, "I am the great liberal. I stand for liberalism."[42]

Intent to marginalize political opponents, Roosevelt set a rhetorical trap into which pro-Franco anticommunists had little choice but to step. Paradoxically, Roosevelt's liberalism became the casualty of its own discourse. As letter writer Elmer Pendell observed and historian John Patrick Diggins has written, instead of being an ideology to challenge dogma, liberalism became "a dogmatic fixation that led people to assume that what they believe is simply what is good and useful." A letter by R. C. Wardel in the *New York World-Telegram* of 15 July addressed the problem facing many dissenters: "Now that we are all seeking a definition of 'Liberal,'" what was the matter with "a liberal is one who has decided not to decide." Yet for those whose angst drove them to seek alternative solutions, deciding not to decide must have seemed a poor option.[43]

Pro-Franco Americanism as Conservative Ideology

Franco lobbyists like W. Cameron Forbes and Ellery Sedgwick, both progressive modernizers, and Kelly, who had been a grass-roots activist for La Follette's Progressive Party presidential candidacy in 1924, must have found it galling that Roosevelt's militant liberalism had so successfully coopted their progressive principles. Had they not been anticommunist Franco supporters, then they might conceivably have thrown in the towel, for they were close to Roosevelt on other principles too, from social security to a more equitable tax code that would cut big business down to size. But lobbying for Franco's Spain as a paradigm for initially exposing and then finally defeating America's Communist International was their fundamental precept, just as they cast Roosevelt as a sort of distracted dupe rooting for Madrid while his cabinet went soft on communism. In the climate of such a powerful discourse, therefore, Franco lobbyists could hardly oppose their pro-Madrid president as liberals, for Roosevelt's New Deal now stood for liberalism. They confronted a dilemma, and its simplest if uncomfortable solution was to change labels. Sedgwick's *Atlantic* published a preponderance of commentators who increasingly billed themselves as conservatives. Whereas Kelly had earlier used *conservatism* as a synonym for *capitalism* in the fight against "Sovietism," in 1938 he began labeling himself a conservative. Kelly's writings became more overtly derogatory toward New Deal liberals and praiseworthy of "rightists." In June 1941 he wrote a provocative article for *America* entitled "Stupid, Wishful Liberals Forget That Stalin Hates Us," and by 1943 he routinely clipped out newspaper columns by conservative commentators such as Westbrook Pegler and George E. Sokolsky.[44]

Red-fascist discourse and Roosevelt's discourse of liberalism backed Franco lobbyists into the conservatives' corner. At the outset of their figurative shift, they sat there awkwardly—none more so than Kelly, who at heart was a multilingual cosmopolitan, a liberal progressive, and an atheistic humanist, aside from the evident malice as well as racist stereotyping he displayed toward those who already were, or he thought might become, un-American communist revolutionaries. Evaluating the extent to which Franco lobbyists either belonged on or became comfortable with the political Right is challenging. After all, their defense-mechanism argument sanctioned authoritarian regimes, and through their quarrel with pro-Loyalists, they sought to strengthen, if not reshape, national identity in order to withstand external threat. Interpretive confusion arises because it is the modernist project of nationalism—as "imagined" by political elites, transmitted through mass media, inscribed by immigration laws, and exaggerated by imperialism and total war, all of which engender the deepest of psychological resonances—which scholars so often associate with the right wing.[45]

Eric Hobsbawm's *The Age of Extremes* dwells at length on the "ideological threat to liberal civilization" that developed during the interwar years before becoming a global reality in 1939. As a "potentially world-wide movement," this terrifying danger to liberal institutions came "exclusively" from the reactionary and authoritarian right and was above all "nationalist." Yet it is only by glossing over the causes of civil war in Spain—a backward, "peripheral" European country that nonetheless "became the symbol of a global struggle in the 1930s"—that Hobsbawm can assert so categorically that there were no threats to liberal government from forces of the left during the interwar years. For Hobsbawm, Spain's Second Republic of 1931 was a government of "well-meaning liberals" that conservative reaction "pushed aside" in 1933 but that triumphed again in February 1936 as the "effective government" of the (implicitly liberal) Popular Front before tragically succumbing to a reactionary and fascistic military coup. Absent from Hobsbawm's synthesis is the reality of full-scale anarcho-communist revolution by 20,000 militiamen in Asturias in

1934, which included the murder of several dozen priests, abolition of money, dynamiting of parts of central Oviedo, theft of 15 million pesetas ($60 million) from local banks, and imposition of a workers' state, the first in the West since the 1871 Commune of Paris. According to Hobsbawm, who mentions Asturias only to illustrate the rightists' policy of "repressing agitations," this was a spontaneous "rising" by discontented miners. Absent, too, is any sense that Spain lacked civil order in the spring of 1936. Rather, as Franco lobbyists worked so hard to explain and historian Stanley G. Payne has recently reiterated, there was widespread, systematic government-tolerated anarchy and anticlericalism, culminating in the murder of opposition leader José Calvo Sotelo by the Popular Front's own security forces. By this time, Spain's radicalized climate nourished the "broadest and most intense panoply of revolutionary movements of any country in the world." Militant socialist Francisco Largo Caballero was rooted in local *madrileño* culture, yet he drove his vast Union General de Trabajadores (UGT) headlong toward Bolshevization, thereby embracing a truly worldwide movement, to use Hobsbawm's words, that posed a serious "ideological threat to liberal civilization."[46]

Political historian Elie Kedourie is equally emphatic that "nationalism and liberalism" are "antagonistic principles," although he does believe that it is a "misunderstanding to ask whether nationalism is a politics of the right or left." As Hobsbawm's interpretation suggests, Kedourie feels that the misunderstanding derives from the success of Bolshevism in Stalinist Russia. As long as nationalists struggled against capitalists and imperialists, theirs was a progressive movement; but when capitalists used nationalism to curb the advance of socialism, they became retrogressive. Kedourie maintains that nationalism is "a doctrine invented in Europe at the beginning of the nineteenth century," and he is careful to distinguish post-Enlightenment nationalism from ancient patriotisms and xenophobia. For Kedourie, then, modern nationalism is a "comprehensive doctrine" that produces a "distinctive style of politics." After dividing humankind into distinct, sovereign nation-states, the doctrine of nationalism is able to promise "freedom and fulfillment" to member citizens in return for their unquestioning submersion in the will of the state. It defines *nation* in terms of language, race, and religion; it requires that all members belong to the state or else depart; and it demands that all citizens merge their will with that of the community. Because such thinking by Americans "is marginal and insignificant," Kedourie considers American nationalism to be little more than patriotism.[47]

Yet through their increasingly vitriolic argument with pro-Loyalists, Franco lobbyists were turning Americanism into a political doctrine, the power and promise of which adheres closely to Kedourie's conception for European states. Rather than evaluating this doctrine in Left/Right terms, where the two poles stand for social progress and retrogressive coercion, it will be better to detach the anticommunist Americanism of Franco lobbyists from the political spectrum and situate it instead in a more organic or spiritual explanation of national self-determination, "the lasting fulfillment which comes to man when he lives as a member of a sovereign nation." Party-line anti–national communism during the era of Stalin's purges was, in all practical terms, a doctrine of the Right. Despite harping on traditional values, Americanism, as Franco lobbyists conceived it, was dynamic and progressive. When Kelly drafted "A Programme for American Nationalism" in the spring of 1939, a constructive manifesto he later circulated in pamphlet form through his network of elites, he called for equitable social and economic reconstruction for U.S. citizens, including worker representation on corporate boards and the sharing with labor of profits over a fixed percentage. As argumentative defenders of Americanism, Franco lobbyists emerge not as reluctant fascist coconspirators intent on polarizing political debate at the cost of the Center but, rather, as concerned citizen-activists who sacrificed previously held political positions—for the most part liberal, progressive, or even progressive socialist, like Kelly's in 1924—in order to adopt a new oppositional politics of anti–New Deal, pro-Franco anticommunism.[48]

3

Roosevelt's Mental Map

March of Time's newsreel of President Roosevelt's "Quarantine" address from the isolationist heartland of Chicago on 5 October 1937 captured his characteristic head waggles and expressionless eyebrows, the wind-blown notepaper, and his liturgical monotone delivery. In the newsreel's introduction, Edward Herlihy called it a "bombshell declaration against the policy of isolation and neutrality"; the declaration had brought the "nations of this earth" to attention. But might it lead to war, Herlihy wondered.[1]

It was an alarming speech. Secretary of State Hull and roving ambassador Norman H. Davis, who wrote the first draft of the speech, intended to scare Americans into backing international sanctions against expansionist nations, principally Japan. Roosevelt explained how the world had fallen into a "state of international anarchy." Without justification of any kind, "civilians, including vast numbers of women and children," were "being ruthlessly murdered with bombs from the air," a reference to the bombing of Guernica by Spanish Nationalists and of Shanghai by the Japanese. Submarines were sinking ships without warning. Nations were taking sides in other nations' civil wars. Were such things "to come to pass in other parts of the world," he intoned, "let no one imagine that America will escape." Americans must not think they could "continue tranquilly and peacefully to carry on the ethics and the arts of civilization" immune from the spreading contagion. Peace-loving nations—headed implicitly by America—"must make a concerted effort" to quarantine the epidemic of lawlessness. "We are determined to keep out of war," he assured listeners, "yet we cannot insure ourselves against the disastrous effects of war and the dangers of involvement." "America hates war," he nodded reassuringly as the crowd applauded, "America hopes for peace. Therefore America actively engages in the search for peace."[2]

Roosevelt probably thought the speech would have educational value, function as a trial balloon, and placate calls for action from internationalists like Hull and Davis. When he wrote the concluding phrases, which he delivered with emphatic wags of his head, he no doubt sought to reinforce the notion that U.S. foreign policy only ever had peaceful intentions. But isolationists read it as a dangerous blueprint for intervention writ large, while internationalists felt cheated once they realized that Roosevelt's active search for peace still lacked a concrete agenda. Instead of gaining support for coordinated sanctions against aggressor nations, the address solidified public opinion around isolationism. Historian Dorothy Borg's influential interpretation sees the speech as part of a "groping and intermittent" effort by Roosevelt to avert war, part of an ongoing "nebulous" plan "for warding off catastrophe." Yet while Roosevelt's thinking on Spain was nebulous, his Asian policy built aggressively on decades of U.S. military as well as missionary involvement in China, from gunboats patrolling the Yangtze, to expanding troop levels in Shanghai's international settlement, to shipping boatloads of war matériel to Chinese Nationalists.[3]

During 1938—a pivotal year for geopolitics, the Neutrality Act, and Spain's civil war in particular—Roosevelt's approach to foreign policy making was as eclectic as the theories advanced by historians to explain it. Most agree that he shifted focus from domestic to foreign affairs, moved from isolationism to internationalism, and acted decisively in spite of congressional and public constraints. Still, overarching explanations tend to be unsatisfying, because Roosevelt might say one thing but do something else, just as his policies were inconsistent from one region to another. He told friends he wanted to arm Spain's Loyalists but avoided doing so; he appeased Germany while antagonizing Japan, America's enemy and ally, respectively, in 1917. Given the specter of Axis expansionism in the spring of 1938, along with the growing intensity of the Great Debate over arms to Spain and Gallup polls running three to one in favor of the Loyalists, realpolitik suggests that a decisive, internationalist Roosevelt should have moved Congress for the act's repeal, abrogated it by executive fiat, or, at least, actively encouraged its circumvention. Official support for Loyalist Spain would have enabled reticent Nazi generals—Werner Freiherr von Fritsch, Ludwig Beck, and, later, the cautious Walter von Brauchitsch—to challenge the Führer's insistence that there was nothing to fear from isolationist America in the event of general war over an invasion of Czechoslovakia. Although there were at least two initiatives by individuals within or close to Roosevelt's administration to circumvent the Neutrality Act, and Roosevelt did belatedly investigate its abrogation post-Munich in November, virtually no U.S. war matériel reached the beleaguered Loyalists, the act remaining in force until after Gen. Francisco Franco's victory. Why did Roosevelt sidestep this crucial issue?[4]

One compelling reason was isolationism, a sentiment central to the way Americans had understood their place in the world ever since George Washington counseled that long-term political entanglement in Old World squabbles would prove to be the bane of republican governance. And after the findings of a 1935 Senate committee implied that profiteering munitions makers had encouraged America's entry into the Great War, isolationism had become a mantra. Nevertheless, as historian H. W. Brands has shown, U.S. policy makers have always balanced their parochial "exemplarist" sentiments against the attractions of physical intervention abroad, which in the latter case has enabled them to become "vindicators" of American exceptionalism on the world stage. Idealist presidents, from Thomas Jefferson during the Barbary Wars, to Woodrow Wilson and his seven foreign interventions around the globe, through to George W. Bush's efforts at state building in Afghanistan and Iraq, have lived out this Jekyll/Hyde personality. Roosevelt, arguably the master vindicator by 1940, was no exception. His Good Neighbor Policy precluded military action in Latin America in support of U.S. geobusiness interests, and although he did revive diplomatic relations with the Soviet Union in November 1933, he gave Europeans the coldest of shoulders five months earlier at the London Economic Conference. Isolationism was an important factor, and the 1930s marked the ideology's high-water mark. But in light of the rapid naval expansion program that Roosevelt began in 1933 and sold as economic revitalization amid accusations he had started an arms race and his eager interventionism across the Pacific, especially military aid to the Chinese during the Sino-Japanese conflict of 1937, it is necessary to investigate other causes.[5]

White House contemporaries and historians ever since have agreed that fear of alienating Catholic voters in an election year was Roosevelt's primary reason for inaction over Spain. And yet, while it may have been convenient to blame Catholics for the administration's failure to assume a position of leadership on Europe, with all that implies for the appeasement of Hitler and Holocaust guilt, the evidence hardly supports the Catholic factor argument. Indeed, documents in State Department files make clear that the Loyalist lobby—the Comintern factor—had the upper hand. Consequently, I argue here for a denouement of two more plausible scenarios: at the executive level, Roosevelt gave scant attention to what he saw as the decadence of Franco's Old World Spain at a time when his heart lay with a romanticized view of Chiang Kai-shek's otherworldly China; at the legislative level, activism by pro-Franco lobbyists did prove decisive on Capitol Hill, but Catholic votes per se were a secondary issue. When it came to Spanish foreign policy, the interplay between Roosevelt's Sinophilia and his dislike of Spaniards led him to abdicate his control to contending forces within his administration and in Congress, forces that were in thrall either to Comintern propaganda or to Franco lobbyists, men like W. Cameron Forbes and John Eoghan Kelly, neither of whom were Catholic.[6]

Roosevelt Besieged: Pro-Loyalist Appeals

Roosevelt was only fifty-six in 1938, yet his health was deteriorating under the strain of office. After rolling seas and an abscessed tooth forced him to curtail a fishing cruise through the Gulf of Mexico in December 1937, Interior Secretary Harold L. Ickes, who vacationed with him, recorded in his diary that the president appeared listless and despondent, as if he had "more or less given up." With so much left unaccomplished—and with his cousin Theodore's vigorous legacy unfulfilled—a gloomy anxiety now suffused his administration. *Washington Post* columnist Franklyn Waltman noticed this enervation spreading "from the White House to Capitol Hill," leaving "all officialdom" drifting in an "atmosphere as murky and muggy as the weather." According to Waltman, Roosevelt had "decided to leave Capitol Hill to its own devices," abdicating his leadership responsibilities to legislators who were now usurping "the President's job of directing foreign policy." Franco lobbyists also learned to exploit this leadership vacuum. Although historian Barbara Rearden Farnham has identified the Munich crisis—specifically 25 September 1938—as the "turning point" in Roosevelt's foreign policy activism, his malaise did not lift until December 1941, when wartime exigencies provided justification for massive government spending, a possibility of U.S. global hegemony after victory, and the further expansion of his executive powers, especially in the arena of foreign affairs.[7]

As the third session of the Seventy-fifth Congress opened in January 1938, Roosevelt's was an administration under siege. He faced gathering storm clouds abroad as well as economic decline at home, the falling business indices and rising unemployment of the so-called Roosevelt Recession foreboding social unrest. He could not forget that Washington's calendar was unusual, with Congress set to adjourn in June for a seven-month hiatus, culminating in November midterm elections that were already promising to be a crucial referendum on the second term of his presidency. And he was still smarting from the resounding defeat of his ill-conceived court-packing scheme. "When you wanted to pack the supreme court," New York Life Insurance executive Warren R. Evans of Shelby, Montana, later wrote to him, "you turned me from a steady supporter of yours into a cynical and disallusioned [sic] antagonist." Fearful of "dictatorial" tendencies (although he was careful not to implicate the president), Evans reminded Roosevelt that "all stable progress in a democracy must be careful and slow."[8]

Evans's critique of his president's meddling with the Supreme Court was an introduction to his real reason for writing: arms for Loyalist Spain. Although he stacked his prose with snipes at the Old World, Evans had no trouble identifying the issues. Great Britain had "browbeaten" France into refusing to aid Spain, its natural ally, because of the interests of "bankers and industrialists." But these "English financial barons" could not see that they stood to "loose [sic] infinitesimally less in Spain than from a triumphant Germany." Evans nonetheless discounted Britain's influence on American policy makers, who had historically demonstrated their capacity for independent action. At the outset in 1936, Evans presumed that Roosevelt's embargo was standard wartime practice, but, after realizing that arms were still flowing to China, he abandoned that theory too. What caught his attention was presidential "hobnobbing" with such Catholics as ambassador to Britain Joseph P. Kennedy, former mayor of Detroit Frank Murphy, and Chicago's Cardinal George Mundelein. Evans concluded that Roosevelt was a "political opportunist," someone who "professes liberalism" in order to "gain political power," someone who "professes democracy" only to "knuckle under to the greatest foe of democracy": "It looks like you are doing the bidding of the Catholic Church." Here was a ring of truth, but if it did touch a chord with the president, then it was likely one of indignation, not shame, for there was little substance behind Evans's Catholic factor accusation.[9]

Evans's letter was one of eighty-odd pro-Loyalist appeals that Assistant Secretary to the President Col. Marvin Hunter McIntyre passed on to the presidential desk between January 1938 and February 1939. These varied in format from boilerplate telegrams, to summaries prepared by McIntyre, to petitions from hundreds of signatories. Roosevelt's files indicate that he saw about two dozen personal letters—from notepad scrawls to congressional felicitations—urging that he abrogate the Neutrality Act in favor of Loyalist Madrid. "For Gods sake! Lift that embargo to Spain. Look what happened to us," scribbled the "Ghost of Czecho-Slavakia [sic]" in January 1939. Congressman Jerry J. O'Connell (D-MT), a communist sympathizer and a Catholic, wrote several times asking that Roosevelt lift the embargo. Pro-Madrid appeals arrived through other channels, too, such as when Undersecretary of State Sumner Welles forwarded a terse memorandum from President Lázaro Cárdenas of Mexico or when German playwright and onetime communist revolutionary Ernst Toller brought a petition for aid to Madrid sponsored by Britain's Lord Halifax, the Archbishop of York, and the Dean of Canterbury (whom Toller pretended was the Archbishop of Canterbury). Toller wanted to deliver the petition in person, but Roosevelt was at his Warm Springs, Georgia, retreat in late November 1938, so Toller settled for lunch with First Lady Eleanor Roosevelt.[10]

Historians of the Great Debate speak in terms of floods of appeals to lift the embargo from constituents around the country throughout 1937–38, before peaking in January 1939. Robert Dallek says that during the important spring months of 1938, "calls for repeal of the Spanish arms embargo became a constant din." Wayne S. Cole states that the White House was "inundated with mail," and F. Jay Taylor implies that Roosevelt read "hundreds" of pleas. Yet, while it is accurate to say that appeals inundated the White House—its mailroom received an average of 3,000 letters a day, of which several hundred may well have been embargo related—few of those appeals ever landed on Roosevelt's desk. From 11 January to 12 February 1937, McIntyre processed for Roosevelt's perusal only thirty-seven pleading letters and telegrams from various individuals and groups, reducing most of them to a one-sentence summary that he then listed on single-page memoranda. But this rate of just over one pro-Loyalist appeal per day exceeded by far the average for January 1937 to February 1939 of one appeal every four days.[11]

It is instructive to examine Taylor's *The United States and the Spanish Civil War* (1956), which laid the groundwork for later studies and which Leo V. Kanawada

Jr., the Catholic actor's leading advocate, calls "the most authoritative source" on the embargo controversy. To support his case for the sheer volume of pro-Loyalist appeals reaching Roosevelt in April and May 1938, Taylor provides an extended footnote that references a petition from the University of Chicago. This was a hefty, inch-thick telegram bearing the names of fifty-seven faculty and 1,500 students expressing their "heartfelt demand for the immediate lifting of the embargo from Loyalist Spain." After dating the telegram to 4 May 1938—the week before a fateful decision by Senate Committee on Foreign Relations chairman Key Pittman (D-NV) to abandon an effort to reverse the Act before Congress's seven-month recess—Taylor adds that it "was only one of *hundreds* of such communications examined by this author at the Roosevelt Library." Taylor's statement is misleading: first, because Chicago's faculty actually sent their telegram more than eight months later, on 28 January 1939, by which time lifting the embargo was moot; and second, because File 422-C, Roosevelt's Official File on the Spanish Civil War, which covers all the general correspondence reaching the president, contains just sixty-two appeals for the whole of 1938.[12]

Still more remarkable is the virtual absence of pro-Franco appeals in the presidential files, especially given Kanawada's claim that for the second week of May 1938 alone, "the White House, the State Department, and members of Congress received *thousands* of [pro-Franco] messages denouncing any attempt to lift the embargo." File 422-C does contain the National Catholic Welfare Council's (NCWC) "Keep the Spanish Embargo!" flier of January 1939, but only because Roosevelt's friend Michael Francis Doyle forwarded it to McIntyre "in order that [the president] may be promptly informed as to what is going on." Roosevelt had come to rely on Doyle, a Philadelphia lawyer and prominent layman in Catholic hierarchy circles, for an inside track, so in this context he would have understood that Doyle was referring to what was going on within the hierarchy. Yet, not only was Doyle an influential Catholic, he was also a Loyalist sympathizer. During the whole of 1938, Roosevelt saw just three pro-Franco letters from American Catholics, and only one of those pushed the arms embargo. A single keep-the-embargo message is a far quieter voice than the thousands claimed by historians advocating the Catholic factor thesis.[13]

Franco supporters, of course, were actively lobbying Roosevelt's administration, both to maintain the embargo and to recognize Franco's Nationalist government. Sometimes they targeted the State Department rather than the White House. When Kelly urged on 15 September 1937 that ALB volunteers who had enlisted in Madrid's foreign army automatically forfeit their American citizenship, it was to Secretary of State Hull that he presented his argument. (Assistant Secretary George S. Messersmith, who leaned toward the Loyalists, brushed off Kelly's letter by citing a technicality.) When Merwin K. Hart, chairman of the American Union for Nationalist Spain, recommended on 3 April 1939 that America should recognize Franco's new government, it was also to Hull whom he appealed. Franco lobbyists did try to appeal directly to Roosevelt, and with considerable force. A petition to the president of 14 November 1938 commended the U.S. government for "consistently refusing to lift the embargo," trusted that it would "rigidly adhere" to neutrality and "discourage Communist propaganda," and hoped that "misguided American 'liberals'" under the "cunning tutelage" of communists would finally accept that a majority of "thinking [Spaniards] of all classes" supported Franco's Nationalist government. Kelly, who prepared the letter at Hart's midtown office, networked sixty-five prominent Americans—including eighteen professors or doctors, two diplomats, six writers or artists, six company directors, and one of the world's richest women, Anne Tracy Morgan—to sign it. Of those practicing a religion, there were almost as many Protestants as Catholics. (Kelly actually attracted 130 signers, but the secretary to whom he delegated the mailing of the petition to the White House and *New York Times*—probably Gladys Rountree, who later became an FBI informant—failed to enclose four of its seven mimeographed sheets.) This weighty pro-embargo appeal from American elites did appear in the *Times,* but I could find it neither in File 422-C nor anywhere in the Roosevelt Papers.[14]

Explaining why Roosevelt never read Kelly's petition, along with hundreds (perhaps thousands) of other salient appeals mailed to him by Franco supporters during 1938, requires an overview of White House mailroom protocol as well as Roosevelt's own proclivities about general correspondence. In her memoir, Grace G. Tully, one of Roosevelt's three personal secretaries along with Marguerite A. "Missy" LeHand and McIntyre, described beginning her day around ten o'clock, when she would "quickly thumb through the incoming mail" in the mailroom. Roosevelt's executive clerk, Rudolph Forster, and his assistants would already have been busy opening the letters and sorting the correspondence into rough piles by category, working at a hurried pace. Four hundred fifty pieces per hour was the upper limit for one person to open, scan, and stack letters, a chore that the busy personal secretaries happily delegated to White House clerks and interns. No president could deal meaningfully with even a few hundred letters per day, so the secretaries had to make decisions about whether to direct correspondence to a particular governmental department or to the president's desk. In the case of Spanish arms embargo appeal letters or telegrams, they culled a tiny proportion for presidential perusal, perhaps one in every three to five hundred. In her thumbing through the mail, Tully decided which letters the president should see, a task she shared with LeHand and McIntyre, with McIntyre having the final veto.[15]

With a busy day of organizing, typing, and general office work ahead of them, the secretaries would have made snap decisions based on the legitimacy of the addressor, the style of the letterhead, the readability of the handwriting, and the shortness of the message. If the letter was from a correspondent with whom they were familiar—Socialist Party leader Norman Thomas, say, who was also a pacifist, Loyalist campaigner, and a visitor to Madrid in 1937—or for whom Roosevelt had previously expressed an interest, then that alone might have provided a criterion for selection. When McIntyre saw the scribbled note from the Ghost of Czecho-Slavakia, it likely elicited a laugh, making him think his boss would have a chuckle over it too, so he selected it in preference to a few of the more humdrum pro-Loyalist appeals from the hundreds on the mailroom table. When the secretaries noticed a letter that, to them, seemed important, they would mark it with a red tag and place it on top of the pile that went to Roosevelt's desk. Still, Tully noted, Roosevelt habitually ignored their prioritizing, attacking the pile "at random, sometimes beginning from the very top, sometimes from the bottom." On days when he was fatigued, he might push the whole pile aside to work on it later, but Tully nevertheless felt he was "very conscientious about his mail," giving "at least a quick once-over even to letters that did not require specific instruction or dictation," as was the case with embargo appeals. Once he had read his daily correspondence, the secretaries filed every piece, for Roosevelt, who founded the first presidential library, intended to create a historic legacy. Therefore, if an appeal is in 422-C, then Roosevelt read it, or at least gave it a once-over.[16]

Why was it that Roosevelt read virtually no pro-Nationalist appeals in 1938, excepting, perhaps, those, like Kelly's petition, that made it into the national newspapers? Based on their annotations, memoranda, and a few albeit oblique published references, it is my conjecture that Tully and LeHand were resolute pro-Loyalists or, at the very least, vehemently anti-Franco. In a sentence in her memoir mentioning the Spanish Civil War, Tully talked in the same breath about the "ranting" of "Hitler and his stooges." LeHand wrote a memorandum, which she attached to a June 1937 letter to Roosevelt from the Catalan radical Jaume Miravitlles, reiterating that the Catalans were "fighting for the ideals of Democracy." Given their understanding, too, that the "Boss," as they called Roosevelt, was pro-Loyalist, as was the overwhelming majority of New Deal officials, White House visitors, and the First Lady, with whom the secretaries brushed shoulders, it would seem probable that they culled the pro-Franco correspondence, directing it instead to the State Department. Perhaps, too, they could tell that Roosevelt had little patience for Spain, sensing the contours of his mental map.[17]

Secretary Marvin McIntyre, a journalist and the *Washington Times*'s city editor before joining Roosevelt's staff, was apparently a strong supporter of Loyalist Madrid. Of the thirty-eight summaries of embargo-related appeals that he prepared for Roosevelt from 1 January 1937 to 31 January 1939, only one urged maintenance of the embargo. Documenting McIntyre's politics has proved problematic, although Representative Martin Dies (D-TX) had little doubt where McIntyre's sympathies lay, for on two occasions, according to Dies, McIntyre proudly posed for photographs at the White House with CPUSA members, including its financial secretary, William Weiner. To whatever extent McIntyre liked communists, it seems he disliked Catholics. Of the seventeen embargo-related letters that

Roosevelt saw during this same period, several were antipapist. While it is not possible to attribute the selection of these letters to McIntyre, it is unlikely that LeHand or Tully picked them, for they were both pious Catholics.[18]

Horace W. O'Connor, for instance, wrote from Chicago on 12 February 1938 in a similar vein to Warren Evans. "Since when," O'Connor asked his president cynically, had it become necessary for U.S. senators to obtain "advance approval" from Catholic priests before showing solidarity with a peaceful "government properly constituted in accordance with law," by which he meant Madrid's Loyalist government. O'Connor despised the Ku Klux Klan, yet he wondered whether Rome's Catholic Action had become so insidious a foreign ideology that there was now a "need for some organized method of combating it." Americans did not want fascism or communism, O'Connor asserted, "but neither do we need or want Catholic Actionism. Plain Americanism, which means real democracy, is all we need." Real democracy, for O'Connor, evidently meant strict conformity to a rather undemocratic package of Anglo-Protestant core values. It is ironic how many of those on both sides in the Great Debate over arms for Spain became sufficiently angry as to advocate extra-legal—or "organized"—methods to oppress an opinion they saw as subversive of the very freedoms that made their argument over Americanism possible.[19]

An alternative variant on the theme of secretarial bias as explicator for the lack of pro-Franco appeals is that Roosevelt may have conveyed to his staff that he would give "a quick once-over," as Tully put it, to a few selected pieces from pro-Loyalists, but he had no interest in seeing anything from the other side. When Roosevelt "attacked at random" his pile of mail, Tully was sitting by his side ready to take dictation. Even if Roosevelt never gave an explicit indication, and even if Tully never consciously culled mail because of her own political bias, then from Roosevelt's grunts, chuckles, and general body language she would have developed an acute instinct for his tastes in correspondence, for what pleased the Boss she adored. She knew that when he was fatigued he pushed the mail pile, with all its nagging appeals to lift the Spanish embargo, to one side. She would have wanted the Boss to be happy. Subliminally, if nothing else, when she was thumbing through the incoming mail at ten o'clock every morning in the White House mailroom, she would have sidelined the pro-Franco appeals and put the odd red sticker on choice appeals from prominent pro-Loyalists. A combination of active and subconscious censorship explains the relative paucity of pro-Loyalist appeals as well as the absence of pro-Franco appeals. Yet whatever the explanation, it is clear from File 422-C that the Spanish Civil War letters and telegrams in Roosevelt's daily mail pile were overwhelmingly—and, throughout the most crucial first half of 1938, entirely—pro-Loyalist, including several appeals from pro-Loyalist Catholics, and that all of them shouted for an end to the embargo.

Appeals to the State Department: The Comintern Factor

Missing from the foregoing discussion of White House mail handling is the fate of the hundreds of appeals left on the mailroom table by the president's secretaries. Where they went raises the issue of appeals sent to Capitol Hill in general and the State Department in particular, an issue less important only because of the relative power wielded by Roosevelt over foreign policy in comparison to the ineffectiveness of State. Confronting what is not in archives—but ought to be—is the researcher's bane. Thankfully, in this case, the volume of correspondence became so great that for August and September 1938, State Department clerks prepared summary sheets that not only shed light on the absent appeals but also point to standard mail handling practices at other departments of government, including the White House.[20]

State's term for important correspondence requiring an official reply was "black ink," while letters or telegrams of a general nature, from protests to congratulations, were deemed "red ink" correspondence. For red inks, State, like the White House, practiced culling. With postcards, clerks tallied them by category before packing them off to "DCR [Division of Communications and Records] for filing"; postcard writers, therefore, received at most a preprinted acknowledgment card. With letters and telegrams, clerks culled a small proportion (1:20 to 1:1,000, depending on topic and volume) for an official response, marking the rest for either a preprinted receipt or a mimeographed letter. Only the culled red inks entered State's filing system, and, of those, the majority received a boilerplate letter from a second-tier officer. In following Taylor's research, generations of historians have presumed that if sacks full of keep-the-embargo appeals arrived at the State Department from pro-Franco Catholics, then State Department officials were cognizant of them and consequently feared the Catholic factor. Yet State's summary sheets, reinforced by the letters that made it to the files, point instead to the power and reach of the Comintern factor, as do the White House's.[21]

Tallies for September and October 1938 indicate a base level of around six hundred letters and telegrams per month, plus about a thousand postcards. In March, State received 1,788 letters and telegrams, rising to 7,856 in April, peaking at 12,349 during the critical month of May when Senator Gerald P. Nye (R-ND) proposed a joint resolution to lift the arms embargo unilaterally to Loyalist Spain, then falling to 4,586 in June, 1,089 in July, and 973 in August. During the week 9–14 May, State's mail sacks bulged with 5,271 letters and telegrams and 3,105 postcards. Spanish embargo appeals accounted for "practically all" of this massive influx of correspondence, as clerk R. V. Haig noted, with an overwhelming majority being pro-Loyalist: for the two months, incoming appeals averaged 23:1 in favor of lifting the embargo.[22]

Yet in evaluating the relative effectiveness of pro-Loyalist and pro-Nationalist lobbying on the State Department, the issue becomes not so much the volume

Spanish embargo letters and telegrams received by the State Department

Month	Lift Spanish embargo pro-Loyalists	Keep Spanish embargo pro-Nationalists	Japan embargo (for comparison)
August 1938	645	31 or 20:1	(264)
September 1938	256	10 or 26:1	(282)

of letters received but the criteria used by mailroom clerks doing the culling. Although State officials could gauge opinion from the summary sheets, in terms of the persuasiveness of the correspondence, they, like Roosevelt, only read those appeals that a clerk had selected. As opposed to the White House, where virtually everyone from Roosevelt down was strongly anti-Franco, State Department officials held mixed opinions on Nationalist Spain. A majority was anticommunist, but many officials—especially George S. Messersmith, Stanley K. Hornbeck, and to a lesser extent Hull—simultaneously advocated a hard line against fascist aggression, which translated into a loathing of Franco, for Comintern propaganda had merged Spanish Nationalism with German Nazism. While it is likely that most lower-level State employees would have been anti-Franco, just as at the White House, some would have felt the influence of their bosses or tried to please them by selecting the type of letters their bosses liked to read. Such a selection bias explains why the pro-Loyalist to pro-Nationalist ratio of response letters in State's files is half that of the incoming mail, though still extreme at 11:1. From 3 May to 18 May, officials from Joseph C. Green and Charles W. Yost at the Office of Arms and Munitions Control to Counselor R. Walton Moore and Secretary Hull signed thirty-three written responses to red inks, thirty of which were in response to pro-Loyalist appeals to lift the embargo. These personalized responses were in answer to more than 10,000 letters and telegrams, or one for every three hundred pieces of incoming correspondence.[23]

Appeals selected by clerks at State were often those from large organizations or ones with a congressional endorsement, as well as those selected perhaps for their novelty, style, or cachet. Alrose Andryski, chairman of the University of Wisconsin alumni's Summer School for Workers in Industry, wrote to Representative Dewy Johnson (Free Labor–MN) to say that the arms embargo discriminated against "the Spanish people who are engaged in a life and death struggle to preserve their liberty." Florence Bean James, of Seattle, blamed Sumner Welles for placing millions of Americans "in the position of murderers of thousands of helpless children, old men and women" in Spain. James was "sick" of America's nonintervention, which "really intervenes for the monstrous brutalities" of fascist aggressors. Among the handful of appeals from pro-Nationalists was one from *America* editor Francis Talbot and three from Protestants: *Patriot Digest* editor R. Caldwell Patton, W. Cameron Forbes, and Dr. Joe C. A. Eckhardt of Austin, Texas.

Eckhardt billed his family as "average citizens." To the extent that they were, his claim to represent an ordinary Joe American hardly fits the prevailing profile of a Franco lobbyist, the more so because his letter came with an endorsement from his congressman and family friend, Lyndon Baines Johnson (D-TX). Eckhardt, who, according to his granddaughter, was anticommunist but otherwise "had very liberal leanings politically," worked as a boy with Mexican *braceros,* spoke fluent Spanish, and had many Hispanic patients, which suggests why he was no friend of Loyalist Spain. In 1938, lobbying for Franco as an anticommunist was quite compatible with satisfying the tenets of Americanism as a liberal Presbyterian multiculturalist.[24]

Lobbying by Franco supporters from the rural Northwest and Midwest also complicates the profile. Compton I. White (D-ID) forwarded a petition to Hull signed by 414 "prominent citizens" of Cottonwood, Idaho. As Cottonwood's population was barely a thousand, and two of its three churches were Protestant, it is unlikely that Catholicism was the primary determinant of activism. George J. Griffin of Mendon, Ohio, wrote to Welles, arguing that if the sentiment in his state was any indication, then at least 90 percent of Americans wanted to keep the embargo. Yet there was more here than midwestern pacifism or isolationism. "Out this way, the conviction grows that the demand for repeal comes mostly from a certain racial group," by which Griffin meant East European Jews, "and an assortment of varying hued radicals." For the Methodists of Mendon, the issue was Americanism in its most nativist and anticommunist form.[25]

State officials also had to cope with a dramatic increase in the number of delegations, virtually all of which were pro-Loyalist. James Clement Dunn, Walton Moore, and Carlton Savage received twenty-three during April and May, the largest being a contingent of thirty from the International Workers Order. Dunn complained that while he had "willingly given all the necessary time desired by these delegations," hearing their arguments before explaining State's policy, delegates took advantage of the occasion "for purposes of organized publicity." Instead of reiterating to the press what they had discussed with State officials, delegates issued political statements "from their own point of view."[26]

As early as 4 May 1938, it was apparent to State officials that the "recent flood of red ink letters protesting against the embargo" was not a "spontaneous" outburst of public indignation but rather the result "of a campaign initiated by the American League for Peace and Democracy," a pro-Loyalist Popular Front organization, which "furnished the 'protest' forms to the various union locals." It was no accident, Raymond E. Murphy advised his colleagues, that the protests arriving at the department failed to "include communism with fascism as the greatest threats to the development of free trade unions." For five years, the Comintern-backed American League for Peace and Democracy (ALPD), under its former title the American League Against War and Fascism, had "consistently upheld Soviet peace policies and was formerly pledged to defend the Soviet Union." Murphy attached a 3 May clipping from the CPUSA's *Daily Worker* organ which claimed that 612 local unions around the country had already endorsed the ALPD's call to lift the embargo to Spain.[27]

For the critical period 1 May 1938 to 30 January 1939, McIntyre forwarded at least thirteen pro-Loyalist but just five pro-Nationalist appeals to the State Department. In almost every case, they came either from a major organization such as the ALB or the Washington Friends of Spanish Democracy, or they arrived from Capitol Hill with an endorsement signed by a member of Congress. Of the pro-Nationalist appeals, all five came via the office of a House or Senate member. It seems reasonable to conclude that the pro-Loyalist McIntyre—with reluctance, no doubt—forwarded these particular appeals only because, had he neglected to do so, congressmen could have learned from their constituents that the appeals were unacknowledged and blamed him. Included with the unknown hundreds of keep-the-embargo appeals mailed to Roosevelt that his mailroom clerks consigned to the trash was the potentially influential "Mr. President" petition from sixty-five prominent Americans that Kelly organized, for it is not in State's file 852.24. To reiterate the weakness of the Catholic factor argument, throughout the entire period when the Neutrality Act was most at risk, Roosevelt saw no appeals to keep the embargo, and State officials saw fourteen, the five forwarded from McIntyre and nine from their own mailroom.[28]

Roosevelt Besieged: Pro-Loyalist Friends and Associates

Virtually all of Roosevelt's friends and associates added their voices to pro-Loyalist letter writers like Evans, O'Connor, or the Ghost of Czecho-Slavakia. Among the most persistent were ambassador to Spain Claude G. Bowers, cabinet members Ickes and Henry Morgenthau Jr., and his wife, Eleanor. Roosevelt had a special affection for Bowers, who in 1925 authored *Jefferson and Hamilton*, which portrayed founder Thomas Jefferson as the shining star of American history. When Roosevelt reviewed the work for the *New York World*, he deemed it "thrilling." Foreign affairs scholar John Lamberton Harper emphasizes the impact that Bowers's interpretation had on Roosevelt, for Jefferson "had seen European society first hand and had found it 'rotten to the core.'" Bowers bombarded Roosevelt with memoranda, running eight or ten pages, on the tragic fate of Spain's democratic Second Republic, the abominations of Franco's Nationalists, and why he must lift the iniquitous arms embargo. On 20 February 1938 Bowers raged that because the embargo was prolonging the war—by which he meant it was denying the Loyalists their certain victory—it was "responsible for the lives of hundreds of thousands of men, women, and children." Fascist bombs were "slaughter[ing] hundreds of women and children," but

"Spanish democracy" would never "capitulate before the fascist salute." Lifting the embargo would "end this savage, barbarous slaughter," for then Spanish democracy could defend itself. Franco, who had exhausted his hard currency and sources of taxation, "cannot win," Bowers was convinced, unless "Italian and German armies" arrived or America failed to lift the embargo.[29]

Ickes also felt the moral burden of U.S. foreign policy. Americans will view "our embargo," he wrote in his diary, as "a black page in our history." To Ickes, a Franco victory implied far more than an Old World regime change, or even fascist dominance of Europe; American liberal exceptionalism would suffer irreparable harm. In 1938 Ickes politicized his Loyalist sympathies by joining the North American Committee to Aid Spanish Democracy, ostensibly a legitimate aid organization headed by Methodist Episcopal bishop Francis J. McConnell but in reality a Popular Front umbrella organization. Twenty-two thousand New Yorkers attended the flagship event, a 9 June 1938 "Lift the Embargo: All Aid to Spain!" mass meeting at Madison Square Garden, at which Loyalist Spain's premier Juan Negrín spoke by transatlantic cable, Manhattan borough president Stanley M. Isaacs gave a speech, and four Spanish communists served as guests of honor. Ickes later praised ALB veterans for being "in the forefront of all the battles for democracy."[30]

Like Ickes, Morgenthau viewed Loyalist Spain as a democracy fighting bravely against Franco's fascist tyranny. He felt so strongly about the righteousness of Madrid's cause that in 1938 he schemed to circumvent the U.S. Neutrality Act, purchasing thirty-five million ounces of devalued silver peseta coins in return for hard-currency dollars, which the Loyalist government could then use for purchasing weapons on the black market. National Guard units secured the Treasury Department's clandestine silver importations, one of which occurred at 2 A.M. on the night of 5 September at the Port of New York, and might have gone undetected were it not for a pro-Franco dock laborer who reported the incident to the *Catholic Worker*. Even at a discounted rate for silver of 43 cents per ounce, Morgenthau's initiative generated $15 million ($450 million) for the Loyalists. While this hard currency was certainly useful, it could not buy embargoed U.S. aircraft and spare parts. Morgenthau "had long harbored an admiration for the Soviets," his son commented later, so his efforts to check fascist aggression in Spain may have been ideological as much as national security oriented. "Although Morgenthau was not a Communist," notes international relations scholar John Dietrich, "many of his views coincided with those of [Harry Dexter] White's," Morgenthau's deputy and a Soviet spy. Morgenthau and White enjoyed an intimate working relationship, with White being the "major architect" of the punitive Morgenthau Plan for postwar Germany. Whatever his motivation, Morgenthau could not have expected the treasury to recoup his investment, for even Spain's democratic government of 1931 had begun the process of nationalizing U.S. investments, and he had no way of knowing when—or even if—the world price for silver would return to pre-

Depression levels. "Among those in the Cabinet," writes cultural historian John Morton Blum, "no one was closer to the President" than Morgenthau, and few were closer to Morgenthau than Roosevelt's wife.[31]

Eleanor was one of Loyalist Madrid's most powerful lobbyists, constantly badgering her husband to lift the arms embargo, lending her name to pro-Loyalist causes, and socializing with ALB volunteers. On 24 February 1938 she entertained at tea at the White House Louis Fischer, a U.S. foreign correspondent and champion of Soviet Russia. Fischer had left Moscow in 1936 to defend the "liberal, enlightened, legally-elected government" of Spain on its "front line against Fascism," as he put it in 1949. Eleanor listened in fascination as Fischer spoke of the "murderous raids" on Madrid and Valencia, the Republic's lack of antiaircraft guns, and how "Nazi and fascist airmen in the service of Franco" could therefore "slaughter Loyalist citizens with impunity." Although the Loyalists "possessed some bombers," Fischer noted that they "refused to use them against civilian targets." Eleanor promised to pressure her husband to lift the embargo. But as she confided in a letter that reached Fischer as he sailed back to Spain on the *Queen Mary,* she could not move Roosevelt. "He agrees with you," Eleanor explained disappointedly, "but feels that it would be absolutely impossible" to repeal an act the American people believed "was designed to keep us out of war." Roosevelt, nonetheless, had implied to her that "a period of education" might sway public opinion toward a lifting of the embargo.[32]

Many others expressed their pro-Loyalist sympathies to Roosevelt, most vocally Socialist Party leader and frequent White House visitor Norman Thomas. Neither did admiration for authoritarian rulers preclude support for the Loyalists. Roosevelt's trusted undersecretary of State, Sumner Welles, who let slip to Morgenthau that Benito Mussolini "was the greatest man that he had ever met," nevertheless felt that "in the long history of the foreign policy of the Roosevelt Administration," there had been "no more cardinal error" than the arms embargo to Loyalist Spain. All these key players in Roosevelt's court saw Loyalist Madrid as a refuge of democratic republican governance imperiled by Franco's fascist aggression, and most of them pestered him to raise the embargo. It is therefore remarkable that there is no evidence to show that Roosevelt seriously contemplated doing so until November 1938, and then with a half-hearted telephone call to Attorney General Francis Biddle to query his executive prerogatives. Even if he believed it was "absolutely impossible" to repeal the act, either through congressional initiative or by executive fiat, then he certainly had the option of circumventing it by encouraging the illicit routing of U.S. war matériel to the Loyalists, a course of action that he did decide to follow in the case of China, and avidly so. While he may well have schemed with his alcoholic half-brother G. Hall Roosevelt to transship twenty-two U.S. Bellanca aircraft to Loyalist Spain via France in spring 1938, as historian Dominic Tierney argues, this could simply have been an indifferent gesture designed to get Hall off his back and please Eleanor.[33]

Roosevelt's policy on warring Spain, therefore, raises two fundamental questions. First, why did he not take decisive action to arm the Loyalists covertly while
they still had the possibility of negotiating a settlement or even defeating Franco?
Roosevelt's own answer, or at least the one he gave to Ickes at the end of April 1938,
was that it would be a futile exercise because the shipments "would never reach the
Loyalists"; Franco interdicted the sea routes, while the French policed the overland
route. Yet, as Eberhard von Stohrer, the German ambassador to Spain, noted in a
dispatch to Berlin of 4 May, "lately the amount of matériel reaching Red Spain via
France was really tremendous." In addition to the various land routes across or
around the Pyrenees, of which the border crossing at Puigcerdá and the Mediterranean littoral south of Perpignan were the most popular with arms traffickers,
bringing matériel through the ports of Barcelona or Valencia was an option too.
Despite some losses to dive bombers, mines, and Italian submarines, the Russians
still managed to dock at least fifteen 3,000–12,000-ton merchantmen during the
first six months of 1938. Roosevelt's stated reason was weak. As Ickes remarked in
his diary, "It seemed to me that he was evading the issue."[34]

Another reason that Roosevelt sometimes gave was that sending arms would
make little difference to the outcome, for Franco was going to win anyway. This apathetic assessment had some military validity after the Nationalists retook Teruel
in February 1938, although even at this nadir renowned British strategist Capt. Ba-
sil Henry Liddell Hart stated optimistically in a *Time* interview of 14 February that
the Loyalists had superiority in motor transport, and their "fighting spirit seems to
be stronger." Providing the Loyalists did not run out of food, Liddell Hart expected
that "Franco's prospects may have definitely faded by the summer," yet even if
Franco were to retain the upper hand, a negotiated settlement and a Spain divided
along its present battle lines would be "the most probable outcome." Liddell Hart's
view aside, by the time the Loyalists mounted their daring Ebro offensives of the
summer, Roosevelt's reasoning was sounding more like another excuse.[35]

An ebullient Bowers could now write to Roosevelt on 18 August from his cross-
border refuge in Saint-Jean-de-Luz to describe a "radical, almost sensational"
improvement in the Loyalists' military prospects. What previously had been in-
experienced, ill-disciplined militias were now armies of seasoned veterans. Auda-
cious young generals, whom Bowers likened to Napoleon's finest, had "completely
flabbergasted" the Nationalists. Because the Non-Interventionist prescription denied the Loyalists arms, yet did not protest Germany's and Italy's ready supply of
planes, tanks, artillery, and soldiers to Franco, Loyalist strategy, Bowers explained,
was to fight holding actions until international opinion swung in favor of lifting
the iniquitous embargo. In addition to pushing the Nationalists back across their
Ebro lines, these new Loyalist offensives were exacerbating long-standing resent-
ments and frustrations within Nationalist forces. Bowers expected that "bitter
hostility" between German and Italian contingents would soon send one or both

packing. Dissension among Spanish noncombatant elites, moreover, suggested that Nationalist Spain was ripe for a negotiated settlement. Bowers closed with an impassioned plea to his friend Roosevelt to restore to the "legal, constitutional, democratic Government of the Spanish people its right under international law to buy arms for its defense" and so end the "thoroughly dishonest 'Non-Intervention' scheme" now utterly caked with the blood of innocent women and children. In light of the assessments by Stohrer, Liddell Hart, and Bowers, prevailing explanations for Roosevelt's lack of active circumvention are unsatisfying.[36]

In addition to asking why Roosevelt failed to pursue circumvention, the second question is why did he not lift the embargo either through legislative initiative or by executive fiat? Ickes had no doubt it was "fear of the Catholic sentiment in this country" that was inhibiting Roosevelt's cabinet from doing its moral duty, and historians ever since have agreed. Kanawada makes the strongest case for the Catholic factor, insisting that "it was obvious to Roosevelt that to lift the embargo" would have meant losing "the support of the Catholic-American community." Kanawada is adamant that "losing the Catholic vote" was Roosevelt's primary concern. It was obvious to Roosevelt—primarily from the "thousands of messages denouncing any attempt to lift the embargo" pouring into the White House from Catholics, which Kanawada presumed Roosevelt was reading—that most Catholics were pro-Franco and therefore would be furious were he to lift the embargo. Kanawada then concludes eo ipso that Roosevelt could not afford to scrap the embargo, for by doing so he would lose the crucial Catholic vote.[37]

Yet Kanawada's first step is already faulty, for not only did Roosevelt fail to see any pro-Franco appeals in 1938, he instead saw several pro-Loyalist appeals from prominent Catholics, such as lawyer Michael Doyle and Congressman Jerry O'Connell. Indeed, many of the pro-Loyalists with whom he came into contact were devout Catholics, including two of his three personal secretaries, LeHand and Tully. Historian George Q. Flynn understates his claim that "the only outspoken Catholic supporter of the Loyalists was [New York attorney] Frank P. Walsh," although as head of the Lawyers' Committee for Loyalist Spain (a Popular Front organization), Walsh was certainly a vocal advocate for Madrid.[38]

Kanawada's second step is also unconvincing. He cites Gallup poll data showing that 58 percent of Catholics supported Franco, which means 42 percent did not, so there was a potential electoral swing of 16 percent, or 1,297,000 votes, but he fails to mention that a third of Catholics in the poll expressed sympathy for neither side in the Spanish conflict. This statistical oversight reduces the swing vote to 869,000, presuming that every pro-Franco Catholic would have switched party allegiance based on Roosevelt's decision to lift the embargo. Furthermore, because 30 percent of Catholics voted Republican anyway (a percentage that would have been higher for pro-Franco Catholics), the maximum swing vote, which Kanawada implies was so crucial to Roosevelt's success at the polls, was 608,000. Granted, Democrats did lose eighty-one House and eight Senate seats in the November midterms, yet Republican gains came in industrial states with powerful unions, a pro-Loyalist constituency that surely would have been less likely to desert had Roosevelt lifted the embargo. Granted, too, Roosevelt's share of the popular vote did fall from 61 percent in the 1936 election to 55 percent in 1940, but he still beat Wendell L. Willkie by five million votes. It is unclear, therefore, why Roosevelt needed to lose sleep over 600,000 Catholic votes, especially when balanced against the pressure he was under to lift the embargo from his inner circle, the pro-Loyalist correspondence flowing across his desk from Catholics, and his sense of destiny, his longing to create "a favorable historical reputation," as Patrick J. Maney puts it. Even if Catholic votes were paramount, he could have worked to ameliorate the risk, say, by asking his ally, Chicago's powerful Cardinal Mundelein, to sell his decision to the laity, a strategy he did implement in October 1939 in the context of the Nazi invasion of Catholic Poland. Mundelein might not have been pro-Loyalist, but neither was he any fan of Franco, and it was Mundelein who assisted Roosevelt by derailing Father Charles E. Coughlin's bid for the presidency in 1935. If not the Catholic factor, then what explains Roosevelt's inertia?[39]

Roosevelt's Loathing of Spain

Despite efforts by scores of researchers, President Roosevelt remains an enigma. Because he kept no diary, refused to allow secretaries to take minutes, wrote little and then in ambiguous phrases, and even tampered with the documentary record, historians have either remained puzzled or read into his thinking whatever has suited their arguments. Commenting on Roosevelt's habit of saying "Yep, yep" when someone was talking to him, historian Wayne S. Cole believes this was a ploy to convey interest and understanding but not necessarily agreement. "Many left White House conferences," Cole notes, "confident that Roosevelt shared their views—even when he really did not." Waldo Heinrichs's evaluation is that Roosevelt was the "most elusive and dissembling of presidents," and Mark A. Stoler talks about his "notorious secrecy and deviousness." "Even when FDR did break down and say something meaningful for the record," Stoler concludes, "one was often unsure if it was what he really thought, or even of what it meant." Kenneth S. Davis's magisterial *FDR: A History* goes further, suggesting that he liked to "indulge in deviousness and indirection for the sheer fun of it." And the voluminous Roosevelt Library can be just as unenlightening. Roosevelt's adviser, Rexford Tugwell, thought that the president deliberately archived huge quantities of documents to set a "gigantic trap for historians," who would then be too preoccupied "to ask embarrassing questions." Therefore, what follows is necessarily a tentative interpretation, reliant as it is on anecdotal evidence as well as inspired leaps of faith; yet even if it fails to convince, then perhaps it will serve to stimulate further research.[40]

There is a corpus of material, especially from the pre–White House years, that casts light on Roosevelt's disposition toward foreign affairs. Historians of Roosevelt's policy making often refer to his dislike of the Old World. "Roosevelt's opinion of the French," comments Thomas Fleming, "was almost as low—and as hostile—as his opinion of the Germans." Frederick W. Marks observes that he "harbored little admiration or respect for any of the European powers." John Lamberton Harper stresses Roosevelt's aversion to the backwardness and moral turpitude of Europe, a "distancing" from Old World "decadence" that Harper terms "Europhobic-hemispherism." Perhaps because Roosevelt never visited the Iberian Peninsula, historians pass no comment on his cognitive image, or mental map, of decadent Spain, but circumstantial evidence, when taken in sum, indicates that it was negative.[41]

As a young man, Roosevelt held few individuals in higher esteem than his cousin Theodore Roosevelt, and, as Harper notes, few events "reinforced his sense of the distinctness of the Old and New Worlds—and the decadence of the former" than those of 1898. While at Groton School at the still impressionable age of sixteen, and already a devotee of naval warfare, he would have read newspaper accounts of the sinking of the wondrous battleship USS *Maine* and the ensuing Spanish-American War. A letter in the *New York Times* by Samuel Essmond Shipp was one of many on the subject that might have caught his eye. Old enough to remember the horrors of the Civil War, Shipp implored Americans to maintain a dignified peace rather than rush into conflict against an "arrogant and emasculated race, a race entirely unworthy [of] a great nation's hostile anger." Shipp spoke for many Americans who did not even count effeminate Spain among the civilized nations. "Barbarous and treacherous," "she" was simply unworthy of America's attentions. It was the "brutalizing effects of her Sunday bull fights" and long familiarity with "murder and rapine in her distressed colonies" that had debased Spain to its current level. "When civilization passed over the world, it looks as if it left Spain untouched." If the country must have a war, Shipp mused, then let it be on equal terms, let it be fought with honor in respectable combat, not against an "effervescent and quixotic race, whom it would be no credit to ourselves to thrash."[42]

For their honeymoon, the Roosevelts went on a three-month European grand tour. He took her to see the famous sites of England, France, Italy, Germany, and Switzerland, but they did not venture across the Pyrenees. During the Great War, Roosevelt again traveled between France and England, and he visited Italy. As with all his other European trips, he never went near Spain. (Though, as he sailed home in September 1918, an almost fatal virus struck him, a deadly strain of influenza called the Spanish flu.) Shortly after he became president, he had the opportunity to hear about the opulence of Madrid's haut monde from his son Franklin Jr., who vacationed there. Ambassador Bowers reported in glowing terms how Franklin attended a bullfight, met President Niceto Alcalá Zamora at the sumptuous Royal Palace, and dined in the best restaurants in town. In 1935 Roosevelt backed a policy of high tariffs in a trade war with Spain. William Phillips at the State Department recommended two concessions as a means to reestablishing mutually beneficial trade: reducing Washington's punitive tariffs of 200 percent on cork stoppers and onions. In a memorandum to Phillips, Roosevelt said that he was "inclined to go along" with the recommendation on stoppers, but he baulked over the onions: "Is not this essential commodity grown in almost every county of the United States?" Just like potatoes, he said matter-of-factly, "there is no good reason why we should not grow them here at a reasonable price." His understanding that cork trees did not grow in North America was correct, and he was right about potatoes; but when it came to onions, his mental map was faulty. Phillips pointed out that before the tariff war two years earlier, 64 percent of onions consumed by Americans—Roosevelt included—had always been best-quality Spanish onions. Yes, domestic producers were now planting a larger acreage of Bermuda onions; but even with new imports from Chile and Egypt making up part of the huge shortfall, demand on either side of the short spring growing season far exceeded supply, and prices had skyrocketed.[43]

Individually, these anecdotes mean little, but taken together they do underpin a rare documented instance of an opinion suggesting that Roosevelt's mental map of Spain was prejudicial. French ambassador Doynel de Saint-Quentin wrote to his foreign minister Joseph Paul-Boncour in March 1938 observing that Roosevelt derided the Spanish as "naturally indolent." Because of Spaniards' inherent lethargy, Roosevelt expected that in the event of victory by Franco's Nationalists, they would have to turn to the Germans for help in rebuilding their country. Indolence, for Roosevelt, was a sin, the enemy of the cult of strenuous manhood he imbibed from his cousin Theodore, who had charged up San Juan Hill in 1898 to avenge the sinking of the *Maine*. Mastering indolence through vigorous activity—the sailing, fishing, swimming, and jogging; the fall overboard; the extinguishing of a brush fire at Campobello—had been the reason for the exhaustion that compromised his resistance to the poliomyelitis that paralyzed his legs. Masculine vigor was Roosevelt's faith just as it had sealed his doom. Effeminate Spaniards propped up decrepit colonies, surreptitiously sunk U.S. battleships, fled before Colonel Theodore's Rough Riders, tortured hapless bulls, undercut American onion growers, had killer viruses named after them, and, when they did fight, waged a bloody civil war with atrocities committed by both sides. Worse still, for Roosevelt, they were all indolent. Indeed, Spaniards occupied an unloved, distant corner of Roosevelt's global mental map, one for which he had little time and less patience.[44]

Roosevelt's Love of China

By contrast, Roosevelt had a positive mental map of exotic China. He knew by heart from his mother, Sara Delano, who doted on her only child, the story of how his grandfather Warren had twice made a fortune in the China trade (she might not have mentioned that the second fortune was from opium dealing). He knew the stories of her five luxurious years in Hong Kong as a young girl and of her return visit there in 1876 via the newly opened Suez Canal. (Perhaps she told him, too, how during her only visit to Spain with husband James they both fell ill with a fever.) Warren himself, who did not die until his grandson was sixteen, would have reminisced about his China adventures, from the estate in Macao to the clipper ships that brought his tea across the Pacific to America, fast ships that made distant China seem like a near neighbor. At Groton, Roosevelt—no doubt biting his lip—had to argue in a school debate against a resolution that the United States should guarantee Chinese sovereignty. But he did enjoy the "most interesting" lectures on China by Edward S. Morse, curator of Salem's Peabody Academy of Science, even though he was upset that Morse "ran down the poor Chinamen" and thought "too much of the Japs."[45]

Rosy admiration of China could reduce Roosevelt's policy making to a kneejerk reflex. When Herbert Hoover's secretary of State, Henry L. Stimson, announced a hawkish policy against Japan over Manchuria in January 1933, President-elect Roosevelt signed on without consulting Rexford Tugwell or Raymond Moley, the two Columbia University professors who comprised part of his "brain trust" of close advisers. Convinced (rightly, as it turned out) that the Hoover-Stimson Doctrine would force America into a Pacific war, Tugwell and Moley asked Roosevelt why he had not consulted them first. After mentioning that his ancestors had been China traders, Roosevelt replied unthinkingly, "I have always had the deepest sympathy for the Chinese. How could you expect me not to go along with Stimson on Japan?"[46]

A comparison of Spain's Franco with China's Chiang Kai-shek offers a window onto Roosevelt's mental map of their respective countries in 1938. Aside from the obvious difference that Roosevelt tarred Franco's Nationalists and Chiang's enemy, Japan, with the same fascist/expansionist brush, there were interesting similarities. Both were strongmen with iron wills and great courage in battle who called themselves Generalísimo and their popular movements *Nationalist*. Both presided over countries with extensive economic ties to the United States through trade and direct investment. Both led vigorous lifestyles, which in Franco's case included a passion for sailing and fishing, Roosevelt's favorite leisure activities. Both were dedicated fighters of communism and pious Christians, although whereas Chiang was a Methodist, Franco was a Catholic. Still, Roosevelt backed a ruthless Catholic strongman in Nicaragua, Anastasio Somoza García; indeed, as historian Seth Jacobs argues in the context of South Vietnam's Ngô Đình Diêm, U.S. presidents and State Department officials could view Catholicism as an asset, for it implied deference to hierarchy and appreciation of order.[47]

Yet Roosevelt loathed Franco just as he revered Chiang (at least, that is, until November 1943 when he met Chiang in person). Although Roosevelt did find the time to send a nineteen-word telegram of greeting to Loyalist president Manuel

Azaña on 14 April 1938 on the anniversary of Spain's Second Republic, he avoided any communication with Franco until the commencement of Operation Torch, the U.S. landings in North Africa in November 1942, almost four years after his government begrudgingly recognized Franco as head of state. At the same time as Secretary McIntyre was sending form letters to Americans stating that the president was far too busy to read their appeals for lifting the Spanish arms embargo, the president was writing to Chiang with warm appreciation for a signed photograph. And at the same time that Roosevelt was claiming the impracticability—not to mention the illegality—of sending war matériel to Loyalist Spain, he was actively arming Nationalist China and would shortly be imposing sanctions on America's longtime friend and World War I ally, Japan.[48]

Between July 1937 and December 1938, the State Department granted export licenses for arms, munitions, and military equipment to China totaling $16 million ($480 million). In April 1938, Roosevelt saw a confidential memorandum detailing shipments to Hong Kong of "15 cases of machine guns for aeroplanes" and "500 tons of gunpowder and other explosives." Two months later, he read a similar memorandum specifying the "airplanes, airplane machinery and parts" along with "machine guns and small arms" that had arrived in Hong Kong from the United States. State Department officials approved these shipments, which were illegal under the meaning, if not the strictest letter, of the same Neutrality Act that embargoed arms to the belligerents of Loyalist Spain. In November 1938, Eleanor read newspaper reports indicating that American-made aircraft bombs had been leaving the country on German ships and became distressed, concluding that their destination was Franco's Nationalists. When Sumner Welles checked with Charles W. Yost, Yost investigated only to discover that 69,000 bombs had indeed left Delaware River ports on German vessels during the first five months of 1938, but the purchasing agent was a K. C. Li of the Wah Chang Trading Corporation and their ultimate destination was Hong Kong. It is a compelling irony of Roosevelt's duplicitous neutrality policy—a policy that I argue was a product of his biased mental map—that in his enthusiasm to arm Chiang's Guomindang army against the Japanese, Roosevelt was shipping war matériel through Nazi Germany during the Austrian *Anschluss*. Three months after Munich—as Welles noted to Roosevelt in December—Germany was still supplying "more arms than any other country" to Chiang's China. When it came to China in 1938, Roosevelt's mental map and Hitler's desire to trade weapons for strategic materials made them unlikely partners in the international arms business.[49]

While arming Chiang, Roosevelt was cognizant that his actions contravened the provisions of the Neutrality Acts of 1935 and 1936—legislation he had signed—dealing with the export of arms to belligerents and the use of export credits to finance such shipments. In October 1938, he hatched a scheme with his equally Sinophilic treasury secretary. Assistant Secretary of the Treasury, Wayne Taylor, wrote a "strong recommendation" to Morgenthau, which Morgenthau directed to Roosevelt, urging the scheme's abandonment. "Regardless of the technicalities which appear to surround modern conflicts," Taylor began, "it is obvious that Japan and China are engaged in a bitter war." "In the absence of a specific expression by the American people on the specific points," it was Taylor's "conviction" that if the president approved the tung oil transaction then he "would stretch to the breaking point any authority hitherto delegated to him by Congress." Roosevelt and Morgenthau went ahead anyway, regardless of Taylor's charge that they were going behind the backs of the American people to break the law.[50]

Arms for Nationalist China, Not Loyalist Spain

Despite overwhelming pressure from all sides to raise the embargo on arms to Loyalist Spain, Roosevelt left it in place. He made only token gestures, moreover, toward its circumvention. He may well have been fearful of upsetting the Catholic hierarchy, and there were borderline congressional districts that Democrats might have lost in the November midterms were he to have lifted it. Yet from all the pro-Loyalist correspondence passing across his desk, he should have realized that he actually stood to make more friends by raising the embargo than enemies. Leaving aside the Catholic factor argument, which the evidence presented here calls into doubt, along with the weak reasons that Roosevelt himself gave—practicalities of delivery, the Loyalists had as good as lost anyway—there are at least two other quite plausible reasons for Roosevelt's inaction. First, for the sake of the special relationship, he was probably concerned to keep in step with Britain's lead, although as one letter writer, Evans, noted, American policy makers had long displayed their independence, and Roosevelt was scarcely more partial toward imperial Britain than any other Old World power.[51]

Second, and most significantly, Roosevelt could see from opinion polls (of which he was a devotee) that 70 percent of Americans supported a policy of strict neutrality. Lifting the embargo to Spain, carte blanche, could well have cost him ten times more than the half-million-plus Catholic votes. Yet he could see, too, from the same polls, that over a third of Americans sympathized with the Loyalist cause (allowing for the fact that half of those polled expressed no opinion). Had he so desired, turning public sympathy for the Loyalists into a compelling argument for making Spain an exceptional case should not have been too challenging, especially for a president who could project such enormous influence through press conferences and fireside chats. Even if he had reasoned that abrogating the Neutrality Act was too risky going into the midterm elections, then he still had the option of aiding the Loyalists covertly, as he did so successfully with Chiang's Nationalists.[52]

Ickes's casual remark to his diary of 1 May 1938 may well have been closest to the truth: "It seemed to me that he [Roosevelt] was evading the issue." When it came to the Spanish issue, Roosevelt was evasive. He obfuscated, he procrastinated;

he really did not want to be bothered with decadent Spain. Morgenthau, admittedly, bought Madrid's silver pesetas, but that was an independent initiative with Roosevelt out of the loop.[53]

China was another matter. Roosevelt worked with Morgenthau to arrange a massive credit against tung oil, despite the strong censure of Assistant Secretary Taylor. He badgered Welles for updates on arms shipments. He did everything he could to ensure that American arms flowed to China. When he wrote to an embattled Chiang in January 1938, his brief letter, despite being a masterpiece of diplomatic obfuscation, nonetheless indicated his strictest attention: "We are giving constant study and thought to the problem of ways and means of promoting peace." Decoded, he was saying, first, that China was much on his mind and, second, that he was doing everything he could to send China war matériel while simultaneously curbing exports to Japan. Chiang replied with a five-page letter, also in code, underscoring their "traditional . . . unexcelled Sino–American friendship," but his purpose was to make a somewhat oblique yet "urgent wish" that Roosevelt would "enable us to continue our resistance." Writing from Chungking in December 1938, minister H. H. Kung, who had spent time with Roosevelt in 1937, was able to acknowledge how "our national resistance against the invader" had received "much encouragement" from America's "unfailing friendship." During World War II, Roosevelt continued the unexcelled friendship, elevating Chiang to the status of one of the world's Four Policemen and, for three months over the winter of 1942–43, sharing first his Hyde Park home and then the White House with Madame Mei-ling Chiang Kai-shek while she was convalescing from an operation. Meanwhile, Roosevelt continued his loathing of Nationalist Spain, isolating Franco as a Nazi pariah, despite the strategic advantages—most obviously over Gibraltar and access to the crucial Mediterranean theater—of wooing this particular Generalísimo to the Allied side.[54]

Roosevelt visited neither Spain nor China. Perhaps having no direct experiences made it easier for him to develop his own distorted mental maps of each country. China was farther away, yet from his Hyde Park home it was thousands of miles closer than Spain. There a magnificent Chinese dresser with carved oriental dragons occupied pride of place in his entrance hall. As he rolled his wheelchair from the hall, he passed a pair of Chinese stools with a ceramic tea table in the form of a flat-topped elephant, and in the family room a pair of massive Chinese standing candle sconces framed the fireplace. Among other Chinese curiosities brought back by his grandfather Warren and his mother, Sara, were the watercolors in the music room, the bronze bell on the half-landing, and several large porcelain vases, two of which stood on the mantelpiece in his study. Indeed, China was never far from Roosevelt's mind during the late 1930s. But when he thought of Spain, it was to complain to his clerk Forster in January 1937 that he had not received any Spanish postage stamps for his collection in months. It was almost as if he had relegated Spain's five-month-old civil war to a philatelic incon-venience. But had he received stamps, he might have found their commemora-tions informative. Stamps from the Nationalist zone typically carried religiously inspired images of Queen Isabella or the Spanish patron saint, James, while Loy-alist stamps, such as a set of four issued in Barcelona in 1937, carried the words "Homage to the Soviet Union" and featured pictures of Maksim Gorky or Red Guards in the characteristic style of socialist realism.[55]

Any one of three scenarios would have allowed U.S. arms to reach Loyalist Spain in 1938: First, the State Department could have circumvented or otherwise turned a blind eye to export licenses, which admittedly was trickier than with China, for the Neutrality Act of 1937 stated explicitly that Spain was off limits. Licensing arms sales to France on the pretext of counterbalancing German re-armament was the most obvious of possible workarounds. An ideal opportunity for transshipment existed during the last weeks of Léon Blum's Popular Front government in April and May, when leftists were especially keen to ignore the Non-Intervention Agreement of August 1936 and aid their comrades in Loyalist Spain, so much so that Franco seriously considered the possibility of the French army marching over the Pyrenees. Because State Department officials held di-vided sympathies for each side in warring Spain, only Roosevelt could have sup-plied the necessary impetus for such circumvention, much as he did in the case of China. Yet his heart was not in it. Second, Roosevelt could either have lifted the embargo by fiat or actively encouraged congressional leaders, such as Key Pittman, to raise it through legislation. Again, his heart lay elsewhere. Third, Con-gress itself needed to enact rather than merely propose legislation, and here the efforts of Franco lobbyists, in concert with a general public sentiment for isola-tionism toward Europe, decisively outweighed those by pro-Loyalists.[56]

At the end of September 1938, once Hitler's Sudetenland gambit had stretched appeasement ideology to the limits of credulity, Roosevelt probably realized, as he later admitted to Ickes, "that the embargo had been a grave mistake." Historian Bar-bara Rearden Farnham uses sophisticated political decision-making modeling tech-niques to argue that Munich switched Roosevelt from an uncertain conciliator to a committed interventionist. In the case of Spain, nevertheless, he dawdled for eight weeks until the end of November before putting any effort into investigating the practicalities of overturning the Act by executive order, writing first to Ickes about the "desirability of making a change" and then telephoning Welles to ask about the legality of immediate executive action. Then, after receiving a legalistic treatise from Assistant Solicitor General Golden W. Bell, he abandoned the attempt. By the end of the year, he was urging Pittman to move the upcoming Seventy-sixth Congress for repeal, but again, this belated and half-hearted attempt by Roosevelt met with overwhelming legislative resistance. Franco's forces paraded triumphantly through Madrid in May 1939, and fifteen weeks later, Hitler invaded Poland.[57]

Just as Neville Chamberlain thought Hitler's intentions were peaceful, until the Nazi blitzkrieg, so historians who make assumptions about policy makers' opinions have to contend with not only what they said—or what little they said, as in Roosevelt's case—but also what they subsequently did about it. Robert Dallek's exhaustive study of presidential foreign policy making states that Roosevelt was sympathetic to Spain's Loyalists. Dominic Tierney goes further, arguing that by the spring of 1938 Roosevelt had become an ardent Loyalist benefactor. It seems evident as well as logical that Roosevelt was indeed pro-Loyalist. Yet *seems* is a necessary proviso, for Roosevelt left virtually nothing to the documentary record, leaving historians to either make inferences or rely on third-party accounts, and those invariably recount Roosevelt telling someone what he thought they wanted to hear rather than what he necessarily believed. A month or two after the civil war's outbreak, Roosevelt's interest in preserving Spain's Republic "was either small or nonexistent," as Dallek puts it, his objective being "simply to keep the conflict from becoming a general European war." Roosevelt may have been more concerned for the Loyalists' plight by July 1937, when Joris Ivens, a Dutch communist who made documentary films for the Comintern, previewed *The Spanish Earth* at the White House. Even here, the initiative for the event was Eleanor's, while Roosevelt, who sat next to Ivens at the screening, was primarily interested in the performance of the Loyalists' French and Russian tanks, although he did ask Ivens to stress the feudal state of Spanish agriculture. (Ivens did incorporate Roosevelt's suggestion in the final soundtrack: Ernest Hemingway, speaking as a peasant, complained bitterly, "For fifty years we've wanted to irrigate, but *they* held us back.") All Ivens could tell reporters was that Roosevelt thought the picture had "fine continuity." When it came to decadent feudal Spain, Roosevelt had enthusiasm for the Loyalists' stamps and tanks, but little else. Historians who argue otherwise are stuck, trying to reconcile what Roosevelt said—or, more often, what others heard him say—with his disinterested actions, a tricky prospect, because when it came to assisting the Loyalists, those amounted to nothing.[58]

4

Keeping the Embargo

Twin factors ensured that arms did not flow from the United States to Loyalist Spain. On one hand, President Franklin D. Roosevelt put little effort into either circumventing or lifting the Neutrality Act–imposed arms embargo because his heart lay in aiding exotic China rather than decadent Spain. On the other, a pro-Franco lobby was mobilizing both public and congressional opinion behind maintenance of the act. Roosevelt's reticence over Spain in particular, along with his indecisiveness over Europe in general, combined with a malaise exacerbated by enervation, most obviously his own paraplegia and Secretary of State Cordell Hull's tuberculosis. A sort of miasma settled on the White House, creating a petty-squabbling, heavy-drinking administrative culture that left a leadership vacuum, throwing the onus for foreign policy making onto Congress and, hence, public opinion. It would be neither the White House nor the State Department but, rather, a mixed bag of American lobbyists, those who honed their skills and carved out their positions through the Great Debate over arms to Spain, who steered America's European policy during the pivotal year of 1938.

There were three periods when the Act appeared most vulnerable, and three matching initiatives by Franco lobbyists to ensure its continuance: first, an effort in May by Senate Committee on Foreign Relations chairman Key Pittman to overturn the act before the Seventy-fifth Congress disbanded; second, momentum during the summer recess to abrogate the act either by executive fiat or through congressional recall; and third, a massive campaign in January 1939 by both sides in the Great Debate when the Seventy-sixth Congress opened. Despite the view of Roosevelt contemporaries, as well as prevailing historiography, that pressure from the Catholic hierarchy and Roosevelt's consequent fear of losing the Catholic vote proved decisive in every case, it was only that of January's NCWC's "Keep the Embargo!" campaign in which the hierarchy played a determinative role.

While it examines each of these three initiatives, this chapter's primary focus is on the efforts of Franco lobbyist John Eoghan Kelly during the latter part of

1938, and it addresses the troublesome question among diplomatic historians of whether the public has the power to influence foreign policy. Robert C. Hilderbrand, in analyzing the early twentieth century, speaks for the consensus: "No real power has ever been given to the people"; rather, executive officials have choreographed America's steps across the international stage. In taking a contrary stance, I document here a case where a single private citizen learned to tap into real power, directing it through elites and then to policy makers. Kelly not only swayed public opinion but also influenced the course of U.S. foreign affairs.[1]

Ickes and the Nye Resolution

Of the three periods when it appeared to contemporaries that Congress was ready to lift the embargo, historians have given the most attention to Key Pittman's effort in May 1938. Pittman was the architect of the original 1935 Neutrality Act, negotiated for its eighteen-month continuation as the Act of 1936, and designed its cash-and-carry provision and extension to Spain's civil war in the Act of 1937. Pro-Loyalist legislators were therefore as pleased as they were surprised to discover in April 1938 that Pittman was ready to work for its repeal. Friction that began on 31 January after sixty legislators sent a telegram to Loyalist Spain's Cortes supporting its "fight for democratic institutions" smoldered on in the House during the spring, then ignited in the Senate on 2 May after another surprise when arch isolationist Gerald P. Nye (R-ND) proposed a joint resolution to lift the arms embargo unilaterally on Loyalist Spain while continuing to embargo Franco's Nationalists. In 1935, the findings of Nye's committee, that bankers and munitions makers reaped millions from the shell-pocked fields of the Great War, had led to the first Neutrality Act; but since 1937, a growing sense of injustice over the Loyalist cause had prompted Nye to rethink the merits of such a rigid policy. Nye, who was one of the signatories on the pro-Loyalist telegram, may have considered his timing propitious, for both Hull and Roosevelt were taking curative vacations to address fatigue and ill health, and there was enough time to pass the resolution before Congress recessed in June for its seven-month summer break and fall campaigning. Circumstances between 2 May and 13 May, when Pittman abandoned the Nye resolution, are unclear, but it may be that retired diplomat and Franco lobbyist W. Cameron Forbes played a significant—and previously overlooked—role.[2]

Roosevelt returned to Washington from a Sargasso Sea fishing trip on Monday, 9 May, and began what a *New York Times* reporter called "one of the busiest mornings at the executive offices in months" by meeting with House Speaker William B. Bankhead (D-AL), Majority Leader Samuel Rayburn (D-TX), and Representative Edward Taylor (D-CO). As Roosevelt made clear to reporters the day before, the "chief topic of discussion" was to be the Fair Labor Standards Act, a central plank of New Deal legislation as well as the last to become law because the House had stalled its progress since the previous summer. Still, at some point during this long, trying meeting, the subject of Nye's resolution evidently cropped up. When pressed on the point by reporters as he left the White House, Rayburn conceded that they had talked about the arms embargo but only "incidentally." Rayburn then added vaguely that, in his opinion, the House should leave the issue alone, for it would be a "funny thing" to change the Act after such a "short operation."[3]

Ickes, thick necked, heavy browed, and looking more like a long-retired prize-fighter than secretary of the Interior, marched in to see Roosevelt as soon as the House delegation had left. Intent on forcing Roosevelt's hand on the embargo issue, Ickes stressed that they should never have imposed it in the first place, pointing out that it constituted "a black page in American history," and he urged for its immediate lift. Roosevelt then tried to put a lid on the topic, explaining that House Democrats were "jittery" about lifting the embargo and that it "would mean the loss of every Catholic vote" in the November elections. Roosevelt had finally let the Catholic cat out of America's embargo bag, Ickes realized excitedly, and it was "the mangiest, scabbiest cat ever." Ickes's account of the meeting, from a 12 May entry in his *Secret Diary,* formed the basis for historians' Catholic factor argument.[4]

It is certainly possible that Bankhead, Rayburn, and Taylor warned Roosevelt not to tamper with the Neutrality Act during an election year because they were fearful of losing the pro-Franco segment of the Catholic vote. Still, if Democratic leaders considered these votes crucial, then it is odd that so many Democrats were prepared to upset their pro-Franco constituents by signing the telegram of support to the Loyalist Cortes three months earlier, two of whom were Taylor's fellow Coloradans, Representative John A. Morrison and Senator Edwin C. Johnson. Rayburn's Texas delegation was predominantly pro-Loyalist, with Senator Thomas Connally and Representatives George H. Mason and W. R. Poage, all signers. Also relevant is Bankhead's, Rayburn's, and Taylor's internationalism. In all likelihood, with such a critical piece of New Deal labor legislation to pass before the end of the session in June, neither Roosevelt nor the House leaders had much time that busy morning, 9 May 1938, to bother with arms for distant Spain. Roosevelt's remark to Ickes was a clever excuse for presidential foot-dragging rather than an expression of genuine concern over the repercussions of upsetting America's Catholic hierarchy.[5]

Ickes wrote too much into his diary entry. Roosevelt that Monday morning was trying hard to maintain his "tanned and invigorated" appearance acquired during the Caribbean cruise, on which he hoped journalists would report. "Glowing from Rest at Sea," the *New York Times* dutifully subheaded its front page, noting the president's "tanned complexion" offset by white flannel trousers and a cream sport coat. "It was just what the doctor ordered," an official remarked within earshot of both Roosevelt's personal physician and the *Times* reporter. Yet no amount

of sun and fishing could ameliorate the deterioration of the body due to hyperten-
sion or the tension of the mind due to the stress of having the nation's top job.
After the difficult and lengthy meeting with his party's leaders, Roosevelt surely
felt fatigue returning and the sunny resolve weakening when Ickes entered, once
again eager to pressure Roosevelt on his pet project: arms for Loyalist Spain.[6]

During their last meeting on 23 April, when Roosevelt began his vacation by
taking a few friends for a weekend cruise to the Chesapeake Bay on the presidential yacht *Potomac*, Ickes had similarly nagged him about Spain. It was widely
known that outside of the Oval Office, Roosevelt disliked talking shop, and once
embarked on his favorite of all escapes, a boat trip, "serious affairs of state," as
Ickes grumbled to his diary, "are barely mentioned." It was a damp and dreary
day aboard the *Potomac* with little to do, and Ickes had gone to Roosevelt's cozy
cabin, where the latter was engrossed in another favorite activity, cutting foreign
stamps from a stack of State Department envelopes and mounting them on album
pages. But Ickes did not want to chat about philately. He launched instead into a
monologue about amendments to the pending executive branch Reorganization
Bill, during which Roosevelt "listened but didn't say much." Undaunted, Ickes
then tackled Roosevelt on the Spanish arms embargo. No doubt resenting the
intrusion in the first place and not wanting to discuss the affairs of an Old World
country he loathed, Roosevelt told Ickes how pointless it was to lift the embargo
because the arms would simply not reach the Loyalists. Ickes confided to his *Secret Diary* that what he had just heard sounded like a weak excuse from someone
who "was evading the issue."[7]

Back in Washington, and with the president embarked on an eight-day fishing cruise to the Caribbean and Sargasso Sea aboard the USS *Philadelphia*, Ickes
learned that Nye had presented his embargo-lifting resolution to the Senate and
that Pittman was prepared to press ahead with it before the June recess. Jay Allen,
a former *Chicago Tribune* foreign correspondent who was now a Madrid lobbyist,
paid Ickes a visit. Allen was "outraged" over the embargo and intent on urging a
sympathetic Ickes to do his utmost to help lift it. During their meeting, Allen happened to mention that the French, who had been turning a blind eye along their
border so that arms could flow to the Loyalists, would comply with British pressure
and close the frontier unless U.S. matériel arrived soon to justify their stratagem.
Allen was correct about the flow of arms: the French let 25,000 tons of matériel into
Loyalist Spain during April and May, and even cut down trees along the roads of
Aquitaine to allow the passage of trucks transporting 300 Russian aircraft.[8]

Ickes must have been incensed at Allen's information, for it showed him that
Roosevelt either was out of touch or had been giving him the run-around. It is
not surprising, therefore, that as soon as the House delegation left the Oval Office
on the morning of 9 May, Ickes could not wait to raise the matter with renewed
determination. Roosevelt reiterated that the Loyalists could neither afford to buy

munitions from America nor find a way to transport them to their zone. But Ickes now knew otherwise. In a combative mood, he countered, pointing out what Allen had told him: the French wanted to leave their frontier with Spain open but would close it if no U.S. arms arrived soon. Ickes was no doubt angry, as well as puzzled, that his friend the president would not act to save the democratic Republic of Spain, especially in the face of mounting Nazi aggression in Europe.[9]

Roosevelt, for his part, did not want to talk about Spain. Perhaps he wanted to talk to Ickes, a fellow deep-sea angler, about his invigorating trip around the Sargasso Sea or, failing that, the pending labor legislation. Roosevelt trotted out the same excuse about Madrid's credit and difficulties of delivery, but this time he could see that Ickes was having none of it. He needed to give Ickes—his card-playing, hard-drinking, fishing pal—a valid reason for why he was not encouraging Pittman to debate the Nye resolution in committee. If Bankhead, Rayburn, or Taylor had mentioned the potential problem of Catholic votes, then they might have planted the seed in Roosevelt's mind of a justification that would make sense to Ickes. Biographers Graham White and John Maze show how Ickes, traumatized as a child by his mother's strict Calvinism, grew up more like his loose-living father, secular with an ingrained distrust of organized religions but governed by an "unwavering belief in his own moral rectitude." In 1937, New York's mayor Fiorello La Guardia told Ickes about a legislative hearing on a child labor amendment at which Catholic prelates expressed such vocal opposition that their behavior reminded the mayor of the Spanish Inquisition, a prejudicial comment with which Ickes could find no fault. As an antipapist liberal, therefore, Ickes was predisposed to buy Roosevelt's new Catholic factor excuse on that busy morning in early May, and historians have been sold on it ever since.[10]

Forbes and the Nye Resolution

On 2 May 1938, Cordell Hull returned to Washington from his curative vacation "looking really rested for the first time in many months," according to J. Pierrepont Moffat, one of Hull's evening croquet opponents and the chief of the State Department's European Affairs division. Hull might have looked rested, but his tuberculosis was no better, and neither were matters in Europe. That day Nye submitted his resolution, and Hull's worries returned. Moffat sounded out two members of the Senate's Committee on Foreign Relations, the isolationist Arthur H. Vandenberg (R-MI), who "just shrugged his shoulders," and the internationalist chairman Pittman, who "had rarely seen so powerful a lobby" in favor of a resolution. Not only did this crucial legislative committee suffer from serious differences of opinion; it is also significant that it had caught a breath of White House miasma. Pittman's alcoholism was chronic by 1938, impairing his judgment as well as his leadership of the committee. One biographer noted that alcohol often caused him "to act on rash impulse, failing to grasp the importance of what he was doing." To supply the ice he needed to cool down his daily intake of over a pint of whiskey, Pittman installed a refrigerator in the committee room.[11]

Hull called an emergency conference the following day with top aides Adolf A. Berle, legal adviser Greene H. Hackworth, counselor R. Walton Moore, Undersecretary Sumner Welles, and European affairs adviser James Clement Dunn. Commentary from informed sources—syndicated newspaper columnists Drew Pearson and Robert S. Allen, as well as journalist Robert Bendiner and Moffat— indicates that at the urging of the pro-Loyalists Welles and Moore, a consensus emerged. With the exception of the pro-Franco Dunn, "the entire Department appeared to have swung over" and was now prepared to back a neutrality law that would grant the president greater flexibility over foreign policy. Moore communicated the results of the conference to Pittman the following day, 4 May, to the effect that Hull advised lifting the embargo subject to two conditions: first, the lift applied to both Loyalist and Nationalist zones; second, the executive retained discretionary powers over the shipments of matériel. May 5's *New York Times* carried a startling front-page headline: "ROOSEVELT BACKS LIFTING ARMS EMBARGO ON SPAIN." Its author, Arthur Krock, the dean of Capitol Hill journalists, had canvassed senators and found that, with Roosevelt's support, a wide majority would now vote for the Nye resolution with the expectation that Congress would pass an amended version before the June recess.[12]

Kanawada hangs much of his Catholic factor argument on the assumption that either Hull or Welles leaked a bogus report to Krock with the intent of deliberately provoking a national Catholic backlash so that the Nye resolution would perish in Congress. Although he describes the leak theory as fact, his evidence comes from a 1963 interview with Krock by historian Hugh Thomas. who wrote that, "so far as he [Krock] could recall," either Hull or Welles gave him the information for his article, and "that was the policy his informant wished to achieve." Thomas implies a policy of scuttling the resolution, thereby placating the Catholic hierarchy. Presuming Thomas correctly understood Krock, and Krock—who was uncertain if the informant was Welles or Hull—correctly remembered the incident after twenty-five years, this evidence is as puzzling as it is unlikely. Welles makes an unusual suspect: he was solidly pro-Loyalist and would have had to face the First Lady's ire at his duplicity in the event that Krock disclosed his source. Hull, too, despised Franco and his Nationalists. More problematic, though, is why Hull— suffering from tuberculosis, depression, and stress—would bother to convene a conference, thrash out a consensus, and then give a green light to Pittman only to meet with Krock the same day to leak a false report with the intention of undermining all that work. Simple explanations may fit the evidence better than conspiracy theories.[13]

Krock might have been planning an embargo article anyway, but its timing and content do point to a high-level source within State. There were "some" in the administration, Krock's report mentioned, who saw neutrality as a matter of international law and who, "from the first," "felt that the neutrality legislation was a mistake." Because of the administration's failure to embargo arms to Japan and China, Spain's Loyalist government had made numerous protests, which were "embarrassing to the State Department." Impetus for these remarks point to Hull, for whom the effects of the Act he had always opposed were not merely an embarrassment but a constant source of anxiety. For Hull, increasingly feverish and fatigued, an elementary reason for leaking the report, which he presumably anticipated would sway congressional opinion behind lifting the embargo, was that the intensified lobbying by both sides in the Great Debate was literally sickening him. Krock held Hull in high esteem; Hull had a history of using Krock whenever he needed to go public with State policy, and they routinely dined together. Rather than intending a leak per se, Hull was probably enjoying a frank dinnertime chat with Krock, one tinged with relief at clearing his in-tray of another irritation.[14]

Moffat's diary entry for 4 May argued that Hull was still opposed to Congress tampering with the Neutrality Act on the rather passive grounds of preserving "the power of the Executive," of the Act having thus far "kept us out of a European mess," and of not wanting to "take the lead in a European matter but leave this to France and Britain." Yet Moffat was not present at the meetings, his diary is sometimes inaccurate, and he seems to have dictated his notes for the typed diary with the benefit of several days'—if not weeks'—hindsight. In all likelihood, as Pearson and Allen stated in their "Washington Merry-Go-Round" insiders' column, "an abrupt and sudden hitch" occurred after Hull's decision to back a modified Nye resolution and support Krock's article of 5 May. That hitch was Roosevelt, who, while fishing in the Caribbean, "put out his hand and said, in effect, 'Stop,'" pending his return to Washington. Always preoccupied with controlling his department and presenting a united front, Hull now looked powerless, as Roosevelt once again pulled the rug out from under him. It had all "finally got to be too much for him," according to Moffat, and a frustrated Hull "blew up at press conference." Again, if Hull had leaked to Krock with the intention of sabotaging the Nye resolution, then his anger over Roosevelt doing the job for him was odd, to say the least. At about 12:30 on Monday, 9 May, not long after Ickes left the Oval Office, but nonetheless last on the list, a "resentful" Hull met with Roosevelt. Leaving aside the validity of Krock's comment during Thomas's interview, it is necessary to consider whether Roosevelt had a legitimate reason for stalling the Nye resolution, and, if so, then appeasement is the likely explanation, with the Catholic factor offering the perfect excuse.[15]

Appeasement in May 1938 was not the dirty word it would become by September 1939. Krock himself, who had long been a critic of the New Deal at home, was a consistent advocate of the administration's foreign policy, especially the policies of his friend Hull. After initial disappointment over Roosevelt's isolationist abandonment of the 1933 London Conference, Krock enthused about all of Roosevelt's efforts to push hard for a peace short of war. An interventionist who saw America as the world's policeman, Krock favored the peacemaking style of Theodore Roosevelt's judicious big stick. Yet realpolitik, not exceptionalist ideology, lay behind Krock's championing of appeasement. Krock opposed the arms embargo, but not out of any love for the Loyalists. In his article of 5 May, he stated that senators' clamor to lift the embargo had been a "psychological reaction" for "sentimental reasons," because they felt—erroneously, Krock implied—"that the Loyalists are fighting a battle for democracy." His son, T. A. Ashby-Poley-Krock, perhaps for sentimental reasons, was one of the few Americans who enlisted with Franco's army, rising to the purported rank of general. But Krock remained unmoved by the motives of either side in Spain. At this late stage in the conflict, he held that allowing Loyalists and Nationalists to purchase arms would make little difference in military terms anyway, especially to the Nationalists, who received matériel from Germany and Italy. Rather, Spain's interest for Krock, as it should have been for Roosevelt, too, was as an opportunity to demonstrate the decisiveness of U.S. foreign policy by brokering an agreement to disengage forces in return for not lifting the embargo, essentially as a carrot-and-stick to check Nazi aggression.[16]

On 16 April 1938, Neville Chamberlain and Benito Mussolini concluded an Anglo–Italian pact, which in addition to encouraging cooperation between the two imperial powers in the Mediterranean also suggested the possibility of reductions in Italian troop levels in Spain. Nye's resolution came at a time when the ink on Chamberlain's pact was still drying, and following that was Krock's *Times* report trumpeting Roosevelt's intention to support the U.S. embargo's annulment. Ambassador to Britain Joseph P. Kennedy, who was both pro-Franco and a proponent of appeasement, cabled a frantic protest to Roosevelt against meddling with the embargo, but as historian Michael R. Beschloss suggests, there is no evidence that Kennedy's plea moved Roosevelt. It is likely, nonetheless, that Roosevelt decided that stalling on the embargo would give Chamberlain's pact time to settle: dragging his feet on this issue, over a decadent country for which he had little time, would both keep the British happy and maximize the chances for appeasement in Europe to work. This scenario explains Hull's odd reversal of a position he reached just a week before: because Roosevelt instructed him to reverse. Throughout 10 May, Hull and Moffat worked on a letter to Pittman, which he received in committee on the 13 May, cautioning that lifting the embargo entailed "unnecessary risks" and was against America's "best interests," by which historians have incorrectly understood Hull to mean the interests of Catholic voters.[17]

Hull's letter, the outcome of Roosevelt's dislike of Spain and his acquiescence over Chamberlain's appeasement of Mussolini, may well have been sufficient to cause Pittman to postpone his efforts to lift the embargo. But there is another ingredient in the mix that historians have overlooked. Kanawada, F. Jay Taylor, and other scholars of the Great Debate have noted that there was considerable public lobbying of senators during the days following Krock's report, but their preoccupation with the Catholic hierarchy has obscured any finding that the most effective pressure came from the efforts of Protestants. Either because he had seen Krock's *New York Times* article or because another Franco supporter had solicited his help, W. Cameron Forbes decided to lobby Congress. Forbes wrote to his senator, David I. Walsh, recommending maintenance of the arms embargo and urging immediate diplomatic recognition of Franco's government. Forbes posted the letter to Washington on Saturday, 7 May; it arrived in Monday's mail, and Walsh read it into the *Congressional Record* during morning business on Tuesday, 10 May.[18]

As befitted a former ambassador and Boston Brahmin, Forbes's message was a model of decorum and common sense. Because the "policy of the Reds" had been to "liquidate" any Spaniards of "wealth, standing and training," the Loyalists had few natural leaders, thus rendering their cause hopeless. In Franco's zone, by contrast, which now comprised four-fifths of the people, Forbes had found "peace, orderliness, good feeling, high spirits," and a certainty of victory. Sending arms to support Madrid's "so-called 'Loyalists'" would only prolong a hopeless struggle, dooming "additional thousands" to "fight or get shot" for a revolutionary cause that many had no desire to join. A powerful pragmatic argument underscored Forbes's humanitarian concerns. Franco would interpret a lifting of the embargo as an act of hostility. With Nationalist victory, in Forbes's judgment, just a matter of time, such a "blow in the face" made no sense when the United States would soon be living with Franco's Spain "as a neighbor and friend."[19]

Lack of documentary evidence precludes any direct linkage between Forbes's initiative and Pittman's climb down, although there is a circumstantial connection, for the Senate referred Forbes's adroit letter to Pittman's Foreign Relations Committee on 10 May, two days before Hull gave Pittman his written opinion. Those on Pittman's committee who read Forbes's letter, regardless of their sympathies for either side in Spain, surely found its balanced cogency impressive. Forbes had devoted his life to public service as governor of the Philippines and ambassador to Japan, through his chairmanship of such investigative committees as the Hoover Commission to Haiti, and as board chairman of the Carnegie Institution. His letter resonated with the authority of one who understood Spanish culture and had visited Franco's Spain. Although Forbes was disparaging toward "Reds," he nonetheless exonerated regular or "natural" Spaniards, as he put it, from the revolutionary actions of their communist leaders. His argument for keeping the embargo as a means to hastening the war's end, and thereby reducing suffering, meshed well with the State Department's interest in giving appeasement some breathing space. Forbes, moreover, was not a silver-tongued Irish Catholic prelate, but a demure old-stock Protestant. Whether his letter made any difference is unclear and may be unknowable, but Forbes and his fellow Franco lobbyists at least had the satisfaction of seeing Nye's resolution die in Pittman's committee.

"Making Neutrality the Big Issue"

No sooner had Congress recessed for the summer than Franco lobbyists had to re-group for a new legislative challenge to the arms embargo, which this time would take all the concerted efforts of John Eoghan Kelly to overcome. In addition to the kind of tactical lobbying for Nationalist Spain throughout 1938 at which he excelled, Kelly also operated strategically. He gathered information, considered options, took initiatives, planned operations, and, above all, networked his fast-expanding web of contacts among influential elites.

In a letter of 23 August expressing alarm, but tempered with optimism for his latest "plan," Kelly intruded on the summer vacation of his primary contact in the Catholic hierarchy, Father Francis X. Talbot. There was a "drive of rapidly increasing momentum" among Washington's "radical new dealers," who, according to Kelly's Capitol Hill contact (perhaps Brooklyn's representative, Andrew L. Som-ers), were now insisting that Roosevelt had the power to lift the arms embargo to warring Spain by executive fiat, and must do so forthwith. So not only was there an immediate crisis, but there was also another worrying period looming, between November's midterms and the seating of Congress, when the Act's origi-nal backers would be distracted by new business. But Kelly had an idea. On 19 September in Los Angeles, the American Legion was holding its twentieth annual convention. Might the Legion's Foreign Policy Committee be amenable to passing a resolution condemning any attempt to tamper with the Neutrality Act–imposed embargo that so favored Franco? Kelly intended mobilizing his network of con-tacts to that end. He explained to Talbot how adding the voices of one million Legionnaires to those of America's pro-Franco Catholics would create an unchal-lengeable pro-Neutrality bloc, especially in so important an election year. Kelly knew that to challenge the American Legion, as National Commander Ralph T. O'Neil put it in 1931, was "to condemn the American people, for we are a repre-sentative cross section of the nation."[20]

Considering Kelly's plan in context requires a brief update of Spain's war, Eu-ropean grand strategy, and the Act itself, all of which were at turning points. First, the Loyalists' recently launched Ebro offensives indicated that the war was far from an inevitable Franco win, as it had seemed in January. In his monograph of the Ebro theater, historian Chris Henry notes that the Loyalists "only narrowly missed" their objectives during summer 1938, a time when they had welded their Popular Army into "an effective fighting force." Hindsight indicates that Nationalist air superiority, combined with Joseph Stalin's Spanish pullback in favor of preparations to battle Adolf Hitler across Eastern Europe, foredoomed Loyalist success, yet this is beside the point. For contemporaries, there were plenty of variables militating against a Franco victory, not least of which was whether Édouard Daladier, France's radical socialist prime minister, would ask his General Staff officers to implement their plan to cross the border to relieve Catalonia (as a prelude to seizing Spanish ports and attacking Spanish Morocco). Commentators such as the ambassador to Spain, Claude G. Bowers, had observed a growing frustration among and dissension between Nationalist generals, German and Italian contingents, and noncombatant elites, which boded well for a negotiated settlement. Unsurprisingly, therefore, newspaper and magazine reports during August and September spoke of Loyalist prospects in euphoric terms.[21]

Second, whether Roosevelt would lift the arms embargo, or even lend official diplomatic or material support to Republican Madrid, may have factored into Hitler's expansionist calculus, although this counterfactual scenario is hard to evaluate. Opinion ranges from ambassador to France William C. Bullitt's observation to Roosevelt on 17 August that fear of the United States was "unquestionably" uppermost in Hitler's machinations over Czechoslovakia to historian Gerhard L. Weinberg's assessment that Hitler's only fear was for his own declining health, which might compel him to unleash the Wehrmacht before it reached sufficient strength. Hitler, for his part, seems to have been as contemptuous of America's weak foreign policy and "'military inefficiency'" as he was disparaging of the "grasping materialism" and "social inequality" of its "half Judaized half negrified" people. In 1922 his Harvard-educated friend Ernst Hanfstaengl asked him why Germany lost the Great War. "Because America came in," Hitler answered, to which Hanfstaengl added, "If there is another war it must inevitably be won by the side which America joins." Hitler apparently forgot this counsel as well as his own Western Front experiences, for in 1938 he discounted intervention from an America "incapable of conducting war." Nonetheless, as historian James V. Compton's analysis shows, Hitler predicated his assumptions on U.S. isolationism. "America is still not a danger to us," he assured staffers in November 1939, "because of her neutrality laws." Hitler "clearly counted on American isolationism." Just as Hitler respected Roosevelt in 1933 for marching "straight toward his objective over Congress, over lobbies, over stubborn bureaucracies," so would he have taken notice of a resolute, internationalist foreign policy—had Roosevelt chosen to project one.[22]

Executive or congressional lifting of the embargo would have sent a strong hands-off signal to reticent Nazi military leaders—from Ludwig Beck to Wilhelm Canaris—who were opposed to courting war against European powers, and it would have embarrassed Chamberlain's parliament over its quid pro quo appeasement of Hitler's Axis partner, Mussolini. Writing to Roosevelt from Rome, Ambassador William Phillips agreed with Bowers that the Italian pole was wavering;

Mussolini was at the end of his tether over Spain and staying well "out of the [Sudetenland] picture." Most historians are skeptical that a U.S. U-turn on Spain in mid-1938 would have stiffened British and French resolve against Nazi aggression enough to avoid September's Munich debacle. Arnold A. Offner rates the probability of Hitler backing down no higher than "perhaps," although one skeptic, Richard P. Traina, acknowledges the contingency of "psychological uplift." Lifting the embargo, in other words, would have brokered an emotional boost to Loyalist spirits and a concomitant blow to Nationalist hopes.[23]

Elevated by the Great Debate to a weighty public discourse, the embargo had come to symbolize official anti-Loyalist partisanship rather than impartial neutrality. That Spanish, French, and British debaters showed so much enthusiasm for writing articles for American magazines and even crossing the Atlantic to present their opinions in person is indicative that America's embargo policy had become a matter of transatlantic consequence. Here was a pivotal démarche: had a special session of Congress during the latter part of 1938 lifted the embargo with the explicit intent of checking Nazi expansionism, then American resolve may have redressed Europe's unstable balance of power sufficiently to promote diplomatic solutions over military preemptions. At the same time, Spain's war would have dragged on— for another year or more, given sufficient Soviet and U.S. aid—wearing down and distracting the contending powers, namely Russia, Germany, and Italy. A negotiated settlement, as Bowers predicted, could have divided Spain Cyprus-like along the Tagus-Ebro or even Tagus-Turia lines. Therefore, if lifting the embargo might have forestalled the tragedy of Poland, then it would have created a Soviet client south of the Pyrenees, bolstering a Popular Front bloc in Western Europe. But such is sophistry, for Congress was enjoying a seven-month recess until January 1939, and Roosevelt, for whom "the challenge and the fun of power lay not just in having, but in doing," was not the type of man to call it back for a special session, especially when the issue involved decadent Spain.[24]

Third, Kelly had correctly intimated to Talbot that there was a mounting "drive" by New Dealers to goad Roosevelt into waiving the embargo as well as an "increasing momentum" for repeal by the forthcoming Congress. Among the most active embargo-lifters were the interventionist senators Hamilton J. Lewis (D-IL), William H. King (D-UT), and Pittman. Indeed, no sooner had Congress recessed on 16 June than on 19 June the *Washington Post* reported that Pittman was once again calling for "complete revision of our neutrality pronouncements." That Pittman spoke out so quickly and so loudly is indicative of the dissent that prevailed among the members of his Foreign Relations Committee over the decision to stall the Nye resolution and perhaps, too, that it had taken more than Hull's letter for them to arrive at a majority consensus. It is notable that while opinion on the committee split eight to eight between isolationists and interventionists, with four moderates on the fence, the 13 May vote had been seventeen to one in favor of rejecting Nye's resolution.

Then on 10 July, and most worryingly for Franco lobbyists, the *New York Times* carried a demand by Pittman for greater presidential latitude regarding neutrality. But pro-Nationalists could find encouraging signs too, for Hull at the State Department had thrown up his hands in abject frustration. According to the *Post,* Hull stressed the "gravity of world affairs," spelled out a clear choice between "greater isolation" or "giving support to the democracies," and proposed to "consult the 'Man in the Street'" in order to decide which policy to follow.[25]

In contrast to the depressed and exhausted Hull, Kelly had energy and enthusiasm for convincing the man on the street that a pro-Nationalist arms embargo was in America's best interests. He determined to focus all his efforts on Los Angeles and the American Legion's Foreign Relations Committee. His overriding objective was to stymie any attempts by the Legion's leftist delegates to recommend an immediate lifting of the embargo. That fear allayed, he then intended to mobilize conservative delegates to pass a resolution recommending a strengthening of the Neutrality Act in order to protect it from any executive tampering. Franco's representative, Juan Francisco de Cárdenas, with whom Kelly had first broached the plan, was, like Talbot, enthusiastic. Kelly set about networking. He put Talbot to work writing to a list of twenty-one prominent regional Legion commanders whom Kelly felt had "distinguished themselves in the fight against communism," advising him to incorporate the phrase "in the hope that you will bring the matter to the attention of the Resolutions Committee." On the list was Homer L. Chaillaux, director of the Legion's National Americanism Commission. Chaillaux and Kelly had met at the 1937 New York convention, and the two had corresponded over the necessity of exposing "revolutionary radical groups." Talbot took further initiative, writing to his own political contacts as well as clergy. Before Kelly entrained for St. Louis, he badgered other contacts into service. A return letter shows that he wrote to R. Caldwell Patton, chairman of Manhattan's Republican Committee for Safety and editor of the short-lived *Patriot Digest,* both of which promoted "Constitutional Americanism," defined as "the defense of the American ideal of government as defined by the founders of the nation," although that was a rhetorical front for an elitist brand of libertarian isolationism that Patton claimed was as antifascist as it was anticommunist. Patton, in turn, solicited support from Brooklyn's building commissioner and Engineers' Club president, Edwin Thatcher, and probably others in his circle of Protestant elites, including banker Thomas Jewett Hallowell and city alderman Lambert Fairchild.[26]

From the Hotel Jefferson on 12 September, Kelly sent Talbot a progress report, explaining how he hoped for audiences with St. Louis's archbishop, mayor, and other local leaders. Kelly must have had a busy day, for he also called on several old acquaintances. As he reported to Talbot the next evening, his call on Luke E. Hart, Supreme Advocate of the Knights of Columbus, turned out to be a "stroke of very good luck." Hart lent all his enthusiasm to Kelly's project and wrote to Legion leaders, including National Commander Daniel J. Doherty and Chaillaux, as well as to John J. Cantwell, archbishop of Los Angeles. Hart's letter to Cantwell, a testament to Kelly's networking skills, demonstrates the ability of a single appealing idea to grow in the public domain. "From many sources," Hart explained, it was apparent that Roosevelt's embargo resolve was weakening. Because public opinion guided the administration, an American Legion resolution that upheld its "present Neutrality stand" and "clamped down tighter" on the Spanish arms embargo would be of "tremendous value" in preempting "Communist-led liberals" from lobbying the White House. Hart was confident that Cantwell could bring his weight to bear on convention delegates through both priests and laity.[27]

Luke Hart went further: he decided to throw a dinner party on 14 September for civic dignitaries, including Archbishop John Glennon, Mayor Bernard F. Dickman, and his star guest, Massachusetts senator and Naval Affairs Committee chairman David Walsh, the latter en route to Los Angeles as the convention's principal speaker. Although Kelly was leaving for Los Angeles on the thirteenth, Hart assured him that he would discuss the plan with Walsh. Kelly felt sure that Hart would be successful in persuading Walsh to either "incorporate it [Neutrality] into his address to the Legion Convention" or raise the matter with Commander Doherty "or both." Hart also promised to ask his dinner guests to write to any fellow townsmen who were going to Los Angeles. In a farewell thank-you letter to Hart, Kelly reiterated that it was those two great conservative groups—Catholics and veterans—who alone possessed the power to sustain America's "traditional policy of nonintervention in European quarrels." With someone as respected by the Legion as Walsh on their side, the Act would be safe, for the Legion was "one of the great cross sectional voices of public opinion." Maybe the letter lent Hart extra impetus, for he arranged an after-dinner press conference, where, leaning back in one of Hart's chairs, Walsh expounded to a *St. Louis Globe-Democrat* reporter why "neutrality is the most important policy of America today." Between puffs on a long cigar, the senator called for a further tightening of the existing neutrality laws so that "this nation will have no trade relations with any belligerent." Cutting off trade to Spain was the last thing Kelly and his fellow Franco lobbyists would have wanted, but at least they now had Walsh pitching for their team.[28]

With such resolution coming from a Democrat whose party, according to the *Globe-Democrat,* considered him presidential material, Kelly could not have wished for a better advocate. Kelly never read the *Globe-Democrat*'s 15 September edition. Had he done so, he would have found vindication for his plan. An editorial titled "Futile Neutrality Law" noted that House Foreign Affairs Committee chairman Sam D. McReynolds had just predicted that Congress's next session would overturn the Act. Despite characterizing an ongoing move to invest the president with broader discretionary authority as "alarming powers for hurling the country into dangerous if tacit alliances," the pro-Madrid editor nevertheless recommended abandoning the Act forthwith.[29]

Legionnaires were already thronging Los Angeles when Kelly detrained, and he had difficulty finding accommodation. While he was used to temperatures in the nineties, apathy among Legion delegates and ominous press reports from the Ebro front proved more troubling. He must also have been worried about surveillance, for his 16 September letter to Talbot referred mysteriously to "contacts" and to "our man in [place name]." Such subterfuge was not altogether silly; detectives tracked his movements, Popular Front stenographers attended his lectures, and, the month before, Talbot warned him of an apparent Franco supporter who was probably "an agent of some sort." Although he had encountered no open opposition to a resolution supporting the Neutrality Act, several delegates were indifferent. "We have good men in Washington. They will know what to do." Or, "We should not tell them what to do, but wait for them to do what is needed." Not intending to rely on "the good start in St. Louis," Kelly determined to work round the clock to overcome the delegates' "let Washington do it" lethargy. Funds were also a pressing problem, so he asked Talbot to wire him $100; Talbot duly sent the money but considered it a loan.[30]

Press clippings among Kelly's papers indicate that he read from three to six newspapers on any given day. Both the *Los Angeles Times* and *Examiner,* which he took while in Los Angeles, carried troubling news: "Spain Government Claims Victory" told how Loyalists had seized seventeen strategic hilltops; "Spain Drive Gains, Says Government" claimed that Franco had been forced to throw reinforcements into the Javalambre Mountains; and "Spain Drives upon Cordoba" explained how a new offensive was even threatening the Nationalists' southern stronghold. This was largely Loyalist propaganda; but unable to chat with Cárdenas over lunch, Kelly could not easily verify the situation.[31]

Kelly's letters to Talbot reveal a counterculture that was alien to East Coast politicians like Walsh, but Kelly was at home in the Hispanic milieu of L.A.'s barrios. There was Father García in the San Joaquin Valley, who had escaped Loyalist Spain's murders of priests only to lose a brother in the Nationalist Army. There was millionaire supporter Jaime del Amo, who claimed to be for Franco, although his multimillionaire father, Don Gregorio, was for Loyalist Madrid. And there was Father Zapato, Kelly's intermediary, who had insulted Jaime by not bringing with him an introductory letter from "Senor - - - - - - - - - -" (de Cárdenas), so now Jaime had withdrawn his offer to give $20,000 to Kelly's neutrality preservation campaign. How electric L.A.'s atmosphere must have felt. Quite apart from the convention itself, with all its West Coast hoopla and razzmatazz, newspaper stalls were soon buzzing with new excitement over the frightening Great Hurricane of '38 that walloped the Northeast and a crisis in Europe over Czechoslovakia.[32]

On the seventeenth, Kelly sent Talbot another lengthy report full of regained optimism. He had just received a press cutting from St. Louis detailing Walsh's strong advocacy of neutrality during Hart's press conference. Now, he enthused, he wanted to do more "than just get a resolution drafted." If he could reach every state delegation, making them "understand the issues involved," then each "home-going group will be missionaries for the truth and we will reach public opinion in every city of the country." He was also emboldened to realize that he was "quite well known" on the West Coast, for the *Tidings,* Los Angeles's Catholic organ, had just reprinted one of his *Spain* articles. In his last report from the convention, he teased Talbot to not mind if the $100 loan had become a donation, for he could now report that his efforts had borne spectacular fruit: "We have succeeded in making Neutral-ity the big issue of the convention." Even more significantly, a final draft of a firm resolution to retain the embargo was pending passage through committee.[33]

Weary, no doubt, when he left Los Angeles on 25 September, Kelly was none-theless surely elated that the Legion's policy makers had resolved to support the arms embargo to Spain, with all that implied about the Legion's official stance being not merely anticommunist but also pro-Franco. Now he wanted to lock in those gains before a final effort to lobby the incoming Congress against repeal-ing the Neutrality Act. He spent the next ten days traveling, covering almost four thousand miles over about seventy-two hours of train time. While the documen-tary record is fragmentary, it appears that he discussed American Legion policy in Tyler, Texas, debriefed Luke Hart in St. Louis, met with Congressman Martin Dies in Washington to discuss methods for combating communist subversion, and visited parties unknown—Legionnaires, perhaps, as he wired Talbot about an "approval"—in Chicago before returning to New York.[34]

Kelly's Influence on U.S. Foreign Policy

But was it Kelly's networking plan that made the difference? Had it influenced a broad sector of public opinion? Did it, moreover, affect an important aspect of U.S. foreign policy? Attributing a chain of causation to an outcome that may have occurred anyway is always problematic. It is important, first, to reiterate Kelly's paramount fear in August that the American Legion would resolve to lift the em-bargo. As in any large organization, the Legion had its share of leftist delegates, a preponderance being West Coasters, and Iowa's Ray Murphy (a recipient of one of Talbot's Kelly-inspired letters) was not its only left-leaning commander. Fight for Freedom, Inc., which supported Spain's Loyalists, was one of several interven-tionist groups lobbying in Los Angeles during the convention. When Roosevelt finally repealed the Act, albeit after the Nazi blitzkrieg of Poland in September 1939, two-thirds of Legionnaires backed him. Kelly's fear, then, was well founded, and the fact that no delegate presented a resolution to so much as soften the Act is testimony that correlates well with his networking efforts. Correlation with a non-event, though, hardly supports a causational argument. Requiring substantiation are Kelly's twin claims to have facilitated the drafting of a pro-embargo resolution and to have made "Neutrality the big issue."[35]

In its *Reports*, the American Legion convention's National Committee worried that the Roosevelt administration would lift the arms embargo "so that the Spanish Loyalists might procure such implements of war." Darrell T. Lane, chairman of the World Peace and Foreign Relations Committee (of the National Executive Committee), reported studying the 1937 convention's strict neutrality mandate "at great length," but he recommended no further legislative action, judging it to be a "proper neutrality policy" integral to the Legion's general peace objective. Legion records do indicate, nonetheless, that its Foreign Relations Committee (FRC), chaired by Charles Hann Jr., considered Resolution 627, filed by Wisconsin's department adjutant, Gil Stordock. While the *Proceedings* shows that 627 recommended strengthening the Act, unfortunately neither the resolution text nor details of its deliberation are extant. Although the FRC decided in October that 627 was superfluous, it nevertheless recommended that "the 1938 convention reaffirm the position of the 1935 and the 1936 conventions with respect to Resolution No. 72 [of 1937] on the policy of non-intervention." Yet without further evidence to connect Kelly with Stordock, this particular causational trail soon goes cold.[36]

Evidence does substantiate Kelly's other claim, though. When Walsh addressed 6,600 delegates representing 974,957 Legionnaires packed into the seats and aisles of Los Angeles's Shrine Auditorium on 19 September, he delivered a four-point manifesto: a powerful two-ocean navy, vigilance against foreign subversives, Americanism, and, primarily, neutrality. In order to prevent another world conflict, America must follow "unquestioned and affirmative neutrality." In case the sweating delegates missed his point, Walsh reiterated, wagging his finger, "American neutrality must be real and genuine, fearlessly asserted and meticulously enforced." Strict neutrality, coupled with strong national defense, was the "best and perhaps only assurance of peace," for, as proved by the Czech crisis, weakness encouraged aggression. East Coast papers, which tended to be interventionist, downplayed this latter point, but L.A. editions were on the mark. Captioning Walsh's center-front-page photograph "Pleads for U.S. Neutrality," the *Examiner* also covered his speech in full on page two, under the headline "Sen. Walsh Urges Neutrality."[37]

Would Walsh have delivered the same speech if Kelly's activism had not set in motion the chain of events that led to Hart's dinner party and press conference in St. Louis? Possibly. Walsh was certainly an ardent isolationist, and he tried to be sensitive to the policies of the Catholic hierarchy. Going into Los Angeles, nevertheless, he had no reputation for outspoken public advocacy of neutrality—neutrality, that is, as a synonym for the arms embargo to Loyalist Spain. He had presented Forbes's letter on the Senate floor in May, but he was not even present for the Senate's crucial 29 April 1937 vote for the Neutrality Act. Walsh's public renown essentially stemmed from his promotion of a two-ocean navy, Theodore Roosevelt's doctrine of military preparedness, and that was why the Legion chose him to be its keynote speaker. Dorothy Wayman devotes a full chapter of her biography of Walsh to his navy policy, and while she does mention how Legionnaires "applauded wildly" when Walsh called on them to "shun war as we would a poisonous reptile," she neither mentions neutrality nor connects Walsh to the raging embargo controversy of 1937–39. Yet Walsh's Legion speech skimmed over a big navy in a single paragraph and instead devoted five paragraphs to neutrality, virtually half of his message (given that seven of the nineteen paragraphs were introductory flimflam). Neutrality was a new hobbyhorse for the Walsh of Los Angeles.[38]

At a press conference the day before his address, Walsh told reporters that Congress should further strengthen existing neutrality laws, strict though they were, to ensure a "definite legislative policy of neutrality without power left to any department of government to take a course, unconsciously or intentionally, that may draw us into war." In other words, in acknowledging that power over foreign affairs resided in departments of government, which reported to and were under the final control of the president, Walsh was insisting that Roosevelt must not tinker with Congress's 1937 Neutrality Act, especially during an election-year recess. Kelly could—and often did—make statements like Walsh's, but they did not enthrall 6,600 Legion leaders, echo down the corridors of Capitol Hill, or reverberate around the Oval Office. Yet in Los Angeles, it was as if Kelly was Walsh's speechwriter; and in Washington, it is likely that the import of Kelly's plan reached Roosevelt's desk. Roosevelt met regularly during 1938 with Walsh—whom he addressed as "Dear Dave" in their frequent correspondence—to discuss their shared ambition for a two-ocean navy and particularly Roosevelt's efforts in mid-October to finance $150 million worth of naval construction by raising income taxes. Walsh was responsible for the preparation of a report on naval appropriations for the upcoming session of Congress, and hence Roosevelt's principal ally, so it is likely that during their talks Walsh stressed the necessity for maintaining the embargo on arms to Spain.[39]

Because Roosevelt avoided committing his thoughts to paper, historians know little of what influenced "this most elusive and dissembling of presidents," to borrow Waldo Heinrichs's assessment. Yet open to influence Roosevelt surely was, for his policies toward European nations lacked an agenda, at least until after Munich. Hiram W. Johnson, California's progressive Republican senator and ranking member of the Senate Committee on Foreign Relations, watched the president "drifting without the slightest idea of what to do or how to do it." As Johnson wrote to his son during Congress's 1938 session, Roosevelt did "not know what his foreign policy" was, made statements that he did not "mean a word of," and had "a confused mind" that did not "know which way to go." Johnson, though, was convinced of three points: first, it was the president who made all the decisions and not Secretary Hull, who was "simply a 'dumb Dora.'" Second, Roosevelt was an internationalist who dreamed of an "alliance with the English" and an even more "outrageous" entanglement in a league of nations. Third, Roosevelt craved a "big Navy" because he was a warmonger, a cynic like Napoleon, who, when his people became "discontented, or unhappy," would "amuse them with a foreign war." Roosevelt may well have calculated that by accommodating Walsh's newfound zeal for neutrality he could buy support in the Senate for his expansionist navy. At the same time that Roosevelt's Jeffersonian heart harbored sympathy for the idealism of Spain's democratic if decadent Second Republic, his Napoleonic mind was looking forward to ballots and battleships. By claiming that the Act's fate was now in the hands of January's upcoming Congress, he could placate pro-Franco Catholic swing voters without upsetting too many pro-Madrid Popular Fronters.[40]

Embargo Retained

Franco lobbyists' last major initiative of 1938 was ensuring that the incoming Seventy-sixth Congress would not lift the arms embargo to Spain. Even though Franco was advancing on Barcelona and seemed certain to crush the last Loyalist resistance within weeks, both sides in the Great Debate threw their all at Capitol Hill during the first days of January. Through an extraordinary effort that flooded Washington with two million petitions, the NCWC's "Keep the Embargo!" campaign prevailed. To explain this phenomenon, historians point to the infamous Radio Priest, Father Charles E. Coughlin and cite his sixteen million listeners as proof of his influence on public opinion. Coughlin's broadcasts, Albert Fried maintains, were "instrumental in killing the [January 1939] attempt to repeal the embargo." Yet this explanation is unsatisfactory.[41]

Apart from the fact that only 39 percent of Catholics who expressed an opinion to pollsters on the Spanish Civil War supported Franco, less than a third of Coughlin's listeners were Catholics. Coughlin's popularity, moreover, had been declining for some time. By December 1938, over half of Coughlin's audience disapproved of him: most Americans tuned in simply because they liked the sound of the Radio Priest's sonorous voice. Eight hundred thousand Jewish Americans listened to Coughlin, but according to Gallup pollsters, just a quarter of them "approved." Because Coughlin's "The Hour of Power" broadcasts interested— perhaps even uplifted—Americans on a Sunday does not necessarily mean that he influenced workaday public opinion, let alone affected policy makers' actions. How instrumental was Coughlin at this time, when many listeners understood him to be an egotistical Jew-baiter, when the Nazis were menacing Prague and he had moved past veiled fascist sympathies to open support for the Rome-Berlin Axis, and when fans hearing him in person realized that his melodious radio persona belied the red-faced screaming demagoguery once he stepped on stage? As one biographer put it, his followers "drifted away in droves."[42]

Kelly did not need to be a demagogue to convey his message. As a shy, somewhat awkward, self-effacing individual who preferred to put others in the spotlight, he appreciated that his activist ideology—support for Spain's cultural heritage,

virulent anticommunism, unwavering Americanism—was most effective when expressed through reputable third parties. His effectiveness, indeed, could have been
no greater than when those third parties chaired key congressional committees,
as Walsh did. Kelly reached Americans—not all Americans, to be sure, but those
Americans he felt might make a difference. He affected foreign policy, too—not
directly, but through a complex web of elites, through decision makers who often
did not know the source of their own impetus.

Kelly was one of several activists who orchestrated the NCWC's national
letter-writing campaign, his part mostly preparing promotional materials, distributing fliers, and soliciting signatures through his network of contacts. More
importantly, he spent the previous year laying much of the campaign's ideological
groundwork. During 1938, he delivered at least fourteen speeches to mixed audiences totaling five thousand plus concerned citizens. He wrote more than thirty
articles for seven different magazines read by upward of 200,000 Americans. He
published a pamphlet on Franco for distribution through Catholic churches. His
exposé of Loyalist ambassador Fernando de los Ríos's abuse of diplomatic franking privileges reached the *New York Times*'s front page. He organized a petition
by sixty-five leading American figures that did not make it to Roosevelt's mail pile
but nonetheless received coverage in numerous newspapers. He took part in a nationally syndicated radio debate. He operated behind the scenes, too, observing,
organizing, and networking through the Manhattan offices of well-placed elite
organizations, including the Constitutional Educational League, American Defense Society, and especially Merwin K. Hart's New York State Economic Council,
a potent 17,000-member organization principally concerned with lobbying for
greater deregulation of private enterprise. Through Hart's office, he prepared and
distributed 20,000 keep-the-embargo fliers, timed to coincide with the NCWC
campaign; copies went to every member of Congress. He also acted as executive
secretary for the American Union for Nationalist Spain, a pro-Nationalist organization to counter the Comintern's pro-Loyalist propaganda, and by February
1939 he was screening the dramatic documentary *Spain in Arms* to large audiences around the country. All these narrowly focused, carefully targeted activities
spread the message from the committed to the uncommitted that the cause of Nationalist Spain was the cause of patriotic anticommunist Americanism. It would
be Kelly's consistent coaching, not Coughlin's frothy fulminations, that led many
prominent elites as well as broad publics to believe that sticking up for Franco's
Spain meant standing up for Americanism.[43]

Kelly's tactical activism and strategic networking acumen helped ensure that
arms to Loyalist Spain remained embargoed throughout 1938. Because Kelly's networking had convinced influential blocs of public opinion that neutrality was a
"big issue," the NCWC's campaign of January 1939 was able to raise more than
enough public support to persuade the Seventy-sixth Congress to "Keep the Em-

bargo!" A hundred thousand communist-led Loyalists would perish before Franco drove over the Ebro and on to Madrid. Thousands more died by Nationalist firing squad after summary courts martial found them guilty of murder or treason. Prescient though he was of international affairs, Kelly had no crystal ball in the fast-moving fall of 1938. He could not foresee how his successful advocacy of Franco might affect geopolitical diplomacy. In part, through Roosevelt's inaction over Spain and with Hitler's increasing confidence that isolationist Americans would not intervene to check German expansion, Kelly's work facilitated a pact between the archenemy of Soviet communism and the Nazism that he and his mother had credited in 1933 with transforming their bankrupt, rebellious homeland.[44]

5

The American Union for Nationalist Spain

American supporters of Nationalist Spain came from different backgrounds, had varying interests, and held wide-ranging opinions. A loathing of international communism was their most fundamental unifier, followed at some remove by suspicion of the New Deal as a leviathan state encroaching on individual liberties. While it would be a truism to say that they shared a liking for traditional Spain, Spain for pro-Nationalists was a romanticized construct, a mental map onto whose contours they had imprinted a set of attributes—from Christian reconquest to castanets—and which may or may not have had a factual basis. American activists, though, those lobbyists who were devoting much of their lives to General Franco's cause, not only held a deeper attraction toward Spain as a country but also believed they had a more authentic conception of Spain as a historical-cultural reality. Most had visited Spain at least once, and several spoke Spanish; they were—or, rather, had become—*españolistas*. Nationalist officials recognized the propaganda benefits of having foreigners experience Franco's Spain firsthand, for by June 1938 they had a brochure in English advertising nine-day guided tours of the war zone for £8 ($1,000), including all expenses. In addition to golf, fly-fishing, chamois stalking, and unsurpassed beauty—"the skies at sunset, streaked with silver clouds, and the green moss and ivy clinging to the dark walls of romantic houses"—War Route 1, through the Basque country, from San Sebastián to Bilbao and finishing in Oviedo, promised the drama of "history in the making." "Form your own judgment of the real situation in National Spain to-day," was the brochure's challenge.[1]

One American determined to form her own opinion of Nationalist Spain was renowned art deco muralist Hildreth Meière, whose iconic modernist plaques still enliven the 50th Street elevation of Manhattan's Radio City Music Hall. Meière's experience so moved her that, on returning to New York, she began networking an informal support group, and by December her local activism had helped spawn a nationwide promotional and lobbying organization, the American Union for Nationalist Spain (AUNS). From a detailed diary of her trip that she transcribed as an unpublished memoir, her amateur cine films, and interviews with surviving family and friends, it is possible to reconstruct Meière's impressions of Franco's zone. This chapter locates Meière in the art world of 1930s Manhattan; analyzes her motives for visiting Nationalist Spain; connects her to other women fundraisers and activists, such as old-stock philanthropist Anne Tracy Morgan, Spanish American opera singer Lucrezia Bori, and Polish American homemaker Clare Singer Dawes; and documents her association with John Eoghan Kelly, Merwin K. Hart, and the other Franco lobbyists of the AUNS. While the paramountcy of checking communists in Spain before they could sweep away the Christian bedrock of American civilization was the idea that drove all Franco lobbyists, women lobbyists further emphasized assistance for the poor, widows, and especially orphans of Nationalist Spain. Yet their focus on humanitarian aid, just as with their fight against communism, was not a principal motivation per se. Rather, their singular brand of pro-Franco anticommunist ideology, which lobbyists formulated in the face of both peer and federal censure, was ultimately about adapting as well as strengthening the core values that comprised American identity at a time of national crisis unprecedented since 1861.

While several Franco lobbyists noisily claimed to have ancestors that arrived on the *Mayflower* in 1620, a majority were immigrants or the children of immigrants; and in two cases, lobbyists who stressed their old-stock heritage had a foreign-born relative or spouse about whom they kept noticeably quiet. At a more general level, pro-Nationalists were often of immigrant stock, as, for that matter, were their most outspoken antagonists in the Great Debate, those socialists, Marxists, and fellow travelers who predominantly were of eastern or southern European descent. I borrow from cognitive dissonance theory to suggest that identity insecurity may inform not only the exaggerated preoccupation with Americanism versus communism evident among pro-Nationalists but also the transatlantic crossings made by Franco lobbyists in an effort to mentally map a notional Spain onto their beloved, and often adopted, homeland in order to enhance their case in the argument over the soul of American ideology. Visiting the Nationalist zone helped Franco lobbyists—all of whom prized historical knowledge, conflated *history* with *civilization,* and, in three cases, had even written academic histories—to legitimate their representation of the True Spain, as they called it. Their trips to the Nationalist zone, validated through the texts they constructed on their return home, enabled them to contrast Loyalist Madrid with all they saw as wrong with New Deal America, select those values of a historicized Spain that suited their particular neo-mugwump reformist agendas, and then imprint those values onto what would become a reworked cold war national consciousness.

As with Ellery Sedgwick's enthusiasm for Seville's affordable housing, Meière was always keen to see how workers on the other side of the Atlantic lived. During a 1936 trip to study the twelfth-century mosaics at Kiev, she found impressive apartment blocks in Warsaw and made a point of inspecting a block of flats in Moscow, the modern plumbing and ample-sized rooms of which she could see put New York's squalid tenements to shame. Meière considered herself a latter-day mugwump, a fence-sitter who championed the civil rights and progressive reforms of a Democrat like Alfred E. Smith but who might vote Republican to stop the kind of big government, mass-leveling statism of Franklin D. Roosevelt. While admitting that mugwumps have often invited derision, historian Larry Carl Miller places them in the vanguard of a twentieth-century "professional reformation." As Miller shows, they were individualistic intellectuals who avoided sweeping political ideologies—laissez-faire, bureaucratic centralization, the welfare state—to concentrate instead on improving American society through specific, tailored, and, above all, practical reforms. Eschewing machine politics, they promoted their ideas via the media they understood best: writing letters to newspaper editors, articles for periodicals, or consultative works. As a "self-conscious . . . professional intelligentsia," they supported associations in their own fields, whether in academia, medicine, social work, art, engineering, or matters of public or foreign policy. Although Meière was the only AUNS member to identify herself as neo-mugwump, it is an apt—if foolish sounding—descriptor for the seemingly idiosyncratic yet well-intended progressive politics of Franco lobbyists like Sedgwick, W. Cameron Forbes, Hart, Morgan, and Kelly.[2]

Morning in a Manhattan Studio

Hildreth Meière began the memoir of her trip to Spain by narrating a debate among fellow artists over the meaning of the foreign ideologies then competing for Americans' attention. Because their dialogue provides important insight into political opinion among a group of New York intellectuals in 1938, I have excerpted it here, rounding it out with corroborating information from Meière's daughter. Meière described the scene at her studio at 200 West 57th Street, Manhattan, a typically bohemian artists' colony, in which she climbed on a scaffolding to sketch a figure on a massive canvas—a commission for the 1939 New York World's Fair—that stretched across one wall. Active, prepossessing, and of confident posture, Meière naturally assumed center stage. Even at forty-six, she was still good looking, with rich black hair swept back into a bun, high forehead, Nordic nose, and dark clothes set off with a brooch or string of pearls. Robert Johnson, Meière's friend who taught at the Art Students League across the street, lounged back on a paint-speckled couch to ask why she was not at the previous night's party. Meière began explaining her attendance at an America Spanish Relief Fund (ASRF) meeting to raise aid contributions for the sick, poor, and orphans of Nationalist Spain, when her twenty-year-old assistant, Nina Barr Wheeler, working below her on another area of the canvas, interrupted hotly.[3]

"Wouldn't you think she had troubles enough with all the Mural Painters' fights, without getting mixed up in the Spanish War?" Wheeler, a practicing Catholic like Meière, was no friend of Franco's Nationalists.

"I guess I'm several fights behind," drawled Greenwich Village artist Ethel Howe as she reached for another cigarette. "What's the new one?"

"I think it's all the same one," replied Meière. "A group of Communists have made our trouble in the Mural Painters' and Communists have made the war in Spain. It all hooks up."

"Oh hold on!" Johnson protested. "You're seeing red, if I may say so."

This initiated a serious and at times heated argument. Meière was the only pro-Nationalist of the group, which soon swelled to five with the arrival of Moira Flanagan, a tall, thin, Irish Catholic artist.

Meière tried to explain to Johnson why she was not so much seeing red as experiencing Red. A motion by the National Society of Mural Painters to align with Spain's Loyalists in the summer of 1936 had failed to carry by a single vote; soon after, the recently formed American Artists' Congress began raising money for Loyalist Madrid. When Meière realized the Congress was actually "a very nice, Red Party–line" organization, she resigned in protest that her professional body had become "camouflage" for communist fund-raising.

Johnson interjected that many caring Americans who contributed aid to Loyalist Spain were not left-wingers. Meière conceded the point but stressed that credulous Americans had fallen for the Comintern's ploy of "throwing the word 'Democracy'" into all its propaganda; what had happened in Spain was patently "instigated and steered by Russia as a planned step in the great Red World Revolution." Religion, too, was a factor in Meière's abhorrence of Spain's Loyalist government, which she felt went against not just Catholicism but all faiths. "I don't see how any Catholic can possibly support the principles of a Red Government," she added, looking at Flanagan.[4]

Flanagan agreed that the war was between "two fundamentally opposed philosophies . . . Christianity and Communism," but she nonetheless suspected that Franco's reliance on military assistance from Germany and Italy meant Nationalist Spain would be "Fascist and Totalitarian." Military intervention could do nothing but breed hatred, while communism, because it was materialistic, was inherently flawed. But neither scenario need pose an insurmountable difficulty, for Flanagan noted that there was already a perfect solution: the corporatist, communitarian system of Catholic social justice. Johnson commented wryly that, after two thousand years of trying, Christianity could hardly claim perfection.

Meière then surprised everyone by admitting that Christianity had not worked, but she blamed Catholics for failing to practice the Church's teachings. There followed a discussion of when and if a religious organization had a moral obligation to meddle in politics. But sensing they would soon be lost in a philosophical maze, Meière brought the debate back to Flanagan's point about hatred. Exhibiting a deeper concern on this issue than did many Franco supporters, Meière found that the "cheap, rabble-rousing tactics" of anticommunist organizations offended her intelligence and taste, just as she could see how a fanatical loathing of communism might have the unintended consequence of pushing anticommunists into the open arms of fascists. Indeed, she admitted that after listening to the venom of some of the "Antis," she sometimes felt drawn to the communist cause. She suspected that they all agreed that communism and fascism were equally bad, yet she did not share the others' fears that Spain would become fascist. Her travels there in 1925 had taught her that Spaniards were "complete individualists, and not mass-minded."[5]

Howe ventured into the fray to raise the issue of Nationalist bombing of civilians, for it was over these air raids that most Americans faulted Franco. Meière agreed with Howe that there could be no ethical justification for killing noncombatants, and she condemned the bombing of civilian centers during the Great War as well as the U.S. naval bombardment of Veracruz in 1914. She wondered whether the issue was instead one of modernity, of "what's cricket and what isn't." Aerial bombing cried out for international codification, especially now that everyone behind the lines was involved in some kind of war-related work, and she also noted how the latest antiaircraft guns pushed aviators to such heights that they could not bomb with any hope of accuracy. Bombing of civilians had been a public relations disaster for Franco, Meière agreed; along with the deployment of German and Italian troops, it played into the antipapist prejudices of American Protestants, leaving them a "pushover for the Red side." Her reasoned assessment of this complex sociopolitical issue nonetheless catalyzed the discussion into an argument.[6]

Wheeler protested Meière's use of Red as a slur. Meière countered by objecting to "'Rebels' for the Nationals." And Johnson twisted the knife further, declaring, "Franco is a Fascist and a dictator." These were strong words among intimate friends. "He is Hitler's and Mussolini's straw-man. I want to see them all licked."

Just as Meière was thinking that without firsthand knowledge of what was happening in Spain there was nothing more she could say to convince Johnson and the rest of her circle, the doorbell rang. Franco's unofficial ambassador, Juan Francisco de Cárdenas, who resided two blocks away at the Ritz-Carlton, entered. After climbing down from the scaffold and wiping her charcoaled hands, Meière made the introductions.

Trim for fifty-seven, Cárdenas had a full head of graying hair, moist blue eyes, and a thin-lipped quizzical smile for everyone. In his dark suit and habitual spotted bowtie, he probably felt uncomfortable in the paint-spattered studio. He sat down with the group and, as they smoked, explained how the concert he and Meière were organizing to aid destitute Spanish children could not go ahead. He told them that managers of the three Spanish musicians who were to top the billing had advised their clients that appearing for a Nationalist benefit would result in their being blacklisted and forfeiting all future engagements. "Is this a free country, or isn't it?" he exclaimed. "Do you mean to say the Reds have *everything* sewed up their way?"

This reopened the argument, although Cárdenas's attempts to sway Johnson and the beautiful blonde Wheeler fared no better than Meière's. "It has always been so hard to get a hearing for our side here," he said despondently, half to himself.

"I still think," Meière said, "that small groups working for and talking about Nationalist Spain" could overcome Americans' Loyalist bias.

"Why don't you go, Hilly?" Wheeler chipped in. "You like excitement."[7]

Meière Tours Nationalist Spain

A few months later, with a passport certifying her as one of Father Francis X. Talbot's ASRF aid workers, Hildreth Meière left her eight-year-old daughter with a French governess in Tourraine, took a train to Saint-Jean-de-Luz, and, after a last-minute hitch over a special entry visa that required the intervention of U.S. ambassador Claude G. Bowers, she crossed the border at Irún on 8 August 1938. Instead of depending on official guides and chauffeured automobiles—as Forbes and Sedgwick did during their tour in January—Meière planned her own itinerary, out of which she spent five days and 800 miles with a Valladolid taxi driver. Meière's memoir of her two-week trip inevitably carries a pro-Nationalist bias; yet, it is unusual for its detachment, candid observations, and the corroboration provided by thirty minutes of 16-mm film footage, half of it in color. Still, Meière was a well-heeled traveler whose official and familial connections ensured VIP treatment, and while she did meet Spaniards from a range of social backgrounds, she drew much of her information from members of Spain's bloated petty aristocracy who had suffered at Loyalist hands. Meière's memoir, nonetheless, backed up by images from her films, offers a unique window into the Nationalist Spain of the summer of 1938.[8]

Despite coming across war-shattered buildings, Meière found the Nationalist zone's normalcy surprising. Whereas she had expected a sullen populace clothed in rags, she noted "perfectly normal-looking people going about in a perfectly normal-looking way." In the Basque border town of Irún, subject both to bombardment during the Nationalist assault of the prior August and then to arson attacks by anarchists fleeing into France, there were girls in neat summer clothes, soldiers buying ice cream, and sports cars on the streets. She was exhausted on arrival at the María Christina Hotel in San Sebastián but in time for a late dinner of soup and fish with salad but no third course, for Monday was "Dessert-less Day," ostensibly to support a soldiers' fund but, as someone explained to her later, intended to maintain a climate of war awareness. Not that María Christina customers needed reminders. There were Spanish flags aplenty, soldiers' collection boxes for cigarettes or the money to buy them, and posters of good "artistic quality" hanging in the corridors

(Meière liked one of a frowning man with a hand cupped behind his ear, the caption reading, "In time of war we must distrust everybody. Anyone may be a spy"). Images of Franco and Gen. Emilio Mola Vidal took pride of place in the hotel lobby, flanked by posters of Adolf Hitler and Benito Mussolini.[9]

Well rested and breakfasted, Meière set off the next day to see Luis Antonio Bolín, director of Nationalist Spain's new bureau of tourism, who had been the London correspondent for the monarchist *ABC* newspaper before the war and the man responsible for flying Franco from the Canary Islands to Morocco in July 1936. As well as the opportunity to meet social workers and artists, Meière explained to the "tall, good-looking" Bolín that she hoped for an audience with Toledo's Cardinal Isidro Gomá, requests that Bolín and the nearby Propaganda Office had no difficulty arranging. An Auxilio Social soup kitchen was Meière's first stop of what would be a busy day; there she filmed scenes of care-worn mothers and their children carrying special three-tiered food containers clipped into a metal frame.[10]

Founded in October 1936 by the dynamic Mercedes Sanz-Bachiller—whom Meière interviewed and filmed—the all-women's Auxilio Social counted 300,000 members spread across 1,265 branches, and its Brotherhood Kitchens catered to the needs of tens of thousands of poor, orphans, and war refugees. During her trip, Meière visited several Auxilio Social facilities, including a kitchen in Valladolid serving a thousand meals a day and a children's dining room with "gay tablecloths" and flower arrangements. Auxilio Social was a branch of the Falange Española Tradicionalista y de las JONS, and while Meière was uncomfortable with the political connotations of Franco's umbrella party—her diary at one point refers to the Falange as "the Coalition Party"—she delighted in filming the fascist-style yoke-and-arrows insignia of its premises and the straight-arm salutes of its women members. Toward the end of her trip, she toured a summer camp for 120 girls ages eight to eighteen and filmed the staff and campers in their smart uniforms enthusiastically saluting while they sang the Spanish national anthem and gave the Falange exhortation "¡Arriba España!" followed by "¡Arriba América!" for their visitor's benefit. Perhaps it was the girls' neat freshness, their youthful energy, that impressed her, their evident sense of place in a chaotic world, an innocent vitality that always bubbles from membership of a uniformed group and that her filmed sequences convey so well. Maybe, too, she tried to capture on film what she saw as the Falange's marriage of tradition with modernity, the kind of classical-modern synergy she distilled into her own art deco murals.[11]

Her next stop was San Sebastián's 350-bed General Mola Military Hospital for post-trauma patients. It was an unsettling experience. With Rosa de Mandivil and Lupe de los Arcos, two petty aristocrats turned social workers, she went from ward to ward passing out cigarettes. Amputees greeted them in the first ward, where Meière learned that soldiers preferred losing a leg to an arm. A youth without a right leg and a "fevered, desperate face" reduced Meière to tears, and at one point she handed a pack of cigarettes to a man without an upper lip and a "small hole in a great healed scar" for a nose. On reaching the top floor, she found soldiers guarding a ward for Loyalist prisoners. Her companions would not enter, for their families had suffered personal and financial loss because of the war, especially Rosa, still heartbroken over the death of her only son. Other than the guards, Meière determined that conditions for Loyalist patients were no different, and she received the same warm smiles as she handed out her smokes. So this was what war did to the flower of youth, Meière mused, as the trio walked in silence back to town. Yet she could neither see the suffering as useless nor war as the worst evil. Surely it was better to fight, "at whatever cost, than to submit tamely to the horrors that the Reds deliberately create." As she continued her tour, she could find no Spaniard who disagreed with her evaluation.[12]

Later that day, Meière satisfied a second objective: meeting Ignacio Zuloaga, Spain's greatest contemporary artist alongside Pablo Picasso, at Zuloaga's beachfront estate at nearby Zumaya. On introduction, the feisty sixty-eight-year-old painter exclaimed, "Why are all Americans against us? Why don't they understand?" American artists whom he had once counted friends were always sending him letters "full of Red lies" and abuse for taking Franco's side. How could his friends despise him so, he asked, when he had "always been a staunch Republican." Meière tried to persuade him to travel to the States to plead Franco's cause in person, to which Zuloaga replied that he had given all his money to Auxilio Social and could not afford the trip. As they looked over the folksy portraits of peasants and gypsy girls that were Zuloaga's hallmark, he noted that of the two hundred most distinguished Spanish intellectuals in the six academies of medicine, history, philology, fine arts, mathematics, and science in 1936, 125 were now in the full- or part-time service of the Nationalist government, 25 were abroad and sympathetic to the Nationalists, 25 were in the Loyalist zone, 15 had disappeared, 8 sympathized with the Loyalists, and just 2 were working for Madrid.[13]

Meière learned more about disappearances the next day while she awaited the completion of travel formalities. Through her paternal ancestor, Thomas McKean, signer of the Declaration of Independence for Delaware, whose daughter had married the first Spanish minister to the United States, Meière was a distant cousin to several members of Spain's outmoded aristocracy, including Pedro, the Duque de Sotomayor, and it was at the duke's villa that she lunched. Pedro was lucky to be alive. Loyalists had imprisoned him in July 1936 and then began systematically shooting 220 of his cellmates, usually in batches of five, though one morning Pedro went out to the exercise yard to the sight of 52 machine-gunned bodies. He survived a fire that gutted the floor below him, an attack on the prison by an angry mob, and four sleepless nights on his knees praying as he heard guards opening cell doors and calling names. Loyalists then transferred him to a prison ship in Bilbao harbor, where he suffered through the winter with inadequate clothing and nourishment while a further 480 of his fellow political internees died from disease or execution. Loyalists in San Sebastián, Meière learned, had targeted middle-class *nacionalistas* as well as aristocrats, the former accounting for the majority of executions.[14]

For the trip to Burgos en route to Toledo, Bolín provided a chauffeured car and a traveling companion, Elizabeth Dilling, author of *The Red Network*, an anticommunist and anti-Semitic polemic published with financial backing from Henry Ford. Meière did not enjoy Dilling's company, for she periodically launched into "tirade[s]" against "the Reds," although it was probably Dilling's priggish Protestant moralizing that soured the relationship. From Burgos, Meière took a train to Valladolid and then, for the journey to and from Toledo, hired a taxi, whose unshaven driver, Santiago Pérez, "met everyone on equal terms, with courtesy but assurance." She soon warmed to the affable Pérez, pronouncing him a "true Spaniard," an "individualist from the word 'Go!'" Franco lobbyists liked to stress the individualism of true Spaniards, for such a proud, independent people, they argued, could accept military aid from a Mussolini or a Hitler without falling prey to the accompanying ideologies of fascism or Nazism. Yet, why they believed that several million *madrileños* and *barcelonés* had succumbed so easily to a Soviet-led communist revolution was a paradox they never thought necessary to explain, presumably because they dismissed Loyalist leaders as alien Muscovites and their followers as gullible automatons of the industrialized factory floor. Hence, the distinction Franco lobbyists drew between true Spaniards on one hand and those anarcho-communists who had inadvertently strayed into falsity on the other. Spaniards who held true to the traditions of their birthright, to their country's rich history, were self-willed characters (just like true American individualists)—Franco lobbyists made sure to find all over real Spain—whether working on wheat farms, helping in soup kitchens, painting gypsy girls, or driving noisy taxis. Spain's anarchic communists, by contrast, were faceless factory workers, a mobocracy of modernity that American elites feared but could thankfully forget, unless they strayed into inner-city ghettos or became embroiled in unseemly Old World revolutions.[15]

From Segovia, Meière detoured to Navas de Riofrío, host to a popular royal hunting lodge in a bygone era but by then a dusty depopulated village on the Madrid-Valladolid rail line. There she visited Isabel, the Duquesa de Vistahermosa (Pedro's sister), and her English-speaking family of five. As they strolled in the garden after lunch, Isabel pointed to a hillside half a mile distant, where, quiet in the hot glare of the afternoon sun, ran a section of the Loyalist trenches. Were they not fearful for their lives, Meière asked in amazement. Perhaps, Isabel implied, but this was their home, which Nationalist soldiers would requisition if they moved. Anyway, fear was relative: she had one son recovering from a shrapnel wound and another sheltering in the Norwegian embassy in Madrid, where she prayed he would remain, since many who had walked out of embassies armed with safe conduct passes had disappeared.[16]

Ávila, birthplace of Saint Theresa, was their next stop, and there Meière visited another distant cousin, María, the Marquese de la Romana, whose house was integral with the town's medieval walls. María took Meière for a drive to a Carmelite convent, where Meière learned that the nuns, far from living in style on accumulated wealth, were bankrupt and dependent on local charity for food. That evening, Meière dined with María and her husband, the Conde de Villamediana, who had served in Spain's diplomatic corps before the war. A thoughtful, cosmopolitan couple, they surprised Meière by observing that the social programs of Spain's warring governments were analogous, and it was only "the why and the how of carrying them out" that was so different. Walking back to her hotel, Meière experienced the surrealism that often strikes travelers to Spain. Villamediana had told her of his two brothers, one shot on the roadside by a Loyalist assassination squad and the other shot by a Nationalist sentry after failing to notice a signal to stop the car. Yet now, as she marveled at the moonlight bathing Ávila's ancient walls and cathedral, the "saints and the Middle Ages seemed much nearer than the war." Her film sequences of Ávila also have a dreamlike quality: panoramas of the walls; passersby with black berets or long black dresses; Pérez enjoying a cigarette, standing proudly by his Renault taxi as he chatted to a smiling matriarch in a print frock; close-ups of the dry stone walling; three fine-looking youths showing off for Meière, a flower in each of their jacket buttonholes, joking and singing while one played a guitar; more shots of the walls as a lone spindly tree waves about in the wind; a man sitting outside a house engrossed in a newspaper.[17]

Sunday, 14 August, the American artist and Spanish taxi driver attended mass together at the twelfth-century Romanesque church of San Vicente. Whether Meière asked Pérez to accompany her, or vice versa, is unclear, but she did write, "I am sure that he felt better about me," just as their shared spirituality "reassured me about him." With a hitchhiking soldier in the back seat, they were soon on the road, reaching Leganés, a front-line village three miles from Madrid, in time for lunch. Captain Arteaga, who was expecting them, drove Meière to the vantage point of an abandoned radio transmitter, from where she filmed a half-minute panoramic sequence of Madrid's University City, telephone building, and royal palace shimmering in the midday heat just over a mile away. Arteaga gave her a demonstration firing of a rocket system capable of raining propaganda leaflets on the Loyalists' lines, one reading, "This war is lost: prolonging your resistance will only sacrifice more lives unnecessarily." Over a meal of an omelet and beefsteak tough enough to be mule, but lubricated by plenty of Spanish wine, Meière chatted with army officers and the staff of Radio National AZ, who were especially interested to hear about her 1936 trip to the Soviet Union. Station AZ's English-speaking announcer, Carlos Paz, joined Pérez and Meière for the hot, dusty drive to Toledo.[18]

After checking into a hotel and washing off the road grime, Meière had her long-anticipated audience with Cardinal Gomá, himself weary from a day spent sick in bed. This large, jovial man blessed with a phenomenal memory was a scholar thrust into the political spotlight, the stress of which was aggravating his kidney cancer. Having earned three doctorates by the age of twenty-seven, Gomá had lectured at Catholic universities for thirty years and written treatises on Thomist philosophy before his peers nominated him for their highest office. By dint of being in Pamplona for a rest cure, Gomá survived the Loyalists' anticlerical rampage of July–August 1936, although virtually his entire staff—twenty-three members—perished; militia had even sought out and murdered the cathedral organist and the lay lawyer of his ecclesiastical tribunal. Gomá achieved international notoriety for his *Spanish Bishops' Collective Letter,* published in its entirety in the *New York Times* of 3 September 1937, which mounted a 10,500-word point-by-point justification of the generals' rebellion against communist revolution and Franco's subsequent administration of the Nationalist zone. Yet since then, Franco's authoritarian governance and adoption of fascist trappings had become Gomá's biggest worry, leading to an August 1939 pastoral letter cautioning against "exaggerated modern statism that makes the State the ruler of morals and the educator of the people." Despite his sickness, Gomá received Meière warmly, offering his sincerest thanks for the ASRF aid contributions and explaining that, without the donations, he would have been unable to provide poor relief as well as traveling expenses to send priests into the recently retaken towns of Extremadura. He then instructed his secretary to show Meière around his ransacked gothic cathedral.[19]

As the sun was setting, Meière stumbled through the looted sacristy, saddened by the broken crosses, vandalized reliquaries, and slashed paintings. She reached a small room under the tower where, stacked against the wall, were fourteen El Grecos, a large Goya, and two works by Diego Velázquez. Lost in wonder, she picked up the canvases, turning them toward the dimming light, marveling at the quality of the brushwork, the brilliance of the composition. It was the high point of her trip. "Only an artist," she wrote, could understand what those moments meant. Amid her joy, she missed the irony of handling such priceless artworks at a time when aid contributions from America were the lifeline of Spain's impoverished Catholic Church. During the next morning, she toured Toledo's shattered Alcázar, no less massive for lying half-ruined. For seventy days following July 1936, 520 women, 50 children, 100 old or infirm men, and 1,028 men capable of firing a weapon had held out against air raids, artillery bombardment, infantry assault, and massive charges placed in tunnels dug under the walls by Loyalist miners from Asturias. For Franco lobbyists, the Alcázar was doubly emblematic: through its wreckage, it evidenced the nihilism of Marxist revolution; through the heroism of its beleaguered garrison that survived against all odds in an austere fortress redolent of Philip II's regal monasticism, it symbolized the valiance as well as the virtue of Western civilization. Meière celebrated the event by shooting six minutes of film through her Bell & Howell Filmo-70DA.[20]

After lavishing a fifth of her film stock on the Alcázar, Meière began the return journey. From Salamanca the following day, 16 August, Pérez drove to visit the

3,400-acre estate of another relative, María de Martínez y Irujo, a former lady-in-waiting to Alfonso XIII's Scottish-born Presbyterian wife, Queen Ena. A plucky gray-haired woman in her sixties, Martínez rented out half her acreage for sheep grazing but managed the rest herself, employing thirty laborers. Threshing was in progress. Meière filmed a beaming boy of eight or ten riding an ox-drawn sled over the wheat stalks. She panned her Filmo past a worker with a pitchfork, another leading a cart, huge mounds of grain drying in the sun, cattle snuffling through the chaff with young boys minding them—all set against an endless horizon blank except for a Dali-esque stand of cypress. Here was the epitome of traditional Spain, a dreamy bucolic flashback to the methods of a bygone era. Was Martínez the kind of rapacious *latifundista* (hereditary owners of large estates) historians like to blame for Spain's rural poverty and backwardness? Possibly, though she claimed she had invested in machinery only to discover that her workers preferred the pace of oxen, forcing her to scrap further plans for mechanization. Perhaps the villagers rationalized that it was better to have thirty hands employed than to suffer the unemployment and resulting dislocation to an urban environment that tractors entailed.[21]

At Burgos, Meière bid farewell to Pérez. Before leaving for Bilbao, she interviewed Pilar Primo de Rivera, the young sister of the executed Falange leader who headed the Sección Femenina women's organization, but she thought Pilar shy and did not learn much from her. From Bilbao, Meière visited the Iron Ring, an impressive yet futile circuit of defenses built by the Basques in 1936, and then Guernica, where she filmed fire-gutted buildings as well as the intact parliamentary hall and legendary oak tree, under which generations of Spanish monarchs had sworn to uphold Basque privileges. She estimated the destruction at about five square blocks over an area of houses and factories in the lower part of town near the train station, an estimate borne out by a panoramic sequence she shot from the balcony of a house on the nearby hillside. Unlike other pro-Nationalist visitors to Guernica, Meière did not try to perpetuate the myth that retreating Basques had destroyed the town with dynamite and gasoline. From what she saw and learned by talking to witnesses, she concluded that the "Reds had troops and munitions concentrated" in the downtown area and "the Nationals bombed it." This was correct. Basque president José Antonio Aguirre had ordered his soldiers to stand and fight at Guernica, and the commander of his Loyola Battalion that occupied the town, Capt. Juan de Beiztegi, intended it to be "our Alcázar, which we shall defend to the last brick." There were two arms factories, the larger being the Astra-Unceta complex, which a closet Franco supporter owned. And on the afternoon of 26 April 1937, fifty-seven German Condor Legion aircraft dropped 500 tons of explosives and incendiaries. Still, Meière had seen Irún, where retreating Loyalists had burned many buildings, so she was prepared to admit the possibility that some of the gutted edifices in Guernica, like a warehouse whose intact roof structure she filmed, might have been the work of arsonists, as some of the townspeople claimed.[22]

Before returning to Paris and sailing home, Meière wrote to Ambassador Bow-ers. After thanking him for assistance with visas, she offered her observation that throughout her 1,400-mile trip, she had encountered a "marvelous spirit of cour-age and patriotism, with a constructive attitude towards the future that argues well for the new Spain." She then questioned U.S. policy pertaining to Bowers's ambassadorship. Why, during the massacres of July–August 1936, had the U.S. embassy refused sanctuary to refugees without U.S. passports, when Madrid's other foreign embassies—excepting Britain's—had opened their doors to desper-ate noncitizens? Mexico's embassy, she noted, sheltered 1,200 refugees by virtue of renting extra housing. Why, too, had the U.S. embassy refused to offer any hu-manitarian aid? And why was Bowers maintaining his office at Saint-Jean-de-Luz, across the border in France, when all other embassies had established headquar-ters in either Valencia or Burgos? Perhaps because he realized that Meière's letter exposed his pro-Loyalist bias, Bowers never replied.[23]

Meière Networks Manhattan's Pro-Franco Elites

Back in Manhattan at the end of September, Meière caught up on her studio's commissions for the upcoming New York World's Fair of 1939, which included *Science the Healer* for the Medicine and Public Health Building, featuring a thirty-foot-high modernist doctor; a pair of sixty-foot-tall panels of a linesman and a switchboard operator for the entrance to the Bell Telephone Building; and a stunning 150-foot-long art deco tableau, *Man, Between the Past and the Future, Reaches for the Ever-Advancing Lamp of Human Knowledge*. With massive murals such as these, artists typically produced full-sized paintings on canvas of figures and other principal elements, along with a scaled-down rendition of the entire work. Commercial painters then reproduced the artist's conception on site, with the artist painting in critical detail as required. In the case of the World's Fair, Meière would later be frustrated to learn that she could not work on her own murals without first joining the Paper Hangers' Union, but, as an artist, she would be a Class-B nonvoting member, so she refused on principle to pay to join a trade union in which she would have no franchise.[24]

Once Meière had these projects on track again, it was with newfound enthusi-asm that she went fund-raising for Talbot's ASRF. She gave at least one lecture about her trip, at Kenwood, Convent of the Sacred Heart, a Catholic girls' boarding school in Albany, which netted a $50 ($1,500) collection, and she probably spoke about her experiences of Nationalist Spain at Manhattanville College of the Sacred Heart in New York City, as Louise Meière Dunn remembers her mother giving frequent lectures there. Who attended these lectures and how influential they were is hard to estimate, but elite Catholic New Yorkers considered Kenwood and Manhattanville to be premier girls' schools, and an interesting lecture about Spain would have been a good excuse for a visit. Meière soon transitioned from fund-raising, parlaying her energy and organizational skills into networking her pro-Franco women friends as well as professional elites for more overtly politicized lobbying activities.[25]

Meière was in regular contact with Anne Morgan, daughter of financier John Pierpont Morgan and one of the world's richest women, whom Meière may have known for some years through their memberships of the elitist yet left-leaning Cosmopolitan Club, though more personally after attending a party at Morgan's Three Sutton Place apartment in May. During the 1900s, Morgan established a sailors' center at the Brooklyn Navy Yard, became a sanitary inspector in order to identify social and public health issues in industry, started a program to provide vacations for working girls, and contributed to the Women's Trade Union League, and in the 1930s he was a principal backer of several organizations to improve pay, conditions, and opportunities for women in the workplace. A professional philanthropist as well as a social reformer, Morgan became internationally famous for assisting French victims of both world wars. As an Episcopalian who held left-wing sympathies and loathed Nazi Germany, Morgan would seem an unlikely lobbyist for Franco's Spain. But closer investigation indicates three reasons for her pro-Nationalist activism, which also inform the motivation of some other Franco supporters: peer pressure from a close circle of *españolista* friends, neo-mugwump ideology, and humanitarian fund-raising.[26]

First, Morgan spent much of her adult life socializing within a group of wealthy women artists and intellectuals, all of whom enjoyed—at varying levels of affectionateness—close friendships. Within this close-knit circle, there would have been pressure to share political opinions. In addition, the members of this group had all developed a love of Spain, of the romantic Spain of Moorish castles, Renaissance paintings, Baroque churches, and picturesque villages; of the sensual Spain of the dinner party hosted by a grandee in a fine old villa or a famous artist on a beachfront estate; and of the dangerous, climactic Spain of the Sunday *corrida*. During a trip to Paris in 1904, Morgan met Elisabeth Marbury, a voluptuous theatrical agent of forty-eight, and in the words of biographer Alfred Allan Lewis, fell "madly in love." For her part, as she wrote in her *Reminiscences,* Marbury thought there was "something pathetic" about Morgan, a "splendid girl, full of vitality and eagerness" yet trapped in a conservative environment who "had never been allowed to grow up." It was time, Marbury determined, for Morgan's thirty-one-year-old mind to have its "spark plugs . . . adjusted." Over the next ten years of summers, the newly emancipated Morgan bankrolled Marbury's Villa Trianon at Versailles, adding a Morgan Wing in 1912, and the two would take pleasure in "purposeless motoring" as they "gadded about sightseeing" over much of France "under conditions of self-indulgent comfort." In 1924, with her mental spark plugs firing on all cylinders, Morgan fulfilled her "independence of spirit" to the point where no woman in

America was of "finer fibre, of higher vision, of more disinterested conduct or of more persistent achievement." Morgan drew close to Marbury's protégé and companion since 1884, actress turned interior designer Elsie de Wolfe.[27]

De Wolfe was an aficionado of the Spanish vacation, touring the country on a number of occasions, including in 1914 when she motored to Barcelona with a maid and two dogs, whereupon the outbreak of war and the call-up of her French chauffeur caused Marbury and Morgan to gad down to Biarritz to collect her. In *Reminiscences,* Marbury does not specify the year of her own first Spanish vacation, but she does describe driving to Madrid in her Panhard limousine and checking into the Ritz Hotel with her maid to await the arrival of De Wolfe and Morgan, who had been traveling together by train through Seville and Granada. It is also unclear if this was Morgan's first visit to Spain—or even her last—although it is apparent that the three American ladies had a marvelous time. "Rarely shown" private art collections "were the excuse for many an afternoon tea to which we were invited by the stately owners." In Toledo, where they were "delightfully entertained," all the "beautiful tapestries, furniture," and other "priceless treasures" that yet remained in the "land of their birth" left an "indelible impression" on them. On the Feast of Corpus Christi, Marbury, De Wolfe, and Morgan attended a private mass in Toledo's Royal Chapel. Marbury thought it "profound" how the courtiers formed such a "natural part of their historic surroundings," while King Alfonso XIII's private cortège was "the most brilliant thing I have ever witnessed." As they drove back to France, Morgan, noted that "nowhere can one see such red and purple, blue and yellow" as in the "picturesque" villages of northern Spain. Although Marbury did not record Morgan's impressions, they were no doubt similarly profound.[28]

Second, Morgan's support for Franco should not be so unexpected, for she fits the neo-mugwump profile. Morgan voted Republican and was an active member in the Women's National Republican Club of Manhattan, yet she supported Roosevelt's New Deal during its early years and admired the First Lady, whom she knew personally. She commended New Deal policies that produced a climate favorable to job growth, but she opposed Roosevelt's Works Progress Administration because the creation of new jobs was none of the government's business. Morgan's support of left-wing women's labor organizations was no less ambiguous. As reported in the *New York Times* during the 1910 strike by shirtwaist workers, while she was "heartily in favor of the strikers" and upset by their treatment in the courts, she also thought it "dangerous to allow socialistic appeal to emotionalism," just as it was "reprehensible" for New York's socialists to take advantage of the strike "to preach their fanatical doctrines." Morgan's mugwumpism allowed her to sit firmly on the fence, taking a principled stand for women's legal rights and improved working conditions yet demarcating the line between social reformism and what she judged to be fanatical socialism. In the same way, Morgan could support the fight by Nationalists to preserve Spain's cultural heritage from similarly fanatical Soviet doctrines while drawing her line at Franco's Falangist leanings and recourse to military support from Nazi Germany.[29]

Third, she was predisposed to lobby politically for Franco because of her ongoing humanitarian support for the Nationalist zone. Along with her most intimate of companions, Anne Harriman Vanderbilt, Morgan had been a founding member of the Spanish Nationalist Relief Committee (SNRC), which had registered with the State Department on 10 February 1938 but taken some months to become operational. Morgan's membership in the SNRC may have been at the behest of its chairman, Alexander Hamilton Rice, whom Morgan knew well. On 21 November 1938, Morgan wrote to Meière, telling her "what an angel you were about the photographs" of her Spain trip, which, despite Meière's apparent reservations about their artistic quality, were "really the loveliest things I have seen in many a long day," and recommending that she contact another pro-Franco fund-raiser, Lucrezia Bori.[30]

A descendent of the Italian Borgias and the daughter of a Valencia army officer, Bori capped an illustrious career as lead soprano of New York's Metropolitan Opera by becoming its grande dame and first woman director. Bori had been organizing benefit concerts through the SNRC, but Morgan felt that Bori would do better to pool her efforts with Meière through Talbot's ASRF. Talbot's organization, Morgan realized, operated with minimal overhead, ensuring that a high percentage (82 percent) of funds raised reached Spain, whereas the SNRC, according to a regulatory filing that Morgan spotted in the *New York Times,* had collected $8,616 but spent $7,806 on administration and advertising. As the SNRC's secretary, Joseph F. Moore, later explained to Morgan, the published figures were anomalous, with expenses running around 20 percent of donations. Rice had given a generous $4,835 ($145,000) to cover startup costs, and the filing lumped that amount in with contributions, $2,725 of which were awaiting transmittal to Spain. Still, as a veteran fund-raiser herself, Morgan was right to be apprehensive. Unlike Talbot's conscientious shoestring operation, the SNRC's committee employed a professional fund-raiser and included a number of wealthy philanthropists in addition to Vanderbilt, who may have lent the SNRC an air of benign profligacy.[31]

Meière, Bori, and Talbot began collaborating soon after Morgan's letter, coordinating their fund-raising concerts during meetings in Meière's studio and the homes of Manhattan socialites and opera buffs, several of whom moved in the same circles as Morgan and Vanderbilt. One of Bori's friends was portrait painter Viva Vidal-Quadras, daughter of music critic Leonard Liebling. Vidal-Quadras, who had lived in Spain for ten years as the wife of a banker, until he died in an automobile crash in 1938, wrote a series of articles for *Spain* on Spanish dance, music, and art. Morgan's earliest recorded lobbying activity is her signing of Kelly's November 1938 petition to "Mr. President" to maintain the arms embargo. It is possible, therefore, that the politicization of her activism was a direct consequence of Meière's tour of Nationalist Spain in August.[32]

On 10 October, Meière attended a lecture at the Cosmopolitan Club that no doubt caused her to raise an eyebrow. Britain's so-called Red Duchess of Atholl, who was still masquerading as a Conservative member of Parliament, was promoting Loyalist Madrid and her propagandistic best seller *Searchlight on Spain*. It was "ludicrous" to say that Spain was "under 'Communist domination'"; no one, Atholl noted, had yet produced "reliable evidence of any planned Communist rising." Indeed, according to a Loyalist she quoted, the struggle in Spain was "not between socialism and capitalism, but between bourgeois democracy and fascism." Also attending—at the invitation of one of the Cosmopolitan's centrist members, Mary Benjamine, and with prompting by Talbot—was Kelly, who subsequently wrote an exposé for the Catholic monthly newspaper *Wisdom* in which he queried Atholl's decision to site her hospital/orphanage next to the train station in Puigcerdá, the border town through which the bulk of Loyalist war matériel arrived from France. Surely, he said, it was the height of hypocrisy to "gamble with the lives of children to protect the Red munitions" from air strikes when she had been so vocal in claiming that Nationalist bombings were atrocities.[33]

On the evening of Thursday, 20 October, Meière invited a dozen pro-Nationalist friends and acquaintances to her studio for an informal meeting, including Talbot, Cárdenas, Chase National Bank assistant cashier Mary Vail Andress, Fordham University English professor Francis X. Connolly, and Merwin K. Hart, a well-connected Harvard-educated lawyer who ran the influential New York State Economic Council. An Episcopalian, a Great War veteran, and a Freemason, Hart moved in a community of anti–New Deal elites that included former undersecretary of State William R. Castle, philanthropist John B. Snow, and John B. Trevor, architect of the 1924 Immigration Restriction Act. Ten days later, Meière attended a rally at the Hotel Commodore to hear Elizabeth Dilling speak about her experiences in Spain, and there Meière may have again met Kelly, although whether Kelly also addressed the rally is unknown (he spoke to large crowds at the Commodore at least twice, on 21 July and 4 December 1938).[34]

Meière invited a larger group of nineteen to her studio the following Thursday, for a debate about how best to promote Franco's Spain and counter Comintern propaganda. Among those present were Marie-Therese Marique, a Belgian American schoolteacher who wrote a book review page in *Spain* called "The Pen and the Sword"; Talbot and Connolly from the prior meeting; Meière's assistant, Nina Wheeler, whom Meière had presumably converted to Franco's cause; Gerdt Wagner, manager of Ravenna, the U.S. factory of the German company that installed Meière's mosaics; Walter M. Walters, a banker in Barcelona for eighteen years who was joining the Foreign Service; Kelly; and Ogden H. Hammond, a former ambassador to Spain (1925–29). There is no way of knowing specifics of the evening's discussion, but participants decided that Meière should regularize the Thursday meetings, which continued through December and then became more intermittent until

May 1939. According to Maj. John V. Hinkle, a *New York Times* staffer and National Council of Catholic Men official who dropped in several times, the studio meetings were always casual, and Meière would sometimes show her films of Spain.[35]

One of the attendees at Meière's informal sessions was Clare Singer Dawes, the Franco lobbyist from Massachusetts and publisher of Kelly's *Christian Soldier* pamphlet. Born to Polish immigrants around 1879, Dawes had enjoyed a career in advertising, been an intelligence officer during the Great War, and traveled extensively, although she saw herself primarily as a homemaker, mothering two children before settling down with her second husband, an engineer. Motivated by dual concerns for the rising popularity of communism at home and the plight of Catholic clergy in Spain, she had, since the summer of 1936, promoted Franco's cause by organizing guest speakers for and giving addresses at women's forums throughout the East Coast and Midwest. Locally, she was active in Boston's Women's National Republican Club and the Florence Crittenden League as well as her parish church, St. Mary's of the Assumption in Brookline. Her most enthusiastic endorser was Boston College president William J. McGarry.[36]

Sometime over the winter of 1937–38, Dawes went to a talk on Spain by Meière at Manhattan's Young Catholics' Club; their first meeting had been at Meière's studio in early December 1938, when they discussed their shared fund-raising and promotional interests. In January, Dawes wrote to Meière in a letter bubbling over with excitement that there was so much "in the air" that "one is dizzy watching and listening." Newspapers and radio were "hammering away on the Spanish situation," with much of the hammering, Dawes observed, drawing parallels with Latin America. She had listened to a review by a Mr. FitzGerald of Edwin Rolfe's *The Lincoln Battalion,* which she thought was "deadly," but what "amazed" her most was a full-page advertisement in her December *American Mercury*— an ostensibly conservative, anti–New Deal literary digest—for a book by Joseph Lewis entitled *Spain: A Land Blighted by Religion.* Dawes evidently did not know that the *Mercury's* editor, Eugene Lyons, and a sizeable number of its writers were either ex-communists or fellow travelers; still, she had presumed that Lewis's agenda was communistic when in fact his Freethought Press Association evangelized atheism. Behind Dawes's letter was a request for Meière to give a lecture and show her film on her Spanish tour to an audience of Boston schoolteachers, billed as a fund-raiser for Spanish children and sponsored by Bishop Richard T. Cushing. Meière declined, preferring dinner at Morgan's Sutton Place apartment to addressing teachers in distant Boston, so a Miss Solano, head of Boston City Schools' foreign languages department, showed lantern slides and spoke of her travels through Spain instead. These talks, slide shows, and fund-raisers, many of which women lobbyists organized, were the kind of unpretentious local affairs that historians seldom document, yet in sum they constituted a groundswell of activism that kept the Great Debate in the public mind.[37]

The American Union for Nationalist Spain

Franco's cause kept Meière busy. "Hy went to Spanish debate," records the 15 December diary entry of Louise Benedict Harmon, a sixty-three-year-old socialite with whom Meière, Meière's daughter, and a governess shared an apartment at 620 Park Avenue. "Hy Spanish party in evening 50 there," records the entry for 31 January 1939, after what was presumably a hectic evening at the studio. It is unfortunate that Harmon's diary catalogs so few of Meière's pro-Nationalist lobbying engagements, making no mention, for instance, of the inaugural AUNS meeting held at Merwin Hart's midtown office on 5 December 1938.[38]

Before discussing the role that Meière and Kelly played in the formation of the American Union for Nationalist Spain, it is important to contrast these two lobbyists. Whereas Meière moved solely among Manhattan's artistic and social elites, Kelly was just as comfortable with blue-collar union members as he was with affluent old-stocks. He could transition from listening to a lecture at the Cosmopolitan, to a beery crowd at Donovan's bar-and-grille in Hell's Kitchen, where on at least three noisy Friday nights he hung up his suit jacket, rolled up his sleeves, and gave a rousing speech. In this era before television, sound bites, and the commodification of politics, it is interesting to observe the alacrity with which concerned citizens wrote articles, sent letters to publishers and politicians, addressed large and sometimes hostile audiences, screened documentary films, and formed associations.

Meière, Talbot, Kelly, Ogden Hammond, and Merwin Hart constituted the inaugural meeting of AUNS; all of them were regular attendees at Meière's Thursday-evening discussion sessions, from which had come the decision to form a nationwide organization to "co-ordinate the efforts of those friendly to Nationalist Spain." as Meière put it. Kelly typed the meeting's minutes. By unanimous decision, the committee conferred on him the hard-working though often unappreciated position of secretary, which he took willingly, for through this role he could better expand his networking of Franco supporters around the country. Pending approaches to public figures such as Gen. Henry Joseph Reilly, Hart assumed the chair, a position he was to retain. As for a name, Hammond suggested that of a similar organization in London, Friends of National Spain, or, alternatively, Friends of True Spain. Kelly proposed either Committee for Christian Spain or General Committee for Spain. Talbot offered the winning title, American Union for Nationalist Spain, for which a mission statement was then required. Humanitarian aid, so well covered already by Talbot's ASRF, would be outside the scope of the AUNS. Rather, this organization would "serve to orient and coordinate all American efforts to tell the American people the truth about Spain," to which end it would never be defensive but "aggressive," carrying "the publicity battle to the reds."[39]

They aimed high, shooting for one thousand members drawn from every state, including such pro-Franco candidates as Calvin Bullock, an Episcopalian and New York investment banker; Robert Ignatius Gannon, Fordham University's president; William Joseph Donovan, a decorated Great War colonel, lawyer, Catholic, and Republican candidate for New York state governor in 1932; William J. Houston, of Pennsylvania; Atwater Kent, the pioneer manufacturer of radio sets; Mrs. Dorrance, an Episcopalian socialite married to the president of Campbell Soup; J. Frederick Byers, ex-president of the U.S. Golf Association; and Richard Montgomery Tobin, a Catholic diplomat turned banker. (Tobin was also vice president of San Francisco's Japan Society, which is significant because most Franco supporters favored Japan over China, the former being a far more natural ally ever since the Japanese had looked to the West following the Meiji Restoration of 1868.) Talbot offered his wholehearted support; but because either he considered it wise not to have Catholic priests on the letterhead or he feared politicizing his Jesuit order, he declined a place on the committee, suggesting Wall Street attorney and ex-judge Alfred Joseph Talley instead. Talley may have been unacceptable, or perhaps he also declined, for the six-person committee was comprised of Hart, Kelly, Meière (treasurer), Sedgwick, Hammond, and Ignatius M. Wilkinson, dean of Fordham University Law School. Though its membership never reached a thousand, the speed with which the AUNS recruited leading citizens coast to coast was impressive; its first mass mailing in early January sent a hand-signed and -addressed letter to 530 presumed pro-Franco American elites.[40]

Rice, who had spent most of his life alternating between teaching at Harvard, where he created the Institute of Geographical Exploration and lectured on tropical diseases, exploring South American rivers, and socializing from his 5th Avenue apartment (his friends quipped that he knew headwaters like they knew head waiters), did not serve on AUNS's committee, but he was an active associate. In September 1938, he toured the Nationalist zone, becoming the only Franco lobbyist to meet the Generalísimo in person. During the frantic 1938–39 efforts to maintain the arms embargo, Rice worked full time with AUNS members such as Meière, Kelly, or Hart, and especially through his SNRC, to raise funds, keep the arms embargo, and gain diplomatic recognition for Nationalist Spain. He held musical recitals followed by fund-raising receptions in his Manhattan home, and on 1 December he staged a rally at Philadelphia's Academy of Music, packing 3,500 into the auditorium plus 500 into the foyer, leaving the police to turn away more than 2,000 disappointed pro-Franco Philadelphians. "Nationalist Spain," he told the crowd, "is carrying on a fight against Communism for the whole world." Franco had granted the interview with him as "a gesture of friendship" to the United States, he explained, despite the fact that Republican Madrid's official Washington embassy was the "No. 1 Communist Propaganda Dissemination Station" in the country, followed by the Loyalist North American Committee to Aid Spanish Democracy. But, he assured the crowd, Franco's intention was to "restore peace and prosperity to Spain," so Americans need have no further worries. Whatever inklings Rice had gleaned of the Nationalist regime's repressive character, his glowing portrayal gave no hint.[41]

At the end of January 1939, the AUNS's committee delivered to the State Department a petition to recognize Franco, bearing the signatures of 126 respected Americans, including those of twenty-nine editors, nine university presidents or deans, twenty-five PhDs or LLDs, and six presidents of major corporations. In addition to several prominent diplomats, artists, and educators, other standouts included John Moody of Moody's Investor Services, San Francisco's postmaster and Pacific Coast Baseball League president William H. McCarthy, and 1928 Democratic presidential nominee Alfred E. Smith. Although Franco's near-triumph was fast rendering the petition moot, it may have smoothed the path to recognition on 1 April 1939 and guided the selection—probably through the aegis of the State Department's European affairs adviser James Clement Dunn—of the pro-Franco Alexander W. Weddell as ambassador to Madrid. On behalf of the AUNS's committee, chairman Hart cabled Franco its congratulations, and on 3 April Hart sent a telegram to Secretary of State Cordell Hull ensuring him of their continuing effort "to work toward a good understanding between New Spain" and America, because close relations were "in the best interests of both countries" as well as the "cause of international peace."[42]

AUNS and the Affirmation of National Consciousness

Other than Ignatius Wilkinson, all AUNS committee members had made at least one trip to Spain and, with the exception of Hart, could converse in Spanish. Of the group, Hart was the last to go, probably at Kelly's prompting. For some months, Kelly had been a regular at Hart's 17 East 42nd Street office, a central Manhattan location with secretaries, telephones, and the latest mimeographic equipment from where he could efficiently network business and political elites. Whether out of discomfort with Hart's pretentious self-assurance or Hart's drift into political Christianity (to the point of running New York City's John Birch Society eighteen years later), or simply a personality clash, Kelly grew to dislike him, ending the relationship in February 1940, but for two years he made full use of every opportunity that their collaboration as Franco lobbyists afforded.[43]

Determined to find out "what really was going on" in Spain, Hart spent September and October of 1938 touring the Nationalist zone. His connection to Cárdenas assured him VIP treatment, although he insisted nevertheless that he had come with an open mind "to get the truth." Once he had gained the confidence of his guides, Nationalist officials saw him as a valuable promoter. On 29 September they allowed him to broadcast an address from Radio Málaga, "America—Look at Spain: The Agony Will Be Repeated Here," which reached across the Atlantic to Americans via shortwave radio and through publication in the widely read journal *Vital Speeches of the Day*. "I came to study economic conditions," Hart began, to "learn whether closer trade relations might in future exist" between America and Spain. But, he went on to say, he found it impossible to ignore what he judged to be the impressive social and political changes sweeping through the Nationalist zone, from the thousands of women running the Auxilio Social welfare organization, to the five hundred affordable houses completed in Seville alone, to the general sense of well-being and order. He learned that Franco, far from falling under the hegemony of Germany or Italy, had surrounded himself with "the best talent in Spain," including "a quarter of all the members of the six Spanish Academies." Franco, Hart admitted, had led a military revolt, but it was a "rising to end a reign of murder and violence," a "movement by all decent people in Spain" to set up a government capable of effective governance. Propaganda had convinced Americans that the "so-called 'Loyalists'" were "fighting for 'democracy,'" which was "one of the greatest hoaxes ever attempted in America." Here in Spain, Hart asserted with hyperbolic flourish, "was the main battle-front of the world against one of the greatest threats to civilization in all human history," the menace of Russian Marxism.[44]

On his return, Hart, with Kelly's assistance, wrote a similarly titled book. *America, Look at Spain!* contrasted Spain's warring zones as an opening gambit through which to draw parallels with the United States. A final showdown between the post-Enlightenment materialistic ideologies of Marxism and capitalism was inevitable, he felt, and while he expected the clash to take the form of a bloody insurrection on home turf, he correctly predicted that it must center on America as the world's industrial superpower. Americans, Hart fretted, were just too naive. "In subtle ways through the press, the theater, the movies, the radio," they had fallen prey to "international influence," to "alien philosophy." Communists had "convinced millions that the American system is cruel and unjust." Through their "soft-sounding" front organizations and insidious propaganda, communists had won over "high dignitaries in the churches," "professors and executives in colleges," even some business owners. British propagandists of a different stripe drove Americans into the Great War. Now a second war was looming, the consequence of which could only be further dictatorial controls by big government that would prove impossible to shake off. Hart believed, therefore, that the survival of American republicanism depended neither on intellectuals enamored of "fine-spun theories" nor on business leaders who were "too cautious, too intimidated by Washington," and certainly not on "press and pulpit," where fondness for alien philosophy ran deep. Hart was sure that American survival depended on the growth of an educated, informed middle class.[45]

Hart stressed that a Nationalist victory in Spain offered the best insurance against further revolutions south of the Mexican border and for the protection of U.S. investments there. Because sentiment among Latin American elites favored the Nationalists, and given the United States' *primus inter pares* role in the Western Hemisphere, Hart advocated State Department support for Franco. Sedgwick and Kelly, both of whom had traveled throughout Central and South America, had voiced similar concerns. In a letter Hart received before leaving for Spain, Sedgwick observed how "the drift in Mexico toward Communism is unsettling the masses of the south," so it was likely that "a Bolshevist victory in Spain would make most of South America lurch to the left." Sentiment south of the border was in fact as divided as it was to the north, although at least in the case of Colombia, say, Hart's remarks had some validity. Historian David Bushnell notes the pro-Loyalist *El Tiempo*'s admission that when Colombians watched newsreels about Spain there were more cheers for the Nationalists, and while Bushnell can find little evidence that Franco's victory caused the rightward shift in Columbian politics, Liberal Party members nevertheless thought it had.[46]

Americans, Hart concluded, faced two example-setting "duties." First, to "keep out of all foreign wars of every nature, while building up our national defense." Second, "to put our own house in order" by curbing reckless public spending, reducing national debt, unshackling government from private enterprise, and reestablishing "peace and tranquility at home." Hart did not specify a method for the reestablishment, but his analysis of Franco's Spain implied that social upheaval justified recourse to authoritarian rule, even though such a brief was at odds with his principled stand against unchecked executive power. Similarly, Hart was uncomfortable reconciling the "so-called vertical syndicates, each composed of an entire industry or profession," of Franco's corporatist economic policies with the business deregulation that his New York Economic Council championed in the face of Roosevelt's comparably statist New Deal policies. Still, in posing the question, "Would you favor this Spanish [authoritarian] plan for the United States?" he answered emphatically, "I would not." In America's case, republican government had "worked well on the whole," providing the "greatest liberty and the greatest material well-being for the average person, as well as the greatest development of philanthropy, the world has ever seen." His belief, rather, was that "in view of history"—the kind of Spanish history he had romanticized in the initial fifty-four pages of *America, Look at Spain*—"Spain at the present time" was not yet "adapted" to U.S.-style republicanism. If Americans wanted to preserve their unique system, which had "produced a higher standard of living for a greater part of the population" than any other, then they must look at Spain but never be like Spaniards.[47]

Seeing the Old Masters was the high point of Meière's trip. Hart worked to strengthen business ties for New York entrepreneurs. And Sedgwick, when he toured Nationalist Spain in January 1938, drew inspiration from Gen. Gonzalo Queipo de Llano's progressive public housing polices. And for them all, an exciting vacation to a romantic land was an enticing prospect. Still, these reasons alone hardly explain the lengths to which Franco lobbyists went in order to make their trips. While their endeavors back home ranged from keeping in place the arms embargo that so favored the Nationalists, to gaining diplomatic recognition for

Franco's new government, to raising aid for Spanish orphans, their stated aim was informational: fellow-traveling propagandists, working throughout the popular media, had blinded Americans to the true level of Comintern subversion; compounding Soviet infiltration into New Deal departments was a White House that sympathized with Soviet-run Loyalist Spain; and a Red Spain was but a precursor to a Red Western Hemisphere. With no end in sight to a deteriorating economy, with its corollary of social unrest, their argument, therefore, was that unless Americans learned the truth, Washington would fall to a communist coup. Yet even Kelly, at his gloomiest in the spring of 1939, having traveled through virtually every state of the union during the Great Depression and having felt the pulse of regular folks at so many fraternal clubs in smokestack cities, must have sensed that his prognostications of doom were overdrawn, that Americans had acquired sufficient confidence in their political system to obviate wrecking it. Maybe a more fundamental overarching interpretation of their concern, of their angst, is required—an additional motive, one that perhaps affected them at an unconscious level.

Through their unpopular stand, Franco lobbyists alienated many of their friends and colleagues. Moreover, they were in open opposition to their own government. But by cutting loose from their society's ascendant New Deal–based ideology, they created intellectual space for themselves. Franco lobbyists either had ample funds or, like Kelly, resigned themselves to debt. They had time on their hands, too. They were as much idealistic thinkers as they were pragmatic doers. Complacency was not their character; rather, there were issues, and their duty was to care about them. And care they would—with a passion. For them, politics was not an activity of some remote government but a process in which active citizens immersed themselves. Franco lobbyists were typically cosmopolitan, multilingual, and widely read and had a detailed knowledge of and a sincere respect for America's history. Sedgwick, Kelly, and Forbes had even published academic histories. So they sought answers in history, just as they looked to history for an explanation of themselves. Who were they, these self-styled superpatriots? Is there a relationship between who they were, what they sought, and the solution on which they settled?

Franco lobbyists were vocally *American,* both in the patriotic tone of their political writings and through their professional endeavors, whether it was Forbes's managerial technocracy, Sedgwick's New World philology, Hart's abhorrence of big government, Kelly's free-market entrepreneurialism, or Meière's art deco modernism. Yet as much as they promoted their American-ness, several of them seemed troubled by their own foreignness. Sedgwick kept quiet about his German cousin Ernst "Putzi" Hanfstaengl, the publisher of the Nazi Party's *Völkischer Beobachter* illustrated weekly magazine. Despite asserting in correspondence that Hanfstaengl was only "a very remote connection of mine," Sedgwick knew him well, even paying $200 ($6,000) so that Ernst's son, Egon, could attend Harvard in 1939. And Meière could, and often did, trace her ancestors back to the *Mayflower,* yet her father, Ernest Meière, was the grandson of a French immigrant from Alsace-Lorraine and her ex-husband Richard Alexander von Goebel was an Austrian who lived in Kitzbühel, and she told few friends about her Spanish relatives. To whatever extent Franco lobbyists accepted that America was the land of the immigrant, they never celebrated their Old World ties, none less so than the most committed lobbyist, the half-Irish half-German Kelly, whose sole claim to American heritage rested on his birth in Pittsfield, Massachusetts. Foreignness was an undesirable trait in the elite circles within which these actors moved. Therefore, the self-conscious promotion of their American-ness at a time when their pro-Franco anticommunism was the source of so much social discord enhanced not only their credibility as lobbyists and their acceptability within society but also their own feelings about their identity as patriotic citizens.[48]

Cognitive dissonance theory, as propounded by psychologist Leon Festinger, predicts that the psyche abhors discord and therefore works to minimize it. After Joe, say, allows a salesperson to sell him a Jaguar when his original intention was to buy a Buick, Joe will now be particularly interested to spot Jaguar advertisements in magazines and will point when he sees a Jaguar on the street, "Look! There's another one!" (especially if it's the same color as his own). Joe was uncomfortable that he had made a bad choice, but the presence of the other Jaguars reinforces his decision, and his cognitive dissonance subsides. Joe's fear of dissonance had a counterintuitive effect. His close reading of Jaguar advertisements followed rather than preceded his purchase, making it contingent on an important and irreversible decision.[49]

As detailed so well in Robert A. Gross's *Minutemen*, Americans have always abhorred disharmony and striven to build consensus within their communities. By 1938, a number of concerned intellectuals felt strongly enough about the way they saw communism undermining the core values that defined their identity as Americans as to commit wholeheartedly to saving their Depression-mired system. Their commitment to Franco, necessitated by the evidentiary value of Madrid's Soviet-inspired revolution, became problematic, as Nazism in Germany turned inhumanely totalitarian and Franco's regime adopted fascist imagery. Despite their belief that altruism drove them to act in the interests of their fellow citizens, Franco lobbyists inexorably alienated themselves from the sentiments of their pro-Loyalist friends and the whole tenor of their New Deal society. But theirs was an irreversible commitment. Their solution to reducing their cognitive dissonance was threefold: first, to build consensus among their group and expand the group to include a wider membership; second, to try to convince pro-Loyalist Americans of the merits of what they were soon touting as the New Spain; and third, to map the values of that New Spain onto what they saw as the rottenness of New Deal America, which of necessity implied a modification of the core values they assumed were immutable and touted as sacrosanct. After 1945, their efforts

would underpin a fourth solution, as they discovered that their unique and so-
cially unacceptable brand of pro-Franco anticommunism had somehow become
a desirable, state-backed project: the consensus-building anticommunism of the
McCarthy era. Sure enough, the cold war brought a redefinition of Americanism,
but one with which they would be uncomfortable.[50]

6

Spain in Arms

City dwellers with a quarter in their pocket and a longing for entertainment had plenty of choices in the late 1930s. In addition to plays, concerts, and dances, they could choose from dozens of venues, from five-thousand-seat theaters to halls that rented a flickery 16-mm projector for an evening of motion picture viewing. Few feature films ran longer than ninety minutes, so patrons typically watched newsreels or a stage act before the main attraction. Documentaries were popular too, both in movie theaters and at social gatherings, fund-raisers, and political meetings, the larger of which might be true multimedia events, with film, slides, addresses by amplified telephone, and a band or stage show in addition to the speeches. Pro-Loyalist groups in mid-1938 could pick from at least five documentaries—*The Spanish Earth, Spain in Flames, Heart of Spain, Fire in Spain,* and *Spain Fights On!*—and two feature films, Paramount Pictures's *Last Train from Madrid,* starring Dorothy Lamour, and United Artists' *Blockade,* boasting Henry Fonda. But pro-Nationalists, with enemies in Hollywood and limited funds, had nothing on celluloid with which to counter such Popular Front agitprop. Although their efforts to block pro-Madrid pictures while finding a documentary of their own met with limited success, these dual strategies exposed a mass audience of Americans to the Great Debate over the Spanish arms embargo, and hence the deeper argument over the meaning of Americanism.[1]

In this chapter, I interpret *Blockade* blockers' street-level activism in the New York metropolitan area as an alarmist response by patriotic Catholic immigrants to the Comintern's more organized and better-funded efforts to position New Deal America as a Popular Front ally of Spain's Moscow-directed revolution. It goes on to document the campaign by AUNS committee members to counter *Blockade* with their own propaganda film, *Spain in Arms.* Even though two-thirds of this vivid documentary is unavailable, the discovery and transfer to digital medium of twenty-nine minutes of film, together with a detailed shooting script of the entire movie, makes possible the first analysis since its last screening sixty-five years ago.

The chapter closes by investigating the claim disseminated in the early 1940s by New York's Jewish antifascist organizations and perpetuated by John Roy Carlson's best-selling *Under Cover* that Franco supporters led by "storm-trooper" John Eoghan Kelly instigated anti-Semitic "violence and terror" on the streets of New York.[2]

Unlike the government-run regulatory boards of most European countries, America's film industry has always been self-censoring, with cutting or outright bans being a matter for local jurisdictions. Hollywood producers voluntarily complied with the recommendations of the Production Code Administration, presided over by Joseph I. Breen from 1934 to 1954, which decided what words were offensive and held films to his own Catholic standard of morality. Non-Hollywood documentaries, therefore, such as *The Spanish Earth* or *Spain in Arms,* were not subject to any form of control unless they were banned by town or city councils. There was no official censorship even during wartime, although Lowell Mellett at the Office of War Information made clear to studios the kind of films he wanted moviegoers to see.[3]

Blockade

As exemplified by *Blockade,* public context rather than media content drove the Great Debate. On face value, *Blockade* was standard-fare melodrama, tedious at times, with a threefold message that spies were everywhere, war harms noncombatants, and American good ultimately triumphs over foreign evil. Intent on promoting his film as apolitical, and in the hope of avoiding local bans, producer Walter Wanger costumed warring parties in nondescript uniforms, disguised place names, and omitted political references. Castelmare, the setting, resembled a quaint Italian fishing village rather than the industrialized port-city of Bilbao, site of the actual blockade. Yet anyone who had so much as glanced at a newspaper front page during the previous year would have had no difficulty identifying the dreamy peasants with their Basque berets and flintlock rifles as good democratic Loyalists, while the coldhearted spies with their leather jackets, fast cars, bombers, and submarines were obviously the evil fascist Nationalists.[4]

This was not yet the fifth column scare of 1939, but, with plenty of mass media prompting, the public mind was already conflating spying and Nazism. Communists found it useful to propagate this myth. To much fanfare, the FBI had broken a New York–area German ring in February 1938, although Abwehr (Nazi intelligence) recruited few Americans. By contrast, Soviet espionage was spreading through most government agencies, reaching even the highest levels. Henry Morgenthau Jr.'s Treasury Department harbored at least nine Soviet spies under the aegis of Assistant Secretary Harry Dexter White. While Abwehr had to rely on conspicuous noncitizens with thick accents shipped over from Germany, Comintern officers found a ready supply of American recruits. As well as "scoring dramatic successes in recruiting agents" during the 1930s, Soviet communications intelligence was "the world's largest and richest." In Spain, ironically, spies were most likely to be Loyalists gathering intelligence on rival factions. Interestingly, one of *The (London) Times*'s two correspondents in the Nationalist zone was Soviet master spy H. A. R. "Kim" Philby, who in the summer of 1937 was looking for an opportunity to assassinate General Franco.[5]

Wanger was left-wing, director William Dieterle was a radical socialist, and screenwriter John Howard Lawson was a CPUSA member (on trial in 1947 as one of the Hollywood Ten), although film critics invariably depicted the production team as enlightened American liberals not anticapitalist communists. In *Liberty*, a traditionalist magazine with a middle-class readership two million strong, Ruth Waterbury's *Blockade* review referred to Lawson as a "radicaliberal." As subtle as its hidden messages were repetitive, Lawson's screenplay, like all effective propaganda, reached viewers on a subliminal level. Lines such as "spies and traitors are spreading false rumors" and "you can't trust anybody" blended seamlessly with references to "foreign newspapers" and cautions not to "believe everything you read in the newspaper." Pro-Nationalists could have seized on this message to suggest that Loyalists were untrustworthy; indeed, the only character who spread false rumors was the Loyalist shepherd Luis. Yet, because it was so obvious which side was good and which evil, "war psychology"—a catch phrase of the movie's war correspondent Edward Grant—worked to convince the viewer that rumor-mongering foreign newspapers were lying to American readers about naturally honest Loyalists. American newspapers that said good things about Loyalists were telling the truth, Lawson's script implied, but whenever they had something bad to say, readers should dismiss such information as false rumor spread by fascist spies. When the movie's General Vallejo (who turned out to be a traitor, an irony easily missed on first viewing) explained warmly to heroine Norma, "Perhaps you'll tell your friends abroad that we're not such barbarians as they've heard," the audience received a signal to discount newspaper stories of Loyalist atrocities. Following Lawson's script a priori, Nationalist atrocities were ever-present realities for Spaniards, but Loyalist atrocities were false rumors spread through foreign newspapers by fascist spies.[6]

Director Dieterle emphasized shots of haggard mothers praying in Castelmare's Catholic church for relief ships to bring food for their starving children. While in the real Spain Basques were devout Catholics who tragically picked the Loyalist side in the hope of achieving national autonomy, Dieterle's was propaganda at its best, for it was anticlerical Loyalists who had destroyed churches and massacred priests and nuns. Encouraged by British propaganda in 1915, Americans had read the worst of inhuman frightfulness (*Schrecklichkeit*) into German submarine warfare, which newspapers turned into a fixation after *U-20* torpedoed *Lusitania*. In the

1930s, Comintern propagandists built on the *Schrecklichkeit* legend to conflate aerial bombardment of cities with fascist barbarity. Perhaps because he appreciated the romantic appeal of aviation at this time, Dieterle never showed attacking aircraft. Instead—and more effectively—his cameras focused on people's faces as air raid sirens wailed, and on extended scenes of bomb devastation. The only time viewers saw "the enemy" soldiers was as the crew of a submarine. It is also notable that the film's dramatic scene of the sinking of a relief ship featured a lingering shot of a submarine-fired torpedo. While Italy did have submarines stationed in the Mediterranean during 1937, Germany deployed no U-boats in Spanish waters after December 1936. So to mount what was actually a halfhearted—and therefore porous—blockade of Bilbao, the Nationalists used surface vessels and mines, not submarines.[7]

To amplify the *Schrecklichkeit* message, Lawson—or perhaps Dieterle, who was German—used two cinematographic devices. As *Blockade* built to a climax, the camera zoomed to a page of correspondent Grant's typed report: "As I sit here, I see a nightmare vision of air raids sweeping over great cities . . . London . . . New York . . . San Francisco." And in the movie's hyperbolic close, hero Marco (Henry Fonda) spoke directly to the camera: "Our country's been turned into a battlefield." Moviegoers would have had little doubt that invading fascists had done the turning, and if good Americans, such as the Abraham Lincoln Brigade volunteers, did not stop the fascists in Spain, then New York would be the next battlefield. When churches, schools, and hospitals were targets, Marco continued plaintively, "It's murder! Murder of innocent people." *Blockade*'s "the enemy"— anonymous but self-evidently Nationalist—was so evil that it had even corrupted the glorious nature of warfare itself. "There's no sense to it. The world can't stop it. Where's the conscience of the world?" Marco's direct address retrospectively gave the entire picture a documentary quality. Audiences witnessed in scene after tearful scene how the enemy blockade was starving women, children, and old people. Lifting the blockade could only be right and humanitarian. Even though logic dictated that more arms would cause more suffering, there could have been few among *Blockade*'s audiences who did not equate the words *embargo* and *blockade*. Would not lifting America's iniquitous arms embargo be lifting the murderous blockade of Castelmare/Bilbao? Where was America's conscience?

Fonda, as did most of the cast, made no effort at speaking with a foreign accent. (Andre Gallinet, *Blockade*'s villain, spoke with a plummy British voice, a long-standing Hollywood device.) Fonda reached his audience as an all-American hero. And when the relief ship *Fortuna* docked in Castelmare harbor in the penultimate scene, the expectant crowd, especially the children, would not have looked out of place on the streets of Manhattan. By its close, *Blockade* had acquired a familiar, down-home quality brought nearer still to the viewer by the extra distance of the unseen enemy, an enemy that could swoop down unexpectedly from the skies or pop up from the ocean at periscope depth. In Wanger's presentation, quaint Loyalist Spain had become traditional friendly America, imperiled by the mechanized menace of impersonal, foreign fascism. For American moviegoers, Wanger drew the two countries on a single mental map. It is important to realize how both sides in the Great Debate preached—and practiced—the same teleology: What was happening in Madrid could happen in Manhattan and no doubt would, quite soon, unless Americans organized to stop it.

"Blocking Blockade*"*

United Artists spent $125,000 ($4 million) on newspaper advertising before *Blockade*'s 17 June 1938 release. It opened at Rockefeller Center's glitzy six-thousand-seat Radio City Music Hall and was preceded by a Mickey Mouse cartoon and followed by a symphony orchestra. In his *New York Times* review, Frank S. Nugent thought the film itself could have developed "greater dramatic power" but left no doubt that its context would make it highly "controversial." While Wanger failed to mention "Loyalist and Rebel, Franco or Mussolini," Nugent praised producer Wanger's "rare courage in going even so far." (*Courage* became ubiquitous in leftist *Blockade* reviews, serving as a trope for Madrid's virtuous stand and tying the antifascist heroism of Wanger to the battlefield sacrifice of ALB volunteers.) *Blockade,* Nugent was careful to explain, did not identify its heroic villagers and townsfolk. But in the very next sentence he artfully quoted a woman he overheard after the performance saying, "But it is obvious they were the Loyalists; after all, it was their cities that were bombed."[8]

A week later, Nugent's Sunday column, entitled "Blocking 'Blockade,'" feigned surprise that *Blockade*'s "mild" protest "against wholesale murder" could possibly have caused such a public "outcry." For "if the picture *is* pro-Loyalist"—a question of no little temerity on Nugent's part—then it could only be because those "with whom it sympathizes have been bombed in their homes and left to starve among the ruins." Nugent had no doubt that "the guilty party" was not *Blockade* but the viewing public, by which he really meant an intolerant Catholic public. Although Nugent did quote a Catholic source claiming that *Blockade* was a "historically false and intellectually dishonest" polemic for the "Marxist controlled cause in Spain" and a Trojan horse for "subtle foreign political propaganda," this was not so much an intent to demonstrate his column's impartiality as it was a ruse to make the identity of the guilty party obvious. Quoting his Catholic source, too, allowed him to counter with a block quote from a "courageous" defense by Wanger, in which the producer aligned his film with the "American spirit" and an "uncompromising devotion to democracy." For Wanger and Nugent, Spanish Loyalists and the Popular Fronters across the Atlantic who supported them were acting in the spirit of democratic Americanism.[9]

It was the same sentiment for Franco lobbyists, who believed they too were defending democratic Americanism. Talbot's *America* was at the forefront of the outcry in the Catholic press. Reviewer Thomas J. Fitzmorris thought that Hollywood had betrayed the trust of Catholic Americans through *Blockade*'s sly portrayal of Franco's Nationalists as fascist persecutors of Spanish Catholic victims. In his editorial, Talbot asked not just Catholics but all Americans who objected to the propaganda of "Communist and Marxist ideologists" to boycott the film. An adjacent editorial pointed out that Franco, who held the upper hand militarily, had once again offered an honorable peace to all combatants, with the exception of those who had committed common-law crimes. Yet the doomed "die-hard fanatics" defending Madrid, Valencia, and Barcelona rejected Franco's initiative, thereby forcing the hapless residents of these cities to suffer needlessly. In part because of Talbot's call for a boycott through organizations like the Knights of Columbus or his contacts at institutions such as the University of Detroit, *Blockade* was a box office flop.[10]

Although Knights in Omaha successfully pressured the Omaha Theatre to cancel its booking of *Blockade,* Wanger's avoidance of explicit political references prevented all but a handful of outright bans. In Kansas City authorities compromised with K-of-C leaders and required Wanger to cut Fonda's closing speech. *Blockade* even went ahead in censorship-prone Boston. Following a request by Mrs. David J. Johnson, an executive of the League of Catholic Women that represented fifty local Catholic organizations, the city council voted unanimously to request a ban by Boston mayor Maurice J. Tobin, who had watched the film but found it inoffensive. After Wanger promised to delete the opening caption, "Spain—1936," Tobin allowed *Blockade* to open at Loew's State and Orpheum theaters on 21 July 1938. Historian Vincent A. Lapomarda acknowledges that Tobin was "sympathetic" to Franco but suggests that this "loyal New Dealer" with a "personal affiliation with organized labor" sought broad appeal—from Boston's Jews as well as Catholics, from workers as well as business elites—as a fusion politician similar to New York City's La Guardia. Tobin's decision "excited a storm of comment," as one newspaper reviewer put it. Mrs. Johnson fumed that minor deletions could never correct the "whole trend of [a] picture," while the Massachusetts CPUSA branch wired its congratulations to the mayor for his "courageous stand." Boston's *Traveler* agreed with the communists that Tobin was "right and courageous," and after asking, "What is communistic and what is not communistic [anyway]?" answered fatuously, "Even Stalin and Trotsky cannot agree on that subject." Still, Mrs. Johnson did derive a measure of satisfaction a week later when her efforts prompted Mayor John M. Lynch of Somerville, Massachusetts, to ban the film.[11]

There were public protests—pro and con—all across America, several of which became heated affairs. Three smartly attired employees of the *Catholic Worker* holding politely worded placards that read "Boycott 'Blockade': Keep war propaganda off the screen," "Please do not patronize this theatre, the picture is a lie," and "This picture is an insult to Catholics, please do not see it" paced along the sidewalk outside Manhattan's Radio City as moviegoers arrived on the fifth day of screenings. *Life* magazine carried a picture of the three picketers above a critical commentary on the Catholic "crusade" against *Blockade* and its "courage[ous]" producer. When John Eoghan Kelly spotted the article, he dashed off a terse memorandum to Talbot: *Life*'s "attack on Catholics" was "Pure Bigotry." What *Life* failed to mention, though, was the violent reception awaiting the three picketers when they returned at 3:45 the following afternoon.[12]

New York's *Evening Post*—avowedly pro-Loyalist, with its own Madrid correspondent, George Seldes, a radical leftist if not a communist—had no qualms about reporting the 22 June incident, even appearing to gloat over the pickets' fate, although it did gloss over the brutality they suffered. According to the *Post*'s reporter, who was evidently present, whether by happenstance or forewarning, after just ten minutes of the picketers' silent protest, a man began shouting at one of them, "You are nothing but a Fascist. You are a Franco-Fascist." A crowd that quickly grew to five hundred surrounded the pickets, "pushed them about," and destroyed their placards. An alert traffic policeman at a nearby intersection rushed over and managed to extricate the picketers. Someone presumably telephoned the precinct three blocks south, for the *Post* reported that three radio cars and a patrol wagon containing ten officers soon arrived, but after the picketers had already left.[13]

Looking back on the incident almost fifty years later, picketer Stanley Vishnewski had a different recollection. As he approached Radio City on that fateful afternoon, he noticed there were no police on duty, and, unlike the previous day when several police cars appeared within minutes to keep the crowd in check, none came. It seemed to him that the toughs who first surrounded them acted as an organized group. Furious faces, hemming in closer, mesmerized him. He found it difficult to believe that he was "on the streets of New York and not in some far-off jungle facing a horde of grimacing savages." "Etched out against the mob," against a wall of arms waving like "wind mills," Vishnewski retained a vivid memory of a sharp-faced woman with a gaping lipstick-smeared mouth screaming "Fascist Bastard!" supported in her "ecstasy of hate" by a "giant of a man" like a "huge hunk of beef." One of the windmills punched him, but adrenaline anesthetized the pain; another wrenched the placard from his grip. In the spirit of nonviolent resistance, Vishnewski, Joseph Zarella, and managing editor William M. Callahan took their beating as silently as they had been protesting. Vishnewski's account mentions nothing about rescue by a lone officer but does recall the welcome sound of wailing sirens as he tried to protect himself from further injury. After police drove back the incensed mob, a woman took pity and led him to a coffee shop. In this interpretation, it is clear the crowd was so large and ugly that the lone officer had dared not intervene, instead telephoning the precinct for backup.[14]

Two weeks later, another incident moved the *Brooklyn Tablet* to observe that "only the Reds can picket" on New York's sidewalks without having their literature "taken up and thrown into the gutter." Half a dozen women of the International Catholic Truth Society (ICTS) had met outside Loew's Metropolitan Theatre for *Blockade*'s first Brooklyn screening, with the intention of distributing leaflets advocating peace and urging Americans to stay out of any European war. On arrival, they found a large group of pro-Loyalist picketers already occupying the sidewalk, handing out literature, and soliciting contributions for the ALB. One of the police officers on duty at the cinema confronted Mrs. Edna Garde, president of the ICTS Women's Auxiliary, explaining that he had orders to prohibit the ICTS from distributing literature. Some of the picketers then tried to grab the women's leaflets, in one case forcing a circular into a woman's mouth. Another officer told a Mrs. Troyes to "get into the gutter where [you] belong." This, to a New Yorker of the 1930s, was a severe insult. A bystander, Patrick O'Beirne, concerned by the police officers' partisan indifference, intervened to protect Troyes from "violent handling" by the "Reds." "Fulton Street," the *Tablet* commented wryly, "might well have been a street in Madrid after the Red controlled Loyalist Government" came into power.[15]

It is beyond the resources of this study to verify the Metropolitan Theatre incident or to document the complaints to Mayor La Guardia and the New York Police Department (NYPD) that Troyes claimed to have filed. There is a need here for further research, because the starting premise of prevailing historiography is that police officers are uniformly reactionary, showing indifference to the illegal or violent behavior of conservative political activists while resorting to excessive force when dealing with radical leftists. Marilynn Johnson's *Street Justice* praises as "truly significant" the implementation by NYPD commissioner Lewis Valentine during the late 1930s of La Guardia's policy of political tolerance, noting that "repression of Communist political activities dropped dramatically in 1937." Yet Johnson still assumes that whatever police indifference or violence continued to occur was politically unidirectional. In a force of 18,314 culled from the neighborhoods of cosmopolitan New York, there would have been officers who were leftists, officers who disliked Catholics, and officers who believed that Loyalists were fighting for American-style democracy.[16]

Blockade as a touchstone of political protest evidences a deepening national identity crisis during the summer of 1938, when the economy deteriorated at home, tensions mounted abroad, and *Blockade* moved out into New York's poorer, tougher neighborhoods. Supporting *Blockade* came to indicate a belief that international communism could uplift the downtrodden at home just as it took a courageous stand against fascist aggression abroad. Opposing the film showed a concern that Comintern propaganda was hoodwinking honest Americans as well as a willingness to oppose the New Deal order as something strangely alien. Fascism and communism in Spain—for both sides, respectively—became tropes for everything that was wrong in Depression-era America. With the greater confidence that the Spanish example of godless mobocracy running amok lent their arguments, Catholic immigrants, with the Irish in the vanguard, were claiming the high ground of Americanism, as a close reading of the *Tablet* report on the Fulton Street incident reveals.

New York's sidewalks belonged to "American citizens," and it was as "American citizens" that the ICTS's "Catholic-American" women intended to "exercise every one of their civil rights." When the women came under attack by a "Red mob," and police officers acted indifferently, "decent American bystanders" intervened. How far could America have descended, the *Tablet* asked, when "Reds could distribute their literature" but "American women" could not? ICTS auxiliaries were attempting to distribute "American literature" that called for "American Peace" and that urged "all Americans to unite in the task of keeping the United States out of war." As "every *real* American" ought to understand, the *Tablet* challenged, it was "the Reds and the Leftist Propagandists who wish to plunge this country into war." *Blockade* blockers were essentially arguing that the film's message was topsy-turvy: Marco's plea to the "conscience of the world" at the film's close was not an appeal to peace but to arms. Were not real Americans those who saw standing armies as anathema and war as the barbarism of Old World monarchies? Franco-supporting Irish Catholics, the *Tablet* implied, now represented real America, while those who would lift *Blockade*'s blockade and its synonymous arms embargo were un-American dupes of "[Earl] Browder, the Charlie McCarthy of Stalin" (who, like Edgar Bergen's popular ventriloquist dummy, drew listeners into a "safe little world of small boys' pranks" where there were "no unemployed men, no budget deficits, no marching dictators").[17]

In September, a protest almost turned violent outside Ditmar's Theatre in Queens, where a much larger group of a hundred pro-Franco picketers was trying to persuade moviegoers that *Blockade* was "communistic." Members of the Frente Popular Español de Queens provoked the confrontation by marching past the theater ahead of an ambulance they had purchased for shipment to the Loyalist zone holding placards attesting to the truth of "fascist bombing." Pro-Nationalists reacted angrily, shouting to let the air out of the ambulance's tires, and there was some minor "pushing and jostling" between partisans until a squad of nineteen police officers intervened. Still, during the time it took police to arrive from their precinct, the pro-Franco picketers—who may have outnumbered the pro-Loyalist marchers—never deflated the tires, let alone "vandalized" the ambulance, as the *New York Times* report insinuated. These incidents over *Blockade* demonstrate the deepening animosity and widening polarization between both sides in the Great Debate in the latter half of 1938.[18]

When F. Melder of the West Side News Agency in Grand Rapids, Michigan, wrote to the *Catholic Worker* to complain about the newspaper's picketing of Radio City, he stressed that "where the struggle of the Spanish people" was concerned, there could be "no such thing as working class neutrality." Melder would no longer distribute the "pro-fascist" *Catholic Worker* because, despite its title, it was not "in concurrence with the best interests of the working people nationally and internationally." American workers, Melder's language suggested, must understand the imperative of acting in the interest of international working-class solidarity. It was the duty of every exploited worker of the world to support embattled Madrid: Spain's cause was nonnegotiable. By contrast, since the civil war's outset, editor Callahan had translated distant Spain into a parochial context for his laboring Catholic readership, predominantly of metropolitan New Yorkers and most first- or second-generation immigrants, as were his two copicketers, Vishnewski and Zarella. They had crossed the Atlantic—metaphorically or physically—because America held promise that the lowest laborer could climb out of the gutter and make good.[19]

Callahan, Vishnewski, and Zarella, along with thousands of their fellow Irish, Lithuanian, and Italian Americans, found solace and developed working-class solidarity at first in the comforting rituals of the Catholic Church and later in their growing enthusiasm for, faith in, and politicization of traditional American values. Spain, for them, did not demonstrate the hope of liberal democracy but the despair of godless revolution, and unless they acted to expose the insidious fallacy of films like *Blockade,* then Madrid's slaughter of priests and destruction of churches was coming to their new home in New York City. Both sides of the Radio City incident assuredly missed its ironies. Marco's closing speech in *Blockade*—at least at face value—was a plea to end all wars, and Vishnewski and his fellow picketers were actually strict pacifists who advocated a neutral stand on Spain. Dorothy Day, moreover, the *Catholic Worker*'s founding inspiration and a former communist, espoused the French philosophy of personalism, which offered a compassionate, spiritual, and dynamic alternative to the harsh materialistic enjoinders of both capitalism and socialism. Far from being profascist, as Day explained to author Studs Terkel in 1970, the *Worker*'s staff espoused "more the anarchist's point of view." They had been "the first ones in the Church to oppose Mussolini and Hitler," and they had picketed the SS *Bremen* when it docked in Manhattan flying the Nazi flag.[20]

Spain in Arms

According to a *New York Times* report headed "Support [for] Social Films," Columbia University screened *Blockade* before a thousand students and faculty, after which an "overwhelming majority" voted that the picture was neither anti-American nor "subversive to democratic principles." Voters in Columbia's postscreening questionnaire also called for more films devoted to "social problems." Of concern to Franco lobbyists, though, was not the shortage of social films but their abundance. *Spain in Flames,* a compilation of newsreel footage by Dutch communist

Helen van Dongen with narration by John Dos Passos, was one of several documentaries available to pro-Loyalist groups for their fund-raising and promotional events, whereas pro-Nationalists could do no better than a few slide shows. Typically billed as mass meetings and held under the auspices of a principal association, events pushing one side or the other in Spain gained in grandness and frequency as well as bellicosity during 1938, especially in the New York–Jersey City area. On 21 March, for instance, New York's Italian Anti-Fascist Committee hosted a "Mass Protest Meeting" at West 55th Street's 2,750-seat Mecca Temple. "First Ethiopia and now Spain!" their handbill proclaimed and called for a protest against Benito Mussolini's "Invasion of Democratic Spain." Along with a screening of *Spain in Flames,* a panel of American political leaders gave speeches.[21]

When John Eoghan Kelly popped the handbill into his files, he might have wondered about the committee's understanding of the term *democracy.* Speakers included former International Workers of the World (IWW) poet-activist Arturo Giovannitti, radical socialist and Amalgamated Clothing Workers organizer Girolamo Valenti, former IWW and CPUSA member (later honored with a state funeral in Red Square) Elizabeth Gurley Flynn, and CPUSA member and Representative John T. Bernard of Minnesota's proto-communist Farmer-Labor Party. (In January 1937, Bernard cast the only vote in both houses against emergency provisions to the Neutrality Act, which embargoed arms to Spain.) But Kelly and other Franco lobbyists were soon to have cinematographic ammunition of their own.[22]

On 1 October 1938, Talbot and two colleagues, Maurice Ahern of Fordham University and Talbot's lawyer, John J. M. O'Shea, met with Konstantin Maydell, a German-speaking Estonian who had fled his homeland after fighting the Red Army in 1919. Maydell explained that he was working with the Berlin office of a Spanish outfit, Hispano Films, to import a pro-Franco documentary, *Spain in Arms,* which he felt would be ideal to show at Talbot's America Spanish Relief Fund gatherings. Talbot expressed interest, so Maydell cabled Berlin, and a 16-mm print of the film duly arriving via diplomatic pouch a week later. Under an atmosphere of secrecy, Cárdenas, publisher of *Spain* magazine Miguel Echegaray, Talbot, O'Shea, and Ahern attended a private screening on 11 October in Manhattan. Although the film had a German soundtrack, the assembled company agreed that its visuals worked well. Talbot deemed it "excellent for the purpose" and "magnificent, on the whole" and thought the "impact of the propaganda" was "terrific." Even though Cárdenas had sent the film back to Berlin by the following day, Maydell persuaded a group of investors, primarily Col. Pierpont M. Hamilton, great-great-grandson of Alexander Hamilton and the son-in-law of banker/industrialist John Pierpont Morgan, along with another Morgan relative, nephew Morehead Patterson, to finance a company, Film Facts, Inc., to handle the importation and distribution of a version with an English soundtrack. While Maydell surely inflated a claim to have spent $17,000 by December, start-up costs were at least $8,000 ($250,000), including $950 for a 35-mm negative.[23]

Financing for *Spain in Arms,* a private endeavor by necessity, highlights an important contrast between the propagandizing capabilities of the Great Debate's contending parties. Cárdenas's unofficial embassy kept up appearances with a suite at the Ritz-Carlton, and there was sufficient funding to make *Spain* magazine a high-quality production, but other than incidentals, like lecturers' stipends, Cárdenas's budget allowed for little else. Pro-Loyalist endeavors, though, enjoyed almost unlimited funds. In a *Boston Advertiser* article of January 1939, Kelly estimated that Loyalist ambassador Fernando de los Ríos alone had handled $45 million ($1.35 billion). Adding the 175 million pesetas wired by the Bank of Spain to Ríos Urruti before January 1938 ($12–20 million at a deteriorating conversion rate of 8.7–14), $14 million in confiscated gold and jewelry redeemed in America, $2 million in fund-raising, and the $14 million of illicit silver purchases by Henry Morgenthau Jr.'s Treasury Department indicates the reasonableness of Kelly's figure.[24]

Spain in Arms had two European progenitors, a Spanish version, *España Heroica* (Heroic Spain), and a German version, *Helden in Spanien* (Spanish Heroes). Soundtracks took the form of one or two narrow celluloid strips carrying a black-on-clear analog wave pattern, which the engineer spliced to one edge of the main filmstrip with acetone cement. This technology allowed Film Facts to retain the original German orchestral score but replace the German-language narration; the engineer would have cut off the outer strip, and then spliced back on a new strip with the prerecorded English commentary. Although no complete copy of *Spain in Arms* has survived, it is nonetheless possible to evaluate this unique Spanish Civil War artifact. Three full reels and two half-reels of a 35-mm print of *Spain in Arms* (probably seized from Maydell by the FBI in 1943) passed into the files of Martin Dies's House Un-American Activities Committee, so a digitized copy of one-third of the film is now available for viewing. Reconstructing the content of the missing footage is also possible. A detailed shot-by-shot list of the entire film is extant, as is a script by foreign correspondent H. E. Knoblaugh for a new soundtrack added in 1940 when then-owner Michael P. Grace donated the film to the University of Notre Dame.[25]

As Talbot had appreciated, overall production quality was high, facilitated by a German budget that extended to annotated maps and a full orchestral score. Short, fixed-focal-length clips of rarely more than five seconds interspersed crowd adulation with marching troops, or generals at plotting tables with frontline sniping. Alternating scenes of high contrast and varied lighting, while rousing martial music played in the background, created a style similar to Leni Riefenstahl's *Triumph of the Will* (1935). What set *Spain in Arms* apart was its riveting live-action footage, much of it captured from Loyalist camera crews. Many Americans had some exposure to Movietone newsreels of the fall of Shanghai's International Settlement to the Japanese in November 1937, as well as newsreels from Spain's civil war; yet, while audiences no doubt found Movietone's shots of "sky bombing" or "aerial terrorism" disturbing in their realism, scenes of actual combat were rare. Audiences surely noticed that a camera crew had staged a clip of a Loyalist soldier struck by a Nationalist bullet during the defense of Madrid, for, apart from the bright lighting and absence of blood, few people killed instantly by a .303 slug to the head can think to put their hand to their face before falling. *Spain in Arms'* director emphasized the distinction between what Franco supporters often called the "Two Spains," contrasting the history, culture, and pastoral tranquility of a traditional Spain with the anarchic modernity of a communist Spain. Reel I featured Spanish castles, winding roads on "rugged terrain," and "rugged royal palms," as the shot-by-shot list described them, followed by scenes of plowing, reaping, and threshing. Reel II, by contrast, showed communist rallies, street mobs, corpses of rightist victims, church burnings, and a six-man firing squad symbolically executing Christ in the Statue of the Sacred Heart on Madrid's Hill of Angels. Such sensational material must have provided a stark contrast with the make-believe world of *Blockade*.[26]

Audiences must have found the many scenes of actual combat especially gripping to watch. Shots of Franco's forces advancing on the Madrid University campus in November 1936 alternated with captured footage taken by an International Brigade cameraman on the other side of the lines. Perfect lighting and a tripod-steady picture are evidence that the director posed a shot or two of Nationalist riflemen but that the bulk of the footage was live action. It was grainy, jittery, sometimes washed out, and loud. Anxious-looking Loyalists burst from dugouts still smoking cigarettes. Nationalist infantry with tank support scampered over open ground under heavy fire. Loyalists fired through sandbagged loopholes and popped up to toss grenades. A wounded soldier fell off a parapet onto a dead comrade. Loaders jammed clips into smoking machine guns. Nationalists leaped over a berm and down into the trench below, running past the doomed cameraman who continued filming. A shell exploded between two Loyalist gun crews, wounding or killing at least one of the gunners.[27]

There was no mistaking the destruction in Teruel (a crossroads city in southern Aragón that changed hands three times during the winter of 1937–38) in reel VIII or the devastation around Madrid's University City in reel V, yet panoramic shots of Madrid itself, with no damage to be seen, skillfully conveyed the message that Franco had been careful to preserve Spain's national heritage. International Brigade volunteers inevitably emerged from the film in a poor light. Shots taken by their own photographers showed them eating heartily while haggard *madrileñas* foraged for firewood; they relaxed while civilians—"pressed into service," according to the narrator—dug fortifications. Volunteers slugged port straight from a cask as a muted trumpet from the orchestra mocked the slack-jawed laughter of inebriated soldiers. Throughout the film, the orchestral score acted as a cue to the identity of the combatants, switching from pleasant melodies and patriotic refrains when Nationalists were on camera to comical discords and irritating riffs whenever Loyalist troops appeared. Effective, too, no doubt, were the director's efforts to counter charges in the mass media of Nationalist atrocities. Live footage showed the Loyalist bombing of a civilian target and its tragic aftermath. Franco's police lowered casualties from the windows of shattered homes, a woman clutching her baby wailed in a debris-strewn street, and Sisters of Mercy tended to the victims in a hospital with broken windows. This air raid seems to have been after the taking of Málaga in February 1937 by Gen. Gonzalo Queipo de Llano's army, when a Loyalist squadron led by André Malraux, the French Marxist writer, attempted to slow—or punish—Nationalist units in their pursuit of fleeing Loyalists.[28]

Mass support from Spaniards in liberated urban areas appeared genuine enough in the film. Dense crowds thronged Seville's streets as Nationalists paraded past amid much clapping, waving, and exultant cheering. Only in the Basque country— where Catholics had made the fateful decision to cast their lot with Madrid's Republic in the hope of achieving independence—did the film show windows bereft of cheering women and glum pedestrians padding the sidewalk as a Nationalist army streamed through a town, probably Bilbao after its fall in June 1937. Yet even here, *Spain in Arms* could still stand in counterpoint to *Blockade,* for one extended sequence of eighteen shots showed Basque children, whom the Loyalists had destined for evacuation to England, reuniting with their joyful parents, followed by a short clip of "refugees returning to their homes loaded with household goods." Street scenes—and increasingly so toward the war's end—depicted straight-arm, fascist-style waving from the crowd; during a sequence showing Franco visiting the fleet at Castellón, near Valencia, in June 1938, sailors in the crowd greeted their Generalísimo's cavalcade with right arms raised. Fascist imagery was also apparent in the annotated maps featured in the film; to indicate Nationalist advances, the director used the Falangist yoke-and-arrows, a symbol appropriated by the Falange Española Tradicionalista y de las JONS from 1469 when it represented the marriage of Queen Isabella (*yugo*) to Ferdinand (*flechas*).[29]

Yet if the intention of Berlin's Hispano-Film-Produktion company was to portray Nationalist Spain as a proud and willing member of Europe's Axis, then its director ultimately failed, for no amount of crowd adulation could compensate for Franco's self-evident lack of charisma as well as his apparent distaste for Nazi propriety. Far from a studied Hitler or a theatrical Mussolini, Franco—short, dumpy, his arms flaccid at his sides—waddled ducklike from shot to shot, with a warm yet prosaic smile here and a wooden handshake or regular army salute there. From the many candid shots of Franco and his officers, it was clear that Nationalist forces habitually saluted in traditional manner, with the palm to the eyebrow. Only once in the film was there any inkling of the sort of cult of personality that so characterized the totalitarian regimes of Germany or Italy, and that was when Queipo de Llano paraded his men through the thronged streets of Seville and a woman wrapped an arm around the tall, handsome general's neck and kissed him.

Enhancing the film's documentary quality was its English narration. Hammond, who wrote the script with Maydell, pulled off a coup in hiring Edward Herlihy, whose clipped elocution, resonant baritone, hint of an Irish brogue, and studious narration of Henry Robinson Luce's documentary series *The March of Time* had made his voice one of the most well-known and respected of the 1930s. In developing the soundtrack, which they recorded at the Ritz-Carlton, Hammond and Maydell were careful to avoid polemics, to match observations to visual content, and, in general, to convey a sense of detached objectivity. Shortly after Herlihy narrated "Málaga is liberated—a jubilant populace greets Franco's army," the camera swiveled from a crowd overview to focus on three women wildly clapping and cheering. When Herlihy stated matter-of-factly "Men, women, and children driven out of the city by Red anarchy return to Málaga," the camera showed proud Spaniards leading laden-down mules and then moved in for an appealing close-up of a young boy hugging his baby brother.[30]

Philip Liebmann's Crisis of Americanism

By December 1938, Konstantin Maydell's Film Facts had a midtown office, funding from backer Hamilton, versions of *Spain in Arms* in both 16-mm and 35-mm formats (for rent at $25–60 a showing and for sale at $300 [$9,000] a copy), and John Eoghan Kelly working as a commissioned salesman. When Kelly described the film to fellow AUNS committee member Ellery Sedgwick, he enthused about its "remarkable battle scenes outdoing anything that ever came from Hollywood" and noted that Loyalist forces had killed in action three of its fifty-five cameramen. For a one-man promoter working part time, Kelly had considerable success, selling at least three prints to institutions and individuals, arranging more than thirty showings at meeting halls across the country, and screening *Spain in Arms* to mass audiences in Boston and New York. Upward of 23,000 pro-Franco Americans watched the film between January and July of 1939.[31]

Woolworth Donohue, an heir to the Woolworth five-and-dime fortune, purchased a 16-mm print of *Spain in Arms*. Boston's Bishop Richard T. Cushing bought a copy, intending to show it in diocesan schools; but, as Cushing explained during an FBI interview in 1942, the film's excessive "blood and thunder and shooting" rendered it unsuitable for small children. A third customer was the flamboyant brewery executive Philip Liebmann, who spent $300 so that he could show the film at home.[32]

Brewing and advertising were two of the most profitable sectors of the economy during the late Depression, and Liebmann Breweries excelled at both. Twenty-one-year-old Philip Liebmann joined the family firm founded by great-grandfather Samuel, who fled Germany after the failed revolutions of 1848, in 1936 straight out of the University of Pennsylvania's Wharton business school. Liebmann's flair for marketing was the perfect complement to the production expertise of Dr. Hermann Schülein, formerly of Munich's Löwenbräu and a refugee from the Nazi Party's anti-Semitic persecution. Their brainchild was Rheingold

Beer and an annual Miss Rheingold beauty contest, which together generated revenues that expanded the Brooklyn plant to cover seven city blocks with buildings as high as sixteen stories by 1950. Liebmann was a tall, well-built man with eccentric habits, expensive tastes, and a smile for everyone. Never having learned to shave, he visited a barber daily, and when not marching through the city with breathless executives in tow, he traveled in his chauffeured Rolls Royce. After discovering chocolate mousse while vacationing in Paris, he had a fifty-pound tub of it hauled onto his liner so he could gorge himself all the way back to Manhattan. Prone to emotional outbursts, his mood might swing from raucous laughter to floods of tears and back to smiles a minute later. Liebmann's romantic attachments were no less colorful, with one-year marriages to starlet Dorothy Temple and actress Linda Darnell.[33]

Liebmann's parents socialized in a narrow circle of moneyed and largely secular Jewish families and groomed their son for success in the family business, a recipe for a classic Eriksonian identity crisis. Soon after college, Liebmann began to find it "very distasteful to be a Jew," as his sister recalls. He did everything he could to "separate himself from the Jewish point of view," even if he could "never deny" the Jewishness "in his heart." At some point in 1937 or early 1938, he heard Fulton J. Sheen on the radio, met the charismatic preacher with the deep black eyes and captivating voice soon after, and converted. Catholicism became Liebmann's new persona, and most publicly, too, much to the chagrin of his family and friends. Striding up crowded 5th Avenue a few yards behind his father Alfred one day, Liebmann threw his hands in the air and screamed, "F-a-t-h-e-r!" Alfred swung around, expecting a rapprochement, but son Philip was already running past him toward a shocked-looking Catholic priest further up the block. Supporting Franco was a natural progression, for Liebmann loved to hold court, arguing politics with all comers. His loud harangues against President Roosevelt and praise of Franco angered his left-leaning and vehemently antifascist father, just as they were naturally "alien to the rest of the family," as his sister remembered with evident regret sixty-seven years later. At the same time, Liebmann was so gregarious, so much larger than life, that people could not help but be drawn to him.[34]

It is tempting to interpret Liebmann's motives as his way of striking back at domineering parents, or identifying with Catholic workers at the brewery, or even winning over Catholic customers. But this would be too cynical. Liebmann's sister recalled her brother's "mystical" streak and reverent Catholicism. Although he exhibited a typical playfulness in his support for Franco (as in naming his string of dogs Carmencita after Franco's daughter), Liebmann devoted most of his pro-Nationalist energies to the organization and funding of an aid organization for the supply of medicine and hospital equipment to Spain. That he did this after the conclusion of hostilities in May 1939 suggests a genuine altruism in the tradition of Jewish philanthropy. While Liebmann is the only Jewish—or ex-Jewish may be more apt—Franco lobbyist I have been able to identify, a Gallup survey on 16 December 1938, one month after Kristallnacht, indicated that there were upward of 8,000 Jewish Franco supporters.[35]

There may yet have been a deep ulterior motive—deeper than distaste for Jewishness or spiritual yearning—behind Liebmann's conversion to Catholicism and concomitant support for Franco's Christian crusade. Considerable evidence thus far has shown that Franco lobbyists seized every opportunity to contrast their American virtues on one hand with the alien characteristics of pro-Loyalists on the other. Pro-Franco Catholics, in particular, could push this national identity–bolstering project to rhetorical banality, as with the repetitious use of *American* in the *Tablet* report on the Fulton Street *Blockade* protest. Catholic immigrants, this evidence suggests, were coming to realize the possibilities within their adopted culture for conflating Catholicism with Americanism. They were beginning to appreciate that by parlaying their religious heritage into pro-Franco anticommunism, they could raise Catholicism to the level of patriotic endeavor: arguing for Franco was their ticket to superpatriotism.[36]

Local Screenings of Spain in Arms

Spain in Arms, which was typically accompanied by a lecture, reached audiences in church halls, civic auditoriums, and clubhouses across the country. While attendance at these thirty-plus screenings is difficult to gauge, an average of three hundred attendees a night is a conservative estimate. Whenever Kelly took responsibility for a screening, he arranged with a local Bell & Howell representative to supply a projector equipped for sound and a folding screen, along with a projectionist to run the equipment and load the reels. He made sure that local organizers had adequate publicity and had invited dignitaries from the area. He would also give a short lecture before the showing on either communism in Spain or the war's military aspects, depending on his audience. For a screening in Washington, D.C., on 7 March 1939, through the auspices of the National Catholic Welfare Conference, he reminded the NCWC's Michael J. Ready to invite former ambassador to Spain Irwin Laughlin and diocesan chancellor Joseph M. Nelligan, and he telephoned Archbishop Michael J. Curley with a view to arranging a subsequent screening in Baltimore.[37]

Joseph Markoe of the Men's Club of St. Luke's Church, St. Paul, Minnesota, and Mary Elizabeth Dunn of the United Christian Platoons, Hartford, Connecticut, must have anticipated large audiences for their showings, for they rented spacious halls and screened *Spain in Arms* twice on consecutive evenings. Not all the screenings were open to the public. Liebmann showed his personal copy to a group of mostly White Russian Americans at the Women's National Republican

Club of Manhattan. Brother P. Rosenecker showed the film at the priests' residence of St. Joseph's College, Philadelphia. *Spain in Arms,* Rosenecker told an FBI agent three years later, "vividly portrayed with unforgettable realism the fate of a republic that permits Communism to gain a foothold in its government." And Capt. Edward J. F. Glavin, who later ran the U.S. Army's psychological warfare operations during the Korean conflict, showed the film to officers of New York's Second Corps Area on the Governor's Island army base.[38]

Sometimes church, military, and student interests combined, as when the Reverend N. A. Steffan screened *Spain in Arms* in the 375-seat St. Joseph's Auditorium at Loras College, Dubuque, Iowa, under the auspices of the local Knights of Columbus, and the speaker was the Reverend Dr. Mathias Martin Hoffman, a professor of modern European political science and a U.S. Army chaplain with the rank of major. Loras College's students promoted *Spain in Arms* on the front page of their newspaper as "the first film giving both sides of the Spanish war," by which *The Lorian* meant the Nationalist side. Unlike *Blockade,* which had "omitted facts unfavorable to the Red cause," students would now be able to see "Moscow provocateurs preaching class hatred among the Spanish workingmen," the distribution of Soviet arms "to inflamed, bloodthirsty mobs and the resultant anarchy," such as the "public desecration of sacred images"—the symbolic execution of the Sacred Heart on Madrid's Hill of Angels—and "whole city squares covered with the bodies of patriots, priests and civilians, women and children," just some of the "40,000 slaughtered immediately after the Red coup d'etat in 1936." Although director of public relations Father Harry Long oversaw *The Lorian*'s publication, its editor, Joseph Egelhof, and his twenty staff members were students. Sentiment among Loras College's 950 male undergraduates evidently backed the Nationalists in the Great Debate.[39]

William B. Disco of Watertown, Connecticut, exemplifies an organizer who screened *Spain in Arms* to church-based groups. During an interview in January 1943 by FBI agent Edward S. Pritchard, Reverend Disco explained that he showed the film at St. John's School to the local Holy Name Society not only out of an interest in the Spanish Civil War but also because he had visited Spain as a tourist and wanted to see how it had changed. Disco paid the $25 rental ($750) out of his own pocket. He recalled that the film "struck him as being an attack on Communists," because it showed that "Communists had injured the Catholic religion," destroyed old Spanish missions, and abused priests and nuns. In response to Agent Pritchard's leading questions about the film being Falangist, fascist, or Nazi propaganda, Disco agreed that were he to view it now—a year after Pearl Harbor—he might construe it as such, but at the time of the showing in May 1939 he "did not think of it in that light," since the United States was not yet at war and Americans were "not thinking along those lines."[40]

The Great Pro-American Mass Meeting, February 1939

By far the largest audiences to see *Spain in Arms* were at the Boston Opera House on the evenings of 15 and 16 February and at Manhattan's 7th Regiment Armory on Sunday, 19 February 1939. Around six thousand Bostonians and eleven thousand New Yorkers attended these events, which organizers timed to coincide with the patriotic celebrations of Washington's Birthday. Clare Singer Dawes was the event organizer in Boston, at which both Kelly and Alexander Hamilton Rice gave speeches to capacity audiences. For Manhattan's Great Pro-American Mass Meeting, as the event's Committee for Americanism and Neutrality billed it, Merwin K. Hart acted as chairman, although Kelly as secretary did much of the legwork and AUNS handled finances. Included among the thirty-four leading sponsors, whose names crowded the left margin of the event's promotional stationary, were philanthropists (Anne Morgan, Theodore Starr Jr.), lawyers (Arthur T. O'Leary, Knowlton Durham), business executives (Philip M. Allen, Walter M. Walters), editors (Ward Clarke, Patrick F. Scanlan), and educators (Ross J. S. Hoffman, Vincent F. Holden). Boasting the event as New York's "largest and the most interesting patriotic meeting" since the Great War, and *Spain in Arms* as the "most exciting" war picture ever filmed, handbills touted a threefold message: "Keep America out of War," "Preserve Neutrality," and "Combat Communism." Manhattan's landmark 7th Regiment Armory, built in 1877 as an imposing citadel from which National Guard militia could set off to quell civil unrest, was the ideal venue for a pro-Franco rally. Kelly, whose reserve officer rank the army had just elevated to major, was instrumental in obtaining permission from Col. Ralph C. Tobin, the 7th's commanding officer, whose sole condition was that promotional material satisfied an army regulation prohibiting any mention of a foreign nation's name. When Tobin wrote to Hart confirming the booking, he added personally that he was "very happy to grant your request."[41]

As an Episcopalian and a brigadier general in France after the Normandy landings, Tobin might not seem the most natural of Franco supporters in the spring of 1939. Energetic, outspoken, individualistic, yet fiercely patriotic, Tobin epitomized the Jeffersonian producerist American. He thought of his thousand-strong "Old 7th"—the oldest National Guard in the country, with its elegant historic headquarters and its eighteenth-century uniform of white trousers, gray frock coat, white cross belts, and brass-studded shako—as an independent militia and certainly not as a standing army. When he paraded his Old 7th down 5th Avenue in 1938 en route to its annual divine service at St. Thomas's Protestant Episcopal Church, he did not march at its head but followed behind the regiment's crucifer sergeant, who bore a large silver cross. He paraded his militia through Manhattan with colors flying and band playing, but without rifles or side arms. Tobin openly tangled in the press with Mayor La Guardia, to whom he made clear that his only allegiance was to the state governor as commander-in-chief. Not content with politicizing his leadership of the 7th, he parlayed his military standing into the civil arena, becoming president of the Retail Wine and Liquor Guild to lobby against the monopolistic practices of large distillers. Neither was he any friend to the New Deal, which he saw as oppressing entrepreneurs with burdensome taxation. In a letter printed in the *New York Times*, Tobin quarreled with the city planning commissioner for blaming the international economy for America's ills when the problem really lay at home. "One outrageous tax situation after another" was the real reason that small businesses were fleeing the city, he claimed, their interests "victimized by [the] power politics" of "noisy, articulate and highly organized minorities," by which Tobin meant the kind of noisy minorities that Franco was battling in Spain.[42]

Tobin's faith in his country's founding past—its struggles and accomplishments, myths and heroes, ideals and laws—explains his empathy with Franco. Tobin conflated Franco's effort to save historic Spain with his own mission to safeguard historic America from the ravages of the Great Depression and the subversive activities of a highly organized Communist International. In trying to explain U.S. intervention in Vietnam, Frances FitzGerald claims that "Americans ignore history, for to them everything has always seemed new under the sun." Yet history had so steeped Tobin's psyche—as it had the thousands of New Yorkers who watched his Old 7th on parade, its silver cross and archaic brass-studded hats glinting that bright October morning in 1938—as to become a civil religion. Americans, furthermore, FitzGerald persists, have never known "serious ideological struggle." Yet it was precisely because the historically constructed Americanism of patriotic pro-Nationalists was so fundamentally at odds with the futuristic communism of pro-Loyalists that the Great Debate over Spain became such a serious ideological struggle—so serious, in fact, that its cold war synthesis actually embroiled America in Vietnam two decades later. Yes, Tobin was reacting against communism, just as he sought to preserve traditional values. But where Tobin, Kelly, and perhaps even Merwin Hart, whom historian Justus D. Doenecke labels "an arch-rightist," were conservative thinkers, it was in the narrow context of preserving the vitality of Depression-era America from what they judged to be the dogma of illiberal communism.[43]

Police estimated that more than ten thousand New Yorkers had packed into the armory's cathedral-like Drill Hall by 4:00 P.M., and the number was probably closer to the twelve thousand estimated by the *Herald Tribune*. Eleven hundred paid $1.10 for seats on a platform that ringed the perimeter and in galleries at each end, and the rest—paying 40¢ for reserved or 25¢ for general admission—stood shoulder to shoulder in roped-off areas on either side of an aisle leading to the speaker's platform. After commissions to ticket agencies, receipts generated $1,834, and because the band never presented a bill, this covered $1,828 ($55,000) of expenses. Hart, who presided, as well as Hammond, Rice, and Catholic educator Joseph F. Thorning all gave speeches. Hart spoke first, with an attack on communism. His mention that Adolf Hitler and Mussolini had driven Marxists out of their countries drew applause, but he was quick to condemn Nazism as un-American. "American people will never long tolerate in [their] midst uniformed persons"—a pointed reference to New York Bundists—"who openly take their cue from the head of any foreign government." Now that the Nationalists had virtually won, Hart linked the necessity of recognizing Franco's regime to the continued success of the Monroe Doctrine, for America's (presumably weak) "neighbors to the south" needed the example of resolution in the north in their fight against encroaching communism. Hammond then took the microphone to describe the social anarchy and political infighting of prewar Spain, stressing that Franco would finally unite Spaniards under a stable government. Rice's speech expanded on the civil war's origins, which he summarized as Christianity and civilization against communism and atheism. Rice was explaining how Franco's new government of Spaniards would restore law and order when Christian Front activists carried in a large picture of Father Charles E. Coughlin. Whether the Fronters had only just arrived or became bored with Rice's scholarly presentation is unclear, but the response elicited by Coughlin's picture drowned out the speaker for several minutes. Still, the *New York Times* journalist was sufficiently objective to report that the applause "did not seem to be general."[44]

Thorning, a professor of sociology and a contributor to *Spain* magazine, gave the concluding speech, in which he called for genuine neutrality and urged Americans to adopt a "peace psychology." Although Thorning probably intended the phrase at face value, peace psychology in the context of the pro-Nationalist *Spain in Arms* made a nice counterpoint to the war psychology of correspondent Edward Grant in the pro-Loyalist *Blockade*. Hart then proposed resolutions that Congress must adhere to strict neutrality, prohibit secret agreements that privileged foreign powers, and recognize Franco's government, each of which received a unanimous show of hands. He also read a telegram of greeting from pro-Franco New York transit workers.[45]

At this point, according to newspaper reports, a Christian Front leader strode to the speaker's stand and shouted, "There is a telegram here from General Franco. We want it read." In fact, it was not a Fronter but a member of Cárdenas's staff, and it was Cárdenas, no doubt, who had asked Franco to send the congratulatory telegram. Hart, as well as Hildreth Meière, who as AUNS treasurer was handling the event's finances, had heard about the telegram and knew that it constituted a political message, which if given at a public hearing would compromise their arrangement with Tobin. Hart therefore denied that any such telegram existed. There was some shouting when friends of Cárdenas's staffer came to the stand in his support, but Hart prevailed on the police to escort them from the armory, leaving the press to conclude, falsely, that they were rabble-rousing Christian Fronters. This marked the only incident of the rally, and it is noteworthy for such a large political gathering that Monday's newspapers could report no rowdy behavior associated with the event. Also of note is that the only speeches listed in newspaper accounts were by Hart, Hammond, Rice, and Thorning.[46]

Yet *New York Herald Tribune* reporter Bob Shaplen told a different story in a press release he prepared for the New York Coordinating Committee for Democratic Action (an antifascist organization backed by B'nai B'rith and headed by Maurice Rosenblatt), which Shaplen addressed to the U.S. attorney general and leaked prematurely to FBI assistant director P. E. Foxworth. After mentioning—somewhat correctly—that Kelly "organized" the mass meeting, Shaplen stated that Kelly had "consolidated the persons attending" into "storm-trooper platoons" and then "launched a campaign of violence and terror on the streets of our city." What makes Shaplen's claim to be presenting "facts" and "evidence" all the more suspect is that Kelly was actually in Boston at the time, where he had remained after the opera house screenings to deliver a series of lectures. At 8:00 P.M., at about the moment when he was supposedly launching his campaign of terror against New York's Jews, he was launching into a major speech, entitled "Subversive Elements," at an event organized by Mrs. Dawes at Boston College's Chestnut Hill auditorium.[47]

During their prosecution of the Kelly case, FBI chiefs, from J. Edgar Hoover down, never bothered to corroborate or crosscheck witness testimony, so they consistently reported speculation as evidence and hearsay as fact. Konstantin Maydell told Agents Joseph T. Boston and Albert H. Cote that Kelly was not only present at the armory but also gave a speech "on the background of the Spanish War" that "definitely favored the Franco side." Boston and Cote took the deposition in February 1943 while Maydell was imprisoned in Maryland's Fort Howard "as a dangerous enemy alien" and was no doubt fearful for his future. On the false assumption that organizer Kelly would have been at his own meeting, Maydell presumably concocted the story to please his interrogators, basing it on other Kelly speeches that he had heard. Evidence also shows how Hoover's FBI, under pressure from Roosevelt to smother dissenting opinion, relied on biased and invariably erroneous reports by pro-Loyalist informants and at least two agents provocateurs to build its case against Franco lobbyists. These reports, taken at face value by three generations of scholars, have hitherto provided the sole basis for the accepted historical account.[48]

7

Franco Lobbyists and the Christian Front

In the electric geopolitical environment of 1938–39, when so many anxious underemployed Americans had time on their hands, there was an explosion of social activism, soapbox oratory, mimeographed newssheets, and politicized organizations. Labels of all kinds proliferated, from Bundists to Trotskyites, Peace Crusaders to Christian Defenders. A label became a badge of honor, a part of one's identity, easy to acquire by tagging along to a meeting with an enthusiastic friend yet hard to slough off once social commitments were in place. Activists might join an organization without fully understanding its ideology only to discover that aspects of its ideology clashed with other positions they espoused, or the organization might harden or change its position soon after they joined. So much seemed at stake. So much was in flux. Activists at the time struggled to reconcile their conflicting opinions, and historians ever since have wrestled to force their actors into neat boxes—none more so than the Franco supporters and Christian Fronters of metropolitan New York, many of whom were transit workers, longshoremen, or musicians. When an Irish Catholic trade unionist argued with a Jewish communist trade unionist over U.S. foreign policy toward Spain, both staked their claims on being thoroughly American, just as both hoped to become more American in the process.

When American Union for Nationalist Spain committee members organized the screening of *Spain in Arms* at their Great Pro-American Mass Meeting at Manhattan's 7th Regiment Armory in February 1939, they arranged to sell tickets through four independent agencies around the city, one of which their handbill advertised as "The Christian Front, Manhattan." Kelly spoke at another Great Pro-American Mass Meeting in Manhattan in May, when one of twelve sponsoring organizations was, again, "The Christian Front." Also in May, Kelly screened *Spain in Arms* and gave a speech to three hundred New Yorkers at the Tri-Boro Palace in the Bronx, a meeting held under the auspices of "The Christian Front." According to an FBI informant, Kelly addressed a Christian Front meeting at Donovan's Bar on West 59th Street, where he urged Fronters to "get ready for action to take con-trol of the Federal Government." And he joined a mixed group of several hundred men, women, and children, many of whom were Christian Fronters, to picket the premises of WMCA after that radio station refused to air Father Coughlin's weekly address. Prevailing historiography conceives only of a monolithic Coughlin-directed organization called the Christian Front, whose predominant characteris-tic was violent anti-Semitism, so it is important to evaluate the substance behind these connections.[1]

Historians understandably condemn Christian Fronters. After Pearl Harbor, Americans invested $318 billion and 405,000 lives fighting "the Good War," as Studs Terkel put it, against Nazis whose defining crime was the Holocaust, and Americans have taken pride in their society's record of combating anti-Semitism through legislation, in backing the Jewish state of Israel, and by instituting mul-ticulturalism ever since. When Coughlin broadcast his populist "Declaration of Independence" from "financial Toryism" in 1935, he blamed Protestant "Morgans" alongside Jewish "Rothschilds" and "Baruchs" for the country's poverty and social unrest, but by the summer of 1938, his harangues were singling out Jewish bank-ing houses. Coughlin then lent his support to the concept of a Christian Front at a time when some Irish American Catholics calling themselves Christian Fronters, primarily in New York but also in Boston and a few other cities, began distributing anti-Semitic literature, boycotting Jewish-owned businesses, insulting Jews with soapbox oratory, engaging in street corner altercations with Jews, and even form-ing a Nazi-inspired militia. Yet, extrapolating from these observations a blanket condemnation of all Christian Fronters would be as erroneous as concluding that all Popular Fronters were card-carrying communist revolutionaries.[2]

Rather than contrasting bigoted hooligans on one side with rational liberals on the other, it is productive to appreciate that this small window provides a refresh-ing, if disturbing, view of grass-roots American democracy at its best and brashest, with both sides passionate in their beliefs and both sides flinging invective as well as the odd rotten tomato. Christian and Popular Fronters alike were fighting for the soul of Americanism, although they had quite different ideas of what its char-acter ought to be. Both sides, too, had to think on their feet and adapt their posi-tions to fast-changing international events. Kristallnacht, the Nazi seizure of the Slovakian rump state, and especially the Nazi-Soviet Non-Aggression Pact were just three of the watersheds that complicated the snug preexisting division be-tween anticommunist isolationists and pro-socialist interventionists, who, in the vital East Coast metropolises, were predominantly of either Catholic or Jewish im-migrant stock, respectively. Pro-Nationalists' defense mechanism argument—that fascism abroad, a benign polity rejuvenating economies and keeping order, only arose as a welcome antidote to godless communism—was looking untenable. Pro-Loyalists found their case—that Soviet communists had built a model workers' paradise while single-handedly rolling back fascist aggression—equally problematic. Activists on both sides had invested so much of their lives staking out these opposing claims that their identities had taken on the character of their positions. With pro-Loyalists fearing fascist aggression abroad and pro-Nationalists sensing communist revolution at home, they now had to work doubly hard to justify their positions. Tensions mounted, rhetoric edged from provocative to confrontational, debaters switched their attentions from elite magazines to street corners, and the political Center fell away.[3]

Some Franco lobbyists, like Ellery Sedgwick, tired of this public and acrimonious Great Debate. Those that remained, none more so than Kelly, delighted in its political energy. In striving to defend Americanism from what he saw as the fast-growing menace of Soviet communism, Kelly began occupying an increasingly radical position. Or, rather, he took conservative positions that appeared radical—both at the time and to himself, were he honest about it—but which, within a decade, would become the mainstream cold war liberal consensus. In reacting to the Comintern's pro-Loyalist propaganda, AUNS lobbyists became a vanguard for those who unwittingly remade interwar Americanism into a modern, globally hegemonic ideology.[4]

Justus D. Doenecke, the leading historian of isolationism, describes the Christian Front as "Father Coughlin's paramilitary group." While this is an accurate representation of Joseph E. McWilliams's two dozen or so armed Christian Mobilizers of the summer of 1939, it oversimplifies the activities of a wide range of faith-based anticommunist groups, comprising some quarter-million patriotic Americans who briefly adopted "Christian Front" as a catchphrase or claimed to belong to a Christian Front of such-and-such an area. There never was a cohesive national Christian Front organization in the United States, nor was there any kind of central committee, fund-raising mechanism, or membership structure. What it meant to be a Christian Fronter varied across groups and over time, from the concept's faint beginnings in the spring of 1938 to its marginalization just two years later. Adoptees of the Christian Front label in the New York area—who were always anticommunist, predominantly Catholic, and typically pro-Franco, but sometimes in a nominal sense—tended to follow either an intellectual religious or a blue-collar lay path. These began in parallel but soon diverged, as groups treading the latter path lost whatever ideological relevance they had earlier claimed. In the crisis-ridden atmosphere of mid-1939, some lay groups seeking power and legitimacy found it convenient to overlap with or borrow from Nazi Bundists, themselves eager to muscle in on Front activity, just as they tended to attract the unemployed and disillusioned who reduced complex political issues to basic ethnic rivalries. Yet given New York's record of gang warfare, and the transatlantic backdrop that linked communists and Jews statistically as well as through the fabled *Protocols of the Elders of Zion*, there was surprisingly little serious trouble and even less actual violence. Anti-Semitic "hoodlums," the term used by journalists and police, were often bored teenagers or preteens acting out their parents' ancient prejudices on the street.[5]

Christian Front historiography has relied uncritically on reports filed at the time by investigators working for Jewish organizations, such as the American Jewish Committee (AJC) or Samuel Untermyer's Non-Sectarian Anti-Nazi League to Champion Human Rights, who made sure to find rabid anti-Semitism lurking wherever they looked. Further hindering objective analysis are the motives and behavior of the FBI itself. Even the case against Joseph McWilliams's Mobilizers, or, to be more precise, the seventeen defendants of John (Jack) F. Cassidy's fresh-faced, business-suited militia arrested by the FBI in January 1940, may not have been quite what it seemed. An editorial in *The Nation*—no friend to forces of reaction—pointed out that an FBI agent had "admittedly bought them [Cassidy's men] ammunition with FBI funds." In comparing these reports with Kelly's own writings and speeches, documents in Kelly's FBI file, and materials in Mayor La Guardia's papers, this chapter argues toward a revision of Christian Front activism in particular and street-level anticommunism more generally.[6]

Revision, though, cannot excuse Kelly, Talbot, and other AUNS members for not doing more to speak out against Nazi persecutions of Jews, especially after Kristallnacht in November 1938. Who better than Kelly, a German speaker who visited Berlin at the end of 1937, or Talbot, whose *America* office was a collecting house for trans-European reportage, to expose the rising tide of virulent anti-Semitism. Yet it behooves the historian not to prejudge a contemporary context with the foreknowledge of hindsight, however shocking the outcome. While there were ample precedents for genocide in the Darwinian age of New Imperialism the half-German, half-Irish Kelly was predisposed to believe that National Socialism was well-intentioned, just as he had been so outspoken against English terrorism in Ireland during the Black and Tan era. It is a sad irony that Kelly looked the other way in Berlin, when, along with his father, he had celebrated German assistance in the effort to free Ireland of British racism in the 1916 Easter Rising. Moral confusion along ethnic-religious lines plagued late-1930s Americanism. According to opinion polls, 83 percent of Americans opposed any increase in immigration quotas. President Franklin D. Roosevelt might have talked about raising quotas, but he did nothing, and many Jewish organizations were themselves opposed to the admittance of thousands of Jewish refugees. In his analysis of Jews' self-interested "public silence" over Kristallnacht, historian Gulie Ne'eman Arad cites an AJC position paper that worried about intensifying "the Jewish problem here," concluding that, "as heartless as it may seem, future efforts should be directed toward sending Jewish refugees to other countries instead of bringing them here." It is sobering to reflect on a post-Kristallnacht Gallup poll of 9 December 1938, which found 6 percent of Americans (some five million citizens) approved of Nazi persecution of Jews.[7]

Transatlantic Origins of Christian Front Ideology

In response to the Comintern's Popular Front and the Spanish Civil War, Ireland's Catholics formed a nationwide Irish Christian Front (ICF) as early as September 1936 under the presidency of Patrick Belton. Belton's ICF raised funds for its Dublin treasury, had a standing committee, and counted thirty-one branches throughout Ireland by December, although it lacked a written constitution or formal membership. A serious mass movement, if only for six months, the ICF attracted 40,000 people to a rally in Cork at which the mayor was an officiating dignitary and more than 120,000 (600 by train from Belfast) to an event in Dublin with the lord mayor presiding. An "immense gathering," according to the *Irish Independent,* of many thousands demonstrated in Clonmel, and 12,000 marched in Waterford to hear ICF speakers urging Catholics to "steal the Communists' thunder by remedying social evils," as the *Irish Press* put it. Ireland's primate, Cardinal Joseph MacRory, lent little more than tacit approval to the ICF, whose local leaders tended to be laity: trade union representatives, business professionals, politicians, and some Jesuit intellectuals. Ideologically, it espoused Catholic Social Action as an alternative to communism, and in practice it devoted much of its energy to supplying uniforms, surgical dressings, and ambulances for Gen. Eoin O'Duffy's Blue Shirts, an Irish volunteer contingent that fought briefly for Franco's Nationalists. While Irish society of the 1930s was latently anti-Semitic, the ICF held no particular brief on the subject; when Irish newspapers were not focused single-mindedly on the threat of communism, they were pondering the dangers of Masonry.[8]

England also had a faith-based organization dedicated to combating Popular Front propaganda and supporting Franco's Nationalists, although this United Christian Front (UCF) was quite different from its Irish namesake. Upset by the Church of England's pro-Loyalist stance, and with the expectation that popular revulsion over anticlerical atrocities by Spanish communists would boost Christianity in England, two evangelical Methodists, Sir Arnold T. Wilson and Sir Henry Lunn, founded the UCF in 1937. Wilson and Henry Lunn, both colonial administrators, and Lunn's son Arnold, who was born in Madras, were all apostles for the liberalizing mission of Christian empire. A World War I colonel and pioneer colonialist in India, Wilson was a gifted individual who served as a member of Parliament (MP) for Hitchin, Hertfordshire, for seven years until antiaircraft fire shot down his bomber over France in 1940. In common with many U.S. Franco lobbyists, Wilson visited the Nationalist zone, where he befriended Cambridge graduate Peter Kemp. Kemp, who received two life-threatening wounds while fighting in the Spanish Legion, addressed a group of MPs in the House of Commons, convincing them, according to Wilson, that the British press had "swallowed the propaganda of one side and ignored those aspects of truth which told against it." Unlike the ICF, the UCF was an elitist lobbying group, not a mass political movement, and it was successful in appealing to Christian anticommunists across religious lines.[9]

Lunn's son, Arnold H. M. Lunn, toured Nationalist Spain over the winter of 1936–37 and then carried the UCF's message—that Christians must stand together in the face of Popular Front revolution—across the Atlantic. He became a University of Notre Dame visiting professor, learned how to appeal to Americans by quoting Alexis de Tocqueville, and wrote articles as well as a popular book, *Spanish Rehearsal* (1937). An atheist who turned to Catholicism in his forties, Lunn detested the "mediaeval territorial" Church of England almost as much as Soviet communism. Although his publications give no indication, anti-Semitism colored his politics. From Notre Dame, he wrote to a friend how curious it was that "any Catholic who has Jewish blood or Jewish affiliations is invariably anti Franco," with French philosopher Jacques Maritain, who had "married a Jewess," being "a case in point." After addressing an audience on the Spanish Civil War in December 1938, "at least half" of whom "were violently antagonistic," Lunn observed to a friend that "Jewish faces predominated." Lunn felt that the press exaggerated the incident, and he considered the crowd's behavior to have been mild compared to similar meetings he had addressed in Glasgow.[10]

A ski mountaineer who originated the slalom and later received a knighthood for his services to British skiing, Lunn was a Jeffersonian at heart. He disliked the "megapolitan civilization of giant cities," admired the "small men working on their own land or in their own businesses," and believed in the "wide distribution and redistribution of private property." *Spanish Rehearsal* tried to whitewash the bombing of Guernica as a Loyalist hoax but otherwise mounted a convincing argument. One of Lunn's more telling quotations was from English historian Arthur Bryant, who after the Spanish elections of February 1936 had wondered in *The Observer* how "a liberal like Franco, who supported [Spain's] republican revolution of 1931," could justly be accounted a "Fascist and a reactionary" simply because he risked his own life to lead a popular rising of the "more responsible elements" against a government that encouraged mobs to burn churches and that condoned a Marxist "reign of terror." "What Englishman," Bryant asked, as if feeling the weight of Rudyard Kipling's civilizing burden, "would not have done the same?" Lunn also wrote a pamphlet, *Spain and the Christian Front,* published by the Paulist Press in October 1937, with the subtitle *Ubi Crux Ibi Patria* (Where Cross, There Home), and sold it from a rack of five-cent booklets at the back of Catholic churches throughout America. Lunn's pamphlet was probably the first exhortation for a Christian Front in the United States.[11]

Paulist Fathers, an evangelical Catholic order based at Manhattan's Church of St. Paul the Apostle, produced liturgical and inspirational pamphlets, issued the *Catholic World,* and, for a while, operated a radio station, WLWL. Soon after General Secretary Georgi Dimitrov unveiled the Popular Front strategy at the Comintern's Seventh World Congress in 1935, the Paulists, through their Trinity League publishing subsidiary, began a new monthly newspaper, *Wisdom: The Catholic Front.* No hole-in-the-wall outfit, in addition to three editorial staff, seven staff correspondents, twenty-six executive staff, and Paul B. Ward as editor-in-chief, the newspaper had an advisory board of twenty-eight, including five Paulists and the radio preacher Fulton J. Sheen. *Wisdom* enjoyed an influence that belied its circulation of around 5,000 copies, through Catholic missionaries as far away as Kenya, and, at eight twelve-by-seventeen-inch pages (with no advertising), it was high in content. Despite *Wisdom's* clear anti–Popular Front message, the Paulist Fathers' principal purpose was Catholic outreach. As its title suggests, Paulists called for a Catholic not a Christian Front, and even at the height of Christian Front activity in the spring of 1939, they exhibited little ambition to run any sort of local, let alone national, Christian Front organization.[12]

If there is anything remarkable, therefore, about the formation of a Christian Front in America, it is that it did not happen sooner, and then only as uncoordinated, narrowly Catholic endeavors rather than as a true cross-denominational front. In February 1938, seventeen months after the formation of the ICF and five months after Lunn's *Christian Front* booklet, Edward Lodge Curran, a Brooklyn priest and publisher of the International Catholic Truth Society's anticommunist pamphlets, proposed an American version. Three months later on 30 May, the "Co-Operation Coupon" included in each weekly edition of Coughlin's *Social Justice* newspaper asked readers to write for information on how to start a "Social Justice Platoon of 25 among your friends." Readers should not forget, the coupon cautioned, that communism was not hammering at the gates, "COMMUNISM IS WITHIN THE GATES!" "Spawn of Oriental hatred of Christianity"—*Social Justice* was never shy of melodrama—communism "is coiled for its final thrust into the heart of the America we once knew." In the 20 June edition, the Co-Operation Coupon explained how "the 'democratic front' is the new, polished up name of Communism." In the following edition, 27 June, the coupon for the first time stated that, "the saving of America must be done by a Christian Front." Then, on 25 July, Coughlin put these pieces together, claiming that every Platoon was now "an integral part of the Christian Front." Yet this was hardly the case; like Mary Dunn's United Christian Platoons in Hartford, they were autonomous associations of concerned churchgoers. Only in metropolitan New York—and perhaps Boston, but to a far lesser extent—did Christian Front groups attain anything like cohesiveness as a political movement, and they were still only local, not national.[13]

Genesis of New York's Christian Fronts

Some three dozen New Yorkers gathered at the Paulists' rectory at 415 West 59th Street on the evening of 14 July 1938 for an informal meeting to discuss the increasing radicalization of their work places by communists. Father John E. Burke, the Paulists' pastor, acted as moderator, but it was probably his lay secretary, Walter D. Ogden, who arranged the meeting and persuaded Burke to allow the use of the rectory. As historian Evelyn Savidge Sterne's research shows, synagogues and churches of the 1920s and 1930s acted as "alternative political spaces," and when it came to mobilizing immigrants, none could rival Catholic churches for the size of their constituencies and the extent of their resources. A network of parish activities provided forums through which members learned to be organizers and orators. Immigrants used parish-based associations as springboards to their larger political communities, where they found that they could speak out "with the moral authority that religion provided," as Sterne puts it. In communities where lobbying for Franco did become a largely Irish Catholic endeavor— Brooklyn, say, or Manhattan's Lower West Side—the process was not so much the hierarchy dictating policy through parishioners, but the parishioners using religious affiliation to make an argument about the meaning of American citizenship. Because they happened to be Catholics, they could point to the persecutions of priests in Spain to argue that communists in New York were thwarting their ambitions for employment and political representation, essentially their hopes of fulfilling the American Dream.[14]

Although speakers at the rectory included Jack Cassidy, a recent law school graduate from Brooklyn, and Angel González Palencia, a visiting professor from Spain who delivered a lecture two weeks later at Stanford University on the aesthetics of traditional Spanish culture, most attendees at this first meeting were Catholic trade unionists. There was a union worker named Schneider from the city's power department, someone called Neefro from the Garment Workers' Union, and at least two members of, but probably a contingent from, the American Federation of Musicians' Union, Local 802, oboe virtuoso Marcel Honoré and a man named Cooper. These men were angry that communists had gained control of their unions. Yet leaving the union meant losing the ability to work, while staying in the union and objecting to matters of political policy had resulted in recriminations and loss of income. Devout Catholic anticommunists in Local 802 were particularly incensed because their union officials, along with bandleaders and orchestral conductors, were all supporters of anticlerical Loyalist Madrid. In addition to circulating pro-Loyalist leaflets and soliciting contributions for the Abraham Lincoln Brigade, 802 officials had organized several large concerts in Manhattan to benefit the Lincolns, at which they expected union musicians to play for free.[15]

Inevitably, the political issue for union musicians like Cooper and Honoré shaded off into ethnic rivalry, if not animus, for most of the pro-Loyalist activists in 802 were recent Jewish immigrants, although assessing the extent to which the Catholic unionists were anti-Semitic, and whether their ethnic biases fueled their anticommunism, or vice versa, is problematic. Because all Christian Front historiography to date has relied unquestioningly on anonymous reports filed by informants and investigators employed by Jewish organizations, a veil of doubt shrouds analysis. One of the attendees at the 14 July meeting was an informant of the AJC, or an affiliated organization, whose report provides the only extant source, whose raison d'être was to document anti-Semitism. So, as in this case, whenever the informant heard the word *Jew,* he reported that the "entire trend of [——'s] comments was anti-Semitic." At one point in the meeting, Father Burke intervened to cool partisan criticisms of both Freemasonry and the Holy Name Society, pointing out that there were Masons as well as Protestants attending and that they were just as anticommunist as the Catholic sitting next to them. Cooper then said, "I don't care if there are any Jews here," for it was Jews who "are making the trouble in our union." In context, it is unclear whether Cooper's isolated remark (presuming the quote to be verbatim) demonstrated a hatred of Jews, yet the AJC informant's intention was to show that the entire trend of the meeting was anti-Semitic.[16]

It is possible that there was more than one informant at this first gathering. Evidence presented here identifies by name four out of a number of undercover investigators who attended Christian Front meetings; working independently, for either Jewish organizations or the FBI, they would have been unaware of each other's real identity. FBI informant Harold Neff, for instance, reported that he had attended several Front meetings in early 1939, raising the intriguing possibility that the unusually named Neefro in one informant's report was the alias of Neff. On the occasions when two or more informants attended the same meeting, it is easy to see how there would have been an escalation in rhetoric, as each informant strove to protect his cover by being the most outspoken.[17]

Leonard Dinnerstein's landmark synthesis *Antisemitism in America* (1994) and monographs such as Ronald H. Bayor's *Neighbors in Conflict* (1978) rely on a Columbia University master's thesis by Edward C. McCarthy, "The Christian Front Movement in New York City" (1965), which relies on AJC reports. When Dinnerstein says that Christian Fronters "were likely to be anti-Semitic, bellicose and vulgar," he quotes McCarthy, and to back up a statement that meeting organizers routinely called on Fronters to "liquidate the Jews in America," he cites a page in McCarthy's study claiming that Front meetings "often ended in disorder and violence." Yet for the weight Dinnerstein places on it, McCarthy's study contains surprisingly little evidence. McCarthy describes the 14 July meeting, stating that fifty mostly blue-collar trade unionists gathered to hear "lectures on Communism and tirades against the Jews." McCarthy does not document his claim, presumably because the only source available is the informant's report, and Cooper's aside from the floor scarcely qualifies as a tirade by a lecturer. When McCarthy does evidence anti-Semitism two pages later it is to reference the arrest of another disgruntled anticommunist union musician, Joseph Bono of Brooklyn, in October 1938 for posting in a New York subway an anti-Semitic caricature of the Statue of Liberty that Bono had obtained at a Christian Front meeting. Bono served six months' hard labor for this offense. It is also instructive to consider McCarthy's evidence in support of his claim that Front meetings often ended in violence.[18]

McCarthy provides a statistic that for the whole of 1939 the New York Police Department arrested 112 persons "who expressed anti-Semitism or physically attacked Jews," although he does not offer a breakdown between expressive and physical acts, state how many of those arrested were Christian Fronters, or compare the 112 figure to arrests for anti-Semitism in, say, 1935, before the Spanish Civil War and the Christian Front. At the same time, McCarthy admits that vendors of Coughlin's *Social Justice* banded together in groups of ten because of the "likelihood" of assaults by "Jews and other passersby," that violence "was as much the work of heckling opponents as it was of the Coughlinites themselves," and that it was "virtually impossible to tell just who was responsible for a street brawl" anyway. In a later, and less partisan, chapter, McCarthy does get down to evidence, informing his readers that there were just four cases of serious injury connected to Front activity, and of those, "in only two cases, one of rather dubious authenticity, was this the result of an assault by Coughlinites." Having led readers to believe in prior chapters that Christian Fronters were thoroughgoing anti-Semitic hoodlums, McCarthy then makes the remarkable admission that "more typical of the violence" was an incident involving three middle-aged housewives who "rolled their copies of *Social Justice* and routed their 'Communist' opponents with spirited blows upon the head."[19]

Throughout 1939, telegrams from Jewish organizations complaining of violent attacks by Christian Fronters deluged the mayor's office. Abraham Cahan, editor of the *Jewish Daily Forward,* telegraphed La Guardia in June that he had received "any number of reports from eye witnesses regarding vicious antisemetic [*sic*] attacks at open air meetings," which Jewish residents portrayed as "incitements to pogroms." On 15 August La Guardia received fifteen identical telegrams from leaders of Jewish organizations claiming that "physical attacks upon citizens incited to riot and race hatred" had characterized "*all* previous meetings" of the Christian Front. These telegrams, along with scores of similar letters from individuals in the mayor's files, make for shocking reading. Yet, as La Guardia tried to explain to several other Jewish constituents, they were "typical of the exaggerated accounts circulated from some quarters." Since the spring of 1939, New York police commissioner Lewis Valentine had been saturating street corners frequented by Fronters with details of six to twenty-five officers. A confidential "Final Report" of 6 November by La Guardia's committee of investigation into anti-Semitic groups in New York City concluded that, because of the heavy policing tactics and prosecutions of soapbox orators on charges of disorderly conduct, "the problem assigned to us has been solved." Valentine's heavy-handed approach would explain the court's harsh sentencing of musician Bono.[20]

Neither McCarthy nor Dinnerstein cite Robert Morton Darrow, author of yet another Columbia University dissertation on the Christian Front era, although other scholars do. Darrow devotes six pages to a discussion of Catholic reactions to *Blockade,* commenting, "Occasionally, violence broke out," by which he means that

Catholics resorted to violence. Then, to prove his contention, he then uses the *New York Times* report of the "Loyalist sympathizers" who paraded their ambulance past Ditmar's Theatre and how the "provocative sight inflamed the mob spirit" of the Catholic pickets, "and they attempted to smash the ambulance." "Street fighting," Darrow continues, "broke out," and only the arrival of the police "saved the machine from complete destruction." Darrow talks in terms of "smashing," "destroying," and "fighting," yet the article—his sole source—states clearly that "no blows were struck," although there was some "pushing and jostling." As for the ambulance, picketers shouted how someone should deflate its tires, though no one did so. Darrow's interpretation of this incident, which extrapolates from "jostling" and the suggested removal of a tire valve to mob brawling and the smashing of property, is indicative of the distortion of evidence that pervades his study.[21]

In critiquing these scholars' well-meaning interpretations, I do not imply that all Fronters were paragons of civility. Many were active participants in a vibrant culture of street politics, which, on a hot summer's night, after young men had downed one too many glasses of beer, could easily shade off into heated confrontation. I do propose that a more nuanced history emerges once the pro-Franco side of the Great Debate receives a fair hearing.

After explaining how the Bono incident so alarmed the Paulist Fathers that they banned Christian Front meetings from their premises, McCarthy then mentions that meetings resumed at the rectory sometime thereafter. What seems to have occurred was that the New York Fronters split into at least five overlapping yet distinct groups, with Honoré leading a formal Christian Front organization in Brooklyn; Cassidy making forays into the Bronx and then forming the Mobilizers militia with McWilliams in 1939; the unionists, headed by the brothers Harry and Joseph Thorne, adding an "L" to their "CF" logo signifying that theirs was henceforth the Christian Labor Front (CLF); and the Paulist Fronters splitting into two groups, a blue-collar/lay group and an intellectual/religious group associated with the publication of *Wisdom,* which soon distanced itself from, and by the fall of 1939 had repudiated any connection with, both Coughlin and Christian Front activism. Anti-Semitism in these five broad groups seems to have varied from unabashed racism at the Thornes' Christian Labor Front to Jewish outreach at the Paulists' *Wisdom.* While individual Paulists such as Father Burke and Ogden may well have been anti-Semitic—it would have been extraordinary among any sample of New Yorkers in 1938 to find no ethnic prejudice—it is a historical distortion to suggest that anti-Semitism was the Paulists' stock-in-trade. Then, as seventy years later, the Paulist Press was at the forefront of ecumenicalism between the Catholic and Jewish faiths.[22]

It is beyond the scope of this study to investigate Christian Front groups with only tenuous connections to Franco lobbyists, although it is worth noting the heterogeneity of and fluidity among the various splinter groups. Honoré, for instance, found Cassidy's militancy and advocacy of militia tactics unpalatable, and he moved back to Ogden's meetings at Donovan's Bar. Honoré was a full-time faculty member of the Chatham Square Music School, a primarily Jewish-staffed and endowed nonprofit institution, so the fact that he continued his employment there while briefly leading the Brooklyn Christian Fronters suggests he may not have been as anti-Semitic as AJC reports claimed. If the Thornes were not reticent about expressing their anti-Semitism, then it was because they saw a clear divide in their Local 802 between the bulk of musicians and conductors who were pro-Loyalist Jews and a minority of Catholic musicians who were pro-Nationalist. Charles Lichter directed the hundred-piece Modern Symphony Orchestra in an Aid Spanish Democracy benefit concert at the Mecca Temple on 23 April 1937; Max Goberman conducted the New York Symphony Orchestra on 1 July 1937 in a benefit for Loyalist Basque refugees; Leon Barzin led the National Orchestra Association on 28 November 1937 in a program supervised by the North American Committee to Aid Spanish Democracy—and these were just some of the engagements at which Local 802 officials expected pro-Franco union musicians to play for free in support of Loyalist Spain. A June 1939 CLF pamphlet entitled "The Pro-Semitic Persecution of Harry Thorne" explained how communist union officials finally expelled Thorne from the union after finding him guilty of playing a Christmas engagement at a Catholic church for less than the union pay scale. Thorne consequently lost his position of ten years' standing in the Goldman Band to a pro-Loyalist activist. "Race friction," the pamphlet observed, stemmed from the bigotry of the Jewish union officials, not from Catholics like Thorne, whose crime was to play "an engagement in a Christian Church, in a Christian Nation, on Christmas Day."[23]

Perhaps it was inevitable that charges of anti-Semitism—to whatever extent valid or inflated—would, at the local level, taint and quickly poison the Paulists' well-intended *Wisdom*. Located on the corner of Columbus (9th) Avenue and 60th Street, their Church of St. Paul the Apostle stood at the upper end of Hell's Kitchen, home turf to Irish American gangs during Prohibition. As journalist Richard O'Connor noted, the second-generation Irish and Germans who populated Hell's Kitchen in the 1910s intermarried, so there were "frequently such christening oddities as, say, Herman O'Brien or Michael Vincent Schultz." By the 1930s, upwardly mobile Irish Americans had moved on, often to outlying boroughs to be closer to the bus and subway terminals as many were transit workers. Those who remained in the aging neighborhood competed for scarce jobs with ethnic Italians and East Europeans, many of whom were Jewish, and after La Guardia's political machine overcame Tammany Hall's influence in the 1933 mayoralty election, the Irish lost their traditional political influence and lucrative patronage appointments. Ethnic animosities, steeped in the myths of shootouts between Irish and Italian or Jewish mafiosi, found fresh fuel when La Guardia's Republican Fusion ticket opened up rewarding city government posts to the newer ethnic groups that were predominantly Jewish.[24]

In addition to making full use of their enhanced access to the mayor's office, New York's Jewish groups gained strength as an ironic consequence of the worsening persecutions in Nazi Germany, not only from an influx of often well-heeled immigrants but also from the insecurity that fear of anti-Semitism engendered. While many organizations served bona fide aims, the motivations of others were not always clear. In November 1938, Stanley Howe, La Guardia's personal secretary, received a telegram from an organization at The Hague called the International Jewish Colonization Society, which was seeking to raise bonds in New York to assist in the resettlement of refugees from central Europe. Suspicious, Howe contacted the U.S. consulate in Holland, where officials could find no trace of such a society. Howe then talked with three Jewish community leaders who shared his concern that "overnight organizations" and "racketeering organizations" intent on "exploiting the cause of the refugees" would erode sympathy for the plight of oppressed Jews as well as encourage "mushroom organizations" and floods of letters from "excited individuals." In fact, the Colonization Society, formed by Daniel Wolf, was legitimate.[25]

Howe may have been nearer the mark with his assessment of the Non-Sectarian Anti-Nazi League. During the first year of La Guardia's administration, Samuel Untermyer had persuaded La Guardia to become a vice president of the League, and Howe felt that while Untermyer was "well and active," his organization had been "honest and performed some valuable service." But by December 1938, with Untermyer in retirement, Howe doubted if the League was "either honest or useful." In drawing La Guardia's attention to its pending application in Pennsylvania for a license to solicit funds, Howe charged the League with operating a "money-raising racket" and suggested the mayor resign his vice-presidency. With the Paulists holding public meetings in Hell's Kitchen, and a dozen or more undercover investigators from the AJC, Anti-Defamation League (ADL), Anti-Nazi League, and other Jewish organizations trying to justify their pay, it was predictable that anti-Semitism would become the lens through which generations of commentators would interpret Christian Front groups in New York City.[26]

Father Burke's lay assistant, Ogden, who assumed the secretarial functions of West Side Christian Fronters, acted as liaison between other Front groups, arranging regular weekly meetings at the Paulists' rectory throughout the summer. After Bono's arrest, and concerned by the militant polemics of Fronters like Cassidy, the Paulist Fathers told Burke (whom they transferred to the Midwest soon after) and Ogden that their open public meetings held on church premises were attracting undesirables and had become an embarrassment. Paulists must have realized, too, that the Nazi Bundists who had been distributing literature at Front meetings for some weeks were not merely gatecrashers but area organizers seeking a Front takeover. Columbus Circle, one block east on 7th Avenue, always a favored spot for soapbox orators, became the gathering place for Christian Fronters looking to let off steam or purchase a copy of Coughlin's *Social Justice* from one of several street hawkers. Ogden's group moved its meetings to Arthur W. Donovan's bar at 310 West 59th Street, on the corner of Columbus Avenue adjacent to St. Paul's.[27]

Kelly's "Right Side"

For the Paulists' *Wisdom* of March 1938, Kelly wrote a front-page article, "Free Speech in Jersey City: A Defense of Mayor Hague," which chronicled an escalation by Congress of Industrial Organizations (CIO) agitators from New York City following a challenge of municipal ordinances prohibiting mass picketing and the arrest on 1 December 1937 of thirteen CIO organizers for distributing leaflets without a permit. Stressing that these ordinances were "of long standing, sustained by the highest courts of New Jersey," Kelly explained how it was not so much Frank Hague as the "citizens of Jersey City, in overwhelming majority," who were determined to prevent the CIO from provoking "riot and civil commotion" and importing "its red allies to destroy the peace." Tensions had reached fever pitch after a letter from "fellow traveler" Roger Baldwin of the American Civil Liberties Union (ACLU) to Jersey's CIO leaders referencing a "plan" to test Hague's resolve appeared in the *Jersey Journal* and after CIO counsel Morris L. Ernst, who was also the ACLU's cofounder and counsel, told members of Congress and Secretary of Labor Frances Perkins that unless the CIO had its way, "there will be machine guns in Jersey City." Three thousand worried American Legion veterans assembled at the city's National Guard Armory to pass a resolution that they would "forcibly prevent the intrusion of the lawless C.I.O. and red elements." Kelly felt this showed the true "spirit of our citizens." A subsequent veterans' rally on 6 January attracted 20,000 people into the armory, and as many as 50,000 more stood outside "roaring their approval of the actions of their mayor." Kelly's office-cum-lodgings were seven blocks to the northeast on Brinkerhoff Street, so he probably witnessed the enthusiastic turnout.[28]

Ernst, in fact, never threatened violence, although both the CIO and Hague camps employed inflammatory language. Addressing the National Lawyers Guild in Washington, D.C., Ernst said that the CIO was "determined to keep after Jersey City and Hague until they are licked," and he accused Hague of being "the worst dictator," the kind that would use "spies, machine guns and tear gas." Seizing the phrase, the *Jersey Journal* then bannered its front page "CIO LEADER TALKS OF 'MACHINE GUNS'" and quoted Ernst as wanting to "cut Hague down." Whether CIO activists intended insurrectionary action was beside the point. What mattered was the usefulness of the story to Franco lobbyists. Tens of thousands of Jersey citizens had rallied to protect themselves from an "Invasion" of Tommy-gun-wielding New York communists. Here was an opportunity for Kelly to map the anticlericalism of

Madrid and Barcelona onto America's major metropolis. His logic was that there had been a Red revolution in Spain with 6,800 religious murdered, and now there was talk of CIO machine guns in down-home Jersey City. Therefore, if the spirited citizens of New Jersey had faced down the lawless Red elements, then he had an example to use in his speeches of what civic action could achieve.[29]

Kelly's article, with its confident prose and matter-of-fact journalistic style, impressed *Wisdom*'s editors, and they asked him to write a regular column, "The Right Side," which appeared on the paper's front page for the next eighteen editions. His second article tried to woo uncommitted Catholics by convincing them that pro-Loyalist New Yorkers were motivated as much by their hatred of Catholicism as by their communist sympathies. "Catholic Americans must realize," he wrote, that, in common with Catholics in Nationalist Spain, they were targets of an "envenomed propaganda." Were they to preserve their American form of government, which was the very "sanctity of home and religion," they "MUST fight back." He said that Catholics should spend two minutes a day snipping out Loyalist articles from their newspaper, underlining any names, and then filing the clippings in a folder or pasteboard box. Once a month, they should go through the clippings, look for the reappearance of names, and draw up a list of those occurrences. This was the first step, for they had now learned "to distinguish America's enemies." Next, they should discuss their list with friends and members of their clubs and societies. Now they could pool their efforts. "Some of them [the pro-Loyalist enemies] hold public office: You have votes. Some of them teach in school or college: Your societies can make effective protest. Some of them are in business: take your trade elsewhere." Here, then, was Kelly's twelve-column-inch primer on how to become a productive lobbyist.[30]

In common with all *Wisdom*'s columnists, Kelly contributed his articles free of charge, so he would have felt less beholden to editorial oversight. Editor-in-chief Ward encouraged a range of opinion, which may explain why "The Right Side" contained Kelly's most outspoken anticommunist rhetoric. By April 1938 he was sounding as committed to polarizing the Great Debate as the pro-Loyalists were. "Examine yourself," he challenged *Wisdom*'s readers. "How many of your acquaintances that you welcome in your home express subversive opinions?" This was no time to be "broadminded," to be "hearing all sides." When "bigots" took the floor at meetings, it was the Catholic American's duty to speak out. "In the crisis that is approaching," Kelly warned, the crisis "the reds are frantically accelerating, no man can remain neutral." This was the time for choosing. American Catholics "must choose between civilization and Stalin." If *Wisdom*'s readers chose not to fight now "in words," but "in deeds if need be later," then they did not deserve to "enjoy the freedom that past generations died to establish and to preserve." Communists, Kelly was arguing, sought world revolution; they sought to replace American democracy with a workers' dictatorship, so the preservation of that democracy might require undemocratic means, particularly when the Comintern's influence in Washington was growing.[31]

All "Right Side" topics, which ranged from "La Guardia Encourages Communism" to "Duchess of Atholl Raises Money for Red Spain," followed Kelly's standard theme of communist revolution in Loyalist Spain necessitating anticommunist vigilance at home. With his columns proving so popular, Ward provided a biographical snapshot in the September edition, noting how Kelly had an "astounding" knowledge of the "machinations of radical forces" and boosting him as "one of the ablest, if not the ablest, champion of democracy in the east." By *democracy*, Ward really meant opposition to an ideology he believed to be un-American and support for the Americanism of the Founding Fathers, which had actually been an intolerant meritocracy that abhorred factions.[32]

In January 1939 Kelly judged the recent Kristallnacht pogrom in Nazi Germany to be "infinitesimal compared with the mass terror and massacre perpetrated by the Reds in Mexico, Spain, and Russia." In statistical terms, he was correct, yet he could neither find the heart to condemn Germany's snowballing anti-Semitism nor divorce the Nazis' inhumane means from their anticommunist ends. His justification came in the next paragraph, which evidenced Kurt Rosenfeld (Prussia's justice minister at the outset of the Weimar Republic), who was then in America "instructing us how to combat Nazism, with never a word against communism." Germans had the right idea, Kelly implied, for after the Spartacist uprising in 1919, they "threw off the octopus represented by Rosa Luxembourg [*sic*], Karl Liebknecht, Walter Rathenau, and Matias [*sic*] Erzberger." Kelly then took to task Roosevelt, who, according to press reports, had agreed with visiting British statesman Anthony Eden that a "victory for General Franco would be inimical to American interests." To the contrary, Kelly averred excitedly, a Franco victory was "a victory for peace, freedom of conscience, Christianity, equality before the law, work, charity." Were Roosevelt to have his way, the alternative would be "a Spanish Soviet, dominated by Moscow." Kelly was roaring now. Were Franco's Nationalists to lose, the certain consequence would be "a peninsula drenched with the blood of new massacres, Christianity extinguished, communist agitators exported by thousands to subvert Latin America and bring communism to the Western World." Confronted by what he saw as a cresting Comintern wave about to crash over his cherished American breakwater, Kelly's once-liberal center fell away.[33]

Kelly's "Right Side" apologia notwithstanding, *Wisdom* scrupulously avoided anti-Semitic language, and almost every edition included pro-Jewish pieces, albeit written with a patronizing tone. Adjacent to Kelly's January 1939 column was an article by the Reverend Gregory Feige, entitled "Anti-Semitism." Feige castigated German National Socialism as univocally racist, and he tackled Coughlin's *Social Justice* for its blatant anti-Semitism and false claim that Nazism could somehow be justified on the grounds that it was a "defense mechanism" against communism. Through a letter printed in *Wisdom*'s March edition, Feige also attacked Kelly's January 1939 column for its sloppy reportage and implicit racial slur. Rathenau and Erzberger, Feige pointed out, had not only been "vigorous opponents" of communism but also "conscientious public servants," sincere democrats, and "God-fearing and devoted patriots." Feige was particularly incensed because Erzberger was Catholic.[34]

In May 1939 Kelly had to take more of his own medicine from "Fourth Estate," a *Wisdom* letter writer. Kelly's April column criticized the *New York Times* for showing a bias toward Loyalist Spain and hinted at the value of press censorship in the case of communist propaganda. Fourth Estate was indignant because the *Times* had been the most balanced of any American daily, and talk of censorship was "in utter contradiction to Major Kelly's hope that we can rebuild America in the dreams of the founders." This was a reference to Kelly's call not merely for a negative-sounding defense against communism but a positive new "programme for the restoration of normal conditions" for the reestablishment of Americanism, "a non-political platform" about which all "sane elements of our population" could gather "to rebuild America in the dreams of the Founders." Elements of Kelly's program appeared in subsequent "Right Side" columns, his articles for magazines like *America,* and a nine-point mimeographed pamphlet entitled *A Programme for American Nationalism.*[35]

Part nativist, part statist, part progressive, *Programme*'s domestic proposals called for the cessation of European immigration either for ten years or until unemployment fell below 1.5 million; the fingerprinting by federal authorities of all aliens and the deportation of those with criminal records. It also proposed the suspension of federal taxes for one to two years, which, supported by an inflationary issuance of gold-backed Treasury notes, would encourage private enterprise and jump-start the economy. On one hand, labor unions would have to incorporate (thereby rendering them liable for any illegal actions by their agents), only workers employed at the plant in question could call strikes, strikers could not interfere with the rights of non-striking workers, and there should be a repeal of the Wagner Act. On the other hand, labor would gain representation on all boards of corporations with assets over $1 million, and corporations with earnings in excess of 8 percent on equities would share the surplus profit with labor in a proportion determined by a government board. A "cardinal tenet" of America's national policy would be efforts to reduce the costs of distribution, although Kelly gave no details on how to minimize the "role and compensation of middlemen." (He would have approved, no doubt, of Internet commerce.)[36]

Most controversial among *Programme*'s domestic policies was a plan for curtailing the inroads of communism into "education, labor, press, motion pictures, government and other phases of our national life." Having seen the results of communism in Spain, Kelly believed that Stalinist Russia's most expedient path to world revolution was to attack capitalism in its American heartland. He therefore proposed legislation to make the advocacy of communist revolution a crime, punishable by death if necessary. For a liberal humanist like Kelly to recommend such a draconian measure indicates the seriousness of his argument with communists. *Programme*'s foreign policies were seemingly conventional, supporting the Monroe Doctrine, neighborliness in the Western Hemisphere, and the Open Door in Asia. Still, at a period when isolationism was a powerful impulse in American society, and Kelly himself was opposed to U.S. military intervention both in the Old World and in support of American interests in Latin America, his foreign policy was internationalist: he called for an end to Western imperialism and the elimination of all global trade barriers. When Talbot read *Programme,* he scribbled a note to a secretary that it was full of "sweeping 'nut' ideas" and best ignored. Yet with the exception of mandatory profit sharing with employees, much of what Kelly proposed found resonance in the cold war consensus of 1950s America.[37]

Kelly and the Christian Front

On 18 February 1943, FBI special agents Gust A. Koski of Newark and Eugene Coyle of New York City interviewed confidential informant T-3. T-3 explained how he had known Kelly since 1920 (presumably in their joint capacities as U.S. Army Military Intelligence investigators into communist activity), and in cultivating this acquaintance he had obtained a considerable amount of information about Kelly. T-3 testified that Kelly was "the actual leader of the Christian Front," which at that time (1939) had "35,000 members in the metropolitan district." Kelly, moreover, had organized and trained "400 New York City policemen for the purpose of making a special elite guard," and Kelly intended to merge this guard with other regional groups, such as the Silver Shirts and Knights of the White Camellia, to form a national anticommunist militia under the nominal leadership of Maj. Gen. George Van Horn Moseley, but with Kelly as its real commander. FBI report 65–1461:304 escaped censorship, giving the identity of T-3 as Frank Bielaski, then the director of the Domestic Investigation Division of the recently formed Office of Strategic Services (OSS, the CIA's precursor). Bielaski later achieved notoriety for uncovering a major security leak by Comintern spies in the OSS itself when, during the midnight hours of 11 March 1945, he led a team of five agents to burgle the office of the leftist magazine *Amerasia* and found more than three hundred classified documents.[38]

Despite his credentials as a professional investigator, Bielaski's statement was speculation based on hearsay. While membership would have been a logical move, there is nothing in Kelly's papers to suggest that he even joined a Christian Front group, let alone acted as a principal organizer and elite guard trainer. Neither does it seem as if any of the other Franco lobbyists discussed in this study joined. Kelly, nonetheless, skated energetically around the edges of Front activity. Coughlin, during his scheduled broadcast on station WMCA on 20 November 1938, decried Nazi persecution of Jews but then spoke about persecutions of German Catholics, restated his defense mechanism argument, and linked Jews to a communist conspiracy. When Coughlin refused a request by WMCA management to submit his scripts in advance, WMCA rescinded his contract. A group of Coughlin supporters, primarily Patrick F. Scanlan of the *Brooklyn Tablet*, Queens lawyer Bernard T. D'Arcy, and Allen Zoll, called a mass meeting for 15 December to plan a response. Scanlan and D'Arcy were both Catholics, but Zoll, a World War I veteran, Harvard graduate, sales consultant, and president of his own anticommunist organization, American Patriots, Inc., was a Presbyterian. Zoll asked the six thousand attendees to help man a picket line at WMCA every Sunday at the time of Coughlin's regular slot. From then until September 1939, when the outbreak of war presented Mayor La Guardia with an excuse to ban all demonstrations, five hundred or more people showed up every Sunday afternoon to picket, with more than two thousand on the picket lines during the first few weeks.[39]

These affairs seem to have been closer to social gatherings than street protests, in part because many of the picketers were clergy and their congregants, including mothers with young children. Picketers carrying placards, portraits of Coughlin, or the American flag paraded up and down the sidewalk; there was some singing and chanting but few incidents. According to a rather eclectic list in the AJC files, "John Kelly—of Jersey City, an engineer," was "active on the picket line." Picketing was hardly Kelly's style, and his frequent speaking commitments on Sunday evenings would have curtailed his activity, but he was a popular and well-known figure and no doubt boosted the picketers' solidarity. It is less clear whether it was "Kelly—A man with that name" whom AJC investigators claimed had called a WMCA advertiser "with threats." In addition to *Kelly* being a common enough name for a Christian Fronter, had John Eoghan placed a menacing telephone call, it is odd that he would have given his real name.[40]

He did, however, speak at several Front meetings. During the first six months of 1939, documents record that Kelly delivered twenty-two major speeches, of which five were to Front groups of between fifty and three hundred or more, although he probably spoke forty or more times at venues from American Legion halls to elite clubs up and down the East Coast. Non-Sectarian Anti-Nazi League informant Mario Buzzi attended a large Christian Front rally held in the thousand-seat ballroom of Brooklyn's Grand Prospect Hall on 22 May, organized by D'Arcy and chaired by the Reverend Edward Lodge Curran, at which Kelly gave the keynote speech. Yet in recalling the event in testimony to FBI agents four years later, Buzzi implied that Kelly spoke not as a Christian Fronter but as a guest speaker of Zoll's American Patriots. Kelly's speech, Buzzi remembered, concentrated on "the fight which America had on her hands against Communism," the reasons for the Spanish Civil War, and "atrocities committed by the Reds against the Catholic Church" in Spain.[41]

According to FBI informant Neff, Kelly was also the principal speaker at Donovan's Bar on 5 May 1939. It must have been a rousing speech, for Kelly "inspired his listeners to the point of intense enthusiasm." Sensing from political tensions that insurrection or war of some kind was imminent, Kelly's was a fighting talk "in the language of a soldier." Fronters, Kelly recommended, should work to build support in the countryside because, in Spain, revolution broke out in the cities, and Franco ultimately triumphed because he had won over "folks from the rural areas." This was a Friday evening at a smoky pub in Hell's Kitchen during the worst of the Great Depression, and Kelly evidently pitched a populist message, lambasting "cafe society and those of the idle rich." Elite society was degenerating, and this would only lead to further despair among the unemployed and fuel the fires of the coming revolution. Therefore, it was time "to get ready for action to take control of the Federal Government." Whether Kelly actually used those words is unknowable, but Neff thought it was "probably the toughest speech ever delivered to the Christian Front."[42]

One of Kelly's toughest speechmaking assignments was his address at the Great Pro-American Mass Meeting in Behalf of Free Speech and Americanism, an event held in midtown Manhattan on 24 May 1939. Organizers, principally Zoll and the representatives of a dozen self-styled patriotic organizations, including Ogden's Christian Front, had booked the 2,800-seat Carnegie Hall and were expecting to fill it. But, under pressure from an unidentifiable source, Carnegie's management backed down eight hours before the event. Organizers then hired the Shriners' domed 2,750-seat Mecca Temple, but, again, persons unknown— Mayor La Guardia, Police Commissioner Valentine, perhaps a member of one of the Popular Front or Jewish organizations—pressured management to cancel the booking. This left Pro-American organizers scrambling. With just two and a half hours to go, they convinced management of the nearby Great Northern Hotel to hire out the ballroom, and they staged an overflow meeting for earlier in the evening at Columbus Circle. Because there are four separate accounts of Kelly's speech at this meeting, one of which Neff wrote for the FBI, and because the text from which Kelly read is extant, it is possible not only to recreate a sense of what actually happened but also to see how the historical record has distorted the event. But before undertaking this analysis, it is first necessary to identify another of the informants who attended and to consider whether he was an FBI agent.[43]

A popular genre of the late Depression and early war years was the exposé of conspiratorial networks. Unlike the muckrakers of the Progressive Era, who pitted their populist reformism against the robber barons of interlinked corporate trusts, these authors faced off along Red-fascist lines. One exponent from the anticommunist side was Elizabeth Dilling, whose *Octopus* (1940) linked 2,300 people and organizations to argue that an international Zionist-Marxist hydra was throttling free speech and driving the country into war. Only through "knowing the facts" (facts being the genre's stock-in-trade) could Americans begin to understand why

B'nai B'rith, the ADL, and other Jewish organizations were spending millions on propaganda and working so hard to gag the press and "truth tellers." American Jewry, Dilling explained, was "grounded and soaked in imported Marxism, which is totally opposed to Christianity and American principles." Dilling did fill her account with factual details, but her connections relied on innuendo, as when she claimed that the "war mongering" Dean G. Acheson was Felix Frankfurter's "'Hot Dog Boy'" on the strength of Acheson's Jewish law partner having taught at Harvard with Frankfurter. From the antifascist side in 1943 came John Roy Carlson's classic *Under Cover: My Four Years in the Nazi Underworld of America,* which, the following year, became the best-selling nonfiction book and was sufficiently influential to push the Justice Department into a mass sedition trial against thirty suspected fascist conspirators, including Dilling. Kelly emerges in *Under Cover* as a sordid "promoter of Franco-Nazism in America," the "organizer" of Manhattan's "Jew-baiting" Christian Front, and an un-American "fascist collaborator."[44]

To gain the confidence of Nazi Bundists and Christian Front "storm-troopers," and eventually to infiltrate their "goon squads," Carlson assumed the guise of Italian American fascist George Pagnanelli. As Pagnanelli, Carlson scripted, mimeographed, and distributed the weekly *Christian Defender,* which he "deliberately designed" to be "one of the coarsest" anti-Semitic sheets in print. Now having become Pagnanelli the "convincing actor," Carlson explained in *Under Cover* how in May 1939 he spent a typical evening with a group of fellow Christian Fronters distributing *Social Justice* and anti-Semitic newssheets (such as the *Christian Defender*) in the Bronx. "Heiling Hitler" and "screaming anti-Jewish slogans," they then "marched in formation" as a "mob" to a subway station, where they split into groups and "pushed" their way into separate cars, "ramming their way between the strap hangers [and] stepping on toes." Once the doors had closed, they "started up and down the aisle shouting insults at Jews . . . deliberately kicking out at anyone who appeared to be Jewish."[45]

An Armenian immigrant born in Greece, Carlson was twenty-nine in October 1938 when he went undercover to root out fascists, Nazis, and anti-Semites on the streets of New York. Carlson uncovered everything he expected to find—and far more than was actually there. Five years earlier he had witnessed a traumatizing event: the gory murder by two "swarthy, pock-marked" knife-wielding assailants of Armenian archbishop Leon Tourian before the altar during High Mass. Historian Benjamin L. Alpers considers that Carlson had a psychological fixation with "frightening foreignness." Emerging into Times Square on the night of the subway incident, Carlson, as he wrote guiltily in *Under Cover,* was "in mortal fear of being recognized by my respectable friends," so he grabbed a placard from "one of the girls" to hide his face. He then talked with a "pimply youth in his early teens" about how to solve the Jewish question. It would seem from these two remarks that several members of the Hitler-heiling, toe-squashing mob were not so much hardened goons and storm troopers as adolescent grade-schoolers. Carlson and Dan Walker, a "thin scarecrow of a youth with a sharp, pimply face," went to a bar for two beers and then returned to Times Square to sell more newssheets. A "youth with thin features and large eyes" (whom Carlson presumed to be Jewish) had apparently been "goaded by the insults" that Carlson's fellow "hawkers were screaming," for this youth came over and knocked the newspapers from Walker's hand. Walker swung back, which prompted the "goon squad" that "loitered in the darkened entrances of shops" to come running, "eyes blazing, fists ready to pummel the Jewish youth into a bloody pulp." "By the Grace of God," police officers "got there first" and took the pimply sparring partners into custody.[46]

Carlson's subway incident suggests three plausible scenarios: first, it was merely bizarre fiction; second, it actually happened and Carlson actively participated, for he could scarcely have maintained his cover by sitting out and pretending not to notice; and third, in order to enhance his credibility, Carlson deliberately incited the others in the group. Indeed, when describing his participation on the Sunday evening WMCA picket lines, Carlson let slip that he "shouted louder than the others, eager to impress the strong arm boys that my 'allegiance' was second to none." Presuming that *Under Cover*'s narrative reflects a modicum of truth, his presence, at minimum, would have lent confidence to the other Christian Fronters. But Carlson was no pimply-faced teenager. He was a thirty-year-old refugee from ethnic conflict and a convincing actor, and, as a role model and Walker's drinking partner, he no doubt elevated tensions during the altercation at Times Square. He was not only a writer/distributor of coarse anti-Semitic literature, but he was also an instigator of—and probably an active participant in—racially motivated street fighting between Irish Catholic and Jewish youths.

Kelly's FBI file contains a seven-page report of the Great Northern meeting; its phrasing matches text in Carlson's *Under Cover,* and its coversheet bears the annotation "AD 5/24/39." Carlson's real name was Avedis (or Arthur) Derounian, so it was no doubt Carlson who compiled the report. At the very least, therefore, Carlson was simultaneously an instigator of and an investigator into anti-Semitism who submitted reports that found their way into the FBI's files. To decide if Carlson was an agent provocateur for the U.S. government begs a final question: Was he working, paid or unpaid, for the FBI while so engaged.[47]

At least two historians have hinted that Carlson was more than a biased observer whose book ADL staff edited. Wayne S. Cole and Kenneth O'Reilly both mention that Carlson, while working as an investigator for Leon M. Birkhead's Friends of Democracy in the mid-1940s, was briefly on the FBI's payroll. O'Reilly's source is a letter from FBI director J. Edgar Hoover to syndicated commentator Westbrook Pegler, an extract from which Pegler quoted in his column in 1947. Hoover wrote that he "utilized" informant Carlson at the "specific request of a special assistant [O. John Rogge, a fellow traveler] to the attorney general from

July 18, 1942, to October 12, 1942," which was Carlson's "only connection" with the FBI. Might Carlson have been working for Hoover earlier, say in May 1939?[48]

Identical in style, composition, layout, and typeface to Carlson's Pro-American Mass Meeting report in FBI file 65–1461 is a three-page report of a meeting on 3 May 1939 at the Tri-Boro Palace in the Bronx, held under the auspices of the Christian Front. Three hundred men and women attended, whom Carlson described as a "dominantly Irish American crowd with a sprinkling of German faces, and a few Italians." Kelly gave a talk and screened *Spain in Arms*. Carlson thought the film made "a profound impression on the audience," acted as a "valuable emotionalizing agent," and speakers like Kelly used it to "prove" their contention that "what happened in Spain can also happen in this country unless we organize to do something about it." At the beginning of his report, Carlson noted that it was "very difficult to crash these meetings," that he took flash pictures of the signs tacked over the entrance door, and that he had missed "your own man." There was a bank on the ground floor with darkened windows, he offered, "[so] perhaps your investigator thought this was the hall" and presumably left, thinking the meeting was cancelled. Carlson also mentioned he had "phoned you of the proposed meeting" the night before "in order to give you time to make whatever arrangements you regarded wise." Perhaps the missing investigator was an ADL informant, since Carlson was addressing an official of a Jewish organization, such as the ADL, and the wise arrangements referred to the possibility of pressuring the management of the Tri-Boro Palace to cancel the booking. Yet, the Palace was a regular Front venue, copies of Carlson's four FBI reports are not in the ADL's files, and it is noteworthy that FBI informant Harold Neff, who made a point of crashing the other Christian Front meetings in May, made no report on the meeting.[49]

Although this analysis does not constitute proof, it does provide compelling linkage between Carlson and either Hoover himself or New York bureau chief P. E. Foxworth. It is also evident that Carlson was not the only agent provocateur. During an interview with FBI Agent Robert F. X. O'Keefe in April 1943, Frank Evans, who was then employed by Lt. Col. William C. Godfrey of military intelligence on New York's Governor's Island army base, stated that he had earlier been an Anti-Nazi League investigator. Evans then made a casual—though nonetheless extraordinary—admission: While working undercover for the Anti-Nazi League, he was "Chairman of the Propaganda Committee for the Christian Front movement during its initial stages." Evans also stated that Kelly "was not a regular member but more in the capacity of a paid lecturer." So while there is independent evidence that Kelly was not a Christian Front official, it also appears that a Jewish organization informant (Evans) was the Front's senior propagandist and that at least one other undercover informant (Carlson) was spreading virulently anti-Semitic literature throughout metropolitan New York and inciting impressionable adolescents to engage in acts of violence against Jews. Interesting ironies underlie the process of democracy and discourses of political power in twentieth-century American history.[50]

Great Pro-American Mass Meeting, May 1939

For the Pro-American Mass Meeting of 24 May 1939, Kelly decided to deliver a speech entitled "John L. Lewis, Public Enemy No. 2," a version of which he had given five days earlier to fifty-plus elite New Yorkers at one of Allen Zoll's American Patriots weekly luncheon meetings at the Hotel Iroquois. Kelly's FBI file contains a single-page report of this meeting, also submitted by Carlson. Zoll, who "struck a handsome figure in the dim light" of the dining room, urged those present to buy tickets for the upcoming Mass Meeting, and then Kelly related his personal experiences of CIO agitation among the miners of Harlan County, Kentucky. References to crowds and mobs occur repeatedly in Carlson's reports as well as in *Under Cover.* "This crowd," Carlson observed, "gulped everything which 'Major' Kelly pumped into them," and "tsk-tsk-tsked all over the place." "I fell in," Carlson remarked, "tsk-tsking at them, though they didn't know it. Tsk. tsk. tsk." Carlson despised elites—the "upper strata of moneyed class," the "well dressed" men "of wealthy appearance," the "mostly dried up" women, "Old Americans out to redeem their country from the enemy knock-knock-knocking at the door"—yet he could find no "exciting . . . Jew-baiting" at this "very mild" and "pleasant gathering of Babbitt men and women."[51]

Carlson might have been disappointed with the lack of exciting Jew-baiting at the Iroquois, but he would find plenty five days later at the Great Northern Hotel. "To prevent disorder," said the *New York Times,* implying the inevitable outcome of patriotic mass meetings, more than a hundred police officers patrolled the street as eight hundred American Patriots, Christian Fronters, and members of a dozen other anticommunist and Franco-supporting groups packed their way into the Great Northern's lobby. Carlson arrived to find "the mob" boiling "like a broken hornets' nest," "buzzing around carping and biting the 'kikes,'" and he pushed his way in with it. He found the ballroom "choked with a sweating, steaming mob in an ornery mood, ready to rip up anybody on enough provocation." One of the "dried-up Old Americans" for whom Carlson held a particular dislike was the "ever-present" Leonora Rogers Schuyler, who was more than a "comic figure" because she had been an "officer of the Daughters of the American Revolution and her ancestors had come here in 1682." Carlson wrote in *Under Cover* that Schuyler was close to "many important anti-Americans and spread her propaganda in respectable circles." Schuyler was one of several representatives of the sponsoring organizations who sat on the dais while a thirty-six piece band played patriotic favorites. At about 8:30 P.M., a baritone led the audience, "which reflected some wealth and influence," in singing "The Star Spangled Banner." (It is difficult here, as with much of Carlson's writing, to reconcile his statements that the audience was wealthy and respectable yet sufficiently ornery to rip up innocent bystanders.) Following a prayer by Father John J. Murphy, Kelly delivered the keynote speech.[52]

As was shown earlier in the case of his community forum address at St. Stephen's Protestant Church in Philadelphia, Kelly's speech notes compare verbatim with quotes reported in the *Brooklyn Tablet*. While Kelly surely ad-libbed at venues like Donovan's Bar, the evident care he spent preparing notes for major speeches suggests that he stuck to his script. No doubt he revised his earlier speech at the American Patriots luncheon and then prepared a draft before typing it, for the nine, double-spaced sheets headed "Speech of John E. Kelly at Carnegie Hall [the original venue], 24 May 1939" are well crafted with few typos. "John L. Lewis, Public Enemy No. 2" (enemy number one being Roosevelt) was powerful yet balanced and was supported by plentiful evidence, much of which had a ring of truth.[53]

Basing his account on his own experiences as a mining engineer in Harlan County, Kelly first explained how nonunion Harlan miners earned more per hour than in Lewis's United Mine Workers of America union. Driven by ambition and greed, Lewis determined to unionize Harlan at whatever cost. At $3 a month, union dues brought Lewis $18 million a year ($540 million), "for which he need give no accounting to anyone." "Half a million dollars," Kelly stated, "went as a contribution to the New Deal," a shrewd investment that "paid dividends many times over." Under White House pressure, coal companies had agreed to "enslave the independent American worker," but not in Harlan County. Operators there were naturally prepared to accept union hours and wages, "which were lower than they had originally paid," but they were not prepared to accept a closed union shop. Amply supported by Lewis's war chest, and urged on by his "agitators and organizers," many workers struck. Others, though, preferred to keep working, so to protect these self-reliant individuals from intimidation by Lewis's snipers in the wooded hillsides, Governor Ruby Laffoon sent in the National Guard. Kelly stressed his own advocacy of trade unions, but of the kind that protected workers, selected staff from local members, accounted for union dues, and acted lawfully.[54]

He then compared Lewis to Spanish labor leader Francisco Largo Caballero, the self-styled "Lenin of Spain," who seized control of the government and for a year "drenched the unhappy peninsula with the blood of 300,000 of its best citizens." Yet, as always "in times of great human failure, when tyranny or selfishness saps the will of men," providence supplied an instrument of salvation "fitted to the need: a Lincoln, a Franco." Here, Kelly tied the piety of his audience to U.S. history through the example of Franco's God-fearing Spain. "As one among millions of peace-loving Americans," Kelly hoped Lewis would put aside "Marxist blandishments and the urgings of his own ambitious nature." There could be no future for either Lewis or America under "Red dictatorship. That way lies chaos." Listeners, though, could rest assured that patriots were "organizing defenses of our heritage and faith." Kelly closed—"with all the emphasis and sincerity of my being"—by stressing that were communists to attempt to set up a dictatorship in America, "THE CHRISTIAN FRONT will tear it down."[55]

These closing remarks, building to a crescendo that he tailored to suit his audience, were the only inflammatory touches of Kelly's entire twenty-five-minute speech. Then again, Kelly's was no call to unseat a functioning, democratic government but, rather, a statement of hope that patriotic Christian Americans stood ready to thwart any attempt by Stalinist revolutionaries to replace such a government with a Madrid-style workers' dictatorship. He had mentioned "siren voices in alien accents" cooperating with the Third International, but his speech was devoid of anti-Semitism. Yet the *New York Times* reporter felt that "repeated references to 'Christian America'" by Kelly or the following speaker, silver-haired New York state senator John J. McNaboe, had indicated a "definite anti-Semitic tinge." FBI informant Neff, who had earlier heard Kelly at the overflow meeting at Columbus Circle make a "bitter harangue against the Jews," was also present in the hot and crowded ballroom. Despite having praised Kelly's oratorical skills at Donovan's Bar, Neff thought Kelly's speech was "impromptu and shabby," an odd comment given Kelly's meticulous preparation and experience as a public speaker. Carlson, in his FBI report, had no such reservations, pointing out that the speech received "thunderous applause." After admitting that "the word 'Jew' was used little during the meeting," Carlson nonetheless claimed that by laying their emphasis on "Christian civilization and the American way of doing things," speakers had "slurred [the Jews] by the use of innuendo."[56]

When Carlson typed out the manuscript for his best-selling *Under Cover* in 1943, slur and innuendo filled every page, while fact served only for flights of fancy. All he had heard while undercover was hate. "Hate! Hate the Niggers, the Jews, the Polacks . . . Hate anything, but hate!" And on the night of 24 May 1939, he had heard nothing but "hate preached at a meeting which started with a prayer tendered by Father John J. Malone [*sic,* Murphy]." Having said in his FBI report that Senator McNaboe "spoke softly, with an air of reasonableness," Carlson now explained that McNaboe had given regular addresses at Zoll's "fascist meetings." Carlson had reported to the FBI that Jack Cassidy, the meeting's last speaker, was a "magnificent orator" who urged Americans to "forget differences in religion and to organize on a common front against Communism." Yet for his 800,000 American readers, he now wrote in terms of the "fiery and intense" speech of "Jack Cassidy, fuehrer of the Christian Front." In his FBI report, Carlson stated that when a woman objected to a derogatory line about Roosevelt in an address given by Joseph McWilliams, chairman Zoll signaled to McWilliams to either cut short or tone down the speech. Now, in *Under Cover,* Carlson wrote luridly how "the goon squad hauled her out as bony hands were clamped tight against her mouth. Her feet did not touch the floor." (Neither Neff nor the *Times* reporter mentioned any such incident.) *Under Cover* left no doubt in readers' minds that this had been a "regular Christian Front meeting," a meeting full of anti-Semitic hate and Nazi-inspired calls to violence masquerading as patriotic Americanism. As the subtitle of his book indicates, having spent *Four Years in the Nazi Underworld of America,* Carlson/Pagnanelli could confidently make *The Amazing Revelation of How Axis Agents and Our Enemies*

Within Are Now Plotting to Destroy the United States. Kelly, the leading "promoter of Franco-Nazism in America" and "organizer" of the violent, anti-Semitic Christian Front, consequently lurked in every imagined alleyway of Carlson's hate-filled alien underworld.[57]

Carlson and Kelly had much in common. Both were children of European immigrants, worked as journalists, and dedicated their lives to full-time activism for their new country, rooting out un-American fascists and un-American communists, respectively. Yet they saw America and their identity as Americans quite differently. Carlson's America was a sordid, grubby place. "I walked past garbage cans," he wrote of his first foray into U.S. Nazidom, into a "shabby, dim-lit" room. "Cigarette butts littered the floor. In one corner stood a battered steel cabinet." Every page of *Under Cover* continues this baleful litany. His Americans were sordid, hate-ridden people. "I had thought myself inured to the display of prejudice," he wrote in the preface to his second best seller, *The Plotters* (1946), "but even I was alarmed at the scope of anti-Catholic, anti-Semitic, anti-Negro, anti-foreign-born bigotry which I discovered." Throughout the thousand-odd pages of his two books, Carlson could find nothing good to say about anyone.[58]

Whereas Carlson wrote only to denigrate, to despise, Kelly filled his writings with a celebration of America and its multiculturalism. In a later article for the magazine of the Jonathan Club (a large hotel-cum-business association in Los Angeles), for instance, Kelly waxed Whitman-like about Humboldt County's foresters, those "tall brawny Swedes," and its fishermen, "lithe Latins . . . fast men with hook and net." "Coffee and old-fashioned courtesy" were unlimited in Humboldt, as were the wildflowers. "Nature stipples the marshes navy and white with iris, carpets the meadows in lupins cream and yellow. . . . Impatient redbud sets the thickets ablaze before its leaves appear. Azalea borders forest trails, bleeding heart lines pasture paths." Carlson was too angst-ridden over what he judged to be America's loss of democracy to fascism to smell its wildflowers. Kelly, rather, was naturally egalitarian, as comfortable among the dried-up old Babbitters at a ritzy luncheon as he was with the well-lubricated Fronters at Donovan's Bar. Whereas Carlson was mean spirited, vindictive, as if trying to repay others for the persecutions that he, his family, and his fellow Armenians had suffered in the Old World, Kelly was ever the optimist, looking forward to a post-Depression America. Kelly's *Programme for American Nationalism* might have been full of sweeping nutty ideas, as Talbot put it, but at least he had sat down to think through a constructive plan. For sure, his "Free Speech in Jersey City" article maligned machine-gun-toting CIO agitators, but the thrust of the piece nevertheless served to praise what Kelly understood to be the true American spirit of Jersey's anticommunist citizens.[59]

Carlson's *Under Cover* became the best-selling nonfiction title of 1943, and Kelly, America's principal "promoter of Franco-Nazism," appeared in it a dozen times. When Kelly read the book, he inscribed "Either *Superman* or ONE BIG

DAMN LIAR!!!" on the front cover and annotated page 360 with "A wizard at memorizing." Kelly had reason to be cynical. He would spend most of 1943 fighting to stay out of jail on a serious federal charge, and *Under Cover*, by its own admissions, identified Carlson as an informant.[60]

8

Un-American Americanism

Gen. Francisco Franco's face adorned *Time*'s front cover on 27 March 1939. With much reluctance, five days later Franklin D. Roosevelt's State Department recognized Spain's new government. For America's Franco lobbyists, preoccupation with the arms embargo was over. But with the Loyalists defeated, their cause was now ill defined, and with Adolf Hitler poised for European expansion, their support of a regime that had just signed a bilateral Treaty of Friendship with Germany was becoming harder to justify. Some lobbyists tired of the Great Debate's growing rancor. Others, like Merwin Hart and Hildreth Meière, stressed humanitarian aid and support for ambassador to Spain Alexander W. Weddell. A few, most notably John Eoghan Kelly, saw that Franco's victory over communism in Spain was generating complacency among anticommunists at home, so they heightened their rhetoric to convince Americans of the probability of social collapse and communist accession. At the same time, Roosevelt was stepping up his campaign to convert Americans from isolationists to interventionists, and he was intolerant of critics. Kelly reacted to the new climate of apathetic anticommunism and warlike internationalism by radicalizing his message. A collision between activist and state was inevitable.[1]

At the end of a grueling three-week trial in May 1943, which followed a five-year investigation involving some eighty FBI agents spread across twenty-two states deposing two hundred witnesses, a jury convicted Kelly of being an unregistered agent of a foreign power. He thereby became one of the first U.S. citizens whom the federal government convicted on charges relating to un-American activities, the first as an anticommunist. Kelly was stunned. For fifteen years he had held a U.S. Army commission and gathered intelligence on seditious activity, as when on 16 October 1938 he reported to Col. J. T. Ross from one of his contacts—Edwin G. Banta, "a patriotic citizen" who had joined the CPUSA as a mole—that a communist named Gabriel Taken was working at the Brooklyn Navy Yard through the Federal Writers Project and was apparently spying. On several occasions, he had pushed Martin Dies, chairman of the Special House Committee for the Investigation of Un-American Activities, to act against communist subversives and spies. And for five years, until December 1941, he had worked virtually full time to inform Americans of the threat he thought Soviet communism posed to their republican system. He considered himself the truest of patriots. Yet his country had now decided that he, too, was guilty of sedition.[2]

This chapter examines the FBI's extraordinary prosecution of the Kelly case, documenting the circumstances of his trial and showing the perils that await individuals who dare to confront a state's prevailing ideology. In arguing that antifascism rather than anticommunism was Roosevelt's preferred tactic for marginalizing opponents, and hence the Justice Department's primary modus operandi during 1938–43, this chapter describes a powerful nexus between J. Edgar Hoover's FBI and two unlikely law enforcers, Walter Winchell's *Jergens Journal* radio show and the Popular Front tabloid *PM*.

"Little Red Schoolboys"

By January 1939, Franco's Nationalists were near victory in Spain, but Kelly was even more convinced that the still-deteriorating U.S. economy would lead to societal breakdown and some sort of Popular Front takeover of the federal government. He worried that Roosevelt's indecisive administration was trending further leftward, which he evidenced in its dogged refusal to recognize Franco's New Spain and in the company kept by First Lady Eleanor Roosevelt. Certain that foreign and domestic tensions were reaching a crisis, and frustrated by his fellow citizens' apparent indifference, Kelly's rhetoric became harsher and his targets more public. Because his leftist adversaries exerted so much influence through the mass media, as well as having powerful friends in the Justice Department, and because he was attacking prominent figures, Kelly would soon discover the limits of his government's tolerance for criticism and its respect for the rights of free speech.[3]

In December 1938 he attended the American Student Union's (ASU) fourth national convention and then wrote a provocative article for *America* magazine entitled "Little Red Schoolboys," arguing that although ASU leaders claimed the high ground of democracy in the name of the Founders, they were actually "little commissars" intent on turning naive students into communists. Roosevelt, Kelly explained, had sent ASU executive secretary Joseph P. Lash a letter of greeting— reproduced on the back of the convention itinerary—in which Roosevelt heralded Lash's mantra to make "the Campus a Fortress of Democracy." After pledging the convention's theme to "Keep Democracy Working by Keeping It Moving Forward," Lash opened the ASU business sessions by advocating a "Primer for Democracy" course in every college as an answer to Germany's "Nazi Primer." Alongside *freedom,* there can be nothing stronger in an American citizen's dictionary of core values than *democracy,* and Kelly was duly impressed by the two huge banners that hung either side of the speaker's rostrum proclaiming "Democracy" and "Americanism." But after listening to delegates' speeches, Kelly realized that the ASU was "mouthing" democracy while it indoctrinated "immature minds" with socialism; it was nothing less than the "Comintern's youth outpost." As he toured the display stalls, he was shocked to find "everywhere" an "open, brazen, accepted, praise of the Soviet Union." ASU officials—those privileged "beneficiaries of the Founders' sacrifices"—were proclaiming democracy and Americanism at the same time as they were sending delegations "to Russia, ambulances to Red Spain," and openly deriding "the Founders of Americanism." Kelly quoted an advertisement for the ASU's fourth-annual European tour, which assured students that "in Moscow and Leningrad youth leaders will expound Soviet life as it appears to the first socialist generation." Still, Kelly wondered what kind of "Workers' Paradise" the Soviet Union had become when "hot running water and a bath on five minutes notice cannot always be guaranteed." Red, Kelly concluded, was the predominant color in the "crazy quilt" of Student Union thinking, "Moscovite [*sic*] red," that "magnet of the ambitious, the unscrupulous, the 'do-gooders,' the atheists, the haters, the unfit."[4]

Whereas previously the ASU had opposed military spending to advocate peaceful cooperation, it now declared its peace program to have been a misguided "prowar policy" whose only beneficiaries were the fascists. In "Little Red Schoolboys," Kelly reserved his most biting cynicism for this change of heart by the ASU, which he interpreted as a Moscow party line directive. Presumably because they were "faithfully heeding" Lash, their "little Commissar," delegates had no qualms about reversing their previous stand, which had never been about principles, Kelly implied, but Stalinist realpolitik. Kelly discerned three factors behind the delegates' call for a "great army and navy for 'national defense.'" First, Americans would buy the scheme because Comintern propaganda had "forced down [their] throats" the notion that Russia was a fascist-fighting democracy. Second, the delegates clamored for a huge military establishment because they were convinced it would soon be used in a "foreign adventure," namely for "the Soviets' aid in a planned Russo-German war." Third, CPUSA leader Earl Browder was now so confident of his "control of the machinery of government" that, come the revolution, he no longer needed to confront the U.S. Army with his own workers' militia. In strident tone, Kelly closed with an appeal to all those "instinctively anti-Communist" students— ROTC officers, athletes, Catholics—he knew existed on every campus. They were a "nucleus" from which would grow a militant undergraduate movement that would be "America's pride, a bulwark of true democracy—not the Stalinite variety." If such patriotic students could only drive communism from colleges, then they would be taking a great step toward returning "America to the ideals of the Founders." But as well as trying to make friends, "Red Schoolboys" made dangerous enemies, for it fingered a dozen of the prominent figures who gave convention speeches as communist dupes. Kelly went further with Aubrey Williams, the government's National Youth Administration executive, mentioning a public denunciation of her as a CPUSA member. Dubbing Lash a "little Commissar" and singling him out as director of the Student Leadership Institute, "a sort of training camp for future commissars," was Kelly's riskiest assertion. Roosevelt had personally endorsed Lash, and *America* was a respected, influential magazine with a circulation of 35,000.[5]

Moreover, within a year Lash was close friends with Eleanor Roosevelt. Although they had first met at a White House tea party in 1937, they did not begin corresponding until after 1 December 1939, when Eleanor helped Lash prepare to testify before the Dies Committee. By February 1940, they were seeing each other regularly. During one conversation, Lash told her that since leaving the Socialist Party in 1937, he regarded himself "as a non-party Communist," had joined a "Marxist study circle organized by the party," and was only waiting to leave the ASU before formalizing his membership. Eleanor showed no concern for Lash's frank admission, for, as Lash noted, she "was not afraid of the Communists or Communism." In November 1940 she helped furnish Lash's New York apartment, and for Christmas he gave her a little bronze Loyalist militiaman, which she kept on her desk as a cherished reminder of noble courage. By the following year, Lash had a key for her New York apartment, and she bought him a Pontiac convertible for Christmas. There is no evidence that Eleanor or Lash had any influence on the Justice Department's prosecution of Kelly, although Eleanor would no doubt have been pleased to read about the trial, which featured almost daily in *PM*, the Popular Front workers' tabloid to which she subscribed.[6]

In addition to "Red Schoolboys," during the first seven months of 1939, Kelly published twenty-six articles and delivered at least twenty-four speeches, typically to audiences of two or three hundred in clubs and hotel ballrooms. As in Boston, where he gave six speeches at the invitation of Clare Singer Dawes, he spoke on either the Comintern's subversive activities, how Latin American regimes were combating communists, or—as at the Women's National Republican Club, where he packed the ballroom—the importance of the Dies Committee at a time when the Justice Department leaned left. Franco's victory was cause for celebration in pro-Nationalist circles, yet, as Kelly urged Talbot in a letter of 7 April, there was still "much to be done to educate the American people and eradicate the red poison." Just as the "various red committees" would re-form as aid organizations to keep their message alive, Kelly recommended changing the American Union for Nationalist Spain into the American–Spanish Institute to stress culture and friendly relations.[7]

Despite his determination to keep up the pressure, in the summer Kelly had an unexpected six-month hiatus, which he needed. (He was only forty-three, but hunching over a typewriter, lecturing in smoky halls, hustling around crowded train stations, and eating fatty food in lonely hotel restaurants was a telling lifestyle for someone with a genetic predisposition for heart disease.) The U.S. Army called him to Plattsburg for military training in the last two weeks of August. Then, on 20 September 1939, he left for Spain, via Lisbon, with sixteen other passengers aboard the beautiful Pan American Airways *Yankee Clipper* flying boat. On behalf of its subsidiary, Consolidated Edison Company, the Stone & Webster utilities company wanted Kelly to ascertain what products—mercury, wine, olives, almonds—it might import in lieu of foreign exchange to help pay down a debt incurred by the Second Republic before undertaking any new infrastructural investments. His mother later recalled how happy he was to be making the trip, to have an engagement again in a worthwhile business activity as well as to be doing something productive for his country. Because the State Department was not authorizing business trips to Spain, Kelly obtained a visa from Ruth B. Shipley, his contact in the passport division, as a correspondent for Talbot's *America*. Once in Spain, he was disappointed that Franco would not grant him an appointment, but he did meet Gen. José Enrique Varela Iglesias, minister for army affairs. He also delivered letters from the War Department to the U.S. military attaché and Spanish general staff in Madrid.[8]

After his return to New York, detectives employed by his ex-wife, Frances Mae McBee, arrested him on a civil warrant for alimony arrears of $73,400 ($2.2 million), and he spent a month in jail, until 15 January, when his brother-in-law, E. Russell Cameron Jr., managed to raise the $2,500 bond ($75,000). Although Stone & Webster paid him a handsome $5,000, his expenses had been high—Pan American charged an astonishing $675 for a round-trip flight—so after paying his court costs, he was once again without money. He continued writing articles, publishing fifteen mostly cultural pieces about Spain during 1940, and barely covered the bills. Twin initiatives consumed the bulk of his time: first, with the backing of Talbot and Spain's reinstated ambassador Juan Francisco de Cárdenas, he hoped to form Friends of the New Spain, a promotional organization to overcome Americans' anti-Franco prejudice while lobbying the State Department to reestablish commercial ties; second, he pushed the importation of Spanish products, primarily mercury, through his consultancy arrangement with Stone & Webster. But in part because Spain's embassy seemed reluctant to commit precious funds to independent ventures, and in large measure because New Deal officials in Washington wanted nothing to do with Franco's Spain, both of Kelly's endeavors ended in frustration.[9]

Franco Lobbyists, Postrecognition

On Franco's victory and establishment of a government of reconstruction—though not reconciliation—in Madrid, AUNS members cabled Cordell Hull their fervent hope that the State Department would "work toward a good understanding between New Spain and the United States" in the belief that this would be in "the best interests of both countries and for the cause of international peace." They would be disappointed. Even though Franco did maintain his policy of official neutrality throughout World War II, and the critical strategic outpost of Gibraltar remained in Allied hands, it was no thanks to Washington's policy makers. Indeed, Roosevelt's first communication with Franco was not until the North African Operation Torch landings in November 1942, almost four years after his begrudging recognition of Nationalist Spain. And White House loathing did not abate under President Harry S. Truman, who, according to Assistant Secretary of State Dean G. Acheson, "held deep-seated convictions on many subjects," most notably "a dislike of Franco and Catholic obscurantism in Spain." Far from offering humanitarian aid to desperate Spaniards with a view to preserving their neutrality, Hull "turned a deaf ear" and would even hinder efforts by a new pro-Franco aid organization.[10]

In August 1939, Ambassador Alexander Weddell cabled Undersecretary of State Sumner Welles warning that Spaniards faced famine over the winter. A "gift of wheat and corn might spell a benevolent neutrality," he suggested, boding well for the impending conflict with Germany. But under pressure from Eleanor, who on 8 July threw a luncheon party for former Loyalist prime minister Juan Negrín and Loyalist Spain's principal U.S. lobbyist Jay Allen, Roosevelt wanted to make all dealings with Franco contingent, including the release of U.S. prisoners held in Spanish jails and the dismissal of Franco's request for compensation from Henry Morgenthau's Treasury Department for its purchases of silver from the Loyalists. Welles, who was keen to "recapture the Spanish market," was even having difficulty arranging export credits for surplus cotton that "we are exceedingly anxious to dispose of in the world market." At least in the case of Spain, Yankee moralism rather than useful realpolitik drove Roosevelt's foreign policy making.[11]

Because the Italian and German governments were pressing for payments on war matériel, and the Soviet Union had taken Spain's gold reserves, Franco's regime had to sell olive oil to raise hard currency, further exacerbating the nutritional crisis. While an increasingly discouraged Weddell was pestering the State Department to send wheat, the chronic shortages of vitamins, anesthetics, antibiotics, and other medicines were disturbing his wife, Virginia. In May 1940 she wrote for help to Franco lobbyists whom she had met through Hart and Meière's studio parties, pointing out that doctors were performing Caesarean deliveries on unanesthetized patients. Hart, Meière, and Ogden Hammond quickly founded the Committee to Send Anesthetics and Medicines to Spain (CSAMS). Through networking seventeen leading Americans, including Alexander Hamilton Rice, Philip Liebmann, opera star Lucrezia Bori, plastic surgeon J. Eastman Sheehan, Talbot, and Jewish philanthropist Maud J. Seligman, the CSAMS had shipped or was processing for shipment $2,836 ($85,000) of medicines by August 1940.[12]

But after Spanish farmers suffered widespread crop failures in 1940, conditions only worsened. Virginia Weddell rationed precious medical supplies arriving from the CSAMS, pleaded with the American Red Cross for blankets, and supplied Hart with harrowing tales of suffering for his press releases. On 3 December she told Hart that in "many districts . . . there has been no bread for six weeks" and worried that malnutrition could trigger an epidemic. She prayed for help from the United States: "O, for some of our golden wheat or flour." She was convinced that Spain was "doing everything in her power to stay neutral," but "rioting brought on by hunger *might* bring the Germans charging in 'to help.'" Yet instead of helping, Washington officials were hindering aid. After CSAMS members resorted to sending their medicines to Weddell in five-pound packages via diplomatic pouch to circumvent formalities, James Clement Dunn wrote to Hart indicating that the State Department "was not particularly favorable" to the CSAMS's work; this was probably at Hull's insistence, because Dunn was one of Hull's most pro-Franco subordinates. With Virginia Weddell experiencing delays in shipments, and her husband "increasingly frustrated with what he perceived to be a dangerous lack of [State] cooperation," Hart called a special CSAMS meeting for 2 October 1941 to discuss the situation. Anxious not to antagonize State, committee members considered disbanding their organization but decided to keep going after Hart received assurances from Dunn that if they acted as private individuals and sent all their medicines to Virginia Weddell care of the Madrid embassy, then the State Department would not object.[13]

In May 1939, Meière and Hart, along with Father Albert I. Whelan, *America*'s associate editor, also participated in a half-hour radio interview on New York's WQXR, the transcription of which Meière preserved. Father Philip A. Dillon, who played the uncommitted spectator with no knowledge of Spain, moderated the discussion. Because Whelan, Meière, and Hart had firsthand experience of Spain, were focused on humanitarian issues, and were accomplished public speakers, the program may well have left listeners with a favorable impression of New Spain. Dillon voiced concern about newspaper reports of postwar reprisals. Whelan countered by citing William P. Carney, the *New York Times* correspondent in Madrid. Of 4,500 cases handled by forty-seven courts, there had been fifty death sentences, with just seven executions in Madrid over the past four weeks. This belied the reality of *franquista* repression, but it sounded convincing. Whelan remarked that after the "cold-blooded killing of many tens of thousands of defenseless civilians by the Loyalists," it would be neither surprising nor unfair if "some of those guilty should pay the penalty." After detailing the extent of Soviet involvement in Loyalist Spain, compared to the social welfare programs of Nationalist Spain, the panel explained how New Spain would retain its independence and never become a fascist state. No Europeans feared war more than Spaniards, Meière remarked. After three years of desperate civil strife, their longing for peace would ensure neutrality. Hart then advocated a rapprochement with Franco, if only to support that cornerstone of U.S. foreign policy, the Monroe Doctrine. Every Central and South American state except Brazil looked to Spain, their mother country, "with respect and a good deal of veneration." What better way for the United States to promote its Good Neighbor Policy, Hart suggested, than by demonstrating that it had the "good will and friendship" of New Spain.[14]

Fourteen thousand New Yorkers packed into Madison Square Garden on 29 November 1939 for Franco lobbyists' final political extravaganza. Although their Mass Meeting for America said little about Franco's Spain, the meeting's agenda was a natural outgrowth of their "Look at Spain!" anticommunism, along with their conviction that Roosevelt's animosity toward Franco was illustrative of the New Deal's reluctance to tackle communist subversion. Neither would the meeting have been possible without the efficient organizational network they had built to lobby for Franco. Kelly was in Spain, leaving Hart and Meière to develop the concept, sell the seats, and raise funds. As their handbill explained, they had a threefold agenda: to pay tribute to the work of Congressman Martin Dies, who would be the meeting's principal speaker; to "urge the American people to forget all foreign isms (Communism, Nazism, Fascism)"; and to foster a "return to American concepts and ideals." Event sponsors included the New York Board of Trade, the American Jewish Federation to Combat Communism and Fascism, and Col. Theodore Roosevelt Jr.[15]

After the Metropolitan Opera's Frederick Jaegel sang "The Star-Spangled Banner," Hart introduced the speaker. As press publicity advertised, Dies did not "pull any punches." Basing his speech on President George Washington's warning that Americans must guard "against the insidious wiles of foreign influence," Dies explained how his HUAC hearings were only just beginning to scratch the surface of communist infiltration. "Hooded as 'liberals' and 'New Dealers,'" Joseph Stalin's agents had penetrated America's free institutions as well as its labor unions. But unionists should look to the dictatorships of Stalin and Adolf Hitler to see how foreign isms meant the abrogation of collective bargaining and "certain enslavement for the laborer." Americans must realize that the CPUSA was "a *conspiracy* organized in Moscow for the purpose of undermining and eventually destroying our national security." Americans should understand, too, that their government was part of the problem. He beseeched Roosevelt's administration "to come out openly and say whether it is for or against" the Dies Committee, and if *for* then it was time he received "the necessary funds" as well as "other assistance," implying the cooperation of the Justice Department. "God gave us America," he shouted confidently, and "the Marxists shall not take it away." Other speakers—Jeremiah H. Cross, American Legion; George U. Harvey, Queens borough president; Joseph P. Ryan, International Longshoremen's Association; Jean Mathias, Jewish War Veterans—reiterated the same points. As the band closed with a rousing patriotic medley, Dies led the company out of the Garden through a 7th Regiment guard of honor.[16]

By June 1940, with the Wehrmacht at Dunkirk, Roosevelt quarantining Spain, and Hitler pressuring Franco to commit to the Axis, Franco lobbyists realized their position was untenable. They decided to cable Franco, pledging their continuing support while pleading with him to stay neutral. As an indication of how wartime exigencies were straining their relationships, the wording of the cable caused a split in their once-single-minded ranks. Hart's original statement proposed the "earnest hope that Spain will not be drawn directly or indirectly into the present war, on the side of Germany," but when he asked the Spanish embassy for approval before transmittal to Franco, Cárdenas objected to the "on the side of Germany" clause. Although Ellery Sedgwick and Kelly agreed to the removal of the offending clause, Meière refused to lend her name to the amended version.[17]

Making Enemies

Throughout the late 1930s, Kelly was dodging McBee's detectives, who were hounding him for huge alimony payments when it was all he could do to make rent. As something of an investigator himself, he suspected that parties unknown were monitoring his political activities, but he did not have proof until he went to deliver his 21 July 1938 speech at Manhattan's Rotary Club. Jay Allen, a former *Chicago Tribune* foreign correspondent turned Loyalist defender, had sent a telegram to challenge his facts behind Nationalist executions of noncombatants at Badajoz in August 1936; in passing, Allen mentioned that a stenographer had transcribed his entire "Spanish Red Propaganda in the United States" speech to the Center Club in February. That same week, Talbot cautioned him against an apparent Franco supporter who was probably "an agent of some sort." Kelly, therefore, was no stranger to surveillance. Still, months later, on 13 February 1939, it would have shocked him to know that the FBI had just opened file "65–1461, John Eoghan Kelly." For on that particular day he was addressing officers of the U.S. Army's 316th Infantry at the Hotel Robert Morris in Wayne, Pennsylvania, on revolution in Spain and Comintern subversion at home. Col. Clifton Lisle judged the lecture "perfectly splendid," could "never recall an evening in which more interest was shown," and felt Kelly's "presentation of the Spanish situation was amazingly well done." Once over the shock, Kelly might have laughed had he been able to read the report from FBI's agent George J. Starr. A bureau veteran since at least 1929, Starr believed his investigation of Kelly was "probably the most sensational development in connection with subversive activities" that he had encountered during his career.[18]

Agent Starr based his report on interviews with a young woman named Gladys Rountree, whom he had met after an introduction from Morris Leon Radoff. What Dr. Radoff, who by 1940, if not then, was Maryland's state archivist, was doing in Manhattan and how he knew Rountree is unknown; perhaps they shared a romantic interest or membership in an organization. Rountree related to Starr how AUNS chairman Hart had needed an assistant writer for his book *America, Look at Spain!* Mary Vail Andress, a pro-Franco executive at the Chase Manhattan Bank, recommended to Hart that he hire Rountree, but after typing in Hart's midtown office for three months, Rountree became so worked up about her employer's pro-Franco politics that it was having an "effect on her nervous system," as Starr put it, and she had considered quitting. Once FBI director J. Edgar Hoover learned of Starr's investigation, Hoover advised her to stay and become an informant. Rountree was convinced that Kelly was a Nazi spy plotting to overthrow the U.S. government and that Hart's office was a hub for subversive activity, with Kelly as its ringleader.[19]

According to Rountree, Hart's New York State Economic Council was "devoting fully 90% of its time" to disseminating pro-Franco propaganda, "pamphlets and circulars" were mailed "in quantities of two and three million copies," and those coming and going were either "strongly Anti-Communist, outstanding so-called Patriots, or just plain every day American Fascists," all of whom wanted "what would amount to a totalitarian form of Government." Kelly, she was sure, "exerted the most influence" on the council's "extra-curricular activities," which aimed to "keep a 'Red scare' constantly before the public." Although there were "constant telephone calls back and forth," many were to set up meetings, "later or at some other place," and so far she had been "unable to learn anything of value." Kelly received calls "twenty and thirty times a day," and she said that "no move is made without his approval." She claimed that Kelly's "hatred" of the democratic U.S. government was "so violent that he actually loses control of himself" and had to "go into German for words sufficiently vile to describe his opinion of our form of government." Rountree did state—presumably in response to questions by Starr—that during all the "plotting" by the group, their "pronouncements" "did not condemn the Jews, and in fact make appeal to their allegiance to this country." She had no doubt, nevertheless, that the group was "seeking to undermine these Jewish people."[20]

Evaluating Rountree's assessment of Kelly in the plotters' den is difficult without considering its context. A year earlier, amid considerable publicity, the FBI exposed a Nazi spy ring operating in metropolitan New York, and the pro-Loyalist *Blockade* was just one of several spies-are-everywhere movies that Rountree may well have seen. In the fall of 1938, Leon G. Turrou, an FBI agent who helped to crack the German ring, published *The Nazi Spy Conspiracy in America*. At just the time that Radoff persuaded Rountree to talk to Starr, moreover, Warner Brothers launched prerelease publicity for its April 1939 blockbuster *Confessions of a Nazi Spy*, based on Turrou's book, which portrayed Nazism as a contagious mental illness. This was a time of international crisis, a time when thousands of angst-filled Americans heard Orson Welles's radio dramatization of H. G. Wells's *War of the Worlds* and concluded that the Martians had landed. In the mind of a young woman with a nervous disposition, it is easy to see how Kelly grew into a Nazi. It is possible, but unlikely, that he behaved and spoke as Rountree claimed. There is nothing to indicate poor self-control—his temperament was easygoing, placid even—or that he lapsed into German. His mother, who emigrated at age

twelve, retained German fluency but must have had little accent, for her husband's acquaintances took her for Irish; Kelly's brother Domnall, according to his
daughter-in-law, only ever spoke English, and then with an educated East Coast
elocution. While Kelly no doubt enjoyed practicing his German, he would have
had few opportunities in Hart's office, with the exception of discussing business
relating to *Spain in Arms* with Konstantin Maydell, a German speaker whose English was poor. At a time when so many Americans were recent immigrants, it was
easy to link an accent to foreignness and un-Americanism, a standard tactic of
Hollywood films to distinguish good Loyalists from bad Nationalists.[21]

It would be March 1940 before P. E. Foxworth, New York chief and later the FBI's
assistant director, forwarded another Kelly report to Hoover, but the delay was not
so much from any lapse in the investigation as from the conflicting nature of the
evidence at hand. Agent J. A. Sizoo heard from one informant that Kelly was "a
very brilliant crook," "in contact with many gangsters," and "very dangerous" and
learned that Kelly had "a connection in the State Department," was an "authority"
on intelligence with the U.S. Army reserve at the rank of major, and had even made
an appointment to see Agent J. B. Little after hearing that the FBI was investigating
Maydell. But with the international crisis worsening and Kelly's enemies closing in,
Hoover and his agents would soon be dismissing puzzling evidence to dwell on the
incriminations. Kelly's lobbying for Franco combined with his relentless attacks
on communists had made him too well-known, too successful, too dangerous for
Comintern officials to tolerate. Informants—including some two dozen at Jewish
organizations and the FBI's Rountree and Carlson—were gathering incriminating
evidence. In March 1938, when he ran out of money for salaries, Kelly had laid off
his last office assistant, James Finucane. Either from animosity at being unable to
find other employment, out of some political belief, or perhaps because of his dalliance with Kelly's ex-wife McBee, Finucane began collaborating with McBee and
later the FBI. On 4 June 1940, McBee walked into the FBI's Manhattan office to
make a statement, much of which she reiterated in a letter to Sumner Welles at the
State Department that landed on the attorney general's desk.[22]

McBee's claims stressed Kelly's foreign connections and seditious activity at the
highest levels, beginning with his father, who had worked with the Irish nationalist
Roger Casement until Casement's "execution for treason" and who had made his
home a meeting place for "all the Anti-English agitators from Ireland and India."
For years, she claimed, Kelly was "bootlegging war supplies" to "revolting Latin-
American countries" and even Japan and had financed "several revolutions." In 1937
he traveled to Berlin "to contact HITLER and was designated by him to represent
the Gestaop [Gestapo] in this country." In 1939, she said, Kelly flew to Spain "to
see Franco, and make a contract," whereby he would be the purchasing agent "for
all American goods to be shipped through Spain for the Axis." After Italy's 10 June
1940 declaration of war, Kelly called steamship companies about leasing a fleet of oil

tankers for shipment to Spain, and the following day National City Bank received $2.8 million. Piece by piece, over two pages of testimony, McBee assembled a "jekyl [*sic*] and Hyde" character. Kelly was "a very brilliant man," but one with "absolutely no idea of the truth"; a "great linguist . . . possessed of perfect manners"; "the brains behind the Christian Front" and the "leader of a revolution in the United States." Because he surrounded himself with "influential people as a shield," she claimed, with "HIGHER-UPS," including "many of our diplomats," it would be hard for the government to prosecute him. (While it was standard FBI procedure to uppercase names, this is an intriguing example of the cult of professionalism then in vogue as well as of class-consciousness in America's supposedly egalitarian society.) Even though Agent J. A. Ruehle admitted in his report that McBee "had no definite proof of any of her accusations," he agreed with her that "it was impossible to underestimate" Kelly's capabilities. He concurred that Kelly was "certainly a most dangerous man to have in this country in time of war." From Kelly's viewpoint, it would prove the adage that hell hath no fury like a woman scorned.[23]

The Winchell-PM-Hoover Antifascist Nexus

Pro-Franco anticommunism of 1937–43 stands in contradistinction to its state-sponsored bookends, the 1920s Red Scare and 1950s McCarthyism. It was an effort to defend Americanism against communists by citizens who found themselves in opposition to their state. Effort and opposition alike stemmed from their observation that the state was as indifferent to communism as it was hostile to their brand of anticommunism. During the early war years, if not by the end of 1938, Roosevelt sought to discredit his isolationist opponents. He took advantage of the Winchell-*PM*-Hoover nexus, the principal product of which, especially after June 1941, when the USSR became a U.S. ally, was a prevailing climate of antifascism rather than anticommunism.

After World War I, radicals posed a real threat to capitalist order, although hindsight suggests it was containable without recourse to heavy-handed measures. By the summer of 1919, President Woodrow Wilson was castigating opponents of his League of Nations as "Bolshevistically inclined" and explaining how "the poison of disorder, the poison of revolt, the poison of chaos" was spreading to the "free people" of America. Wilson, though, was neither an exploiter of popular anticommunist hysteria nor a possessor of an unwarranted fear of communism. To the contrary, as Regin Schmidt argues, Wilson's administration engineered the Red Scare in order to nip a budding menace. After followers of anarcho-communist Luigi Galleani mailed thirty bombs to government officials, and dynamite blew the porch off Attorney General A. Mitchell Palmer's house, secretary Joseph P. Tumulty advised Wilson in Paris of a "terrible unrest stalking about the country." Attacks peaked in

1920 with a massive blast on Wall Street that killed thirty-eight and wounded four hundred. Wilson's foremost anti-Bolshevik was Robert Lansing at the State Department, who saw a "very real danger in view of the present social unrest," whether from a pending wave of strikes or a growing agitation against capitalism, and he no doubt factored in the IWW's efforts to disrupt wartime production.[24]

Palmer's new appointee at his Radical Division Department, J. Edgar Hoover, was eager to implement Lansing's program. Schmidt identifies the scare over white slavery in 1912 as a precedent for Hoover's tactic of whipping up popular feelings against a threat to order. But it is important here to note that Hoover was not so much concerned with stamping out vice—or, as with the Red Scare itself, sedition—as with increasing both the powers and budget of his fiefdom. With postwar cutbacks looming, the newly reorganized Bureau of Investigation pounced on anticommunism "to safeguard its bureaucratic interests" as well as consolidate its hold over internal security. Schmidt's interpretation dovetails with Hoover's behavior in later years. Alexander Stephan notes how Hoover, during investigations into German émigré writers such as Thomas Mann and Bertolt Brecht in the early 1940s, was uninterested in and made few distinctions between their political ideologies, lumping them all together as "Communazis." What seemed to fascinate Hoover were his suspects' sexual dalliances, for, as Stephan suggests, he judged immorality as un-American and thus conflated "perversion" with sedition. Wilson's Red Scare successfully repressed America's neophyte radical anarcho-communist movements. John Earl Haynes observes that over the 1921–31 decade, the CPUSA "remained a small movement without influence" staffed by "immigrants who spoke little English." But Hoover's methods worried legislators. In 1924, as a condition of his acceptance of the Bureau's directorship, Hoover had to promise Attorney General Harlan Fiske Stone that he would henceforth restrict his investigations to breaches of federal law, and Stone in turn promised Congress that the FBI would no longer concern itself with "political or other opinions of individuals."[25]

There was, of course, anticommunism in America during between 1922 and 1946. William Randolph Hearst was not the only reactionary press mogul, several midwestern cities had conservative mayors, and patriotic organizations such as the American Legion were officially anticommunist even if a substantial proportion of their memberships was left-wing. Nine states required loyalty oaths of public school teachers. Chicago's Memorial Day Massacre was but the most notorious of several bloody confrontations between police and strikers. And pro-Franco Americans were resolute anticommunists. Still, in comparison to the bookends of the Red Scare and McCarthyism, anticommunism was as much a minor concern society-wide as it was a low priority for Roosevelt's federal government. As a leading historian of U.S. anticommunism admits, during the 1930s, "Congress itself officially discounted the idea of a Communist menace," while across the nation, according to M. J. Heale, "antiradicalism enjoyed neither the government nor the public support" of other periods.[26]

After World War II, with the economy booming and society united in the glow of victory, Truman might not have faced a communist threat at home, but he was eager to convince Americans to back his doctrine of aiding anticommunist regimes in Greece and Turkey. Hoover happily dusted off his Red Scare tactics, which through the acquiescence of President Dwight D. Eisenhower and at the further encouragement of Republican legislators became the hysterical witch-hunting of McCarthyism. Anticommunism during 1919–22 and 1947–54 was a state project, whereas from 1937 to 1943 antifascism was the principal modus operandi of the New Deal state.

According to Sumner Welles, Roosevelt saw little "need to fear Communism," an indifference, perhaps, that explains why so many Comintern agents managed to infiltrate his government and compromise its security. Welles recounted a conversation during which Roosevelt discussed the narrowing gap between the systems of U.S. democracy and Soviet communism. At the outset in 1917, Roosevelt placed the two systems at "opposite pole[s]," with America at a nominal value of 100 and Russia at 0. But by the early 1940s, the "Soviet system had advanced materially toward a modified form of state socialism," to the point where he expected that it would soon "reach the figure of 40." Revealing, too, is Roosevelt's stated hope that "American democracy might eventually reach the figure of 60," an albeit cryptic yet presumably serious insinuation that he wanted a substantially socialist American system.[27]

With the exception of State, Roosevelt's key departments did not seem to fear communism either. Morgenthau at Treasury "had long harbored an admiration for the Soviets," as his son put it. According to historian Richard W. Steele, Interior secretary Harold L. Ickes, who was the administration's "chief anit-Nazi [sic]," readily approved of "dissidents on the left." More importantly, Justice, as Ted Morgan suggests, may well have been "soft on Communism." In 1940, Attorney General Robert H. Jackson apologized for remarks by Assistant District Attorney O. John Rogge, which a panel of state governors understood to be "'Commy in tenor." Rogge had complained to the panel that HUAC was persecuting communists and fellow travelers (of which Rogge was one) while ignoring the true threat, fascism. Jackson's predecessors, Homer S. Cummings, and then Frank Murphy, who was Detroit's mayor in the early 1930s, were probably Loyalist sympathizers. FBI agents in Detroit had been reporting since 1937 on a Young Communist League recruiting drive for the Abraham Lincoln Brigade, but the Justice Department had ignored Hoover's requests for instructions.[28]

Then, on 1 September 1938, Justice's Criminal Division advised Hoover to reopen his investigation. But this was in response to intervention by Cordell Hull, who was in part motivated by a letter he received from Kelly at the end of June alerting him to the repatriation from the Loyalist zone of large numbers of "warhardened communists." Yet no sooner had Hoover sent his agents' findings to Justice in April 1939 than the Criminal Division told him once again to shelve the investigation. There were two more flip-flops before Hoover ordered the arrest of a dozen ALB veterans in February 1940, only to see a flurry of protests from communist organizations and leftist legislators such as Senator George W. Norris (I-NE), after which Jackson ruled that ALB recruiting was a technical violation unworthy of prosecution.[29]

Schmidt and others have stressed that apart from a "few isolated instances" when the White House asked the FBI to investigate communist activities, Roosevelt was far more concerned with "extreme right wing elements and fascist sympathizers." In May 1942, Attorney General Francis Biddle relayed to Hoover the president's annoyance that the FBI seemed to be "ignoring the Fascist minded groups both in the Government and out," by which Biddle meant that Roosevelt wanted to see more fascists behind bars. Roosevelt appropriated $50,000 for FBI countersubversive surveillance in late 1938, to which Congress in 1939 added a further $250,000, with the intention of encouraging Hoover to repress anti–New Deal rightists not interventionist pro-Roosevelt leftists. Indicative of Roosevelt's reluctance to prosecute communists was his contemptuous attitude toward Dies's committee. In November 1939, when Congress debated HUAC's dissolution, House Rules Committee chairman Adolph J. Sabath (D-IL) wrote three letters to Dies insisting that he "stick to the Nazis," by which Dies understood him to mean "leave the Communists alone."[30]

Prevailing historiography considers Dies's HUAC to be the bad boy of American anticommunism. One popular college textbook disparages its "crusade" as "viciously anti–New Deal." For sure, in its form as a permanent committee under a different chairman in 1947 (Dies, who had been running HUAC as a one-man show since 1941, retired in 1944), HUAC did commit "shameful" excesses of McCarthyism. But following its inception in 1938, when Dies's hearings commanded front-page news, its investigations proved more effective than the FBI's and its accusations rarely lacked substance. In October 1941, Dies accused 1,121 federal employees of membership in subversive organizations, embarrassing the FBI into investigating 601 cases, of which the Bureau completed 455 and brought just two charges. As Morgan puts it, "Dies cried whitewash, not without cause," for in addition to those who were merely members of communist-affiliated groups, at least seventy-six federal employees were spying for Soviet intelligence at the time, as proven in 1995 when the CIA released its Venona Project transcripts. Several of these spies occupied high-level posts. Privy to the Trident conference of May 1943 to discuss the opening of a second front was "Source No. 19," a top-ranking U.S. official whom Herbert Romerstein and Eric Breindel argue was Harry L. Hopkins, Roosevelt's closest confident, although other historians are skeptical. Still, of HUAC's hearings and the FBI's sedition cases, those receiving most press coverage during 1938–45 involved right-wing not left-wing groups, most notoriously the New York German spy ring (1938), the preemptive anticommunist coup-plotting of Maj. Gen. George Van Horn Moseley and George E. Deatherage (1940), the pro-German propagandizing by editor George Sylvester Viereck and U.S. aviator Laura Ingalls (1941 and 1942), and the Great Sedition Trial of 1944.[31]

Following the London Blitz of September 1940, Roosevelt's fireside chats stressed how Americans were "living at the point of a gun." By May 1941, he was popularizing the phrase "second World War" and by July was provoking German U-boats to fire the first shot at U.S. destroyers on escort duty near Iceland. Driven by Wilsonian internationalism, a yearning to deploy the latest in sea and air power, an impatience to create a historic legacy, and an expectation, perhaps, that only total war could fix the broken economy, Roosevelt was eager to draw Americans into global hazard. There was, of course, a major war in Europe, and Nazi leaders were explicit about acquiring *lebensraum* in the Slavic east. It was also the case that once Stanley K. Hornbeck, Hull, and other U.S. policy makers who saw the Pacific as an American lake abandoned diplomacy in favor of saber rattling, Pearl Harbor may have been inevitable. Yet as late as mid-September 1940, Japanese policy makers were undecided whether to ally with Germany or America. Had a less ideological Roosevelt persuaded them in favor of a realpolitik deal over Manchukuo, then a range of counterfactual scenarios suggest that global catastrophe was avoidable.[32]

Largely at the administration's prompting, which built easily on the Popular Front's antifascist propagandizing, war fever swept the nation, becoming a pandemic after Pearl Harbor. Anxious Americans of the early war years flocked to cinemas to see *Confessions of a Nazi Spy* and other Hollywood blockbusters that likened fascism to a psychotic contagion. On Sunday evenings, around twenty million Americans tuned in to Walter Winchell's radio show, *Jergens Journal*, to listen to his shocking catalogs of sabotage and sedition, made the more dramatic by the host's staccato delivery. Putting to use a talent for showmanship honed by a decade in vaudeville, Winchell mesmerized listeners with his own lingo, coupling words—*debutramp, Chicagorilla*—and popularizing others, *making whoopee, pash.* Some eight million Americans could also catch up on Winchell's Nazi witch-hunts in his daily syndicated newspaper exposés, "On Broadway" and "In New York." With so much talk of a so-called German fifth column, it was no wonder that Americans dutifully filed more than two hundred reports of parachute landings, none of which turned out to be Hitler's saboteurs.[33]

No mere egotistical windbag, Winchell was a powerful man with high-level connections; his office became a collecting house for War Department leaks and Capitol Hill rumormongers. Apart from his inside track to Columbia Broadcast Systems (CBS)—his secretary, Rose Bigman-Fox, being the wife of a CBS executive—Winchell was a friend of Hoover's. Hoover socialized with him at the after-hours Stork Club (of which Winchell was a part owner), *spoke as "guest columnist" on his radio show or submitted briefs for "On Broadway,"* and considered Winchell so well informed on matters of national security that he assigned a senior agent to report on his weekly broadcast. In August 1940, courtesy of Hoover, at Winchell's pleading, Bigman-Fox enjoyed a "special tour" of the FBI's facilities with her husband, John, during which they both "fired the tommy gun." Winchell and Hoover, along with many Americans it would seem, were living vicariously in a bizarre frontierlike world of secret agents, gunrunners, and gumshoes. Just as Stephan has shown for the FBI's investigation of German émigré writers that Hoover was more interested in the sexual liaisons of his suspects than the substance of their supposed subversion, it is similarly clear from the Kelly case that it was the investigatory means—wiretaps, mail searches, interrogations, tests for invisible ink—FBI agents lived for, not the prosecutorial end.[34]

Winchell worked closely with Ralph McAlister Ingersoll, editor/publisher of *PM*. To launch *PM*, Ingersoll acquired financial backing from Marshall Field III, the inheritor of a dry goods empire who sold his holdings in order to devote his life to philanthropy and newspaper publishing, principally the *Chicago Sun*. After lumping together Benito Mussolini's conquest of Ethiopia, Hitler's remilitarization of the Rhineland, and Franco's rebellion in Spain, Field concluded that he must throw his support behind the Loyalists, which he did by trying to raise $250,000 ($7.5 million) in food aid for Madrid and by promoting the Loyalist cause through Ingersoll's *PM*. Although *PM* sold out of its first 500,000-copy print run on 18 June 1940, and Field sometimes resorted to purchasing thousands of copies, circulation rarely exceeded 100,000 for much of the paper's short life. Still, *PM*'s marketing hype and radical reportage raised media interest, and it enjoyed an influence that far surpassed its sales. Willard L. Beaulac, counselor at the U.S. embassy in Madrid from June 1941 to March 1944, lamented that whereas many State Department officials did not read his dispatches, "nearly everyone" read the press—"including such papers as *PM*, which was conducting a private war against Franco"—and remembered what was said, especially when it came to Spain.[35]

While Ingersoll promoted *PM* as liberal-socialist, it was thoroughly Popular Front, right down to its internal squabbles between staff who had joined the CPUSA and those who joined Norman Thomas's Socialist Party. Ingersoll, nevertheless, was critical of Joseph Stalin's August 1939 accommodation with archenemy Hitler. When Ingersoll visited Soviet ambassador Constantine Oumansky five days after the Nazi invasion of 22 June 1941 to ask for an appointment to meet Stalin and travel to the war zone, Oumansky granted both requests but not before lecturing Ingersoll on his failure to follow the party line over the Nazi-Soviet Non-Aggression Pact.[36]

A heavy drinker, Ingersoll frequented New York's Yale Club on Vanderbilt Avenue, where since 1925 he often met Winchell to trade news stories and a glass of scotch. Once Ingersoll had *PM* running, the two shared leads from undercover informants as well as Justice Department leaks. At one point in 1942, an angry Biddle asked Hoover about an FBI report on subversives that Biddle had sent to Capitol Hill, details of which appeared in both *PM* and on Winchell's radio show before any congressional officials had seen it. In an equally brusque tone, Hoover cynically suggested to Biddle that he "give consideration to subpoenaeing [*sic*] Mr. Walter Winchell."[37]

Winchell, a Russian American Jew, reserved special reproach for Germans in general and Nazis in particular, calling them "Ratzis." He still found fault with un-American communists, but during 1939–45 this would seem to have been a smokescreen. Writing in the CPUSA's *Daily Worker* organ, George Daugherty appeared concerned that while Winchell "usually strikes out at Hitler and the Nazis," he also "slanders labor." Yet the gist of Daugherty's two-part article was that his readers should tolerate Winchell, as the slander was insincere. When he first began attacking Nazis, Winchell realized that he "stood in the line of fire of those red-baiters who were then declaring that all Jews who spoke out against fascism were Communists." In order "to prove he was not a Red," he therefore "decided to attack the Reds," which helped curry favor with his employer, William Randolph Hearst. Daugherty implied, too, that Winchell was a cynical opportunist, a "supreme egoist" who would always side with the most popular cause as a path to enhancing his "power, prestige, and personality."[38]

As an ardent supporter of both the New Deal and U.S. military intervention against the fascist powers, Winchell ingratiated himself with Roosevelt, who eagerly reciprocated. Winchell was one of a handful of columnists, along with Arthur Krock and Anne O'Hare McCormick, whom Roosevelt favored with invitations to the White House or his Hyde Park home for exclusive interviews. Winchell even assisted with administration speechwriting. No journalist, writes Steele, was "more determined, less restrained in his advocacy, or more closely aligned with the administration propaganda effort" than Roosevelt's "favorite," Winchell. According to Morgan, the White House used Winchell "to attack its enemies," slipping him leads through operatives Tommy Corcoran and Ernest Cuneo. Roosevelt was not only eager to stifle critics of his domestic polices but also, after the spring of 1940, to raise support for beleaguered Britain among an isolationist public. Steele explains how Roosevelt drew on the "fifth column myth" to promote "an education campaign that portrayed his domestic critics as part of the Nazi conspiracy." Secretary of the Navy Frank Cox sponsored a four-part newspaper series that appeared in editions nationwide, explaining how Hitler's European triumphs were a direct consequence of an inherent weakness by democracies to internal subversion from within. Roosevelt, already possessed of an "intolerant, conspiratorial outlook," skillfully cultivated an American "disposition to view dissent on foreign policy matters as subversion." By encouraging the Winchell-*PM*-Hoover nexus, Roosevelt could satisfy his twin objectives of building interventionist sentiment while silencing critics and at the same time mollifying labor.[39]

After June 1941, when the Soviet Union became a U.S. ally, and especially after Pearl Harbor, when the Comintern could claim the moral high ground even more self-righteously, the nexus's antifascism became the dominant force. By 1942, CPUSA membership was back to 1938 levels. To increase support for Russia's Great Patriotic War, Stalin—the Uncle Joe who smiled benevolently from four of *Time's* front covers—resurrected Russian Orthodoxy, and to appease his allies, he disbanded the Comintern in May 1943. With Earl Browder's "Americanization" of the CPUSA in full swing and Winchell joking that the CPUSA's next move would be to change its name to the American People's Party, Red baiting became an unpopular national pastime, at least until after VJ Day. Winchell's Sunday radio spot, reinforced with his daily newspaper columns, was so effective in the wartime climate of fear that the Winchell-*PM*-Hoover nexus produced an antifascist hysteria.[40]

Pro-Franco anticommunists were obvious targets, and Kelly provided the perfect scapegoat. René Girard's surrogate victim theory of scapegoating states that the purpose of sacrifice is always "to restore harmony to the community, to reinforce the social fabric." In Greek mythology, Kelly would have been "a mysterious savior who visits affliction on mankind in order subsequently to restore it to good health." In 1943, to paraphrase Girard, his trial symbolized the change from passionate and destructive debate to unanimous accord and the construction of the cold war.[41]

Kelly Faces the Nexus

Winchell first went after Kelly in a prime-time broadcast of 19 January 1941. Basing his attack on information he received from McBee and the Non-Sectarian Anti-Nazi League to Champion Human Rights, Winchell charged Kelly with being a longtime Nazi agent whom Mexican authorities had arrested twenty years earlier as a German spy. On the next day, Newark's lieutenant of police, James Fitzgerald, and Detective Riccardi drove to Kelly's lodgings at 14 Brinkerhoff Street, Jersey City, to interview him. Winchell repeated the charges against Kelly the following Sunday. Because Winchell had broadcast Kelly's address, claiming it to be a gathering place for Nazis, irate listeners stopped by his lodgings or called on the telephone. With his landlady upset and his privacy gone, the stress proved too much. Kelly collapsed. A doctor came and diagnosed angina pectoris, explaining that he must stay in bed for at least a month. Unable to pay his bills, he wrote in desperation to Talbot, asking if he might prepare an article or take any other work that he could do while convalescing.[42]

Talbot was predisposed to sympathy, as he had just read a letter from a concerned *America* subscriber, William M. Ryan of Flushing, New York. While Ryan appreciated that Major Kelly could take care of himself, Winchell had "hurled such a vicious charge" that Catholics must rally to Kelly's defense. "While not of our faith," Kelly had done "magnificent work for the Catholic church in spreading the truth about Mexico and the Spanish Civil War." No one except *America*'s own staff had contributed more articles over the past four years, and all his articles had been "splendid." "Undoubtedly," Ryan determined, the reason "these Jews are trying to smear him and destroy his character before the gullible American people" was his "forthright condemnation of the Communist forces in Spain." If Kelly, a "splendid American Protestant gentleman," was willing to "go all the way in defending Catholic ideals and principles," then the very least that Catholics could do was make it plain to "these contemptible Jews of the Anti-Nazi league and their degenerate spokesman Winchell" that Catholic publications were ready and willing to defend him. Ryan apologized for the "strong language" but said that he felt it was "no time to remember the proprieties" when "Anti-Christian forces" were attempting to destroy someone in the "foremost ranks of the army of Christ." Ryan knew neither Talbot nor Kelly, but he had heard Kelly speak at a communion breakfast and felt compelled to come to his aid. Talbot assured Ryan that he held Kelly "in the highest esteem," and he may have been gratified to hear that there were still *America* readers who appreciated its anticommunist message, but, in truth, Talbot was losing his nerve.[43]

Angina forced Kelly to take days off work for the first time ever, he remarked to a friend; yet even convalescing in bed he was productive, typing out two articles, a poem, and drafts for two books. "Traveler's Reference Guide to the Provinces of Spain" was a detailed 270-page compendium, complete with references to Spanish Civil War sites, that he hoped Peninsular Press would publish. But with no American tourists traveling to Spain, the project lapsed. "Can Democracy Survive?" which exists only as a 22,500-word cut-and-pasted draft, presented an economic survey of American capitalism since the Industrial Revolution. "As an individualist of liberal heritage," Kelly explained how his thinking had passed through three stages: from shock in 1929, to a faith in American resiliency, now—with ten million unemployed and a further twelve million on the New Deal's payroll—to the "settled conviction that something fundamental is the matter" with capitalism and that "political democracy cannot cure it." Following the European war, which Kelly incorrectly assumed was no cure but "merely a palliative that is followed by a relapse, leaving the patient worse off than before," he expected that unemployed Americans would clamor for a lasting solution. He considered two equally unpalatable options: Soviet-style socialism or an authoritarian government with an imperialistic foreign policy. He concluded gloomily that by taking the second path, America could survive, but its democracy would be unrecognizable.[44]

After four weeks in bed, Kelly felt sufficiently rested to attend an Army Field and Staff School training session. But his troubles were only beginning. Hoover's agents were accumulating lurid reports. One *Jergens Journal* listener, George Schlager Welsh, wrote to Winchell from Miami Beach to say that he had once met Major Kelly in the Village Square, a Greenwich Village "beer joint" frequented by "pro-Nazi and anti-British" undesirables. A report bearing the designation "Stott, 2–7–41" pointed out that Kelly's father "was an intimate friend of [Irish nationalist] Sir Roger Casement," while his mother lived in Pittsfield, Massachusetts, "a centre of I.R.A. activity." An undated, anonymous report, typical for its use of the passive voice—"It has been learned from responsible sources"—implicated Kelly in the purchase of magnesium and other strategic minerals "now being sent to South America and Russia" but with an "ultimate destination" that was "unquestionably Germany." Kelly, moreover, "was intimate with Martin Dies," yet—troublingly, one would think, for the report did not reconcile the two statements—"almost every individual subpoenaed before the Dies Committee would come to see Kelly for instructions before appearing." Capt. Peter Rodyenko, who had attended maneuvers with Kelly at the army's Plattsburg facility in 1939, wrote to Winchell describing Kelly's "very obvious snooping around," the "mean look on his face," and the disturbing fact that he "swiped my daily paper." Whether Hoover considered newspaper swiping an un-American activity is unclear, but in a memorandum of 8 April 1941 he recommended Kelly "for custodial detention in the event of a national emergency." Then in May the army discharged Kelly's commission on the grounds of an "incompatible vocation." Winchell's broadcast of 18 May gloated over the news of Kelly's discharge. McBee, who was listening to the radio at a friend's house on Long Island, "shouted for joy."[45]

Next to weigh in was *PM*. The magazine employed "crusading tactics," as Marshall Field put it, with Ingersoll imbuing his staff with "the importance of getting mad, and staying mad." And nothing got *PM* staff madder than fascists, especially American Franco-fascists. Over a multipage spread that included a rogue's gallery of photographs, on 12 June 1941 *PM* called for Congress to act against a "Working Fascist Front," within which it included "Known Christian Fronters" such as Senator Robert A. Reynolds (D-NC), "professional 'patriot'" Elizabeth Dilling, "upper class citizens with access to Park Avenue drawing rooms" such as Hart, and "U.S. Army" Fronter Kelly. While it claimed to be saving America from communism, the "real role" of the "Fascist Front" was to "promote Fascism at home, patterned after the Franco crusade in Spain and using anti-Semitism as its chief weapon of disunion." Intriguingly, *PM* launched its attack ten days before Operation Barbarossa broke the Nazi-Soviet Non-Aggression Pact. Despite the probability, if not inevitability, of a German invasion of Russia, though, *PM* was still careful to avoid the problematic word *Axis,* claiming only that U.S. Fascist Fronters aimed to wreck America's "defense effort" and, "under the Franco flag," use Spain as a fascist "bridgehead to South America." But after Barbarossa, with the Soviet Union officially on the Allied side, *PM* threw off the gloves and went after pro-Axis American fascists with a vengeance.[46]

On 3 November 1941, *PM* mounted a three-day multipage "Inside Story" of "John Eoghan Kelly as Paid Madrid Stooge," or, as its headline cried, "How the Axis Uses Spain as Its N.Y. Mouthpiece." It was a masterful witch-hunt, interweaving Dies Committee revelations and photographs of arms' shippers and Kelly at the signing of the 14 November 1938 petition to Roosevelt with spicy testimony from McBee's alimony hearing and even reproductions of two of Kelly's letters to editors. Setting the tone of the exposé was the text of a telegram sent the night before to Attorney General Francis Biddle from the New York Coordinating Committee for Democratic Action. Since 1938, the telegram began, a "ruthless campaign" inspired from abroad that "seeks the destruction of our American democracy" had been "waged on the streets of New York and other cities," and Kelly was "one of its most important and dangerous chiefs." Kelly was a prime mover, "dominating the anti-democratic forces as publicity agent, propagandist, military advisor, contact man and master strategist." He had visited "leaders" in Spain and Germany, created "pressure organizations," was "actively engaged in influencing [U.S.] foreign policy," and, despite working for Franco's Spanish Library of Information, he was not registered with the State Department as an "agent of a foreign government." And especially, the telegram charged, he had "consolidated the persons attending numerous rallies into storm-trooper platoons which then launched a campaign of violence and terror on the streets of our city." Despite talking about "evidence," "documents," and "facts," there was little of substance in the telegram. It correctly stated that Peninsular News Service had paid Kelly $1,200 ($36,000), but it did not say that the sum represented multiple payments for over fifty-five freelanced articles. There was much, too, that was sheer fabrication or innuendo. It claimed that Germans held the rights to *Spain in Arms,* when in reality Film Facts had bought the U.S. rights, a corporation whose major stockholder, Col. Pierpont M. Hamilton, was a descendent of Alexander Hamilton.[47]

In a similar vein, *PM* reporter Victor H. Bernstein built his article around words like *transcript, record,* and especially *testimony,* which he used ten times. Bernstein admitted that he did not know whether Kelly was "America's No. 1 stooge of fascism abroad, or the No. 2 or No. 3"—indeed, Kelly's work had been "one of organization rather than execution"—but whatever place Kelly held, he trafficked with "nearly every native fascist in this country." Bernstein impressed on *PM* readers the "vital importance" of prosecuting Kelly. Americans might have "thrown out the Nazi and Italian consular services and with them a complex Fascist espionage system," but the "Spanish Phalanx," directed from Spain "at Berlin's bidding," had taken its place. As the "hireling" of "Hitler's stooge government," Kelly earned his "Spanish gold" by operating a "vast network of Fascist propaganda." Working in ways that "the Nazis and Italian Fascists have long since made familiar," Kelly sought to "propagandize the American people" and destroy their democracy. Worse, the Kelly situation showed that those "inside the Government and out" had stood idly by for years suffering "the siege of democracy to go on unmolested."[48]

One of the people who read *PM*'s Kelly exposé was Ulrich Bell, an Abraham Lincoln Brigade supporter and the executive chairman of Fight for Freedom, Inc. With the feisty old senator Carter Glass (D-VA) as honorary chairman, and southern Ohio Episcopal bishop Henry Hobson as its chairman, Fight for Freedom was a powerful ultrainterventionist lobbying organization that, naturally, enjoyed Roosevelt's favor.

Bell put down his copy of *PM* on 3 November and wrote to Secretary of State Cordell Hull, pointing out that Kelly had "received more than $1,200 from the Franco government for his propaganda services" yet was "not registered with you as an agent of a foreign government." It was Kelly's care to serve "the anti-democratic forces" inconspicuously, Bell explained, that had made him such an effective Axis agent; now, to make amends, Bell said, Hull must bring a prosecution.[49]

As the attacks mounted, Kelly tried to keep writing, although his publishing friends were distancing themselves, and it became harder for him to earn a living. During the last half of 1941, *Spain* published ten Kelly pieces mostly on Spanish history and culture, and *America* published four political articles, including "For the Defense of America Against the Communist Threat." But after publishing "Taxes Mount and Mount as America Girds for Defense" in November, Talbot accepted nothing more. Kelly wrote a number of reports for Lawrence Dennis's influential *Weekly Foreign Letter,* including an astute analysis of Rudolf Hess's flight to Scotland (Hess had earlier flown to Madrid, where he confided to Gen. José E. Varela that "he was fed up to the neck" with Joachim von Ribbentrop's pact with Russia). One of Kelly's last political endeavors was speechwriting. Congressman Andrew L. Somers (D-NY) delivered an address to the Committee for a Jewish Army that Kelly wrote for him just after Pearl Harbor, which argued for an all-Jewish U.S. Army corps on the basis that through a sacrifice in blood, Zionists could better press their case postwar for a state in Palestine. Kelly's speech for Somers had a double agenda, for its intention was not only to mend bridges between Brooklyn's Irish and Jewish communities but also to conflate the Jewish and Irish causes for full republican independence. Kelly had become so desperate to maintain his writing career that he sent resumes to both the New York and Washington offices of the Works Progress Administration. Officials there regretted to inform him that congressionally mandated budget cuts precluded any further allocation of projects. On 24 October he filed for bankruptcy, recording $10,340 in unsecured claims plus accrued alimony to McBee of $96,000.[50]

By October 1941, Agent J. M. Tennant was coordinating the efforts of FBI offices in Huntington (WV), Richmond (VA), Boston, Newark, and Washington, D.C.; had placed a "mail cover" as well as a telephone log on Kelly's Brinkerhoff Street address; and had compiled for Hoover a thirty-seven-page report on Kelly's activities as a suspected Nazi agent. In addition to reiterating the litany of charges leveled by McBee and Anti-Nazi League informants, Tennant included a memorandum dating from May 1940 entitled "The Fifth Column in the United States: The Christian Front—John Eoghan Kelly," from the director of naval intelligence, Commander D. B. Downer. Downer stated as fact that Kelly was "the actual leader of the Christian Front," which included "35,000 members in the Metropolitan district," of which four hundred were police officers; "the actual directing leader of the American Confederation Against Communism"; "the directing leader of the affiliated organization, American Women Against Communism"; organizer of the 36,000 strong Reserve Officers Association for the "dissemination of anti-Communist and anti-Semitic propaganda." He also claimed that Kelly maintained contacts with naval reserve officers that were similarly political; was "welding [these] and other organizations together"; had "offered leadership of the anti-Communist, anti-Semitic movement to General Moseley"; and that he expected a crisis in 1940–41, at which point he proposed "the elimination of party politics." To this extraordinary catalog Tennant added startling claims of his own, including British suspicion that Kelly was a German agent during the Great War and was now a Nazi agent supplying both Germany and Spain with war materials and even that Kelly was "one of the world's greatest military minds." Tennant's report is typical of all those that Hoover saw concerning the Kelly investigation. Even though Downer stated his claims as fact, he mentioned in his preamble that the information had reached him through "an intimate personal friend" and that the friend had gathered the information from Kelly himself. Downer, moreover, admitted the possibility that Kelly had been "playing a part" in his capacity as an official of U.S. military intelligence.[51]

Hoover was now involved with the Kelly case on a daily basis, writing two hundred directives pertaining to one of the FBI's most extensive investigations before the McCarthy era. Some eighty agents from thirty regional offices would question more than two hundred witnesses, assembling a file of 1,800 pages. To put this in perspective, Kelly's dossier exceeds those of Bertholt Brecht, Erika Mann, Heinrich Mann, and Klaus Mann combined, each of which Alexander Stephan considers a product of a major investigation. From the reports he was reading, Hoover must have discerned two difficulties. First, to bring an indictment, he needed hard evidence, whether of espionage or propagandizing for a foreign power. He asked Assistant Attorney General Wendell Berge about Kelly's articles in *Spain,* but Berge regretted that they "cannot be considered propaganda" under the Foreign Agents Registration Act (FARA) of 8 June 1938. Second, Hoover could see that the reports not only mentioned suspects with Irish- or German-looking names but that they also pointed to important old-stocks, to "HIGHER-UPS." Through the simple expedients of planting evidence and scapegoating, FBI agents would solve these problems; but in the meantime, Hoover noticed that McBee had listed Kelly's "sweethearts," so he instructed his agents to interview them.[52]

Yet just as Hoover was moving the investigation into high gear, Kelly's pro-Franco anticommunist campaigning was in decline. McBee's alimony proceedings had ordered Kelly to pay her $65 per month ($2,000), and to meet the obligation he had taken a job as manager of a disused platinum-iridium mine near Eureka, California, which aimed to supply metals for the war effort. Although he did publish four articles in January, he wrote only one during the rest of 1942, "Spain's Role in South America" for the March edition of *Catholic World.* Even though his heart pained him frequently, he brought energy and enthusiasm to the mine. But on 7 July, he fell off a wooden trestle, breaking his right leg at the knee. While lying in traction, he probably heard Winchell talking about him on the radio.

Although they had helped put half a dozen Nazi-paid German-alien propagandists behind bars, Winchell and *PM*'s editors exposed few so-called native fascists, let alone any real Axis spies or saboteurs. To keep the pot boiling, they returned to their witch-hunt of Franco lobbyists. As Winchell reminded his listeners on Sunday, 19 July 1942, Kelly was a "propaganda agent" for "Nazi-dominated" Spain who the FBI should have jailed long ago. Had the FBI forgotten about Kelly, Winchell wondered? "Why is that?" It was time to put these "Joe McNazis" behind bars. Kelly might not have heard the broadcast, but Eureka's mineworkers and police officers had. Humboldt County's deputy sheriff, Adrian Anderson, told an FBI agent that Kelly employed a Chinese cook, insisted that people dress for dinner, and clicked his heels Nazi-style. Mineworker Ben Kimsey thought Kelly's real business was checking coastal soundings, though his wife believed Kelly's interest was submarine landing sites. Kimsey's brother-in-law, Charles Holber, said that Kelly paid him to make a mapping table, took unexplained "trips around Humboldt County," snooped around a lighthouse, and even "stayed up until two o'clock in the morning ostensibly to work on minutes pertaining to the mine." As if all this suspicious activity was not proof enough, so FBI agent Arthur V. Hart implied, liquor enforcement officer Wallace M. Stryker quoted Kelly as saying, "Hitler's strong; the world doesn't realize how strong he is." Presumably in response to Hart's leading questions, Stryker then stated, "[Kelly said that Hitler is] getting rid of the Jews and that's what we ought to do in this country," but after reading over this portion of his statement, Stryker added in retraction, "I can't recall the exact phraseology he used." Hart claimed to have interviewed two witnesses who stated that Kelly tried to talk them out of enlisting.[53]

Agent Hart's report reads like the tittle-tattle of a backwoods community made fearful by war fever and Winchell's accusation that Kelly was a Nazi spy. In casual conversation, Kelly probably portrayed Germans as resourceful, Jews as socialists, and war as dangerous. Yet it is unlikely that he tried to talk anyone out of enlisting. After a second round of interviews at the mine, the only evidence that Agent Robert Earl Gocke could pinpoint was a government notice explaining that war-related mining work was grounds for deferment, posted by Kelly in the hope of retaining his skilled workers. And as his regular correspondence with his brother-in-law Sgt. E. Russell Cameron Jr. makes clear, Kelly was writing letters of recommendation so that Cameron could attend officers' school before a posting to the Pacific. Some of the witnesses also harbored personal reasons to disparage Kelly. Ben Kimsey, the mine's discoverer and foreman in the 1930s, likely resented Kelly's professional expertise and decision to hire someone over him as foreman. And now, with Kelly in hospital, the mine had once again closed, leaving everyone without work. Hart did depose two friendly witnesses. U.S. Forest Service ranger Wesley Houghtelling, despite having had frequent contact with Kelly, was "unable to furnish any information as to possible seditious utterances or subversive activity"; whatever Hart had heard in the community was "gossip" occasioned by Winchell's broadcast, he said. Forest Service investigator Stuart M. Schick noted that in maintaining a payroll of fifteen, Kelly had made "outstanding efforts to please everyone," and in all his dealings in the locality had been "very prompt in meeting obligations."[54]

With his heart still bothering him, his leg in a brace, and Col. H. Harrison Smith closing the Eureka mine and withholding payment of his salary, the fall of 1942 could not have been a happy time for Kelly. Although he had found work as a field engineer for a war-related materials company in San Francisco, he had to file in New York State Court for an extension of his alimony payments. Celia M. Cameron, his second wife and true love, who was now largely bedridden with tuberculosis, decided after several exhausting interviews with FBI agents over four months, during which time agents opened her mail and illegally tapped her telephone, that it was in both their interests to divorce. This was a defensive tactic to throw off the FBI, as the two kept close, with Kelly visiting whenever he could and choosing clothes and books for her, which he sent regularly by mail. After the war, Celia helped him revise his fiction writing, including working with him on a 376-page manuscript, "Sonora: A Novel of Victorian Mexico." Then, in February 1943, he began receiving airmail letters from friends startled by grand jury summonses in *United States v. Kelly*, so he went to the FBI's office in San Francisco.[55]

Agent Starr had rated Kelly "the most sensational development in connection with subversive activities" of his career. It is striking, therefore, that the climax of the FBI's investigation came when, some four and a half years later, the suspect presented himself voluntarily to ask if he might be of assistance. Yet this would be the least astonishing aspect of the case. At no point did FBI agents take the trouble to analyze, let alone report on, Kelly's supposedly subversive propagandizing, either as speeches or as published articles. Far from attempting to nip Kelly's activities in the bud at the outset—by issuing a warning, interrogation, filing a restraining order, trumping up a charge—Hoover's FBI created a climate more favorable for sedition through agents provocateurs such as John Roy Carlson and Harold Neff. Had Hoover's procrastination stemmed from a belief in upholding free-speech rights, then the oversight might seem laudable. But the real explanation was self-justification. Hoover and his agents needed Kelly in circulation as long as possible. Not only did Kelly validate the FBI's role in society, but he also provided fodder for the Winchell-*PM* component of the nexus, and not merely by boosting newspaper sales and listener ratings. Kelly was a perfect fascist Other: an intelligent, middle-class American with connections to the higher-ups. He was really a German wolf in superpatriot clothing, a walking example of how fascists had ingratiated themselves into every level of elite society and why workers must rise to stamp out the upper classes.

Guilty of Un-Americanism

When it came on 10 March 1943, forty-one months after Kelly's first appearance in the FBI's "Agents of the Fascisti" dossier, *United States v. Kelly* was a show trial, an indictment not of a dangerous subversive intent on overthrowing democracy but of the criminal justice system that undergirds that democratic ideal. Journalists from *PM* covered every day of the three-week event, as if they understood that it symbolized the final argument in the Great Debate over the soul of Americanism. Reporter Victor Bernstein was interviewing Kelly's defense team at one point when a lawyer asked if *PM* was responsible for the indictment. Bernstein replied nonchalantly, "Well, yes and no . . . We brought pressure to bear and obtained it." To convince the grand jury to try Kelly, an FBI agent colluded with an informant to plant evidence, which itself was circumstantial. Witness testimony at the trial was anecdotal or based on hearsay. Jurors received instructions to disregard contradictory evidence brought by the defense. And the charge, which hinged on a technicality, depended on subjective interpretation by an expert witness. It was an exercise, too, in scapegoating, for after the inevitable guilty verdict, a plea bargain ensured that Kelly waived his appeal in order to protect the higher-ups, who could now forget that they were ever Franco lobbyists.[56]

Three agents arrested Kelly at the Jonathan Club Hotel in Los Angeles on 1 March 1943, taking him into custody along with two overnight bags, a briefcase, and a typewriter. Kelly spent two weeks in jail while he hired a lawyer and raised bail, after which he traveled to Washington, D.C., to prepare for trial. Having already exhausted his earnings on legal and bond fees, he had no money left for a hotel room, let alone his defense, so he wrote to Talbot. He need not have worried, for news of his indictment had sent Franco lobbyists running to their lawyers, none quicker than Talbot, who had already testified to Kelly's grand jury and feared the government would prosecute him next. On the advice of Talbot's lawyer, John J. M. O'Shea, and working through his own lawyer in Jersey City, Robert H. Wall, Kelly contacted James V. Hayes, who agreed to take the case for $3,000 ($90,000), on the understanding that Talbot would cover the bill. Hayes filed for an adjournment and began examining the government's case.[57]

Hayes, with Wall on his defense team, made three important discoveries. First, ever since Kelly's first articles for *Spain,* Miguel Echegaray and Javier Gaytan de Ayala, the two Spaniards who ran Peninsular News Service (Spanish Library of Information after May 1940), had presumed he was a U.S. government informant—

a double agent—and so they had never trusted him. Not only did the irony of this revelation shock Kelly, and had him thinking back through all his dealings with Echegaray and Gayton, but it also had the potential to demolish the prosecution's argument that Kelly was using Peninsular as a front for his Nazi activities.[58]

Second, the FBI had found incriminating materials in Kelly's office safe, proving to Hayes's satisfaction that agents had resorted to evidence planting. Hayes's suspicions were well founded. Classified documents in file 65–1461 show that an FBI agent conducted an illegal search. James Finucane, Kelly's office assistant until March 1938, had become a hostile witness, probably because of his dismissal and his relationship with McBee, for whom he testified at Kelly's alimony hearing. Finucane evidently informed Agent Gust A. Koski that Kelly's safe was in a storage warehouse and he knew the combination. When Berge wrote to Hoover on 1 April 1943 authorizing a search warrant, he mentioned that Koski knew "the combination of the safe" and had "already examined the contents thereof." An FBI memorandum acknowledged Berge's authorization, similarly stating that Koski had noted the contents of the safe "some weeks ago." Armed with the warrant, Koski duly seized five items: an October 1940 letter from Kelly to Cárdenas proposing an embassy-funded counterpropaganda agency, with Kelly as its director, along with a reply; Kelly's *The Christian Soldier* Franco booklet and his "Spanish Gold for Propaganda Purposes" article for *America;* and a reprint of Joseph Goebbels's 1937 Nürnberg rally speech, "The Truth About Spain," which portrayed Spain as the archetype of "Bolshevik World Revolution," unmasked the "parasitic" Jew as Bolshevism's "chief agent," and questioned why there was silence over Stalin's extermination of dissenters yet uproar whenever a German gave a Jew a "well-earned box on the ears." Kelly may have owned this pamphlet, but, as he stated to Hayes, none of the seized documents were in the safe. He "carefully checked" its contents before delivering it to the warehouse, and only he and Finucane knew the combination. Anyway, Kelly pointed out, when there were so many folders of Spain-related correspondence boxed up in the storage facility, why keep those particular documents in a safe. Kelly was convinced that Finucane and Koski had rummaged through the folders, selected the most damaging-looking materials they could find, and planted them in the safe to imply that Kelly considered them incriminatory. A further indication of collusion between Finucane and Koski was the FBI's justification to Hayes that they requested the warrant based on "advance knowledge" from an informant that two documents dated October and November 1940 were in the safe, when Kelly had employed no office staff since hiring Finucane in 1938.[59]

Third, Hayes realized that to convict, the Justice Department must first show how FARA applied to Kelly, after which it had to prove he was guilty under one of the act's provisions, both being contentious points. When Kelly first read about FARA in the fall of 1938, he expected that he would have to register, because Franco's Nationalist regime was the principal (a legal term under the act) of Peninsular

News Service, so he visited Charles W. Yost, chief of the State Department's Office of Arms and Munitions Control, who stated explicitly that there was no requirement for him to register under the act as an agent of a foreign principal because, first, Peninsular had already registered and, second, he was a freelance journalist. When the trial began on 10 May, the government's young, blond prosecuting attorney, Isaiah Matlack, who implied his impartiality by stressing he had graduated from Washington's Catholic University, never tried to deny the substance of the Yost conversation, nor did he challenge Yost's opinion in a written clarification that while an "agent of a foreign principal" had to register, a "subagent does not," defining a subagent as "a person who acts under the direct supervision of a registered agent." Matlack argued nevertheless that because Kelly received regular payments from Peninsular while also acting independently as a Franco propagandist, he was an agent in his own right and was therefore required to register. On hearing Hayes move for a dismissal on the grounds of Yost's statement that independent journalists need not register, Judge George F. Morris rejected the fact as irrelevant. Hayes had better luck with the evidence in Kelly's safe, successfully protesting its admissibility, although it no doubt influenced both Morris and the jury. *PM* also made hay with it. Reporter Bernstein stressed that the Goebbels pamphlet was "anti-Bolshevik and anti-Semitic, in the usual Goebbelsian vein," implying by extension that Kelly's *Christian Soldier* was Goebbelsian; Bernstein emphasized that it proved "that Kelly was in Germany in November 1937," thereby incriminating him as anti-Semitic by association.[60]

To prove that Kelly was a propagandist, Matlack called on the testimony of a government expert, Princeton University's Harwood L. Childs. After a day haggling over Childs's qualifications, Judge Morris admitted Childs as an expert witness. A social scientist and expert on pressure-group research, Childs had theorized links between public opinion and propaganda in the "public mind," receiving government funding for his endeavors. With his associates Peter Odegard and Harold D. Lasswell, Childs was eager to demonstrate how the new science of quantitative content analysis could assist prosecutors in convicting citizens suspected of un-American activities. Kelly became Childs's first guinea pig. Using data from three independent coders, who turned out to be Justice Department employees, Childs certified statistically that Kelly used the word *red* at least once every two thousand words in his articles, a rate ensuring that the entire article classified as propagandistic. Morris overruled Hayes's objection that Kelly often wrote "Red Army," Joseph Stalin's own term and one in common usage. After analyzing 420 paragraphs from fifty articles, Childs's coders had certified 209 paragraphs as containing one or more pro-Franco statements, 218 with anti-Loyalist statements, and only three paragraphs with anything anti-Franco. To "write of Francisco Pizarro or Hernando de Soto, dead these 400 years, is to praise General Franco," Kelly observed sardonically to Talbot, adding that "if there was ever an

American Dreyfus case, this is it." Kelly was convinced the government was fram-
ing him as a German spy to cover its failure to lift the Spanish arms embargo.[61]

After an exhausting three-week trial, during which Matlack called more than
forty witnesses, on 28 May 1943 the jurors—eight Protestants, one Jew, one Catholic, two nonchurchgoers, and five who worked or intended to work for the government—deadlocked for four hours but nonetheless brought in a guilty verdict.
Judge Morris set 3 August as the date for sentencing, with Kelly facing a prison
term of up to five years and/or a $5,000 fine. A bitterly disappointed Hayes, who
had never expected to lose the case, filed a motion to set aside the verdict while
he tried to help his client raise funds for an appeal he was sure would succeed. But
Kelly's colleagues and friends were deserting the sinking *franquista* ship. Several,
including Hart, had declined to testify during the trial as character witnesses.
Even Talbot disowned Kelly, at least in private, writing in an internal memorandum, "We are trying to wean ourselves away from the link with Kelly." "Of course,"
he confided brusquely to one attorney, Kelly had "exaggerated our friendship and
the dealings that we have had." Privately, too, Talbot was a worried man. "These
people," by which he meant *PM* and "various groups" stung by Kelly's accusations,
"are determined to involve everyone possible, including Cordell Hull, Ambassador [to Spain] Carlton Hayes, etc."[62]

Armed with a guilty verdict, the Winchell-*PM*-Hoover nexus could drive dissenting pro-Franco anticommunists to the margins of society, where, tarred as fascist crackpots, they would lose all influence. Winchell was soon crowing. His 6 June
broadcast implied that he was the one who first exposed Kelly, resulting in the U.S.
Army revoking Kelly's commission, while the FBI dragged its heels for three more
years before convicting him. This trial revealed that Kelly had "associates," Winchell
continued juicily, "several Americans," no less, "but nothing up to this time has
been done about it." Hinting that influential policy makers were fascist sympathizers, Winchell wondered in signature rhetorical style, "Why is that?" Throughout
its almost daily trial coverage, *PM* had emphasized the same theme. "Franco Propagandist's Trial Shows How Fascists Duped Us," ran one headline, followed by
"Washington Yawns as Testimony Exposes Ways of '100% Americans,'" suggestive
of Rome burning while emperors fiddled. All through the summer, FBI agents kept
interviewing pro-Franco suspects, causing many to lose heart. When Agent C. E.
Hennrich telephoned the prestigious St. Paul's School in Concord, New Hampshire,
to ask why Dr. Kenneth Scott was too ill to comply with a subpoena to testify about
the showing of *Spain in Arms*, he learned that Scott was in the infirmary with a case
of systemic dysentery brought on by an anxiety attack. On hearing about the subpoena, Scott "went to pieces," according to the infirmary's physician, experiencing
"delusions that the newspaper 'PM' and the Communists are after him."[63]

After the trial, everyone from whom Hayes solicited advice found the conduct of the case shocking, and convinced him that an appeal must succeed, even

though at $5,000 ($150,000) it would be costly. Talbot, who also thought the verdict was "utterly outrageous" and "a miscarriage of justice," agreed with Hayes that
an appeal was essential. During early June, Hayes began soliciting funds through
Talbot's connections in the Catholic hierarchy and other benefactors, and Wall
left Washington saying, "my job is to raise the money." Then, in mid-June, everything went quiet, and neither Wall nor Talbot would reply to Kelly's telegrams.
There was something else strange. Kelly learned that his mother, Helen, who had
guaranteed Hayes's trial fees, would now have to pick up the tab because Talbot,
having contributed just $250 of the $3,000, was stalling. What could have happened? Throughout the trial, Talbot had fretted that a guilty verdict would set a
precedent, enabling the Justice Department to prosecute other Franco lobbyists,
especially himself, for as *America*'s editor he had never registered under FARA
either. Kelly reasoned that there could only be one explanation for Talbot to back
away from an appeal: Matlack and Hayes, with Talbot's complicity, had struck a
deal. At the outset, Matlack had never expected to win the case, but he was lucky
with Childs's testimony, and the ten or so pro-Loyalist jurors had been able to
convince their pro-Franco member (or possibly two members) to convict. Because Matlack knew that an appeal would overturn the verdict, he was prepared
to bargain with Hayes.[64]

Events bore out Kelly's theory. Matlack probably signaled to Hayes that as long
as there was no appeal, and provided that Talbot and his other pro-Franco friends
behaved, he would not press any further charges. All that remained was to ensure that Kelly stayed destitute. Helen had written to say that she could not stand
the shame of her son going to jail and would sell her house to fund an appeal;
this information would have been a factor in the negotiations between Hayes and
Matlack. On 3 August 1943, Kelly walked into court expecting a long jail sentence;
in that event, he had instructed his mother to take his plea-bargain theory to the
newspapers. Judge Morris denied Hayes's motions to set aside the verdict and call
a new trial. Morris then admitted that Kelly's articles, though they undoubtedly
"were intended to serve a purpose in enhancing the prestige of the Spanish government," were "not contemplated by the statute [FARA] in question," so impris-
onment would not be a suitable penalty "for acts of such content and character."
To Kelly's relief if not astonishment, Morris fined him $500. Noting that Kelly had
no money, Morris gave him forty-eight hours to pay, placing him in the custody
of his lawyer Hayes.[65]

It was a slap on the wrist, a sweetheart deal so Kelly would go quietly. Because the FBI had Informant C-282 in the Spanish Library of Information's offices
inside the Spanish embassy (the FBI was also tapping the library's telephones,
it appears), it is possible to reconstruct what followed. Hayes telephoned Teresa
Mezquita, the library's secretary, asking her to inform Javier Gaytan de Ayala,
then serving as the Spanish embassy's press attaché but who previously had been

Peninsular News Service's codirector, that Kelly's sentence was a $500 fine with no jail time. At 12:25 P.M. the next day, Kelly telephoned Gaytan de Ayala from the nearby Hotel Washington asking if they might meet. A few minutes later, Kelly and Gaytan entered the LaSalle Dubois Restaurant for lunch. Kelly's FBI Report 388, by Agent Logan J. Lane, records neither what they ate nor the exact time they left, but an hour or two later, Kelly walked up to the district court bailiff and paid his $500 fine ($15,000) in cash.[66]

Over the next eleven years, the *Times* printed seven of Kelly's letters, though none of them railed against communism. He delivered at least four more speeches and published well over twenty-five magazine articles, but only one promoted Franco's Spain, a piece in the Catholic *Sign* of March 1948, which argued cogently for Spain's strategic importance within the framework of the Marshall Plan. As several bulging packets of newspaper clippings in his papers suggest, he never lost interest in Spain. Neither did he lose faith in his vision of Americanism. Rather, the federal conviction for un-American activities knocked the political wind out of his typewriter.[67]

Political activism aside, Kelly stayed as busy as ever, as if through overwork he could forget the trial's shameful trauma. He traveled extensively, from Venezuela to Vancouver, surveying mine workings, networking investors for gas fields and iron deposits, and writing technical articles for mining engineering journals. Acting on his own initiative, and with no financial incentive, he became an unofficial promoter of America's gold industry. In the first of at least five articles he wrote for the business weekly *Barron's* during 1947–49, Kelly presented his case for the upward revaluation of gold toward its world market price; gold's artificially low U.S. dollar exchange rate, he demonstrated, was retarding the domestic economy while stifling world trade. Deluged by "more letters," most of them critical, "than on any topic which has engaged our readers' attention for several months," *Barron's* editor came to Kelly's defense, stressing that the government's current regime distorted international currency rates while creating a flourishing black market. When not moving from one hotel room to another, he visited his mother in Pittsfield and, his wife, Celia, who was dying of tuberculosis at a sanitarium in the West Virginia hills, or he stayed at a rented apartment in Washington, D.C. With his federal conviction at least pardonable in the climate of McCarthyism, in 1947 he consulted for the House Committee on Mines and Mining, and the following year he became a lobbyist for the Steel Committee of the New England Council (NEC), an association that promoted business deregulation and private enterprise.[68]

Deep ironies pervade American history. In 1946—if not in 1943, when Cardinal Francis Spellman visited Madrid—the State Department began a slow rehabilitation of Generalísimo Franco as a cold war bulwark. And in 1949 Kelly stood at a podium in a packed ballroom at Boston's Hotel Statler delivering the keynote address of the NEC's twenty-fifth conference on industrial development, during which he outlined the strategic cold war imperative for establishing an independent steelmaking plant in New England. For Kelly, though, the steel plant initiative meant far more than simply defense. Canvassing support throughout the region had reminded him of how often "the public's instinct is right on basic issues." State officials, labor leaders, business associations, bankers, farmers, professionals, homemakers—all could "sense that a major steel mill of our own will infuse new prosperity into the lifeblood of New England's economy." He had come across few critical voices, excepting scattered cries of "Socialism!" Yet Kelly could defend his project from this ironic charge, for while he admitted the necessity of asking public agencies to secure bonds during the initial funding process, he insisted that the mill would operate in the best traditions of American private enterprise. In closing his speech, he urged his listeners to lobby hard for the mill project, for it would prove to be a "test of our determination to retain the system that has made America great." Secretary of Defense Louis A. Johnson, notorious for drastically downsizing the military, was on stage with Kelly and no doubt one of those who gave him a standing ovation.[69]

A few months before he died of heart failure at age fifty-eight, Kelly's last published thoughts appeared in a letter to the *New York Times* in response to an article by Edith Efron entitled "Haiti's Happy 150th New Year." How could Efron, Kelly wanted to know, celebrate the triumphs of the Haitian people in the face of such adversity without mentioning Toussaint L'Ouverture, "who was the spirit of the revolt," playing a far larger part than, say, "Simon Bolivar in Venezuela's liberation." When it came to struggles for national independence from colonial regimes, Kelly was on the same page as the Trotskyite historian of the Haitian revolution, C. L. R. James, whom the U.S. government deported at the height of McCarthyism in 1953 for his radical politics.[70]

Conclusion

After a counterrevolutionary insurgency by Gen. Francisco Franco's Nationalists in July 1936 degenerated into a brutal, protracted civil war, many Americans for whom Spain seemed closer than 3,600 miles away took interest in the conflict. There were those who had no particular ideological axe to grind—entrepreneurs hoping to recover investments, vacationers with romantic attachments, immigrants worried about relatives, officers keen to evaluate the latest weaponry—but their concerns soon became subsumed into a divisive political argument that would have major repercussions. Millions of Americans identified with the attitudes, if not necessarily the aims, of Popular Front socialism—perhaps as journalists, feminists, social workers, pacifists, civil rights leaders, WPA job beneficiaries, or trade unionists—and this constituency empathized with Spain's Loyalists not only as fellow Fronters but also as front-line surrogates in their own fight against exploitative forces of reaction. That so many Americans became passionate backers of the Loyalist cause was in part because the disciplined CPUSA, in conjunction with the well-funded Spanish embassy, so successfully propagandized the Spanish Civil War as a moralistic struggle between fascism and democracy.

Article 26 of the Second Republic's constitution of December 1931 marginalized the Catholic Church in Spain by abolishing the parochial school system on which middle-class parents depended; there was an escalation of church burnings in the months after the February 1936 election, over which the Popular Front government acquiesced, and then an anticlerical onslaught followed the Nationalist insurgency of July, resulting in the systematic murder of 6,800 religious. It was natural, therefore, that America's Catholic hierarchy, along with many parishioners, saw the conflict in different but equally moralistic terms, as a struggle between Christian civilization and atheistic communism. To exemplify this position, historians have dwelt on Father Charles E. Coughlin, stressing both his influence as the Radio Priest and his anti-Semitism. Still, while *America,* the *Pilot,* and other hierarchy organs were as dogmatically partisan as any *Daily Worker* or

PM, the Catholic lay newspaper *Commonweal* under George N. Shuster's editorship opposed Franco, Dorothy Day's *Catholic Worker* sympathized with the Loyalists, and at the *Catholic World* editor James M. Gillis was critical of both sides.[1]

German American Bundists and self-styled American fascists such as William Dudley Pelley's Silver Shirts also held an ideological position on the conflict, which they saw as a struggle between fascism and communism. Though their rhetoric was no less dogmatic, they had little time for Spain, as their primary political philosophy was race-based nationalism. Isolationists represented a fourth category of Americans interested in the Spanish Civil War on political grounds, for they saw a struggle among Old World powers that threatened to entangle the United States. Because they insisted on embargoing arms to Spain, isolationists could appear to be in the pro-Nationalist camp even if their sympathies lay with the Loyalists. Robert M. La Follette Jr., the Senate's foremost isolationist, upheld the arms embargo while supporting the Loyalist cause against fascism.[2]

There was a fifth ideological grouping of Americans hitherto ignored by historians but documented here: those who lobbied for Franco's Nationalists because they saw a struggle in Spain between dictatorial communism and the kind of middle-class liberal republicanism they enjoyed at home, and they worried that the Comintern's agitprop was replicating that struggle in America. While they associated with the crude Christianity versus communism argument made by the Catholic hierarchy, and even exploited it, their interest in Spain was essentially as concerned liberals, as individualistic professional intellectuals, as reformers, as Progressives, as neo-mugwumps, and even as erstwhile socialists. Had they lived in Spain in April 1931, they would have cheered the departure of Alfonso XIII and the establishment of the Second Republic, as did most professional, intellectual, and middle-class Spaniards.[3]

Theirs was a complex as well as a conflicted position, which they tried to simplify and ultimately failed to reconcile. Franco lobbyists could hardly argue that communism had snuffed out Christian civilization in the Loyalist zone without allying with Spain's Catholic Church and its antediluvian reputation. Yet many lobbyists were Protestants or atheists for whom hierarchical Catholicism was inimical to individualistic Americanism. They could not emphasize that a communist revolution meant the end of civil liberties without downplaying Nationalist repression. Yet they recognized that eradicating communism in America would be equally difficult while maintaining constitutional rights to free speech. They could not advocate Franco's stand against communism without backing an authoritarian regime. Yet their hopes that Franco's New Spain would institutionalize Christian corporatism seemed hypocritical when they attacked Franklin D. Roosevelt for supersizing government. Indeed, their efforts to defend Americanism against communism by supporting Franco forced them to confront the inconsistencies inherent in their own national ideology, which they had always presumed was as exceptional as it was immutable, at a moment when it was in crisis and disjuncture.

When Franco lobbyists asked their fellow Americans to "Look at Spain!" and when they stressed that what was happening there "must not happen here," their mission was educational, or, in the jargon of the day, propagandistic. Three points of qualification are required, for theirs was always a counterpropaganda campaign. First, they were anticommunists because there were communists who in fact were growing in numbers, visibility, and influence. CPUSA enrollment might only have been 75,000 by 1938, but "many figures" in the Popular Front "thought of themselves as generic 'communists,' using the term with a small *c*," notes Michael Denning, who also enthuses over a *Fortune* magazine poll of 1942 that found a quarter of Americans favored socialism and another third had an open mind. Second, Franco lobbyists would never have bothered about distant Spain had not the CPUSA, by casting the revolution there as an antifascist crusade, used it so brilliantly as an ideological touchstone, a recruiting drive, and a vehicle to steer the Popular Front toward state socialism. Spain, of course, enthralled American communists and socialists not so much as a fight against fascism but, rather, as a proletarian revolution in progress. A comparison with their ineffectual response to Fascist Italy's invasion of imperial Ethiopia in 1935 makes this point clear. Third, what set Franco lobbyists' propaganda apart, and raised the intensity of the arguments they cocreated, was that they were both pro-Franco and anticommunist at a time when a majority of Americans, beginning with Roosevelt's administration, were pro-Loyalist and at least open minded about socialism if not necessarily attracted toward small-*c* communism, as were Roosevelt's wife, Eleanor, his confidant Harry L. Hopkins, and his Treasury, Interior, Agriculture, and Labor secretaries, Henry Morgenthau Jr., Harold L. Ickes, Henry A. Wallace, and Frances Perkins.[4]

Would small-*c* communists have countenanced a revolution in the United States? Would Franco lobbyists have backed a military junta to preempt one? Could socioeconomic conditions have deteriorated to the point of provoking enough Americans into beginning one? Mass disaffection among communists over Joseph Stalin's alliance with Adolf Hitler in August 1939, followed by a global war that lifted the U.S. economy out of recession, rendered these questions moot, just as it may seem ridiculous to pose them subsequently. Nonetheless, in 1938— the year before the Nazi and Soviet invasions of Poland and on which this study rests—plenty of Americans argued over them with a serious intensity. A more productive as well as a less contentious frame for historical analysis is to consider that participants in the Great Debate over arms for Loyalist Spain, despite what they claimed, were not actually arguing over Spain or even over communism; they were arguing over Americanism, over not only the composition of their national ideology but also who exactly would do the composing. An exchange of correspondence among John Eoghan Kelly, Francis X. Talbot, and Jay Allen, the Spanish embassy's principal U.S. lobbyist, is instructive.

When Kelly arrived at Manhattan's Rotary Club in July 1938 to address five hundred Rotarians, a telegram from Allen awaited him. Allen challenged Kelly's version of the Nationalists' capture of Badajoz in August 1936, based on a stenographer's transcript of a "preposterous speech" Kelly had given at the Center Club in February. "As an expert on propaganda," Allen chided, "you must know that good propagandists get their facts straight." When Kelly reported to Talbot, he judged the Rotarians to have been "a very good audience and receptive." After the address, "a young red headed Jew named Ahrendt, son of a Rotary member, who had lived in Russia," rose to complain that all Kelly's statements were wrong, but "the audience gave him short shrift." Kelly enclosed the text of Allen's telegram and commented that Allen's real name "it is alleged in Philadelphia is Ginsberg." Kelly also mentioned to Talbot that the day after the speech he received a "long violent letter" from Allen. "I wonder if he considers himself the keeper of the world's conscience," Kelly mused. "I intend to ignore him, as it is communist tactics to involve a speaker in side fights."[5]

In the context of this study, it is beside the point whether Loyalists or Nationalists perpetrated more atrocities, whether Allen embellished his eyewitness account of reprisals nine days after Badajoz's fall, whether Kelly whitewashed his version of events, or whether Ahrendt was Jewish. Neither is it relevant that Allen's distinctly un-Jewish grandfather, Gen. R. T. P. Allen, was a first-generation Irish American patriot who founded the Kentucky Military Institute in 1845. What matters is that Kelly, whose writings in the 1920s had attacked the anti-Jewish racism of southern Klansmen, was by 1938 conflating communism with Judaism and jumping at rumors that his chief adversary was Jewish. For Franco lobbyists, increasingly desperate to save Americanism from communism, dalliance in Soviet Russia or a Jewish-sounding surname suggested the potential for what they saw as un-Americanism, just as pro-Loyalists tended to profile Franco supporters as un-American Irish or White Russian immigrants. What does matter here is that there was an argument at the end of Kelly's Rotary Club address and that the two principal lobbyists on either side of the Great Debate accused each other of being lying propagandists. What matters especially is that their argument over distant Spain was moral: They both saw themselves as keepers of the world's conscience.

Unsettled by modernity, puzzled by recession, disturbed by immigration, convinced of the scientific truth of social Darwinism, frightened by German and Japanese expansionism, and intrigued by the promise of new political philosophies, Americans in 1938 were even more anxious than usual about themselves, about their national ideology as Americans, and their role in the world. Americans—not all, for sure, but certainly those caught up in the Great Debate—were as preoccupied with their moral rectitude as they were dizzy over their democratic freedoms. Yet at the same time, they worried about what might happen to those freedoms were they to embrace, or have forced on them, some sort of fascistic or communistic system, even if those systems were successful elsewhere. In their angst, they enthusiastically created an argument about the meaning of a civil war in Spain, which proved to be as intense yet safely voyeuristic as it was oddly productive.

Events allowed both pro-Loyalists and pro-Nationalists to claim a moral victory, thereby reducing their cognitive dissonance, restoring national consensus, and pointing to a stronger, more rewarding, and newly self-righteous America. Once the Nazi-Soviet Non-Aggression Pact was an embarrassing complication of the past, and especially in 1945 when newsreels of death camps so vividly exposed Nazi inhumanity, pro-Loyalists became the ignored prophets of a fascist world conquest that sending arms to Madrid would surely have prevented. It would take longer for pro-Nationalists to declare victory, for the nihilist reality of Nazism's final years was confounding. But their discomfort at recognizing the USSR as an ally in June 1941 had turned to elation by 1947, when they became the ignored prophets of a communist world conquest that enforcing the arms embargo surely delayed by a decade. Both these victories shouted for the imperative of interventionist U.S. foreign policies and the concomitant maintenance of a military-industrial complex. Pro-Loyalists were even able to reconcile the irony that America's expanded role as global cop was communist containment, for as the New Left they could blame Stalin for perverting Marxism-Leninism into the totalitarian horrors of the Gulag. With the cold war liberal consensus established, Americans could enjoy the suburbanization, domesticity, and mass consumption of the postwar boom.

To the extent that after 1945 he lobbied for the exploitation of America's minerals on geostrategic grounds, and was unwaveringly watchful of international communism, Kelly was a committed cold warrior. Yet whether Kelly, along with his fellow Franco lobbyists, looked admiringly on the consensus that emerged from their argument with pro-Loyalists is another matter. Unfortunately, the documentary record offers few hints. By the time the U.S. Senate censured Joseph R. McCarthy on 2 December 1954, W. Cameron Forbes, Ellery Sedgwick, and Ogden H. Hammond were octogenarians in quiet retirement; Talbot and several other prominent lobbyists were dead; and Kelly's correspondence from 1950 onward is not extant. It seems likely, nonetheless, that they would all have been critical of the Eisenhower era, but for different reasons. From the perspective of Merwin K. Hart, who went on to lead the Manhattan branch of the libertarian John Birch Society with remarkable vigor for a seventy-seven-year-old, American society was still insufficiently Anglo-Protestant, at least if the reports of his unreformed anti-Semitism in the American Jewish Committee's files are any indication. At the other extreme was Hildreth Meière. A friend of Meière's daughter recollects how Meière detested the whole cold war climate, not least the intellectual repression of McCarthyism. For his part, Kelly was probably no less critical of Eisenhower's burgeoning national-security state than he had been of Roosevelt's New Deal statism, as, like Hart, Kelly had always advocated a limited government role in the private sector.[6]

In as much as Franco lobbyists had criticized the Roosevelt administration for its softness on communism and called on it to take seriously the findings of Martin Dies's House Un-American Activities Committee, hindsight vindicated them, for the FBI belatedly uncovered Stalin's spies in virtually every government agency, most gravely—and not without irony, for the Soviet A-bomb became the primary intensifier of Americans' cold war anticommunist angst—in the Manhattan Project. Contemporaries, though, vilified them. George Seldes's *Lords of the Press* charged Sedgwick with "becoming the chief defender of the child-murderer Franco"; John Roy Carlson's *Under Cover* smeared Hart as the world's greatest devotee of "Spanish Nazism," Kelly as a "fascist collaborator," and the AUNS as anti-Semitic Christian Front leaders. By ignoring them, historians have left their odious reputation intact. Richard Gid Powers's *History of American Anticommunism* has only three paragraphs on the Spanish Civil War, and then in the context of Catholic bishops and the Knights of Columbus, before dwelling for five pages on Father Coughlin's "anti-Semitic anticommunism." Powers mentions only one actor who was an AUNS lobbyist—Merwin Hart, part of a "potential brown network"—though had he discussed Kelly and his associates, it would probably have been in a paragraph including Gerald L. K. Smith, Elizabeth Dilling, and "all of the country's other notorious anti-Semitic anticommunist crackpots."[7]

Although this study has concentrated on only a handful of the most active Franco lobbyists, these actors networked larger circles, each of which had its own character and influence; in the process, they made arguments with neighboring circles of pro-Loyalists. Clare Singer Dawes distributed Kelly's *Franco* pamphlet through Catholic churches in New England and the Midwest, where she would have chatted with sympathetic priests and parishioners, but she also organized speakers, including herself, for meetings of Republicans, engineers, and college students, some of whom would have expressed disapproval. Philip Liebmann showed his copy of *Spain in Arms* to a meeting of Russian Americans at the Women's Republican Club in Manhattan, he argued Franco's cause with his Jewish family and friends, and his views no doubt percolated among the employees of his vast Rheingold brewery. Sedgwick championed Franco in the national press, just as his advocacy turned heads at Boston's elite Tavern Club and Cambridge's scholarly Harvard Club and made enemies among leftist *Atlantic* contributors, none more so than his most famous protégé, Ernest Hemingway, whose *For Whom the Bell Tolls* popularized the hero myth of the idealist American battling evil fascism in Spain. Through the speeches they delivered, the articles they wrote, and the mass meetings they organized, the actors discussed here presented their pro-Franco anticommunism to upward of a million Americans. Yet their significance lies not so much in those they directly propagandized as in those they indirectly antagonized, for millions more Americans developed their pro-Loyalist antifascism through hearing about the un-American activities of Franco lobbyists like Kelly in Popular Front mass media, such as *PM* or Walter Winchell's newspaper columns and radio broadcasts.[8]

Franco lobbyists' story is ultimately one of troubling counterfactuals, unintended consequences, and compelling ironies. Determined to convince their compatriots that communists posed a valid threat to Americanism, lobbyists pointed to Spain's revolution. To give their argument authenticity as well as urgency, they promoted Franco as a Christian crusader and worked successfully to maintain the arms embargo, on one hand through their networking, publishing, and speechmaking endeavors and on the other by capitalizing on Roosevelt's loathing of decadent Spain, an enervating miasma that pervaded the White House, and a year when Congress convened for only 118 days between 3 January and 16 June. Had Roosevelt lifted the embargo and officially backed the Loyalists, then the French would have left open their frontier, Ambassador Fernando de los Ríos would have purchased over $18 million of U.S. weaponry (especially aircraft and aero engines), a second wave of international volunteers would have enlisted, and Loyalist morale would have soared. It is thus probable that the Spanish Civil War would have become a protracted stalemate, bogging down Nazi aircraft and troops and consuming ordnance; and Stalin would not then have needed to stall for time by signing the Nazi-Soviet Non-Aggression Pact, which more than anything else discredited communism and caused the CPUSA's enrollment to plummet. By the same token, it seems likely that Hitler would have delayed his plans for Poland, perhaps precluding world war, which would have left Americans mired in recession, thereby increasing the chances of social unrest at a time of growing, not shrinking, CPUSA membership. Although the embargo remained and Poland fell, the argument that Franco lobbyists made with pro-Loyalists helped convince Roosevelt that Franco was a Nazi pariah. Had he not been so prejudiced against Spain in general and Franco in particular, Roosevelt would surely have thawed relations by swiftly recognizing the new government, sending aid, and then pressuring Franco into a British-leaning neutrality, a realpolitik strategy that was obvious to Assistant Secretary of State Sumner Welles, who in July 1939 urged Roosevelt not to "treat the Franco Government as an outcast," for that would only "strengthen the hands of the Falangist element" and increase the odds of a "watertight agreement with the Axis powers." And yet, had a different Roosevelt brought Spain into the Allied fold, it is instructive to ponder the likelihood that the Wehrmacht would have deposed Franco and seized Gibraltar, interdicting the Mediterranean and changing the outcome of World War II.[9]

Because they had backed Franco in the run-up to the Nazification of Europe, and then continued to attack Roosevelt's wartime administration as sympathetic to communism, pro-Franco anticommunists isolated themselves as a political force and tarnished their well-meant patriotic ideology as un-American. At the same time, through their argument with pro-Loyalists, they had popularized the Red-fascist discourse that empowered the shrill rhetoric of 1950s McCarthyism. So instead of a pragmatic, law-enforcement approach to compromised national security, ousting communist spies from government agencies became a noisome witch hunt that undermined civil liberties. Having slurred Franco lobbyists as fascist collaborators and ridiculed their exaggeration of the communist threat, former Popular

Front journalists, writers, and academics had a precedent for similarly scorning McCarthy and then joining the cold war consensus as liberal intellectuals.

Liberal humanistic Americans like Sedgwick, Meière, or Kelly could have ignored the revolution in Spain and the Popular Front at home and simply edited a literary magazine, designed modernist murals, or prospected for natural gas. Instead, overcome by a moralistic angst rooted in their transatlantic Enlightenment heritage, aroused by an intellectual curiosity common to mugwumps and progressives, and compounded by their own insecurities as Americans, they devoted much of their time and energy to making an argument with pro-Loyalist Popular Fronters over U.S. foreign policy and the meaning of American democracy. To build their case for the strict neutrality of pro-Franco anticommunism, they drew from their historically informed mental maps, which integrated an array of pictures—from conquistadors to Puritans, from the Inquisition to the Constitution—into their shining-city image of American exceptionalism. They knew their history: Kelly, after all, had written *Pedro de Alvarado, Conquistador,* Forbes *The Philippine Islands,* and Sedgwick *Thomas Paine.* Had not George Washington cautioned against entangling political alliances? Had not Thomas Jefferson advocated a meritocracy derived from the property accruing from the honest labor of yeoman farmers? Surely, they argued, arms must remain embargoed, and communism was anathema to the natural rights enshrined in the Declaration of Independence. Inevitably, therefore, their response to revolution in Spain and communism at home was alarmist and after Pearl Harbor struck most Americans as misguided and, by the 1990s, seemed irrational. Liberal anticommunism, nevertheless, would be the defining characteristic of U.S. ideology for four decades.

Appendix

Data

This study references the following spreadsheets I compiled, all of which are available in electronic format on request:

- *Atlantic* Data: A spreadsheet of the 422 authors whose 718 articles and poems appeared in the *Atlantic* from edition no. 157 (beginning January 1936) to no. 163 (beginning January 1939), sortable by author, sex, religion, genre, subject matter, number/frequency of articles, and political orientation, if ascertainable.
- *Atlantic* Pro/Con: A spreadsheet of 114 letter writers who expressed either support for or criticism of Ellery Sedgwick's stand on Franco (44 pro and 70 con) during 1938, sortable by date, name, sex, religion, city, and state, if ascertainable.
- JEK-FBI, 65–1461: A spreadsheet of 24 FBI field agents, 54 reporting FBI agents, and 201 witnesses interviewed, sortable by name, file number, religion, category, city, and state, if ascertainable.

Content Analysis

This study references my analysis of above-the-fold, front-page column headlines from the *New York Times* during the Spanish Civil War, July 1936–March 1939.

Each *NYT* late city edition front page during the 1930s carried eight columns. Stories and their respective headlines were generally of single-column width; more newsworthy stories carried a two- or three-column headline that either overlapped a less important story in the column(s) below or, less commonly, stretched over two adjacent columns. Because of imaging constraints, my quantitative headline analysis ignores any headlines in the lower third of the page, although such headlines were rare and typically of little importance. I performed the coding, although statistical analysis generally supports single coding for headline analysis, which is far less subjective than textual analysis.

New York Times front-page column headlines by topic, July 1936–March 1939

	July–Sept. 1936	Oct.–Dec. 1936	Jan.–Mar. 1937	Apr.–June 1937	July–Sept. 1937	Oct.–Dec. 1937
Spanish CW	197	171	88	138	88	64
Economy	80	83	74	87	82	158[a]
Unions/strikes	40	78[b]	214[c]	184	58	71
NY politics	90	49[d]	54	48	131[e]	104
Violence/crime	56	55	107	65	29	71
Germany/Nazis	43	51	48	46	27	39
Roosevelt	87	85	56	65	49	74
China/Japan	21	51[g]	25	8	231[h]	133[i]
Great Britain	8	19	30	26	22	27
Supreme Court	13	2	120[j]	71	81[k]	28
Natural disaster	63[l]	4	61[m]	1	27	8
France	30	22	16	18	6	21
Russia	20	17	19	43[n]	30	23
Transport accidents	25	22	26	41[o]	12	18
Neutrality/Hull	6	41[p]	18	5	7	35
Sports	40	28	3	21	25	28
British monarchy	13	80[q]	8	39[r]	1	18
Italy	8	12	11	14	5	12
Landon	76	58	1	0	0	4
Coughlin	17	7	0	0	0	0
World's Fair	1	3	0	0	0	0
Amelia Earhart	0	0	2	0	11	0
Ethiopia	6	0	2	0	1	0
All other	158	137	123[s]	165	141	169
Total column headlines	1,090	1,075	1,106	1,085	1,064	1,082
Spanish CW, as %	18	16	8	13	8	6

Notes: [a]Congressional debates over taxes, budget balancing, wages. [b]Strikes in shipping. [c]Sit-down strikes. [d]Totals for July–October noticeably higher due to election. [e]Elections and Tammany Hall. [f]Austrian Anschluss. [g]Rising tensions in China; capture and release of Chiang Kai-shek by Japanese. [h]Japanese bombing of Shanghai. [i]Japanese capture of Nanjing and sinking of *Panay*. [j]Roosevelt's fight to pack the Supreme Court. [k]Appointment of Justice Black and his alleged Klan membership. [l]Drought. [m]Midwest floods. [n]Soviet show trials.

Jan.–Mar. 1938	Apr.–June 1938	July–Sept. 1938	Oct.–Dec. 1938	Jan.–Mar. 1939	Total No.	Total %
74	77	38	21	113	1,069	8.9
79	111	31	74	87	946	7.9
36	66	54	52	41	894	7.5
82	81	80	108	60	887	7.4
57	89	120	82	77	808	6.7
97[f]	73	144	132	103	803	6.7
86	79	86	62	58	787	6.6
48	55	31	43	18	664	5.5
59	44	90	77	64	466	3.9
18	45	33	14	26	451	3.8
26	18	47	14	15	284	2.4
26	26	28	54	24	271	2.3
32	14	23	7	11	239	2.0
8	19	27	13	27	238	2.0
30	8	17	35	31	233	1.9
4	22	10	21	0	202	1.7
1	0	0	7	1	168	1.4
13	26	13	19	14	147	1.2
0	1	2	3	1	146	1.2
0	0	0	2	0	26	0.2
0	5	1	0	4	14	0.1
0	0	0	0	0	13	0.1
0	1	0	0	0	10	0.1
305	242	239	260	285	2,224	
1,081	1,102	1,114	1,100	1,002	11,990	
7	7	3	2	11	8.9	

[o]*Hindenburg* airship disaster. [p]Buenos Aires Conference. [q]Mrs. Simpson affair; abdication of Edward VIII and succession of George VI. [r]Coronation of George VI. [s]Texas school gas explosion. Full-banner headlines similarly counted on a per-column basis: "Roosevelt Sweeps the Nation," 4 Nov. 1936; "Edward VIII Renounces British Crown," 11 Dec. 1936; Hindenburg Burns in Lakehurst Crash," 7 May 1937; "La Guardia Is Re-Elected by 454,425," 3 Nov. 1937.

Notes

Introduction

1. Roosevelt's "moral embargo" originated in a 5 Aug. 1936 State Department meeting. See Cordell Hull, *The Memoirs of Cordell Hull*, 2 vols. (New York: MacMillan, 1948), 1:477–78; F. Jay Taylor, "Great Debate," in *The United States and the Spanish Civil War, 1936–1939* (New York: Bookman, 1956). For the debate on military intervention following the German invasion of Poland in Sept. 1939, see Michael W. Miles, *The Odyssey of the American Right* (New York: Oxford Univ. Press, 1980), 50.

2. In July 1936 the Loyalists had some twenty-two Douglas transports, including four modern DC-2s. Engines and mechanical parts were more critical than airframes, for 1930s engines wore out quickly, sometimes failing in under 100 hours of flight and requiring an overhaul after about 250 hours. Barcelona-based Hispano-Suiza provided engines for French aircraft, such as the Loyalists' Nieuport 52s and Breguet XIXs; but even before the dislocations of July 1936, they could never build enough, so they had subcontracted production to what became Curtiss-Wright in Buffalo, NY. Wright's ubiquitous Cyclone-9 air-cooled rotary engine powered, among other aircraft, the Tupolev SB-2 twin-engine bomber and Polikarpov I-15 fighter (German pilots called the I-15 a Curtiss), of which ten SB-2s and twenty-five I-15s arrived in the Loyalist zone from the USSR as early as mid-Oct. 1936. While the potent I-16 single-wing fighter came with a Shevetsov ASh-62 engine, this was a modified Cyclone, with which it would have been interchangeable had Curtiss-Wright shipped engines to Spain. Howson (app. 3) documents the arrival of fifty-one Tupolevs and 400 Polikarpovs by boat during the conflict, although the total that the Soviets delivered—whether by land from France or by other flagged vessels—was three times higher. Gerald Howson, *Arms for Spain: The Untold Story of the Spanish Civil War* (New York: St. Martin's Press, 1999). Reina Pennington gives a figure of 1,500, and Tom Alison and Von Hardesty give 1,400 flown by 700 Russian pilots, in Robin Higham, John T. Greenwood, and Von Hardesty, eds., *Russian Aviation and Air Power in the Twentieth Century* (London: Frank Cass, 1998), 44, 92–93. A measure of the importance of engines is that after Apr. 1937, the USSR shipped at least 380 replacement engines, which is the number in Howson (*Arms for Spain*), so the total number of engines could well have been three times that.

3. For a discussion of Soviet exchange rate manipulation, see Howson, *Arms for Spain*. After Aug. 1937 the Soviets abandoned shipments from the Black Sea, which had to run a gauntlet of Italian submarines off Sicily. Helen Graham, *The Spanish Republic at War, 1936–1939* (Cambridge: Cambridge Univ. Press, 2002), xi–xii, 158, 389.

4. Diary entry for 12 May 1938, Harold L. Ickes, *The Inside Struggle, 1936–1939*, vol. 2, *The Secret Diary of Harold L. Ickes* (New York: Simon & Schuster, 1954), 390; Allen Guttmann, *The Wound in the Heart: America and the Spanish Civil War* (Glencoe, NY: Free Press, 1962), 119; Leo V. Kanawada Jr., *Franklin D. Roosevelt's Diplomacy and American Catholics, Italians, and Jews* (Ann Arbor, MI: UMI Research Press, 1982), 65; for data, see chap. 3 below.

5. For examples of "Catholic hierarchy," see David M. Kennedy, *Freedom from Fear: The American People in Depression and War, 1929–1945* (New York: Oxford Univ. Press, 1999), 399; and for "fascist crackpots," see Arthur M. Schlesinger Jr., *The Age of Roosevelt: The Politics of Upheaval, 1935–1936* (Boston: Houghton Mifflin, 2003), 82. A term of 1930s leftists, "lunatic fringe" denoted right-wing extremists. Exemplifying the conflation of rightists with "pathological" "crackpots" is Daniel Bell, ed., *The Radical Right*, 3rd ed. (New Brunswick, NJ: Transaction, 2002), esp. intro.; Peter N. Carroll and James D. Fernandez, eds., *Facing Fascism: New York and the Spanish Civil War* (New York: New York Univ. Press, 2007).

6. America's leading authority on the Spanish Civil War, Stanley G. Payne concludes that "Franco was never a 'core Fascist' or a genuine Falangist." Payne, *Fascism in Spain, 1923–1977* (Madison: Univ. of Wisconsin Press, 1999), 477. He notes that following the civil war, there was "a growing expression of the fascist style in politics and an increasing political 'vertigo of fascism,' even though [Franco's] regime was eclectic in its personnel and origins, and culturally and spiritually depended as much or more on Catholicism." Payne, *Franco and Hitler: Spain, Germany, and World War II* (New Haven, CT: Yale Univ. Press, 2008), 16. Payne charts the consistent and effective revolutionary aims of Spain's tiny but fast-growing Communist Party (PCE), although after Feb. 1936 its strategy was effectively counterrevolutionary, as several million anarcho-syndicalists (CNT), *Caballeristas* in the Socialist Party (PSOE), and militant Marxists (POUM) sought rapid revolutionary collectivization and/or nationalization. Payne, *The Spanish Civil War, the Soviet Union, and Communism* (New Haven, CT: Yale Univ. Press, 2004), and *The Collapse of the Spanish Republic, 1933–1936* (New Haven, CT: Yale Univ. Press, 2006). For supporting documentation, see Ronald Radosh, Mary R. Habeck, and Grigory Sevostianov, eds., *Spain Betrayed: The Soviet Union in the Spanish Civil War* (New Haven, CT: Yale Univ. Press, 2001). For a single-paragraph summary of incipient revolution in Feb.–July 1936, see Payne, *Franco and Hitler*, 4. Pío Moa's controversial revision, *Los mitos de la guerra civil* (Madrid: La Esfera de los Libros, 2003), stresses the "strategic benefit of the very first order" to the Allies of Franco's neutrality in World War II (esp. 509–10) and argues that Franco's liberalizing social and economic reforms after 1959 facilitated rapid modernization and growth, paving the way for stable parliamentary democracy (519–21, 529–31). Unless otherwise noted, all translations here and throughout the book are mine.

7. National Industrial Conference Board reports, published periodically in newspapers like the *New York Times* (*NYT*), showed jobless numbers fluctuating around 10 million for much of 1938 (a rate of 18 percent), rising to 10.65 million and 10.76 million in Jan. and Feb. 1939, respectively. Franco lobbyists noted the growing numbers employed by the government's emergency labor force, which totaled 3.4 million by the end of 1938, as well as by local, state, and federal government agencies, which had risen from 2.1 million in 1929 to 2.6 million by 1938, or one-sixteenth of the workforce. In a Mar. 1938 newspaper article, the government's own deputy WPA administrator, Aubrey Williams, estimated effective unemployment at over 12 million and worried about the "tremendous problem, a problem more complex and vital than any which this nation has had to face in times of peace," that a "standing army of paupers" was causing. See *NYT*, 30 Jan. 1939, 20; 18 Aug. 1938, 21; and 27 Mar. 1938. Jobless numbers over 10.75 million equated to an unemployment rate in excess of 20 percent.

Data places the average unemployment rate for the whole of 1938 at 17.8 percent. Robert M. Coen, "Labor Force and Unemployment in the 1920s and 1930s: A Re-Examination Based on Postwar Experience," *Review of Economics and Statistics* 55, no. 1 (1973): 52. John Eoghan Kelly (JEK), *The Christian Soldier* (Brookline, MA: Mrs. Herbert N. Dawes, 1938).

8. Michael Denning, *The Cultural Front: The Laboring of American Culture in the Twentieth Century* (London: Verso, 1997), xvi.

9. Merwin Kimball Hart, *America, Look at Spain!* (New York: P. J. Kenedy & Sons, 1939).

10. In Federalist Paper No. 10 (*Daily Advertiser*, 22 Nov. 1787), Madison explained the problem of factions, or what might be termed a "mobocracy": "Either the existence of the same passion or interest in a majority . . . must be prevented, or the majority . . . must be rendered . . . unable to concert and carry into effect schemes of oppression." He noted how a pure democracy, "by which I mean a society consisting of a small number of citizens, who assemble and administer the government in person, can admit of no cure for the mischiefs of faction," but that "a republic, by which I mean a government in which the scheme of representation takes place, opens a different prospect." And he made clear that a meritocracy would administer the republic, a Congress of "men who possess the most attractive merit and the most diffusive and established characters." Http://thomas.loc.gov/home/histdox/fedpapers.html.

11. Henry Kamen estimates 2,000 executions for the Spanish Inquisition's 356-year reign. Kamen, *The Spanish Inquisition: A Historical Revision* (New Haven, CT: Yale Univ. Press, 1998), 60. E. William Monter lists 1,500 killed for the "Converso period" (1480–1530), of which 95 percent were Jews; 1,000 for the "Aragonese period" (1530–1630); and 250 for the final "Portuguese period" (1630–1730), when, again, 95 percent were Jewish. Monter, *Frontiers of Heresy: The Spanish Inquisition from the Basque Lands to Sicily* (Cambridge: Cambridge Univ. Press, 1990), 53. In 1987, less than 2 percent of Spain's fifty million tourists were Americans. Theodore Roosevelt—with his parents in 1868 and 1872 and his wife in 1881—was one of several presidents who toured Europe but did not visit Spain. [John Adams,] *Diary and Autobiography of John Adams*, ed. L. H. Butterfield, vol. 2, (Cambridge, MA: Belknap Press, 1962), 419, 417, 419, 430. For Bilbao's relative prosperity and registered ships (as of 1800), see David Ringrose, *Spain, Europe, and the "Spanish Miracle," 1700–1900* (Cambridge: Cambridge Univ. Press, 1996), 228.

12. Daniel Webster, *An Address Delivered at the Laying of the Corner Stone of the Bunker Hill Monument, June 17, 1825* (Boston: Tappan & Dennet, 1843), 69; and *An Address Delivered at the Completion of the Bunker Hill Monument, June 17, 1843* (Boston: Tappan & Dennet, 1843), 11, 12–13. Reprinted into dozens of editions by fifteen major publishing houses, Webster's *First Bunker Hill Oration* was required reading for the College Entrance Exam, alongside George Washington's "Farewell Address."

13. *NYT*, 19 Feb. and Mar. 1898.

14. Antonio Machado popularized the phrase "las dos Españas—una España que muere y otra España que bosteza" (the two Spains—a Spain that dies and another that yawns) in a short poem from circa 1936; his brother Manuel, who fought for Franco, had a different interpretation of Spanish politics.

15. Raymond Carr, *Spain, 1808–1939* (Oxford: Oxford Univ. Press, 1966), 407, 405; Harry Browne, *Spain's Civil War* (London: Addison Wesley Longman, 1996), 6; Paul Preston, *The Spanish Civil War: Reaction, Revolution, and Revenge* (New York: W. W. Norton, 2006), 18; Ringrose, "*Spanish Miracle*," 389.

16. Michael Seidman, *Republic of Egos: A Social History of the Spanish Civil War* (Madison: Univ. of Wisconsin Press, 2002), 8, 10, 13.

17. Alan K. Henrikson, "The Geographical 'Mental Maps' of American Foreign Policy Makers," *International Political Science Review* 1, no. 3 (1980): 495–530, esp. 498–99. I admit to violating Henrikson's strict "systems of orientation" approach to imply cognitive "impressions of particular places."

18. Johan Galtung, "The Basic Needs Approach," in *Human Needs: A Contribution to the Current Debate,* ed. Katrin Lederer (Cambridge, MA: Oelgeschlager, Gunn & Hain, 1980), 65.

19. Survey of thirty-four countries by the University of Chicago's National Opinion Research Center summarized in *Boston Globe,* 28 June 2006. For the destructive arrogance of Americans' obsessive guilt, see Bernard Lewis, *Cultures in Conflict: Christians, Muslims, and Jews in the Age of Discovery* (New York: Oxford Univ. Press, 1995), 75; David Campbell, *Writing Security: United States Foreign Policy and the Politics of Identity* (Minneapolis: Univ. of Minnesota Press, 1998), 3.

20. JEK to Talbot, 15 Jan. 1938, and Talbot to JEK, 17 Jan. 1938, in folder (f.) 38, John Eoghan Kelly Papers (JEKP), in author's possession, Charlestown, MA. For a concise discussion of American core values in the context of national security, see Melvyn P. Leffler, "National Security," in *Explaining the History of American Foreign Relations,* ed. Michael J. Hogan and Thomas G. Paterson (Cambridge: Cambridge Univ. Press, 1991), 202–13; Samuel P. Huntington, *Who Are We? The Challenges to America's National Identity* (New York: Simon & Schuster, 2004), esp. 17–20, 59–80. *Core values* as a term has passed into common usage, as in the front-page headline "Day of Renewal for Core Values," *Boston Globe,* 21 Jan. 2009, 1.

21. Michael H. Hunt, "Chinese National Identity and the Strong State: The Late Qing–Republican Crisis," in *China's Quest for National Identity,* ed. Lowell Dittmer and Samuel S. Kim (Ithaca, NY: Cornell Univ. Press, 1993), 78–79; JEK, *Christian Soldier;* Prasenjit Duara, "Historicizing National Identity: or, Who Imagines What and When," in *Becoming National,* ed. Geoff Eley and Ronald Grigor Suny (Oxford: Oxford Univ. Press, 1996), 151. Debaters talked in terms of taking sides, as in, for instance, *Writers Take Sides: Letters About the War in Spain from 418 American Authors* (New York: League of American Writers, 1938).

22. President Dwight D. Eisenhower went so far as to state that the "purpose of America" was to "defend a way of life rather than merely defend property, homes, or lives." Reclaiming lost traditional values was the aim of the Reagan Revolution of 1981, as epitomized in the Traditional Values Coalition. In his inaugural address, President Barack Obama did provide a list of "values upon which our success depends—hard work and honesty, courage and fair play, tolerance and curiosity, loyalty and patriotism," noting that "these things are old. These things are true." *Boston Globe,* 21 Jan. 2009, 10. Robert A. Gross, *The Minutemen and Their World* (New York: Hill & Wang, 1976), 28.

23. Some translators prefer the "concept of dread" to the "concept of anxiety." Søren Kierkegaard, *The Concept of Anxiety: A Simple Psychologically Orienting Deliberation on the Dogmatic Issue of Hereditary Sin,* ed. and trans. Reidar Thomte (1844; repr., Princeton, NJ: Princeton Univ. Press, 1980), 41–42, 61.

1. Pro-Franco Anticommunism

1. *NYT,* 14 July, 1936, 1.

2. *NYT,* 17–23 July 1936. For data table, see the appendix. Test analyses for single-month periods in editions such as the *Chicago Tribune, Louisville Courier-Journal,* and *Boston Globe* yield comparable results. Kennedy (*Freedom from Fear,* 398), makes a common claim that "most Americans could not have cared less" about Spain's civil war, yet he rests his

assumption on a Jan. 1937 Gallup poll that asked Americans whether their sympathies lay with the Loyalists or the "Rebels," by implication communists and fascists. Sixty-six percent chose "Neutral, no opinion" not from any lack of interest, I suggest, but because the poll's choices were both unpalatable. George H. Gallup, *The Gallup Poll: Public Opinion, 1935–1971* (New York: Random House, 1972), 49.

3. For an astute reading of Brahmin society, see David Strauss, *Percival Lowell: The Culture and Science of a Boston Brahmin* (Cambridge, MA: Harvard Univ. Press, 2001), esp. 1–68; note particularly Strauss's comments on the dilettantism—but in a positive sense—of polo and gentlemen's clubs. For American liberal exceptionalism, see N. Gordon Levin Jr., *Woodrow Wilson and World Politics: America's Response to War and Revolution* (London: Oxford Univ. Press, 1968), 2. At the Tavern Club, Sedgwick socialized with William Sturgis Bigelow, an expert on, as well as promoter of, Japanese art, culture, and philosophy.

4. For the pragmatism that undergirded New England's Anglo-Protestant ideology, see Gillis J. Harp, *Brahmin Prophet: Phillips Brooks and the Path of Liberal Protestantism* (Lanham, MD: Rowman & Littlefield, 2003), esp. 33–37.

5. In two separate statements written in 1943, JEK wrote "Colonel Infante"; his memory was generally excellent, but he was almost certainly referring to Col. William A. Alfonte, General Staff Corps, Chief of Staff, Fifth Corps Area Headquarters, Fort Hayes, Columbus, OH; JEK's commanding officer was Col. W. H. Waldron. See Memorandum re Military Service, ca. Mar. 1943, JEKP, f. 4; statement of JEK, ca. 24 Mar. 1943, JEKP, f. 8; Alfonte Memorandum re Flood Activities, 18 Feb. 1937, JEKP, f. 4.

6. Biographical sketch compiled primarily from Domnall Forrest Kelly, "John Forrest Kelly," typed memoir, folder 6, JFKP. John F. Kelly worked with Thomas A. Edison at Menlo Park. During the 1880s he was a regular contributor to anarchist newspapers, especially *Liberty* and *The Alarm*. For his philosophy, see Frank Brooks, "Egoist Theory and America's Individualist Anarchists: A Dilemma of Praxis," *History of Political Thought* 15, no. 3 (1994): 403–22; and Paul Avrich, *Anarchist Portraits* (Princeton, NJ: Princeton Univ. Press, 1988), 155. Always an outspoken champion of women's rights and civil liberties, Bride had several clashes with the police, including a disorderly conduct arrest in 1919 while leading a parade urging amnesty for political prisoners. *NYT*, 26 Dec. 1919, 1. Mayor Fiorello H. La Guardia dedicated a playground to Bride in 1936, the Dr. Gertrude B. Kelly Recreation Center, on 17th Street west of 8th Avenue.

7. According to either Pittsfield's police chief or Col. William C. Godfrey, U.S. Army Intelligence, Helen told Chesney that in 1890 she was the secretary of New York's Anarchist Party. I have not been able to verify the existence of such an organization. See JEK, FBI, file 65–1461 [JEK-FBI], 2:68, 31 National Archives, College Park, MD. An abstract of JEK's birth record (middle name spelled Eoghin) is in JEKP, f. 1. , JEK-FBI, 2:98, 10. In addition to Spanish travel materials from the 1910s found in the family library, John Forrest was unusually interested in Spanish culture, and he surely would have included the Iberian Peninsula in the itinerary. JEK apparently visited Spain before 1933, and his schedule left little opportunity after 1914. Southland Products Co., capitalized at $2 million, processed and packaged a wide range of Cookellized dehydrated vegetables. See Michael E. Chapman, "'How to Smash the British Empire': John Forrest Kelly's *Irish World* and the Boycott of 1920–21," *Éire-Ireland* 43, nos. 3/4 (2008); obituary, *Irish World*, 28 Oct. 1922.

8. I am grateful to Katie Burns for alerting me to JEK's school anecdote, found in a letter of 22 June 1910 from his aunt Bride to Leonora O'Reilly, found in Leonora O'Reilly Papers, reel 5, frame 106, Papers of the Women's Trade Union League, Schlesinger Library, Cambridge, MA. Felix Gras, *The Reds of the Midi: An Episode of the French Revolution* (New York:

D. Appleton, 1897); Rensselaer Polytechnic's *The Transit* (1914–15). Although executors sold the library's most valuable editions in 1956, Domnall, also an avid reader, bought from used bookstores in an effort to replace the missing works. Frances Kelly, interview by author, 9 Aug. 2003, Lanesboro, MA. I have examined the remnants of the library, around a thousand titles, several of which bear John Forrest's or John Eoghan's signature on the flyleaf.

9. Passport, JEK-FBI, 2:98, 11. Biographical information is from JEK's statement to the FBI, 1943, JEKP, f. 8; Memorandum for attorney John O'Shea, 30 Sept. 1941, and divorce affidavits, JEKP, f. 5; miscellaneous correspondence, JEKP, ff. 2–9. JEK may have worked for the Compañía Minera de Peñoles, Mexico's primary producer of lead and silver, which by the mid-1920s was a subsidiary of American Metals Co.

10. In a follow-up letter to *Leslie's*, he praised Mexico for conceding more liberty to the individual than any of the countries he knew, including America. JEK to Manuel Prieto Jr., 8 Nov. 1919, and to the editor of *Leslie's Weekly*, 7 and 14 Nov. 1919, JEKP, f. 19. See also JEK to the editor, *Irish World*, 14 Oct. 1920, in which he pointed to the hypocrisy of a *Nation* staffer who stressed liberty yet called for intervention in Mexico, adding, "The man who wants to crush liberty in Mexico must uphold tyranny in Ireland." JEKP, f. 20. For JEK's thoughts on anti-imperialism, see, for instance, "North Africa and Arab Asia Are Needed to Win the War," *America* 65, no. 4 (1941): 90; and for a cynical pro-Arab critique of the mandate system in a provocative analysis of Norwegian parliamentarian Carl Joachim Hambro, see "England's Quisling," ca. Aug. 1940, JEKP, f. 84.

11. JEK, "The White Reaction in Ireland," *The Nation* 115, no. 2978 (1922): 118–20; and "The Enemy Unmasked," 12 Oct. 1922, written for the *Irish World* but rejected, presumably as too radical, in JEKP, f. 80. Where JEK did employ biblical themes in a poem, it was in a cultural sense.

12. The Passerby [JEK], "Glimpses of the 'Klan,'" 20 Nov. 1923, St. Louis, MO, JEKP, f. 80; I have yet to locate this piece in print, although a majority of the typed drafts in JEK's papers did find publication. Western Union telegram, 7 May 1946, JEKP, f. 46. Even though he hunted for the stockpot while in Central America, his humanism extended to being a conscientious member of the Anti-Vivisection Society. See antivivisection materials, JEKP, f. 78.

13. His Newark speech was on 2 Nov. See JEK to Helen Kelly, 22 Oct. 1924 and (on official "La Follette-Wheeler Campaign: Conference for Progressive Political Action" stationery) 3 Nov. 1924, and Mrs. Aileen Reilly to JEK, Assistant to Regional Director, La Follette-Wheeler Campaign, 25 W. 43rd Street, New York City, all in JEKP, f. 24. JEK to the editor, *NYT*, 25 Oct. 1928, 28. Coined from a Native American word meaning mug on one side of the fence and wump on the other, mugwumps were righteous, idealistic Republicans who sat on the sidelines during the 1880s and 1890s.

14. To adjust for inflation over the last seventy years, this study employs a rule-of-thumb multiplication of thirty, which works well for a basket of commonplace items, including cinema tickets ($0.25–$8), a loaf of bread ($0.07–$2), laundering a shirt ($0.10–$3), and a room at New York's Hotel Commodore ($3.50–$105). Adjusting for inflation will always be problematic because price increases vary widely and goods change in both content and quality, as these items indicate (1938–2011 = multiple): popular magazine (newsstand), $0.05–$4.00 = 80; gentleman's tailored suit, $17–$1,100 = 64; pint of draught beer, $0.09–$5.00 = 55; women's sports shoes, $1.30–$60 = 46; family sedan, $685–$17,000 = 25; toothpaste, $0.25–$3 = 12; refrigerator, $90–$800 = 9. Yet today's car is an incomparably more advanced and reliable machine, while an off-the-rack suit on sale for $120 would fit most people and is a bargain at a multiple of 8. Passport, 1927, JEKP, f. 1; "Increases Gas Output," *NYT*, 25 Aug. 1929, N9; "Midland Gas Pays $2,000,000 for Oil Leases," *Chicago Daily Tribune*, 12 July 1930, 17.

15. For McBee, see Memorandum for Mr. O'Shea, alimony proceedings, 30 Sept. 1941, JEKP, f. 5. Diggs capitulated on 24 Oct. 1930. Portfolio calculations, JEKP, f. 30. A trick of many police officers whose sidearm is a revolver is to keep an empty chamber in the firing position; if someone seizes their weapon, then they know that time is safely on their side.

16. JEK, *Pedro de Alvarado, Conquistador* (Princeton, NJ: Princeton Univ. Press, 1932), esp. 170, 29; book reviews, from Princeton University Press flier, JEKP, f. 1; Dean Ivan Lamb, *The Incurable Filibuster: Adventures of Col. Dean Ivan Lamb* (New York: Farrar & Rinehart, 1934); JEK, "The Stewardess Wore Furs," draft, 24 Feb. 1948, JEKP, f. 177; JEK, "Sandy McGrew's War," *Zane Grey's Western Magazine* 5, no. 7 (1951): 119–32. *Encomienda* was a grant by the Spanish crown of trusteeship over a group of Amerindians to a New World conquistador; *encomenderos* could tax natives and compel labor, although natives retained land rights.

17. JEK to Helen, 21 July 1923, JEKP, f. 23; correspondence between John Forrest Kelly and USSR Commercial Department director A. A. Heller, Heller's brother-in-law Spectovsky, and Ella Tuck[?], JFKP, f. 40.

18. JEK, *A Programme for American Nationalism* (N.p., 1940); "A Programme for American Nationalism," JEKP, f. 102, and Francis X. Talbot Papers (FXTP), box (b.) 22, f. 37, Lauinger Library Special Collections, Georgetown University, Washington, DC; see also chap. 7 below. JEK, "Wanted: A Conservative Counter Attack," June 1932, JEKP, f. 80.

19. JEK, "Counter Attack." Exports to the USSR reached an unremarkable $43 million by 1937.

20. Madison, a protégé and close friend of Jefferson's, described his fear of factions and preference for a government administered by men of merit in Federalist Paper No. 10. *Daily Advertiser*, 22 Nov. 1787.

21. My thanks to Jared Bjornholm for stressing individualist anarchists' distrust of communists.

22. Lamb, *Incurable Filibuster*, preface and 175. For a sense of Lamb in action, see where he recounted of killing sixteen horsemen with one drum of his Thompson submachine gun, taking a bullet in the thigh, riding miles to the next village, and then requiring hot water to loosen the blood that stuck him to his saddle (228–30).

23. JEK to Talbot, 13 Sept. 1938, JEKP, f. 38. For JEK's talk on 16 Jan., see testimony of Maj. John T. West, JEK-FBI, 3:112. JEK to the editor, *NYT*, 15 Jan. 1929, 28. Carranza's assassination was in Apr. 1920, and JEK was in Tennessee for much of 1919.

24. For payments to Cameron, see JEK-FBI, 2:94. During the first nine months of 1938—after which JEK's secretary James Finucane no longer had access to his papers—JEK wired an impressive $1,985 ($60,000) to Cameron, suggesting that he was sending her all his income rather than keeping it in his New Jersey account where McBee might be able to seize it. *Investigation of Un-American Propaganda Activities in the United States, Hearings Before a Special Committee on Un-American Activities: House of Representatives*, 16 vols. (Washington, DC: GPO, 1939), 5:3458–60, 3483–84. Deatherage testified to HUAC that JEK was in regular contact with Moseley, yet there is nothing in JEK's papers or the FBI's investigation to substantiate the link. Deatherage named his organization after the officers' wing of the Reconstruction-era Ku Klux Klan (officers joined the Knights while enlisted men joined the KKK), although he denied any connection with the KKK. Ibid., 3460. Moseley, a veteran of the Philippines and of John J. Pershing's expeditionary force in Mexico, was Douglas MacArthur's chief of staff until 1933, commander of Fifth Corps Area during 1934, and commander of the U.S. Third Army until 1938, when he retired from military service to politicize his concern over the expansion of communism during the New Deal. See, for

instance, "Moseley Proposes Use of the Army to Drive Out Reds," *NYT*, 1 June 1939, 1, 4. For Moseley in his own virulently anticommunist and anti-Semitic words, see his *Major-General George Van Horn Moseley: American Patriot*, ed. N. W. Rogers (N.p., 1940).

25. Report of Agent Andrew K. Ogden, 9 Jan. 1942, JEK-FBI, 3:112; report of Agent Ralph V. Reed, 13 Aug. 1943, JEK-FBI, 11:482. For more on Winchell, see chap. 8 below.

26. JEK to Helen Kelly, Oct. 1933, JEKP, f. 30. JEK also commented that the *American Hebrew* had denounced him as a Nazi propagandist, although he had not been able to verify the accusation. This weekly did feature articles on Nazi propagandists such as William Dudley Pelley, and it printed a list of thirty-two "Nazi Conspirators," but after scanning issues for 1 Apr–10 Nov. 1933, I find no mention of JEK. List of conspirators, *American Hebrew* 133, no. 22 (1933): 355. *North America Program*, JFKP, f. 151. This was among Helen Kelly's correspondence for 1938, so I presume it was hers rather than her son's. Programs featured news and commentary in both English and German, sports and magazine reviews, light music, folk singing, brass bands, and symphony concerts. Director of wartime broadcasting to Britain, Eduard Roderich Dietze, cited in Horst J. P. Bergmeier and Rainer E. Lotz, *Hitler's Airwaves: The Inside Story of Nazi Radio Broadcasting and Propaganda Swing* (New Haven, CT: Yale Univ. Press, 1997), 38.

27. For the "strenuous life" doctrine and the turn-of-the-century cult of masculinity, see E. Anthony Rotundo, *American Manhood: Transformations in Masculinity from the Revolution to the Modern Era* (New York: Basic Books, 1993), 226, 227–44.

28. See, for instance, JEK's comment that the Securities and Exchange Commission (SEC) was a "Death Sentence . . . which prevented further utility expansion" in statement made to the FBI, ca. Mar. 1943. JEKP, f. 8.

29. JEK, "Propaganda: Civil War in Spain," notes for speech delivered to Reserve Officers, JEKP, f. 70.

30. At 17 Battery Place, a classic art deco office block, JEK initially worked in a space rented by the Rock Asphalt Export Corporation before taking a small office himself. JEKP, ff. 7, 8; JEK-FBI, 2:94, 6. JEK's detractors liked to point out that the German consulate's address was 17 Battery Place, but the complex comprised upward of 1,200 rooms and probably around a thousand separate offices. Thomas P. Abello to Talbot, 7 Sept. 1937, Abello to Alonso, 8 Sept. 1937, and Abello to JEK, 9 Sept. 1937, JEKP, f. 37.

31. JEK, "The Cause of the Nationalist Government in Spain," speech delivered at Bar Harbor, ME, 3 Sept. 1937, JEKP, f. 70. Abello later had something of a checkered career in Spain; after a spell in a Nationalist jail in 1938, he apparently went over to the Loyalist side. See *Daily Worker*, 4–6 May 1938, cuttings in FXTP, b. 37, f. 17.

32. Abello to Talbot, 7 Sept. 1937, Abello to Alonso, 8 Sept. 1937, and Abello to JEK, 9 Sept. 1937, JEKP, f. 37.

33. "Father F. X. Talbot, Ex-Head of Loyola," obituary, *NYT*, 10 Dec. 1953, 47. An official obituary by John LaFarge is in FXTP, b. 64, f. 21. Francis X. Talbot, *Saint Among Savages: The Life of Isaac Jogues* (New York: Harper & Brothers, 1935), esp. 194–207; also see Talbot, *Saint Among the Hurons: The Life of Jean de Brébeuf* (New York: Harper, 1949).

34. Talbot to Gomá, 27 May 1937, FXTP, b. 21, f. 29. From May 1937 to Nov. 1938, in compliance with the Spanish Embargo Act, the U.S. State Department recorded total gross collections for the Loyalists of $1,734,809, of which, after advertising and administrative costs, $1,251,950 went to Spain; sundry organizations collected $181,622 for the Nationalists, with $179,533 actually sent. FXTP, b. 37, f. 10; and see *America*, 27 May 1939, 147; FXTP, b. 37, f. 14. For each issue his magazine tackled, Talbot accumulated press clippings, articles, pamphlets, National Catholic Welfare Conference (NCWC) reports, along with voluminous

personal correspondence, and—thankfully for the historian—he was meticulous about filing everything away.

35. For Talbot's bias toward the moralistic propaganda value of all literary forms, see William M. Halsey, *The Survival of American Innocence: Catholicism in an Era of Disillusionment, 1920–1940* (Notre Dame, IN: Univ. of Notre Dame Press, 1980), 110; Henri Massis and Robert Brasillach, *The Cadets of the Alcazar,* foreword Francis X. Talbot (New York: Paulist Press, 1937), 7–11; and Francis X. Talbot, "Foreword," 15 Mar. 1937, FXTP, b. 21, f. 29.

36. Francis X. Talbot, "The Attitude of Organized Religion Toward Government," address delivered at the Poughkeepsie Civic Forum, Poughkeepsie, NY, 3 Apr. 1938, reprinted in the *Catholic Mind* 36, no. 850 (1938): 189–90, 195, 196.

37. Ibid., 189; Eric J. Hobsbawm, *Nations and Nationalism Since 1870: Programme, Myth, Reality* (Cambridge: Cambridge Univ. Press, 1990), 146–47.

38. JEK's statement for counsel at the time of his trial, ca. Mar. 1943, JEKP, f. 8.

39. Cárdenas to JEK, 17 Apr. 1937, and JEK to Cárdenas, 29 Apr. 1937, JEKP, f. 37.

40. JEK to Shipley, 1 May 1937, and see, for instance, J. G. to JEK, 28 July 1937, JEKP, f. 37; attached note, box 6429, 852.2221/391, State Department, General Records, Central Decimal File (SD-CDF), 1930–39, Record Group (RG) 59, National Archives, College Park, MD. For Golos, see, for instance, Don Whitehead, *The FBI Story: A Report to the People* (New York: Random House, 1956), 173. Commonly called the Abraham Lincoln *Brigade,* its correct army designation was battalion. Earl Browder, "The American Communist Party in the Thirties," in *As We Saw the Thirties: Essays on Social and Political Movements of a Decade,* ed. Rita James Simon (Urbana: Univ. of Illinois Press, 1967), 235.

41. JEK to Shipley, 8 June 1937; R. E. Wall[?] to JEK, 5 Aug. 1937; JEK to Hull, 15 Sept. 1937, all in JEKP, f. 37. JEK to Hull is also in SD-CDF, b. 6430, 852.2221/559. JEK to Shipley, 24 June 1937, JEKP, f. 37. For verification, see Hugh Thomas, *The Spanish Civil War,* 3rd ed. (New York: Modern Library, 2001), 665, from *Bajo la bandera de la España republicana* (Moscow, ca. 1970).

42. Cárdenas capitalized *Spain* at $37,500 ($1.1 million). Francis X. Connolly replaced Bayo as editor. In May 1939, Echegaray became Consul General, while Gaytan de Ayala ran the Spanish Library of Information. To compare JEK's "Military Operations" series, see Luis María de Lojendio, *Operaciones militares de la guerra de España, 1936–1939* (Barcelona: Montaner y Simon, 1940). JEK, "Foresworn Americans Serve Red Cause in Spain," *America* 57, no. 29 (1937), 55–56.

43. "Journal of W. Cameron Forbes" (WCFP-J), compiled ca. 1946, 2 series, 5 vols., II:V, 355A, W. Cameron Forbes Papers, Houghton Library, Harvard College, Cambridge, MA. Sedgwick and Forbes's tour is a condensed and revised version of Michael E. Chapman, "Pro-Franco Anti-Communism: Ellery Sedgwick and the *Atlantic Monthly,*" *Journal of Contemporary History* 41, no. 4 (2006): 641–62.

44. W. Cameron Forbes, *The Philippine Islands,* 2 vols. (Boston: Houghton Mifflin, 1928), 1:30. For a balanced overview of Forbes's administration, see Artemio R. Guillermo and May Kyi Win, eds., *Historical Dictionary of the Philippines* (Lanham, MD: Scarecrow Press, 1997), 92; Robert M. Spector, "W. Cameron Forbes in Haiti: Additional Light on the Genesis of the 'Good Neighbor' Policy," *Caribbean Studies* 6, no. 2 (July 1966): esp. 44–45. For an insightful synthesis of the quest for order, see Robert E. Hannigan, *The New World Power: American Foreign Policy, 1898–1917* (Philadelphia: Univ. of Pennsylvania Press, 2002), esp. 10–16. For economic technocrats, see Emily S. Rosenberg, *Financial Missionaries to the World: The Politics and Culture of Dollar Diplomacy, 1900–1930* (Cambridge, MA: Harvard Univ. Press, 1999), esp. 23–30; Rosenberg incorrectly describes Forbes as a governor of New

Jersey. For Forbes's financial acumen, see David Neal Keller, *Stone & Webster, 1889–1989: A Century of Integrity and Service* (New York: Stone & Webster, 1989), 26–27.

45. "Jumped," WCFP-J, II:V, 355A.

46. For the *Atlantic*'s reputation for bold discussion of religious matters and intellectual vitality, see John Tebbel and Mary Ellen Zuckerman, *The Magazine in America, 1741–1990* (New York: Oxford Univ. Press, 1991), 201–3, 318; for circulation, see Ellery Sedgwick Jr., *The* Atlantic Monthly, *1857–1909: Yankee Humanism at High Tide and Ebb* (Amherst: Univ. of Massachusetts Press, 1994), 314. A high percentage of readers were annual subscribers. For the *Atlantic* as a fount of probity, literary brilliance, and liberal progressivism, see ibid., 4. "Facts," WCFP-J, II:V, 384.

47. Sedgwick to O'Connell and Lockwood, 19 Nov. 1937; Sedgwick to Finley, 30 Nov. 1937; Sedgwick to Ford and Merriman, 16 Nov. 1937; Ford to Sedgwick, 17 Nov. 1937, all in carton 15, b. 37 [15:37], f. 13, Ellery Sedgwick Papers (ESP), Massachusetts Historical Society, Boston.

48. Welles to Forbes, 24 Nov. 1937, ESP, 15:37, f. 13; WCFP-J, II:V, 372–73. They arrived in Algeciras on 10 Jan.; Forbes departed from Irún on 22 Jan. 1938, followed by Sedgwick a day or so later. See "Viaje a España de ilustres personalidades norteamericanas," ESP, 15:38, f. 13, and WCFP-J, II:V, 421. "Overjoyed" in WCFP-J, II:V, 373–74. For Queipo de Llano as both "Radio General" and "Social General," see Raymond L. Proctor in James W. Cortada, ed., *Historical Dictionary of the Spanish Civil War, 1936–1939* (Westport, CT: Greenwood Press, 1982), 412. "Red menace" in WCFP-J, II:V, 378–79.

49. For Badajoz, see WCFP-J, II:V, 384–87; William Cameron Forbes, *As to Polo* (Boston: Geo. H. Ellis, 1919). For the rest of the tour, see WCFP-J, II:V, 390–422; and for their itinerary, see "Viaje a España," ESP, 15:38, f. 13. Historians today accept that the Nationalists, primarily contingents of Spanish Moroccan Moors, killed about a thousand Loyalist fighters and sympathizers during the fall of Badajoz in Aug. 1936. Of the eight thousand militia defending the town, few wore uniforms to distinguish them from noncombatants. For a balanced account, see Thomas, *Spanish Civil War,* 360–61. Pro-Loyalists made much of an eyewitness report by correspondent Jay Allen in the *Chicago Daily Tribune* on 30 Aug. 1936, which pro-Nationalists questioned from the outset because it also appeared in the *New York Herald Tribune* but under N. Reynolds Packard's byline, and Packard was in Burgos at the time. See Geoffrey McNeill-Moss, *The Siege of Alcazar: A History of the Siege of the Toledo Alcazar, 1936* (New York: Knopf, 1937), app. 2. Allen visited Badajoz nine days after the Nationalists entered, and his account is largely anecdotal, making it difficult to interpret objectively. "Suddenly we saw two Phalanxists halt a strapping fellow in a workman's blouse and hold him while a third pulled back his shirt, baring his right shoulder. The black and blue marks of a rifle butt could be seen. . . . The report was unfavorable. To the bull ring with him." *Chicago Daily Tribune,* 30 Aug. 1936, 1–2. Leaving aside whether recoil bruising would still be visible nine days later, when Allen suddenly saw the Falangists, he was, by his own admission, driving past in a car. While it is quite possible that Nationalists did stop suspects in civilian clothes, check for telltale bruising, and execute culprits as a reprisal for prior Loyalist murders of civilians, it is hard not to conclude in this case that Allen was recounting hearsay. Memorable for its chilling quality, this incident has nevertheless passed into historiography as fact. See, for instance, "The Massacres," in Robert Payne, ed., *The Civil War in Spain, 1936–1939* (New York: Putnam's Sons, 1962), 85–91; and Preston, *The Spanish Civil War,* 121.

50. *Time* 31, no. 7 (1938): 28. For the politics of *Time*'s Spanish Civil War coverage, see chap. 2 below. Melvin Small notes how Roosevelt was prone to influence by "a few salient but unrepresentative" opinions. See Small, "Public Opinion," in *Explaining the History of American Foreign Relations,* ed. Michael J. Hogan and Thomas G. Paterson (Cambridge:

Cambridge Univ. Press, 1991), 174. "Present Conditions in Spain, Jan. 1938: Speech by W. Cameron Forbes, Delivered before the University Club, Baltimore, Maryland, on Feb. 23, 1938," pamphlet, copies in ESP, 15:37, f. 7, and WCFP-J, II:V, following 423. "U.S. Recognition of Franco Regime Urged Here by W. Cameron Forbes," *Boston Globe,* 4 May 1938, 1, 15. It is unclear whether proceeds went directly to Nationalist Spain's Red Cross or to SNRC. Other speakers included plastic surgeon J. Eastman Sheehan and Irish lecturer Aileen O'Brien. See *Boston Herald,* 4 May 1938, 19. Letter from SNRC secretary Joseph F. Moore to Anne Morgan, 3 Dec. 1938, in b. T1, Spanish Papers, Correspondence, Committee to Send Anesthetics and Medicines to Spain, Hildreth Meière Papers (HMP), Archives of American Art, Smithsonian Institution, New York. Essentially the U.S. fund-raising wing of the Falange's Auxilio Social women's aid organization, the SNRC drew its membership predominantly from Manhattan elites, many of whom were Protestants. See chap. 5 below.

51. Forbes, "Present Conditions," 15–16, 5; Forbes to Sedgwick, 24 May 1838, ESP, 17:42, f. 25.

52. Memorandum of Conversation, 16 Mar. 1938, SD-CDF, b. 6425, f. 3, 852.01/377. For Hornbeck's realpolitik, see Richard P. Traina, *American Diplomacy and the Spanish Civil War* (Bloomington: Indiana Univ. Press, 1968), 81, 124–26.

53. Ellery Sedgwick, "Life Found Normal in Insurgent Spain," *NYT,* 13 Feb. 1938, 19, and "Franco Is Shrewd in Political Acts," *NYT,* 15 Feb. 1938, 12; both were advance wire dispatches from London written by Sedgwick before his return. For recent scholarship concluding that Spain's Falangists were "interested in Nazi Germany and Fascist Italy, but in thrall to neither," see Wayne H. Bowen, *Spaniards and Nazi Germany: Collaboration in the New Order* (Columbia: Univ. of Missouri Press, 2000), 16. Falangist ideology, which always espoused Catholic piety, emphasized its Hispanic character, opposed communism and Freemasonry and coopted its imagery from Italian Fascism, evolved from the revolutionary national syndicalism of the movement's founder, José Antonio Primo de Rivera, in 1933 to the statist conservatism of Franco's administration by 1945. As with many political movements, Falangists held a range of sentiments, including those of hard-core street-thug fascists. Here, I am thinking more about the women activists of the Auxilio Social in Spain, and especially the FET-JONS in Puerto Rico, who raised large aid contributions for Talbot's ASRF.

54. *New York Herald Tribune,* 6 Mar. 1938, and *Spokane Catholic,* 25 Mar. 1938, from Romeike Press Clipping Bureau, ESP, 15:38, f. 16. *Boston Globe,* 13 Feb. 1938, 1; Ellery Sedgwick, "On Franco's Side in Spain," *Reader's Digest* 32, no. 193 (1938): 27–29.

55. *NYT,* 27 Feb. 1938, IV:9, and 8 Mar. 1938, 11. *Syracuse American,* n.d.; *Milwaukee Sunday News and Sentinel,* 27 Mar. 1938; *New York Evening Journal,* 28 Mar. 1938; *Brooklyn Tablet,* 2 Apr. 1938, all in Romeike Press Clipping Bureau, ESP, 15:38, f. 16.

56. Letter from Rev. Dr. Joseph B. Code, *Washington Post,* 14 Apr. 1938, 8; and see Robert Davis, "A Vermonter in Spain: What Sort of Government Do the Spaniards Want?" *New York Herald Tribune,* 23 June 1938, 18.

57. Data are from a spreadsheet compiled by the author of *Atlantic* articles during July 1936–June 1939, along with profiles from *Who's Who, 1938–39* and *1944–45* (London: A. & C. Black, 1939, 1945), and *World Authors, 1900–1950* (New York: H. W. Wilson, 1996). Wilson Follett, "Letter to a Communist Friend," *Atlantic* 162, no. 4 (1938): 461; Albert Jay Nock, *Our Enemy the State* (Caldwell, ID: Caxton Printers, 1950), and *Memoirs of a Superfluous Man* (New York: Harper & Brothers, 1943), 25. A good history of the modern movement is Jonathan M. Schoenwald, *A Time for Choosing: The Rise of Modern American Conservatism* (Oxford: Oxford Univ. Press, 2001). For Ortega and Suñer, see Paul Preston, *Franco: A Biography* (New York: Basic Books, 1994), 544, 647. Franco actually disliked Ortega, whom he considered a member of the liberal intelligentsia. For Falangists, see chap. 1, n. 53 above.

58. *Current Biography* (Bronx, NY: H. W. Wilson, 1941); George E. Sokolsky, *Labor's Fight for Power* (1934; repr., Port Washington, NY: Kennikat Press, 1971), 275, 218; *Time* 32 (1 Aug. 1938): 22. "Arbiter" (237), "entanglements" (209), and foolish "alliances that lead inevitably to war" (221) in Sokolsky, *Labor's Fight.* At the height of the cold war, Senator J. William Fulbright (D-AR) articulated the folly of American exceptionalism in *The Arrogance of Power* (New York: Random House, 1966). For a thoughtful treatment of Wilson's seven interventions, see Frederick S. Calhoun, *Power and Principle: Armed Intervention in Wilsonian Foreign Policy* (Kent, OH: Kent State Univ. Press, 1986); and for an alternative interpretation of the American way of war as typified by the Powell Doctrine, see Max Boot, *The Savage Wars of Peace: Small Wars and the Rise of American Power* (New York: Basic Books, 2002). For an analysis of Taft's selective interventionism, see Russell Kirk and James McClellan, *The Political Principles of Robert A. Taft* (New York: Fleet Press Corporation, 1967), 162–63. Still, fueled by a fanciful understanding of the operational capabilities of the latest submarines and aircraft, many Americans of the late 1930s did have a genuine fear that "Hitler's legions (or the Japanese hordes) would come marching down Main Street" at any moment. David M. Esposito, "Franklin D. Roosevelt and American Strategic Vulnerability," in *Franklin D. Roosevelt and the Formation of the Modern World,* ed. Thomas C. Howard and William D. Pederson (Armonk, NY: M. E. Sharpe, 2003), 45–56. For Coughlin as "radio priest," see, for example, *Broadcasting,* 15 Nov. 1936, 38. Richard M. Ketchum, *The Borrowed Years, 1938–1941: America on the Way to War* (New York: Random House, 1989), 124.

59. Ellery Sedgwick, *The Happy Profession* (Boston: Little, Brown, 1946), and "The Patron Saint of Andalusia," *Atlantic* 161, no. 6 (1938): 784.

60. Ellery Sedgwick, "The Fan and the Sword," *Atlantic* 158, no. 2 (1936): 136, 130, 131, 135, 137.

61. Ian D. Colvin, "The Case for Franco," ibid. 161, no. 3 (1938): 399, 402; John Langdon-Davies, "The Case for the Government," ibid., 406–7.

62. For isms, see, for instance, Homer L. Chaillaux, *Isms: A Review of Alien Isms, Revolutionary Communism, and Their Active Sympathizers in the U.S.* (Indianapolis, IN: American Legion, 1937). Word counts of *communism* and *fascism* include derivatives (*communist, fascist*). Although Sedgwick had effectively retired by the time Hitler grabbed the remaining half of Slovakia in Mar. 1939, Sedgwick's successor, Ted Weeks, did little to increase coverage regarding the imminent perils of Nazi expansionism; articles continued to stress U.S. nonintervention in European squabbles for empire.

63. For a discussion of typical letter writers, see Hillier Krieghbaum, *Facts in Perspective: The Editorial Page and News Interpretation* (Englewood Cliffs, NJ: Prentice-Hall, 1956), 283–84. I am grateful to Cromwell Schubarth, business editor for the *Boston Herald,* for explaining the vagaries of letter selection; editors may publish letters supportive of their own opinions, or they may print strongly opposing views in order to make an editorial position appear less radical.

64. For an example of the discourse of aggression, see Harold B. Hinton, *Cordell Hull: A Biography* (Garden City, NY: Doubleday, Doran, 1942), 323 and passim. According to a *Times* editorial, America was engaged in "wholly peaceful trade" as an "innocent bystander" in the face of Japanese "aggression," *NYT,* 14 Dec. 1937, 24. Modern references to the *Panay* incident are no less sycophantic: Robert Dallek only talks in Roosevelt's voice of the "deep shock at the indiscriminate bombing of an American vessel" in *Franklin D. Roosevelt and American Foreign Policy, 1932–1945* (Oxford: Oxford Univ. Press, 1995), 153. Also see "deliberately and wantonly sunk," in Charles A. Jellison, "A Prelude to War," *American History* 34, no. 5 (1999), 64; and see the "gunboats" of "neutrals" in Harlan J. Swanson "The *Panay* Incident: Prelude to Pearl Harbor," *U.S. Naval Institute Proceedings* 93, no.

12 (Dec. 1967): 32. Sedgwick, introduction to "Under Thirty" column, *Atlantic* 161, no. 6 (1938): 840; Tambussi, "Challenge from Italy," ibid. 162, no. 1 (1938): 112–13. Ella Grasso, née Ella Rosa Giovanna Oliva Tambussi, was governor of Connecticut from 1975 to 1980. I am indebted to Peter Holloran for alerting me to the Tambussi/Grasso connection.

65. James's letter, "The Coming War," *Atlantic* 161, no. 6 (1938): 842–43; Davis's letter, "The Open Mind," ibid. 162, no. 3 (1938): 405–6; Elizabeth——'s letter, "Father, Husband, and Son," ibid. 161, no. 6 (1938): 841–42.

66. Benjamin L. Alpers, *Dictators, Democracy, and American Public Culture: Envisioning the Totalitarian Enemy, 1920s–1950s* (Chapel Hill: Univ. of North Carolina Press, 2003), 11, 15–17, 33.

67. Ellery Sedgwick, *Thomas Paine* (Boston: Small, Maynard, 1899); Alan Brinkley, *Voices of Protest: Huey Long, Father Coughlin, and the Great Depression* (New York: Vintage Books, 1983), xi.

68. Moses to Sedgwick, 25 Mar. 1938, ESP, 15:37, f. 1; Sedgwick to Cárdenas, 14 Apr. 1938, ESP, 15:37, f. 2. Laughlin, *Washington Post,* 28 Mar. 1938, 7.

69. Officials at the Commerce Department probably backed the Loyalists too, especially after Dec. 1938 under Harry L. Hopkins, although I have not yet found supporting documentation. For Murphy's sympathies with Franco representative, Eduardo Propper de Callejon, see Robert Murphy, *Diplomat Among Warriors* (Garden City, NY: Doubleday, 1964), 31. For Wiley, see Douglas Little, *Malevolent Neutrality: The United States, Great Britain, and the Origins of the Spanish Civil War* (Ithaca, NY: Cornell Univ. Press, 1985), 87. David Mayers, *The Ambassadors and America's Soviet Policy* (New York: Oxford Univ. Press, 1995), 140. For investments, see especially John H. Morgan to R. Walton Moore, 10 Nov. 1936, in *Franklin D. Roosevelt and Foreign Affairs,* ed. Edgar B. Nixon, 1st series, 3 vols. (Cambridge, MA: Belknap Press, 1969), 3:478–80; *American Direct Investments in Foreign Countries–1936,* ed. Paul D. Dickens (Washington, DC: GPO, 1938), 9, 16.

70. Sedgwick to Brown, 10 June 1938, ESP, 15:37, f. 9; see Sedgwick to Brown concerning sympathetic officials connected with "embassies, consulates, etcetera," 11 July 1938, ESP, 15:37, f. 10; Cabot to Sedgwick, 30 Dec. 1938, ESP, 15:37, f. 10.

71. Schoonmaker to Sedgwick, 23 Mar. 1938, Hibbard to Sedgwick, 27 Mar. 1938, ESP, 15:37, f. 17. *The American Travelers' Guide Book, Spain* (New York: Simon & Schuster, 1932).

72. Allin to the editor, 12 Mar. 1938, ESP, 15:38, f. 2; Hill to the editor, 16 Mar. 1938, ESP, 15:37, f. 3; Holt to the editor, 26 Mar. 1938, ESP, 15:38, f. 4; Mrs. Richard Edsall to the editor, ca. 21 Apr., and Sedgwick to Edsall, 22 Apr. 1938, ESP, 15:38, f. 5.

73. Robert Warshow, *The Immediate Experience: Movies, Comics, Theatre, and Other Aspects of Popular Culture* (1946–54; repr., Cambridge, MA: Harvard Univ. Press, 2002), 3–4; Jacobs to the editor, 7 June 1938, and Holdt to the editor, 21 June 1938, ESP, 15:38, f. 6; Michael Denning, *The Cultural Front: The Laboring of American Culture in the Twentieth Century* (London: Verso, 1997), esp. xiii–xx, xvi.

2. Defending Americanism

1. "Boring from within" was a tactic of leading U.S. communist William Z. Foster to penetrate conservative American Federation of Labor (AFL) unions in the early 1920s; anticommunists of the 1930s hurled the phrase back at the CPUSA to evidence the insidious nature of communism. Theodore Draper, *American Communism and Soviet Russia: The Formative Period* (New York: Viking Press, 1963), 63, 67; Merwin K. Hart, "America—Look at Spain: The Agony Will Be Repeated Here," speech, Málaga, Spain, 29 Sept. 1938, printed

in *Spain* 3, no. 1 (15 Oct. 1938): 5, 7, 20, and in *Vital Speeches of the Day* 5, no. 2 (1 Nov. 1938): 57–58; Merwin K. Hart, *America, Look at Spain!* (New York: P. J. Kenedy & Sons, 1939).

2. For communism as Americanism, see, for instance, Mary McCarthy, *Intellectual Memoirs: New York, 1936–1938* (New York: Harcourt Brace Jovanovich, 1992), 2.

3. Once he closed his Battery Place office, JEK rented a second room at his lodgings in Jersey City, from where his office assistant James Finucane worked until Mar. 1938. *America* generally paid $25 for an article, occasionally $30 or $20 for better or worse quality and/or length. See "Honoraria Paid John E. Kelly," JEKP, f. 8. Correspondence among JEK, Talbot, Shipley, and the Berlin consulate in JEKP, f. 51; memorandum for O'Shea, ca. Mar. 1943 JEKP, f. 8.

4. JEK arrived in New York on 16 Dec., so the *Bremen* probably left Hamburg on the tenth. JEK to Talbot, 15 Jan. 1938, and Talbot's reply of 17 Jan. 1938, JEKP, f. 38. I am grateful to Frank Turnbull at *America* for his estimates of circulation figures for 1938.

5. "World Revolution's Next Objective," draft article in JEKP, f. 82, published as "World Revolution's Objective," *Sign* 17, no. 9 (1938): 552–53. For membership, see Harvey Klehr, *The Heyday of American Communism: The Depression Decade* (New York: Basic Books, 1984), 240, 413. Membership may have peaked slightly higher in mid-1938. Enrollment figures minimize the number of communists because of the party's revolving door of 50 percent per annum; onetime membership in Jan. 1938 would have been 160,000–200,000; there was a brief second peak after the German invasion of the Soviet Union in June 1941.

6. "Private property," from "Communism" speech outline, delivered 25 Jan. 1938, Worcester, MA, JEKP, f. 70; JEK may well have given the same speech in the New York area.

7. "Spain: The Issues Behind the Conflict," broadcast on WEVD, 13 Feb. 1938, JEKP, f. 71. Polling returns gave the following numbers of votes cast: Popular Front, 4,654,116; the Right, 4,503,505; center parties, 400,901; Basque Nationalists (pro-Left), 125,714. From Javier Tusell, in Ramón Salas Larrazábal, *Los datos exactos de la guerra civil* (Madrid: Colección Drácena, 1980), 255. For an excellent analysis of the election results, see Stanley G. Payne, *The Collapse of the Spanish Republic, 1933–1936* (New Haven, CT: Yale Univ. Press, 2006), 174–81.

8. Dolores Ibárruri, *They Shall Not Pass: The Autobiography of La Pasionaria* (New York: International Publishers, 1966), 68. Compare JEK's claims with Payne, *The Spanish Civil War*, 11–15, 29–31, 53–55. Denning, *The Cultural Front*, xvi. Arlo Guthrie, "Jarama Valley," recorded variously, released 1938. For Ortiz González, see JEK-FBI, 7:297; WEVD letters and correspondence from the WPA Adult Education Program, JEKP, f. 71; Mrs. Herbert N. Dawes to Station WEVD, 15 Feb. 1938, JEKP, f. 71. Unfortunately, a recording of the broadcast appears not to be extant. Sheen taught at Catholic University, Washington, DC; he became Bishop of Rochester in 1966 and Archbishop of the Titular See of Newport (Wales) in 1969. His Sunday "The Catholic Hour" broadcast, which reached four million listeners, ran from 1930 to 1952. For further information on Clare Singer Dawes, see chap. 5 below. Judeo-Christian in character, the Florence Crittenden League of Compassion ran homes for women and arranged for the adoption of orphans. It is beyond the scope of this study to catalog and interpret the hundreds of cultural works inspired by the Popular Front/Comintern line on Loyalist Spain and fascist aggression, but some of the more obvious examples are Orson Welles's *War of the Worlds* radio broadcast, along with his Mercury Theatre productions; Ernest Hemingway's *The Fifth Column and the First Forty-Nine Stories* (New York: P. F. Collier & Son, 1938); the glossy biweekly magazine *Ken;* and the documentary film, *The Spanish Earth*. After the announcement of the Nazi-Soviet Non-Aggression Pact, it is notable how these same artists flip-flopped to follow official CPUSA policy; Guthrie (with Pete Seeger and the Almanac Singers) switched virtually overnight from popularizing noninterventionist antiwar folksongs to churning out patriotic pro-war songs after the Nazi invasion of the Soviet Union in June 1941.

9. JEK's speech reconstructed from *NYT,* 23 May 1938, 20; "Spain," speech notes, Communion Breakfast, 22 May 1938, JEKP, f. 70; text of two similar speeches delivered three weeks prior to the Knights of Columbus, the Bronx, and at St. Joseph's College, Philadelphia, JEKP, f. 70. Also see JEK, "His Excellency the Spanish Ambassador," *America* 59, no. 9 (1938): 197–98.

10. JEK's speech reconstructed from *NYT,* 23 May 1938, 20; "Spain," speech notes, Communion Breakfast, 22 May 1938, JEKP, f. 70; text of two similar speeches delivered three weeks prior to the Knights of Columbus, the Bronx, and at St. Joseph's College, Philadelphia, JEKP, f. 70. Also see JEK, "His Excellency the Spanish Ambassador," *America* 59, no. 9 (1938): 197–98.

11. "The Situation in Spain," delivered to 300 attendees under the auspices of St. Stephen's Protestant Episcopal Church, St. Stephen's Forum, Philadelphia, JEKP, f. 70, emphasis added but consistent with JEK's note cards. Coverage of JEK's Saturday, 6 Aug. speech, "Non-Catholics Hear Spain Talk," *Brooklyn Tablet,* 13 Aug. 1938, 2; his speech notes compare verbatim with quotes printed in the *Tablet.*

12. "The Situation in Spain," delivered to 300 attendees under the auspices of St. Stephen's Protestant Episcopal Church, St. Stephen's Forum, Philadelphia, JEKP, f. 70, emphasis added but consistent with JEK's note cards. Coverage of JEK's Saturday, 6 Aug. speech, "Non-Catholics Hear Spain Talk," *Brooklyn Tablet,* 13 Aug. 1938, 2; his speech notes compare verbatim with quotes printed in the *Tablet.*

13. JEK never discarded receipts and expense sheets; his papers contain selected examples, indicating clothes, books, stationary, presents, laundry, hotels, travel, and so forth; see JEKP, ff. 170–71. "The Situation in Spain," delivered to 500 attendees of the Rotary Club, Hotel Commodore, New York City, 21 July 1938, JEKP, f. 70. JEK was referencing Roosevelt's Good Neighbor Policy for Latin America, which Roosevelt first announced in his inaugural address of 4 Mar. 1933, although credit for the initiative belongs with Herbert Hoover, for it was he who had laid the groundwork for improved relations during his Latin American tour in Nov. 1928.

14. By far his most rewarding trip was to Boston in Jan. 1939, where he delivered three lectures in a single day, earning $50, $35, and $40 ($3,750 today), less expenses for train, taxis, and hotel. See JEKP, f. 7, addresses arranged by Mrs. Herbert N. Dawes.

15. Fredrick B. Pike, "The New Corporatism in Franco's Spain and Some Latin American Perspectives," in *The New Corporatism: Social-Political Structures in the Iberian World,* ed. Fredrick B. Pike and Thomas Stritch (Notre Dame, IN: Univ. of Notre Dame Press, 1974), esp. 184; Howard J. Wiarda, *Corporatism and Development: The Portuguese Experience* (Amherst: Univ. of Massachusetts Press, 1977), esp. 55–56; Sebastian Balfour, "Spain, from 1931 to the Present," in *Spain: A History,* ed. Raymond Carr (Oxford: Oxford Univ. Press, 2000), 266–68.

16. John MacCormac, "Quebec Makes First Test of Its Anticommunist Law," *NYT,* 14 Nov. 1937, 74; George T. Eberle, "Portugal's Progress," WNAC radio address, reprinted in *Catholic Mind* 36, no. 854 (1938), 283, 285, 287. WNAC became WRKO Talk Radio. For a popular contemporary presentation, see Charles E. Coughlin, "The Birth of a Corporatist State," *Social Justice* 2A, no. 5 (1938): 3, 19, and 2A, no. 7 (1938): 3, 23; for another presentation of corporatism in the U.S. Catholic press, see Irene Hernaman, "Portugal's Corporative State," *Catholic Mind* 36, no. 843 (1938): 52–55.

17. Charles J. McFadden, *The Philosophy of Communism* (New York: Benziger Brothers, 1939), xvi, 150, 152; Fulton J. Sheen, "Preface," in ibid., vii–viii; Joseph Patrick Dalton, "Is Christian Corporatism Compatible with Democracy?" (master's thesis, Boston College, 1942).

18. Emil Ludwig, *Emil Ludwig's Life of Roosevelt: A Study in Fortune and Power*, 12 vols. (New York: McFadden, 1937–38); *Liberty* (New York), 5 Feb. 1938, 33, 35; *NYT*, 31 Mar. 1938, 1.

19. Speech text, delivered 1 May 1938 to the Knights of Columbus, the Bronx, and St. Joseph's College, Philadelphia, JEKP, f. 70; Ronald H. Bayor, *Neighbors in Conflict: The Irish, Germans, Jews, and Italians of New York City, 1929–1941* (Baltimore: Johns Hopkins Univ. Press, 1978), esp. chaps. 4 and 5; Leonard Dinnerstein, *Antisemitism in America* (New York: Oxford Univ. Press, 1994), 113.

20. *Brooklyn Tablet*, 25 June 1938, 7, 11, including extracts from "Dr. Scanlan: Successful Candidate for Office of Jew Baiter No. 1," *Jewish Examiner*, n.d. Although its readership was primarily Catholic, the *Tablet's* serious political content ensured an influence both throughout and beyond metropolitan New York. Circulations from *ABC Blue Book, Publisher's Statements: Newspapers* (Chicago: The Bureau, 1945).

21. Nathan Glazer, *The Social Basis of American Communism* (Westport, CT: Greenwood Press, 1961), 130, 220; Robert A. Rosenstone, *Crusade of the Left: The Lincoln Battalion in the Spanish Civil War* (New York: Pegasus, 1969), 370, 110, 112–13. Rosenstone considered that ALB volunteers were at least a third Jewish and two-thirds CPUSA members. ALB historian Peter N. Carroll is only prepared to say that "a large majority of the volunteers were party members," but he does add that "most of the others had been screened by party committees in America" in *The Odyssey of the Abraham Lincoln Brigade: Americans in the Spanish Civil War* (Stanford, CA: Stanford Univ. Press, 1994), 108. Kevin McDermott and Jeremy Agnew, who stress that Stalin was "heavily embroiled" in events in Spain "from the start," state matter-of-factly that "most [volunteers were] communists," in *The Comintern: A History of International Communism from Lenin to Stalin* (New York: St. Martin's Press, 1997), 140–41. For the extent of ALB recruitment in America, see R. Dan Richardson, *Comintern Army: The International Brigades and the Spanish Civil War* (Lexington: Univ. Press of Kentucky, 1982), esp. 34–35. Speech text, delivered 1 May 1938 to the Knights of Columbus, the Bronx, and later that day to St. Joseph's College, Philadelphia, JEKP, f. 70.

22. For unemployment in mid-Nov. 1937 at 10,870,000, see *NYT*, 2 Jan. 1938, 1, and see introduction, n. 7, above. "Socialized," in Lash, *Love Eleanor*, 280–81; "communist-controlled," in Klehr, *Heyday*, 172, 320–22. For Lash as ASU head, see Richard Gid Powers, *Not Without Honor: The History of American Anticommunism* (New York: Free Press, 1995), 127–28.

23. Jefferson to Thomas Law, 13 June 1814, in *The Portable Thomas Jefferson*, ed. Merrill D. Peterson (New York: Viking Press, 1975), 540; Jefferson to Benjamin Rush, 23 Sept. 1800, *The Papers of Thomas Jefferson*, vol. 32, ed. Barbara B. Oberg (Princeton, NJ: Princeton Univ. Press, 2005), 168; "A Bill for Establishing Religious Freedom," 1777 draft, in *The Portable Thomas Jefferson*, ed. Merrill D. Peterson (New York: Viking, 1975), 251; G. K. Chesterton, *What I Saw in America* (New York: Dodd, Mead, 1922), 7.

24. Samuel P. Huntington, *American Politics: The Promise of Disharmony* (Cambridge, MA: Belknap Press, 1981), esp. 25. For a history of Dies's HUAC, see August Raymond Ogden, *The Dies Committee: A Study of the Special House Committee for the Investigation of Un-American Activities, 1938–1944* (Washington, DC: Catholic Univ. of America Press, 1945). Harvard's Andrew Gordon provided input on the *hikokumin*. For the eccentricity of Britishness, and Britons' chuckles over political radicalism, I am thinking of George Orwell's dismissal of the Far Left, P. G. Wodehouse's playful mockery of Moseley in his character Sir Roderick Spode in *The Code of the Woosters* (1938; repr., Mattituck, NY: Rivercity Press, 1976), and, more recently, skits in the *Monty Python* and *Faulty Towers* BBC-TV series. My thanks to Peter Weiler for his assistance on this point.

25. Homer L. Chaillaux, *Isms: A Review of Alien Isms, Revolutionary Communism, and*

Their Active Sympathizers in the U. S. (Indianapolis, IN: American Legion, 1937), 11; Joseph K. Carson Jr. to the editor, *Life* 5, no. 5 (1938): 6. For an excellent analysis of American exceptionalism as "a core element of American national identity" in the context of recent foreign affairs, see Trevor B. McCrisken, *American Exceptionalism and the Legacy of Vietnam: U.S. Foreign Policy since 1974* (Basingstoke: Palgrave Macmillan, 2003).

26. See, for instance, *A Little Book for Immigrants in Boston* (Boston: Committee for Americanism of the City of Boston, 1921), or Hubert Beckwith Groves, *Americanism* (Portland, OR: Boyer, 1923); ed. Winthrop Talbot, *Americanization: Principles of Americanism; Essentials of Americanization; Technic* [sic] *of Race-Assimilation,* 2nd rev. ed. (New York: H. W. Wilson, 1920), 1. Emory S. Bogardus, *The Essentials of Americanization* (Los Angeles: Univ. of Southern California Press, 1919), 16, 59; Massachusetts Acts (1935), 258:306, "I pledge allegiance to the Flag of the United States of America and to the republic for which it stands, one Nation indivisible, with liberty and justice to all." "Ford English School Melting Pot," Henry Ford Museum and Greenfield Village, Dearborn; "1919: Golda Meir as Liberty in Poale Chasidim pageant," WHi (X3) 22831, University of Wisconsin–Milwaukee Libraries. It seems the first Americanization Day was the designation of Washington's Birthday by the Hebrew Sheltering and Immigration Aid Society in 1919, "to bring home the necessity for complete Americanization." *NYT,* 26 Jan. 1919, 16. Later advocates included Governors Alfred E. Smith (NY) and Harold G. Hoffman (NJ) and Mayor Frank Hague (Jersey City, NJ).

27. For America's Anglo-Protestant ideal, see Samuel P. Huntington, *Who Are We? The Challenges to America's National Identity* (New York: Simon & Schuster, 2004), chap. 4; Israel Zangwill, *The Melting-Pot: Drama in Four Acts* (New York: Macmillan, 1911), 37, 29; C. C. Chapman, "Just What Is Americanism?" *Catholic Mind* 37, no. 877 (1939): 748.

28. Duara, "Historicizing National Identity," 152.

29. For a first-person account of revolutionary songs at May Day parades, see Mary McCarthy, *Intellectual Memoirs: New York, 1936–1938* (New York: Harcourt Brace Jovanovich, 1992), 1–3; for mine-related violence and submarginal pits, see Harriet D. Hudson, *The Progressive Mine Workers of America: A Study in Rival Unionism* (Urbana: Univ. of Illinois, 1952), 43–45, 71–72, 99–101; for CIO/UMWA intimidation, see, for instance, "a crowd of 2,000, armed with stones, bottles, and guns," in "Mine Labor Inquiry Demanded by A.F.L," *NYT,* 31 Aug. 1938, 16. JEK's speech outline, "Communism," delivered 25 Jan. 1938 at Worcester, MA, JEKP, f. 70. Lewis consistently rejected socialism as well as communism, but his organization was beholden to communists to such an extent that he toed the CPUSA line in the 1940 presidential election by backing the antiwar Republican candidate Wendell Willkie. I have not yet been able to corroborate JEK's description of the stamp selling. Blanshard saw himself as a "crusading liberal," but he was actually a Protestant crusader against Catholic political power. Paul Blanshard, *God and Man in Washington* (Boston: Beacon Press, 1960), 9; for his views on Franco, see ibid. 108, 126. According to a 13 Aug. 1943 report by FBI agent Ralph V. Reed, sometime in 1937–38 JEK and others had sought a loan from Hayes Pickelsimer, at Charleston's Kanawha Valley Bank, so that local mine operators could buy guns to protect themselves against "labor trouble." JEK-FBI, 11:482. Gerson's Dec. 1937 appointment and ensuing controversy is in Ronald H. Bayor, *Neighbors in Conflict: The Irish, Germans, Jews, and Italians of New York City, 1929–1941* (Baltimore: Johns Hopkins Univ. Press, 1978), 38, 89–90. Antonio Montero Moreno, details 6,832 individual murder victims, including 283 nuns, in *Historia de la persecución religiosa en España, 1936–1939* (Madrid: Biblioteca de Autores Cristianos, 1961), 762–883.

30. John M. Muste, *Say That We Saw Spain Die: Literary Consequences of the Spanish Civil War* (Seattle: Univ. of Washington Press, 1966), 24; Frederick R. Benson, *Writers in Arms: The Literary Impact of the Spanish Civil War* (New York: New York Univ. Press, 1967), 3.

31. *Spain,* Joseph M. Bayo, ed.; for Peninsular's corporate summary, see JEKP, f. 57. For lunch, see trial testimony by Merwin Hart's secretary, Gladys Rountree, *PM,* 23 May 1943, 3, xx, 8. "The Christian Soldier," draft, 31 July 1938, JEKP, f. 82; JEK, *The Christian Soldier;* Dawes to Talbot, 29 Oct. 1938, FXTP, b. 20, f. 12.

32. JEK, "Should Relief Vote?" *Patriot Digest* 1, no. 1 (1938): 3–7; for Mencken, see M. K. Singleton, *H. L. Mencken and the* American Mercury *Adventure* (Durham, NC: Duke Univ. Press, 1962), 237–38.

33. "Franking Abuse Laid to Spanish Embassy," *NYT,* 11 Feb. 1938, 1.

34. *NYT,* 27 June 1938, 6; JEK to Sloan, 29 June 1938; Sloan to JEK, 7 July 1938; JEK to Talbot, 9 July 1938, all in JEKP, f. 52.

35. Seth Jacobs, *America's Miracle Man in Vietnam: Ngo Dinh Diem, Religion, Race, and U.S. Intervention in Southeast Asia, 1950–1957* (Durham, NC: Duke Univ. Press, 2004), esp. 197, 221; and see also T. Christopher Jespersen, *American Images of China, 1931–1949* (Stanford: Stanford Univ. Press, 1996), chap. 2; Denning, *The Cultural Front,* xvi, 83–84. *Time,* 14 Feb. 1938, 15, and 28 Mar. 1938, 15. Historians still contest the figures, but in the spring of 1938, on the Loyalist side there were about 25,000 foreign volunteers, 1,000 Russian pilots and advisers, and 10,000 aid workers; for Franco, Italian forces had fallen far past their spring 1937 peak of 40,000–50,000, and there were less than 10,000 Germans, roughly 36,000 on each side. Thomas, *The Spanish Civil War,* 941–43, 937–39; Joseph Lash, notes on Spain, 21 June 1938, b. 27, Youth Organizations and Activities, f. Spain, 1937 (Spanish Civil War), Joseph Lash Papers, Roosevelt Library, Hyde Park, NY.

36. For a discussion of the depoliticization, or "technologization," of ideology and Slavoj Žižek's discursive social "'fantasy,'" see Jenny Edkins, *Poststructuralism and International Relations: Bringing the Political Back In* (Boulder, CO: Lynne Rienner, 1999), esp. 8–11.

37. Franklin D. Roosevelt, "Fireside Chat on Reorganization of the Judiciary," 9 Mar. 1937, in *FDR's Fireside Chats,* ed. Russell D. Buhite and David W. Levy (Norman: Univ. of Oklahoma Press, 1992), 85, 86, 95.

38. Edward McArdle to the editor, *Time* 31, no. 19 (1938): 2; Walter Lippmann, *An Inquiry into the Principles of the Good Society* (Boston: Little, Brown, 1937) 232–40; Dorothy Thompson, "The Embargo Against Loyalist Spain," *Boston Globe,* 6 May 1938, morning ed., 22.

39. 180 letters, *Time* 31, no. 25 (1938): 9; ibid. no. 23 (1938): 2.

40. "President Roosevelt's Own Story of the New Deal," *Liberty* 15, no. 11 (1938): 4–10; *The Public Papers and Addresses of Franklin D. Roosevelt: The Continuing Struggle for Liberalism,* 1938 vol. (New York: Macmillan, 1941).

41. *Public Papers and Addresses of FDR,* xxix–xxxi, xxiv, xxi, xxix.

42. "Fireside Chat on Party Primaries," 24 June 1938, in ibid., 398–99; Charles E. Coughlin, "Mr. Roosevelt and Liberalism," *Social Justice* 2A, no. 3 (1938): 3.

43. John Patrick Diggins, *On Hallowed Ground: Abraham Lincoln and the Foundations of American History* (New Haven, CT: Yale Univ. Press, 2000), 186; R. C. Wardell to the editor, *New York World-Telegram,* 15 July 1938, 2nd ed., 14.

44. For *conservative* as synonym, see JEK's June 1932 article, "Wanted: A Conservative Counter Attack," JEKP, f. 80; "Stupid, Wishful Liberals Forget that Stalin Hates Us," *America* 65, no. 10 (1941): 257–58; 99 Pegler and 123 Sokolsky clippings, JEKP, f. 124.

45. For the argument that print capitalism has created or "imagined" national consciousness, see Benedict Anderson, *Imagined Communities: Reflections on the Origin and Spread of Nationalism* (London: Verso, 1991), esp. 34–36, 44–45; and see the introduction above.

46. Eric Hobsbawm, *The Age of Extremes: A History of the World, 1914–1991* (New York: Vintage Books, 1994), 112–13 ("exclusively" emphasized but consistent with Hobsbawm's usage and repetition of the word), 157–58 ("peripheral"). Payne, *The Spanish Civil War,* esp.

83–89, 273 ("panoply"); for Asturias, see also ibid., 54–57, where Payne stresses that directing government power in 1934 was a "centrist liberal democrat president and a centrist liberal democrat prime minister." UGT, or Workers' General Union. It is ironic that when nationalist elites from China to Cuba to Egypt to the stateless Basque Country sought solutions to their particular country's dominance by an imperialist power, they turned to statist socialism.

47. Elie Kedourie, *Nationalism,* 4th ed. (Oxford: Blackwell, 1993), 104 ("antagonistic principles"), 84–85 ("misunderstanding"), 1 ("doctrine invented"), 67–69 ("comprehensive doctrine"). In *Nationalism* (New York: New York Univ. Press, 1997), Ernest Gellner considers Kedourie's periodicity extreme but nevertheless "links nationalism to industrialism" (41). A less Eurocentric view might reflect that Lê Lói's army of would-be independent citizens drove Chinese imperialists out of a functioning Vietnamese nation-state in the fifteenth century. And the Elizabethan England of William Shakespeare's plays looks quite nationalistic at the turn of the sixteenth century.

48. JEK, *A Programme;* see chap. 7 below. Kedourie, *Nationalism,* 69.

3. Roosevelt's Mental Map

1. "Roosevelt Warns Nations Against New World War," *March of Time* newsreel, from *Timeline 1937,* DVD (Sebastopol, CA: Whirlwind Media, 2000).

2. What Roosevelt actually said differs from the official transcript, found in *Papers Relating to the Foreign Relations of the United States: Japan, 1931–1941,* vol. 1 (Washington, DC: GPO, 1943), 379–83. For the genesis of the speech, see Dorothy Borg, "Notes on Roosevelt's 'Quarantine' Speech," in *Causes and Consequences of World War II,* ed. Robert A. Divine (Chicago: Quadrangle Books, 1969), 54. Roosevelt claimed the bombings were unprovoked, yet Guernica was a strategic town defended by Basque forces (see chap. 5 below), and the first bombing at Shanghai was of Japanese naval installations by the Guomindang on 14 Aug.; a Guomindang bomb inadvertently fell on the international settlement, killing 1,000 mostly Chinese.

3. Borg, "'Quarantine' Speech," 48. After the 7 July 1937 Marco Polo Bridge incident, Roosevelt sent 1,200 Marines to Shanghai, reinforcing the 2,000 U.S. troops already stationed there and inadvertently aiding Chiang Kai-shek's strategy of baiting the Japanese to attack. For this interpretation, see Stephen R. MacKinnon, "The Sino-Japanese Conflict, 1931–1945," in *A Military History of China,* ed. David A. Graff and Robin Higham (Boulder, CO: Westview Press, 2002), 214.

4. A Gallup poll of 27 Feb. 1938 found that 75 percent of those polled with an opinion on the Spanish Civil War were sympathetic to the Loyalists (52 percent expressed no opinion). Gallup, *The Gallup Poll,* survey no. 111-A, 92.

5. H. W. Brands, *What America Owes the World: The Struggle for the Soul of Foreign Policy* (Cambridge: Cambridge Univ. Press, 1998), esp. 1–4 and chap. 5. Accounts of Roosevelt as a warmongering interventionist range from Charles C. Tansill's Beardian *Back Door to War: The Roosevelt Foreign Policy, 1933–1941* (Chicago: H. Regnery, 1952) to Bruce M. Russett's Vietnam War–inspired *No Clear and Present Danger: A Skeptical View of the United States Entry into World War II* (New York: Harper & Row, 1972); Mark A. Stoler discusses the complexity of Roosevelt's thinking on isolationism versus intervention in Justus D. Doenecke and Mark A. Stoler, *Debating Franklin D. Roosevelt's Foreign Policies, 1933–1945* (Lanham, MD: Rowman & Littlefield, 2005), 119–25. For naval expansion, see Justus Doenecke, "The Roosevelt Foreign Policy: An Ambiguous Legacy," in ibid., 30–31.

6. In *The American Catholic Voter: 200 Years of Political Impact* (South Bend, IN: St. Augustine's Press, 2004), for instance, George J. Marlin includes the oft-quoted line from Ickes's *Secret Diary* that Roosevelt refused to lift the embargo because that would "mean the loss of every Catholic vote next fall" (211). Interestingly, Marlin cites the quote from a study by George Q. Flynn that expressed reservations about the influence of Catholic voters on Roosevelt's decision making. Flynn, *Roosevelt and Romanism: Catholics and American Diplomacy, 1937–1945* (Westport, CT: Greenwood Press, 1976).

7. Diary entry for 6 Dec. 1937, Ickes, *The Inside Struggle*, 260. As Gary Dean Best has pointed out, historians have long overlooked the effect that Roosevelt's disability had on his administration. Gary Dean Best, *The Critical Press and the New Deal: The Press versus Presidential Power, 1933–1938* (Westport, CT: Praeger, 1993), 154, 162–63. Hugh Gregory Gallagher argues that it was "the central key to understanding FDR's personality and motivation." Gallagher, *FDR's Splendid Deception: The Moving Story of Roosevelt's Massive Disability—and the Intense Efforts to Conceal It from the Public* (St. Petersburg, FL: Vandamere Press, 1985). *Washington Post*, 18 Dec. 1937, 2; Barbara Reardon Farnham, *Roosevelt and the Munich Crisis: A Study of Political Decision-Making* (Princeton, NJ: Princeton Univ. Press, 1997), 91, 112. Waldo Heinrichs dates Roosevelt's return to a sunnier optimism a little earlier, to July 1941, following Operation Barbarossa. Heinrichs, *Threshold of War: Franklin D. Roosevelt and American Entry into World War II* (Oxford: Oxford Univ. Press, 1989), 144–45. For Roosevelt's "relish of power and command," see Dean G. Acheson, *Present at the Creation: My Years in the State Department* (New York: W. W. Norton, 1969), 740.

8. Evans to Roosevelt, 22 Jan. 1939, file 422-C, f. Spanish Revolution of 1936–39, 1939–42, Franklin D. Roosevelt, Papers as President, Official File, 1933–45 (FDR-OF), Franklin D. Roosevelt Library, Hyde Park, NY.

9. Evans to Roosevelt, 22 Jan. 1939, FDR-OF, file 422-C, f. Spanish Revolution of 1936–39, 1939–42.

10. Eighty-four appeals for 1 Jan. 1938 to 31 Jan. 1939, FDR-OF, file 422-C, f. Spanish Revolution of 1936–39, 1938, and f. Spanish Revolution of 1936–39, 1939–42; see, for instance, O'Connell to Roosevelt and Roosevelt to O'Connell, 23 June and 6 July 1937, FDR-OF, file 422-C, f. Spanish Revolution of 1936–39, 1937. Ralph Lord Roy discusses O'Connell's proclivities in *Communism and the Churches* (New York: Harcourt, Brace, 1960), 135. Various correspondence between Toller, Welles, and Roosevelt, and Toller to Eleanor, 18 Dec. 1938, in FDR-OF, file 422-C, f. Spain—Misc., 1937–40. For Archbishop Cosmo Lang's fear that foreign officials might assume that Canterbury's Dean Hewlett Johnson was the actual archbishop, see Tom Buchanan, *Britain and the Spanish Civil War* (Cambridge: Cambridge Univ. Press, 1997), 174.

11. Robert Dallek, *Franklin D. Roosevelt and American Foreign Policy, 1932–1945* (Oxford: Oxford Univ. Press, 1995), 159; Wayne S. Cole, *Roosevelt and the Isolationists, 1932–45* (Lincoln: Univ. of Nebraska Press, 1983), 236; Taylor, *The U.S. and the Spanish Civil War*, 170–71, 191n.29. For average mail as well as an overview of White House mail handling, see Fred W. Shipman, "Report on the White House Executive Office," p. 8, 8 Dec. 1943, Franklin D. Roosevelt Library. There are 189 separate appeals for 1 Jan. 1937 to 31 Jan. 1939, in FDR-OF, file 422-C, f. Spanish Revolution of 1936–39, 1936–37, f. Spanish Revolution of 1936–39, 1938, and f. Spanish Revolution of 1936–39, 1939; if McIntyre prepared a single-page memorandum summarizing, say, three telegrams and two letters, then I have counted this as five appeals.

12. Kanawada, *Roosevelt's Diplomacy*, 149n.1; Taylor, *The U.S. and the Spanish Civil War*, 191n.29 (emphasis added); University of Chicago telegram, 28 Jan. 1939, FDR-OF, file 422-C, f. Spanish Revolution of 1936–39, 1939–42.

13. Kanawada, *Roosevelt's Diplomacy,* 65 (emphasis added); Doyle to McIntyre of 15 Jan. 1939 and McIntyre's reply of 18 Jan. 1939, FDR-OF, file 422-C, f. Spanish Revolution of 1936–39, 1939–42. FDR-OF, file 422-C, f. Spanish Revolution of 1936–39, 1938, contains the three pro-Franco letters that Roosevelt saw: William F. Gorman, Ancient Order of Hibernians, 14 June 1938, summary by McIntyre, protesting "[the] President's statement that no American should bear arms against 'legal' government; thinks the statement is obviously designed as an expression of preference for the Spanish Loyalists-to-Moscow and an objectionable dig at the millions of his fellow citizens whose sympathies are with the Nationalists"; William F. Montavon, NCWC, 7 July 1938, concerning fund-raising by a Popular Front group; John W. McCormack (D-MA), 10 Oct. 1938, endorsing an NCWC letter about food aid. I have discounted two or three pieces of peripheral correspondence (aviators, visas) that were nominally pro-Franco but not embargo related. Taylor (*The U.S. and the Spanish Civil War,* 196n.117) also noticed the missing pro-Nationalist appeals, but he chose to ignore the fact for the sake of his argument; tucked away in a footnote, he mentions examining Roosevelt's files and thinking it "strange that while there were hundreds" of pro-Loyalist appeals, there was "not one" pro-Nationalist telegram or letter.

14. JEK to Hull, 15 Sept. 1937, Messersmith to JEK of 24 Sept. 1937, and JEK's reply of 28 Sept. 1937, in JEKP, f. 37; Hart to Hull, 3 Apr. 1939, 15:37, f. 12, ESP; JEK to Talbot, ca. 8 Nov. 1938, and "Dear Mr. President," 14 Nov. 1938, JEKP, f. 61. For omission of sheets, see JEK to Talbot, 26 Nov. 1938, JEKP, f. 38. "65 Protest Lifting Loyalist Embargo," *NYT,* 25 Nov. 1938, 10. I have so far identified eighteen Catholics and fifteen Protestants; spreadsheet available on request. Her name is spelled "Rountree" in FBI reports but "Rowntree" in *PM.*

15. Roosevelt probably noticed JEK's petition in the *Times.* Grace G. Tully, *FDR: My Boss* (New York: Scribner's, 1949), 78. I am grateful to Robert Clark, head archivist of the Roosevelt Library, for an overview of White House letter handling practices. See Shipman, "Report."

16. Tully, *My Boss,* 80–81. Thanks to diplomatic historian J. Garry Clifford for providing observations about Roosevelt's professionalism with correspondence. For Roosevelt's determination to "enjoy a favorable historical reputation," see Patrick J. Maney, *The Roosevelt Presence: A Biography of Franklin Delano Roosevelt* (New York: Twayne, 1992), 194.

17. Tully, *My Boss,* 229; LeHand memorandum to Roosevelt, attached to a letter of 9 June 1937 to Roosevelt from Miravitlles, FDR-OF, file 422-C, f. Spain, Government of, 1936–39. See also LeHand's assiduous handling of a telegram from the editors of the *New Republic* to Roosevelt, which she typed out and forwarded to State. SD-CDF, b. 6454, f. 2, 852.24/891. LeHand's papers are not extant; for a compelling account of her intimate relationship with Roosevelt, see Frank Costigliola, "Broken Circle: The Isolation of Franklin D. Roosevelt in World War II," *Diplomatic History* 32, no. 5 (2008): 686–94. Arguing that White House office culture trended leftward becomes even more tenable in the wake of the Executive Reorganization Act of 1939, for one of the extra administrative assistants Roosevelt acquired from the Treasury Department in June was Lauchlin Currie, a Soviet spy. See John Earl Haynes and Harvey Klehr, *In Denial: Historians, Communism, and Espionage* (San Francisco: Encounter Books, 2003), 169–82.

18. Martin Dies, *Martin Dies' Story* (New York: Bookmailer, 1963), 143.

19. O'Connell to Mr. President, 12 Feb. 1938, FDR-OF, file 422-C, f. Spanish Revolution of 1936–39, 1938. Huntington, *Who Are We?* esp. 17–20, 59–80; see the introduction above.

20. SD-CDF, b. 6453, contains four relevant memoranda: daily tally of letters and telegrams for 3–7 May 1938 and 9–14 May 1938, in f. 1, 852.24/651 and f. 2, 852.24/706, respectively; a breakdown of all red ink correspondence for Aug. and Sept. 1938 in f. 3, 852.24/768 and f. 4, 852.24/787, respectively.

21. See, for example, memorandum, SD-CDF, b. 6453, f. 4, 852.24/787; and for black ink, see note attached to 852.24/669 in SD-CDF, b. 6453, f. 1.

22. Tallies for Aug. and Sept. 1938, in SD-CDF, b. 6453, f. 3, 852.24/768 and f. 4, 852.24/787, respectively. Haig seems to have been either a clerk or a lower-tier official.

23. Letters, SD-CDF, b. 6453, f. 1, 852.24/629–675. I estimate 10,000 because State received 8,417 letters and telegrams by 14 May 1938, with three delivery days left until 18 May 1938, after allowing for 350 non-Spain red inks.

24. Andryski to Dewy Johnson (Farmer-Labor Party), SD-CDF, b. 6453, f. 1, 852.24/654; James to Welles, 24 June 1938, SD-CDF, b. 6453, f. 3, 852.24/740; Eckhardt to Johnson, 10 May, and Johnson to State, 16 May 1938, SD-CDF, b. 6453, f. 1, 852.24/658. Although neither Eckhardt nor Johnson referenced Franco's Nationalists directly, Eckhardt made clear he wanted to keep the embargo to Spain, and State filed his letter in the Spain folder. Eckhardt was a cousin of Richard Mifflin Kleberg Sr. (D-TX), for whom Johnson had been an aide in 1931. Laurel Eckhardt, emails, 22–23 Oct. 2008.

25. White to Hull, 31 Jan. 1939, SD-CDF, b. 6453, f. 3, 852.24/860; Griffin to Welles, 23 May 1938, SD-CDF, b. 6453, f. 3, 852.24/670.

26. For delegations, see SD-CDF, b. 6453, f. 2, 852.24/690A.

27. Murphy to TXA, MBD, Moffat, PA/D, 4 May 1938, and *Daily Worker* clipping, in SD-CDF, b. 6453, f. 2, 852.24/706; see also, for instance, the open letter from the railroad union's president to Congress, "Quarantine the Aggressor!" *Railroad Trainman,* May 1938, 201, SD-CDF, b. 6453, f. 1, 852.24/666.

28. All of the State Department's Spanish embargo appeals' letters are in SD-CDF, b. 6453, ff. 1–4 and b. 6454, f. 1, 852.24/629–874. While I am confident of accurately identifying McIntyre's forwarded pro-Nationalist appeals, it is possible that my tabulation skipped one or two of his pro-Loyalist appeals. There is, of course, a flaw in my reasoning that JEK's petition went into the mailroom garbage; it is possible that Hart's pro-Loyalist secretary decided not to mail it, although she had every reason to expect that it would have worked its way through to Roosevelt, hence she risked a grilling—and her job—were Hart to discover its nonarrival at the White House.

29. "Thrilling," cited in John Lamberton Harper, *American Visions of Europe: Franklin D. Roosevelt, George F. Kennan, and Dean G. Acheson* (New York: Cambridge Univ. Press, 1994), 44. Bowers to Roosevelt, 20 Feb. 1938, b. 50, f. Diplomatic Correspondence: Spain, 1938, President's Secretary's File, 1933–45 (FDR-SF), Franklin D. Roosevelt, Papers as President. This was only a six-pager, but his letters of 9 May and 18 Aug. 1938 were both nine pages.

30. Ickes, *Inside Struggle,* 7 May 1938, 388. A good report of the meeting is in *News of Spain,* 15 June 1938, 4–5. The four guests of honor, in descending order of their radicalism, were social worker Carmen Meana, journalist and union official Ogier Preteceille, Catholic writer José Bergamín, and novelist Ramón José Sender. Ickes cited in Robert A. Rosenstone, *Crusade of the Left: The Lincoln Battalion in the Spanish Civil War* (New York: Pegasus, 1969), 352.

31. [Henry Morgenthau Jr.], *From the Morgenthau Diaries: Years of Crisis, 1928–1938,* comp. John Morton Blum (Boston: Houghton Mifflin, 1959), 506–8. Prices on the New York exchange for bar silver fluctuated between 44.75 and 42.5 cents during 1938, reflecting a world market depressed far below its historic ceiling of about 72 cents, although as a sop to congressionally influential American silver producers, the subsidized purchase price for domestically mined silver was 64 cents. "Silver to Buy Arms for Spain," *Catholic Worker* 6, no. 5 (1938): 1, 2. This shipment was probably a consignment of 180 tons, valued at $2,160,000, that arrived at Cerbère, en route to Le Havre. *New York Herald Tribune,* 22

June 1938, 8. John Dietrich, *The Morgenthau Plan: Soviet Influence on American Postwar Policy* (New York: Algora, 2002), 23–24; [Henry Morgenthau Jr.], *From the Morgenthau Diaries: Years of Urgency, 1938–1941,* comp. John Morton Blum (Boston: Houghton Mifflin, 1965), 3. See Eleanor Roosevelt's preface to ibid.

32. From Fischer, "Louis Fischer," 217–18; Eleanor to Fischer, 28 Feb. 1938, Correspondence and Interviews with Eleanor Roosevelt, Appendix, Louis Fischer Papers, 1938–49, Franklin D. Roosevelt Library.

33. Thomas also wrote several letters to Roosevelt lobbying to lift the embargo, such as on 26 Aug. 1937 when he followed up on a meeting with Roosevelt, stressing that the Loyalists were "doing the real fighting for Fascism" and that the "one sided enforcement of our neutrality is really an active intervention in behalf of Fascism." FDR-OF, file 422-C, f. Spanish Revolution of 1936–39. Welles on Mussolini after his return from Italy in Mar. 1940, as related to Ickes by Morgenthau, is in Harold L. Ickes, *The Lowering Clouds, 1939–1941,* vol. 3, *The Secret Diary of Harold L. Ickes* (New York: Simon & Schuster, 1955), 465. Sumner Welles, *The Time for Decision* (New York: Harper & Brothers, 1944), 61. I have not yet been able to document whether Roosevelt's confident Harry L. Hopkins pushed the Loyalist cause during 1937–38, although it is likely, and Hopkins was present for the screening of *Spanish Earth.* Biographer Henry H. Adams notes merely that in the fall of 1937, "Hopkins had little concern for foreign affairs, but as an interested citizen he watched dismayed the rising challenge to freedom in Europe and Asia." Adams, *Harry Hopkins: A Biography* (New York: Putnam, 1977), 121. Roosevelt to Ickes, 25 Nov. 1938, in *Franklin D. Roosevelt and Foreign Affairs,* ed. Donald B. Schewe, 2nd series, 17 vols. (New York: Clearwater, 1969), 12:1433; Welles's reply to Roosevelt's call of 25 Nov. 1938, in ibid., 1436; also see 1426 (Ickes), 1439, 1445, and 1454 (Assistant Solicitor General Golden W. Bell's determination of 5 Dec. 1938). Dominic Tierney, "Franklin D. Roosevelt and Covert Aid to the Loyalists in the Spanish Civil War, 1936–39," *Journal of Contemporary History* 39, no. 3 (2004).

34. Diary entry, 1 May 1938, Ickes, *Inside Struggle,* 380; Stohrer to the German Foreign Ministry, 4 May 1938, in *Germany and the Spanish Civil War, 1936–1939,* vol. 3, *Documents on German Foreign Policy, 1918–1945: From the Archives of the German Foreign Ministry: Series D (1937–1945)* (Washington, DC: GPO, 1950), docs. 580, 653. For Russian shipments, see Howson, *Arms for Spain,* 296–300; Ickes, *Inside Struggle,* 380.

35. "War in Spain," *Time,* 14 Feb. 1938, 15.

36. Bowers to Roosevelt, 18 Aug. 1938, in *FDR and Foreign Affairs,* 11:1235. In *Malevolent Neutrality: The United States, Great Britain, and the Origins of the Spanish Civil War* (Ithaca, NY: Cornell Univ. Press, 1985), Douglas Little provides useful international context; see esp. chaps. 1, 9, and 10.

37. Diary entry, 5 Mar. 1939, Ickes, *Inside Struggle,* 586; Kanawada, *Roosevelt's Diplomacy,* 50, 60.

38. For LeHand and Tully, who had once been Cardinal Patrick Hayes's secretary, see Robert Morton Darrow, "Catholic Political Power: A Study of the Activities of the American Catholic Church on Behalf of Franco During the Spanish Civil War, 1936–1939" (PhD diss., Columbia University, 1953), 37; Flynn, *Roosevelt and Romanism,* 50. Walsh was an Irish American nationalist as well as a Chicago union leader.

39. Kanawada, *Roosevelt's Diplomacy,* 54. Catholics accounted for 16.25 percent of the population, giving them 8,109,000 of the 49,902,000 votes cast. Gallup, *Gallup Poll,* survey no. 141, 132. Maney, *Roosevelt Presence,* 194. For Mundelein's closeness to Roosevelt and his attitude toward Franco, see Traina, *American Diplomacy,* 212.

40. Cole, *Roosevelt and the Isolationists,* 6; Heinrichs, *Threshold of War,* vii; Mark A. Stoler, "U.S. World War II Diplomacy," in *America in the World: The Historiography of American*

Foreign Relations since 1941, ed. Michael J. Hogan (Cambridge: Cambridge Univ. Press, 1995), 194; Kenneth S. Davis, *The Beckoning of Destiny, 1882–1928,* vol. 1, *FDR: A History* (New York: G. P. Putnam's Sons, 1972), 165; Tugwell cited in Maney, *Roosevelt Presence,* 194. Tugwell also discussed one particularly egregious case of tampering, in which Roosevelt attached a note claiming that an inaugural address written largely by others was his own work.

41. Thomas Fleming, *The New Dealers' War: FDR and the War Within World War II* (New York: Basic Books, 2001), 310; Frederick W. Marks III, *Winds over Sand: The Diplomacy of Franklin Roosevelt* (Athens: Univ. of Georgia Press, 1988), 124; Harper, *American Visions,* 12–18, 19 ("distancing"), 26 ("decadence"), 60 ("Europhobic-hemispherism"). See Henrikson, "The Geographical 'Mental Maps,'" 495–530; and the introduction above.

42. Harper, *American Visions,* 26. "All my life I have loved ships and been a student of the Navy," Roosevelt told Josephus Daniels in 1913. Quoted in Davis, *Beckoning of Destiny,* 305; *NYT,* 24 Feb. 1898, 6.

43. For Spanish flu, see Davis, *Beckoning of Destiny,* 529; Bowers to Roosevelt of 15 Aug. 1933, as well as a translation and clipping from *Heraldo de Madrid,* 12 Aug. 1933, in FDR-SF, b. 50, f. Diplomatic Correspondence, Spain: 1933–36; Phillips to Roosevelt, 26 July, Roosevelt to Phillips, 27 July, and Phillips's reply of 1 Aug. 1935, in FDR-OF, file 422-C, f. Spain, Government of, 1933–39. Phillips became ambassador at Rome in Nov. 1936.

44. French ambassador Doynel de Saint-Quentin to foreign minister Joseph Paul-Boncour, 26 Mar. 1938, in *Documents diplomatiques français, 1932–1939,* series 2, 19 vols. (Paris: Imprimerie nationale, 1974), 9:58, 112 (my translation, in collaboration with Julien Ducret). Marks's research in *Winds over Sand* (215) alerted me to this invaluable source; distinguishing between Saint-Quentin's and Roosevelt's voice throughout the paragraph in question is tricky, although Marks has no doubt that Saint-Quentin was expressing Roosevelt's opinion.

45. Davis, *Beckoning of Destiny,* 41–42, 49, 122–23.

46. Roosevelt to Moley and Tugwell, cited in Charles A. Beard, *American Foreign Policy in the Making, 1932–1940: A Study in Responsibility* (New Haven, CT: Yale Univ. Press, 1946), 142.

47. For strongman ideology, see, for example, David F. Schmitz, *Thank God They're on Our Side: The United States and Right-Wing Dictatorships, 1921–1965* (Chapel Hill: Univ. of North Carolina Press, 1999), 5–6 and passim; and Robert E. Hannigan, *The New World Power: American Foreign Policy, 1898–1917* (Philadelphia: Univ. of Pennsylvania Press, 2002), 12–16. For Somoza and the Roosevelt administration, also see Schmitz, *Thank God,* 84; Jacobs, *America's Miracle Man,* 86–87.

48. For Roosevelt's and Chiang's first face-to-face meeting at Cairo, see Michael Schaller, *The United States and China: Into the Twenty-First Century* (New York: Oxford Univ. Press, 2002), 81–82; Roosevelt to Azaña, FDR-OF, file 422-C, f. Spain, Government of, 1936–39; Roosevelt to Chiang, 14 Feb. 1939, FDR-SF, b. 27, Diplomatic Correspondence, f. China, 1939–40. On 26 July the U.S. government gave Japan official notice of the abrogation of the 1911 commerce and navigation treaty six months hence; under the chairmanship of Henry L. Stimson, the American Committee for Non-Participation in Japanese Aggression had been pressing for sanctions since Aug. 1938.

49. Robert A. Divine gives a total of $15,902,183 in *The Illusion of Neutrality* (Chicago: Univ. of Chicago Press, 1962), 218. Memorandum of 20 Apr., report from Welles to Roosevelt of 24 June, Welles to Roosevelt of 6 Dec., and Roosevelt's memorandum for Eleanor of 12 Dec. 1938, all in FDR-SF, b. 27, Diplomatic Correspondence, f. China, 1938. Yost to Welles, 5 Dec. 1938, 1918–50, b. 150, Major Correspondents, 1920–50, FDR, Apr. 1938–Dec. 1940, f. FDR, Dec. 1938, Sumner Welles Papers. Michael Schaller's first U.S.-China monograph credits Morgenthau, not Roosevelt, with driving "through a new [China] policy," which did

not gather momentum until Aug. 1938, somewhat later than the sources that I have cited here would suggest. Schaller, *The U.S. Crusade in China, 1938–1945* (New York: Columbia Univ. Press, 1979), esp. 24–25.

50. Taylor's memorandum to Morgenthau of 20 Oct. 1938 and Morgenthau's letter to Roosevelt of 11 Nov. 1938 in FDR-SF, b. 27, Diplomatic Correspondence, f. China, 1938.

51. States that swung toward Wendell Wilkie in the 1940 presidential election were primarily in the agricultural Midwest (North and South Dakota, Nebraska, Kansas, Colorado), and voters switched not from isolationist concerns over foreign policy but because they felt that the New Deal had hurt small farmers. Even then, Wilkie picked up only 82 electoral votes to Roosevelt's 449. Similar concerns over New Deal policies influenced voters in the 1938 midterms; see, for instance, James T. Patterson, *Congressional Conservatism and the New Deal: The Growth of the Conservative Coalition in Congress, 1933–1939* (Lexington: Univ. of Kentucky Press, 1967).

52. For Roosevelt's reliance on Gallup polls, see Maney, *Roosevelt Presence,* 181. A Gallup poll of 10 Oct. 1937 asked, "Which plan for keeping out of war do you have more faith in—having Congress pass stricter neutrality laws, or leaving the job up to the President?" and found "Stricter laws, 69%; President's discretion, 31%"; a Gallup poll of 27 Feb. 1938 asked, "Which side do you sympathize with in the Spanish civil war?" and found that 52 percent of those questioned expressed no opinion, but of the 48 percent who did, the result was "Loyalists 75%" and "Insurgents 25%," or 36 and 12 percent, respectively, of the total poll. Gallup, *Gallup Poll,* survey nos. 98, 111-A, 71, 92.

53. Ickes, *Inside Struggle,* 380.

54. For arms shipments, see, for instance, Welles to Roosevelt, 4 Mar., regarding a conversation of 25 Feb. 1938; Roosevelt to Chiang, 17 Jan. 1938; and Chiang to Roosevelt, 30 Jan. 1938, all in FDR-SF, b. 27, Diplomatic Correspondence, f. China, 1938. Kung to Roosevelt, 11 Dec. 1938, FDR-SF, b. 27, Diplomatic Correspondence, f. China, 1939–40. Roosevelt seems to have changed his mind about Chiang after meeting him for the first time in Cairo in Nov. 1943. Schaller, *United States and China,* 81–82.

55. Hyde Park tour guides today point out the exotic quilted silk robe gracing the chaise longue at the foot of Roosevelt's bed, a gift from Madame Chiang. Memorandum from Roosevelt to Forster, FDR-OF, file 422-C, f. Spain—Msc. 1937–40. For stamps, see, for instance, Joaquín Arrarás, *Francisco Franco: The Times and the Man* (Milwaukee: Bruce, 1939), 259. Barcelona's government issued the set of four stamps, and their inscriptions were in Catalan: "Homenatge a la U.R.S.S. 1937."

56. For a brief synopsis of Franco's strategic decision in the spring of 1938 not press on to Barcelona and the French border for fear of sparking an invasion, see Geoffrey Jensen, *Franco: Soldier, Commander, Dictator* (Washington, DC: Potomac Books, 2005), 86.

57. Diary entry, 29 Jan. 1939, Ickes, *Inside Struggle,* 569; Farnham, *Munich Crisis,* 91, 110–13; Roosevelt to Ickes, 25 Nov. 1938, *FDR and Foreign Affairs,* 12:1433; Welles's reply to Roosevelt's call of 25 Nov., ibid., 1436; also see ibid., 1426 (Ickes), 1439, 1445, and 1454 (Assistant Solicitor General Golden W. Bell's determination of 5 Dec. 1938).

58. Dallek, *Roosevelt and American Foreign Policy,* 159, 127; Joris Ivens, *The Camera and I* (New York: International, 1969), 130–31; Malcolm Goldstein, *The Political Stage: American Drama and Theater of the Great Depression* (New York: Oxford Univ. Press, 1974), 193–94. *The Spanish Earth,* dir. Joris Ivens (Contemporary Historians, 1937; DVD, Sherman Oaks, CA: SlingShot Entertainment, 2000), added emphasis consistent with soundtrack, and n.131; John T. McManus, "Down to Earth in Spain," *NYT,* 25 July 1937, section X, 4. Orson Welles narrated the version Ivens screened at the White House. Eleanor invited Ivens, Ernest Heming-

way, and Martha Gellhorn to the White House on 8 July after Gellhorn, a war correspondent and Hemingway's companion, had lobbied Eleanor to show the film. Caroline Moorehead, *Gellhorn: A Twentieth-Century Life* (New York: Henry Holt, 2003), 131–32.

4. Keeping the Embargo

1. Robert C. Hilderbrand, *Power and the People: Executive Management of Public Opinion in Foreign Affairs, 1897–1921* (Chapel Hill: Univ. of North Carolina Press, 1981), 205.

2. *NYT,* 31 Jan. 1938, 1. For an analysis of Nye's thinking, see Wayne S. Cole, *Roosevelt and the Isolationists, 1932–1945* (Lincoln: Univ. of Nebraska Press, 1983), 235–37; and Divine, *The Illusion of Neutrality,* 224.

3. *NYT,* 10 May 1938, 4, and 9 May 1938, 1; Rayburn, ibid., 10 May 1938, 1; "60 in U.S. Congress Greet Spain's Loyalist Government," ibid., 31 Jan. 1938, 1.

4. Diary entry, 12 May 1938, Ickes, *The Inside Struggle,* 390. I base my interpretation of Ickes's behavior on my reading of his personality, gleaned from his diary and biographers; while I cannot be certain he marched, neither do I believe he shuffled.

5. For the Seventy-sixth Congress, all twenty-one Texas congressmen were internationalist Democrats, although several wanted to retain the arms embargo to Spain in 1938, most notably Martin Dies and Lyndon Johnson. See David L. Porter, *The Seventy-Sixth Congress and World War II, 1939–1940* (Columbia: Univ. of Missouri Press, 1979), apps. 1 and 2.

6. *NYT,* 9 May 1938, 1, 4.

7. Accompanying Roosevelt were ambassador to France William C. Bullitt; federal housing administrator Stewart MacDonald; his oldest son's wife, Betsey; his personal secretary "Missy" LeHand; and Ickes (*NYT,* 24 Apr. 1938, 3). Diary entry, 1 May 1938, Ickes, *Inside Struggle,* 379–80. Following the failure of his Judiciary Reorganization Bill in July 1937, Roosevelt continued with his efforts to strengthen the executive branch, resulting in the Reorganization Act of 1939, which created the Executive Office of the President and allowed the president to hire private staff.

8. Diary entry, 1 May 1938, ibid., 388; for Russian aircraft, see Thomas, *The Spanish Civil War,* 823. Despite the unsettled politics of France's Popular Front parliament—under prime ministers Léon Blum (Socialist, June 1936–June 1937), Camille Chautemps (Radical, June 1937–Mar. 1938), Blum (Mar.–Apr. 1938), Édouard Daladier (Radical, Apr. 1938–Mar. 1940)—the French kept the border open for arms and supplies during 17 Mar.–13 June 1938.

9. Diary entry, 1 May 1938, Ickes, *Inside Struggle,* 390.

10. For a psychological profile of Ickes's upbringing, see Graham White and John Maze, *Harold Ickes of the New Deal: His Private Life and Public Career* (Cambridge, MA: Harvard Univ. Press, 1985), 12–15, 25; diary entry, 27 Feb. 1937, Ickes, *Inside Struggle,* 86.

11. Diary of J. Pierrepont Moffat, 2–3 May 1938, Houghton Library, Harvard College, Cambridge, MA; Fred L. Israel, *Nevada's Key Pittman* (Lincoln: Univ. of Nebraska Press, 1963), 114, 132.

12. Pearson and Allen, "The Daily Washington Merry-Go-Round," quoted from *New Orleans States,* 11 May 1938, 1, 10. "Swung over" in Robert Bendiner, *The Riddle of the State Department* (New York: Farrar & Rinehart, 1942), 60–61; Bendiner had also been an associate editor at *The Nation.* Moffat diary, 3–4 May 1938; Krock, *NYT,* 5 May 1938, 1, 15.

13. Kanawada, *Roosevelt's Diplomacy,* 64; Thomas, *Spanish Civil War,* 824–25, 825n.1.

14. Krock, *NYT,* 5 May 1938, 1, 15.

15. Pearson and Allen, "Washington Merry-Go-Round"; "resentful" in Moffat diary, 9

May 1938. Ickes (*Inside Struggle,* 389) wrote in his diary on 7 May 1938 that whereas the pro-Loyalist lobbyist Jay C. Allen thought the report was "a deliberate plant in order to stir up the Catholics to protest against its [the embargo's] lifting and thus make it impossible for the President to act," Drew Pearson "believed that the [*NYT*] story was based on facts."

16. For Krock's view of appeasement, Roosevelt's peacemaking, and "world policing," see Arthur Krock, *Memoirs: Sixty Years on the Firing Line* (New York: Funk & Wagnalls, 1968), 184, 199–200, and "A Little Early for Laurel Wreaths," *The Nation,* 30 Dec. 1938; *NYT,* 5 May 1938, 1. For Krock's son as a Nationalist "general," Traina, *American Diplomacy,* 177.

17. Michael R. Beschloss, *Kennedy and Roosevelt: The Uneasy Alliance* (New York: W. W. Norton, 1980), 164.

18. Forbes to Walsh, 7 May 1938, with memorandum from Walsh to the Senate president, 10 May 1938, series 1, b. 5, Correspondence 1938, David I. Walsh Papers, College of the Holy Cross, Worcester, MA; *Congressional Record,* 75th Cong., 3rd sess., 1938, 72:6, 6521. Forbes also wrote to Cordell Hull, yet while the letter arrived at State's Division of Communications and Records just after midday on 9 May, it did not reach Hull's desk until 20 May, too late to affect the outcome of the Nye Resolution. SD-CDF, b. 6453, f. 1, 852.24/699.

19. SD-CDF, b. 6453, f. 1, 852.24/699.

20. JEK to Talbot, 23 Aug. 1938, JEKP, f. 38. JEK was friendly with Somers by 1941, for he wrote a speech for him in Dec. of that year, although it is not clear if they knew each other in mid-1938. Other possibilities include Senator Burton K. Wheeler and governor of Pennsylvania and later U.S. senator Edward Martin. O'Neil speaking on NBC Radio, 23 Mar. 1931, cited in William Pencak, *For God and Country: The American Legion, 1919–1941* (Boston: Northeastern Univ. Press, 1989), 79.

21. Chris Henry, *The Ebro 1938: Death Knell of the Republic* (Oxford: Osprey, 1999), 6. For a summary of the French plan, see David Wingeate Pike, "France," in Cortada, ed., *Historical Dictionary,* 1982, 218; and for Franco's fear of French invasion, see Jensen, *Franco,* 86. For euphoria, see, for instance, *Los Angeles Examiner* articles cited in n. 31 below; Herbert L. Mathews, "Morale Stays High in Loyalist Ranks," *NYT,* 7 Aug. 1938, 27; and "extraordinary demonstration of strength during the past month [that] has completely changed the outlook for war," in *News of Spain,* 21 Aug. 1938, 1.

22. Bullitt to Roosevelt, 17 Aug. 1938, *FDR and Foreign Affairs,* 11:1231; Gerhard L. Weinberg, *A World at Arms: A Global History of World War II* (Cambridge: Cambridge Univ. Press, 1994), 29; Hitler's comments in James V. Compton, *The Swastika and the Eagle: Hitler, the United States, and the Origins of World War II* (Boston: Houghton Mifflin, 1967), 25, 20, 17, 9–10, 33, 31, 30. Hitler, quoted in *NYT,* 10 July 1933, 1.

23. For Britain's "diplomatic utilitarianism," see Graham, *The Spanish Republic at War,* 316–17; Phillips to Roosevelt, 1 Sept. 1938, *FDR and Foreign Affairs,* 11:1263; Traina, *American Diplomacy,* 142; Arnold A. Offner, *American Appeasement: United States Foreign Policy and Germany, 1933–1938* (Cambridge, MA: Harvard Univ. Press, 1969), 161.

24. For a summary of Stalin's realpolitik cynicism of British and French intentions in the face of increasing Nazi hostility, see George Esenwein and Adrian Shubert, *Spain at War: The Spanish Civil War in Context, 1931–1939* (London: Addison Wesley Longman, 1995), 256; Richard E. Neustadt, *Presidential Power: The Politics of Leadership from FDR to Carter* (New York: Macmillan, 1980), 119.

25. JEK to Talbot, 23 Aug. 1938, JEKP, f. 38. Porter, *Seventy-Sixth Congress,* is useful for classifying the foreign policy sentiments of senators (in totaling isolationist members of the Senate Foreign Relations Committee, I ignored Supreme Court nominee Hugo L. Black). For the committee's vote, see Israel, *Key Pittman,* 157; *Washington Post,* 19 June 1938, 4; *NYT,* 10 July 1938, 21.

26. JEK's list of prominent Legionnaires, to Talbot, ca. 1 Sept. 1938, JEKP, f. 38; Chaillaux to JEK, 16 Dec. 1937, JEKP, f. 37. Only Patton's return letter to JEK of 24 Aug. is extant, JEKP, f. 38. For Republican Committee of Safety and "the example of Madrid," see "La Guardia Assailed as Communist Ally," *NYT*, 19 Oct. 1937, 16; "A Declaration of Policy," *Patriot Digest* 1, no. 1 (1938), 32.

27. JEK to Talbot, from St. Louis, 12 Sept. 1938, JEKP, f. 38; Hart to Cantwell, 13 Sept. 1938, JEKP, f. 38; JEK to Hart, 13 Sept. 1938, FXTP, b. 22, f. 35.

28. JEK's letters of 13 Sept. 1938 to Talbot and Hart, JEKP, f. 38. Hart lived at 6306 McPherson Avenue. *St. Louis Globe-Democrat*, 15 Sept. 1938, 3.

29. A cutting that Kelley later mailed to Talbot came from a contact in St. Louis. *St. Louis Globe-Democrat*, 15 Sept. 1938, sect. 3, 2; cutting, JEKP, f. 38.

30. JEK to Talbot from Hotel Savoy, Los Angeles, 16 Sept. 1938, JEKP, f. 38; see Talbot's 27 July 1938 letter to JEK about "a man named John Doherty," JEKP, f. 38. In addition to ex-wife Frances McBee's detectives, who once rented a next-door office and wired JEK's phone, FBI agents were compiling dossiers on "Agents of the Fascisti" at this time. See chap. 8 below. JEK to Talbot, 17 Sept. 1938, JEKP, f. 38; telegram and letter from Talbot to JEK, 19 Sept. 1938, JEKP, f. 38; Talbot sent JEK $3,000 in current dollars.

31. His benchmark national dailies were the *New York Times* and *Washington Post/ Times-Herald*, supplemented by the *New York Daily News* and/or *Boston Daily/Evening Globe*, as well as a couple of local editions, such as the *Brooklyn Eagle*, *Newark Examiner*, *Jersey Journal*, or, when at his mother's home in Pittsfield, the *Berkshire Eagle* and *Springfield Republican*; he had subscriptions to a number of weeklies, including the *Boston Pilot*, *Brooklyn Tablet*, *Christian Science Monitor*, and *America*. Throughout the 1940s, he routinely clipped out a dozen or two articles a day, each of which he date-stamped before filing away, a month at a time, in old A4-size envelopes; he typed out particularly interesting pieces on multiple carbons and often mailed clippings to friends. *Los Angeles Examiner* (*LAE*), 22, 24, and 25 Sept. 1938.

32. Letters of 20 and 21 Sept. 1938 from JEK to Talbot, JEKP, f. 38.

33. Letters of 17, 20, and 21 Sept. 1938 from JEK to Talbot, JEKP, f. 38.

34. Synthesized from JEK to Talbot, 26 Sept. 1938, and Western Union telegram, 30 Oct. 1938, both in JEKP, f. 38, along with general correspondence and memoranda, in JEKP, ff. 7, 8.

35. For Murphy as "drinking buddy" of the ACLU's Morris Ernst, see Pencak, *God and Country*, 253; for Legion poll, see ibid., 304–5. Fight for Freedom's executive chairman, Ulrich Bell, who worked for the *Louisville Courier-Journal*, edited *Souvenir Book, Third Annual Convention, American Legion of Kentucky, September 1 and 2, 1921* (Lexington, KY: American Legion, 1921). In 1941 Bell wrote to Secretary of State Cordell Hull drawing Hull's attention to JEK's role as an Axis agent. See JEK-FBI, 11:446.

36. In full, the National Convention Foreign Relations Committee and *Reports to the Twentieth Annual National Convention of the American Legion, Los Angeles, Calif., September 19, 20, 21, 22, 1938* (Indianapolis, IN: American Legion, 1938), 260, 330; *The Proceedings of the 20th Annual National Convention of The American Legion, Los Angeles* (Indianapolis, IN: American Legion, 1938), 44 (also available as *The Proceedings of the 20th National Convention of The American Legion, Los Angeles, CA, 19–22 September 1938*, 76th Cong., 1st sess., House Document 40, 53). The American Legion Library in Indianapolis has microfiche for Resolutions 626 and 628 but not 627.

37. *LAE*, 20 Sept. 1938, 1–2; and see *American Legion Magazine* 25, no. 5 (1938): 55. Compare the *LAE* and *Los Angeles Times* with, for instance, the *NYT* and *Washington Post*.

38. *U.S. Senate Journal*, 75th Cong., 3rd sess., 29 Apr. 1937, 3961–62; Dorothy G. Wayman, *David I. Walsh: Citizen-Patriot* (Milwaukee: Bruce, 1952), 254.

39. *LAE,* 19 Sept. 1938, 9; JEK sent Talbot a clipping from the almost identical evening edition, JEKP, f. 38. For example, "Dear Dave" letter from Roosevelt of 28 June 1938, series 1, b. 5, f. 1938, David I. Walsh Papers, College of the Holy Cross, Worcester, MA. I do not wish to impart too much significance here, for Roosevelt habitually used first names with political associates. For Walsh and Roosevelt in the context of taxes and naval construction, see, for instance, *NYT,* 22 Oct. 1938, 17.

40. Heinrichs, *Threshold of War,* vii; Hiram W. Johnson to Hiram Jr., 5 Mar., 19 Feb., and 29 Apr. 1938, in[Hiram W. Johnson,] *The Diary Letters of Hiram Johnson, 1917–1945,* ed. Robert E. Burke, 7 vols. (New York: Garland, 1983), vol. 6, n.p.; see ibid. for "Dumb Dora" (19 Feb. 1938), "big Navy" and "dream" (29 Jan. 1938), "Napoleon" and "big navy" (19 Feb. 1938).

41. See, for instance, Traina, *American Diplomacy,* 184–85, and Taylor, *The U.S. and the Spanish Civil War,* 184. Donald I. Warren's *Radio Priest: Charles Coughlin, the Father of Hate Radio* (New York: Free Press, 1996) is one of several manuscripts on Coughlin. Albert Fried, *FDR and His Enemies* (New York: St. Martin's Press, 1999), 155.

42. Catholic support (39 percent) covered in J. David Valaik, "Catholics, Neutrality, and the Spanish Embargo, 1937–1939," *Journal of American History* 54 (June 1967): 85. According to *The Official Catholic Directory* (New York: P. J. Kenedy & Sons, 1937), there were 20,959,134 U.S. Catholics in 1938 (16.25 percent of the population). Coughlin's radio audience in Apr. 1938 was 16 million, with a 52 percent approval rating; by Dec. 1938, his total audience had fallen to 14.5 million, of which about 4 million were Catholics, with a 60 percent approval rating (3 million gave no denomination). Warren, *Radio Priest,* app., charts 1 and 2. For Coughlin's radio voice, see Richard Akin Davis, "Radio Priest: The Public Career of Father Charles Edward Coughlin" (PhD diss., University of North Carolina, 1974), 21–22, 192, 194, 210, 275.

43. A six-page draft of JEK's flier, "Why the Embargo Against the Spanish Republic *Should Not* be Lifted," copies of "Keep the Spanish Embargo!" signature petitions, and a personal letter from NCWC executive secretary Edward J. Heffron to JEK, 27 Mar. 1939, are in JEKP, f. 63; press release, JEK to Sedgwick, 9 Jan. 1939, ESP, c. 16, b. 37, f. 12.

44. Henry (*Ebro 1938,* 24) questions President Manuel Azaña's claim that "almost all of the Army of the Ebro was communist" but states, nevertheless, that every unit had its own political commissar. Historians are still contesting figures for murders, executions, and deaths in custody (torture) by both sides, which may ultimately be as unquantifiable as they are academic to the personal grief and tragedies of any violent conflict. In perhaps the best scholarship to date, Julius Ruiz, gives 50,000 for the Loyalist zone in the initial period until winter 1936–37, of which about 8,800 were in Madrid. Loyalists perpetrated mass killings as well as *paseos,* including the mass execution in Nov. 1936 of more than a thousand political prisoners in a village outside the city by guards under the responsibility of Russian journalist Mikhail Kolstov. Julius Ruiz, *Franco's Justice: Repression in Madrid after the Spanish Civil War* (Oxford: Clarendon Press, 2005), 3, 10; see also Thomas, *The Spanish Civil War,* 463. Ramón Salas Larrazábal's serious though conservative *Los datos exactos de la guerra civil* (Madrid: Colección Drácena, 1980), estimates that during the war the Nationalists executed and/or murdered 35,500 captives and killed 11,000 noncombatants in military actions, and the Loyalists 72,500 and 4,000 respectively; deaths in combat were virtually the same for both sides, leaving the Nationalists with 55 percent of the total losses and the Loyalists 45 percent (table 57, 310). Some excellent studies, such as Ángel David Martín Rubio's *Los mitos de la represión en la guerra civil* (Madrid: Grafite Ediciones, 2005), unfortunately do not give data for the war itself. Preston (*The Spanish Civil War,* 202–3) implies that Nationalist executions during the war were as high as 180,000, though he provides no supporting data, presumably because "there is still considerable controversy over exact figures." Factors complicating any objective

assessment of *franquista* postwar repression include an invasion from France in Sept. 1941 by a communist army, its defeat, and subsequent guerrilla activities until 1951. Ruiz (*Franco's Justice*, 7, 16) gives a consensus estimate of 50,000 by Nov. 1940; his figure for the province of Madrid during Apr. 1939–Feb. 1944 is a minimum of 3,113.

5. *The American Union for Nationalist Spain*

1. See Henrikson, "The Geographical 'Mental Maps,'" 495–530, and my introduction above. *Visit the War Routes of Spain*, brochure, b. T1, Spanish Papers, Correspondence, Committee to Send Anesthetics and Medicines to Spain (CSAMS), HMP. In Meière's case, the brochure was a souvenir from Luis Bolín's office of tourism in Spain and was not a factor influencing her trip; see Luis Bolín, *Spain: The Vital Years* (Philadelphia: J. B. Lippincott, 1967), 302–6. At $4.80 to £1, the inflation-adjusted cost = $1,150.

2. Hildreth Meière, "Trip to Russia," Aug. 1936, 2–4, 18, in HMP. "I remember [my mother] saying that she considered herself a mugwump," Louise Meière Dunn, interview by author, 29 Oct. 2005, Stamford, CT; Larry Carl Miller, "Dimensions of Mugwump Thought, 1880–1920: Sons of Massachusetts Abolitionists as Professional Pioneers" (PhD diss., Northwestern University, 1969), esp. 1–8. I am grateful to Robert Hannigan for alerting me to the parallels between mugwumps and Franco lobbyists.

3. Hildreth Meière, untitled memoir, "Spain, August 1938," based on a spiral-bound notebook entitled "Diary—Spain, [Aug.] 1938," pp. 1–2, in HMP. The dialogue is quoted directly from the memoir; full names and other corroborating details are from the Louise Meière Dunn interview. Wheeler later married Hastings Blake, becoming Mrs. Nina Wheeler Blake. Today, 200 West is a luxury condominium development.

4. Meière, "Spain, August 1938," 2–3. Flanagan also spelled Flannigan in some documents. Meière was hinting at the pope's recent warning that "communism is intrinsically wrong, and no one who would save Christian civilization may collaborate with it in any undertaking whatsoever." *Atheistic Communism* (Divini Redemptoris): *Encyclical Letter of His Holiness Pope Pius XI* (New York: Paulist Press, 1937), 26.

5. Meière, "Spain, August 1938," 4–11. According to a diary entry, she attended at least one unspecified but "exciting 'Labor' meeting"; diary entry, 11 Nov. 1937, diary of Louise Benedict Harmon, 1936–40, private collection of Louise Meière Dunn, Stamford, CT. Harmon used a Ward's five-year "A Line A Day" diary, with each page headed by a monthly date and ruled horizontally with five bold lines to demarcate the years; conscientious diarist that she was, Harmon wrote down the day of the week, with the space for each day having four lines; because each page is just five by four inches, and Harmon's script flows along, deciphering the diary can be problematic. Meière's observation meshes with Seidman's thesis in *Republic of Egos* as well as with the outcome of Franco's regime. Noting that Spain did not become an Axis satellite of Germany or Italy after May 1939, Payne (*Franco and Hitler*, 45) avers that "Franco was a nationalist whose policy would be based on his judgment of [Spaniards'] best interests."

6. Meière, "Spain, August 1938," 12–19; whether her tone was objectively neutral or deliberately provocative is unclear from the documentary record. "Not cricket" is a British expression for unsporting conduct or, more sarcastically (as here), for ungentlemanly or immoral behavior.

7. Meière, "Spain, August 1938," 19–24; Meière's account pseudonymously called the visitor "Mr. Quesada," but the gentleman's intimate knowledge of Spanish diplomacy and his efforts to organize a benefit concert in Manhattan indicate that he was Cárdenas.

8. Meière, "Spain, August 1938," 24–24c. Meière also shot still photographs, which do not appear to be extant. Compared with the plethora of pro-Loyalist memoirs, firsthand pro-Nationalist accounts by Americans are scarce; in addition to those by W. Cameron Forbes and by Merwin K. Hart, see, for instance, H. Edward Knoblaugh, *Correspondent in Spain* (London: Sheed & Ward, 1937), and an untitled letter from an American to her English friend, written from Seville, ca. Nov. 1936, 10 pp., in FXTP, b. 20, f. 3. There were about 2,450 nobiliary titles in 1931.

9. For arson attacks as well as executions of "right-wing prisoners" by departing anarchists and communists, see Thomas, *The Spanish Civil War,* 366; and the photograph titled "One of the neighborhoods of Irún, after being set on fire by the reds," in Joaquín Tellechea, *La verdad sobre España* (Buenos Aires: Editorial Tor, 1937). Meière, "Spain, August 1938," 37–40.

10. Meière, "Spain, August 1938," 44–46; "My Tour of Nationalist Spain, August 1938, by Hildreth Meière," 16 mm, 3 reels, DVD, 33 min., Reel III, 03:04–05:44, HMP. At least two of the facilities Meière visited were technically Auxilio Invierno, or Winter Aid.

11. Membership, as of Oct. 1938, in Meière, "Spain, August 1938," 46; and Thomas, *Spanish Civil War,* 491n.3. Thomas (*Civil War,* 492) compliments the dedication of Auxilio Social's staff, noting that had these "wives and daughters of the rich" formed their organization earlier, they "might have rendered the war unnecessary." Meière, "Spain, August 1938," 46, 88, 167–69; the summer camp was at Laquito (Lekeitio), on the coast between Bilbao and San Sebastián. "My Tour," Reel III, 05:44–08:04. Paul Preston believes that Sanz-Bachiller was "uncomfortable with the fascist trappings given to her welfare organization"; see Paul Preston's portrait in *Doves of War: Four Women of Spain* (Boston: Northeastern Univ. Press, 2002), quote from photo caption following 310.

12. Meière, "Spain, August 1938," 50–54.

13. Meière, "Spain, August 1938," 56–58. I have not yet been able to locate a source for Zuloaga's statistics, nor verify their accuracy; Merwin Hart made a similar claim during his trip to the Nationalist zone in Sept. 1938.

14. Meière's paternal grandmother was a daughter of the Confederate naval officer Franklin Buchanan, who was a grandson of McKean. Meière, "Spain, August 1938," 68–69. Lupe related much of this account to Meière, the details of which indicate that Pedro's incarceration was in Madrid's Model Prison, where, according to Thomas (*Spanish Civil War,* 391), CNT militia home on leave and angered over reports of Nationalist atrocities at Badajoz shot forty prisoners in the courtyard on the day of the fire, 23 Aug. 1936, and forty more the next morning. Thomas (*Spanish Civil War,* 498) also mentions the confinement of "right-wing prisoners" in a "horrible prison ship" in Bilbao. Meière's cousin, the Duque de Sotomayor, was also the Marqués de Casa Irujo. When *Mankind: The Magazine of Popular History* published "Franco and the Spanish Civil War" by Jules Archer in 1967, it included a photograph of thirty executed male and female civilians, the caption reading, "Despite overwhelming odds, the Loyalists fought on courageously with dreadful losses (above)." Archer was evidently taken in by his own propaganda, for the picture was not of Loyalist corpses but of the pro-Nationalists lying in the Model Prison courtyard.

15. For a scathing portrayal of Dilling, see Glen Jeansonne, *Women of the Far Right: The Mothers' Movement and World War II* (Chicago: Univ. of Chicago Press, 1996), 10–28; Meière, "Spain, August 1938," 70–71, 96.

16. Meière, "Spain, August 1938," 94–96. In Mar. 1938, Franco set up his staff headquarters in the ducal palace of the Vistahermosas at Pedrola, near Zaragoza, but presumably this must have long since passed out of the family, for Isabel stated that the house in Navas de Riofrío was their only property.

17. María de la Piedad Caro y Martínez de Irujo, VIII Marquesa de la Romana, after the death of her brother in 1936; Meière, "Spain, August 1938," 97–100; "My Tour," Reel II, 06:32–09:52.

18. Meière, "Spain, August 1938," 101, 103–7; "My Tour," Reel II, 00:10–00:34. For a discussion of Meière's trip to the USSR via Berlin during the Olympic Games, see Michael E. Chapman, "Arguing Americanism: John Eoghan Kelly's Franco Lobby, 1936–43" (PhD diss., Boston College, 2006), 246–52.

19. Details of Gomá's career are in Luis Casañas Guasch and Pedro Sobrino Vázquez, *El Cardenal Gomá: Pastor y Maestro,* 2 vols. (Toledo: Estudio Teológico de San Ildefonso Seminario Conciliar, 1983), 1:35–76; Isidro Gomá y Tomás, "Lessons of the War and Duties of the Peace," Pastoral Letter, 8 Aug. 1939, in *Por Dios y por España: Pastorales—Instrucciones pastorales y Artículos—Discursos—Mensajes—Apéndice, 1936–1939* (Barcelona: R. Casulleras, Librero-Editor, 1940), 270. Montero Moreno, *Historia,* "Catalog of Victims," 770–883. Meière, "Spain, August 1938," 108–9.

20. Meière, "Spain, August 1938," 110–17. Adding to what is today one of Spain's primary tourist attractions, the cathedral's extensive collection of Old Masters rivals many museums. "My Tour," Reel II, 00:35–06:21. That Meière used a Filmo-70DA is an informed guess; she took her filming seriously, had no budgetary concerns, owned a state-of-the art zoom lens, and was an early pioneer of color film; she would have wanted the best, and the best appeared in 1933 in the form of Bell & Howell's "semi-professional" 70DA, as the company marketed it; selling for about $260 ($7,800) with zoom lens and accessories, Meière's cine camera cost her almost as much as a Ford Model T. At twelve frames per second, she shot three one-hundred-foot cans.

21. Before her marriage, Queen Ena's title was Princess Victoria Eugénie of Battenberg, and she was a niece of Britain's King Edward VII. Meière, "Spain, August 1938," 129–31; Meière, "My Tour," Reel II, 10:49–13:33.

22. She paid Pérez $99 ($3,000 today) for their eight-hundred-mile trip. Another branch of the Falange, Sección Femenina (Meière called it Acción Femenina) included departments for nurses, press corps, leader training, agricultural schooling, and sewing. Beiztegi, cited in Gordon Thomas and Max Morgan Witts, *Guernica: The Crucible of World War II* (New York: Stein & Day, 1975), 189; Thomas and Witts do not estimate the total number of troops, although Lieutenant Dominiguz's platoon was among 300 troops occupying the Augustine Fathers' monastery (197), 200 troops garrisoned battalion HQ at the La Merced convent, and Beiztegi promised 500 troops to aid evacuation (202), so there were probably at least 1,000. Meière, "Spain, August 1938," 161–64; Meière, "My Tour," Reel III, 8:03–10:27. Irún's arsonists were probably anarchists from the Asturias mining region; it seems improbable that local Basques would have resorted to arson, especially when they tried so hard to fight the fires set by the German incendiaries. A photograph (241) in *Guernica* indicates that the structure Meière filmed was the pelota stadium; presuming this identification to be accurate, the town presumably had a central court as well as the stadium, for Meière mentioned an open square with a pelota court down one side, the wall of which bore a shell hole. Nationalist bombing destroyed about three-quarters of the town. For an objective account from the German perspective, which indicates that the raid, while "miscarried," was never intended as a terror attack, see Karl Ries and Hans Ring, *The Legion Condor: A History of the Luftwaffe in the Spanish Civil War, 1936–1939,* trans. David Johnston (West Chester, PA: Schiffer, 1992), 62–64. Forty years later, academic histories still privilege partisanship over objectivity. "Nationalists and their fascist patrons demonstrated their barbarity by carrying out repeated atrocities, including the bombing of undefended cities such as Guernica," writes Dominic Tierney in *FDR and the Spanish Civil War: Neutrality and Commitment in*

the Struggle that Divided America (Durham, NC: Duke University Press, 2007), 4. Preston (*Spanish Civil War,* 5) writes that "Guernica was the *first* total destruction of an undefended civilian target by aerial bombardment." Leaving aside the French destruction of central Damascus in 1925 by a combination of bombing and shelling, Guernica—as Thomas and Witts make clear—was a heavily defended, legitimate military target.

23. Meière to Bowers, 24 Aug. 1938, HMP, b. T1, f. CSAMS.

24. Meière completed six commissions for four buildings at the World's Fair, including the thirty-foot-tall *Science the Healer* for the Medicine and Public Health Building, and a pair of twenty-five-foot panels depicting a linesman and an operator for the Bell Telephone Building. Hildreth Meière, "Working for a World's Fair," *Journal of the Associated Alumnae of the Sacred Heart,* 4 (1939–40), 35–41. Louise Meière Dunn interview.

25. Fifty dollars, Talbot to Meière, 21 Nov. 1938, HMP, b. T1, f. CSAMS. Manhattanville College of the Sacred Heart, located on a hundred-acre campus at Purchase, NY, simplified its name in 1952 to Manhattanville College.

26. Hy [Hilly, Hildreth Meière] to party Anne Morgan, 15 May 1938, Harmon diary. Morgan's biographical information is from an obituary in *NYT,* 30 Jan. 1952, 25; and see Alfred Allan Lewis, *Ladies and Not-So-Gentle Women* (New York: Viking Penguin, 2000), esp. chap. 32. Morgan inherited a trust fund of $3 million ($90 million).

27. Lewis, *Not-So-Gentle Women,* 211; Elisabeth Marbury, *My Crystal Ball: Reminiscences* (London: Hurst & Blackett, 1924), 148, 150, 149.

28. For De Wolfe's tour of 1914, see Marbury, *Crystal Ball,* 244–46 and 181–88 for the trip by the three, which is undated but probably 1907, 1908, or 1910 (while Alfonso still had his "boyishness" and not during the year of Barcelona's Tragic Week). De Wolfe, who could not drive, had persuaded the American consul in Barcelona to arrange for the crating and shipping of her automobile to the States; Elsie de Wolfe, *After All* (New York: Harper & Brothers, 1935), 174.

29. For Morgan's admiration of Eleanor, see Lewis, *Not-So-Gentle Women,* 439, 464; job growth in ibid., 439; *NYT,* 4 Jan. 1910, cited in ibid., 260.

30. For Morgan's passionate involvement with Vanderbilt, see ibid., xv, 363–64, 375; Morgan to Meière, 21 Nov. 1938, HMP, b. T1, f. CSAMS. For background and its committee, see SNRC advertisement in *Spain* 2, no. 12 (1938): 3.

31. Born Lucrecia Borja y Gonzáles de Riancho in 1887, Bori made six hundred appearances for the Met over nineteen seasons; Morgan to Meière, 21 Nov. 1938, HMP, b. T1, f. CSAMS; Department of State filings for Spanish aid agencies, May 1937–Nov. 1938, in FXTP, b. 37, f. 10; correspondence between Morgan and Moore, HMP, b. T1, f. CSAMS. An unpublished study by the author indicates that because of rigid foreign exchange controls, which created a substantial discrepancy between black market and official currency prices, only about a third of the dollar contributions sent by Talbot actually reached Gomá as peseta equivalents, the balance going to Nationalist Spain's treasury in pounds sterling for the purchase of war materiel. See Michael E. Chapman, "Cardinal Gomá and the Crusader's Sword" (honors thesis, Suffolk University, 2001), 51–65.

32. For Vidal-Quadras, see JEK-FBI, 11:459. It is possible that Meière met Morgan in Paris after arriving from her tour of Spain on 21 Aug. Harmon's diary records, "Went to Morgan & camera with Hy [Hilly, Hildreth Meière]," but Harmon means that they went to Morgan & Co., Place Vendome, to collect their mail. While Meière was in Spain, Harmon had been vacationing on a cruise ship in Greece, returning to Paris on 19 Aug. 1938, two days before Meière. Morgan's Paris apartment was at 22 Avenue Montaigne.

33. For Mary Benjamine, see Talbot to JEK, 8 Oct. 1938, JEKP, f. 38; and Hildreth Meière to unstated recipient, 31 Jan. 1940, HMP, b. T1, f. CSAMS. Katherine, Duchess of Atholl,

Searchlight on Spain (Harmondsworth, UK: Penguin Books, 1938), 75, 84. JEK, "The Right Side: Titled Reds [Duchess of Atholl Raises Money for Red Spain]," *Wisdom: The Catholic Front* 3, no. 11 (1938): 1, 6.

34. Summary letter of networking and lobbying activities, from Meière to unstated recipient, 31 Jan. 1940, in HMP, b. T1, f. CSAMS; Meière probably wrote the letter, which is matter-of-fact and somewhat defensive in tone, at the behest of America's new ambassador to Spain, Alexander W. Weddell, with whom Meière corresponded and had met several times. In 1943, Meière stated to FBI agent Walter L. Roethke that she had first met JEK at her studio on 3 Nov. 1938 when JEK came with Walter M. Walters. JEK-FBI, 11:461. For the Council's membership in 1938, see testimony of Gladys Rountree, 3 Feb. 1939, JEK-FBI, 1:1, 1.

35. For background information on Marie Marique and her brother Pierre, see "Memorandum: Re Pierre Marique Jr. and Marie Marique," JEKP, f. 8. Pierre was the assistant editor of Fordham University Press. For Walters, who by 1943 was executive assistant to William Burdett, the State Department's Coordinator of Inter-American Affairs in Miami, see JEK-FBI, 11:450. Also attending was "Mr. Bridge (Sheed and Ward)," implying a connection with the London publishing company by that name, but it might have been James Howard Bridge, an English American editor, author, historian, inventor of water purification equipment, and onetime literary assistant to Andrew Carnegie who had an address on West 67th Street. Hinkle, JEK-FBI, 8:350; and see JEK-FBI, 6:262, 5:240.

36. Compiled from birth and death records and letters such as Dawes to Talbot, 3 Mar. 1938, FXTP, b. 20, f. 12. Dawes had moved to Brookline from Winchester, MA, during the summer of 1938.

37. Dawes to Meière, 6 Jan. 1939, HMP, b. T1, f. CSAMS; 14 Feb. 1939 dinner, Harmon diary; Edwin Rolfe, *The Lincoln Battalion: The Story of Americans Who Fought in Spain in the International Brigades* (New York: Random House, 1939); Joseph Lewis, *Spain: A Land Blighted by Religion* (1933; repr., New York: Freethought Press Association, 1936). For the *Mercury*'s "many writers who were former Communists or fellow travelers," such as William Henry Chamberlin and Max Eastman, see Benjamin L. Alpers, *Dictators, Democracy, and American Public Culture: Envisioning the Totalitarian Enemy, 1920s–1950s* (Chapel Hill: Univ. of North Carolina Press, 2003), 142. During the period from H. L. Mencken's departure in 1933 to the ownership of editor Paul A. Palmer in 1935, the *Mercury* had swung radically to the left; but in early 1939, it was in transition once again, from Palmer's conservatism to a centrist position under business manager Lawrence E. Spivak. See Singleton, *H. L. Mencken*, 238–40.

38. Harmon was the ex-wife of real estate developer turned pioneer aviator Clifford B. Harmon; while her diary does not specify a location for the 31 Jan. party, the summary letter from Meière to an unnamed recipient states, "I had a Spanish evening here [200 W. 57th Street]." 31 Jan. 1940, HMP, b. T1, f. CSAMS.

39. 31 Jan. 1940, in HMP, b. T1, f. CSAMS; confidential memorandum, "Organization Meeting of Working Committee," 5 Dec. 1938, JEKP, f. 62.

40. Three times wounded, Donovan's medals included a Congressional Medal of Honor, a Distinguished Service Cross, a Distinguished Service Medal, and a Croix de Guerre with palm and silver star. I cannot be certain of Dorrance's identity; Elsie Allan Do. was the wife of Arthur Calbraith Do. of Philadelphia, who routinely socialized in Manhattan and summered at the exclusive Fishers Island colony; or, alternatively, she was Helen Holfelder Do., the wife of New York banker Neil H. Do., a Presbyterian, a Republican, and president of the First National Bank & Trust Company. Hart had connections to both circles, primarily through Manhattan's Freemasons. *Who's Who in America, 1938–1939* (Chicago: A. N. Marquis, 1938). Hooven Letters, Inc., invoice of 21 Jan. 1939 for $89.79 ($2,700), in HMP, b. T1, f. AUNS, CSAMS.

41. Rice's trip in *NYT,* 13 Sept. 1938, 12; for concerts, see JEK-FBI, 7:271, 4; *Philadelphia Inquirer,* 2 Dec. 1938, 2.

42. "AUNS, Partial List of Signers," in ESP, 15:37, f. 11. I have not yet located the petition in State Department archives, although Pierrepont Moffat, chief of State's European Affairs Division, wrote personally to Hart acknowledging receipt of a letter from the AUNS to Roosevelt arguing for immediate recognition; Roosevelt never saw the letter, because White House staff forwarded it directly to State. From the AUNS, signed by Hart and JEK, to the president, 26 Jan. 1939, and Moffat to Hart, 15 Feb. 1939, both in SD-CDF, b. 6425, f. 4, 852.01/430. For cable to Franco, see Hart to Sedgwick, 28 Mar. 1939, and telegram to Hull, 3 Apr. 1939, in ESP, 15:37, f. 12;.

43. For JEK at Hart's office, see trial testimony by Gladys Rountree, *PM,* 23 May 1943, 3; "Merwin K. Hart with whom I [JEK] had broken on Feb. 20 1940," in pretrial memorandum, "Re: Witness Liebmann," undated, ca. Mar.–Apr. 1943, JEKP, f. 8. Witnesses interviewed by the FBI had other theories for the split; Miss Sidney Fell thought Hart had become concerned that JEK was attracting adverse publicity to the AUNS. See the report by Robert F. X. O'Keefe, JEK-FBI, 8:344, which also provides another view of JEK in Hart's office, where Fell worked as a secretary. James Welch's John Birch Society promulgated communist conspiracy theories through a network of countrywide chapters.

44. Merwin K. Hart, "America—Look at Spain: The Agony Will Be Repeated Here," speech, broadcast from Málaga, 29 Sept. 1938, printed in *Spain* 3, no. 1 (1938): 5, 7, 20, and in *Vital Speeches of the Day* 5, no. 2 (1938): 57–58. And see Hart, "Modern Housing—In the United States and Spain," *Spain* 4, nos. 1 and 2 (15 Apr.–1 May 1939): 44–45.

45. Hart, *Look at Spain,* 219, 136–40.

46. Ibid., 212–13, 215; Hart to Sedgwick, 28 July 1938, and Sedgwick's reply, in ESP, 15:37, f. 10; David Bushnell, "Colombia," in *The Spanish Civil War, 1936–39: American Hemispheric Perspectives,* ed. Mark Falcoff and Fredrick B. Pike (Lincoln: Univ. of Nebraska Press, 1982), 166, 180, 186.

47. Hart was articulating a foreign policy ideology that Brands conceptualizes as "exemplarist" in *What America Owes the World,* esp. 1–4 and chap. 5; ibid., 217–19, 140, 189.

48. For Ernst and Egon Hanfstaengl, see correspondence in ESP, 18:43, ff. 5, 6; "remote connection," Sedgwick to Francis A. Harding, 1 Feb. 1943. On 17 Feb. 1944, for instance, Sedgwick wrote to Mrs. Henry P. McKean to say that "a year or two ago from a Canadian Concentration Camp [Putzi] Hanfstaengl wrote me saying that he had nothing but bibles to read. . . . He said he would be greatly obliged if I could send him a copy of the Koran. I took some trouble in the matter and found a good old edition which I sent him and which happened to be the same edition as the copy which he had left in London"; and on 20 Feb. 1945, John Franklin Carter wrote to Sedgwick with an appeal for "transmitting funds to our mutual friend Putzi," because "we have a moral obligation to prevent any undue hardship where Putzi is concerned in view of his services to our cause." The cost of a year at Harvard was around $1,200 ($36,000), which was met by five other sponsors in addition to Sedgwick. Ernest's father, Dr. Julius Ernest Meière, was born in New Haven in 1833, where his father, Julius Meière, was an instructor in French at Yale; Goebel was born in Prague but considered himself Austrian. Nina Wheeler, Meière's assistant with whom she worked every day for several years, did not learn about Meière's European family until summer 1938. Meière, "Spain, August 1938," 4–5.

49. Leon Festinger, *A Theory of Cognitive Dissonance* (Stanford: Stanford Univ. Press, 1957), esp. 4–21, 50–51.

50. Gross, *The Minutemen,* esp. 14, 66, 153–54. For the New Spain, see, for example, *New Spain: Its People, Its Ruler* (New York: America Press, 1939).

6. Spain in Arms

1. Dutch communists Joris Ivens and Helen van Dongen produced *Spanish Earth* (shot on location in Spain) and *Spain in Flames* (a compilation of newsreel clips), respectively, with Ernest Hemingway narrating both; see Goldstein, *The Political Stage,* 193–94. Ivens maintained that he relied on private contributions and underwriting from Contemporary Historians (formed by Hemingway, Herman Shumlin, Dorothy Parker, and various writer/artists); to whatever extent he received indirect—if not direct—Comintern funding, it is clear that he benefited from official assistance in Spain, no doubt from the Spanish Communist Party's Film Popular company, which made thirty-seven films in 1937. See Ivens, *The Camera and I,* 103–8; and José María Caparrós Lera, "The Cinema Industry in the Spanish Civil War, 1936–1939," *Film and History* 16, no. 2 (1986): 38–39.

2. *New York Herald Tribune* reporter Bob Shaplen to the Attorney General, 2 Nov. 1941, JEK-FBI, 3:104, 12–14; echoed in newspapers such as *PM,* 3 Nov. 1941, 5; and John Roy Carlson, *Under Cover: My Four Years in the Nazi Underworld of America—The Amazing Revelation of How Axis Agents and Our Enemies Within Are Now Plotting to Destroy the United States* (New York: E. P. Dutton, 1943), 60, 52–53, 67, 160.

3. For an overview of film censorship, see Anthony Slide, *"Banned in the USA": British Films in the United States and Their Censorship, 1933–1960* (London: I. B. Tauris, 1998), 1–9. A voluntary rating system replaced the PCA in 1968. For Mellett, see Walter Wanger, "OWI and Motion Pictures," *Public Opinion Quarterly* 7 (Spring 1943): 100–104.

4. *Blockade,* 85 min., United Artists, 1938 (DVD, Chatsworth, CA: Image Entertainment, 1987). To mollify censors, as in Boston, Wanger edited out the opening frame, "Spain: The Spring of 1936." For a well-researched analysis of *Blockade* as a "contextualizing discourse," see Greg M. Smith, "Blocking *Blockade:* Partisan Protest, Popular Debate, and Encapsulated Texts," *Cinema Journal* 36, no. 1 (1996): 18–38; for a cast list and overview, see Marjorie A. Valleau, *The Spanish Civil War in American and European Films* (Ann Arbor, MI: UMI Research Press, 1982), 20–29.

5. For Frank Coe, Harold Glasser, William Ludwig Ullmann, Sonia Gold, Nathan Gregory Silvermaster, George Silverman, Irving Kaplan, William Taylor, Solomon Adler, and White (an ideological rather than a party communist), see Haynes and Klehr, *In Denial,* 183–84, 189; and Jeffrey T. Richelson, *A Century of Spies: Intelligence in the Twentieth Century* (New York: Oxford Univ. Press, 1995), 88–89. For Spain, see James W. Cortada, "Espionage," in Cortada, *Historical Dictionary,* 186–87; and Richelson, *Spies,* 94.

6. *Liberty* 15, no. 29 (1938): 53; *Blockade.*

7. See Willard C. Frank, "Submarines," in Cortada, *Historical Dictionary,* 446; James Cable, *The Royal Navy and the Siege of Bilbao* (Cambridge: Cambridge Univ. Press, 1979), chap. 3. To put the legend into historical context, it is noteworthy that Americans pioneered submarine warfare, Britons developed the torpedo, Winston S. Churchill's admiralty did nothing to direct *Lusitania* away from *U-20*'s reach, and Prussian generals learned the value of *Schrecklichkeit* from William Tecumseh Sherman.

8. Advertising, *NYT,* 13 May 1938, 28; review, *NYT,* 17 June 1938, 25.

9. *NYT,* 26 June 1938, 9:3 (emphasis added).

10. *America* 59, no. 13 (1938): 312; ibid. no. 12 (1938): 266. See *Knights of Columbus News* 12, no. 26 (1938): 1, 4, a copy of which is in FXTP, b. 20, f. 6. Joseph A. Luther, SJ, at the University of Detroit, notified Talbot on 9 July 1938 of a successful cancellation in Flint, MI; Luther enclosed his letter to United Detroit Theatres, pressuring owner George W. Trendle to cancel their *Blockade* booking.

11. Omaha, *Brooklyn Tablet,* 16 July 1938, 4; Kansas City, *NYT,* 31 July 1938, 3; Johnson, *NYT,* 19 July 1938, 15; Tobin, *NYT,* 20 July 1938, 22; Vincent A. Lapomarda, *The Boston Mayor Who Became Truman's Secretary of Labor* (New York: Peter Lang, 1995), 130, 131, 292, 286; *Boston Globe,* 22 July 1938, 19; *New York World Telegram,* 20 July 1938, 17; *Boston Traveler,* 20 July 1938, 14. Whether the *Traveler's* reporter was a CPUSA member is unknowable, but the Comintern could certainly count on support within Boston's press corps; the *Boston Globe,* for instance, had at least one CP reporter in 1938, Charles Whipple, who joined the paper in 1936, rising through the ranks to take charge of its influential editorial and op-ed pages during 1964–75, a period neatly coinciding with the cold war conflict in Vietnam. See obituary, *Boston Globe,* 13 May 1991, 19. "Women Defend 'Blockade' Ban," *Boston Evening American,* 30 July 1938, 15. Pictured with Johnson are Miss Alice E. Barry, representing the alumnae of Emanuel, Trinity, and Boston colleges; Mrs. James H. Murray, state regent of the Catholic Daughters of America; and Miss Agnes J. Reavey, representing the Cardinal Newman Club of New England.

12. Text on the placards is visible in the *Life* picture and is quoted in the *New York Evening Post,* 22 June 1938, 5; *Life Magazine* 5, no. 3 (1938): 55; JEK to Talbot, ca. 20 July 1938, JEKP, f. 65.

13. *New York Evening Post,* 22 June 1938, 5.

14. Stanley Vishnewski, *Wings of the Dawn* (New York: Catholic Worker, 1984), 141; *Catholic Worker* 6, no. 3 (July 1938): 3; and see *Social Justice* 2A, no. 5 (1938): 8.

15. *Brooklyn Tablet,* 16 July 1938, 4; *Blockade* opened at the Metropolitan on Thursday, 7 July. While the *Tablet* carried a heavy Catholic bias, its detailed reporting of this incident nevertheless has the ring of accuracy.

16. *Brooklyn Tablet,* 16 July 1938, 4. NYPD records are only accessible via Freedom of Information Act requests, and, as a letter sent by Francis Griffith to La Guardia on 26 May 1938 indicates, the mayor only referred complaints to his Department of Investigation when complainants persisted—in Griffith's case following up with a second letter threatening that he would involve the press unless La Guardia acted promptly. Reel 528, documents 1727 and 1717, Mayor Fiorello La Guardia Papers, Municipal Archives of New York City, New York, NY. Marilynn Johnson, *Street Justice: A History of Police Violence in New York City* (Boston: Beacon Press, 2003), 179, 178.

17. Johnson, *Street Justice,* 179, 178 (emphasis added); Frederick Lewis Allen, *Since Yesterday: The 1930s in America, September 3, 1929–September 3, 1939* (1939; repr., New York: Harper & Row, 1986), 276.

18. *NYT,* 5 Sept. 1938, 10.

19. F. Melder to the editor, *Catholic Worker* 6, no. 4 (1938): 5.

20. For personalism, see Mark Zwick and Louise Zwick, *The Catholic Worker Movement: Intellectual and Spiritual Origins* (Mahwah, NJ: Paulist Press, 2005), esp. 97–105; see also, J. David Valaik, "American Catholic Dissenters and the Spanish Civil War," *Catholic Historical Review* 53, no. 4 (1968): 542–43. Studs Terkel, *The Good War: An Oral History of World War Two* (New York: Ballantine Books, 1984), 348.

21. "Social films," *NYT,* 23 July 1938, 10. There are few references to *Spain in Flames,* but for a brief overview, see *NYT,* 19 May 1937, 10. Handbill, in JEKP, f. 68.

22. For Bernard, see Harvey Klehr, *The Heyday of American Communism: The Depression Decade* (New York: Basic Books, 1984), 291; and Harvey Klehr, John Earl Haynes, and Kyrill M. Anderson, *The Soviet World of American Communism* (New Haven, CT: Yale Univ. Press, 1998), 43. *Congressional Record, House Journal,* 75th Cong., 1st sess., 6 Jan. 1937, 99.

23. Talbot memorandum to the AUNS's committee, 31 Oct. 1938, FXTP, b. 38, f. 11; Maydell office memorandum, 22 Dec. 1938, FXTP, b. 38, f. 11; "magnificent" and "propaganda," from

Talbot to Aileen O'Brien, 17 Oct. 1938, FXTP, b. 20, f. 7. Talbot made no mention of JEK's attendance, although Maydell told FBI agents Albert H. Cote and Joseph T. Brown that Talbot introduced JEK to him at an early private showing. JEK-FBI, 5:213. But because Maydell's testimony does not always corroborate other facts, I do not consider it reliable.

24. "Tells of U.S. Funds for Spanish Reds," *Boston Advertiser,* 22 Jan. 1939, reprinted flier, JEKP, f. 6; for Bank of Spain and confiscated valuables, see Thomas, *The Spanish Civil War,* 934–35. ALB recruitment and transportation accounted for part of the funds; the arms embargo ensured that a substantial proportion of the cash was still on deposit in U.S. banks at war's end.

25. Maydell presumably purchased all of the available footage, for his completed version had a run time of ninety minutes and included considerable footage of the siege of Toledo's Alcázar; the German version ran eighty-five minutes and did not include Toledo; and the Spanish version, which included Toledo, ran under eighty minutes. *Spain in Arms,* 35 mm, 90 min., English soundtrack, 1939; Reels 2A (summer 1936, first half of Reel III, soundtrack incorrectly spliced, 4:24 min.), 3B (Málaga, first half and last quarter of Reel VI, 4:12 min.), 5 (University City, Madrid, Reel V, 7:00 min.), 7 (Navarre, Reel VII, 5:40 min.), and 8 (Teruel, Reel VIII, 7:40 min.), NARA 060811, 233 HUAC, Motion Picture, Sound, and Video Records LICON, Special Media Archives Services Division (NWCS-M), National Archives, College Park, MD; DVD, 29:21 min., author's collection. "Spain in Arms" shot-by-shot list and script, b. 18, f. 95, Michael A. Mathis Papers, Theodore Hesburgh Collection, University of Notre Dame, South Bend, IN, with a copy in JEKP, f. 66. *Spain in Arms* appears to be absent from film studies and historiography. For a listing and brief discussion of five German-language films made in Berlin by Hispano-Film-Produktion during 1938–39 (but not including the German version of *Spain in Arms*), as well as fourteen Italian-language documentaries made by the Instituto Nazionale Luce, see Lera, "The Cinema Industry." There is a review as well as a scene synopsis of the German version, *Helden in Spanien,* by Carsten Jørgensen, "A Filmanalysis of German Documentaries on the Spanish Civil War," in *History and Film: Methodology, Research, Education,* ed. K. R. M. Short and Karsten Fledelius (Copenhagen: Eventus, 1980), 153–58. A copy of *Helden in Spanien* is at the Bundersarchiv-Filmarchiv, Berlin.

26. *Triumph of the Will,* dir. Leni Riefenstahl, DVD (Bloomington, IL: Synapse Films, 2001); for "sky bombing," see, for instance, "Shanghai Falls! Chaipei Burns!"; and for the staged "death strikes swiftly" sequence in the trenches of Madrid, see "Inside Madrid Under Fire," both by Movietone News and available on *Timeline, 1937,* DVD (Sebastopol, CA: Whirlwind Media, 2000). Sacred Heart, "Spain in Arms" shot-by-shot list, Reel II, six shots, 9.5 feet of film, in *A Concise History of the Spanish Civil War* (London: Thames & Hudson, 1974), which also includes a photograph of the event, pro-Loyalist historian Gabriel Jackson characterizes the mock execution as "one of the worst excesses of the [Loyalist zone's] prevailing anticlericalism" (66). King Alfonso XIII commissioned the fifty-foot-high monument in 1919, which lies at the geographic center (heart) of Spain, fourteen miles from Madrid. Nationalist Spaniards also used the term Anti-Spain (*Anti-España*) to refer to the anticlerical ideology of Loyalist Spain. See, for instance, Gen. Maurice Duval, *Lessons of the War in Spain,* trans. John Eoghan Kelly, ed. Michael E. Chapman (Reading, MA: Trebarwyth Press, 2006), 7n.31.

27. Effects of the exploding shell become clear in slow motion, when the blast lifts one of the gunners off his feet. *Spain in Arms,* reel V.

28. "Pressed," *Spain in Arms,* reel V; for air raid, see Thomas, *Civil War,* 570.

29. Basque children, "Spain in Arms" shot-by-shot list, reel VII, nineteen shots, 36.9 feet of film; unfortunately, this sequence is missing from NARA 060811, reel 7.

30. In an interview with Agent Gust A. Koski, ca. 7 Apr. 1943, Michael Grace, then the owner of *Spain in Arms,* explained the script-writing role of Maydell and Hammond. JEK-FBI, 7:287. In 1954, over footage of the first H-bomb detonation, Herlihy's rapt voice announced to the world that "the second era—the thermonuclear era—of the atomic age" had begun. Herlihy also spoke the part of the newscaster on *Who Framed Roger Rabbit.* I am grateful to John Michalczyk, chair of Boston College's film studies department, for positively identifying Herlihy's voice.

31. JEK to Sedgwick, 7 Feb. 1939, ESP, 15:37, f. 11, and a copy in JEKP, f. 39. Audience estimate is based on twenty-eight known screenings totaling approximately 22,100, with at least four screenings untallied; there were several further screenings in the Midwest; an unverified account mentions an additional 3,000 attendees at a NYC armory. JEK-FBI, 11:449; and see n. 41 below.

32. Cushing interview by Agent Barron T. Conklin, ca. 1 Oct. 1942, JEK-FBI, 3:146. Liebmann may have been the only Jewish Franco lobbyist in America, so his conversion to Catholicism and advocacy of Nationalist Spain merits study. Because documentary evidence consists of an FBI report and a JEK memorandum, interviews with Liebmann's sister and cousin form the basis of this account.

33. Walter Liebman, interview by author, 28 July 2005, New York.

34. Dorothea Liebmann Straus, telephone interview by author, 7 Oct. 2005; Walter Liebman witnessed the "Father!" melodrama.

35. Dorothea Liebmann Straus interview. For aid, see, for instance, Committee to Send Anesthetics and Medicines to Spain, FXTP, b. 38, f. 10; Donald I. Warren shows that Gallup survey no. 141 estimated that 800,000 Jews listened to Father Coughlin's radio addresses, and 1 percent of Jews surveyed "Support Franco in Spanish Civil War." Warren, *Radio Priest,* 303, 305, charts 2 and 4. Without knowing the exact numbers polled, and given that some respondents could have lied, dividing total listeners by the 1 percent figure is a statistical leap of faith, although 8,000 out of a Jewish population of about 4.7 million is not unreasonable; taking the 8,000 figure at a risky face value, it is possible that the total number of Jewish Franco supporters was even higher, for Jews who backed Franco may, on average, have been ill disposed to listen to a Catholic radio priest.

36. Daniel Patrick Moynihan similarly argues that Catholic principles became one with, and even surpassed, those of Americanism, but in the context of parochial school education and by a later period, the 1960s. Citing a National Opinion Research Center survey, which found, "paradoxically," that Catholic schools came "closer to the American ideal of the 'common schools,' educating all alike, than do the public schools," regardless of race or ethnicity, Moynihan questioned the stereotype of Catholic children as a class of ignoramuses blindly following their priests. Catholic schools of the 1960s—and by extension a whole generation of educated Catholic Americans, when Moynihan was writing in the mid-1980s—had "come closest to the great liberal American ideal" through which "everyone rises and differences tend to disappear." Moynihan, *"Catholic Tradition and Social Change": Second Annual Seton-Neumann Lecture, May 7, 1984, Rayburn House* (N.p.: United States Catholic Conference, 1984), 17. Evidencing the case of Liebmann's conversion, and more generally the efforts of other Catholics to keep America free of atheistic communism, could help not only locate Catholicism-as-Americanism in the late 1930s but also posit more specifically that pro-Franco anticommunism was the phenomenon's engine.

37. JEK to Michael J. Ready, 5 Mar. 1939, JEKP, f. 66.

38. St. Paul, St. Luke's Parish Hall, JEK-FBI, 3:142; Hartford, Knights of Columbus Auditorium, JEK-FBI, 4:160; Liebman interview, ca. 5 Apr. 1943, JEF-FBI, 7:271; Rosenecker

interview, ca. 30 Nov. 1942, JEK-FBI, 4:160, 4:208; Edward J. F. Glavin to JEK, 5 Jan. 1939, JEKP, f. 66.

39. Steffan interview, ca. 5 Oct. 1942, JEK-FBI, 3:145; "Dr. Hoffman Will Lecture Here Sunday," *The Lorian,* 31 Mar. 1939, 1. I am indebted to Loras College's archivist, Michael D. Gibson, for providing detailed background on the college and its newspaper. Further information on Hoffman is on an index card in World War II Chaplain Records, U.S. Army Chaplain Museum, Fort Jackson, SC. For data on executions, see chap. 4, n. 44 above.

40. Disco interview, ca. 16 Jan. 1943, JEK-FBI, 4:172.

41. For Boston, see *Boston Pilot* 113, no. 6 (1939): 1; Rice interview by Agent Robert F. X. O'Keefe, Apr. 1943, JEK-FBI, 7:271. Michael P. Grace provided an audience estimate for Boston of 3,000 per night, in an interview by Agent Gust A. Koski, Apr. 1943, JEK-FBI, 7:287; as the maximum capacity of the Boston Opera House today is 2,500, Grace might have overestimated, although management may have increased capacity with folding chairs or allowed standing in the aisles. Mass Meeting letterhead and handbill in JEKP, f. 64. Fausto Arredondo, proprietor of the Fausto Wine and Liquor Store, 164 Pearl St., NYC, told FBI agent Walter L. Roethke that he saw *Spain in Arms* at the end of 1938 at a Manhattan armory (possibly the 69th Regiment Armory, near 28th and 8th) when three thousand New Yorkers attended, and JEK sat on the platform but did not deliver a speech. I have not yet been able to corroborate Arredondo's account. JEK-FBI, 11:449. For Colonel Tobin's conditions, see JEK to Ellery Sedgwick, 30 Jan. 1939, JEKP, f. 39; Tobin to JEK, 7 Feb., and Tobin to Hart, 14 Feb. 1939, both in b. 1, f. Mass Meeting for America, Merwin K. Hart Papers (MKHP), University of Oregon, Eugene.

42. Parade, *NYT,* 10 Oct. 1938, 16; allegiance, *NYT,* 22 June 1938, 4; tax burden, *NYT,* 11 Apr. 1939, 41.

43. Frances FitzGerald, *Fire in the Lake: The Vietnamese and the Americans in Vietnam* (Boston: Little, Brown, 1972), 7, 15; Justus D. Doenecke, *Storm on the Horizon: The Challenge to American Intervention, 1939–1941* (Lanham, MD: Rowman & Littlefield, 2003), 170.

44. *NYT,* 20 Feb. 1939, 8; *Herald Tribune,* 20 Feb. 1939, 2. For expenses, including government taxes of $46.30, see memorandum from Col. Cosby to Hildreth Meière, 23 May 1939, in HMP, b. T1, Spanish Papers, f. AUNS, CSAMS. The German American Bund, which received official backing from Germany's NSDAP and drew a predominance of its members from the metropolitan New York area, promoted sociocultural events, Nazi propaganda, and paramilitaristic activities. For Coughlin as "radio priest," see, for example, *Broadcasting,* 15 Nov. 1936, 38. Some commentators may have confused distasteful or rowdy scenes with a Nazi Bund rally held the following night, Monday, 20 Feb. 1939.

45. *Herald Tribune,* 20 Feb. 1939, 2.

46. *NYT,* 20 Feb. 1939, 8; for the correct story, see Hildreth Meière's account in JEK-FBI, 11:461.

47. Shaplen's letter of 2 Nov. 1941 to the attorney general is quoted in full in JEK-FBI, 3:104, 12–14. For JEK's speech at Boston College, see Dawes to Talbot, with enclosed list of speeches, 9 Apr. 1939, FXTP, b. 22, f. 36, JEK's copy of speech list, JEKP, f. 7, and Dawes interview by Agent Charles T. Fletcher, JEK-FBI, 7:286.

48. Maydell interview of 3 Feb. 1943, JEK-FBI, 5:213.

7. Franco Lobbyists and the Christian Front

1. Handbills for mass meetings, JEKP, f. 64; report of confidential informant Harold Neff, 6 May 1943, JEK-FBI, 10:420. See, for instance, Chris McNickle, "When New York Was Irish, and After," in *The New York Irish*, ed. Ronald H. Bayor and Timothy J. Meagher (Baltimore: Johns Hopkins Univ. Press, 1997): "In 1938 a group of disaffected Irish in Brooklyn created the Christian Front for the specific purpose of taking up Father Coughlin's call to repress 'Jews and Communists.' . . . It boycotted Jewish stores and plotted violent acts against [Jews]" (354).

2. Terkel, *The Good War*; Charles E. Coughlin, "The Declaration of Independence," Sunday, 10 Mar. 1935, in *A Series of Addresses on Social Justice, as Broadcast by Rev. Charles E. Coughlin over a National Network, March 1935* (Royal Oak, MI: The Radio League of the Little Flower, 1935), 207–18.

3. Jeanne D. Brennan, aged ten in 1938, recalled that mothers gave their children tomatoes to throw at CPUSA soapbox orators who liked to speak at the corner of 22nd Street and 8th Avenue. Jeanne D. Brennan, interview by author, 28 Dec. 2008, New York.

4. Niall Ferguson prefers "empire" to "hegemon"; see his *Colossus: The Price of America's Empire* (New York: Penguin, 2004), 8–11.

5. Doenecke, *Storm on the Horizon*, 272 (emphasis added), 275.

6. *The Nation* 150, no. 18 (1940): 557.

7. David S. Wyman, *Paper Walls: America and the Refugee Crisis, 1938–1941* (Boston: Univ. of Massachusetts Press, 1968), 210; Gulie Ne'eman Arad, *America, Its Jews, and the Rise of Nazism* (Bloomington: Indiana Univ. Press, 2000), 198–99; poll of 9 Dec. 1938, Gallup, *Gallup Poll*, survey no. 139, 128. From a total population of 130 million, I am estimating a pool of 90 million, which would be 5.4 million.

8. TD, or Teachta Dála, member of the Dáil (Irish parliament); Fearghal McGarry, *Irish Politics and the Spanish Civil War* (Cork: Cork Univ. Press, 1999), 116–18; Dublin, *Irish Independent*, 26 Oct. 1936, 3, 11, 13; Clonmel, *Irish Independent*, 5 Oct. 1936, 3, 12; Waterford, *Irish Press*, 12 Oct. 1936, 10; Masonry, *Irish Independent*, 1 Oct. 1936, 14. For an account of overt anti-Semitism, see Dermot Keogh and Andrew McCarthy, *Limerick Boycott, 1904: Anti-Semitism in Ireland* (Cork: Mercier Press, 2005), 3. Ireland's Jewish population in 1936 was 3,749 (0.1 percent).

9. Buchanan, *Britain and the Spanish Civil War*, 89–90, 175–76. For Wilson's appreciation of the complexities of Middle Eastern politics, see, for instance, Arnold T. Wilson, *Loyalties: Mesopotamia, 1914–1917, a Personal and Historical Record* (1930; repr., New York: Greenwood Press, 1969), esp. 236–37 and chap. 16, and *More Thoughts and Talks: The Diary and Scrapbook of a Member of Parliament, from September 1937 to August 1939* (London: Longmans, Green, 1939), 182–83; and for Kemp, see Judith Keene, *Fighting for Franco: International Volunteers in Nationalist Spain During the Spanish Civil War, 1936–39* (London: Leicester Univ. Press, 2001), 110–15. As acting high commissioner in Baghdad during the 1920s, Wilson had warned his government that its pro-Sunni policy would soon provoke a Shi'ite rebellion.

10. Arnold H. M. Lunn, *Spanish Rehearsal: An Eyewitness in Spain During the Civil War, 1936–1939* (1937; repr., Old Greenwich, CT: Devin-Adir Company, 1974); Lunn to unnamed recipient (he addressed similar letters to "Phyllis," "Etta," and "my darling"), n.d., b. 3, f. 20, Sir Arnold Lunn Papers, Lauinger Library Special Collections, Georgetown University, Washington, DC; "f_ces" in original, Lunn to unnamed recipient, and "Train to New Orleans," 5 Dec. 1938, Lunn Papers, b. 3, f. 20. For America's Anglo-Protestant ideal, see Huntington, *Who Are We?* chap. 4.

11. Lunn, *Spanish Rehearsal,* 186, xx, 77; *Spanish Rehearsal* appeared in bookstores shortly before Apr. 1937. Estimating book sales is problematic, but given that two hundred U.S. libraries own *Spanish Rehearsal,* more than twenty online used booksellers were offering the 1937 edition in late 2005, and magazines from *Commonweal* to the *Springfield Republican* to the *Saturday Review of Literature* reviewed the book, it is reasonable to assume that it sold out its print run, which would have been 3,000–5,000 copies. Arnold H. M. Lunn, *Spain and the Christian Front: Ubi Crux Ibi Patria* (New York: Paulist Press, 1937).

12. Paulists designate profession in their order by the suffix CSP, the Congregation of Saint Paul. Based on comparable publications and a sense of *Wisdom*'s readership, the circulation is my conservative estimate. *Wisdom*'s five Paulist advisers were Fathers John B. Harney, Bertrand L. Conway, Joseph I. Malloy, Joseph McSorely, and James Gills; editor Ward was also a Paulist. Letter from Kenyan missionary, as well as a letter from Jamaica, in *Wisdom: The Catholic Front* 3, no. 8 (1938): 4, 7.

13. Edward C. McCarthy, "The Christian Front Movement in New York City, 1938–1940" (master's thesis, Columbia University, 1965), 1, 8; *Social Justice* 1A, no. 13 (1938): 23; ibid. no. 16 (1938): 23; ibid. no. 17 (1938): 23; "America Needs a Christian Front," Co-Operation Coupon, ibid. 2A, no. 4 (1938): 23. At this time, *Social Justice* claimed that there were 2,500 platoons of about twenty-five members each.

14. Untitled AJC report beginning "On July 14," ca. Sept. 1938, f. Christian Front, Blaustein Library, American Jewish Committee (AJC), New York; Evelyn Savidge Sterne, "Beyond the Boss: Immigration and American Political Culture from 1880 to 1940," in *E Pluribus Unum? Contemporary and Historical Perspectives on Immigrant Political Incorporation,* ed. Gary Gerstle and John Mollenkopf (New York: Russell Sage Foundation, 2001), 53–55.

15. AJC report beginning "On July 14"; Angel González Palencia, *The Flame of Hispanicism* (New York: Peninsular News Service, 1938); for Local 802, see, for instance, "The Persecution of Harry Thorne," June 1939, pamphlet, AJC, f. Christian Front.

16. "Entire trend," untitled AJC report beginning "In the fall of 1938," Sept. 1939, AJC, f. Christian Front (2); "I don't care," AJC report "On July 14." There are several other reports in the Christian Front files at the Blaustein Library that mention this first meeting, and I would expect that there are copies of these and similar reports in the archives of Jewish organizations such as the YIVO Institute for Jewish Research, but they all appear to be variants of the informant's "On July 14," which is by far the most detailed. Because the reports are anonymous, it is impossible to tell if reports of subsequent meetings are the work of the same AJC informant.

17. Reports of informant Harold Neff, 5 and 6 May 1943, JEK-FBI, 10:420. E. E. Conroy, special agent in charge at the FBI's Manhattan office, forwarded Neff's report to J. Edgar Hoover on 7 May 1943 for the JEK trial. Conroy's letter to Hoover, in which he described Neff as a "Confidential Informant," gives no indication whether Neff had been an FBI informant for some time or whether he had been working for one of the Jewish organizations in 1938–39. Given the accuracy of his dates and names, Neff must have compiled his reports of 5 and 6 May from either a notebook or previous reports.

18. Leonard Dinnerstein, *Antisemitism in America* (New York: Oxford Univ. Press, 1994), 121. In his twenty-two-page chapter arguing for "Antisemitism at High Tide," Dinnerstein has twenty-two citations to pages in McCarthy's study; McCarthy, "Christian Front," 43 ("disorder and violence"), 11–12 (meeting), 14–15 (Bono). It is a minor detail, but McCarthy inaccurately transcribed his attendance figure from the second Paulist meeting on 4 Aug., at which, according to the informant, "About 40 or 50 men were present"; AJC report "On July 14." "Caricatures Liberty," *NYT,* 30 Oct. 1938, 40. Bono's sentence stands in

counterpoint to the 2006 publication of anti-Islam caricatures of the Prophet Muhammad in Danish newspapers, as well as in at least one American edition (*Philadelphia Inquirer,* 4 Feb. 2006), on the rationale that the exercise of free expression is a Western prerogative.

19. McCarthy, "Christian Front," 36 (112 arrestees), 34 (assaults on vendors), 43 ("heckling opponents"), 36 ("virtually impossible"), 77 ("dubious authenticity"), 78 ("housewives"). In the first incident, a "Coughlinite bricklayer" knocked unconscious an *Equality* (Comintern propaganda masquerading as a Jewish monthly magazine) vendor, and in the second a group of youths stabbed a young Jew on a subway. But McCarthy could see "no discernible connection" between the youths and the Christian Front (103n.26).

20. Cahan to La Guardia, 26 June 1939, La Guardia Papers, 18:2432; Pauline Lipowsky of the Kletzker Young Ladies Society and fourteen other organizations to La Guardia, 15 Aug. 1939, La Guardia Papers, 10:2495 and following (emphasis added); for "exaggerated accounts," see for instance La Guardia to Isadore Freid, 13 Nov. 1939, La Guardia Papers, 19:231; "Final Report: Activities of Anti-Semitic Groups Within New York City," 6 Nov. 1939, La Guardia Papers, 19:223.

21. Darrow, "Catholic Political Power," 154, 155; *NYT,* 5 Sept. 1938, 10. Letting air out of tires in the 1930s was a simple affair, as Schrader valves typically had a notched metal dust cap to facilitate easy valve replacement. These Columbia dissertations still carry weight; Jay P. Corrin's analysis of Catholic intellectual thought cites Darrow, praising the work as a "good study of American rightists and Catholic support for Franco." Jay P. Corrin, *Catholic Intellectuals and the Challenge of Democracy* (Notre Dame, IN: Univ. of Notre Dame Press, 2002), 471.

22. See, for instance, Leon Klenicki and Geoffrey Wigoder, eds., *A Dictionary of the Jewish-Christian Dialogue,* expanded ed. (Mahwah, NJ: Paulist Press, 1995).

23. For Honoré and the Chatham Square Music School, see "Notes of Musicians," *NYT,* 5 June 1938, 158; flier, "Anti-Communism Is Christian Self-Defense!!" 1 Dec. 1938, and "The Pro-Semitic Persecution of Harry Thorne," 26 June 1939, pamphlet, in AJC, f. Christian Front.

24. Richard O'Connor, *Hell's Kitchen: The Roaring Days of New York's Wild West Side* (New York: Old Town Books, 1957), 187; for Jewish political empowerment during La Guardia's administration, see Bayor, *Neighbors in Conflict,* 33–40.

25. Radiogram of 18 Nov. and memorandum from Howe to the mayor of 22 Nov. 1938, in La Guardia Papers, 530:1376–80.

26. Memorandum from Howe to the mayor, 22 Dec. 1938, La Guardia Papers, 530:1477.

27. Burke's transfer, McCarthy, "Christian Front," 40. Donovan, who had been running the bar since at least 1921, when it was popular among Irish nationalists, had just renewed his lease, *NYT,* 24 Sept. 1938, 32.

28. JEK, "Free Speech in Jersey City: A Defense of Mayor Hague," *Wisdom* 3, no.3 (1938): 1, 6; *Jersey Journal,* 1 Dec. 1937, 4 and 7 Jan. 1938; for Baldwin as "fellow traveler," see Klehr, *The Heyday of American Communism,* 286. JEK lodged with Miss Mary Hughes, at 14 Brinkerhoff Street, Jersey City, where he also rented a room as an office. Balanced accounts of Frank Hague's three-decade tenure at City Hall, Jersey City, prove elusive, but for a hint of the public support for his anticommunist stance, see Dayton David McKean, *The Boss: The Hague Machine in Action* (Boston: Houghton Mifflin, 1940), 195–98; Thomas F. X. Smith, *The Powerticians* (Secaucus, NJ: Lyle Stuart, 1982), 126–29; and especially Reinhard H. Luthin, *American Demagogues: Twentieth Century* (Gloucester, MA: Peter Smith, 1959), 143, which explains that "Jersey City citizens saw something wholesome in Hague's rule. When interviewed as to the reasons for their approval, they pointed to the city's 'family life,' . . . and above all, they lauded the Medical Center as the 'best in the world.'"

29. *NYT,* 18 and 19 Dec. 1937; *Jersey Journal,* 18 Dec. 1937, 1; "Invasion," *Jersey Journal,* passim, but esp. 29 Nov. 1937, 1. JEK referenced Jersey City in his "John L. Lewis: Public Enemy No. 2" speech at the Great Pro-American Mass Meeting.

30. JEK's "Right Side" column of Aug. 1939 was an exception, for it appeared on page three; it is a presumption on my part that the column appeared on the front page in Oct. 1938, for my collection is missing this edition, and no other copy has so far proved accessible. JEK, "The Right Side: Spain," *Wisdom* 3, no. 4 (1938): 1, 3.

31. Ibid.

32. Snapshot, ibid., no. 9 (1938): 7.

33. JEK, "The Right Side: Free Speech? [Red Lunatic Fringe]," ibid. 4, no. 1 (1939): 1, 6. Matías is the Spanish spelling of Matthias, suggesting that JEK had culled his information from a Spanish source, perhaps through the Peninsular News Service where he sometimes typed up his articles for *Spain* magazine. JEK's use of the octopus metaphor predates Elizabeth Kirkpatrick Dilling's *The Octopus* of Oct. 1940, a catalog of leading Jewish Americans claimed by Dilling to be part of an international conspiracy. Dilling, *The Octopus* (1940; repr., Frank Woodruff Johnson [pseudonym for Dilling]; Metairie, LA: Sons of Liberty, 1986).

34. Gregory Feige, "Anti-Semitism," *Wisdom* 4, no. 1 (1939): 1, 5, 7, 8; Feige to the editor, ibid., no. 3 (1939): 2. Rathenau was chairman of the AEG electrical conglomerate and the Weimar Republic's foreign minister, and Erzberger was a leftist member of the Catholic Party; right-wing extremists murdered them in 1922 and 1921, respectively. Uncommitted until after the workers' revolt began, Luxemburg and Liebknecht, both communists, advocated violent overthrow of the Weimar government; Freikorps soldiers killed them.

35. "Fourth Estate" to editor Paul Ward, *Wisdom* 4, no. 5 (1939): 2; JEK, "The Right Side: [Liberal 'Tolerance']," ibid., no. 4 (1939): 1, 6, and *Programme;* JEK's office manager, Hubert J. Hannon, to Talbot, 27 Apr. 1939, and "A Programme for American Nationalism," JEKP, f. 102, and FXTP, b. 22, f. 37.

36. "A Programme for American Nationalism," JEKP, f. 102, and FXTP, b. 22, f. 37.

37. "A Programme for American Nationalism," JEKP, f. 102, and FXTP, b. 22, f. 37.

38. Report by Agent Gust A. Koski, 1 Apr. 1943, JEK-FBI, 8:304; for Bielaski, see Ted Morgan, *Reds: McCarthyism in Twentieth-Century America* (New York: Random House, 2003), 274–75; for twelve identified Soviet spies within the OSS and four others whose identities are unknown, see John Earl Haynes and Harvey Klehr, *Venona: Decoding Soviet Espionage in America* (New Haven, CT: Yale Univ. Press, 1999), 194–95.

39. I base my opinion of JEK's knowledge of, attitude toward, and potential participation in plans by George E. Deatherage, Moseley, and others for a military coup to preempt communist takeover of the federal government on available evidence as well as on my assessment of JEK's character; but this could change in light of additional material, as this matter is not clear cut in my mind. For a composite account with a sense of proportion, see Davis, "Radio Priest," 413–14.

40. Ibid., 414; untitled, undated, unsigned list beginning "Father Keeling," ca. Feb. 1939, AJC, f. Christian Front (2).

41. Interviews with Anti-Nazi League informants Mario Buzzi and Dorothy Waring, reported by Agent Robert F. X. O'Keefe, 23 Apr. 1943, JEK-FBI, 8:353.

42. As this property is now a modern development, its layout at the time is unclear. Investigators called it Donovan's Hall or Donovan's Beer Hall (presumably intending Nazi connotations), so it was probably a single, large ground-floor space or, alternatively, a traditional bar layout with a meeting room above. Report of confidential informant Harold Neff, 6 May 1943, JEK-FBI, 10:420.

43. "Great Pro-American Mass Meeting in Behalf of Free Speech and Americanism," sponsored by American Patriots, and the American Federation Against Communism, "With the cooperation of the Christian Front, American Nationalist party and twelve other Patriotic Organizations," handbill, in JEKP, f. 64. Mecca Temple became the New York City Center.

44. Dilling, *The Octopus,* 77, 231; *Octopus* was a sequel to Dilling's *Red Network* (1935). Carlson, *Under Cover,* 59, 52, 458, 468. *Under Cover* sold more than 800,000 copies. For "Jew-baiting," see Carlson's report "American Patriots, Inc., Luncheon-Meeting, May 19, 1939," in JEK-FBI, 11: Documents.

45. For "storm-troopers" and "goon squads," see, for example, Carlson, *Under Cover,* 68, 67, 28; ibid., 28 ("actor"), 72 ("deliberately designed"), 67–58 (subway incident).

46. Ibid., 15–21; Alpers, *Dictators,* 215; Carlson, *Under Cover,* 32, 67–68.

47. Carlson's four reports are in JEK-FBI, 11: Documents. Compare Carlson's FBI report, "'Great Pro-American Mass Meeting in Behalf of Free Speech and Americanism,' May 24, 1939," in JEK-FBI, 11: Documents, in which he stated "[Joseph McWilliams said:] 'Roosevelt is one of the most vicious little men' . . . a woman near me cried out 'Don't say that,'" with "'Roosevelt is one of the most vicious men' . . . 'Don't say that,' a woman shouted," which appeared in *Under Cover* (52).

48. Cole, *Roosevelt and the Isolationists,* 537; Kenneth O'Reilly, *Hoover and the Un-Americans: The FBI, HUAC, and the Red Menace* (Philadelphia: Temple Univ. Press, 1983), 213; Westbrook Pegler's column "Fair Enough," *New York Times-Herald,* 20 May 1947, 15, JEKP, f. 124.

49. Carlson report, "Christian Front meeting, Tri-Boro Palace, Third Ave. and 137th St., Bronx, May 3, 1939," JEK-FBI, 11: Documents. Carlson mentioned (*Under Cover,* 70–71) that he worked as an investigator, "at a modest salary," for one of several "organizations engaged in combating fascist propaganda"; he also stated that he knew that FBI agents had "made use of similar devices" to his *Christian Defender* "to gain the confidence of saboteurs."

50. Report by O'Keefe, 23 Apr. 1943, JEK-FBI, 8:353.

51. Carlson report, "American Patriots, Inc., Luncheon-Meeting, May 19, 1939," JEK-FBI, 11: Documents. At least one other informant attended this meeting, Dero A. Saunders. See JEK-FBI, 9:359. Carlson was referencing the materialistic conformity of George Babbitt, protagonist of Sinclair Lewis's 1922 satire of middle-class, small-town America, *Babbitt.* Lewis may have drawn his character's name from Irving Babbitt, the Harvard professor, conservative radical, and founder of New Humanism of whom Lewis was deeply critical. For an overview of New Humanists as well as a supporting citation from Carlson, see Schlesinger, *The Age of Roosevelt,* 70–72; and Allen Guttmann, *The Conservative Tradition in America* (New York: Oxford Univ. Press, 1967), 135–38, who points out that Babbitt was an atheist.

52. Carlson, *Under Cover,* 44; details from Carlson's report, "'Great Pro-American Mass Meeting in Behalf of Free Speech and Americanism,' May 24, 1939," JEK-FBI, 11: Documents, and *NYT,* 25 May 1939, 3; Leonora Rogers Schuyler, aka Mrs. Livingston Rowe Schuyler.

53. "John L. Lewis: Public Enemy No. 2," speech, 24 May 1939, JEKP, f. 64; creases on these notes are consistent with JEK folding them to fit into his jacket pocket. Ironically, by the Nov. 1940 elections, Lewis was supporting Republican candidate Wendell Willkie; when Lewis espoused isolationism in Sept. 1939, contemporaries concluded that he was following the Stalinist party line, though Lewis continued to oppose U.S. intervention even after the Nazi invasion of the Soviet Union in June 1941.

54. "John L. Lewis: Public Enemy No. 2," speech, 24 May 1939, JEKP, f. 64. For a historical account biased toward Lewis's pickets, see John W. Hevener, *Which Side Are You On? The Harlan County Coal Miners, 1931–39* (Urbana: Univ. of Illinois Press, 1978); influenc-

ing JEK's views on Harlan would have been the Herrin Massacre of 1922 in Williamson County, not far away in the southern Illinois coalfields, where a mob of union strikers brutally murdered sixteen strikebreakers. See Paul M. Angle, *Bloody Williamson: A Chapter in American Lawlessness* (New York: Knopf, 1966).

55. "John L. Lewis: Public Enemy No. 2," speech, 24 May 1939, JEKP, f. 64.

56. *NYT*, 25 May 1939, 3; Carlson report, "'Great Pro-American Mass Meeting,'" JEK-FBI, 11: Documents; report of confidential informant Harold Neff, 6 May 1943, JEK-FBI, 10:420.

57. Carlson, *Under Cover*, 50, 52 (subtitle), 59, 52, 458; and Carlson report, "'Great Pro-American Mass Meeting,'" JEK-FBI, 11: Documents.

58. Carlson, *Under Cover*, 22–23, and *The Plotters* (New York: E. P. Dutton, 1946), vii.

59. JEK, "Redwood Country," *Jonathan Club* magazine, 15 Mar. 1948, 9 pp., JEKP, f. 99; during June 1947–Mar. 1948, JEK wrote seven articles for the club's magazine, no copies of which I have yet located. Carlson began *Under Cover* (16–18) with an account of the persecutions his Armenian family suffered in Greece and Bulgaria during 1913–18.

60. JEK's first-edition copy of Carlson's *Under Cover* is in the author's collection. Carlson, *Under Cover*, 59, 52, 458, 468. While in America's Nazi underworld, Carlson (ibid., 360) had visited the office of the "traveling missionary of hate," Joseph P. Spencer, who allowed him to glance at a letter from Senator Robert R. Reynolds (D-NC), from which he then quoted a hundred-word passage verbatim.

8. Un-American Americanism

1. Gen. Francisco Gómez Jordana signed the five-year treaty at Burgos on 31 Mar. 1939, and it was actually secret; but on 26 Mar. Franco had publicly agreed to join the Anti-Comintern Pact between Germany and Italy.

2. Data spreadsheet compiled by author from JEK-FBI. Before JEK's trial, six U.S. citizens had received convictions under FARA for being propagandists for either Nazi Germany (German immigrant Paul Fehse, aviator Laura Ingalls, and Senator Frank B. Burch) or Japan (ex-China consular officer Ralph Townsend and advertising executives Frederick V. Williams and Warren Ryder). JEK to J. K. Ross (J. T. in other material), "Subject: Communist in Brooklyn Navy Yard," 16 Oct. 1938, JEKP, f. 38; Ross was assistant chief-of-staff, G-2, on the Governor's Island army base.

3. "New Spain" was the term that Franco lobbyists used to distinguish Franco's post–Apr. 1939 Spain from the divided civil war Spain. See Hildreth Meière to Claude G. Bowers, 24 Aug. 1938, HMP, b. T1, Spanish Papers, Correspondence, CSAMS; and cable from Merwin K. Hart to Cordell Hull, 3 Apr. 1939, ESP, 15:37, f. 12.

4. JEK, "Little Red Schoolboys," *America* 60, no. 15 (1939): 344–45; Roosevelt's letter quoted in *NYT*, 26 Dec. 1939, 26; Lash's theme in *NYT*, 27 Dec. 1939, 26. An ALB volunteer told the U.S. consular office in Valencia in Mar. 1937 that the CPUSA had "units . . . in all the colleges and universities in the United States"; quoted from R. Dan Richardson, *Comintern Army: The International Brigades and the Spanish Civil War* (Lexington: Univ. Press of Kentucky, 1982), 34–35.

5. *NYT*, 27 Dec. 1939, 26; JEK, "Red Schoolboys." Roger N. Baldwin, ACLU founder and executive director, never joined the CPUSA, although Michael Quill, a New York City Council member and head of the Transport Workers Union, and Clarence Hathaway, editor of the *Daily Worker*, were both CPUSA members, while James Wechsler of *The Nation* was a Young Communist League member; Williams never joined the CPUSA.

6. Eleanor Roosevelt, *This I Remember* (New York: Harper & Brothers, 1949), 201, 204. Joseph P. Lash, *Love, Eleanor: Eleanor Roosevelt and Her Friends* (Garden City, NY: Doubleday, 1982), 296 ("not afraid"), 315 (meeting), 322–23 (New York apartment), 327, 359 (militiaman), 355 (Eleanor's key), 363 (Pontiac); *PM,* 287–88, 314.

7. Republican Club, Mrs. J. Hasbrouck LeFevre, presiding, 19 Jan. 1939, JEF-FBI, 5:223, and see clippings at back; JEK to Talbot, 7 Apr. 1939, in FXTP, b. 22, f. 35.

8. From Memorandum, one of JEK's pretrial depositions to James V. Hayes, JEKP, f. 8; general correspondence, JEKP, f. 38; Helen Kelly to Talbot, 3 June 1943, FXTP, b. 38, f. 12. JEK's general staff contact was Lt. Col. Taboada, whom I have not yet identified further. Boeing's 314 flying boat made its maiden flight on 7 June 1938, and Pan American did not begin scheduled transatlantic service until 28 June 1939, so JEK was something of a pioneer; he paid about four times the cost of a Concorde transatlantic crossing.

9. For his arrest on 15 Dec. 1939, see Memorandum, JEKP, f. 8; various correspondence, including JEK to Talbot, 12 Mar. 1940, Talbot to JEK, 19 Mar. 1940, George H. Knutson to JEK, 26 Mar. 1940, JEK to L. N. Boisen, Stone & Webster vice president, 3 Apr. 1940, all in JEKP, f. 40. JEK would also seem to have borrowed $1,200 from Seward Bishop Collins, editor of *American Review,* JEK-FBI, 7:293.

10. Merwin K. Hart, chairman of the AUNS, to Hull, 3 Apr. 1939, ESP, 16:37, f. 12; Acheson, *Present at the Creation,* 169; K. Richmond Temple, "Alexander Weddell: Virginian in the Diplomatic Service," *Virginia Cavalcade* 34, no. 1 (1984): 37; and for further background on Weddell and his wife Virginia, see Charles R. Halstead, "Diligent Diplomat: Alexander W. Weddell as American Ambassador to Spain, 1939–1942," *Virginia Magazine of History and Biography* 82, no. 1 (1974): 3–38. Pablo Franky Vásquez, a member of Colombia's National Congress (1958–61) who attended conferences on social security throughout Latin America and Spain during the 1960s–80s, recalled meeting delegates over the years—from across the political spectrum—who had mentioned to him their disgust over Washington's refusal to aid Spain in the 1940s, primarily on humanitarian grounds. Pablo Franky Vásquez, interview by author, 3 Aug. 2006, Charlestown, MA.

11. Weddell to Welles, 29 Aug. 1939, Sumner Welles Papers, b. 57, Office Correspondence, 1920–43, f. 1, Weddell, Alexander, 1939; Allen to Eleanor Roosevelt, 10 July 1939, for contingencies see text of *New York Enquirer,* 17 July 1939, and Welles to Roosevelt, 19 July 1939, all in FDR-SF, b. 50, f. Spain, 1939.

12. Virginia Weddell to Hart, 1 May 1940, and Hart to CSAMS members, 27 Aug. 1940, FXTP, b. 38, f. 10. Maud Jaretski Seligman was the wife of Eustace Seligman, lawyer, member of six corporate boards, and treasurer of the American Association for Labor Legislation.

13. Virginia Weddell to Hart, 3 Dec. 1940, FXTP, b. 38, f. 10; for diplomatic pouch, see, for instance, Virginia Weddell to Hart, 27 Mar. 1941, HMP, b. T1, f. CSAMS; Temple, "Alexander Weddell," 18. Unfortunately, Dunn's letter of 1 Aug. 1941 is not extant, but see Hart to Dunn, 4 Nov. 1941, from which I have quoted, in HMP, b. T1, f. CSAMS.

14. "The Present and Future of Spain," radio interview, Station WQXR, 10 PM, Friday, 12 May 1939, HMP, b. T1, f. CSAMS. International Broadcasting Corporation ran WQXR, which the *NYT* purchased in 1944; it was predominantly a classical music station. Meière recounted asking U.S. ambassador Claude G. Bowers if it was true that Loyalists had murdered 25,000 in Madrid alone, to which Bowers replied, "No, I do not" and then clarified by stating that "he thought the figure was nearer 40,000." For data on executions, see chap. 4, n. 44 above.

15. They raised $8,700 ($261,000), including $3,500 to rent the Garden and $450 for Col. Ralph C. Tobin's 7th Regiment Band. "Mass Meeting: Budget," MKHP, b. 1, f. Mass Meeting. Attendance estimates varied from 10,000–15,000, with the committee's postevent

literature using the 14,000 figure; when the stage was at one end, the seating behind the stage was roped off, and the floor of the arena was open, a capacity crowd was around 15,000; record attendance of 23,190 was for the welterweight boxing match between Fritzie Zivic and Henry Armstrong in 1941. *Program: Mass Meeting for America*, lists 117 sponsoring associations and individuals, in HMP, b. T1, f. CSAMS.

16. From Dies's speech in HMP, b. T1, f. CSAMS; "Dies Hits New Deal As Secret Enemy," was how the *New York World-Telegram* interpreted his remarks, from press clippings in MKHP, b. 1, f. Mass Meeting.

17. Draft cable, and correspondence with Sedgwick of 10 June and 13 June 1940, ESP, 16:37, f. 12; Meière's refusal, in interview with Agent Walter L. Roethke, JEK-FBI, 11:460.

18. Allen to Kelly, 21 July 1938, and JEK to Talbot, 24 July 1938, FXTP, b. 22, f. 37; Talbot to JEK about "a man named John Doherty," 27 July 1938, in FXTP, b. 22, f. 37. Lisle to JEK, 14 Feb. 1939, JEKP f. 4; report by Special Agent in Charge Dwight Brantley to J. Edgar Hoover, 3 Feb. 1939, JEK-FBI, 1:1, 5. For Allen and Badajoz, see chap. 1, n. 49 above.

19. Spelled "Rountree" in FBI reports and "Rowntree" in *PM*. Report by Brantley to Hoover, 3 Feb. 1939, and Hoover to Brantley, 7 Feb. 1939, JEK-FBI, 1:1.

20. Report by Brantley to Hoover, 3 Feb. 1939, and Hoover to Brantley, 7 Feb. 1939, JEK-FBI, 1:1; and report by Brantley to Hoover, 9 Feb. 1939, JEK-FBI, 1:6.

21. Leon G. Turrou, *The Nazi Spy Conspiracy in America* (London: George G. Harrap, 1939), also published as *Nazi Spies in America* (New York: Random House, 1939); for a discussion of *Confessions'* documentary-like poignancy, see Eric J. Sandeen, "*Confessions of a Nazi Spy* and the German-American Bund," *American Studies* 20, no. 2 (1979): 69–81. For other classics of the fifth column genre, see John Louis Spivak, *Secret Armies: The New Technique of Nazi Warfare* (New York: Modern Age Books, 1939); and Michael Sayers and Albert Eugene Kahn, *Sabotage! The Secret War Against America* (New York: Harper Brothers, 1942). "Radio Listeners in Panic, Taking War Drama as Fact: Many Flee Homes to Escape 'Gas Raid from Mars'—Phone Calls Swamp Police at Broadcast of Wells Fantasy," *NYT*, 31 Oct. 1938, 1.

22. Report by Foxworth to Hoover, 30 Mar. 1940, JEK-FBI, 1:27; memorandum by Agent J. A. Ruehle, 11 June 1940, JEK-FBI, 1:28; anonymous letter to Welles, 29 July 1940, JEK-FBI, 1:29. JEK had actually broken the news to Finucane in Nov. 1937 and tried to employ him on a part-time basis until 30 Mar. 1938.

23. Memorandum by Agent J. A. Ruehle, 11 June 1940, JEK-FBI, 1:28; anonymous letter to Welles, 29 July 1940, JEK-FBI, 1:29.

24. Regin Schmidt, *Red Scare: FBI and the Origins of Anticommunism in the United States, 1919–1943* (Copenhagen: Museum Tusculanum Press, 2000), 75 (quoting Wilson from Arthur Link's collected edition), 77 (quoting Lansing from U.S. State Department papers).

25. Ibid., 85; Alexander Stephan, *"Communazis": FBI Surveillance of German Emigré Writers* (New Haven, CT: Yale Univ. Press, 2000), 14, 231, 92–93 (perversions). John Earl Haynes, *Red Scare or Red Menace? American Communism and Anticommunism in the Cold War Era* (Chicago: Ivan R. Dee, 1996), 9–10; Stone to Congress, cited in Athan Theoharis, ed., *From the Secret Files of J. Edgar Hoover* (Chicago: Ivan R. Dee, 1991), 2. It became the Federal Bureau of Investigation in 1935.

26. M. J. Heale, *American Anticommunism: Combating the Enemy Within, 1830–1970* (Baltimore: Johns Hopkins Univ. Press, 1990), 112, 120.

27. Sumner Welles, *Where Are We Heading?* (New York: Harper & Brothers, 1946), 37.

28. Richard W. Steele, "Franklin D. Roosevelt and His Foreign Policy Critics," *Political Science Quarterly* 94, no. 1 (1979): 21; Morgan, *Reds*, 214. For Murphy, see Tully, *My Boss*, 179. For an inside account of the ALB fiasco, see Whitehead, *The FBI Story*, 172–79.

29. JEK to Hull, SD-CDF, b. 6431, 852.2221/974.

30. Schmidt, *Red Scare*, 344, 349; appropriation, Whitehead, *The FBI Story*, 165; Dies, *Martin Dies' Story*, 142.

31. Mary Beth Norton et al., *A People and A Nation: A History of the United States*, 7th ed. (Boston: Houghton Mifflin, 2005), 806–7; Morgan, *Reds*, 219. For Venona, see Haynes and Klehr, *Venona*; Herbert Romerstein and Eric Breindel, *The Venona Secrets: Exposing Soviet Espionage and America's Traitors* (Lanham, MD: Regnery, 2000), 210–19. For skepticism, see Haynes and Klehr, *Venona*, 205–6.

32. "Point of a gun," from a fall 1940 newsreel, *Timeline, 1940* (Sebastopol, CA: Whirlwind Media, 2001); "Proclaiming an Unlimited National Emergency," radio address from the White House, 27 May 1941, which included, "the battle of the Atlantic now extends from the icy waters of the North Pole to the frozen continent of Antarctica"; for "popularized the term," an overview of the historiography, and a synthesis of Roosevelt's thinking, see David Reynolds, *From Munich to Pearl Harbor: Roosevelt's America and the Origins of the Second World War* (Chicago: Ivan R. Dee, 2001) 5, chaps. 1, 7; and see "Undeclared Naval War with Germany," in Ronald E. Powaski, *Toward an Entangling Alliance: American Isolationism, Internationalism, and Europe, 1901–1950* (New York: Greenwood Press, 1991), 104–6. Foreign Minister Yosuke Matsuoka told Japanese leaders on 14 Sept. that to satisfy their vision of a new Asian order they must choose to ally with either America and Britain or Germany; against opposition from the likes of Hiranuma Kiichirō, Fumimaro Konoe, and especially ambassador to Washington Nomura Kichisaburo, Matsuoka pushed for Germany. See Akira Iriye, *The Origins of the Second World War in Asia and the Pacific* (London: Longman, 1987), 115.

33. For a discussion of movies like *Confessions*, see Alpers, *Dictators*, esp. 101–2. Parachutists, in memorandum for D. M. Ladd, "re: Walter Winchell Broadcast," 9 May 1943, FBI file 62–31615, Walter Winchell, part 4c, available through the FBI's Freedom of Information Act website, http://foia.fbi.gov/foiaindex/winchell.htm (accessed 1 July 2006). In 1939 Winchell's syndicated column appeared in about 150 editions with a combined circulation of some 8.57 million copies; see, for instance, Graham J. White, *FDR and the Press* (Chicago: Univ. of Chicago Press, 1979), 30.

34. Stork Club, in O'Reilly, *Hoover and the Un-Americans*, 32; for Winchell's financial interest in the Stork Club, see George Daugherty's column on Winchell, "He Poses as Anti-Nazi, but Slanders Labor," *Daily Worker*, 11 Mar. 1941, 1, in FBI file 62–31615, Walter Winchell, part 3b; Hoover's talk as guest columnist, for release to *Detroit Evening Times*, 7 July 1939, in 62–31615, part 2e; for weekly reports, see for instance, memoranda for Ladd, "re: Walter Winchell Broadcast," by Agent W. A. Johnson, 7 and 21 June 1942 and 19 July 1942, all in FBI file 62–31615, Walter Winchell, part 3e; J. Edgar Hoover, "Crime Doesn't Pay," *On Broadway*, 26 July 1938, 62–31615, part 2a; memorandum "Re: Special Tour," D. L. Keblinger to Hoover, 6 Aug. 1940, in 62–31615, part 3b; Stephan, *Communazis*, esp. 92–93. For laboratory analysis, see, for example, transmittal of expense accounts to the Cryptographic Section for a check on "coded or hidden messages," Agent E. E. Conroy, 4 Mar. 1942, and Laboratory Report, 4 Apr. 1942, JEK-FBI, 3:119.

35. Stephen Becker, *Marshall Field III* (New York: Simon & Schuster, 1964), 160–61, 212–15. Of historiographical interest is Becker's footnote (160) that criticizes as "nonsensical" a congressional statement of 1961 to the effect that in 1936 Franco had launched a popular "uprising against Communism." Becker stated flatly that there were "no Communists in the Spanish government" (the election of Feb. 1936 brought fourteen communist deputies into the Cortes), that no Russian aid reached the Loyalists until "a year after the war broke out" (the

first Soviet freighter, *Campeche,* carrying 20,350 rifles, docked on 4 Oct. 1936), and that by contrast Franco "had Italian aid from the beginning." Franco's coup, Becker went on to stress, was "an antirepublican military revolt" and an "unmistakable prelude to Hitler's inhuman adventures." Willard L. Beaulac, *Career Ambassador* (New York: Macmillan, 1951), 189.

36. For Oumansky and for Ingersoll's visit to the Soviet Union in July 1941, see Roy Hoopes, *Ralph Ingersoll: A Biography* (New York: Atheneum, 1985), 251.

37. Winchell in ibid., 68, and see 53; memorandum from Biddle to Hoover of 31 Aug. 1942, and Hoover's reply, in 62–31615, part 4a.

38. *Daily Worker,* 11 and 12 Mar. 1941, in 62–31615, part 3b.

39. White, *FDR and the Press,* 18–19, 29–30; Richard W. Steele, *Propaganda in an Open Society: The Roosevelt Administration and the Media, 1933–1941* (Westport, CT: Greenwood Press, 1985), 142–43, 61; speechwriting, Steven Casey, *Cautious Crusade: Franklin D. Roosevelt, American Public Opinion, and the War Against Nazi Germany* (Oxford: Oxford Univ. Press, 2001), 32, 38; Morgan, *Reds,* 220; Steele, "Roosevelt and His Foreign Policy," 19, 18, 32.

40. For 1941 membership and "Americanization," see Hugh Wilford, "The Communist International and the American Communist Party," in *International Communism and the Communist International, 1919–42,* ed. Tim Rees and Andrew Thorpe (Manchester: Manchester Univ. Press, 1998), 227; "People's Party," in memorandum from Agent J. P. Hanratty to Ladd, "Re: Walter Winchell Broadcast," 6 June 1943, 62–3165, part 4d. During the war, Stalin appeared on *Time*'s front cover on 1 Jan. 1940, 27 Oct. 1941, 4 Jan. 1943, and 5 Feb. 1945.

41. René Girard, *Violence and the Sacred,* trans. Patrick Gregory (Baltimore: Johns Hopkins Univ. Press, 1977), 8, 2–3, 18, 86, 99, 100–102, 309–10.

42. JEK to Talbot, n.d.; Talbot to JEK, 4 Feb. 1941; and JEK to Talbot, 6 Feb. 1941, all in JEKP, f. 41. For Fitzgerald, see report by Agent Gust A. Koski, 13 Nov. 1941, JEK-FBI, 2:94.

43. Ryan to Talbot, 20 Jan. 1941; Talbot to Ryan, 4 Feb. 1941; and Ryan to Talbot, 11 Feb. 1941, all in JEKP, f. 41.

44. JEK, "Traveler's Reference Guide to the Provinces of Spain," draft guidebook, ca. Mar. 1941, JEKP, ff. 105–6; JEK, "Can Democracy Survive?" draft book, ca. Feb. 1941, I:A, I:J, V:I, JEKP, f. 104. JEK had actually started the reference guide project before his angina attack.

45. School on 28 Feb. 1941, JEK to Lt. Col. Luis M. Cianchini, 1 Mar. 1941, JEKP, f. 4; Welsh to Winchell, 27 Jan. 1941, JEK-FBI, 1:39; Stott, JEK-FBI, 1:42x; magnesium, JEK-FBI, 1:44; Rodyenko to Winchell, JEK-FBI, 1:38; detention, Hoover to L. M. C. Smith, 8 Apr. 1941, JEK-FBI, 1:49; discharge, War Department to JEK, 8 May 1941, JEKP, f. 4; "shouted for joy," letter from Betty Schenelzel to Winchell, 27 May 1941, JEK-FBI, 2:57.

46. Field is quoted at length in Becker, *Marshall Field,* 221; *PM,* 12 June 1941, 9–10, 16–20.

47. *PM,* 3 Nov. 1941, 5, 7, 13.

48. Ibid.

49. Ulrich Bell to Hull, 3 Nov. 1941, JEK-FBI, 11:446; for background on Fight for Freedom, see Cole, *Roosevelt and the Isolationists,* 427–28.

50. "Memorandum re Rudolf Hess," 13 May 1941, JEKP, f. 93; this was written on the same day the story broke but containing key observations not found in national newspapers. JEK's content is in "L'Affaire Hess: Our Theory," *Weekly Foreign Letter* [*WFL*] 146 (15 May 1941). Doenecke (*Storm on the Horizon,* 6) notes that Dennis was *WFL*'s sole author, yet JEK wrote ten memoranda for Dennis. JEK to Somers, 28 Dec. 1941, and "Why a Jewish Army" speech, prepared for House Representative Andrew L. Somers, 28 Dec. 1941, JEKP, f. 53; and see extension of remarks of Rep. Somers, *Congressional Record, Appendix,* 77th Cong., 2nd sess., 21 Apr. 1942, 1496–97. For Somers's strategy, see Deputy Dillon, *Dáil Éireann* 106 (20 June 1947), Committee on Finance, vote 65, 2334–35. Robert W. Allan, WPA

Newark, to JEK, 27 Nov. 1941, and Florence Herr, WPA Washington, DC, to JEK, 1 Dec. 1941, both in JEKP, f. 41.

51. Report by Agent J. M. Tennant, 2 Oct. 1941, JEK-FBI, 2:68; for details of mail cover, see JEK-FBI, 3:114. FBI agents had been monitoring JEK's telephone calls since at least Jan. 1941, see JEK-FBI, 2:94. Downer was probably referring to the American Federation Against Communism, which had about 175,000 mostly upper-middle-class members, with Allen Zoll as executive vice president; there is nothing in JEK's papers to indicate that he had any official dealings with this organization or its women's auxiliary.

52. Dossiers, from Stephan, "Communazis," 75, 88, 97, 306; Hoover to Berge, 30 Sept. 1941, and Berge to Hoover, 3 Oct. 1941, JEK-FBI, 2:69; "sweethearts," Hoover to New York bureau, 21 Oct. 1941, JEK-FBI, 2:69; "Agents of the Fascisti" was the catch-all file where FBI officials first located reports about JEK in 1938.

53. Justice Department prosecutors took three main paths: income tax evasion, mail fraud, or a specific statute, primarily FARA; tabulation of all prosecutions is beyond the scope of this study. There were thirteen FARA trials before JEK's: two of the first three were of communists, but at least eight of the subsequent trials were against German or Japanese propagandists (of the three unconfirmed, *U.S. v. Transocean News Service, et al.* and *U.S. v. Glicherie Moraru, et al.* are likely to have been Nazis); all eight were aliens, except George Sylvester Viereck (who actually had four separate trials) and Laura Ingalls. "Propaganda agent," from Winchell's broadcast, in memorandum, Agent W. A. Johnson to Ladd, 19 July 1942, in 62–31615, part 3e; Winchell commonly described Nazis as "Ratzis," "Nazzys," and "Joe McNazis," this latter term quoted from a broadcast of 22 Mar. 1942, in L. L. Laughlin to Ladd, 62–31615, part 3e; report of Agent Hart, filed 13 Feb. 1943, JEK-FBI, 5:214; correspondence between JEK and Cameron is in JEKP, f. 15. For an independent, unconnected opinion of Kimsey, see mining engineer W. E. Plank to JEK, 2 Nov. 1944: "This Kimsey is a treacherous man. His wife is just as bad"; JEKP f. 44.

54. Report of Agent Hart, filed 13 Feb. 1943, JEK-FBI, 5:214; report of Agent Gocke, 9 Mar. 1943, JEK-FBI, 5:229; letters between Cameron and JEK, in JEKP, f. 15. Cameron survived Okinawa but developed shell shock.

55. Tapping without a court order, JEK to Hayes, 10 Apr. 1943, JEKP, f. 7; George H. Knutson to JEK, 5 Feb. 1943, JEKP, f. 7; Agent R. H. Cunningham to Ladd, 13 Feb. 1943, JEK-FBI, 4:194; for examples of gifts from JEK to Cameron during 1940–42, and a poem from Cameron to JEK in 1946, see JEKP, f. 14. JEK, "Sonora: A Novel of Victorian Mexico," draft adventure novel, ca. 1944, JEKP, ff. 161–62.

56. Bernstein's response to James V. Hayes, in JEK to Talbot, 20 May 1943, JEKP, f. 8.

57. Report of Agent Peter J. Pitchess, 4 Mar. 1943, JEK-FBI, 5:221; various correspondence between JEK, Talbot, Hayes, and Wall, all in JEKP, f. 7. Legal/bond fees were $1,000 ($30,000 today). JEK had provided an additional guarantee to Hayes from his mother, who was expecting around $3,000 from the sale of her old food dehydration plant in Humboldt, TN; see JEK to Helen Kelly, 16 June 1943, JEKP, f. 9.

58. JEK to Hayes, 11 Apr. 1943, JEKP, f. 7; JEK-FBI, 7:219. For a corroborating view from inside Peninsular, see the testimony of Rosalinda Mallery de Diego Fridley to Agent John Joseph Rooney, 5 May 1943, JEKP-9:388, although Mallery, who had married a navy auditor and was clearly hostile to JEK, may have been FBI informant C-282 (see n. 66 below). For officers, capitalization, and registration information on Peninsular News Service, see James V. Hayes's notes in JEKP, f. 57.

59. Berge to Hoover, and F. L. Welch to Ladd, both 1 Apr. 1943, JEK-FBI, 5:236; Joseph Goebbels, *The Truth About Spain, by Dr. Joseph Goebbels* (N.p., ca. Nov. 1937), 24, 32; JEK to

Cárdenas, 14 Oct. 1940, and Mallery de Diego Fridley to JEK, 7 Nov. 1940, JEK-FBI, 6:237; Trial Memorandum: Re False Evidence, JEK to Hayes, ca. May 1943, JEKP, f. 8. Illogical, too, was keeping a *Christian Soldier* booklet in a safe when there were three dozen copies in one of the boxes; after the trial, JEK moved the boxes to the home of his mother in Pittsfield; from there, on Helen's death in 1956, which was two years after JEK died, they went to the roof of a barn in Lanesboro, where I later found the booklets.

60. Attorney Charles M. Carpenter to Secretary of State, 5 Dec. 1938, and Yost to Carpenter, 8 Dec. 1938, mimeographed copies, in JEKP, f. 38; Carpenter may have been the attorney for Peninsular, or perhaps Merwin Hart. Hayes's objection, *PM*, 24 May 1943, 5. See "Court Rejects Kelly Letter," *PM*, 21 May 1943, 28, and "Kelly, Goebbels Pamphlets Are Ruled Out as Evidence," *PM*, 25 May 1943, 3, clippings also in JEK-FBI, f. Sub. A. For legal aspects of FARA as it related to the JEK case, see *United States v. Kelly*, criminal no. 71560, 51 F. Supp. 362, review (Washington, DC, 3 Aug. 1943); *American Law Reports: Federal, Cases and Annotations*, vol. 67 (Rochester, NY: Lawyers Co-Operative, 1984), 774–96, esp. 787; Michael I. Spak, "America For Sale: When Well-Connected Former Federal Officials Peddle Their Influence to the Highest Foreign Bidder—A Statutory Analysis and Proposals for Reform of the Foreign Agents Registration Act and the Ethics in Government Act," *Kentucky Law Journal* 78, no. 2 (1990): 242–55, esp. 250; Brian C. Costello, "The Voice of Government as an Abridgement of First Amendment Rights of Speakers: Rethinking *Meese v. Keene*," *Duke Law Journal* 654 (1989): 654–58; Burt Neuborne and Steven R. Shapiro, "The Nylon Curtain: America's National Border and the Free Flow of Ideas," *William and Mary Law Review* 26, no. 719 (1985): 719–38, esp. 736. For the act as publicized, see Department of State press release, 6 Sept. 1938, "Rules and Regulations Governing the Registration of Agents of Foreign Principles Under the Act of Congress Approved June 8, 1938," in FXTP, b. 38, f. 3.

61. Content analysis data, from *PM*, 19 May 1943, 4. For examples of Childs's vision of the future, see Harwood L. Childs, ed., *Propaganda and Dictatorship* (Princeton, NJ: Princeton Univ. Press, 1936), and "Public Opinion and Peace," *Annals of the American Academy* 192 (1937): 31–37. Later in 1943, Harold D. Lasswell analyzed William Dudley Pelley's *Galilean* for statements consistent with or contradictory of Nazi propaganda themes; his coders found 1,195 consistent statements against only forty-five contradictory ones (reliability among coders, 99 percent), allowing prosecutors to successfully convict Pelley; two of the statements deemed consistent were: "England has held us up to ridicule and contempt. She has sought to smash the sovereignty of America on three occasions"; and Roosevelt, "at any time within the past year [1941], might easily, by the turn of a phrase or the erasure of a word, have prevented the attack on Pearl Harbor." Lasswell, "Propaganda Detection and the Courts," in *Language of Politics: Studies in Quantitative Semantics*, ed. Harold D. Lasswell (Cambridge, MA: MIT Press, 1949), 181–82, 189, and 393n. For coders Janowitz, Janis, and Drake, see JEK to Talbot, 19 May 1943, JEKP, f. 8.

62. Decliners, JEK to Talbot, 27 May 1943, JEKP, f. 8; "wean," phone message for Talbot, 4 Aug. 1943, FXTP, b. 38, f. 12; "friendship," Talbot to Joseph Scott, 14 June 1943, FXTP, b. 38, f. 12. Hayes's list of jurors is in JEKP, f. 8, and juror profiles are in JEK-FBI, 11: Prospective Jurors; juror no. 8, Alger Lee Irvin, from Woodstock, VA, did not attend a church; juror no. 9, Thomas Joseph Mulliken, was an Irish American but did not attend church; juror no. 11, Mrs. Bernice MacHugh Lawrenson, was a homemaker whose husband worked for the civil service; juror no. 12, Mrs. Anna Wise Lee, had just applied for a position as a government clerk.

63. Agent J. P. Hanratty to Ladd, "Re: Walter Winchell Broadcast," 6 June 1943, 62–3165, part 4d.; tantalizingly, FBI declassification censors blacked out the paragraph following this concluding wording by Hanratty: "When Mr. Winchell remarked that the evidence

brought out at the trial showed that Kelly had several associates in this work." "Duped Us," *PM,* 19 May 1943, 4; report by F. L. Welch to Ladd, 14 May 1943, JEK-FBI, 11:446; in an earlier interview, Scott stated that he had arranged for JEK to lecture and show *Spain in Arms* at Notre Dame College, Euclid, OH; see JEK-FBI, 7:293.

64. Talbot to Scott, 14 June 1943, FXTP, b. 38, f. 12; JEK to Helen outlining his plea-bargain theory, 16 June 1943, JEKP, f. 9. Luckily, Helen had just found a buyer for the old food dehydrating plant in Tennessee, so she could pay Hayes without selling her house. Helen to Talbot, 25 June 1943, FXTP, b. 38, f. 12. I am presuming that at least one of the two Irish American jurors was pro-Franco; judging from the detailed juror profiles, it is highly improbable that any of the other jurors were pro-Franco, and several would have been vociferously pro-Loyalist.

65. Motion to Set Aside Verdict, and "Motion for New Trial," 7 June 1943, both in JEKP, f. 9; report by Agent Logan J. Lane, 6 Oct. 1943, JEK-FBI, 11:484x1. Helen to JEK, 14 June 1943, and JEK to Helen, 16 June 1943, both in JEKP, f. 9; also see Helen to Talbot, 3 June 1943, FXTP, b. 38, f. 12.

66. Report by Agent Logan J. Lane, 6 Oct. 1943, JEK-FBI, 11:484x1. C-282 may have been Rosalinda Mallery de Diego Fridley, who had recently married a navy auditor temporarily stationed in Montauk, NY, and was hostile to JEK; Mallery had left the library in Mar. or Apr. 1943 to have a baby, but the FBI may have paid her to move to Washington to continue her informant role inside the Spanish embassy.

67. JEK, "Petroleum Policy Needed," *NYT,* 24 Sept. 1943, 22; JEK, "The Marshall Plan Without Spain," *Sign* 27, no. 8 (1948): 36–37; there are more than four thousand uncollated clippings in the JEKP; already collated are ninety-six on Spain, from 1943 to 1953, in JEKP, f. 122. It is probable, too, that he tried to keep clear of the FBI's dragnet during the mass sedition trial of 1944, which snared Lawrence Dennis for whom he had written memoranda on U.S. and German foreign policy; reports in JEK-FBI, 11:489–93 indicate that agents were still interviewing witnesses in connection with JEK in early 1944; the last correspondence in JEK's FBI file is dated 13 Dec. 1945. For Dennis's view, see Maximilian J. St.-George and Lawrence Dennis, *A Trial on Trial: The Great Sedition Trial of 1944* (N.p: National Civil Rights Committee, 1945).

68. JEK, "Keeping Gold Price Officially Low Retards Recovery: U.S. Could Raise Quotation to Free-Market Value and Help World Trade," *Barron's* 27, no. 29 (1947): 7; and editor, "Readers Oppose Lifting Gold's 'OPA Ceiling,'" ibid. no. 31 (1947): 7. For a reference to Celia Cameron's treatment for tuberculosis, see, for instance, JEK-FBI, 7:293.

69. See John Cooney, *The American Pope: The Life and Times of Francis Cardinal Spellman* (New York: Times Books, 1984), 125–26; Program of the Twenty-Fifth New England Conference, 17–18 Nov. 1949, JEKP, f. 79; *Boston Globe,* 18 Nov. 1949, 30; *NYT,* 19 Nov. 1949, 3; draft speech, JEKP, f. 70.

70. JEK to the editor, *NYT,* 24 Jan. 1954, SM4; C. L. R. James, *The Black Jacobins: Toussaint L'Ouverture and the San Domingo Revolution* (1938; repr., New York: Vintage Books, 1989); obituary in *Washington Post,* 20 June 1954, M12; attorney William Boraski to Fred H. Bergman in Illinois, 28 July 1955, stating that JEK died of a heart attack in Washington on 18 June 1954, JEKP, f. 1.

Conclusion

1. For the controversy over Shuster's "Some Reflections on Spain," see Rodger Van Allen, *The* Commonweal *and American Catholicism: The Magazine, the Movement, the Meaning* (Philadelphia: Fortress Press, 1974), 60–66. For the *Catholic Worker* and other publications, see Valaik, "American Catholic Dissenters."

2. Patrick J. Maney, *"Young Bob" La Follette: A Biography of Robert M. La Follette Jr., 1895–1953* (Columbia: Univ. of Missouri Press, 1978), 228.

3. Franco's brother Ramón was one of many officers who celebrated. See Preston, *Franco,* 79.

4. Denning, *The Cultural Front,* xviii, 4. For Harlem communists' disgust that Soviet delegate to the League of Nations Maxim Litvinov had sold out the Ethiopian cause, and their split with the CPUSA, see William R. Scott, *The Sons of Sheba's Race: African-Americans and the Italo-Ethiopian War, 1935–1941* (Bloomington: Indiana Univ. Press, 1993), 124–25. During his keynote speech to the National Council of American-Soviet Friendship at Madison Square Garden on 8 Nov. 1943, Ickes mused rhetorically, "We do not like communism? Well, the Russians do not like capitalism. Communism has faults? Capitalism has plenty of them too. We had better not start this kind of an argument, or somebody will be sure to say something about the pot and the kettle." *NYT,* 9 Nov. 1943, 5. I have not yet been able to locate a transcript of Ickes's entire speech, so while he was certainly fulsome in his praise for the Soviet Union and its "great" leader Stalin, it may be apocryphal—but nevertheless in character—that he also said, "In certain respects we could do well to learn from Russia: yes, even to imitate Russia."

5. JEK's typed copy of Allen's telegram, 21 July, and JEK to Talbot, 25 July 1938, FXTP, box 22, folder 37. For Allen and Badajoz, see chap. 1, n. 49 above.

6. For Hart, see, for instance, "Who Backs Merwin K. Hart," *The Facts* (ca. Oct. 1950), and "Merwin K. Hart and the National Economic Council," ca. Dec. 1952, f. National Economic Council, Merwin K. Hart Material, Blaustein Library, American Jewish Committee, New York. Genevieve St. George, a close friend of Louise Dunn since high school, interview with author, 26 July 2006, Cambridge, MA.

7. George Seldes, *Lords of the Press* (New York: Blue Ribbon Books, 1941), 321; Carlson, *Under Cover,* 457, 468, 458. Lester M. Gray, Edward Lodge Curran, Patrick F. Scanlon, Catherine P. Baldwin, Frank W. Clark, Joseph P. Kamp, and Robert Caldwell Patton were never AUNS committee members. Richard Gid Powers, *Not Without Honor: The History of American Anticommunism* (New York: Free Press, 1995), 134–35, 166, 167.

8. Ernest Hemingway, *For Whom the Bell Tolls* (New York: Scribner's, 1940); *For Whom the Bell Tolls,* dir. Sam Wood (Los Angeles: Universal Studios, 1943), 166 min.

9. Memorandum from Welles to Roosevelt, 19 July 1939, Franklin D. Roosevelt, Papers as President, President's Secretary's File, 1933–45, b. 50, f. Spain, 1939. Even with Franco's declaration of nonbelligerence on 12 June 1940, Hitler almost implemented his plan to send the Wehrmacht through Spain in Jan. 1941 to take Gibraltar, holding off in part because of distractions such as Italian problems with their North African campaign and in part because Franco "dug in his heels," as Payne puts it in *Franco and Hitler,* 103. Had Franco's neutrality leaned toward the Allies, Hitler may well have arranged his ouster or elimination in favor of, say, Ramón Serrano Suñer and/or dispatched the Wehrmacht regardless. While Britain's safest supply route for its 8th Army was via Capetown and the Suez Canal, Operation Torch would have been tenuous were supply lines to have extended all the way back to French Morocco. Moreover, interdiction of the Straits by British artillery on Gibraltar hampered U-boat movement and Axis logistics.

Bibliography

Archival Sources and Unpublished Documents

American Legion. National Convention Proceedings. American Legion Library, Indianapolis, IN.

Biddle, Francis. Papers, 1912–67. Franklin D. Roosevelt Library, Hyde Park, NY.

Cárdenas, Juan F. de. Correspondence. *America* Magazine Archive. Lauinger Library Special Collections, Georgetown University, Washington, DC.

Christian Front. Material. Blaustein Library, American Jewish Committee, New York.

Dunn, Louise Meière. Private collection. Stamford, CT.

Fischer, Louis. Papers, 1938–49. Franklin D. Roosevelt Library, Hyde Park, NY.

Forbes, William Cameron. Papers (WCFP). Houghton Library, Harvard College, Cambridge, MA.

Hart, Merwin K. Papers (MKHP). Knight Library Special Collections, University of Oregon, Eugene.

———. Material. Blaustein Library, American Jewish Committee, New York.

Hopkins, Harry L. Papers, 1928–46. Franklin D. Roosevelt Library, Hyde Park.

Kelly, John Eoghan. Papers (JEKP). Author's collection, Charlestown, MA. (A photocopied set of the core collection [folders 1–99] is on deposit at the John J. Burns Library, Boston College, Chestnut Hill, MA)

———. Federal Bureau of Investigation, file 65–1461 (JEK-FBI). National Archives, College Park, MD. (Photocopied set in JEKP)

Kelly, John Forrest. Papers (JFKP). Author's collection, Charlestown, MA.

La Guardia, Fiorello. Papers. Municipal Archives of New York City, New York.

Lash, Joseph. Papers, 1934–78. Franklin D. Roosevelt Library, Hyde Park, NY.

Lunn, Sir Arnold. Papers. Lauinger Library Special Collections, Georgetown University, Washington, DC.

Mathis, Michael A. Papers. Theodore Hesburgh Collection, University of Notre Dame, Notre Dame, IN.

Meière, Hildreth. Papers (HMP). Archives of American Art, Smithsonian Institution, New York.

Moffat, J. Pierrepont. Diary. Houghton Library, Harvard College, Cambridge, MA.

Morgenthau, Henry, Jr. Papers, 1866–1960. Franklin D. Roosevelt Library, Hyde Park, NY.

O'Reilly, Leonora. Papers. Microfilm edition of Papers of the Women's Trade Union League and Its Principal Leaders. Schlesinger Library, Radcliffe College, Cambridge, MA.

Pell, Herbert Claiborne. Papers, 1905–63. Franklin D. Roosevelt Library, Hyde Park, NY.

Roosevelt, Eleanor. Papers, 1884–1964. Franklin D. Roosevelt Library, Hyde Park, NY.

Roosevelt, Franklin D. Papers, 1882–1945. Franklin D. Roosevelt Library, Hyde Park, NY.

Sedgwick, Ellery. Papers (ESP). Massachusetts Historical Society, Boston.

Shipman, Fred W. "Report on the White House Executive Office." Franklin D. Roosevelt Library, Hyde Park, NY.

State Department. General Records, Central Decimal File, 1930–39, Record Group 59 (SD-CDF). National Archives, College Park, MD.

Talbot, Francis X. Papers (FXTP). Lauinger Library Special Collections, Georgetown University, Washington, DC.

Walsh, David I. Papers. College of the Holy Cross, Worcester, MA.

Welles, Sumner. Papers, 1918–50. Franklin D. Roosevelt Library, Hyde Park.

Winchell, Walter. Federal Bureau of Investigation, file 62–31615. Http://foia.fbi.gov/foiaindex/winchell.htm.

Published Documents and Reports

American Direct Investments in Foreign Countries–1936. Ed. Paul D. Dickens. U.S. Department of Commerce, Bureau of Foreign and Domestic Commerce. Washington, DC: GPO, 1938.

American Direct Investments in Foreign Countries–1940. Ed. Robert L. Sammons and Milton Abelson. U.S. Department of Commerce, Bureau of Foreign and Domestic Commerce. Washington, DC: GPO, 1942.

Atheistic Communism (Divini Redemptoris): *Encyclical Letter of His Holiness Pope Pius XI.* New York: Paulist Press, 1937.

Complete Presidential Press Conferences of Franklin D. Roosevelt. 25 vols. New York: Da Capo Press, 1972.

Confidential U.S. State Department Central Files: Spain; Foreign Affairs and Political, 1930–1939. Bethesda, MD: University Publications of America. Microfilm.

Congressional Record: Proceedings and Debates of the Third Session of the Seventy-fifth Congress of the United States of America. Vol. 83, pt. 6. Washington, DC: GPO, 1938.

Congressional Record: Appendix to the Second Session of the Seventy-seventh Congress of the United States of America. Washington, DC: GPO, 1942.

Documents on American Foreign Relations, January 1938–June 1939. Ed. S. Shepard Jones and Denys P. Myers. Boston: World Peace Foundation, 1939.

Documents diplomatiques français, 1932–1939. Series 2 (1936–39), 19 vols. Paris: Imprimerie nationale, 1974.

FDR's Fireside Chats. Ed. Russell D. Buhite and David W. Levy. Norman: University of Oklahoma Press, 1992.

Forbes, William Cameron. *Report of the President's Commission for the Study and Review of Conditions in the Republic of Haiti, March 26, 1930.* Washington, DC: GPO, 1930.

Franklin D. Roosevelt and Foreign Affairs. Ed. Edgar B. Nixon. 1st series, vols. 1–3. Cambridge, MA: Belknap Press, 1969.

Franklin D. Roosevelt and Foreign Affairs: Second Series, January 1937–August 1939. Ed. Donald B. Schewe. Vols. 4–17. New York: Clearwater, 1969.

Gallup, George H. *The Gallup Poll: Public Opinion, 1935–1971.* New York: Random House, 1972.

Germany and the Spanish Civil War, 1936–1939. Vol. 3, *Documents on German Foreign Policy, 1918–1945: From the Archives of the German Foreign Ministry: Series D (1937–1945).* Washington, DC: GPO, 1950.

Investigation of Un-American Activities and Propaganda Activities in the United States: Report of the Special Committee on Un-American Activities. 4 vols. Washington, DC: GPO, 1938–39.

Investigation of Un-American Propaganda Activities in the United States. Hearings Before a Special Committee on Un-American Activities: House of Representatives. 16 vols. Washington, DC: GPO, 1938–39.

The Official Catholic Directory. New York: P. J. Kenedy & Sons, 1937.

Papers Relating to the Foreign Relations of the United States: Japan, 1931–1941. Vol. 1. Washington, DC: GPO, 1943.

The Papers of Thomas Jefferson. Ed. Barbara B. Oberg. Vol. 32. Princeton, NJ: Princeton University Press, 2005.

The Portable Thomas Jefferson. Ed. Merrill D. Peterson. New York: Viking Press, 1975.

Proceedings of the 20th Annual National Convention of the American Legion, Los Angeles. Indianapolis, IN: American Legion, 1938.

Proceedings of the 20th National Convention of the American Legion, Los Angeles, CA, 19–22 September 1938. 76th Cong., 1st sess., House Doc. no. 40, 53.

Public Papers and Addresses of Franklin D. Roosevelt: With a Special Introduction and Explanatory Notes by President Roosevelt. 1938 vol., *The Continuing Struggle for Liberalism.* New York: Macmillan, 1941.

Reports to the Twentieth Annual National Convention of the American Legion, Los Angeles, Calif., September 19, 20, 21, 22, 1938. Indianapolis, IN: American Legion, 1938.

United States Foreign Policy (Supplement). Ed. Julia E. Johnson. New York: H. W. Wilson, 1939.

Newspapers and Magazines

Periodicals are for the period of this study, unless otherwise stated.

DAILY NEWSPAPERS

Baltimore Sun 1938
Boston Daily/Evening Globe
Boston Herald
Brookline Citizen (Brookline, MA) 1938–39
Brooklyn Eagle (Brooklyn, NY) 1938–39
Chicago Daily Tribune
Jersey Journal (Jersey City, NJ) 1937–38
Los Angeles Examiner 1938–39
Los Angeles Times
Louisville Courier-Journal
New Orleans States 1938
New York Daily News 1938
New York Herald Tribune
New York Post

New York Times
New York World-Telegram 1938
Philadelphia Inquirer 1938–39
PM (New York) June 1940–43
Washington Post/Times-Herald

WEEKLY NEWSPAPERS AND MAGAZINES

America: The National Catholic Weekly
American Hebrew and Jewish Tribune (New York) 1933
Appeal to Reason (Becket, MA) 1946
Brooklyn Tablet (Brooklyn, NY)
Commonweal: A Weekly Review of Literature, The Arts and Public Affairs (New York)
Economic Council Letter (New York)
The Freeman, Inc. (New York)
The Hour (New York) 30 April 1939–20 May 1943
In Fact (New York) 1940–43
Ken (Chicago) April 1938–March 1939
Liberty (New York) 1937–39
Life November 1936–39
The Nation (New York) 1935–38
New Masses (New York) 1936–37
New Republic (Washington, DC)
News of Spain (New York) February 1938–February 1939
Social Justice (Royal Oak, MI) 1936–39
Time: The Weekly Newsmagazine November 1936–39
Weekly Foreign Letter (New York) June 1938–July 1942

MONTHLY MAGAZINES AND JOURNALS

Atlantic Monthly (Boston) 1936–39
Catholic Action: A National Monthly (Washington, DC)
Catholic Digest: Of Catholic Books and Magazines (St. Paul, MN)
Catholic Mind (New York)
Catholic Worker (New York)
Catholic World (New York)
Esquire
For Men Only 1937
The Lamp (New York) 1936–41
Modern Monthly (New York) 1936–38
Patriot Digest (Philadelphia, PA)
Protestant Digest (New York) December 1938–September 1941
The Sign (Union City, NJ) 1936–41
Spain: A Monthly Publication of Spanish Events (New York) October 1937–January 1942
Wisdom: The Catholic Front (New York) March 1938–September 1939

Films

Blockade. Dir. William Dieterle. Prod. Walter Wanger. Script. John Howard Lawson. Starring Madeleine Carroll and Henry Fonda. United Artists, 1938. DVD, 84 min. Chatsworth, CA: Image Entertainment, 1987.

Confessions of a Nazi Spy. Dir. Anatole Litvak. Prod. Hal B. Wallis, Jack L. Warner, and Robert Lord. Script John Wexley. Starring Edward G. Robinson, Francis Lederer, and Paul Lukas. Warner Brothers, 1939. DVD, remastered 102 min. Burbank, CA: Warner Archive, 2009.

For Whom the Bell Tolls. Dir. Sam Wood. Adapted from a novel by Ernest Hemingway. Starring Gary Cooper and Ingrid Bergman. Paramount Pictures, 1943. DVD, 166 min. Los Angeles: Universal Studios, 1998.

My Tour of Nationalist Spain, August 1938, by Hildreth Meière. By Hildreth Meière. 16 mm, 3 reels. New York: Archives of American Art, Smithsonian Institution. DVD, 33 min.

Spain in Arms. 35 mm, 90 min. English soundtrack. 1939. Reels 2A (summer 1936, first half of reel III, soundtrack mismatched, 4:24 min.), 3B (Málaga, first half and last quarter of reel VI, 4:12 min.), 5 (University City, Madrid, reel V, 7:00 min.), 7 (Navarre, reel VII, 5:40 min.), and 8 (Teruel, reel VIII, 7:40 min.). NARA 060811, 233 HUAC, Motion Picture, Sound, and Video Records LICON, Special Media Archives Services Division (NWCS-M), National Archives at College Park, MD. DVD, 29:21 min. Author's collection.

The Spanish Earth. Dir. Joris Ivens. Narrated Ernest Hemingway. Contemporary Historians, Inc., 1937. Sherman Oaks, CA: SlingShot Entertainment, Inc., 2000. DVD, 52 min.

Timeline 1937. Sebastopol, CA: Whirlwind Media, Inc., 2000.

Memoirs, Diaries, Contemporary Works

Acheson, Dean G. *Present at the Creation: My Years in the State Department.* New York: W. W. Norton, 1969.

[Adams, John.] *Diary and Autobiography of John Adams.* Ed. L. H. Butterfield. Vol. 2. Cambridge, MA: Belknap Press, 1962.

Allen, Frederick Lewis. *Since Yesterday: The 1930s in America, September 3, 1929–September 3, 1939.* 1939. New York: Harper & Row, 1986.

Atholl, Katherine, Duchess of. *Searchlight on Spain.* Harmondsworth, UK: Penguin Books, 1938.

Beaulac, Willard L. *Career Ambassador.* New York: Macmillan, 1951.

Bendiner, Robert. *The Riddle of the State Department.* New York: Farrar & Rinehart, 1942.

Blanshard, Paul. *God and Man in Washington.* Boston: Beacon Press, 1960.

Bogardus, Emory S. *The Essentials of Americanization.* Los Angeles: University of Southern California Press, 1919.

Bolín, Luis. *Spain: The Vital Years.* Philadelphia: J. B. Lippincott, 1967.

Bowers, Claude G. *My Mission to Spain: Watching the Rehearsal for WWII.* New York: Simon & Schuster, 1954.

Browder, Earl. "The American Communist Party in the Thirties." In *As We Saw the Thirties: Essays on Social and Political Movements of a Decade.* Ed. Rita James Simon. Urbana: University of Illinois Press, 1967.

Carlson, John Roy [(Arthur) Avedis Derounian]. *Under Cover: My Four Years in the Nazi Underworld of America—The Amazing Revelation of How Axis Agents and Our Enemies Within Are Now Plotting to Destroy the United States.* New York: E. P. Dutton, 1943.

————. *The Plotters.* New York: E. P. Dutton, 1946.

Chaillaux, Homer L. *Isms: A Review of Alien Isms, Revolutionary Communism, and Their Active Sympathizers in the U.S.* 2nd ed. Indianapolis, IN: American Legion, 1937.

Colvin, Ian D. "The Case for Franco." *Atlantic Monthly* 161, no. 3 (1938): 397–402.

Coughlin, Charles E. *A Series of Addresses on Social Justice, as Broadcast by Rev. Charles E. Coughlin over a National Network, March 1935.* Royal Oak, MI: Radio League of the Little Flower, 1935.

Dalton, Joseph Patrick. "Is Christian Corporatism Compatible with Democracy?" Master's thesis, Boston College, 1942.

de Wolfe, Elsie. *After All.* New York: Harper & Brothers, 1935.

Dies, Martin. *Martin Dies' Story.* New York: Bookmailer, 1963.

Dilling, Elizabeth Kirkpatrick. *The Octopus.* 1940. Metairie, LA: Sons of Liberty, 1986.

Duval, Gen. Maurice. *Lessons of the War in Spain.* Trans. John Eoghan Kelly. Ed. Michael E. Chapman. Reading, MA: Trebarwyth Press, 2006.

Eberle, George T. "Portugal's Progress." *Catholic Mind* 36, no. 854 (1938): 282–87.

Feige, Gregory. "Anti-Semitism." *Wisdom: The Catholic Front* 4, no. 1 (1939).

Fischer, Louis. In *The God That Failed.* Ed. Richard Crossman. New York: Columbia University Press, 2001.

Follett, Wilson. "Letter to a Communist Friend." *Atlantic Monthly* 162, no. 4 (1938): 460–69.

Forbes, William Cameron. *As to Polo.* Boston: Dedham Country and Polo Club, 1911.

————. *The Philippine Islands.* 2 vols. Boston: Houghton Mifflin, 1928.

————. *Present Conditions in Spain, 1938.* Speech, delivered before the University Club, Baltimore, MD, 23 February 1938. Baltimore: Baltimore University Club, 1938.

Goebbels, Joseph. *The Truth About Spain, by Dr. Joseph Goebbels.* N.p: ca. November 1937.

Gomá y Tomás, Cardinal Isidro. *Por Dios y por España: Pastorales—Instrucciones pastorales y Artículos—Discursos—Mensajes—Apéndice, 1936–1939.* Barcelona: R. Casulleras, Librero-Editor, 1940.

González Palencia, Angel. *The Flame of Hispanicism.* New York: Peninsular News Service, 1938.

Gras, Felix. *The Reds of the Midi: An Episode of the French Revolution.* New York: D. Appleton, 1897.

Groves, Hubert Beckwith. *Americanism.* Portland, OR: Boyer Printing and Advertising, 1923.

Hart, Merwin Kimball. "America—Look at Spain: The Agony Will Be Repeated Here." *Spain* 3, no. 1 (1938): 5, 7, 20; *Vital Speeches of the Day* 5, no. 2 (1938): 57–58.

————. *America, Look at Spain!* New York: P. J. Kenedy & Sons, 1939.

Hemingway, Ernest. *For Whom the Bell Tolls.* New York: Scribner's, 1940.

Hernaman, Irene. "Portugal's Corporative State." *Catholic Mind* 36, no. 843 (1938): 52–55.

Hull, Cordell. *The Memoirs of Cordell Hull.* 2 vols. New York: Macmillan, 1948.

Ibárruri, Dolores. *They Shall Not Pass: The Autobiography of La Pasionaria.* New York: International, 1966.

Ickes, Harold L. *The Inside Struggle, 1936–1939.* Vol. 2, *The Secret Diary of Harold L. Ickes.* New York: Simon & Schuster, 1954.

————. *The Lowering Clouds, 1939–1941.* Vol. 3, *The Secret Diary of Harold L. Ickes.* New York: Simon & Schuster, 1955.

Ivens, Joris. *The Camera and I.* New York: International, 1969.

James, C. L. R. *The Black Jacobins: Toussaint L'Ouverture and the San Domingo Revolution.* 1938. New York: Vintage Books, 1989.

[Johnson, Hiram.] *The Diary Letters of Hiram Johnson, 1917–1945*. Ed. Robert E. Burke. 7 vols. New York: Garland, 1983.

Kelly, John Eoghan. "The White Reaction in Ireland." *The Nation* 115, no. 2978 (1922): 118–20.

———. *Pedro de Alvarado, Conquistador*. 1932. Port Washington, NY: Kennikat Press, 1971.

———. "Foresworn Americans Serve Red Cause in Spain." *America* 57, no. 29 (1937): 55–56.

———. *The Christian Soldier*. Brookline, MA: Mrs. Herbert N. Dawes, 1938.

———. "Free Speech in Jersey City: A Defense of Mayor Hague." *Wisdom: The Catholic Front* 3, no. 3 (1938): 1, 6.

———. "The Right Side: Spain." *Wisdom: The Catholic Front* 3, no. 4 (1938): 1, 3.

———. "His Excellency the Spanish Ambassador." *America* 59, no. 9 (1938): 197–98.

———. "Should Relief Vote?" *Patriot Digest* 1, no. 1 (1938): 3–7.

———. "The Right Side: "Titled Reds [Duchess of Atholl Raises Money for Red Spain]." *Wisdom: The Catholic Front* 3, no. 11 (1938): 1, 6.

———. "Little Red Schoolboys." *America* 60, no. 15 (1939): 344–45.

———. "The Right Side: [Liberal 'Tolerance']." *Wisdom: The Catholic Front* 4, no. 4 (1939): 1, 6.

———. *A Programme for American Nationalism*. N.p.: N.p., 1940. [Mimeographed pamphlet, the last known copy of which is missing at Yale University's Sterling Memorial Library.]

———. "North Africa and Arab Asia Are Needed to Win the War." *America* 65, no. 4 (1941): 89–90.

———. "Keeping Gold Price Officially Low Retards Recovery: U.S. Could Raise Quotation to Free-Market Value and Help World Trade." *Barron's* 27, no. 29 (1947): 7.

———. "The Marshall Plan Without Spain." *Sign* 27, no. 8 (1948): 36–37.

———. "Sandy McGrew's War." *Zane Grey's Western Magazine* 5, no. 7 (1951): 119–32.

Knoblaugh, H. Edward. *Correspondent in Spain*. London: Sheed & Ward, 1937.

Krock, Arthur. *Memoirs: Sixty Years on the Firing Line*. New York: Funk & Wagnalls, 1968.

Lamb, Dean Ivan [and John Eoghan Kelly]. *The Incurable Filibuster: Adventures of Col. Dean Ivan Lamb*. New York: Farrar & Rinehart, 1934.

Langdon-Davies, John. "The Case for the Government." *Atlantic Monthly* 161, no. 3 (1938): 403–8.

Lash, Joseph P. *Love, Eleanor: Eleanor Roosevelt and Her Friends*. Garden City, NY: Doubleday, 1982.

Lewis, Joseph. *Spain: A Land Blighted by Religion*. 1933. New York: Freethought Press Association, 1936.

Lippmann, Walter. *An Inquiry into the Principles of the Good Society*. Boston: Little, Brown, 1937.

A Little Book for Immigrants in Boston. Boston: Committee for Americanism of the City of Boston, 1921.

Lunn, Arnold H. M. *Spain and the Christian Front: Ubi Crux Ibi Patria*. New York: Paulist Press, 1937.

———. *Spanish Rehearsal: An Eyewitness in Spain During the Civil War, 1936–1939*. 1937. Old Greenwich, CT: Devin-Adair, 1974.

Marbury, Elisabeth. *My Crystal Ball: Reminiscences*. London: Hurst & Blackett, 1924.

Massis, Henri, and Robert Brasillach. *The Cadets of the Alcazar*. Foreword Francis X. Talbot. New York: Paulist Press, 1937.

McCarthy, Mary. *Intellectual Memoirs: New York 1936–1938*. New York: Harcourt Brace Jovanovich, 1992.

McFadden, Charles J. *The Philosophy of Communism*. New York: Benziger Brothers, 1939.

McNeill-Moss, Geoffrey. *The Siege of Alcazar: A History of the Siege of the Toledo Alcazar, 1936.* New York: Knopf, 1937.

Meière, Hildreth. "Working for a World's Fair." *Journal of the Associated Alumnae of the Sacred Heart* 4 (1939–40): 35–41.

[Morgenthau, Henry, Jr.] *From the Morgenthau Diaries: Years of Crisis, 1928–1938.* Comp. John Morton Blum. Boston: Houghton Mifflin, 1959.

———. *From the Morgenthau Diaries: Years of Urgency, 1938–1941.* Comp. John Morton Blum. Boston: Houghton Mifflin, 1965.

[Moseley, George Van Horn.] *Major-General George Van Horn Moseley: American Patriot.* Ed. N. W. Rogers. N.p., 1940.

Murphy, Robert. *Diplomat Among Warriors.* Garden City, NY: Doubleday, 1964.

New Spain: Its People, Its Ruler. New York: America Press, 1939.

Nock, Albert Jay. *Memoirs of a Superfluous Man.* New York: Harper & Brothers, 1943.

———. *Our Enemy the State.* Caldwell, ID: Caxton Printers, 1950.

Rolfe, Edwin. *The Lincoln Battalion: The Story of Americans Who Fought in Spain in the International Brigades.* New York: Random House, 1939.

Roosevelt, Eleanor. *This I Remember.* New York: Harper & Brothers, 1949.

Sayers, Michael, and Albert Eugene Kahn. *Sabotage! The Secret War Against America.* New York: Harper Brothers, 1942.

Sedgwick, Ellery. *Thomas Paine.* Boston: Small, Maynard, 1899.

———. "The Fan and the Sword." *Atlantic Monthly* 158, no. 2 (1936): 129–38.

———. "On Franco's Side in Spain." *Reader's Digest* 32, no. 193 (1938): 27–29.

———. "The Patron Saint of Andalusia: Being an Honest Recital of the Incredible." *Atlantic Monthly* 161, no. 6 (1938): 777–84.

———. *The Happy Profession.* Boston: Little, Brown, 1946.

Seldes, George. *Lords of the Press.* New York: Blue Ribbon Books, 1941.

Sokolsky, George E. *Labor's Fight for Power.* 1932. Port Washington, NY: Kennikat Press, 1971.

Souvenir Book, Third Annual Convention, American Legion of Kentucky, September 1 and 2, 1921. Ed. Ulrich Bell. Lexington, KY: American Legion, 1921.

Spivak, John Louis. *Secret Armies: The New Technique of Nazi Warfare.* New York: Modern Age Books, 1939.

St.-George, Maximilian J., and Lawrence Dennis. *A Trial on Trial: The Great Sedition Trial of 1944.* N.p: National Civil Rights Committee, 1945.

Talbot, Francis X. *Saint Among Savages: The Life of Isaac Jogues.* New York: Harper & Brothers, 1935.

———. "The Attitude of Organized Religion Toward Government." *The Catholic Mind* 36, no. 850 (1938): 189–97.

———. *Saint Among the Hurons: The Life of Jean de Brébeuf.* New York: Harper, 1949.

Talbot, Winthrop, ed. *Americanization: Principles of Americanism; Essentials of Americanization; Technic* [sic] *of Race-Assimilation.* 2nd rev. ed. New York: H. W. Wilson, 1920.

Tellechea, Joaquín. *La verdad sobre España.* Buenos Aires: Editorial Tor, 1937.

Tully, Grace G. *FDR: My Boss.* New York: Scribner's, 1949.

Turrou, Leon G. *The Nazi Spy Conspiracy in America.* London: George G. Harrap, 1939.

Vishnewski, Stanley. *Wings of the Dawn.* New York: Catholic Worker, 1984.

Webster, Daniel. *An Address Delivered at the Laying of the Corner Stone of the Bunker Hill Monument, June 17, 1825.* Boston: Tappan & Dennet, 1843.

———. *An Address Delivered at the Completion of the Bunker Hill Monument, June 17, 1843.* Boston: Tappan & Dennet, 1843.

Welles, Sumner. *The Time for Decision.* New York: Harper & Brothers, 1944.

————. *Where Are We Heading?* New York: Harper & Brothers, 1946.

Whitehead, Don. *The FBI Story: A Report to the People.* New York: Random House, 1956.

Wilson, Arnold T. *Loyalties: Mesopotamia, 1914–1917, a Personal and Historical Record.* 1930. New York: Greenwood Press, 1969.

————. *More Thoughts and Talks: The Diary and Scrap-Book of a Member of Parliament, from September 1937 to August 1939.* London: Longmans, Green, 1939.

Wodehouse, P. G. *The Code of the Woosters.* 1938. Mattituck, NY: Rivercity Press, 1976.

Writers Take Sides: Letters About the War in Spain, from 418 American Authors. New York: League of American Writers, 1938.

Zangwill, Israel. *The Melting-Pot: Drama in Four Acts.* New York: Macmillan, 1911.

Secondary Sources: Books, Journal Articles, Dissertations

ABC Blue Book, Publishers' Statements: Newspapers. Chicago: The Bureau, 1945.

Adams, Henry H. *Harry Hopkins: A Biography.* New York: Putnam, 1977.

Alpers, Benjamin L. *Dictators, Democracy, and American Public Culture: Envisioning the Totalitarian Enemy, 1920s–1950s.* Chapel Hill: University of North Carolina Press, 2003.

American Law Reports: Federal, Cases and Annotations. Vol. 67. Rochester, NY: Lawyers Co-Operative, 1984.

Anderson, Benedict. *Imagined Communities: Reflections on the Origin and Spread of Nationalism.* London: Verso, 1991.

Angle, Paul M. *Bloody Williamson: A Chapter in American Lawlessness.* New York: Knopf, 1966.

Arad, Gulie Ne'eman. *America, Its Jews, and the Rise of Nazism.* Bloomington: Indiana University Press, 2000.

Arrarás, Joaquín. *Francisco Franco: The Times and the Man.* Enlarged ed. Milwaukee: Bruce, 1939.

Avrich, Paul. *Anarchist Portraits.* Princeton, NJ: Princeton University Press, 1988.

Balfour, Sebastian. "Spain from 1931 to the Present." In *Spain: A History.* Ed. Raymond Carr. Oxford: Oxford University Press, 2000.

Bayor, Ronald H. *Neighbors in Conflict: The Irish, Germans, Jews, and Italians of New York City, 1929–1941.* Baltimore: Johns Hopkins University Press, 1978.

Bayor, Ronald H., and Timothy J. Meagher, eds. *The New York Irish.* Baltimore: Johns Hopkins University Press, 1997.

Beard, Charles A. *American Foreign Policy in the Making, 1932–1940: A Study in Responsibility.* New Haven, CT: Yale University Press, 1946.

Becker, Stephen. *Marshall Field III.* New York: Simon & Schuster, 1964.

Bell, Daniel, ed. *The Radical Right.* 3rd ed. New Brunswick, NJ: Transaction, 2002.

Benson, Frederick R. *Writers in Arms: The Literary Impact of the Spanish Civil War.* New York: New York University Press, 1967.

Bergmeier, Horst J. P., and Rainer E. Lotz. *Hitler's Airwaves: The Inside Story of Nazi Radio Broadcasting and Propaganda Swing.* New Haven, CT: Yale University Press, 1997.

Beschloss, Michael R. *Kennedy and Roosevelt: The Uneasy Alliance.* New York: W. W. Norton, 1980.

Best, Gary Dean. *The Critical Press and the New Deal: The Press versus Presidential Power, 1933–1938.* Westport, CT: Praeger, 1993.

Boot, Max. *The Savage Wars of Peace: Small Wars and the Rise of American Power.* New York: Basic Books, 2002.

Borg, Dorothy. "Notes on Roosevelt's 'Quarantine' Speech." In *Causes and Consequences of World War II.* Ed. Robert A. Divine. Chicago: Quadrangle Books, 1969.

Bowen, Wayne H. *Spaniards and Nazi Germany: Collaboration in the New Order.* Columbia: University of Missouri Press, 2000.

Brands, H. W. *What America Owes the World: The Struggle for the Soul of Foreign Policy.* Cambridge: Cambridge University Press, 1998.

Brinkley, Alan. *Voices of Protest: Huey Long, Father Coughlin, and the Great Depression.* 1982. New York: Vintage Books, 1983.

Brooks, Frank. "Egoist Theory and America's Individualist Anarchists: A Dilemma of Praxis." *History of Political Thought* 15, no. 3 (1994): 403–22.

Browne, Harry. *Spain's Civil War.* London: Addison Wesley Longman, 1996.

Buchanan, Tom. *Britain and the Spanish Civil War.* Cambridge: Cambridge University Press, 1997.

Bushnell, David. "Colombia." In *The Spanish Civil War, 1936–39: American Hemispheric Perspectives.* Ed. Mark Falcoff and Fredrick B. Pike. Lincoln: University of Nebraska Press, 1982.

Cable, James. *The Royal Navy and the Siege of Bilbao.* Cambridge: Cambridge University Press, 1979.

Calhoun, Frederick S. *Power and Principle: Armed Intervention in Wilsonian Foreign Policy.* 3rd ed. Kent, OH: Kent State University Press, 1986.

Campbell, David. *Writing Security: United States Foreign Policy and the Politics of Identity.* Minneapolis: University of Minnesota Press, 1998.

Caparrós Lera, José María. "The Cinema Industry in the Spanish Civil War, 1936–1939." *Film and History* 16, no. 2 (1986): 35–46.

Carr, Raymond. *Spain, 1808–1939.* Oxford: Oxford University Press, 1966.

Carroll, Peter N. *The Odyssey of the Abraham Lincoln Brigade: Americans in the Spanish Civil War.* Stanford, CA: Stanford University Press, 1994.

Carroll, Peter N., and James D. Fernandez, eds. *Facing Fascism: New York and the Spanish Civil War.* New York: New York University Press, 2007.

Casañas Guasch, Luis, and Pedro Sobrino Vázquez. *El Cardenal Gomá: Pastor y Maestro.* 2 vols. Toledo: Estudio Teológico de San Ildefonso Seminario Conciliar, 1983.

Casey, Steven. *Cautious Crusade: Franklin D. Roosevelt, American Public Opinion, and the War Against Nazi Germany.* Oxford: Oxford University Press, 2001.

Chapman, Michael E. "Cardinal Gomá and the Crusader's Sword." Honors thesis, Suffolk University, 2001.

———. "Pro-Franco Anti-communism: Ellery Sedgwick and the *Atlantic Monthly.*" *Journal of Contemporary History* 41, no. 4 (2006): 641–62.

———. "Arguing Americanism: John Eoghan Kelly's Franco Lobby, 1936–43." PhD diss., Boston College, 2006.

———. "'How to Smash the British Empire': John Forrest Kelly's *Irish World* and the Boycott of 1920–21." *Éire-Ireland* 43, no. 3/4 (2008): 217–52.

Chesterton, G. K. *What I Saw in America.* New York: Dodd, Mead, 1922.

Childs, Harwood L. "Public Opinion and Peace." *Annals of the American Academy* 192 (1937): 31–37.

———, ed. *Propaganda and Dictatorship.* Princeton, NJ: Princeton University Press, 1936.

Coen, Robert M. "Labor Force and Unemployment in the 1920s and 1930s: A Re-Examination Based on Postwar Experience." *Review of Economics and Statistics* 55, no. 1 (1973): 46–55.

Cole, Wayne S. *Roosevelt and the Isolationists, 1932–45.* Lincoln: University of Nebraska Press, 1983.

Compton, James V. *The Swastika and the Eagle: Hitler, the United States, and the Origins of World War II.* Boston: Houghton Mifflin, 1967.

A Concise History of the Spanish Civil War. London: Thames & Hudson, 1974.

Cooney, John. *The American Pope: The Life and Times of Francis Cardinal Spellman.* New York: Times Books, 1984.

Corrin, Jay P. *Catholic Intellectuals and the Challenge of Democracy.* Notre Dame, IN: University of Notre Dame Press, 2002.

Cortada, James W., ed. *Historical Dictionary of the Spanish Civil War, 1936–1939.* Westport, CT: Greenwood Press, 1982.

Costello, Brian C. "The Voice of Government as an Abridgement of First Amendment Rights of Speakers: Rethinking *Meese v. Keene.*" *Duke Law Journal* no. 3 (1989): 654–58.

Costigliola, Frank. "Broken Circle: The Isolation of Franklin D. Roosevelt in World War II." *Diplomatic History* 32, no. 5 (2008): 677–718.

Current Biography. Bronx, NY: H. W. Wilson, 1941.

Dallek, Robert. *Franklin D. Roosevelt and American Foreign Policy, 1932–1945.* Oxford: Oxford University Press, 1995.

Darrow, Robert Morton. "Catholic Political Power: A Study of the Activities of the American Catholic Church on Behalf of Franco During the Spanish Civil War, 1936–1939." PhD diss., Columbia University, 1953.

Davis, Kenneth S. *The Beckoning of Destiny, 1882–1928.* Vol. 1, *FDR: A History.* New York: G. P. Putnam's Sons, 1972.

Davis, Richard Akin. "Radio Priest: The Public Career of Father Charles Edward Coughlin." PhD diss., University of North Carolina, 1974.

Denning, Michael. *The Cultural Front: The Laboring of American Culture in the Twentieth Century.* London: Verso, 1997.

Dietrich, John. *The Morgenthau Plan: Soviet Influence on American Postwar Policy.* New York: Algora, 2002.

Diggins, John Patrick. *On Hallowed Ground: Abraham Lincoln and the Foundations of American History.* New Haven, CT: Yale University Press, 2000.

Dinnerstein, Leonard. *Antisemitism in America.* New York: Oxford University Press, 1994.

Divine, Robert A. *The Illusion of Neutrality.* Chicago: University of Chicago Press, 1962.

Doenecke, Justus D. *Storm on the Horizon: The Challenge to American Intervention, 1939–1941.* New ed. Lanham, MD: Rowman & Littlefield, 2003.

Doenecke, Justus D., and Mark A. Stoler. *Debating Franklin D. Roosevelt's Foreign Policies, 1933–1945.* Lanham, MD: Rowman & Littlefield, 2005.

Draper, Theodore. *American Communism and Soviet Russia: The Formative Period.* New York: Viking Press, 1963.

Duara, Prasenjit. "Historicizing National Identity: or, Who Imagines What and When." In *Becoming National.* Ed. Geoff Eley and Ronald Grigor Suny. Oxford: Oxford University Press, 1996.

Edkins, Jenny. *Poststructuralism and International Relations: Bringing the Political Back in.* Boulder, CO: Lynne Rienner, 1999.

Esenwein, George, and Adrian Shubert. *Spain at War: The Spanish Civil War in Context, 1931–1939.* London: Addison Wesley Longman, 1995.

Esposito, David M. "Franklin D. Roosevelt and American Strategic Vulnerability." In *Franklin D. Roosevelt and the Formation of the Modern World*. Ed. Thomas C. Howard and William D. Pederson. Armonk, NY: M. E. Sharpe, 2003.

Farnham, Barbara Reardon. *Roosevelt and the Munich Crisis: A Study of Political Decision-Making*. Princeton, NJ: Princeton University Press, 1997.

Ferguson, Niall. *Colossus: The Price of America's Empire*. New York: Penguin Press, 2004.

Festinger, Leon. *A Theory of Cognitive Dissonance*. Stanford, CA: Stanford University Press, 1957.

FitzGerald, Frances. *Fire in the Lake: The Vietnamese and the Americans in Vietnam*. Boston: Little, Brown, 1972.

Fleming, Thomas. *The New Dealers' War: FDR and the War Within World War II*. New York: Basic Books, 2001.

Flynn, George Q. *Roosevelt and Romanism: Catholics and American Diplomacy, 1937–1945*. Westport, CT: Greenwood Press, 1976.

Fried, Albert. *FDR and His Enemies*. New York: St. Martin's Press, 1999.

Fulbright, J. William. *The Arrogance of Power*. New York: Random House, 1966.

Gallagher, Hugh Gregory. *FDR's Splendid Deception: The Moving Story of Roosevelt's Massive Disability—and the Intense Efforts to Conceal It from the Public*. St. Petersburg, FL: Vandamere Press, 1985.

Galtung, Johan. "The Basic Needs Approach." In *Human Needs: A Contribution to the Current Debate*. Ed. Katrin Lederer. Cambridge, MA: Oelgeschlager, Gunn & Hain, 1980.

Gellner, Ernest. *Nationalism*. New York: New York University Press, 1997.

Girard, René. *Violence and the Sacred*. Trans. Patrick Gregory. Baltimore: Johns Hopkins University Press, 1977.

Glazer, Nathan. *The Social Basis of American Communism*. Westport, CT: Greenwood Press, 1961.

Goldstein, Malcolm. *The Political Stage: American Drama and Theater of the Great Depression*. New York: Oxford University Press, 1974.

Graham, Helen. *The Spanish Republic at War, 1936–1939*. Cambridge: Cambridge University Press, 2002.

Gross, Robert A. *The Minutemen and Their World*. New York: Hill & Wang, 1976.

Guillermo, Artemio R., and May Kyi Win, eds. *Historical Dictionary of the Philippines*. Lanham, MD: Scarecrow Press, 1997.

Guttmann, Allen. *The Wound in the Heart: America and the Spanish Civil War*. Glencoe, NY: Free Press, 1962.

———. *The Conservative Tradition in America*. New York: Oxford University Press, 1967.

Halsey, William M. *The Survival of American Innocence: Catholicism in an Era of Disillusionment, 1920–1940*. Notre Dame, IN: University of Notre Dame Press, 1980.

Halstead, Charles R. "Diligent Diplomat: Alexander W. Weddell as American Ambassador to Spain, 1939–1942." *Virginia Magazine of History and Biography* 82, no. 1 (1974): 3–38.

Hannigan, Robert E. *The New World Power: American Foreign Policy, 1898–1917*. Philadelphia: University of Pennsylvania Press, 2002.

Harp, Gillis J. *Brahmin Prophet: Phillips Brooks and the Path of Liberal Protestantism*. Lanham, MD: Rowman & Littlefield, 2003.

Harper, John Lamberton. *American Visions of Europe: Franklin D. Roosevelt, George F. Kennan, and Dean G. Acheson*. New York: Cambridge University Press, 1994.

Hayes, Carlton J. H. *The Historical Evolution of Modern Nationalism*. New York: Richard R. Smith, 1931.

Haynes, John Earl. *Red Scare or Red Menace? American Communism and Anticommunism in the Cold War Era.* Chicago: Ivan R. Dee, 1996.

Haynes, John Earl, and Harvey Klehr. *Venona: Decoding Soviet Espionage in America.* New Haven, CT: Yale University Press, 1999.

———. *In Denial: Historians, Communism, and Espionage.* San Francisco: Encounter Books, 2003.

Heale, M. J. *American Anticommunism: Combating the Enemy Within, 1830–1970.* Baltimore: Johns Hopkins University Press, 1990.

Heinrichs, Waldo. *Threshold of War: Franklin D. Roosevelt and American Entry into World War II.* New York: Oxford University Press, 1989.

Henrikson, Alan K. "The Geographical 'Mental Maps' of American Foreign Policy Makers." *International Political Science Review* 1, no. 3 (1980): 495–530.

———. "Mental Maps." In *Explaining the History of American Foreign Relations.* Ed. Michael J. Hogan and Thomas G. Paterson. Cambridge: Cambridge University Press, 1991.

Henry, Chris. *The Ebro 1938: Death Knell of the Republic.* Oxford: Osprey, 1999.

Hevener, John W. *Which Side Are You On? The Harlan County Coal Miners, 1931–39.* Urbana: University of Illinois Press, 1978.

Higham, Robin, John T. Greenwood, and Von Hardesty, eds. *Russian Aviation and Air Power in the Twentieth Century.* London: Frank Cass, 1998.

Hilderbrand, Robert C. *Power and the People: Executive Management of Public Opinion in Foreign Affairs, 1897–1921.* Chapel Hill: University of North Carolina Press, 1981.

Hinton, Harold B. *Cordell Hull: A Biography.* Garden City, NY: Doubleday, Doran, 1942.

Hobsbawm, Eric J. *Nations and Nationalism Since 1780: Programme, Myth, Reality.* Cambridge: Cambridge University Press, 1990.

———. *The Age of Extremes: A History of the World, 1914–1991.* New York: Vintage Books, 1994.

Hoopes, Roy. *Ralph Ingersoll: A Biography.* New York: Atheneum, 1985.

Howson, Gerald. *Arms for Spain: The Untold Story of the Spanish Civil War.* New York: St. Martin's Press, 1999.

Hudson, Harriet D. *The Progressive Mine Workers of America: A Study in Rival Unionism.* Urbana: University of Illinois, 1952.

Hunt, Michael H. "Chinese National Identity and the Strong State: The Late Qing–Republican Crisis." In *China's Quest for National Identity.* Ed. Lowell Dittmer and Samuel S. Kim. Ithaca, NY: Cornell University Press, 1993.

Huntington, Samuel P. *American Politics: The Promise of Disharmony.* Cambridge, MA: Belknap Press, 1981.

———. *Who Are We? The Challenges to America's National Identity.* New York: Simon & Schuster, 2004.

Iriye, Akira. *The Origins of the Second World War in Asia and the Pacific.* London: Longman, 1987.

Israel, Fred L. *Nevada's Key Pittman.* Lincoln: University of Nebraska Press, 1963.

Jacobs, Seth. *America's Miracle Man in Vietnam: Ngo Dinh Diem, Religion, Race, and U.S. Intervention in Southeast Asia, 1950–1957.* Durham, NC: Duke University Press, 2004.

Jeansonne, Glen. *Women of the Far Right: The Mothers' Movement and World War II.* Chicago: University of Chicago Press, 1996.

Jellison, Charles A. "A Prelude to War." *American History* 34, no. 5 (1999): 53–65.

Jensen, Geoffrey. *Franco: Soldier, Commander, Dictator.* Washington, DC: Potomac Books, 2005.

Jespersen, T. Christopher. *American Images of China, 1931–1949*. Stanford, CA: Stanford University Press, 1996.

Johnson, Marilynn. *Street Justice: A History of Police Violence in New York City*. Boston: Beacon Press, 2003.

Jørgensen, Carsten. "A Filmanalysis of German Documentaries on the Spanish Civil War." In *History and Film: Methodology, Research, Education*. Ed. K. R. M. Short and Karsten Fledelius. Copenhagen: Eventus, 1980.

Kamen, Henry. *The Spanish Inquisition: A Historical Revision*. New Haven, CT: Yale University Press, 1998.

Kanawada, Leo V., Jr. *Franklin D. Roosevelt's Diplomacy and American Catholics, Italians, and Jews*. Ann Arbor, MI: UMI Research Press, 1982.

Kedourie, Elie. *Nationalism*. 4th edition. Oxford: Blackwell, 1993.

Keene, Judith. *Fighting for Franco: International Volunteers in Nationalist Spain During the Spanish Civil War, 1936–39*. London: Leicester University Press, 2001.

Keller, David Neal. *Stone & Webster, 1889–1989: A Century of Integrity and Service*. New York: Stone & Webster, 1989.

Kennedy, David M. *Freedom from Fear: The American People in Depression and War, 1929–1945*. New York: Oxford University Press, 1999.

Keogh, Dermot, and Andrew McCarthy. *Limerick Boycott, 1904: Anti-Semitism in Ireland*. Cork: Mercier Press, 2005.

Ketchum, Richard M. *The Borrowed Years, 1938–1941: America on the Way to War*. New York: Random House, 1989.

Kierkegaard, Søren. *The Concept of Anxiety: A Simple Psychologically Orienting Deliberation on the Dogmatic Issue of Hereditary Sin*. 1844. Trans. and ed. Reidar Thomte. Princeton, NJ: Princeton University Press, 1980.

Kirk, Russell, and James McClellan. *The Political Principles of Robert A. Taft*. New York: Fleet Press Corporation, 1967.

Klehr, Harvey. *The Heyday of American Communism: The Depression Decade*. New York: Basic Books, 1984.

Klehr, Harvey, John Earl Haynes, and Kyrill M. Anderson. *The Soviet World of American Communism*. New Haven, CT: Yale University Press, 1998.

Klenicki, Leon, and Geoffrey Wigoder, eds. *A Dictionary of the Jewish-Christian Dialogue*. Expanded ed. Mahwah, NJ: Paulist Press, 1995.

Krieghbaum, Hillier. *Facts in Perspective: The Editorial Page and News Interpretation*. Englewood Cliffs, NJ: Prentice-Hall, 1956.

Lapomarda, Vincent A. *The Boston Mayor Who Became Truman's Secretary of Labor*. New York: Peter Lang, 1995.

Lasswell, Harold D. "Propaganda Detection and the Courts." In *Language of Politics: Studies in Quantitative Semantics*. Ed. Harold D. Lasswell. Cambridge, MA: MIT Press, 1949.

Leffler, Melvyn P. "National Security." In *Explaining the History of American Foreign Relations*. Ed. Michael J. Hogan and Thomas G. Paterson. Cambridge: Cambridge University Press, 1991.

Levin, N. Gordon, Jr. *Woodrow Wilson and World Politics: America's Response to War and Revolution*. London: Oxford University Press, 1968.

Lewis, Alfred Allan. *Ladies and Not-So-Gentle Women*. New York: Viking Penguin, 2000.

Lewis, Bernard. *Cultures in Conflict: Christians, Muslims, and Jews in the Age of Discovery*. New York: Oxford University Press, 1995.

Little, Douglas. *Malevolent Neutrality: The United States, Great Britain, and the Origins of the Spanish Civil War.* Ithaca, NY: Cornell University Press, 1985.

Lojendio, Luis María de. *Operaciones militares de la guerra de España, 1936–1939.* Barcelona: Montaner y Simon, 1940.

Ludwig, Emil. *Emil Ludwig's Life of Roosevelt: A Study in Fortune and Power.* New York: McFadden, 1937–38.

Luthin, Reinhard H. *American Demagogues: Twentieth Century.* Gloucester, MA: Peter Smith, 1959.

MacKinnon, Stephen R. "The Sino–Japanese Conflict, 1931–1945." In *A Military History of China.* Ed. David A. Graff and Robin Higham. Boulder, CO: Westview Press, 2002.

Maney, Patrick J. *"Young Bob" La Follette: A Biography of Robert M. La Follette Jr., 1895–1953.* Columbia: University of Missouri Press, 1978.

———. *The Roosevelt Presence: A Biography of Franklin Delano Roosevelt.* New York: Twayne, 1992.

Marks, Frederick W., III. *Winds over Sand: The Diplomacy of Franklin Roosevelt.* Athens: University of Georgia Press, 1988.

Marlin, George J. *The American Catholic Voter: 200 Years of Political Impact.* South Bend, IN: St. Augustine's Press, 2004.

Martin, John. "In the Beginnings of 'Pacific Service': Early Stages of Hydro-Electric Development in North-Central California." *Pacific Service Magazine* pt. 1, 13 (December 1921): 205–15; pt. 2, 13 (January 1922): 244–50.

Martín Rubio, Ángel David. *Los mitos de la represión en la guerra civil.* Madrid: Grafite Ediciones, 2005.

Mayers, David. *The Ambassadors and America's Soviet Policy.* New York: Oxford University Press, 1995.

McCarthy, Edward C. "The Christian Front Movement in New York City, 1938–1940." Master's thesis, Columbia University, 1965.

McCrisken, Trevor B. *American Exceptionalism and the Legacy of Vietnam: U.S. Foreign Policy since 1974.* Basingstoke, UK: Palgrave Macmillan, 2003.

McDermott, Kevin, and Jeremy Agnew. *The Comintern: A History of International Communism from Lenin to Stalin.* New York: St. Martin's Press, 1997.

McGarry, Fearghal. *Irish Politics and the Spanish Civil War.* Cork: Cork University Press, 1999.

McKean, Dayton David. *The Boss: The Hague Machine in Action.* Boston: Houghton Mifflin, 1940.

McNickle, Chris. "When New York Was Irish, and After." In *The New York Irish.* Ed. Ronald H. Bayor and Timothy J. Meagher. Baltimore: Johns Hopkins University Press, 1997.

Miles, Michael W. *The Odyssey of the American Right.* New York: Oxford University Press, 1980.

Miller, Larry Carl. "Dimensions of Mugwump Thought, 1880–1920: Sons of Massachusetts Abolitionists as Professional Pioneers." PhD diss., Northwestern University, 1969.

Moa, Pío. *Los mitos de la guerra civil.* Madrid: La Esfera de los Libros, 2003.

Monter, E. William. *Frontiers of Heresy: The Spanish Inquisition from the Basque Lands to Sicily.* Cambridge: Cambridge University Press, 1990.

Montero Moreno, Antonio. *Historia de la persecución religiosa en España, 1936–1939.* Madrid: Biblioteca de Autores Cristianos, 1961.

Moorehead, Caroline. *Gellhorn: A Twentieth-Century Life.* New York: Henry Holt, 2003.

Morgan, Ted. *Reds: McCarthyism in Twentieth-Century America.* New York: Random House, 2003.

Moynihan, Daniel Patrick. *"Catholic Tradition and Social Change": Second Annual Seton-Neumann Lecture, May 7, 1984, Rayburn House*. N.p.: U.S. Catholic Conference, 1984.

Muste, John M. *Say That We Saw Spain Die: Literary Consequences of the Spanish Civil War*. Seattle: University of Washington Press, 1966.

Neuborne, Burt, and Steven R. Shapiro. "The Nylon Curtain: America's National Border and the Free Flow of Ideas." *William and Mary Law Review* 26, no. 719 (1985): 719–38.

Neustadt, Richard E. *Presidential Power: The Politics of Leadership from FDR to Carter*. New York: Macmillan, 1980.

Norton, Mary Beth, et al. *A People and A Nation: A History of the United States*. 7th ed. Boston: Houghton Mifflin, 2005.

O'Connor, Richard. *Hell's Kitchen: The Roaring Days of New York's Wild West Side*. New York: Old Town Books, 1957.

Offner, Arnold A. *American Appeasement: United States Foreign Policy and Germany, 1933–1938*. Cambridge, MA: Harvard University Press, 1969.

Ogden, August Raymond. *The Dies Committee: A Study of the Special House Committee for the Investigation of Un-American Activities, 1938–1944*. Washington, DC: Catholic University of America Press, 1945.

O'Reilly, Kenneth. *Hoover and the Un-Americans: The FBI, HUAC, and the Red Menace*. Philadelphia: Temple University Press, 1983.

Payne, Robert, ed. *The Civil War in Spain, 1936–1939*. New York: G. P. Putnam's Sons, 1962.

Payne, Stanley G. *Fascism in Spain, 1923–1977*. Madison: University of Wisconsin Press, 1999.

———. *The Spanish Civil War, the Soviet Union, and Communism*. New Haven, CT: Yale University Press, 2004.

———. *The Collapse of the Spanish Republic, 1933–1936*. New Haven, CT: Yale University Press, 2006.

———. *Franco and Hitler: Spain, Germany, and World War II*. New Haven, CT: Yale University Press, 2008.

Patterson, James T. *Congressional Conservatism and the New Deal: The Growth of the Conservative Coalition in Congress, 1933–1939*. Lexington: University Press of Kentucky, 1967.

Pells, Richard H. *Radical Visions and American Dreams: Culture and Social Thought in the Depression Years*. New York: Harper & Row, 1972.

Pencak, William. *For God and Country: The American Legion, 1919–1941*. Boston: Northeastern University Press, 1989.

Pike, Fredrick B. "The New Corporatism in Franco's Spain and Some Latin American Perspectives." In *The New Corporatism: Social-Political Structures in the Iberian World*. Ed. Frederick B. Pike and Thomas Stritch. Notre Dame, IN: University of Notre Dame Press, 1974.

Porter, David L. *The Seventy-Sixth Congress and World War II, 1939–1940*. Columbia: University of Missouri Press, 1979.

Powaski, Ronald E. *Toward an Entangling Alliance: American Isolationism, Internationalism, and Europe, 1901–1950*. New York: Greenwood Press, 1991.

Powers, Richard Gid. *Not Without Honor: The History of American Anticommunism*. New York: Free Press, 1995.

Preston, Paul. *Franco: A Biography*. New York: Basic Books, 1994.

———. *Doves of War: Four Women of Spain*. Boston: Northeastern University Press, 2002.

———. *The Spanish Civil War: Reaction, Revolution, and Revenge*. New York: W. W. Norton, 2006.

Radosh, Ronald, Mary R. Habeck, and Grigory Sevostianov, eds. *Spain Betrayed: The Soviet Union in the Spanish Civil War*. New Haven, CT: Yale University Press, 2001.

Reynolds, David. *From Munich to Pearl Harbor: Roosevelt's America and the Origins of the Second World War.* Chicago: Ivan R. Dee, 2001.

Richardson, R. Dan. *Comintern Army: The International Brigades and the Spanish Civil War.* Lexington: University Press of Kentucky, 1982.

Richelson, Jeffrey T. *A Century of Spies: Intelligence in the Twentieth Century.* New York: Oxford University Press, 1995.

Ries, Karl, and Hans Ring. *The Legion Condor: A History of the Luftwaffe in the Spanish Civil War, 1936–1939.* Trans. David Johnston. West Chester, PA: Schiffer, 1992.

Ringrose, David. *Spain, Europe, and the "Spanish Miracle," 1700–1900.* Cambridge: Cambridge University Press, 1996.

Romerstein, Herbert, and Eric Breindel. *The Venona Secrets: Exposing Soviet Espionage and America's Traitors.* Washington, DC: Regnery, 2000.

Rosenberg, Emily S. *Financial Missionaries to the World: The Politics and Culture of Dollar Diplomacy, 1900–1930.* Cambridge, MA: Harvard University Press, 1999.

Rosenstone, Robert A. *Crusade of the Left: The Lincoln Battalion in the Spanish Civil War.* New York: Pegasus, 1969.

Rotundo, E. Anthony. *American Manhood: Transformations in Masculinity from the Revolution to the Modern Era.* New York: Basic Books, 1993.

Roy, Ralph Lord. *Communism and the Churches.* New York: Harcourt, Brace, 1960.

Ruiz, Julius. *Franco's Justice: Repression in Madrid after the Spanish Civil War.* Oxford: Clarendon Press, 2005.

Russett, Bruce M. *No Clear and Present Danger: A Skeptical View of the United States Entry into World War II.* New York: Harper & Row, 1972.

Salas Larrazábal, Ramón. *Los datos exactos de la guerra civil.* Madrid: Colección Drácena, 1980.

Sandeen, Eric J. "*Confessions of a Nazi Spy* and the German-American Bund." *American Studies* 20, no. 2 (1979): 69–81.

Schaller, Michael. *The U.S. Crusade in China, 1938–1945.* New York: Columbia University Press, 1979.

———. *The United States and China: Into the Twenty-First Century.* 3rd ed. New York: Oxford University Press, 2002.

Schlesinger, Arthur M., Jr. *The Age of Roosevelt: The Politics of Upheaval, 1935–1936.* 1960. Boston: Houghton Mifflin, 2003.

Schmidt, Regin. *Red Scare: FBI and the Origins of Anticommunism in the United States, 1919–1943.* Copenhagen: Museum Tusculanum Press, 2000.

Schmitz, David F. *Thank God They're on Our Side: The United States and Right-Wing Dictatorships, 1921–1965.* Chapel Hill: University of North Carolina Press, 1999.

Schoenwald, Jonathan M. *A Time for Choosing: The Rise of Modern American Conservatism.* Oxford: Oxford University Press, 2001.

Scott, William R. *The Sons of Sheba's Race: African-Americans and the Italo-Ethiopian War, 1935–1941.* Bloomington: Indiana University Press, 1993.

Sedgwick, Ellery, Jr. *The Atlantic Monthly, 1857–1909: Yankee Humanism at High Tide and Ebb.* Amherst: University of Massachusetts Press, 1994.

Seidman, Michael. *Republic of Egos: A Social History of the Spanish Civil War.* Madison: University of Wisconsin Press, 2002.

Sharer, Elizabeth Jean. "Hildreth Meière, 1892–1961: An Artistic Biography of an American Muralist." PhD diss., University of New Mexico, 2001.

Singleton, M. K. *H. L. Mencken and the American Mercury Adventure.* Durham, NC: Duke University Press, 1962.

Slide, Anthony. *"Banned in the USA": British Films in the United States and Their Censorship, 1933–1960*. London: I. B. Tauris, 1998.

Small, Melvin. "Public Opinion." In *Explaining the History of American Foreign Relations*. Ed. Michael J. Hogan and Thomas G. Paterson. Cambridge: Cambridge University Press, 1991.

Smith, Greg M. "Blocking *Blockade:* Partisan Protest, Popular Debate, and Encapsulated Texts." *Cinema Journal* 36, no. 1 (1996): 18–38.

Smith, Thomas F. X. *The Powerticians.* Secaucus, NJ: Lyle Stuart, 1982.

Spak, Michael I. "America for Sale: When Well-Connected Former Federal Officials Peddle Their Influence to the Highest Foreign Bidder—A Statutory Analysis and Proposals for Reform of the Foreign Agents Registration Act and the Ethics in Government Act." *Kentucky Law Journal* 78, no. 2 (1989–90): 242–55.

Spector, Robert M. "W. Cameron Forbes in Haiti: Additional Light on the Genesis of the 'Good Neighbor' Policy." *Caribbean Studies* 6, no. 2 (1966): 28–45.

———. *W. Cameron Forbes and the Hoover Commissions to Haiti (1930).* Lanham, MD: University Press of America, 1985.

Steele, Richard W. "Franklin D. Roosevelt and His Foreign Policy Critics." *Political Science Quarterly* 94, no. 1 (1979): 15–32.

———. *Propaganda in an Open Society: The Roosevelt Administration and the Media, 1933–1941.* Westport, CT: Greenwood Press, 1985.

Stephan, Alexander. *"Communazis": FBI Surveillance of German Émigré Writers.* New Haven, CT: Yale University Press, 2000.

Sterne, Evelyn Savidge. "Beyond the Boss: Immigration and American Political Culture from 1880 to 1940." In *E Pluribus Unum? Contemporary and Historical Perspectives on Immigrant Political Incorporation*. Ed. Gary Gerstle and John Mollenkopf. New York: Russell Sage Foundation, 2001.

Stoler, Mark A. "U.S. World War II Diplomacy." In *America in the World: The Historiography of American Foreign Relations since 1941*. Ed. Michael J. Hogan. Cambridge: Cambridge University Press, 1995.

Stone & Webster Engineering Corporation in World War II: A Report to the People. New York: Stone & Webster, 1946.

Strauss, David. *Percival Lowell: The Culture and Science of a Boston Brahmin.* Cambridge, MA: Harvard University Press, 2001.

Swanson, Harlan J. "The *Panay* Incident: Prelude to Pearl Harbor." *U.S. Naval Institute Proceedings* 93, no. 12 (1967): 26–37.

Taylor, F. Jay. *The United States and the Spanish Civil War, 1936–1939.* New York: Bookman, 1956.

Tansill, Charles C. *Back Door to War: The Roosevelt Foreign Policy, 1933–1941.* Chicago: H. Regnery, 1952.

Tebbel, John, and Mary Ellen Zuckerman. *The Magazine in America, 1741–1990.* New York: Oxford University Press, 1991.

Temple, K. Richmond. "Alexander Weddell: Virginian in the Diplomatic Service." *Virginia Cavalcade* 34, no. 1 (1984): 22–39.

Terkel, Studs. *The Good War: An Oral History of World War Two.* New York: Ballantine Books, 1984.

Theoharis, Athan, ed. *From the Secret Files of J. Edgar Hoover.* Chicago: Ivan R. Dee, 1991.

Thomas, Gordon, and Max Morgan Witts. *Guernica: The Crucible of World War II.* New York: Stein & Day, 1975.

Thomas, Hugh. *The Spanish Civil War.* 3rd ed. New York: Harper & Row, 1986.

———. *The Spanish Civil War*. Rev. ed. New York: Modern Library, 2001.

Tierney, Dominic. "Franklin D. Roosevelt and Covert Aid to the Loyalists in the Spanish Civil War, 1936–39." *Journal of Contemporary History* 39, no. 3 (2004): 299–313.

———. *FDR and the Spanish Civil War: Neutrality and Commitment in the Struggle that Divided America*. Durham, NC: Duke University Press, 2007.

Traina, Richard P. *American Diplomacy and the Spanish Civil War*. Bloomington: Indiana University Press, 1968.

Valaik, J. David. "Catholics, Neutrality, and the Spanish Embargo, 1937–1939." *Journal of American History* 54 (June 1967): 73–85.

———. "American Catholic Dissenters and the Spanish Civil War." *Catholic Historical Review* 53, no. 4 (1968): 537–55.

Valleau, Marjorie A. *The Spanish Civil War in American and European Films*. Ann Arbor, MI: UMI Research Press, 1982.

Van Allen, Rodger. *The* Commonweal *and American Catholicism: The Magazine, the Movement, the Meaning*. Philadelphia: Fortress Press, 1974.

Wanger, Walter. "OWI and Motion Pictures." *Public Opinion Quarterly* 7 (Spring 1943): 100–110.

Warren, Donald I. *Radio Priest: Charles Coughlin, the Father of Hate Radio*. New York: Free Press, 1996.

Warshow, Robert. *The Immediate Experience: Movies, Comics, Theatre, and Other Aspects of Popular Culture*. 1946. Enlarged edition. Cambridge, MA: Harvard University Press, 2001.

Wayman, Dorothy G. *David I. Walsh: Citizen-Patriot*. Milwaukee: Bruce, 1952.

Weinberg, Gerhard L. *A World at Arms: A Global History of World War II*. Cambridge: Cambridge University Press, 1994.

White, Graham J. *FDR and the Press*. Chicago: University of Chicago Press, 1979.

White, Graham J., and John Maze. *Harold Ickes of the New Deal: His Private Life and Public Career*. Cambridge, MA: Harvard University Press, 1985.

Wiarda, Howard J. *Corporatism and Development: The Portuguese Experience*. Amherst: University of Massachusetts Press, 1977.

Wilford, Hugh. "The Communist International and the American Communist Party." In *International Communism and the Communist International, 1919–42*. Ed. Tim Rees and Andrew Thorpe. Manchester: Manchester University Press, 1998.

Wyman, David S. *Paper Walls: America and the Refugee Crisis, 1938–1941*. Boston: University of Massachusetts Press, 1968.

Zwick, Mark, and Louise Zwick. *The Catholic Worker Movement: Intellectual and Spiritual Origins*. Mahwah, NJ: Paulist Press, 2005.

Index

Abello, Thomas P., 14

Abraham Lincoln Brigade (ALB), 205; as American heroes, 74, 137, 138, 222; composition of, 46, 243n21; embargo appeals from, 73; and First Lady, 75; founding of, 18; fund-raising by, 141; and Musicians' Union, Local 802, 161; and recruitment, 40, 197–98, 265n24; as traitorous aliens, 19, 66, 197–98

Acheson, Dean G., 2, 176, 189

Adams, John, xv–xvi

Adams, John Quincy, xv

aerial bombing, 22, 112, 124; brutality of, xvii–xviii, 53, 61, 142, 147; fear of, 145, 226n–h. *See also* aviation; Guernica, bombing of

Agents of the Fascisti, 210, 255n30

agents provocateurs, 175–78, 209

aggression, discourse of, 16, 29, 103, 239n64; fascist, xiv, xvii, 23, 32, 39, 71, 74, 75, 141, 158; Nazi, 91, 94, 98

Aguirre, José Antonio, 120

Ahern, Maurice, 144

Aid Spanish Democracy, 167

Alcalá Zamora, Niceto, 79

Alcázar, Toledo: siege of, 15–16, 118

Alfonso XIII, 119, 122, 218

Alfonte, William A., 3, 13

Allen, Jay C., Jr., 90, 192, 219–20

Allen, Philip M., 152

Allen, Robert S., 92, 93

Allen, R. T. P., 220

Allin, Bryan, 33

Alonso, Manuel, 13

Alpers, Benjamin L., 30

Alvarado, Pedro de, 7

Amalgamated Clothing Workers of America, 144

Amerasia, 173

America, 15, 19, 37–38, 187, 202–3; and *Blockade*, 139

American Civil Liberties Union (ACLU), 169

American Communist Party (CPUSA), xiv, 33, 144, 196, 217, 219; Americanization of, 202; and *Blockade*, 136, 139; as conspiracy, 191; and international volunteers, xii, xxii, 18, 46; membership of, 14, 38, 201, 219, 223; and NYC government, 51; and *PM*, 54, 200; and Roosevelt's administration, 47, 68

American Defense Society, 106

American Federation Against Communism, 278n51

American Federation of Musicians' Union, Local 802, 46, 163, 167

Americanism, xiv, xv, 35–37, 45, 47–51, 52, 69; and anticommunism, 14, 72, 158, 195, 219, 222–23; Catholicism and, 141–42, 150; and communist threat to, 2; defined, xx–xxi; and democracy, 138–39, 186; and foreignness, 131–32, 159, 194, 220; historicity of, 153; and individualism, 218; and liberal multiculturalism, 72; and meritocracy, 10, 171, 186; and nationalism, 17; as political doctrine, 59–60, 106, 172; redefinition of, 37, 133, 158, 218; right to define, 17, 42, 134, 157, 210, 219; sham patriotism of, 181; Walsh and, 103; Yankee democracy of, 33–34. *See also* core values; un-Americanism

Americanism Commission, American Legion's, 99

Americanization programs, 49

American Jewish Committee (AJC), 159, 164, 167, 168, 174; on Jewish refugees, 159

American League Against War and Fascism, 72

American League for Peace and Democracy (ALPD), 72–73

American Legion, 39, 48, 96, 99–103; and Jersey City rally, 169

American Mercury, 52, 125